Lecture Notes in Computer Science 3953

Commenced Publication in 1973
Founding and Former Series Editors:
Gerhard Goos, Juris Hartmanis, and Jan van Leeuwen

T0180234

Aleš Leonardis   Horst Bischof
Axel Pinz (Eds.)

Computer Vision – ECCV 2006

9th European Conference on Computer Vision
Graz, Austria, May 7-13, 2006
Proceedings, Part III

Springer

Volume Editors

Aleš Leonardis
University of Ljubljana
Faculty of Computer and Information Science
Visual Cognitive Systems Laboratory, Trzaska 25, 1001 Ljubljana, Slovenia
E-mail: alesl@fri.uni-lj.si

Horst Bischof
Graz University of Technology
Institute for Computer Graphics and Vision
Inffeldgasse 16, 8010 Graz, Austria
E-mail: bischof@icg.tu-graz.ac.at

Axel Pinz
Graz University of Technology
Institute of Electrical Measurement and Measurement Signal Processing
Schießstattgasse 14b, 8010 Graz, Austria
E-mail: Axel.Pinz@tugraz.at

Library of Congress Control Number: 2006924180

CR Subject Classification (1998): I.4, I.3.5, I.5, I.2.9-10

LNCS Sublibrary: SL 6 – Image Processing, Computer Vision, Pattern Recognition,
and Graphics

ISSN   0302-9743
ISBN-10   3-540-33836-5 Springer Berlin Heidelberg New York
ISBN-13   978-3-540-33836-9 Springer Berlin Heidelberg New York

Springer is a part of Springer Science+Business Media

springer.com

© Springer-Verlag Berlin Heidelberg 2006
Printed in Germany

Typesetting: Camera-ready by author, data conversion by Scientific Publishing Services, Chennai, India
Printed on acid-free paper   SPIN: 11744078   06/3142   5 4 3 2 1 0

Preface

These are the proceedings of the 9th European Conference on Computer Vision (ECCV 2006), the premium European conference on computer vision, held in Graz, Austria, in May 2006.

In response to our conference call, we received 811 papers, the largest number of submissions so far. Finally, 41 papers were selected for podium presentation and 151 for presentation in poster sessions (a 23.67% acceptance rate).

The double-blind reviewing process started by assigning each paper to one of the 22 area chairs, who then selected 3 reviewers for each paper. After the reviews were received, the authors were offered the possibility to provide feedback on the reviews. On the basis of the reviews and the rebuttal of the authors, the area chairs wrote the initial consolidation report for each paper. Finally, all the area chairs attended a two-day meeting in Graz, where all decisions on acceptance/rejection were made. At that meeting, the area chairs responsible for similar sub-fields thoroughly evaluated the assigned papers and discussed them in great depth. Again, all decisions were reached without the knowledge of the authors' identity. We are fully aware of the fact that reviewing is always also subjective, and that some good papers might have been overlooked; however, we tried our best to apply a fair selection process.

The conference preparation went smoothly thanks to several people. We first wish to thank the ECCV Steering Committee for entrusting us with the organization of the conference. We are grateful to the area chairs, who did a tremendous job in selecting the papers, and to more than 340 Program Committee members and 220 additional reviewers for all their professional efforts. To the organizers of the previous ECCV 2004 in Prague, Vaclav Hlaváč, Jirí Matas and Tomáš Pajdla for providing many insights, additional information, and the superb conference software. Finally, we would also like to thank the authors for contributing a large number of excellent papers to support the high standards of the ECCV conference.

Many people showed dedication and enthusiasm in the preparation of the conference. We would like to express our deepest gratitude to all the members of the involved institutes, that is, the Institute of Electrical Measurement and Measurement Signal Processing and the Institute for Computer Graphics and Vision, both at Graz University of Technology, and the Visual Cognitive Systems Laboratory at the University of Ljubljana. In particular, we would like to express our warmest thanks to Friedrich Fraundorfer for all his help (and patience) with the conference software and many other issues concerning the event, as well as Johanna Pfeifer for her great help with the organizational matters.

February 2006   Aleš Leonardis,
                                                                         Horst Bischof,
                                                                         Axel Pinz

Organization

Conference Chair

Axel Pinz   Graz University of Technology, Austria

Program Chairs

Horst Bischof   Graz University of Technology, Austria
Aleš Leonardis   University of Ljubljana, Slovenia

Organization Committee

Markus Brandner	Local Arrangements	Graz Univ. of Technology, Austria
Friedrich Fraundorfer	Local Arrangements	Graz Univ. of Technology, Austria
Matjaž Jogan	Tutorials Chair	Univ. of Ljubljana, Slovenia
Andreas Opelt	Local Arrangements	Graz Univ. of Technology, Austria
Johanna Pfeifer	Conference Secretariat	Graz Univ. of Technology, Austria
Matthias Rüther	Local Arrangements	Graz Univ. of Technology, Austria
Danijel Skočaj	Workshops Chair	Univ. of Ljubljana, Slovenia

Conference Board

Hans Burkhardt   University of Freiburg, Germany
Bernard Buxton   University College London, UK
Roberto Cipolla   University of Cambridge, UK
Jan-Olof Eklundh   Royal Institute of Technology, Sweden
Olivier Faugeras   INRIA, Sophia Antipolis, France
Anders Heyden   Lund University, Sweden
Bernd Neumann   University of Hamburg, Germany
Mads Nielsen   IT University of Copenhagen, Denmark
Tomáš Pajdla   CTU Prague, Czech Republic
Giulio Sandini   University of Genoa, Italy
David Vernon   Trinity College, Ireland

Area Chairs

Michael Black   Brown University, USA
Joachim M. Buhmann   ETH Zürich, Switzerland

Rachid Deriche   INRIA Sophia Antipolis, France
Pascal Fua   EPFL Lausanne, Switzerland
Luc Van Gool   KU Leuven, Belgium & ETH Zürich, Switzerland
Edwin Hancock   University of York, UK
Richard Hartley   Australian National University, Australia
Sing Bing Kang   Microsoft Research, USA
Stan Li   Chinese Academy of Sciences, Beijing, China
David Lowe   University of British Columbia, Canada
Jirí Matas   CTU Prague, Czech Republic
Nikos Paragios   Ecole Centrale de Paris, France
Marc Pollefeys   University of North Carolina at Chapel Hill, USA
Long Quan   HKUST, Hong Kong, China
Bernt Schiele   Darmstadt University of Technology, Germany
Amnon Shashua   Hebrew University of Jerusalem, Israel
Peter Sturm   INRIA Rhône-Alpes, France
Chris Taylor   University of Manchester, UK
Bill Triggs   INRIA Rhône-Alpes, France
Joachim Weickert   Saarland University, Germany
Daphna Weinshall   Hebrew University of Jerusalem, Israel
Andrew Zisserman   University of Oxford, UK

Program Committee

Motilal Agrawal	Stan Birchfield	Octavia Camps
Jörgen Ahlberg	Laure Blanc-Feraud	David Capel
Miguel Alemán-Flores	Nicolas P. de la Blanca	Barbara Caputo
Yiannis Aloimonos	Volker Blanz	Stefan Carlsson
Amir Amini	Rein van den Boomgaard	Vicent Caselles
Arnon Amir	Patrick Bouthemy	Tat-Jen Cham
Elli Angelopoulou	Richard Bowden	Mike Chantler
Adnan Ansar	Edmond Boyer	Francois Chaumette
Helder Araujo	Yuri Boykov	Rama Chellappa
Tal Arbel	Francois Bremond	Tsuhan Chen
Antonis Argyros	Thomas Breuel	Dmitry Chetverikov
Karl Astrom	Lisa Brown	Ondrej Chum
Shai Avidan	Michael Brown	James Clark
Vemuri Baba	Thomas Brox	Bob Collins
Subhashis Banerjee	Alfred Bruckstein	Dorin Comaniciu
Aharon Bar-Hillel	Andres Bruhn	Tim Cootes
Kobus Barnard	Roberto Brunelli	Joao Costeira
Joao Pedro Barreto	Antoni Buades	Daniel Cremers
Chiraz Ben Abdelkader	Michael Burl	Antonio Criminisi
Marie-Odile Berger	Brian Burns	James Crowley
Marcelo Bertalmio	Darius Burschka	Kristin Dana
Ross Beveridge	Aurelio Campilho	Kostas Daniilidis

Majid Mirmehdi
Anurag Mittal
J.M.M. Montiel
Theo Moons
Philippos Mordohai
Greg Mori
Pavel Mrázek
Jane Mulligan
Joe Mundy
Vittorio Murino
Hans-Hellmut Nagel
Vic Nalwa
Srinivasa Narasimhan
P.J. Narayanan
Oscar Nestares
Heiko Neumann
Jan Neumann
Ram Nevatia
Ko Nishino
David Nister
Thomas O'Donnell
Masatoshi Okutomi
Ole Fogh Olsen
Tomáš Pajdla
Chris Pal
Theodore Papadopoulo
Nikos Paragios
Ioannis Pavlidis
Vladimir Pavlovic
Shmuel Peleg
Marcello Pelillo
Francisco Perales
Sylvain Petitjean
Matti Pietikainen
Filiberto Pla
Robert Pless
Jean Ponce
Rich Radke
Ravi Ramamoorthi
Deva Ramanan
Visvanathan Ramesh
Ramesh Raskar
Christopher Rasmussen
Carlo Regazzoni
James Rehg

Paolo Remagnino
Xiaofeng Ren
Tammy Riklin-Raviv
Ehud Rivlin
Antonio Robles-Kelly
Karl Rohr
Sami Romdhani
Bodo Rosenhahn
Arun Ross
Carsten Rother
Nicolas Rougon
Mikael Rousson
Sebastien Roy
Javier Sanchez
Jose Santos-Victor
Guillermo Sapiro
Radim Sara
Jun Sato
Yoichi Sato
Eric Saund
Hanno Scharr
Daniel Scharstein
Yoav Y. Schechner
Otmar Scherzer
Christoph Schnörr
Stan Sclaroff
Yongduek Seo
Mubarak Shah
Gregory Shakhnarovich
Ying Shan
Eitan Sharon
Jianbo Shi
Ilan Shimshoni
Ali Shokoufandeh
Kaleem Siddiqi
Greg Slabaugh
Cristian Sminchisescu
Stefano Soatto
Nir Sochen
Jon Sporring
Anuj Srivastava
Chris Stauffer
Drew Steedly
Charles Stewart
Tomáš Suk

Rahul Sukthankar
Josephine Sullivan
Changming Sun
David Suter
Tomáš Svoboda
Richard Szeliski
Tamas Sziranyi
Hugues Talbot
Tieniu Tan
Chi-keung Tang
Xiaoou Tang
Hai Tao
Sibel Tari
Gabriel Taubin
Camillo Jose Taylor
Demetri Terzopoulos
Ying-li Tian
Carlo Tomasi
Antonio Torralba
Andrea Torsello
Panos Trahanias
Mohan Trivedi
Emanuele Trucco
David Tschumperle
Yanghai Tsin
Matthew Turk
Tinne Tuytelaars
Nuno Vasconcelos
Olga Veksler
Svetha Venkatesh
David Vernon
Alessandro Verri
Luminita Aura Vese
Rene Vidal
Markus Vincze
Jordi Vitria
Julia Vogel
Toshikazu Wada
Tomáš Werner
Carl-Fredrik Westin
Yonatan Wexler
Ross Whitaker
Richard Wildes
Chris Williams
James Williams

Lance Williams
Richard Wilson
Lior Wolf
Kwan-Yee K. Wong
Ming Xie
Yasushi Yagi
Hulya Yalcin

Jie Yang
Ming-Hsuan Yang
Ruigang Yang
Jingyi Yu
Ramin Zabih
Changshui Zhang
Zhengyou Zhang

Cha Zhang
Song-Chun Zhu
Todd Zickler
Michael Zillich
Larry Zitnick
Lilla Zöllei
Steven Zucker

Additional Reviewers

Vitaly Ablavsky
Jeff Abrahamson
Daniel Abretske
Amit Adam
Gaurav Aggarwal
Amit Agrawal
Timo Ahonen
Amir Akbarzadeh
H. Can Aras
Tamar Avraham
Harlyn Baker
Patrick Baker
Hynek Bakstein
Olof Barr
Adrien Bartoli
Paul Beardsley
Isabelle Bégin
Ohad Ben-Shahar
Møarten Björkman
Mark Borg
Jake Bouvrie
Bernhard Burgeth
Frédéric Cao
Gustavo Carneiro
Nicholas Carter
Umberto Castellani
Bruno Cernuschi-Frias
Ming-Ching Chang
Roland Chapuis
Thierry Chateau
Hong Chen
Xilin Chen
Sen-ching Cheung
Tat-Jun Chin
Mario Christhoudias

Chi-Wei Chu
Andrea Colombari
Jason Corso
Bruce Culbertson
Goksel Dedeoglu
David Demirdjian
Konstantinos Derpanis
Zvi Devir
Stephan Didas
Miodrag Dimitrijevic
Ryan Eckbo
Christopher Engels
Aykut Erdem
Erkut Erdem
Anders Ericsson
Kenny Erleben
Steven Eschrich
Francisco Estrada
Ricardo Fabbri
Xiaodong Fan
Craig Fancourt
Michela Farenzena
Han Feng
Doug Fidaleo
Robert Fischer
Andrew Fitzhugh
Francois Fleuret
Per-Erik Forssén
Ben Fransen
Clement Fredembach
Mario Fritz
Gareth Funka-Lea
Darren Gawely
Atiyeh Ghoreyshi
Alvina Goh

Leo Grady
Kristen Grauman
Ralph Gross
Nicolas Guilbert
Abdenour Hadid
Onur Hamsici
Scott Helmer
Yacov Hel-Or
Derek Hoiem
Byung-Woo Hong
Steve Hordley
Changbo Hu
Rui Huang
Xinyu Huang
Camille Izard
Vidit Jain
Vishal Jain
Christopher Jaynes
Kideog Jeong
Björn Johansson
Marie-Pierre Jolly
Erik Jonsson
Klas Josephson
Michael Kaess
Rahul Khare
Dae-Woong Kim
Jong-Sung Kim
Kristian Kirk
Dan Kushnir
Ville Kyrki
Pascal Lagger
Prasun Lala
Michael Langer
Catherine Laporte
Jean-Marc Lavest

Albert Law
Jean-Pierre Lecadre
Maxime Lhuillier
Gang Li
Qi Li
Zhiguo Li
Hwasup Lim
Sernam Lim
Zicheng Liu
Wei-Lwun Lu
Roberto Lublinerman
Simon Lucey
Gian Luca Mariottini
Scott McCloskey
Changki Min
Thomas Moeslund
Kooksang Moon
Louis Morency
Davide Moschini
Matthias Mühlich
Artiom Myaskouvskey
Kai Ni
Michael Nielsen
Carol Novak
Fredrik Nyberg
Sang-Min Oh
Takahiro Okabe
Kenki Okuma
Carl Olsson
Margarita Osadchy
Magnus Oskarsson
Niels Overgaard
Ozge Ozcanli
Mustafa Ozuysal
Vasu Parameswaran
Prakash Patel
Massimiliano Pavan
Patrick Perez
Michael Phelps

Julien Pilet
David Pisinger
Jean-Philippe Pons
Yuan Quan
Ariadna Quattoni
Kevin Quennesson
Ali Rahimi
Ashish Raj
Ananath Ranganathan
Avinash Ravichandran
Randall Rojas
Mikael Rousson
Adit Sahasrabudhe
Roman Sandler
Imari Sato
Peter Savadjiev
Grant Schindler
Konrad Schindler
Robert Schwanke
Edgar Seemann
Husrev Taha Sencar
Ali Shahrokni
Hong Shen
Fan Shufei
Johan Skoglund
Natalia Slesareva
Jan Sochman
Jan Erik Solem
Jonathan Starck
Jesse Stewart
Henrik Stewenius
Moritz Stoerring
Svetlana Stolpner
Mingxuan Sun
Ying Sun
Amir Tamrakar
Robby Tan
Tele Tan
Donald Tanguay

Leonid Taycher
Ashwin Thangali
David Thirde
Mani Thomas
Tai-Peng Tian
David Tolliver
Nhon Trinh
Ambrish Tyagi
Raquel Urtasun
Joost Van-de-Weijer
Andrea Vedaldi
Dejun Wang
Hanzi Wang
Jingbin Wang
Liang Wang
Martin Welk
Adam Williams
Bob Woodham
Stefan Wörz
Christopher Wren
Junwen Wu
Wen Wu
Rong Yan
Changjiang Yang
Qing-Xiong Yang
Alper Yilmaz
Jerry Yokono
David Young
Quan Yuan
Alan Yuille
Micheal Yurick
Dimitrios Zarpalas
Guoying Zhao
Tao Zhao
Song-Feng Zheng
Jie Zhu
Loe Zhu
Manli Zhu

Sponsoring Institutions

Advanced Computer Vision, Austria
Graz University of Technology, Austria
University of Ljubljana, Slovenia

Table of Contents – Part III

Recognition II

Shape from X

Poster Session III

Tracking and Motion

Multiview Geometry and 3D Methods

Statistical Models and Visual Learning

Face/Gesture/Action Detection and Recognition

Segmentation and Grouping

Visual Tracking

Blind Vision

Shai Avidan[1] and Moshe Butman[2]

[1] Mitsubishi Electric Research Labs,
201 Broadway, Cambridge, MA 02139
avidan@merl.com
[2] Department of Computer Science,
Bar-Ilan University, Ramat-Gan Israel
butmanm@cs.biu.ac.il

Abstract. Alice would like to detect faces in a collection of sensitive surveillance images she own. Bob has a face detection algorithm that he is willing to let Alice use, for a fee, as long as she learns nothing about his detector. Alice is willing to use Bob's detector provided that he will learn nothing about her images, not even the result of the face detection operation. *Blind vision* is about applying secure multi-party techniques to vision algorithms so that Bob will learn nothing about the images he operates on, not even the result of his own operation and Alice will learn nothing about the detector. The proliferation of surveillance cameras raises privacy concerns that can be addressed by secure multi-party techniques and their adaptation to vision algorithms.

1 Introduction

The proliferation of surveillance cameras raises privacy concerns that must be addressed. One way of protecting privacy is to encrypt the images on their way from the camera to the remote server that controls it. However, in some cases this might not be enough. For instance, when the client does not wish to reveal the content of the image even to the server that runs the particular vision algorithm. Consider, for example, a service center offering face detection capabilities over the web. Clients might be interested in the service but reluctant to reveal the content of their images, even to the service provider, either because they don't want the service center to learn the content of the image or they are concerned that virus attacks on the service center will reveal the content of the images. With slight modification the proposed algorithm can be used for blind face recognition. For example, a government agency can have photos of suspects and compare them to images taken from private surveillance cameras without learning anything about the content of the images (so as not to invade privacy), and without revealing the photos of the suspects. The only answer the government agency will learn is either a given suspect appear in a particular image or not. Another application might be in camera phones that does not have the CPU power to run heavy vision algorithms and would like to run the application securely on a remote server. Yet another application is blind OCR

A. Leonardis, H. Bischof, and A. Pinz (Eds.): ECCV 2006, Part III, LNCS 3953, pp. 1–13, 2006.
© Springer-Verlag Berlin Heidelberg 2006

in which the client is not willing to reveal the content of the document to the server. In these cases one can resort to secure multi-party protocols that allow two parties to execute a given algorithm without learning anything about the other party.

Here we investigate the use of secure multi-party protocols for image analysis. This is a challenging task because secure multi-party protocols are known to be computationally intensive and applying them to large data sets, such as images and video streams makes the task even harder. Domain-specific constraints allow us to devise new schemes that are faster to use but might not be applicable to general secure multi-party problems.

As a concrete setup we focus on a surveillance scenario in which Alice owns a surveillance camera and Bob owns a server that runs a face detection algorithm. In our hypothetical scenario Alice and Bob will engage in a protocol that will allow Alice to learn if, and where, are faces in her images without learning anything about Bobs' detector. Bob will learn nothing about the images, not even if faces were detected in them.

We adopt secure multi-party protocols to derive a secure classification protocol. The protocol allows Alice to send Bob a candidate detection window and get a yes/no answer to the question "Is there a face in this window?". This results in a secure protocol that leaks no information to either party, but is slow in practice because of the use of cryptographic primitives. Then we suggest ways to drastically reduce the number of detection windows that Alice needs to send to Bob by using a non-cryptographic protocol that is very fast in practice but is not as secure as the secure classification protocol.

2   Background

Secure multi-party computation originated from the work of Yao [16] who gave a solution to the two-party problem where two parties are interested in evaluating a given function that takes as input private input from each party. As a concrete example consider the millionaire problem: Two parties want to find which one has a larger number, without revealing anything else about the numbers themselves. Later, Goldriech et al. [7] extended the case to $n > 2$ parties. However, the theoretical construct was still too demanding to be of practical use. An easy introduction to Cryptography is given in [14] and a more advanced and theoretical treatment is given in [6].

Since then many secure protocols were reported for various applications. Of particular interest here are those dealing with oblivious transfer [2], secure dot-product [1] or oblivious polynomial evaluation in general [11, 3] and learning decision trees [9]. Oblivious Polynomial Evaluation (OPE) [11, 3] assumes that Bob has a polynomial $P(x)$ and Alice wants to evaluate the polynomial for a particular x, unknown to Bob, without learning anything about the polynomial coefficients. This was later used by [9] to devise an ID3 decision tree learning algorithm where each party holds part of the training data, yet both parties are interested in learning a decision tree that uses all the available training data.

In the end both parties learn the parameters of the decision tree, but nothing about the training data of the other party.

Secure multi-party protocols are often analyzed for correctness, security and complexity. Correctness is measured by comparing the proposed protocol to the ideal protocol where the parties transfer their data to a trusted third party that performs the computation. If the secure protocol is identical to the ideal protocol then the protocol is declared correct (note that one might come up with secure approximation to an ideal algorithm). In security one needs to show what can and cannot be learned from the data exchange between the parties. One often assumes that the parties are *honest but curious*, meaning that they will follow the agreed-upon protocol but will try to learn as much as possible from the data-flow between the two parties. Put another way, one party is willing to trust the other party but is concerned that virus attacks on the other party will reveal the information. Finally, in complexity, one shows the computational and communication complexity of the secure algorithm.

3 Notations

All computations must be done over some finite field F that is large enough to represent all the intermediate results. One can approximate float numbers with fixed arithmetic and represent it as integer numbers in this field. Denote by $\mathbf{X}$ the image that Alice owns. A particular detection window within the image $\mathbf{X}$ will be denoted by $\mathbf{x} \in F^L$ and $\mathbf{x}$ will be treated in vector form. Bob owns a strong classifier of the form

$$H(\mathbf{x}) = sign(\sum_{n=1}^{N} h_n(\mathbf{x})), \tag{1}$$

where $h_n(\mathbf{x})$ is a threshold function of the form

$$h_n(\mathbf{x}) = \begin{cases} \alpha_n & \mathbf{x}^T\mathbf{y_n} > \Theta_n \\ \beta_n & \text{otherwise,} \end{cases} \tag{2}$$

and $\mathbf{y_n} \in F^L$ is the hyperplane of the threshold function $h_n(\mathbf{x})$. The parameters $\alpha_n \in F$, $\beta_n \in F$ and $\Theta_n \in F$ of $h_n(\mathbf{x})$ are determined during training; N is the number of weak classifiers used.

4 Secure Classification

In this section we develop a secure classifier that is based on a linear combination of simple threshold function ('stumps'). However, the ideas presented here can be used to develop other classifiers as well. For example, one can use the OPE protocol mentioned earlier to construct a polynomial-kernel SVM. Work still needs to be done to construct RBF-kernel SVM, or sigmoid-based neural network.

There is an inherent tension between secure multi-party methods and machine learning techniques in that one tries to hide and the other tries to infer. In the extreme case, Alice can use Bob to label training data for her so that she can later use the data to train a classifier of her own. The best we can hope for is to ensure that Bob will not learn anything about Alice's data and that Alice will not help her own training algorithm, other than supplying it with labeled examples, by running the secure classification protocol.

The cryptographic tool we will be using is Oblivious Transfer. Oblivious Transfer allows Alice to choose one element from a database of elements that Bob holds without revealing to Bob which element was chosen and without learning anything about the rest of the elements. In the following we will denote OT_1^M to indicate that Alice needs to chose one out of M elements. We will use OT to develop a series of secure sub-protocols that result in a secure classification protocol.

4.1 Oblivious Transfer

Oblivious Transfer allows Alice to choose one element from a database of elements that Bob holds without revealing to Bob which element was chosen and without learning anything about the rest of the elements. The notion of oblivious transfer was suggested by Even, Goldreich and Lempel [5] as a generalization of Rabin's "oblivious transfer" [13].

Bob privately owns two elements M_0, M_1 and Alice wants to receive one of them without letting Bob know which one. Bob is willing to let her do so provided that she will not learn anything about the other elements. The following protocol, based on RSA encryptions can be used to solve the problem in a semi-honest (i.e. honest but curious) setting.

Algorithm 1. Oblivious Transfer

Input: Alice has $\sigma \in \{0, 1\}$
Input: Bob has two strings M_0, M_1
Output: Alice learns M_σ.

1. Bob sends Alice two different public encryption keys K_0 and K_1.
2. Alice generates a key K and encrypts it with K_0 or K_1. For the sake of argument, let's say she chooses K_0. She sends Bob $E(K, K_0)$; that is, she encrypts K with one of Bob's public keys.
3. Bob does not know which public key Alice used, so he decrypts with both of his private keys. He thus obtains both the real key K, and a bogus one K'.
4. Bob sends Alice $E(M_0, K)$ and $E(M_1, K')$, in the *same* order he sent the keys K_0 and K_1 in step 1. Alice decrypts the first of these messages with the key K and obtains M_0.

Can Alice cheat? She would need to be able to find K', but she cannot do this unless she knows how to decrypt messages encrypted with the public key K_1.

Can Bob cheat? He would have to be able to determine which one of K and K' was the key Alice generated. But K and K' both look like random strings.

4.2 Secure Dot Product

Before diving into the technical details, let us give an intuitive introduction. Our goal is to break the result of the dot product operation $x^T y$ into two shares a and b, where a is known only to Alice, b is known only to Bob and it holds that $x^T y = a + b$. We do this by breaking the product of every pair of elements $x_i * y_i$ into two shares a_i and b_i and then letting Alice and Bob sum the vectors a and b, respectively to obtain shares of the dot product. Observe that a_i and b_i must sum to $x_i * y_i$ where x_i is in the range $[0, 255]$ and $y_i \in \{-1, 0, 1\}$ so the size of the field F should be at least 512 to accommodate all possible cases. The details are given in protocol 2.

Algorithm 2. Secure dot-product

Input: Alice has vector $x \in F^L$
Input: Bob has vector $y \in F^L$
Output: Alice and Bob have private shares a and b s.t. $a + b = x^T y$

1. Bob generates a random vector $b \in F^L$
2. For each i=1...L, Alice and Bob conduct the following sub-steps
   (a) Bob enumerates all possible x_i values and constructs a $256D$ vector a, s.t.

$$a_i = y_i * x_i - b_i \qquad x_i \in [0...255]$$

   (b) Alice uses OT_1^{256} with x_i as her index, to choose the appropriate element from the vector a and stores it as a_i.
3. Alice and Bob sum their private vectors a and b, respectively, to obtain the shares $a = \sum_{i=1}^{L} a_i$ and $b = \sum_{i=1}^{L} b_i$ of the dot-product $x^T y$.

Correctness. The protocol is clearly correct.

Security. The protocol is secure for both parties as we will show next

- From Alice to Bob
  - In step 2(b) Alice uses OT with x_i as an index to choose an element from the vector a. Because OT is secure, Bob can not learn which element she chose and hence can learn nothing about the vector x.
- From Bob to Alice
  - For each element, Bob lets Alice pick one element from the vector a and since a is the sum of the vector y with some random vector b, Alice can learn nothing about y from a.

Complexity and Efficiency. The protocol is linear in L - the dimensionality of the vectors x and y.

4.3   Secure Millionaire

Alice and Bob would like to compare and find which one has a larger number, without revealing anything else about their number [16]. We show here a solution to the problem based on the OT primitive. The idea is to have Alice and Bob represent their numbers in binary format, scan it one bit at a time from left (most significant bit) to right (least significant bit) and then get the result. For each bit Bob should prepare a lookup table that is based on his current bit value and the two possible bit values of Alice. Alice will use OT_1^2 to obtain some

---

Algorithm 3. Secure Millionaire

Input: Alice has a number $x \in F$
Input: Bob has a number $y \in F$
Output: Alice and Bob find out if $x > y$

1. Bob defines three states $\{A, B, U\}$ that correspond to: Alice has a larger number, Bob has a larger number and Undecided, respectively. For each bit, Bob encodes $\{A, B, U\}$ using a different permutation of the numbers $\{1, 2, 3\}$.
2. For the left most bit, Bob constructs a 2-entry lookup table $\mathbf{z}^{(n)}$ using the following table.

	$y_n = 0$	$y_n = 1$
$x_n = 0$	U	B
$x_n = 1$	A	U

where x_n, y_n are the left most (most significant) bit of the numbers x, y, respectively. If $y_n = 0$ then Bob should construct a table from the left column, otherwise he should use the right column.
3. Alice uses OT_1^2 with x_n as her index to obtain $s^{(n)} = z^{(n)}(x_n)$
4. For each $i = n - 1, ..., 1$, Alice and Bob conduct the following sub-steps
   (a) Bob constructs a 6-entry lookup table $\mathbf{z}^{(i)}$ that is indexed by $s^{(i+1)}$ and x_i, s.t.

	$y_i = 0$	$y_i = 1$
$s^{(i+1)} = A \wedge x_i = 0$	A	A
$s^{(i+1)} = B \wedge x_i = 0$	B	B
$s^{(i+1)} = U \wedge x_i = 0$	U	B
$s^{(i+1)} = A \wedge x_i = 1$	A	A
$s^{(i+1)} = B \wedge x_i = 1$	B	B
$s^{(i+1)} = U \wedge x_i = 1$	A	U

where $s^{(i+1)}$ is the state variable from the previous bit. If $y_i = 0$ then Bob should construct a table from the left column, otherwise he should use the right column.
   (b) Alice uses OT_1^6 with $s^{(i+1)}$ and x_i as her indices to obtain $s^{(i)} = \mathbf{z}^{(i)}(s^{(i+1)}, x_i)$
5. Bob sends Alice the meaning of the three states of $s^{(1)}$ of the least significant bit. Alice now knows which number is larger.
6. If she wants, Alice can send the result to Bob.

intermediate result and they both will continue to the next bit. The problem with this approach is that comparing least significant bits is meaningless if the most significant bits were already used to determine which number is larger. Note, also, that Alice and Bob should not abort in the middle of the scan as this might reveal some information about the numbers themselves. To solve this problem we will use a state variable s that can take one of three states: $\mathcal{A}$ Alice has a larger number, $\mathcal{B}$ Bob has a larger number or $\mathcal{U}$ Undecided yet. For each bit Bob constructs a 6-way lookup table that consists of the 3 states of s and the two possible values of the next bit of Alice, the output is the new state after evaluating the current bit. For example, if $s = \mathcal{A}$, Bobs' current bit is 1 and Alice's' current bit is 0 then the output should be $s = \mathcal{A}$ and they both move to the next bit. To prevent Alice from interpreting the state s Bob can use different numbers to represent $\mathcal{A}, \mathcal{B}, \mathcal{U}$ for each bit so, for example, for the first bit $\mathcal{A}$ is represented as the number 1 but for the second bit 1 might represent the symbol $\mathcal{B}$. The details are given in protocol 3.

Correctness. The protocol is clearly correct.

Security. The protocol is secure for both parties as we will show next

- From Alice to Bob
  - In steps 3 and 4b Alice uses x_i as her index in the OT operation. Since OT is secure, Bob can learn nothing about the number x.
- From Bob to Alice
  - For each bit, Bob lets Alice pick one element from the lookup table $\mathbf{z}$ and returns the state s. Since the values of the state s are represented using random numbers for each bit, Alice cannot determine what does a change in s mean and can not learn anything about the number y, other than learning, in the end, if $x > y$.

Complexity and Efficiency. The protocol is linear in the number of bits of the numbers x and y.

4.4 Secure Classifier

We are now ready to present the secure classifier protocol. The protocol relies on the secure dot-product and Millionaire protocols and the details are given in protocol 4.

Correctness. The protocol is clearly correct.

Security. The protocol protects the security of both parties.

- From Alice to Bob
  - In step 2(a) Alice and Bob engage in a secure dot-product protocol so Bob learns nothing about the vector $\mathbf{x}$.
  - In step 2(b) and 3 Alice and Bob engage in secure Millionaire protocol so Bob can learn nothing about Alice's data.

Algorithm 4. Secure Classifier

Input: Alice has input test pattern $\mathbf{x} \in F^L$
Input: Bob has a strong classifier of the form $H(\mathbf{x}) = sign(\sum_{n=1}^{N} h_n(\mathbf{x}))$
Output: Alice has the result $H(\mathbf{x})$ and nothing else
Output: Bob learns nothing about the test pattern $\mathbf{x}$

1. Bob generates a set of N random numbers: $s_1, ..., s_N$, such that $s = \sum_{n=1}^{N} s_n$
2. For each $n = 1, ..., N$, Alice and Bob conduct the following sub-steps:
   (a) Alice and Bob obtain private shares a and b, respectively, of the dot product $\mathbf{x}^T \mathbf{y_n}$ using the secure-dot-product protocol.
   (b) Alice and Bob use the secure Millionaire protocol to determine which number is larger: a or $\Theta_n - b$. Instead of returning $\mathcal{A}$ or $\mathcal{B}$ the secure Millionaire protocol should return either $\alpha_n + s_n$ or $\beta_n + s_n$. Alice stores the result in $\mathbf{c_n}$.
3. Alice and Bob use the secure Millionaire protocol to determine which number is larger: $\sum_{n=1}^{N} \mathbf{c_n}$ or $\sum_{n=1}^{N} \mathbf{s_n}$. If Alice has a larger number then $\mathbf{x}$ is positively classified, otherwise $\mathbf{x}$ is negatively classified.

- From Bob to Alice
  - In step 2(a) Alice and Bob engage in a secure dot-product protocol so Alice learns nothing about Bobs' data.
  - In step 2(b) Alice and Bob engage in a secure Millionaire protocol so Alice only learns if $a > \Theta_n - b$ but since she does not know b she can not learn anything about the parameter Θ_n. Moreover, at the end of the Millionaire protocol Alice learns either $\alpha_n + s_n$ or $\beta_n + s_n$. In both cases, the real parameter (α_n or β_n) is obfuscated by the random number s_n.
  - In step 3 Alice learns if her number $\sum_{n=1}^{N} \mathbf{c_n}$ is greater than Bob's number $\sum_{n=1}^{N} \mathbf{s_n}$. Since $\mathbf{s}$ is a random vector, she can gain no knowledge about the actual parameters of Bobs' strong classifier.
  - Alice can learn the number of weak classifier N from the protocol. This can easily be fixed if Bob will add several fake weak classifiers $h_n(\mathbf{x})$ whose corresponding weights α_n, β_n are zero. This way Alice will only learn an upper bound on N and not N itself.

Complexity and Efficiency. The complexity of the protocol is $O(NLK)$, where N is the number of weak classifiers used, L is the dimensionality of the test vector $\mathbf{x}$ and K it the number of bits in the dot-product $\mathbf{x}^T \mathbf{y_n}$.

Applying the secure classification protocol to face detection is straightforward. Alice scans her image and sends each detection window to Bob for evaluation. Bob learns nothing about the image and Alice only gets a binary answer for every detection window. The problem with the protocol is speed. As we discuss in the experimental section, it might take from a few seconds to a few minutes to classify a detection window (depending on the number of levels in the rejection cascade, see details in the experiments section). This means that the protocol is prohibitively expensive to compute in practice. Therefor we investigate methods to accelerate it.

5   Accelerating Blind Vision

There are three methods to accelerate the above protocol. The first relies on cryptographic methods that leverage a small number of OT operations to perform a large number of OT [12, 8]. We will not explore these methods here.

A second approach would be for Bob to reveal a stripped-down version of his classifier to Alice. This way, Alice can run the stripped-down classifier on her data. This stripped-down classifier will effectively reject the vast majority of detection windows and will allow Alice to use the expansive secure protocol on a relatively small number of detection windows.

Finally, the last method of acceleration is to develop one-way hash functions that will allow Alice to quickly hash her data but still let Bob correctly classify the patterns without learning much about the original image itself. This will be used as a filter to quickly reject the vast majority of detection windows, leaving the "difficult" examples to be classified using the secure classification protocol.

5.1   Image Hashing Using Histograms of Oriented Gradients

There is a large body of literature on one way hash functions [14]. These functions take the input message (detection window in our case) and map it to some hashed vector in such a way that the original message can not be recovered. These one way hash functions are not suitable for our purpose because they map nearby patterns to different locations in hash space. So, two images that are nearby in image space might be mapped to far-apart vectors in the hash space. There is little hope then that a classifier will be able to learn something in the hash space, because the basic assumption that nearby patterns should have similar labels is violated.

We therefor use a domain-specific hash function. Specifically, we use the Histogram of Oriented Gradients (HoG) as our hash function. HoG was proved very useful in a variety of object recognition and detection applications [10, 4], yet it destroys the spatial order of pixels, as well as their absolute values, and is coarsely binned so we assume that recovering the original image patch from a given HoG is impossible. Figure 1 show some examples of face and non-face image patches and their corresponding HoGs.

In our system, Alice computes the HoG for each detection window and store each bin in a response image. We use 18 bin HoG so there are 18 response images used to represent the HoG for every detection window. That is, the 18 bins of the HoG of a particular detection window are stored at the central pixel location of that detection window, across all 18 response images.

By scrambling the order of pixels in the response images we effectively destroy the spatial relationship between the HoGs so Bob can not use this information to reconstruct the original image (the same scrambling permutation must be performed on all 18 response images). Figure 2 show how the response image that corresponds to one of the bins of the HoG looks like with and without scrambling the order of its pixels. Specifically, figure 2b shows a response image that corresponds to one bin in the HoG. Scrambling the order of the pixels (figure 2c)

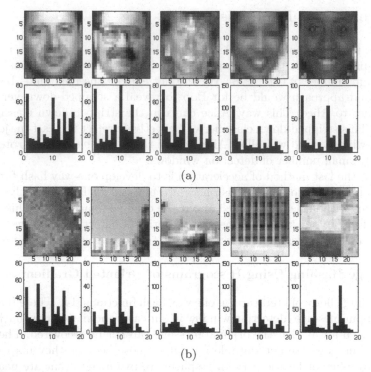

Fig. 1. Image to Histogram of Oriented Gradients (HoG) Hashing. (a) some examples of face images and their corresponding HoG. (b) some example of non-face images and their corresponding HoG. We assume that it is impossible to reconstruct an image from its HoG.

Fig. 2. The importance of scrambling. (a) original image. (b) Image of the first bin of the Histogram of Oriented Gradients (HoG). (c) Same as (b) after pixel scrambling.

destroys the spatial relationship between HoGs. In addition, Alice can bury the scrambled image in a larger image that contain random values (not shown here).

The inclusion of fake HoGs, by burying the response images in a larger image, prevents Bob from recovering the original image, because he does not know if he is using HoGs that came from the original image. Moreover, it prevents Bob from knowing the result of his classification, because he does not know if the

HoGs that he classified as positive (i.e. originated from a detection window that contains a face) correspond to real or fake image patches.

6   Experiments

We implemented the secure classification protocol in C++ using the NTL[1] package for large numbers and used RSA encryption with 128-bit long encryption keys. The HoG detector was implemented in MATLAB. We simulated Alice and Bob on one PC so communication delays are not reported here.

   We converted our Viola-Jones type face detector [15] to a secure detector. In the process we have converted the integral-image representation to regular dot-product operation, a step that clearly slowed down our implementation as we no longer take advantage of the integral image representation. Also, we shifted the values of the filters from the range $[-1, 1]$ to the range $[0, 2]$ to ensure that all values are non-negative integers. We then converted all the thresholds to non-negative integers and updated them to reflect the shift in the filter values. The face detector consists of a cascade of 32 rejectors, where each rejector is of the form presented in equation 1. The first rejector requires 6 dot-product operations and the most complicated rejector require 300 dot-products. There is a total of 4303 dot-products to perform. Instead of computing the secure dot-product for each filter, we use OT to compute the secure dot-product for all the weak classifiers in a given level and allowed Alice and Bob to make a decision after every level of the cascade. This clearly reveal some information to Alice, as she knows at what level of the cascade a pattern was rejected but it greatly accelerates the performance of the program. We found that a single 24×24 detection window can be classified in several minutes using all the levels of the cascade. In most cases the first two levels of the cascade are enough to reject a pattern and they can be processed in a few seconds per detection window. As expected, the main bottleneck of the protocol is the extensive use of the OT operation.

   To accelerate performance we used the HoG based image hashing. Each 24×24 detection window was mapped to HoG as follows. Alice first computes the gradient of every pixel and ignores every pixel whose x and y gradients were below 5 intensity values. Then she binned the gradient orientation into 18 bins and stored the result in a histogram. She then sends the HoGs, in random order and together with some fake HoGs, to Bob. Bob's HoG detector consists of a cascade of 45 levels. Each level of the cascade consists of a feed-forward neural network with 5 hidden units that was trained to reject as many negative examples as possible, while maintaining 98% of its positive examples. The unoptimized HoG detector takes several seconds to process a single 240×320 image. We found that on average the HoG detector rejects about 90% of the detection windows in an image. The remaining 10 percent are classified using the secure classifier protocol described earlier. In a typical case, about 15, 000 detection windows (out of a total of about 150, 000 detection windows) will be passed to the secure classification protocol. This approach accelerates secure classification

---

(a-1)   (a-2)

(b-2)   (b-2)

Fig. 3. Blind Face Detection. (a) result after running the HoG detection. (b) Final detection result.

by an order of magnitude, at the risk of revealing some information. There is clearly a trade-off between the quality of the HoG detector and the amount of information revealed.

Figure 3 show some typical results. The top row shows the result of the HoG detection, as Alice sees them. The bottom row shows the result, as Alice sees it, after the secure classification. A couple of comments are in order. First, note that after the HoG detection the only thing that Bob knows is that he detected several thousands candidates. He does not know their spatial relationship, how they actually look or if they came from the original image or are simply chaff designed to confuse him. Second, the HoG detector is performed in a multi-scale fashion. In our case Alice uses a 3 level pyramid with a scale factor of 1.2 between scales. Finally, all the detection windows that were positively classified by the HoG detector are then scaled to 24×24 windows and fed to the secure classifier protocol.

7   Conclusions

Blind Vision applies secure multi-party techniques to image related algorithms. As an example we have presented a blind face detection protocol that reveals no information to either party at the expanse of heavy computation load. We then suggested image hashing technique, using Histogram of Oriented Gradients (HoG) to accelerate the detection process, at the risk of revealing some information about the original image. There are several extensions to this work. First is the need to accelerate the detection process. Second is the need to develop secure versions to other popular classifiers such as RBF or sigmoid function. Third, we are investigating information theoretic approaches to analyze the amount of information leaked by the HoG hash function, as well as developing better and more secure image hashing functions. Finally we are exploring ways to extend Blind Vision to other vision algorithms such as object tracking or image segmentation.

References

1. M. J. Atallah and W. Du. *Secure multi-party computational geometry*. In WASDS2001: 7th International Workshop on Algorithms and Data Structures, pp 165-179, Providence Rhode Island, USA, August 8-10 2001.
2. C. Cachin. *Efficient private bidding and auctions with an oblivious third party*. In Proceedings of the 6th ACM conference on Computer and Communications Security, pp 120-127, Singapore, November 1-4 1999.
3. Y.C. Chang and C.J. Lu. *Oblivious polynomial evaluation and oblivious neural learning*. In AsiaCrypt: Advances in Cryptology. LNCS, Springer-Verlag, 2001.
4. N. Dalal and B. Triggs. *Histograms of Oriented Gradients for Human Detection*. In IEEE Conference on Computer Vision and Pattern Recognition (CVPR), 2005.
5. S. Even, O. Goldreich and A. Lempel, *A Randomized Protocol for Signing Contracts*, Communications of the ACM 28, pp. 637-647, 1985.
6. O. Goldreich, *Foundations of Cryptography*, 2004.
7. O. Goldreich, S. Micali and A. Wigderson. *How to play any mental game - a completeness theorem for protocols with honest majority*. In 19th ACM Symposium on the Theory of Computing, pp 218-229, 1987.
8. Y. Ishai, J. Kilian, K. Nissim and E. Petrank. *Extending Oblivious Transfers Efficiently*. In CRYPTO 2003, pp 145-161.
9. Y. Lindell and B. Pinkas, *Privacy preserving data mining*. In Advances in Cryptology - Crypto2000, LNCS 1880, 2000.
10. D.G. Lowe, *Distinctive image features from scale-invariant keypoints*. International Journal of Computer Vision, 60(2):91-110, 2004.
11. M. Naor and B. Pinkas, *Oblivious Polynomial Evaluation*. In Proc. of the 31st Symp. on Theory of Computer Science (STOC), Atlanta, GA, pp. 245-254, May 1-4, 1999.
12. M. Naor and B. Pinkas, *Efficient Oblivious Transfer Protocols*. In Proc. of the twelfth annual ACM-SIAM symposium on Discrete algorithms , Washington, D.C., USA pp. 448-457, 2001.
13. M. O. Rabin, *How to exchange secrets by oblivious transfer*, Tech. Memo TR-81, Aiken Computation Laboratory, 1981.
14. B. Schneier, *Applied Cryptography*, 1996.
15. P. Viola and M. Jones, *Rapid Object Detection using a Boosted Cascade of Simple Features*. In IEEE Conference on Computer Vision and Pattern Recognition, Hawaii, 2001.
16. A. C. Yao, *How to generate and exchange secrets*, 27th FOCS, pp. 162-167, 1986.

Object Detection by Contour Segment Networks

Vittorio Ferrari[1], Tinne Tuytelaars[2,*], and Luc Van Gool[1,2]

[1] Computer Vision Group (BIWI), ETH Zuerich, Switzerland
[2] ESAT-PSI, University of Leuven, Belgium
{ferrari, vangool}@vision.ee.ethz.ch,
tuytelaa@esat.kuleuven.be

Abstract. We propose a method for object detection in cluttered real images, given a single hand-drawn example as model. The image edges are partitioned into contour segments and organized in an image representation which encodes their interconnections: the Contour Segment Network. The object detection problem is formulated as finding paths through the network resembling the model outlines, and a computationally efficient detection technique is presented. An extensive experimental evaluation on detecting five diverse object classes over hundreds of images demonstrates that our method works in very cluttered images, allows for scale changes and considerable intra-class shape variation, is robust to interrupted contours, and is computationally efficient.

1 Introduction

We aim at detecting and localizing objects in real, cluttered images, given a single hand-drawn example as model of their shape. This example depicts the contour outlines of an instance of the object class to be detected (e.g. bottles, figure 1d; or mugs, composed by two outlines as in figure 5a).

The task presents several challenges. The image edges are not reliably extracted from complex images of natural scenes. The contour of the desired object is typically fragmented over several pieces, and sometimes parts are missing. Moreover, locally, edges lack specificity, and can be recognized only when put in the wider context of the whole shape [2]. In addition, the object often appears in cluttered images. Clutter, combined with the need for a 'global view' of the shape, is the principal source of difficulty. Finally, the object shape in the test image can differ considerably from the one of the example, because of variations among instances within an object class (*class variability*).

In this paper, we present a new approach to shape matching which addresses all these issues, and is especially suited to detect objects in substantially cluttered images. We start by linking the image edges at their discontinuities, and partitioning them into roughly straight contour segments (section 3). These segments are then *connected* along the edges and across their links, to form the image representation at the core of our method: the *Contour Segment Network* (section 4). By recording the segment interconnections, the network captures the underlying image structure, and enables to cast

---

* T. Tuytelaars acknowledges support by the Fund for Scientific Research Flanders (Belgium).

A. Leonardis, H. Bischof, and A. Pinz (Eds.): ECCV 2006, Part III, LNCS 3953, pp. 14–28, 2006.

object detection as finding paths through the network resembling the model outlines. We propose a computationally efficient matching algorithm for this purpose (section 5). The resulting, possibly partial, paths are combined into final detection hypotheses by a dedicated integration stage (section 6).

Operating on the Contour Segment Network brings two key advantages. First, even when most of the image is covered by clutter segments, only a limited number is connected to a path corresponding to a model outline. As we detail in section 5, this greatly limits the choices the matcher has to make, thus allowing to correctly locate objects even in heavily cluttered images. Besides, it also makes the computational complexity *linear* in the number of test image segments, making our system particularly efficient. Second, since the network connects segments also over edge discontinuities, the system is robust to interruptions along the object contours, and to short missing parts.

Our method accommodates considerable class variability by a flexible measure of the similarity between configurations of segments, which focuses on their overall spatial arrangement. This measure first guides the matching process towards network paths similar to the model outlines, and is then used to evaluate the quality of the produced paths and to integrate them into final detections. As other important features, our approach can find multiple object instances in the same image, produces point correspondences, and handles large scale changes.

In section 7 we report results on detecting five diverse object classes over hundreds of test images. Many of them are severely cluttered, in that the object contours form a small minority of all image edges, and they comprise only a fraction of the image. Our results compare favorably against a baseline Chamfer Matcher.

2   Previous Work

The construction of our Contour Segment Network (sections 3 - 4) is rooted in earlier perceptual organization works [14, 12]. However, unlike these, we do not seek to single out salient edge groups. Instead, we connect all subsequent segments in a single, global network which comprises all possible contour paths. This enables our main contribution: to perform object class detection as path search on the network.

Much previous work on shape matching has focused on class variability. Several measures of shape similarity have been proposed [2, 1]. They can distinguish objects of different classes, while allowing for variations and deformations within a class. However, these works assume the object to be in a clean image, thereby avoiding the problem of localization, and the difficulties of contour detection. Hence, the rest of this review focuses on methods handling clutter.

Our algorithm of section 5 is related to "local search" [4] and "interpretation trees" [11], as it iteratively matches model features to test image features. However, at each iteration it meets an approximately constant, low number of matching candidates (only those connected to the latest matched segment, section 5). Interpretation Trees / Local Search approaches instead, need consider a large number of test features (often all of them [4]). As a consequence, our method is far less likely to be confused by clutter, and has lower computational complexity (*linear* in the number of test segments), thus it can afford processing heavily cluttered images (with typically about 300 clutter segments, compared to only 30 in [4]). Besides, both [4, 11] expect the model to transform rigidly to the test image, while our method allows for shape variations.

Deformable template matching techniques deform a template shape so as to minimize some energy function, e.g. diffusion-snakes [7], elastic matching [5], and active shape models [6]. These approaches require rough initialization near the object to be found. Additionally, several such methods need multiple examples with registered landmark points [6], and/or do not support scale changes [7]. Chamfer matching methods [10] can detect shapes in cluttered images, but, as pointed out by [17, 13], they need a large number of templates to handle shape variations (a thousand in [10]), and are prone to produce rather high false-positive rates (1-2 per image in [10]). Recently Berg et al. [3] proposed a powerful point-matching method based on Integer Quadratic Programming. However, the nature and computational complexity of the optimization problem require to explicitly set rather low limits on the maximal portion of clutter points, and on the total number of points considered from the test image (via a sampling scheme). This is not suitable when the objects' edge points are only a fraction of the total in the image. Besides, [3] uses real images as models, so it is unclear how it would perform when given simpler, less informative hand-drawings. The same holds for [16], whose approach based on edge patches seems unsuited in our setting. Felzenszwalb [8] applies Dynamic Programming to find the optimal locations of the vertices of a polygonal model on a regular image grid. Since the computational complexity is quadratic in the number of grid points, it is intractable to have a high resolution grid, which is necessary when the object covers a small portion of the image (while [8] has a 60×60 grid, taking 5 minutes, using a 180×180 grid would be 81 times slower).

In contrast to previous contributions, our method combines the attractive properties of dealing with highly cluttered images, allowing for shape variations and large scale changes, working from a single example, being robust to broken edges, and being computationally efficient.

3 Early Processing

Detecting and linking edgel-chains. Edgels are detected by the excellent Berkeley natural boundary detector [15], which was recently successfully applied to object recognition [3]. Next, edgels are chained and a smoothing spline curve is fit to each edgel-chain, providing estimates of the edgels' tangent orientations.

Due to the well-known brittleness of edge detection, a contour is often broken into several edgel-chains. Besides, the ideal contour might have branchings, which are not captured by simple edgel-chaining. We counter these issues by *linking* edgel-chains: an edgel-chain c_1 is linked to an edgel-chain c_2 if any edgel of c_2 lies within a search area near an endpoint of c_1 (figure 1). The search area is an isosceles trapezium. The minor base rests on the endpoint of c_1, and is perpendicular to the curve's tangent orientation, while the height points away from c_1[1]. This criterion links c_1 to edgel-chains lying *in front* of one of its endpoints, thereby indicating that it could *continue over* c_2. The trapezium shape expresses that the uncertainty about the continuation of c_1's location grows with the distance from the breakpoint. Note how c_1 can link either to an endpoint

---

[1] The dimensions of the trapezium are fixed, and the same in all experiments.

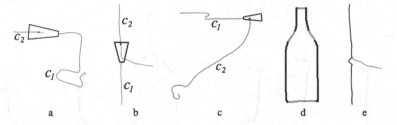

Fig. 1. (a-c) Example links between edgel-chains. (a) Endpoint-to-endpoint link. (b) Tangent-continuous T-junction link. (c) Tangent-discontinuous link. (d) 8 segments on a bottle-shaped edgel-chain. (e) A segment (marked with an arc) bridging over link b.

of c_2, or to an interior edgel. The latter allows to properly deal with T-junctions, as it records that the curve could continue in two directions (figure 1b). Besides, we point out that it is not necessary for the end of c_1 to be oriented like the bit of c_2 it links to (as in figure 1b). Tangent-discontinuous links are also possible (figure 1c).

The edgel-chain links are the backbone structure on which the Contour Segment Network will be built (section 4).

Contour segments. The elements composing the network are *contour segments*. These are obtained by partitioning each edgel-chain into roughly straight segments. Figure 1d shows the segmentation for a bottle-shaped edgel-chain. In addition to these regular segments, we also construct segments *bridging* over tangent-continuous links between edgel-chains. The idea is to bridge the breaks in the edges, thus recovering useful segments missed due to the breaks.

4   Building the Contour Segment Network

Equipped with edgel-chain links and contour segments, we are ready to build the image representation which lies at the heart of this paper: the Contour Segment Network (or just *network*, for short). To this end, we *connect* segments along edgel-chains, and across links between edgel-chains. Thanks to the explicit modeling of the edgel-chains' interconnections, the network supports robust matching of shapes in cluttered images.

Definitions. Before explaining how to build the network, we give a few definitions. First, every segment is *directed*, in that it has a *back* and a *front*. This only serves to differentiate the two endpoints, they have no semantic difference. As a convention, the front of a segment is followed by the back of the next segment on the edgel-chain. Second, every edgel-chain link is directed as well: the edgel-chain c_1, on which the trapezium search-area rests, is at the back, while the other edgel-chain c_2 is at the front. This also defines the front and back endpoints of a segment bridging between two edgel-chains. For clarity, we use the word *links* between edgel-chains, and *connections* between segments.

Rules. The network is built by applying the following rules, illustrated in figure 2. These connect the front of each segment to a set of segments, and its back to another set of

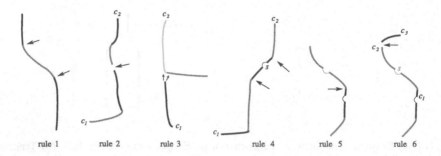

Fig. 2. The six rules to build the Contour Segment Network. They connect (arrows) regular segments and bridging segments (marked with an arc). Rules 2-6 connect segments over different edgel-chains c_i.

segments. Thus the network structure is unconstrained and its complexity adapts to the image content.

1. The front of a segment is connected to the back of the next segment on the same edgel-chain.
2. When two edgel-chains c_1, c_2 are linked at endpoints, the segment of c_1 before the link is connected to the segment of c_2 after the link.
3. Consider a T-junction link (i.e. from an endpoint of c_1 to the interior of c_2). The segment of c_1 before the link is connected to the *two* segments of c_2 with the closest endpoints. As can be seen in figure 2.3, this records that the contour continues in both directions.
4. Let s be a segment bridging over a link from c_1 to c_2. s is connected to the segment of c_2 coming after its front endpoint, *and* to the segment of c_1 coming before its back endpoint.
5. Two bridging segments which have consecutive endpoints on the same edgel-chain are connected. Here 'consecutive' means that no other segment lies inbetween.
6. Consider a bridging segment s without front connection, because it covers the front edgel-chain c_2 until its end. If c_2 is linked to another edgel-chain c_3, then we connect s to the segment of c_3 coming after its front endpoint. An analogue rule applies if s lacks the back connection.

Although they might seem complex at first sight, the above rules are pretty natural. They connect two segments if the edges provide evidence that they could be connected on an ideal edge-map, where all edges would be detected and perfectly chained. Notice how the last three rules, dedicated to bridging segments, create connections analog to those made by the first three rules for regular segments. Therefore, both types are treated consistently.

Since each edgel-chain is typically linked to several others, the rules generate a complex branching structure, a *network* of connected segments. The systematic connections across different edgel-chains, together with the proper integration of bridging segments, make the network robust to incomplete or broken edgel-chains, which are inevitable in real images. Figure 3 shows a segment on a bottle outline, along with all

Fig. 3. Network connectedness. All black segments are connected to S, up to depth 8. They include a path around the bottle (thick).

connected segments up to depth 8 (those reachable following up to 8 connections). Although there is no single edgel-chain going all around the bottle, there is a path doing so, by spanning several edgel-chains. It is the task of the forthcoming matching stage to discover such desired paths.

5   Basic Matching

By processing the test image as described before, we obtain its Contour Segment Network. We also segment the contour chains of the model, giving a set of contour segment chains along the outlines of the object.

The detection problem can now be formulated as finding paths through the network which resemble the model chains. Let's first consider a subproblem, termed *basic matching*: find the path most resembling a model chain, starting from a basis match between a model segment and a test image segment. However we do not know a priori where to start from, as the test image is usually covered by a large majority of clutter segments. Therefore, we apply the basic matching algorithm described in this section, starting from all pairs of model and test segment with roughly similar orientations. The resulting paths are then inspected and integrated into full detection hypotheses in the next section.

We consider the object transformation from the model to the test image to be composed of a global pose change, plus shape variations due to class variability. The pose change is modeled by a translation t and a scale change σ, while class variability is accommodated by a flexible measure of the similarity between configurations of segments.

The basic matching algorithm. The algorithm starts with a basis match between a model segment b_m and a test segment b_t, and then iteratively matches the other model segments, thereby tracing out a path in the network. The matched path $\mathcal{P}$ initially only contains $\{b_m, b_t\}$.

1. *Compute the scale change σ of the basis match.*
2. *Move to the next model segment m. Points 3-6 will match it to a test segment.*

3. *Define a set $\mathcal{C}$ of candidate test segments.* These are all successors[2] of the current test segment in the network, and their successors (figure 4a). Including successors at depth 2 brings robustness against spurious test segments which might lie along the desired path.
4. *Evaluate the candidates.* Each candidate is evaluated according to its orientation similarity to m, how well it fits in the path $\mathcal{P}$ constructed so far, and how strong its edgels are (more details below).
5. *Extend the path.* The best candidate c_{best} is matched to m and $\{m, c_{best}\}$ is added to $\mathcal{P}$.
6. *Update σ.* Re-estimate the scale change over $\mathcal{P}$ (more details below).
7. *Iterate.* The algorithm iterates to point 2, until the end of the model segment chain, or until the path comes to a dead end ($\mathcal{C} = \emptyset$). At this point, the algorithm restarts from the basis match, proceeding in the backward direction, so as to match the model segments lying before the basis one.

For simplicity, the algorithm is presented above as greedy. In our actual implementation, we retain the best two candidates, and then evaluate their possible successors. The candidate with the best sum of its own score and the score of the best successor wins. As the algorithm looks one step ahead before making a choice, it can find better paths.

Evaluate the candidates. Each candidate test segment $c \in \mathcal{C}$ is evaluated by the following cost function[3]

$$q_c = q(m, c, \mathcal{P}) = w_{la}D_{la}(m, c, \mathcal{P}) + w_{ld}D_{ld}(m, c, \mathcal{P}) + w_\theta D_\theta(m, c) \qquad (1)$$

The last term $D_\theta(m, c) \in [0, 1]$ measures the difference in orientation between m and c, normalized by π.

The other terms consider the location of c in the context of test segments matched so far, and compare it to the location of m within the matched model segments. The first such spatial relation is

$$D_{la}(m, c, \mathcal{P}) = \frac{1}{|\mathcal{P}|} \sum_{\{m_i, t_i\} \in \mathcal{P}} D_\theta(\overrightarrow{mm_i}, \overrightarrow{ct_i})$$

the average difference in direction between vectors $\overrightarrow{mm_i}$ going from m's center to the centers of matched model segments m_i, and corresponding vectors $\overrightarrow{ct_i}$ going from c to the matched test segments t_i (see figure 4d). The second relation is analogous, but focuses on the distances between segments

$$D_{ld}(m, c, \mathcal{P}) = \frac{1}{\sigma d_m |\mathcal{P}|} \sum_{\{m_i, t_i\} \in \mathcal{P}} |\sigma\|\overrightarrow{mm_i}\| - \|\overrightarrow{ct_i}\||$$

where d_m is the diagonal of the model's bounding-box, and hence σd_m is a normalization factor adapted to the current scale change estimate σ. Thus, all three terms of function (1) are scale invariant.

---

[2] All segments connected at its free endpoint, i.e. opposite the one connecting to $\mathcal{P}$.
[3] In all experiments, the weights are $w_{la} = 0.7, w_{ld} = 0.15, w_\theta = 1 - w_{la} - w_{ld} = 0.15$.

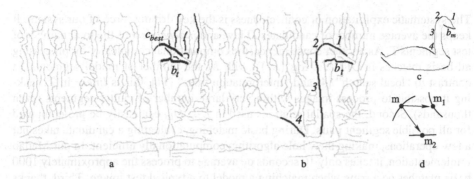

Fig. 4. Basic matching. (a) Iteration 1: basis segment b_t, candidates C with $q_c \leq 0.3$ (black thin), and best candidate c_{best} (thick). (b) Matched path P after iteration 4. (c) Model, with basis segment b_m and segments matched at iteration 1-4 labeled. (d) Example vectors used in D_{la}, D_{ld}.

The proposed cost function grows smoothly as the model transformation departs from a pure pose change. In particular the D_{la} term captures the structure of the spatial arrangements, while still allowing for considerable shape variation. Function (1) is low when c is located and oriented in a similar way as m, in the context of the rest of the shape matched so far. Hence, it guides the algorithm towards a path of test segments with an overall shape similar to the model.

Analyzing the values of q_c over many test cases reveals that for most correct candidates $q_c < 0.15$. In order to prevent the algorithm from deviating over a grossly incorrect path when no plausible candidate is available, we discard all candidates with q_c above the loose threshold $q_{th} = 0.3$. Hence: $C \leftarrow \{c | q_c \leq q_{th}\}$.

In addition to the geometric quality q_c of a retained candidate c, we also consider its *relevance*, in terms of the average strength of its edgels $\nabla_c \in [0, 1]$. Hence, we set the overall cost of c to $q_c \cdot (1 - \nabla_c)$. Experiments show a marked improvement over treating edgels as binary features, when consistently exploiting edge strength here and in the path evaluation score (next section).

Update σ. After extending P the scale change σ is re-estimated as follows. Let δ_m be the average distance between pairs of edgels along the model segments, and δ_t be the corresponding distance for the test segments. Then, set $\sigma = \frac{\delta_t}{\delta_m}$. This estimation considers the relative locations of the segments, together with their individual transformations, and is robust to mismatched segments within a correct path (unlike simpler measures such as deriving σ from the bounding-box areas). Thanks to this step, σ is continuously adapted to the growing path of segments, which is useful for computing D_{ld} when matching segments distant from the basis match. Due to shape variability and detection inaccuracies, the scale change induced by a single segment holds only locally.

Properties. The basic matching algorithm has several attractive properties, due to operating on the Contour Segment Network. First and foremost, at every iteration it must chose among only a few candidates (about 4 on average), because only segments *connected* to the previous one are considered. Since it meets only few distractors, it is likely to make the right choices and thus find the object even in substantially cluttered images.

The systematic exploitation of connectedness is the key driving force of our system. It keeps the average number of candidates D low, and *independent* of the total number of test segments T. As another consequence, the computational complexity for processing all basis matches is $O(TMD\log^2(M))$, with M the number of model segments. In contrast to "local search" [4] and "interpretation trees" [11], this is *linear* in T, making it possible to process images with a very large number of clutter segments (even thousands). Second, the spatial relations used in D_{la}, D_{ld} can easily be pre-computed for all possible segment pairs. During basic matching, evaluating a candidate takes but a few operations, making the whole algorithm computationally efficient. In our Matlab implementation, it takes only 10 seconds on average to process the approximately 1000 basis matches occurring when matching a model to a typical test image. Third, thanks to the careful construction of the network, there is no need for the object contour to be fully or cleanly detected. Instead, it can be interrupted at several points, short parts can be missing, and it can be intertwined with clutter contours.

6 Hypothesis Integration

Basic matching produces a large set $\mathcal{H} = \{\mathcal{P}_i\}$ of matched paths $\mathcal{P}_i$, termed *hypotheses*. Since there are several correct basis matches to start from along the object contour, there are typically several correct hypotheses on an object instance (figure 5b+c+d). In this section we group hypotheses likely to belong to the same object instance, and fuse them in a single *integrated hypothesis*. This brings two important advantages. First, hypotheses matching different parts of the same model contour chain, are combined into a single, more complete contour. The same holds for hypotheses covering different model chains, which would otherwise remain disjoint (figure 5d). Second, the presence of (partially) repeated hypotheses is a valuable indication of their correctness (i.e. that they cover an object instance and not clutter). Since the basic matcher prefers the correct path over others, it produces similar hypotheses when starting from different points along a correct path (figure 5b+c). Clutter paths instead, grow much more randomly. Hence, hypothesis integration can accumulate the evidence brought by overlapping hypotheses, thereby separating them better from clutter.

Before proceeding with the hypothesis integration stage, we evaluate the quality of each hypothesis $\mathcal{P} \in \mathcal{H}$. Each segment match $\{m, t\} \in \mathcal{P}$ is evaluated with respect to the others using function (1): $q(m, t, \mathcal{P}\backslash\{m, t\})$. Whereas during basic matching only segments matched *before* were available as reference, here we evaluate $\{m, t\}$ in the context of the entire path. The score of $\{m, t\}$ is now naturally defined by setting the maximum value q_{th} of q as roof: $q_{th} - q(m, t, \mathcal{P}\backslash\{m, t\})$. Finally, the total score of $\mathcal{P}$ is the sum over the component matches' scores, weighed by their relevance (edgel strength ∇)

$$\phi(\mathcal{P}) = \frac{1}{q_{th}} \sum_{\{m,t\}\in\mathcal{P}} \nabla_t \cdot (q_{th} - q(m, t, \mathcal{P}\backslash\{m, t\}))$$

the normalization by $\frac{1}{q_{th}}$ makes ϕ range in $[0, |\mathcal{P}|]$. In order to reduce noise and speedup further processing, we discard obvious garbage hypotheses, scoring below a low threshold $\phi_{th} = 1.5$: $\mathcal{H} \leftarrow \{\mathcal{P}|\phi(\mathcal{P}) \geq \phi_{th}\}$.

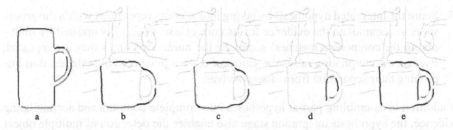

a   b   c   d   e

Fig. 5. Hypothesis integration. a) mug model, composed of an outer and an inner chain (hole). b-d) 3 out of 14 hypotheses in a group. b) and c) are very similar, and arise from two different basis matches along the outer model chain. Instead, d) covers the mug's hole. e) All 14 hypothesis are fused into a complete integrated hypothesis. Thanks to evidence accumulation, its score (28.6) is much higher than that of individual hypotheses (b scores 2.8). Note the important variations of the mug's shape w.r.t the model.

Hypothesis integration consists of the following two phases:

Grouping phase.

1. Let $\mathcal{A}$ be a graph with nodes the hypotheses $\mathcal{H}$, and arcs $(\mathcal{P}_i, \mathcal{P}_j)$ weighed by the (in-)compatibility c_{sim} between the pose transformations of $\mathcal{P}_i, \mathcal{P}_j$: $c_{sim}(\mathcal{P}_i, \mathcal{P}_j) = \frac{1}{2}(c(\mathcal{P}_i, \mathcal{P}_j) + c(\mathcal{P}_j, \mathcal{P}_i))$, with

$$c(\mathcal{P}_i, \mathcal{P}_j) = \frac{|\mathbf{t}_i - \mathbf{t}_j|}{d_m \sigma_i} \cdot \max\left(\frac{\sigma_i}{\sigma_j}, \frac{\sigma_j}{\sigma_i}\right)$$

   The first factor measures the translation mismatch, normalized by the scale change σ, while the second factor accounts for the scale mismatch.

2. Partition $\mathcal{A}$ using the Clique Partitioning algorithm proposed by [9]. Each resulting group contains hypotheses with similar pose transformations. The crux is that a group contains either hypotheses likely to belong to the same object instance, or some clutter hypotheses. Mixed groups are rare.

Integration phase. We now combine the hypotheses within each group $\mathcal{G} \subset \mathcal{A}$ into a single integrated hypothesis.

1. Let the *central hypothesis* $\mathcal{P}_c$ of $\mathcal{G}$ be the one maximizing

$$\phi(P_i) \cdot \left(\sum_{\mathcal{P}_j \in \{\mathcal{G} \backslash \mathcal{P}_i\}} |\mathcal{P}_i \cap \mathcal{P}_j| \cdot \phi(\mathcal{P}_j)\right)$$

   where $|\mathcal{P}_i \cap \mathcal{P}_j|$ is the number of segment matches present in both $\mathcal{P}_i$ and $\mathcal{P}_j$. The central hypothesis best combines the features of having a good score and being similar to the others. Hence, it is the best representative of the group. Note how the selection of $\mathcal{P}_c$ is stable w.r.t. fluctuations of the scores, and robust to clutter hypotheses which occasionally slip into a correct group.

2. Initialize the integrated hypothesis as $\mathcal{G}_{int} = \mathcal{P}_c$, and add the hypothesis $\mathcal{B}$ resulting in the highest combined score $\phi(\mathcal{G}_{int})$. This means adding the parts of $\mathcal{B}$ that match model segments unexplained by $\mathcal{G}_{int}$ (figure 5d, with initial $\mathcal{G}_{int}$ in 5b). Iteratively add hypotheses until $\phi(\mathcal{G}_{int})$ increases no further.

3. Score the integrated hypothesis by taking into account repetitions within the group, so as to accumulate the evidence for its correctness. $\phi(\mathcal{G}_{int})$ is updated by multiplying the component matches' scores by the number of times they are repeated. Evidence accumulation raises the scores of correct integrated hypotheses, thus improving their separation from false-positives.

In addition to assembling partial hypotheses into complete contours and accumulating evidence, the hypothesis integration stage also enables the detection of multiple object instances in the same test image (delivered as separate integrated hypotheses). Moreover, the computational cost is low (1-2 seconds on average).

The integrated hypotheses $\mathcal{G}_{int}$ are the final output of the system (called *detections*). In case of multiple detections on the same image location, we keep only the one with the highest score.

7   Results and Conclusions

We present results on detecting five diverse object classes (bottles, swans, mugs, giraffes, apple logos) over 255 test images[4] covering several kinds of scenes. In total, the objects appear 289 times, as some images contain multiple instances. As all images are collected from *Google Images* and *Flickr*, they are taken under varying, uncontrolled conditions. While most are photographs, some paintings, drawings, and computer renderings are included as well. The target objects appear over a wide range of scales. Between the smallest and the largest detected swan there is a scale factor of 4, while for the apple logos class, there is a factor of 6. The system is given only a single hand-drawn example of each class (figure 7, i2-j3), and its parameters are always kept fixed.

Figures 6 and 7 show example detections. In many test cases the object is successfully and accurately localized in spite of extensive clutter, and even when it comprises only a small portion of the image (e.g. b1, b3, e1, h2). The dominant presence of clutter edges is illustrated in a2, b2, c2, with the edge-maps for cases a1, b3, c3. The object contours form only a small minority of all image edges (about 1/30). The capacity of handling large scale changes is demonstrated in d1 and e1, where the mug sizes differ by a scale factor of 3. Moreover, the individual shapes of the detected objects vary considerably, and differ from the models, hence showing the system's tolerance to class variations. Compare d3 and e2 to the bottle model, or the variations among different mugs. In d1 we overlay the model after applying the best possible translation and scale.

Five of the six mugs imaged in figure c1 are found by the system, proving its ability to detect multiple object instances in the same image. As examples of the accuracy of our method, figures d2 and g2 display the image contours matched to the object for cases d1, d3, and g1 (the other cases are reported as the bounding-boxes of the matched contours).

We quantitatively assess performance as the number of correct detections (bounding-box on an instance of the target object class) and false positives (other detections). All five models have been matched to all 255 test images. The thick curves on plots i2-j3

---

[4] The dataset is available on our website: www.vision.ee.ethz.ch/~ferrari

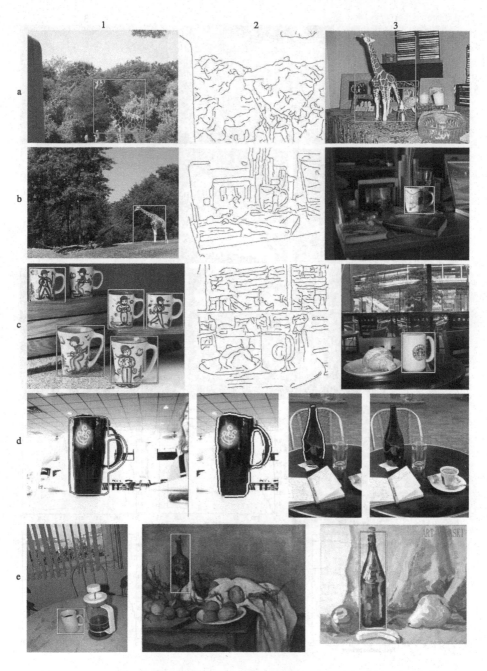

Fig. 6. Results (first page). See text for discussion.

26   V. Ferrari, T. Tuytelaars, and L. Van Gool

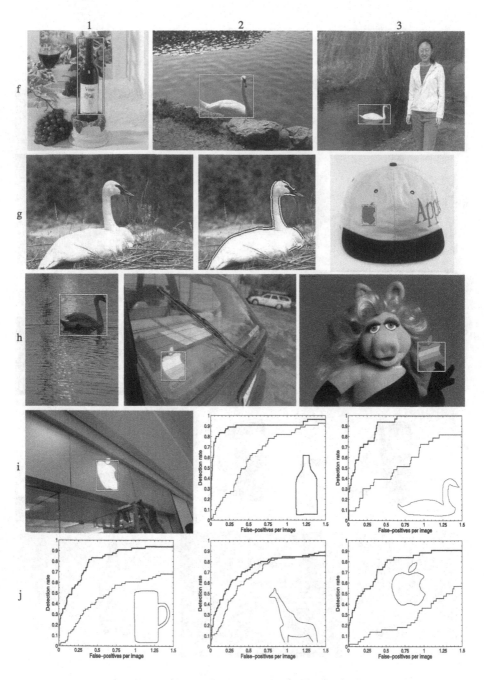

Fig. 7. Results (second page). See text for discussion.

depict the percentage of correct detections (detection-rate) versus the incidence of false-positives (number of false-positives per image FPPI). The system performs well on all five classes, and achieves a remarkable 82% average detection rate at the moderate rate of 0.4 FPPI. For a baseline comparison, we processed the dataset also with a simple Chamfer Matching algorithm[5]. The model is shifted over the image at several scales, and the local maxima of the Chamfer distance give detection hypotheses. In case of multiple overlapping hypotheses, only the strongest one is retained. As the plots show (thin curves) the Chamfer Matcher performs markedly worse than our approach, and reaches an average detection-rate of only 39% at 0.4 FPPI. As also pointed out by [13], the reason is that the Chamfer distance is about as low on clutter edgels areas as it is on the target object, resulting in many false-positives hardly distinguishable from correct detections. The problem is particularly outspoken in our setting, where only a single template shape is given [17]. Our approach instead, is much more distinctive and thus brings satisfactory performance even in these highly cluttered images.

In conclusion, the experiments confirm the power of the presented approach in dealing with extensive clutter, large scale changes, and intra-class shape variability, while taking only a single hand-drawn example as input. Moreover, it is robust to discontinuous edges, and is computationally efficient (the complexity is linear in the number of image segments). As one limitation, models cannot self-cross or branch, therefore excluding some objects (e.g. chairs, text). Nevertheless, every object with a distinctive silhouette can be modeled by a set of disjoint outlines, even if a detailed drawing would feature crossing/branchings (e.g. most animals, tools, and logos). Future work aims at addressing this issue, as well as learning the class variability from a few examples, to apply it for constraining the matching.

References

1. R. Basri, L. Costa, D. Geiger, D. Jacobs, *Determining the Similarity of Deformable Shapes*, Vision Research, 1998.
2. S. Belongie, J. Malik, J. Puzicha, *Shape Matching and Object Recognition Using Shape Contexts*, PAMI, 24:4, 2002.
3. A. Berg, T. Berg and J. Malik, *Shape Matching and Object Recognition using Low Distortion Correspondence*, CVPR, 2005.
4. J. R. Beveridge and E. M. Riseman, *How Easy is Matching 2D Line Models Using Local Search?*, PAMI, 19:6, 1997
5. A. Del Bimbo, P. Pala, *Visual Image Retrieval by Elastic Matching of User Sketches*, PAMI, 19:2, 1997.
6. T. Cootes, C. J. Taylor, D. H. Cooper, and J. Graham, *Active Shape Models - Their Training and Application*, CVIU, 61:1, 1995.
7. D. Cremers, C. Schnorr, and J. Weickert, *Diffusion-Snakes: Combining Statistical Shape Knowledge and Image Information in a Variational Framework*, Workshop on Variational and Levelset Methods, 2001.
8. P. F. Felzenszwalb, *Representation and Detection of Deformable Shapes*, CVPR'03
9. V. Ferrari, T. Tuytelaars, and L. Van Gool, *Real-time Affine Region Tracking and Coplanar Grouping*, CVPR, 2001.

---

[5] While this does not include multiple orientation planes, we believe they would improve performance only moderately [13].

10. D. Gavrila, V. Philomin, *Real-time Object Detection for Smart Vehicles*, ICCV'99
11. W. Grimson, T. Lozano-Perez, *Localizing Overlapping Parts by Searching the Interpretation Tree*, PAMI, 9:4, 1987.
12. D. Jacobs, *Robust and Efficient Detection of Convex Groups*, PAMI, 18:1, 1996.
13. B. Leibe, B. Schiele, *Pedestrian detection in crowded scenes*, CVPR, 2005.
14. D. Lowe, T. Binford, *Perceptual organization as a basis for visual recognition*, AAAI, 1983
15. D. Martin, C. Fowlkes and J. Malik, *Learning to detect natural image boundaries using local brightness, color, and texture cues*, PAMI, 26(5):530-549, 2004.
16. A. Selinger, R. Nelson, *A Cubist approach to Object Recognition*, ICCV, 1998.
17. A. Thayananthan, B. Stenger, P. Torr, R. Cipolla, *Shape Context and Chamfer Matching in Cluttered Scenes*, CVPR, 2003.

Sparse Flexible Models of Local Features

Gustavo Carneiro[1] and David Lowe[2]

[1] Integrated Data Systems Department,
Siemens Corporate Research,
Princeton, NJ, USA
[2] Department of Computer Science,
University of British Columbia,
Vancouver, BC, Canada

Abstract. In recent years there has been growing interest in recognition models using local image features for applications ranging from long range motion matching to object class recognition systems. Currently, many state-of-the-art approaches have models involving very restrictive priors in terms of the number of local features and their spatial relations. The adoption of such priors in those models are necessary for simplifying both the learning and inference tasks. Also, most of the state-of-the-art learning approaches are semi-supervised batch processes, which considerably reduce their suitability in dynamic environments, where unannotated new images are continuously presented to the learning system. In this work we propose: 1) a new model representation that has a less restrictive prior on the geometry and number of local features, where the geometry of each local feature is influenced by its k closest neighbors and models may contain hundreds of features; and 2) a novel unsupervised on-line learning algorithm that is capable of estimating the model parameters efficiently and accurately. We implement a visual class recognition system using the new model and learning method proposed here, and demonstrate that our system produces competitive classification and localization results compared to state-of-the-art methods. Moreover, we show that the learning algorithm is able to model not only classes with consistent texture (e.g., faces), but also classes with shape only (e.g., leaves), classes with a common shape but with a great variability in terms of internal texture (e.g., cups), and classes of flexible objects (e.g., snake).[1]

1 Introduction

The visual recognition problem is currently one of the most difficult challenges for the computer vision community. Albeit studied for decades, we are still far from a solution that is truly generalizable to many types of visual classes. New attention has been devoted to this problem after the influential papers [2,5], where their main contribution was a combination of principled probabilistic recognition

---

[1] This work was performed while Gustavo Carneiro was at the University of British Columbia.

A. Leonardis, H. Bischof, and A. Pinz (Eds.): ECCV 2006, Part III, LNCS 3953, pp. 29–43, 2006.
© Springer-Verlag Berlin Heidelberg 2006

models and (semi-)local image descriptors. The main goal is to represent a visual class with a generative model comprising both the appearance and spatial distributions of those descriptors. This problem has been aggressively tackled lately, where the objective is to provide efficient models (in terms of learning and inference) with good recognition performance [13, 14, 12, 4, 10, 17, 20, 21]. Note that learning is a method to estimate the model parameters, and inference is an approach to classify a test image as being generated by one of the learned models.

In order to make the problem tractable, most of the current approaches make the following assumptions: 1) mutual independence of the appearance of parts given the model; 2) independence of appearance and geometry of parts given the model; 3) restrictive priors in terms of the geometry and number of parts. It is worth noting that we assume a model part to be represented by a local feature, and the geometry of a part to comprise position, scale, and dominant orientation. The third assumption above has two extremes. One extreme is that the geometry of parts is independent given the model [10, 21] (see the bag of features model in Fig. 1), which reduces the number of parameters to estimate during the learning stage. However, this approach leads to a poor model representation that fails to incorporate any information on the relative geometry of parts. The other extreme is to model the joint distribution of the geometry of parts [13] (see the constellation model in Fig. 1), which produces a rich representation. The main challenge with the latter model is that the number of parameters grows exponentially with the number of parts, and learning quickly becomes intractable even with a relatively small number of parts (e.g., less than 10 parts). It is unclear what types of visual classes can be effectively represented with such a small number of parts.

The middle ground between these two extremes has been intensively studied recently, where the goal is to assume restrictive priors in terms of the geometric configuration of parts in order to improve the efficiency of inference (i.e., fewer hypotheses from a test image to evaluate) and learning (i.e., fewer parameters to estimate). For example, the assumption of a star-shaped [9, 14] or a hierarchical prior configuration of local features [12, 4] (see Fig. 1) reduces the number of parameters to estimate, and inference takes advantage of the fact that all these models possess a "special" node (e.g., root in the tree, or center node in the star-shape model), which serves as a starting point for the formation of hypotheses, and consequently reduces the inference complexity. However, it is not clear what the limitations of those models are in terms of which visual classes can be represented using such restrictive priors in terms of the geometry of parts. Also, even though those methods are capable of dealing with more parts, there is still a limit of 20 to 30 parts, which clearly represents an issue if more complex classes are to be represented. A notable exception is the hierarchical model [4] that is able to deal with hundreds of parts, but it assumes an embedded hierarchical model with a small number of nodes, which might impose limits in the visual classes that can be represented with it. Finally, most of these models' parameters are learned using a (semi-)supervised off-line learning approach. This learning approach decreases the flexibility of those methods in dynamic

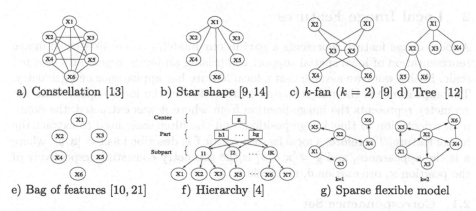

a) Constellation [13]   b) Star shape [9, 14]   c) k-fan (k = 2) [9] d) Tree [12]

e) Bag of features [10, 21]   f) Hierarchy [4]   g) Sparse flexible model

Fig. 1. Graphical geometric models of priors. Note that Xi represents a model part.

environments where new unannotated training images are continuously presented to the learning system.

In this paper we propose: 1) a new model for the visual classification problem that contains a less restrictive prior on the geometry and number of local features, where the geometry of each model part depends on the geometry of its k closest neighbors; and 2) an unsupervised on-line learning algorithm that is capable of identifying commonalities among input images, forming clusters of images with similar appearances, and also estimating the model parameters efficiently and accurately. As commonly assumed in the state-of-the-art works, we also assume that the appearance and the geometry of parts are independent given the model, and that the appearance of parts is mutually independent given model. The main novelty of our model is a prior based on a semi-full dependency of the geometry of parts given model (see Fig. 1-(g)). Note from the graph representing our model that the geometry of each feature depends on the geometry of its k neighboring features, where k is a parameter that defines the degree of connectivity of each part. This prior enables an explicit control on the connectivity of the parts, and it also allows for the object being modeled to have (semi-)local rigid deformation within the area covered by the connected features, and rigid/non-rigid global deformation. Our objective with this new model is to extend the types of classes that can be represented with local image features since the model can potentially have hundreds of parts, tightly connected locally, but loosely connected globally.

We implement a new visual class recognition system using this new model and learning method described above, and demonstrate that our system produces competitive classification and localization results compared to state-of-the-art methods using standard databases. Moreover, we show that the learning algorithm is able to model not only classes with reasonable texture (e.g., faces), but also classes with shape only (e.g., leaves), classes with a common shape but with a great variability in terms of internal texture (e.g., cups), and classes of flexible objects (e.g., snakes).

2   Local Image Features

A local image feature represents a part in our model, and consists of an image representation of local spatial support comprising an image region at a selected scale. In this work we assume that a local feature has appearance and geometry. The appearance is the image feature extracted from the local region, while the geometry represents the image position from where it was extracted, the dominant orientation in that image position, and the filter scale used to extract the image feature. Therefore, a local feature vector $\mathbf{f}$ is described as $\mathbf{f} = [\mathbf{a}, \mathbf{g}]$, where $\mathbf{a}$ is the appearance, and $\mathbf{g} = [\mathbf{x}, \theta, \sigma]$ is the geometry consisting respectively of the position $\mathbf{x}$, orientation θ, and scale σ.

2.1   Correspondence Set

A correspondence set represents a data association between two sets of local features. Let us say we have a set $\mathcal{F}_1 = \{\mathbf{f}_1, ..., \mathbf{f}_M\}$ and another set $\mathcal{F}_2 = \{\hat{\mathbf{f}}_1, ..., \hat{\mathbf{f}}_N\}$. An association is a mapping of the M features from set $\mathcal{F}_1$ to the N feature of set $\mathcal{F}_2$. In this work, a correspondence set is denoted as

$$\mathcal{E} = \{(\mathbf{f}_1, \hat{\mathbf{f}}_{c(1)}), ..., (\mathbf{f}_M, \hat{\mathbf{f}}_{c(M)})\} = \{e_1, ..., e_M\},$$

where $\mathbf{f}_i \in \mathcal{F}_1$, $\hat{\mathbf{f}}_{c(i)} \in \mathcal{F}_2$, and $c(.)$ is a mapping function that associates a feature from $\mathcal{F}_1$ to $\mathcal{F}_2$. When $\mathbf{f}_i \in \mathcal{F}_1$ is not paired with any feature from $\mathcal{F}_2$, then the correspondence is denoted as $(\mathbf{f}_i, \emptyset)$.

3   Probabilistic Model

Assume that there are C visual classes in the database of models, where each class ω_i is represented by a set $\mathcal{F}_i$ of M features, and also by appearance and geometry parameters. Also, consider the presence of a class ω_0 that models general background images. A test image I produces the set $\mathcal{F}_I$ of N features. Then our goal is to first determine the likelihood of the presence of an instance of class ω_i in the test image, and then determine the location of each instance. Hereafter, we refer to the former problem as *classification*, and the latter as *localization*. In order to solve the data association problem, assume that $\mathcal{H}_{iI}$ is the set of all possible correspondence sets from the model features to the test image features. Thus, each correspondence set $\mathcal{E}_{iI} \in \mathcal{H}_{iI}$ has size M (i.e., the number of model features).

The classification of model ω_i given the features $\mathcal{F}_I$ extracted from image I involves the computation of the following ratio:

$$R = \frac{P(\omega_i|\mathcal{F}_I)}{P(\omega_0|\mathcal{F}_I)} = \frac{P(\mathcal{F}_I|\omega_i)P(\omega_i)}{P(\mathcal{F}_I|\omega_0)P(\omega_0)}. \tag{1}$$

The prior ratio $\frac{P(\omega_i)}{P(\omega_0)}$ is assumed to be one, and the likelihood term can be obtained by marginalizing out the variable $\mathcal{E}_{iI} \in \mathcal{H}_{iI}$ that denotes the correspondence set, as follows:

$$P(\mathcal{F}_I|\omega_i) = \sum_{\mathcal{E}_{iI} \in \mathcal{H}_{iI}} P(\mathcal{F}_I, \mathcal{E}_{iI}|\omega_i) = \sum_{\mathcal{E}_{iI} \in \mathcal{H}_{iI}} P(\mathcal{F}_I|\mathcal{E}_{iI}, \omega_i) P(\mathcal{E}_{iI}|\omega_i). \quad (2)$$

Hence, there can be $O(M^N)$ different correspondence sets between $\mathcal{F}_i$ and $\mathcal{F}_I$. However, recall that we aim at a rich visual class representation with hundreds of parts, and possibly thousands of features extracted from a test image, which makes (2) intractable. Therefore, we have to rely on a heuristic that quickly identifies a subset of $\tilde{\mathcal{H}}_{iI} \subset \mathcal{H}_{iI}$ which contains correspondence sets that have the potential to lead to a correct correspondence set. Finally, the likelihood ratio in (1) is then approximated with

$$\frac{P(\mathcal{F}_I|\omega_i)}{P(\mathcal{F}_I|\omega_0)} \approx \max_{\mathcal{E}_{iI} \in \tilde{\mathcal{H}}_{iI}} \frac{P(\mathcal{F}_I|\mathcal{E}_{iI}, \omega_i) P(\mathcal{E}_{iI}|\omega_i)}{P(\mathcal{F}_I|\mathcal{E}_{iI}, \omega_0) P(\mathcal{E}_{iI}|\omega_0)}. \quad (3)$$

First let us concentrate on the term $P(\mathcal{E}_{iI}|\omega)$ in the ratio (3) above. Given the high number of model features, we assume that the prior of having a specific match in the correspondence set is mutually independent of other matches. Therefore, we have

$$P(\mathcal{E}_{iI}|\omega) = \prod_{j=1}^{M} P(e_j|\omega). \quad (4)$$

Basically, $P(e_j|\omega)$ describes the likelihood of detecting model feature $\mathbf{f}_j$ in a test image assuming the presence of model ω.

The term $P(\mathcal{F}_I|\mathcal{E}_{iI}, \omega)$ is computed as follows:

$$P(\mathcal{F}_I|\mathcal{E}_{iI}, \omega) = \left[\prod_{j=1}^{M} P(\hat{\mathbf{a}}_{c(j)}|e_j, \omega) \right] P(\{\hat{\mathbf{g}}_{c(j)}\}_{j=1..M}|\mathcal{E}_{iI}, \omega), \quad (5)$$

where $P(\{\hat{\mathbf{g}}_{c(j)}\}_{j=1..M}|\mathcal{E}_{iI}, \omega) = P(\hat{\mathbf{g}}_{c(M)}|\{\hat{\mathbf{g}}_{c(j)}\}_{j=1..(M-1)}, \mathcal{E}_{iI}, \omega)...P(\hat{\mathbf{g}}_{c(1)}$ $|\mathcal{E}_{iI}, \omega)$, which is the decomposition of the likelihood of feature geometry using the chain rule of probability. The first term $P(\hat{\mathbf{a}}_{c(j)}|e_j, \omega)$ represents the likelihood of having the appearance matching between model feature $\mathbf{f}_j$ and test image feature $\hat{\mathbf{f}}_{c(j)}$. The second term $P(\{\hat{\mathbf{g}}_{c(j)}\}_{j=1..M}|\mathcal{E}_{iI}, \omega)$ denotes the likelihood of having a specific joint geometry of model features that were paired to features in the test image. It is important to mention that the decomposition can happen in all possible ways, which means that feature $\mathbf{f}_1$ does not represent a "special" feature that needs to be found in the test image in order to find all the other model features. As a result, another possible decomposition would be $P(\hat{\mathbf{g}}_{c(1)}|\{\hat{\mathbf{g}}_{c(j)}\}_{j=2..M}, \mathcal{E}_{iI}, \omega)...P(\hat{\mathbf{g}}_{c(M)}|\omega)$. Notice that even though we decompose this joint distribution, its computation still has a high time complexity. Moreover, this joint distribution would make the model sensitive to non-rigid deformations. Therefore, in order to solve these two issues, we approximate $P(\hat{\mathbf{g}}_{c(M)}|\{\hat{\mathbf{g}}_{c(j)}\}_{j=1..(M-1)}, \mathcal{E}_{iI}, \omega)$ to:

$$P(\hat{\mathbf{g}}_{c(M)}|\{\hat{\mathbf{g}}_{c(j)}\}_{j=\arg(\mathcal{K}_{iI}(\mathbf{f}_M, k, \mathcal{E}_{iI}))}, \mathcal{K}_{iI}(\mathbf{f}_M, k, \mathcal{E}_{iI}), \omega), \quad (6)$$

where $\mathcal{K}_{iI}(\mathbf{f}_M, k, \mathcal{E}_{iI}) \subset \mathcal{E}_{iI}$ returns the correspondences containing the k closest model features to feature $\mathbf{f}_M$ in the geometric space of the model. The parameter k denotes how sparsely each model feature is connected to its neighbors and is used to adjust the tradeoff between the richness of representation and the sensitivity of the model to non-rigid deformations. Also the richer the representation is (i.e., larger k), the higher the complexity of computing (6).

3.1 Probabilistic Correspondence Based on Semi-local Geometric Coherence

Equation 6 introduces the likelihood of the geometry of the observed test image feature $\hat{\mathbf{g}}_{c(l)}$ given the geometric information present in the respective k closest model features to $\mathbf{g}_l$ in the space of model geometry. Following up on the idea described in [7], the geometric values of the test image feature $\hat{\mathbf{f}}_{c(l)}$ are predicted using the following pairwise relations:

$$\mathbf{n}_{c(l)c(o)}^T(\mathbf{x}_{c(l)} - \mathbf{x}_{c(o)}) = \|\mathbf{x}_l - \mathbf{x}_o\| + r_{\mathcal{D}}(\mathbf{f}_l, \mathbf{f}_o),$$
$$(\theta_{c(l)} - \theta_{c(o)})_{2\pi} = (\theta_l - \theta_o)_{2\pi} + r_{\mathcal{O}}(\mathbf{f}_l, \mathbf{f}_o),$$
$$\frac{\sigma_{c(l)} - \sigma_{c(o)}}{\sigma_{c(o)}} = \frac{\sigma_l - \sigma_o}{\sigma_o} + r_{\mathcal{S}}(\mathbf{f}_l, \mathbf{f}_o), \qquad (7)$$

where $\mathbf{n}_{c(l)c(o)} = \frac{\mathbf{x}_{c(l)} - \mathbf{x}_{c(o)}}{\|\mathbf{x}_{c(l)} - \mathbf{x}_{c(o)}\|}$, $(.)_{2\pi} \in [0, 2\pi)$, and $r_i(\mathbf{f}_l, \mathbf{f}_o)$ is a Gaussian noise with zero mean and variance $\sigma_i^2(\mathbf{f}_l, \mathbf{f}_o)$ for $i = \mathcal{D}, \mathcal{O}, \mathcal{S}$. The predicted geometry for $\hat{\mathbf{f}}_{c(l)}$, namely $[\hat{\mathbf{x}}_{c(l)}^*, \hat{\theta}_{c(l)}^*, \hat{\sigma}_{c(l)}^*]$ (see Fig. 2), is computed by combining the prediction produced by each one of the k model features assuming that: 1) the variances $\sigma_i^2(\mathbf{f}_l, \mathbf{f}_o)$ are pairwise independent, and 2) the prediction produced by each correspondence is weighted by 1) the distance between these two features in the model space.

Therefore, the likelihood in Eq. 6 can be written as:

$$g([\mathbf{x}_{c(M)}, \theta_{c(M)}, \sigma_{c(M)}]^T - [\mathbf{x}_{c(M)}^*, \theta_{c(M)}^*, \sigma_{c(M)}^*]^T; \Sigma_t), \qquad (8)$$

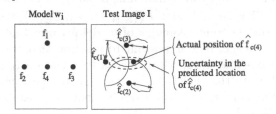

Fig. 2. Example of position prediction. Given the set of model features $\{\mathbf{f}_l\}_{l \in \{1,2,3,4\}}$, suppose we want to estimate the position of test image feature $\hat{\mathbf{f}}_{c(4)}$. The probable location of the feature (represented by an ellipsoid) is based on a Gaussian distribution computed using the position of the correspondences in the test and model images and the pairwise variances $\sigma_{\mathcal{D}}^2(\mathbf{f}_l, \mathbf{f}_o)$ estimated in the learning stage.

where $g(.)$ is the Gaussian function with zero mean, and Σ_t is the weighted covariance computed with the k pairwise variances.

There are two important issues to mention in the computation above. The first issue is the computation of the likelihood of the first match in the correspondence set, which is calculated as $P(\mathbf{g}_1|\mathcal{K}_{iI}(\mathbf{f}_1, k, \mathcal{E}_{iI}), \omega) = \frac{1}{2\pi} \frac{1}{A} \frac{1}{(\sigma_{\mathrm{MAX}}-\sigma_{\mathrm{MIN}})}$, where 2π represents the range of orientation, A is the area of the image in the original image resolution, and $(\sigma_{\mathrm{MAX}} - \sigma_{\mathrm{MIN}})$ denotes the range of scales that the image has been processed. The second issue is the computation of the geometry likelihood assuming the model ω_0. Here we assume that, conditioned on the model ω_0, the likelihood of finding a feature with some specific geometry is independent and uniformly distributed, as follows $P(\{\mathbf{g}_j\}_{j=1..M}|\mathcal{E}_{iI}, \omega_0) = M\frac{1}{2\pi} \frac{1}{A} \frac{1}{(\sigma_{\mathrm{MAX}}-\sigma_{\mathrm{MIN}})}$.

3.2 Probabilistic Correspondences Based on Feature Appearance

The probability of the appearance match between model feature $\mathbf{f}_j$ and test feature $\hat{\mathbf{f}}_{c(j)}$ is denoted in (5) by $P(\hat{\mathbf{a}}_{c(j)}|e_j, \omega)$. According to [8], the distribution of feature similarities between $\mathbf{f}_j$ and $\hat{\mathbf{f}}_{c(j)}$ can be adequately approximated with a *beta distribution* for the cases where this correspondence represents either a correct or a false matching. The beta distribution, denoted as $P_\beta(x; a, b)$, is defined in terms of two parameters a and b. The parameters a_{on} and b_{on} will be learned for each feature $\mathbf{f}_j$ belonging to the model ω_i to explain the observed distribution of feature similarity values given a correct correspondence, and the parameters a_{off} and b_{off} will be learned for the distribution of similarities given a false correspondence. Hence, given the features $\mathbf{f}_j$ and $\hat{\mathbf{f}}_{c(j)}$, and their similarity denoted by $s(\mathbf{f}_j, \hat{\mathbf{f}}_{c(j)}) \in [0, 1)$, the likelihood of having correct and false appearance correspondences are respectively computed with:

$$P(\hat{\mathbf{a}}_{c(j)}|e_j, \omega_i) = P_\beta(s(\mathbf{f}_j, \hat{\mathbf{f}}_{c(j)}); a_{\mathrm{on}}(\mathbf{f}_j), b_{\mathrm{on}}(\mathbf{f}_j)),$$
$$P(\hat{\mathbf{a}}_{c(j)}|e_j, \omega_0) = P_\beta(s(\mathbf{f}_j, \hat{\mathbf{f}}_{c(j)}); a_{\mathrm{off}}(\mathbf{f}_j), b_{\mathrm{off}}(\mathbf{f}_j)). \qquad (9)$$

Finally, recall from Sec. 2.1 that a model feature can remain unmatched. In this case, the term $P(e_j|\omega)$ in (4), which denotes the probability of detecting model feature $\mathbf{f}_j$, works as a penalizing factor. That is, when $e_j = (\mathbf{f}_j, \emptyset)$, then $P((\mathbf{f}_j, \emptyset)|\omega)$ equals one minus the probability of detecting $\mathbf{f}_j$ [8].

4 Matching

The basic matching process consists of finding an initial correspondence set, and iteratively searching for additional correspondences assuming that the previous matches are correct. This process iterates as long as there are still model features available to match test image features. This matching process is not restricted to work with a single type of local feature. As exemplified in [14], this helps in the representation of different types of visual classes. Here, our model uses the following two different types of local image features: SIFT [18], and the multi-scale phase feature [6].

Assuming that the parameters of the distributions above have been learned (see Sec. 5), the matching process selects correspondence sets that produce a ratio $R > \tau_R$, where τ_R is an arbitrary constant (note that we can have more than one correct correspondence set, which means that several classes can be detected in the same test image and also multiple instances of the same class can also be detected in one test image). As explained in Sec. 3, the exhaustive search of correspondence sets is intractable, so we rely on certain heuristics for the matching process. We start the matching process with a nearest neighbor search, which builds the following correspondence set: $\mathcal{E}_{iI} = \{(\mathbf{f}_j, \hat{\mathbf{f}}_{c(j)}) | \mathbf{f}_j \in \mathcal{F}_i, \hat{\mathbf{f}}_{c(j)} \in \mathcal{F}_I, s(\mathbf{f}_j, \hat{\mathbf{f}}_{c(j)}) > \tau_s, \neg \exists \mathbf{f}_k \in \mathcal{F}_i \text{ s.t. } s(\mathbf{f}_k, \hat{\mathbf{f}}_{c(j)}) > s(\mathbf{f}_j, \hat{\mathbf{f}}_{c(j)})\}$, where $s(.) \in [0,1)$ represents the similarity between two features, and τ_s is an arbitrary threshold (here $\tau_s = 0.6$ for the phase feature and $\tau_s = 0.55$ for SIFT, where the similarity measure for SIFT is normalized to be between 0 and 1). The next step comprises a feature clustering step, which assumes that the model suffered a specific type of spatial distortion and groups correspondences that move coherently according to that distortion type. This clustering process can assume rigid distortions (e.g., [18]) or non-rigid ones (e.g., [7, 16]). Similarly to [15, 19, 10], our method does not rely heavily on this initial set of matches produced by the grouping algorithm. In fact, these initial groups are useful as initial guesses for the matching algorithm. Moreover, it does not matter whether this initial grouping is robust to non-rigid deformations since the model, in the process of expanding its correspondence set, is robust to non-rigid deformation because it depends more on nearby features than on far away features for the semi-local coherence presented in Sec. 3.1. Therefore, we adopt a simple Hough clustering approach with a restrictive rigid model (i.e., the bins in the Hough transform space are relatively small) that makes it extremely robust to outliers in the group, but sensitive to non-rigid deformations (see [7]). Specifically, for Hough clustering we used the following bin sizes: 5° for rotation, factor of 2 for scale, and 0.05 times the maximum model diameter for translation. This restrictiveness results in a high number of groups, with each one having just a few correspondences.

4.1   Expanding the Correspondence Set

Given the groups built by the nearest neighbor search and clustering scheme, the expansion of each group is based on the following algorithm:

Algorithm 1 (Matching). *Assuming that G groups have been formed by the clustering process, where each group is denoted as $\mathcal{E}_{iI}^g$, the process of expanding this initial correspondence set is based on the following steps:*

1. For each set $g \in \{1, ..., G\}$, do
   (a) Select the closest model feature $\mathbf{f}_j$ to any of the model features in $\mathcal{E}_{iI}^g$,

$$j = \arg \min_{(\mathbf{f}_j \in \mathcal{F}_i), (e_j \notin \mathcal{E}_{iI}^g)} \{\|\mathbf{x}_j - \mathbf{x}_l\|\}_{e_l \in \mathcal{E}_{iI}^g}$$

*(b) Select the the next correspondence to include in $\mathcal{E}_{iI}^g$ according to $c(j) =$
arg max$_{\hat{\mathbf{f}}_{c(j)} \in \mathcal{F}_I} P(\hat{\mathbf{f}}_{c(j)} | \mathcal{E}_{iI}^g, \omega_i)$ (see Eq. 5). Note that this computation
does not have to be run over all test image features, since only a very
small percentage of test image features lie sufficiently close to the predicted position, orientation, and scale of model feature $\mathbf{f}_j$;*

*(c) If $P(\hat{\mathbf{a}}_{c(j)} | e_j, \omega_i) P(\hat{\mathbf{g}}_{c(j)} | \{\mathbf{g}\}_{j=1..,(j-1)}, \mathcal{E}_{iI}^g, \omega_i) P(e_j | \omega_i) > \tau_P$ (here, τ_P is
dynamically determined based on the appearance parameters of the fea-
ture in 9 and the pairwise variances in (7), then include the correspon-
dence $(\hat{\mathbf{f}}_{c(j)}, \mathbf{f}_j)$ in $\mathcal{E}_{iI}^g$, else include $(\emptyset, \mathbf{f}_j)$ in $\mathcal{E}_{iI}^g$;*

(d) Return to step 1 above until all model features are included in $\mathcal{E}_{iI}^g$.

An example of the matching between two images containing faces (of different
people) is shown in Fig. 3. Note that the matching algorithm tends to expand significantly the initial set $g \in \{1, ..., G\}$ when it contains correct
correspondences.

Step 1(a) has complexity $O(M)$ if performed with linear search, where M
is the number of model features. However, approximate nearest-neighbor search
algorithms [3] can find the nearest neighbor with high probability (which is
sufficient for our purposes) in $O(\log(M))$ time. Both the number of groups to
try, G, and the number of test features to consider in step 1(b), K, are bounded
by constants. Therefore, the complexity of the Alg. 1 is $O(M \log(M))$. Recall that
the models leading to the most efficient matching procedures in the literature
are the k-fans [9] and the star shape [14]. The former method has complexity

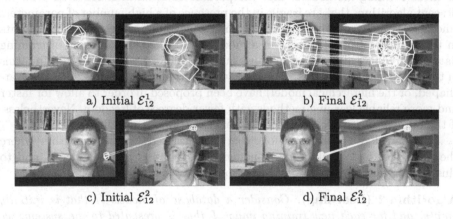

a) Initial $\mathcal{E}_{12}^1$ b) Final $\mathcal{E}_{12}^1$

c) Initial $\mathcal{E}_{12}^2$ d) Final $\mathcal{E}_{12}^2$

Fig. 3. Matching a pair of images using Algorithm 1. The first column shows the initial
group from the heuristic based on nearest neighbor and Hough clustering. The next
column illustrates the final group after the process of expanding this initial group. The
group in the first row is a correct match that can be considerably expanded, while the
second row shows a false initial match. The octagonal shaped features represent the
multi-scale phase feature [6], and the square shaped features represent SIFT [18]. The
white line connecting features from the left to the right image shows the correspondence.

$O(MH^K)$, where H is the total number of places in the image, where $H \gg M$, and $K >= 1$. The latter method has complexity $O(NM)$, where N is the number of parts detected in an image, so $N > M$. Hence, both methods would be intractable for large values of M such as those used in our experiments.

5 Learning

In this section we describe the process of learning the following model parameters:

- For each model feature $\mathbf{f}_j \in \mathcal{F}_i$ it is necessary to learn
  - the parameters of the feature conditional similarity distribution given ω_i (i.e., $a_{\text{on}}(\mathbf{f}_j)$ and $b_{\text{on}}(\mathbf{f}_j)$) and ω_0 (i.e., $a_{\text{off}}(\mathbf{f}_j)$ and $b_{\text{off}}(\mathbf{f}_j)$),
  - the probability of feature detection given ω_i and ω_0: $P(e_j|\omega_i)$, and $P(e_j|\omega_0)$, respectively.
- For each pair of model features $\mathbf{f}_l$ and $\mathbf{f}_o$, it is necessary to learn
  - the variance of the Gaussian noise affecting the distance, main orientation, and scale between $\mathbf{f}_l$ and $\mathbf{f}_o$ (see Eq. 7): $\sigma_D^2(\mathbf{f}_l, \mathbf{f}_o)$, $\sigma_O^2(\mathbf{f}_l, \mathbf{f}_o)$, and $\sigma_S^2(\mathbf{f}_l, \mathbf{f}_o)$, respectively.

In the literature, the process of learning model parameters similar to the above consists of, first, clustering features in the feature space (either manually [12], or automatically [13]), and then, estimating the local feature and spatial parameters based on maximum likelihood estimation. The main issue involved in those learning methods is that the parameter estimation relies on gradient descent algorithms that are fragile in the presence of a high number of parameters since it can easily get stuck in local minima, which imposes very restrictive limits in the number of parts present in a model. Also, the time and size of training data required for this estimation grows quickly (e.g., exponential in [13]) in terms of the number of parameters. Therefore, weakly connected models (e.g., the star-shaped, or the hierarchical model) have been proposed in order to allow for faster and more reliable learning methods with fewer degrees of freedom. Nevertheless, if the number of parts exceeds say 20 parts, learning is usually intractable.

In this work, we propose the following unsupervised learning algorithm, where the main idea is to build correspondence sets between pairs of images and to cluster images that have strong correspondences.

Algorithm 2 (Learning). *Consider a database of models Ω that is initially empty, and for each new training image I that is presented to the system, we have the following steps:*

1. *For each $\omega_i \in \Omega$,*
   (a) Run the matching Algorithm 1 to find an instance of ω_i in I, and select the correspondence set that maximizes the following ratio:

$$\mathcal{E}_{iI}^* = \arg \max_{\mathcal{E}_{iI}^g \in \tilde{\mathcal{H}}_{iI}} \frac{P(\mathcal{F}_I|\mathcal{E}_{iI}^g, \omega_i)P(\mathcal{E}_{iI}^g|\omega_i)}{P(\mathcal{F}_I|\mathcal{E}_{iI}^g, \omega_0)P(\mathcal{E}_{iI}^g|\omega_0)}$$

(b) *If the number of matched features in $\mathcal{E}_{iI}^*$ exceeds $\tau_\mathcal{E}$ (i.e., correspondences $(\mathbf{f}_j, \hat{\mathbf{f}}_{c(j)}) \in \mathcal{E}_{iI}^*$, such that $\hat{\mathbf{f}}_{c(j)} \neq \emptyset$; here $\tau_\mathcal{E} = 30$) then update model ω_i using the correspondence set $\mathcal{E}_{iI}^*$ as the initial guess for matching the image I to each image included in model ω_i using the matching Algorithm 1.*

2. *If the image I failed to match any model $\omega_i \in \Omega$, then form a new model containing all image features and default values for the model parameters.*

3. *For every model $\omega_i \in \Omega$, build a graph, where each node represents an image present in ω_i, and the edges between nodes have weights proportional to the number of non-empty correspondences found between these two images, and then run a connected component analysis so that the initial model can be split into tightly connected groups of images.*

4. *Search for common images present in two distinct models, say ω_i and $\omega_j \in \Omega$. If a common image is found between a pair of models, then check for common features in this image that is present both models, and based on that, join the two models into one single model.*

The output of this learning algorithm is a database of models, where each model consists of the images clustered together, the correspondence sets formed between pairs of model images, the features found in those sets, and the appearance and geometric parameters. In order to learn the parameters of the feature conditional similarity distribution given ω_i (i.e., $a_{on}(\mathbf{f}_j)$ and $b_{on}(\mathbf{f}_j)$), we build the

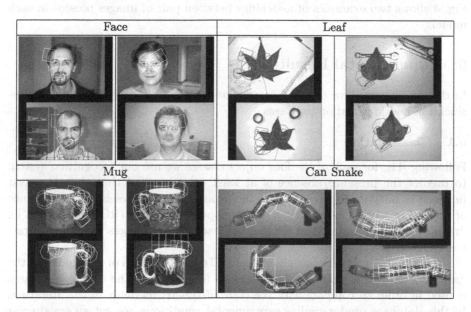

Fig. 4. Illustration of the correspondence sets between two pairs of images for each model. Note that each correspondence set between two images of the same model is shown in a single cell, where the arrangement of the features in the top image must find a similar structure in the bottom image.

histogram of feature similarities of each model feature and, assuming a beta distribution (Sec. 3.2), estimate its parameters [8]. The distribution given ω_0 (i.e., $a_{\text{off}}(\mathbf{f}_j)$ and $b_{\text{off}}(\mathbf{f}_j)$) is then estimated computing the similarities between the model feature and the closest 20 background features (in the feature space)[8]. Note that the background features are extracted from 100 random images (see [8] for more details). The probability of feature detection given ω_i is computed with the detection rate of each model feature in ω_i, and the detection given ω_0 is the probability of detecting a feature in any image (this is done by computing the detection rate of any feature in the database of random images). The variance of the Gaussian noise affecting the distance, main orientation, and scale between pairs of model feature is computed using the correspondence sets in the model ω_i. Finally, it is important to mention that the user has to specify the *upper bound* of the total number of features to be included in the model. Defining this upper bound on the number of model features is important in order to limit the computational complexity of the matching as defined in Sec. 4.1. Note that the model can have any number of features as long as this number is smaller than this user defined upper-bound. Whenever the learner has to eliminate features, it resorts to the classification based on the appearance statistics of the feature [8].

Our learning algorithm is used to build the models of the following databases: a) faces [13] (526 images), b) leaves [1] (186 images), c) mugs (74 images), and d) snake of cans [7] (40 images). For each database, we randomly selected half of the images for training, and the remaining images are used for testing. Fig. 4 shows two examples of matchings between pair of images present in each model.

6   Experimental Results

In this section we show the performance or our recognition system for the classification and localization problems.

6.1   Classification

Following [11], for each of the four object classes we use our recognition system to predict the presence/absence of at least one object of that class in a test image. The output of the classifier is the ratio (1) that represents the confidence of the object's presence so that a receiver operating curve (ROC) curve can be drawn. Note that we use the database of background images from [1] to draw the ROC curve.

In our first experiment, we show the ROC curves for each of the models in the database, and some examples of matchings (see Fig. 5). The database of faces is used in order to compare with the state-of-the-art methods in the literature. In this database, under similar experimental conditions, we get an equal error rate (EER) of 98.2% (recall that EER is the point at which the true positive rate equals one minus the false positive rate). The Face model in this experiment contains 3000 features and connectivity $k = 20$. This represents a competitive result compared to the EER=96.4% in [13] and of 98.2% in [9]. The EER is a

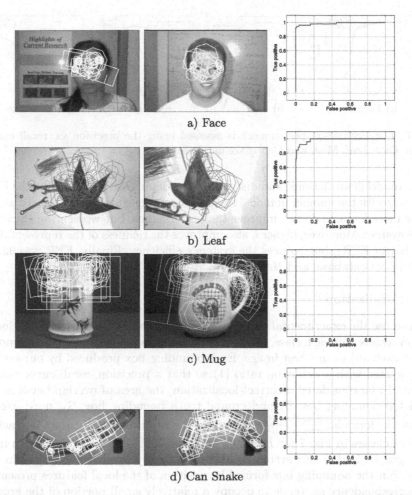

a) Face

b) Leaf

c) Mug

d) Can Snake

Fig. 5. Two examples of correspondence sets found in test images and the ROC curve for each model

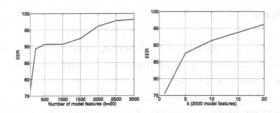

Fig. 6. EER versus number of training features and k for the Face database

function of the following two things (see Fig. 6): a) number of features present in the model, and b) connectivity k. The number of features in the model can be reduced by selecting a subset of the model features that are robust and detectable

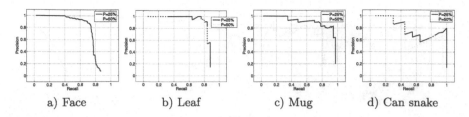

a) Face   b) Leaf   c) Mug   d) Can snake

Fig. 7. The localization performance is assessed using the precision vs. recall curves for the Face, Leaf, Mug, and Can snake databases

under model deformations, and distinctive (for details see [8]). Usually, the EER improves with the number of model features until it reaches a point of saturation, where more features do not improve the performance, but worsen the efficiency of the system. Moreover, higher k also improves the richness of the representation (i.e., better EER), but reduces the system's efficiency. Finally, EER was 92.1% for the Leaf database, and 100% for the Mug and Can Snake databases.

6.2   Localization

We also use the experimental conditions described in [11] to illustrate the localization results. For each class, the task of our classifier is to predict the bounding box of each object in a test image. Each bounding box produced by our system is associated with a detection ratio (1) so that a precision/recall curve can be drawn. To be considered a correct localization, the area of overlap between the predicted bounding box B_p and ground truth bounding box B_{gt} must exceed $P\%$ by the formula: $\frac{area(B_b \cap B_{gt})}{area(B_p \cup B_{gt})}$. We show the precision recall curves for each of the four classes in Fig. 7 for $P = 50\%$ and $P = 25\%$. The main conclusion from these graphs is that our system is able to correctly localize the object in the image, but the bounding box formed by position of the local features present in the correspondence set tends to occupy a relatively small portion of the ground truth.

7   Conclusions

We have shown that it is possible to efficiently derive object class models containing hundreds of features by allowing each feature to depend on only its k closest neighbors. This has the additional advantage that it can represent flexible objects in a natural way because their local geometry is often more tightly constrained than their global geometry. Our novel on-line learning algorithm is able to cluster images with similar appearance, identify consistent subsets of features, and efficiently estimate their model parameters. Experimental results show that this approach can be applied across a variety of object classes, even if they are defined by only a small subset of shared features.

Acknowledgements. The authors would like to thank Kevin Murphy for useful discussions during the progress of this work and to thank Allan Jepson and Sven Dickinson for sharing the Mug database. The authors also wish to acknowledge funding received from NSERC (Canada) to support this research.

References

1. http://www.vision.caltech.edu/html-files/archive.html.
2. Y. Amit and D. Geman. A computational model for visual selection. *Neural Computation*, 11:1691–1715, 1999.
3. S. Arya, D.M. Mount, N.S. Netanyahu, R. Silverman, and A.Y. Wu. An optimal algorithm for approximate nearest neighbor searching. *Journal of the ACM*, 45:891–923, 1998.
4. G. Bouchard and B. Triggs. Hierarchical part-based visual object categorization. In *CVPR*, 2005.
5. M. Burl, M. Weber, and P. Perona. A probabilistic approach to object recognition using local photometry and global geometry. In *ECCV*, 1998.
6. G. Carneiro and A. Jepson. Multi-scale local phase features. In *CVPR*, 2003.
7. G. Carneiro and A. Jepson. Flexible spatial models for grouping local image features. In *CVPR*, 2004.
8. G. Carneiro and A.Jepson. The distinctiveness, detectability, and robustness of local image features. In *CVPR*, 2005.
9. D. Crandall, P. Felzenszwalb, and D. Huttenlocher. Spatial priors for part-based recognition using statistical models. In *CVPR*, 2005.
10. G. Csurka, C. Bray, and C. Dance L. Fan. Visual categorization with bags of keypoints. In *ECCV Workshop on Statistical Learning in Computer Vision*, 2004.
11. M. Everingham, L. Van Gool, C. Williams, and A. Zisserman. Pascal Visual Object Classes Challenge Results. 2005.
(http://www.pascal-network.org/challenges/VOC/voc/results_050405.pdf).
12. P. Felzenszwalb and D. Huttenlocher. Pictorial structures for object recognition. *IJCV*, 61(1):55–79, 2005.
13. R. Fergus, P. Perona, and A. Zisserman. Object class recognition by unsupervised scale-invariant learning. In *CVPR*, 2003.
14. R. Fergus, P. Perona, and A. Zisserman. A sparse object category model for efficient learning and exhaustive recognition. In *CVPR*, 2005.
15. V. Ferrari, T. Tuytelaars, and Luc Van Gool. Simultaneous object recognition and segmentation by image exploration. In *ECCV*, 2004.
16. S. Lazebnik, C. Schmid, and J. Ponce. Semi-local affine parts for object recognition. In *BMVC*, 2004.
17. B. Liebe and B. Schiele. Interleaved object categorization and segmentation. In *BMVC*, 2003.
18. D. Lowe. Object recognition from local scale-invariant features. In *ICCV*, 1999.
19. P.Moreels, M.Maire, and P. Perona. Recognition by probabilistic hypothesis construction. In *ECCV*, 2004.
20. D. Ramanan, D. Forsyth, and K. Barnard. Detecting, localizing, and recovering kinematics of textured animals. In *CVPR*, 2004.
21. N. Vasconcelos. *Bayesian models for visual information retrieval.* PhD thesis, Massachusetts Institute of Technology, 2000.

Differential Geometric Consistency Extends Stereo to Curved Surfaces

Gang Li and Steven W. Zucker

Department of Computer Science,
Yale University,
New Haven, CT 06520, USA
{gang.li, steven.zucker}@yale.edu

Abstract. Traditional stereo algorithms implicitly use the frontal parallel plane assumption when exploiting contextual information, since the smoothness prior biases towards constant disparity (depth) over a neighborhood. For curved surfaces these algorithms introduce systematic errors to the matching process. These errors are non-negligible for detailed geometric modeling of natural objects (e.g. a human face). We propose to use contextual information geometrically. In particular, we perform a differential geometric study of smooth surfaces and argue that geometric contextual information should be encoded in Cartan's moving frame model over local quadratic approximations of the smooth surfaces. The result enforces geometric consistency for both depth and surface normal. We develop a simple stereo algorithm to illustrate the importance of using such geometric contextual information and demonstrate its power on images of the human face.

1   Introduction

Viewing someone's face at about 1 meter provides a rich description of its surface characteristics. While two-view dense stereo vision has achieved remarkable success [22], this success has been limited to objects with restricted geometry. Assuming a rectified stereo pair [7, 8], many stereo algorithms either explicitly or implicitly exploit the *frontal parallel plane assumption*, which assumes position disparity (or depth) is constant (with respect to the rectified stereo pair) over a region under consideration. We seek to move beyond this assumption and to develop richer descriptions of smooth surfaces curving in space (Fig.1).

Traditional area-based stereo algorithms (e.g. SSD) explicitly use the frontal parallel plane assumption by comparing a window of the same size and shape in the left and right images for the similarity measure. Results often exhibit a "staircase" effect for slanted or curved surfaces. To address this problem, [9] uses a parameterized planar or quadratic patch fit; [10] uses variable window size (but fixed shape); [5] uses disparity derivatives to deform the matching window; [2, 16] model each segmented region as a slanted or curved surface while segmentation and correspondence are iteratively performed; [25] seeks correspondence for image regions instead of individual pixels; [23] uses a PDE-based approach for wide baseline dense stereo.

A. Leonardis, H. Bischof, and A. Pinz (Eds.): ECCV 2006, Part III, LNCS 3953, pp. 44–57, 2006.

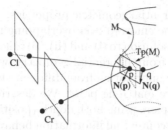

Fig. 1. Given a regular surface $M \subset \mathbb{R}^3$, the tangent plane $T_p(M)$ (in solid lines) and surface normal $\mathbf{N}(\mathbf{p})$ at a point $\mathbf{p}$ are well defined. Traditional stereo algorithms using contextual information (between $\mathbf{p}$ and a neighboring point $\mathbf{q}$) use the frontal parallel plane (in dotted lines) as the local surface model at $\mathbf{p}$. This implicit use of the frontal parallel plane assumption will result in a bias towards frontal parallel plane reconstruction, which is fundamentally flawed for curved surfaces. The correct use of contextual information should encode the change of both position and surface normal (at $\mathbf{p}$ and $\mathbf{q}$) on the surface. A differential geometric account of such contextual information is our contribution in this paper.

Since point-wise geometric constraints (e.g. epipolar constraint) and similarity measure (e.g. SSD) cannot always resolve matching ambiguities, it is natural to explore contextual information, i.e. requiring neighboring matching pairs to be "consistent". However such consistency often implicitly uses the frontal parallel plane assumption: [17] uses a local excitatory neighborhood of the same disparity level to support the current matching pair, while [27] refines local support as the sum of all match values within a 3D local support volume. [1] represents surface depth, orientation, boundaries, and creases as random variables. In the nonlinear diffusion algorithm [21], local support at different disparity hypotheses is diffused iteratively, and the amount of diffusion is controlled by the quality of the disparity estimate. In [3] a smoothness term over neighboring pixels is introduced in an energy functional minimized by graph cuts. In [24, 26] messages (similarity measures weighted by gaussian smoothed disparity differences) are passed between nearby matching pairs in a Markov network by belief propagation. These algorithms implicitly use the frontal parallel plane assumption because the neighboring matching pairs interact in a way such that the frontal parallel plane solution is preferred (Fig.1).

1.1   Our Approach

Systematic errors will be introduced by both the explicit and the implicit use of the frontal parallel plane assumption (see experiment section for details). Although the explicit use of this assumption has been addressed (e.g.[5]), the implicit use in the contextual inference stage has received little attention. To move beyond this assumption and overcome such errors, locally it implies that the tangent plane $T_p(M)$ deviates from the frontal parallel plane. Our geometric observation then arises in several forms: (i) varying the shape of matching patches in the left/right images; (ii) interpolating integer coordinates; (iii) relating disparity derivatives to surface differential geometric properties; and (iv) (at least) surface normal consistency must be enforced over overlapping neighborhoods. Devernay and Faugeras [5] provide a solution to (i) and (ii). To take full advantage of (iii) and (iv), which follow directly from differential geometry, we exploit (Cartan) transport to combine geometric information from different surface normals in a neighborhood around a putative matching point. We describe geometric consistency between nearby matching pairs using both depth (position disparity) and surface normal, thus showing that contextual information behaves like an *extra geometric constraint* for stereo correspondence. To our knowledge this is the first time such geometric contextual constraints among nearby matching pairs have been used explicitly in stereo vision.

2 Background

2.1 Initial Local Information from Deformed Matching Window

Assuming a rectified stereo pair [7, 8], traditional area based methods compare a small window (e.g. 11x11) centered at (u, v) in the left image with a window of the same size and shape at $(u-d, v)$ in the right image using a similarity measure such as SSD, and select a disparity estimate d based on such a measure. When the scene within the window satisfies the frontal parallel plane assumption the above method is valid. But for slanted or curved 3D surfaces such a formulation is incorrect. Consider a small image window of a curved surface: If the correspondence of (u, v) in the left image is $(u - d, v)$ in the right image, then to a first order approximation the correspondence of $(u + \delta u, v + \delta v)$ in the left image is $(u + \delta u - d - \frac{\partial d}{\partial u}\delta u - \frac{\partial d}{\partial v}\delta v, v + \delta v)$ in the right image, with $\frac{\partial d}{\partial u}$ and $\frac{\partial d}{\partial v}$ the partial derivatives of disparity d with respect to u and v, respectively; δu and δv are a small step size in each direction.

With this formulation of the similarity measure, the *local initial correspondence problem* is then: for every (u, v) in the left image, select $\{d, \frac{\partial d}{\partial u}, \frac{\partial d}{\partial v}\}$ that gives the best similarity measure of the deformed window SSD:

$$\arg \min_{\{d, \frac{\partial d}{\partial u}, \frac{\partial d}{\partial v}\}} \sum_{(u+\delta u, v+\delta v) \in \mathcal{N}_{..}} (I_l(u + \delta u, v + \delta v)- \tag{1}$$

$$\hat{I}_r(u + \delta u - d - \frac{\partial d}{\partial u}\delta u - \frac{\partial d}{\partial v}\delta v, v + \delta v))^2$$

where $\mathcal{N}_{uv}$ denotes the window centered at (u, v), and $\hat{I}_r$ is the linearly interpolated intensity of two nearest integer index positions in the right image. We use the direction set method [19], a multidimensional minimization method, initialized with the integer disparity d_I (obtained from traditional SSD) and zeros for the first order disparities. The results are the (interpolated) floating point disparity d and first order disparities $\{\frac{\partial d}{\partial u}, \frac{\partial d}{\partial v}\}$ that achieve the best similarity measure at (u, v). They could also be obtained by enumerating different combinations of these parameters if they are properly quantized, and selecting the set that minimizes deformed window SSD. In [5] such a deformed window was also used. Our contribution is to relate the deformation to surface orientation and to impose geometric consistency over overlapping neighborhoods by using surface orientation, which provides extra geometric constraints for stereo correspondence. We now start to develop our contribution.

2.2 Problem Formulation in Euclidean Space

Using the left (reference) camera coordinate system as the world coordinate system, the depth z at pixel (u, v) is $z(u, v) = \frac{\alpha b}{d(u,v)}$, where $d(u, v)$ is the (positional) disparity at (u, v), α is the focal lengh (in pixels), and b is the stereo baseline. We assume such a model with known α and b; i.e. the pin-hole cameras are calibrated and the stereo pair is rectified. To work in $\mathbb{R}^3$ (not in disparity space) we need the partial derivatives of depth z with respective to x and y, respectively:

$$z_x = \frac{\partial z}{\partial x} = \frac{\partial z}{\partial u}\frac{\partial u}{\partial x} = -\frac{\alpha b}{d^2}\frac{\partial d}{\partial u}\frac{\alpha}{f}, \quad z_y = \frac{\partial z}{\partial y} = \frac{\partial z}{\partial v}\frac{\partial v}{\partial y} = -\frac{\alpha b}{d^2}\frac{\partial d}{\partial v}\frac{\alpha}{f} \quad (2)$$

where $\frac{\partial u}{\partial x}$ and $\frac{\partial v}{\partial y}$ are constants determined by quantization of the image sensor, i.e. the focal length in pixels (α) and in physical unit (f) (we assume the same values in both x and y directions). A typical value is $1200 pixels/12mm = 100$.

Remark 1. Further taking derivatives shows that disparity derivatives (e.g. $\frac{\partial^\cdot d}{\partial u^\cdot}$) are (roughly) related to scaled physical derivatives (e.g. $\frac{\partial^\cdot z}{\partial x^\cdot}$) by $(\frac{f}{\alpha})^n$ (e.g.$(1/100)^n$). □

For physical objects with meaningful higher-order derivative information (e.g. $\frac{\partial^2 z}{\partial x^2}$, normal curvature in x direction), numerically it is difficult to manipulate the related higher-order disparity derivates (e.g.$\frac{\partial^2 d}{\partial u^2}$) in disparity space with image coordinates. This was a problem in [5]. We avoid working in such disparity space and chose to work in Euclidean space $\mathbb{R}^3$. First order derivatives $\{z_x, z_y\}$ are computed using the above equations after getting $\frac{\partial d}{\partial u}$ and $\frac{\partial d}{\partial v}$ from the inital deformed window SSD . A fitting process over a 3D neighborhood yields $\{z_{xx}, z_{xy}, z_{yy}\}$.

Now, for every candidate match we have estimated its depth z (disparity d), first order derivatives z_x and z_y, second order derivatives z_{xx}, z_{xy}, and z_{yy}, based on a local deformed SSD window (followed by fitting). Next we will show what it means for a candidate match with these properties to be *geometrically* consistent with its neighbors. This will enable us to eliminate inappropriate candidate matches and to refine the geometric estimates.

3 Differential Geometry of Smooth Surfaces

Assume the object under view is bounded by a smooth surface that can be described (locally) as a Monge patch. We briefly review the relevant differential geometry following [6, 4, 18] for notation. In particular, M is a regular surface in $\mathbb{R}^3$, $\mathbf{p}$ and $\mathbf{q}$ denote surface points in $\mathbb{R}^3$, $\mathbf{v} \in \mathbb{R}^3$ denotes a tangent vector in the tangent plane $T_p(M)$, $\mathbf{X}$ the position vector field (i.e. $\mathbf{X}(\mathbf{p}) = \mathbf{p}$), and $\mathbf{N}$ the unit surface normal vector field.

3.1 Surface Differential Properties

For a regular surface $M \subset \mathbb{R}^3$ the surface normal (or equivalently the tangent plane) changes as we move over it. This geometric property has been studied as the second fundamental form and the shape operator. They both encode such geometric information. In particular: The *shape operator* $S_p(\mathbf{v})$ encodes the shape of a surface M by measuring how the surface normal $\mathbf{N}$ changes as one moves in various directions from point $\mathbf{p}$ in the tangent plane $T_p(M)$. It is defined as [18]:

$$S_p(\mathbf{v}) = -\nabla_v \mathbf{N} \tag{3}$$

where $\nabla_v \mathbf{N}$ denotes the covariant derivative of the unit normal vector field $\mathbf{N}$ with respect to the tangent vector $\mathbf{v} \in T_p(M)$, i.e. the initial rate of change of $\mathbf{N}(\mathbf{p})$ as $\mathbf{p}$ moves in the $\mathbf{v}$ direction. In other words, it gives an infinitesimal description of the way surface M is curving in $\mathbb{R}^3$.

The *second fundamental form* II_p is defined in $T_p(M)$ as the quadratic form $II_p = -\langle d\mathbf{N}_p(\mathbf{v}), \mathbf{v} \rangle$, where $d\mathbf{N}_p$ is the differential of the Gauss map [6].

For tangent vectors $\mathbf{v}$ and $\mathbf{w}$ (both in $T_p(M)$) these two concepts are related by $II_p(\mathbf{v}, \mathbf{w}) = S_p(\mathbf{v}) \cdot \mathbf{w}$.

3.2 Second Fundamental Form for Monge Patch

We now switch to a convenient form for computation. In the (reference) camera coordinate system we can represent the surface as a Monge patch, $\mathbf{r}(x,y) = (x, y, z(x,y))$. Taking partial derivatives:

$$\mathbf{r}_x = (1, 0, z_x), \quad \mathbf{r}_y = (0, 1, z_y)$$

$$\mathbf{r}_{xx} = (0, 0, z_{xx}), \quad \mathbf{r}_{xy} = \mathbf{r}_{yx} = (0, 0, z_{xy}), \quad \mathbf{r}_{yy} = (0, 0, z_{yy})$$

Unit surface normal $\mathbf{N} = \frac{\mathbf{r}_\cdot \wedge \mathbf{r}_\cdot}{\|\mathbf{r}_\cdot \wedge \mathbf{r}_\cdot\|} = \frac{(-z_\cdot, -z_\cdot, 1)}{\sqrt{1 + z_\cdot^2 + z_\cdot^2}}$, where $\wedge$ is vector cross product.

The matrices of the first fundamental form I and the second fundamental form II are:

$$I : \begin{bmatrix} \mathbf{r}_x \cdot \mathbf{r}_x & \mathbf{r}_x \cdot \mathbf{r}_y \\ \mathbf{r}_y \cdot \mathbf{r}_x & \mathbf{r}_y \cdot \mathbf{r}_y \end{bmatrix} = \begin{bmatrix} 1 + z_x^2 & z_x z_y \\ z_x z_y & 1 + z_y^2 \end{bmatrix}$$

$$II : \begin{bmatrix} \mathbf{r}_{xx} \cdot \mathbf{N} & \mathbf{r}_{xy} \cdot \mathbf{N} \\ \mathbf{r}_{yx} \cdot \mathbf{N} & \mathbf{r}_{yy} \cdot \mathbf{N} \end{bmatrix} = \frac{1}{\sqrt{1 + z_x^2 + z_y^2}} \begin{bmatrix} z_{xx} & z_{xy} \\ z_{xy} & z_{yy} \end{bmatrix}$$

respectively. In the basis $\{\mathbf{r}_x, \mathbf{r}_y\}$, $d\mathbf{N}$ is given by the matrix $-I^{-1}II$, and the matrix of the shape operator S is $I^{-1}II$. This matrix is relative to the tangent vectors $\mathbf{r}_x$, $\mathbf{r}_y$ (as basis vectors) in the tangent plane $T_p(M)$ of M at $\mathbf{p}$. The matrix of the shape operator S is:

$$I^{-1}II : \begin{bmatrix} a_{11} & a_{12} \\ a_{21} & a_{22} \end{bmatrix} = \frac{1}{(1 + z_x^2 + z_y^2)^{3/2}} \begin{bmatrix} 1 + z_y^2 & -z_x z_y \\ -z_x z_y & 1 + z_x^2 \end{bmatrix} \begin{bmatrix} z_{xx} & z_{xy} \\ z_{xy} & z_{yy} \end{bmatrix} \tag{4}$$

$$= \frac{1}{(1 + z_x^2 + z_y^2)^{3/2}} \begin{bmatrix} (1 + z_y^2)z_{xx} - z_x z_y z_{xy} & (1 + z_y^2)z_{xy} - z_x z_y z_{yy} \\ (1 + z_x^2)z_{xy} - z_x z_y z_{xx} & (1 + z_x^2)z_{yy} - z_x z_y z_{xy} \end{bmatrix}$$

Note that this matrix is not necessarily symmetric, unless $\{\mathbf{r}_x, \mathbf{r}_y\}$ is an orthonormal basis. Typical values are given in Section 5.

Remark 2. When the object is a planar surface ($z_{xx} = z_{xy} = z_{yy} = 0$), elements of matrices II and S are all zeros. Observe that S still encodes the geometric property for such planar surfaces. The special case of a frontal parallel plane ($z_x = z_y = 0$) is also encoded in S. □

Remark 3. At the occluding boundaries of the surface (when $\mathbf{N}$ is orthogonal to the line of sight), we can not represent the surface as a Monge patch. As a result matrices of I, II, and S are not well defined in above formulas. This is an implementation limitation but not a theoretical one. □

4   Differential Geometric Consistency for Curved Surfaces

The intuition behind geometric consistency is that the measurement (position, normal) information at each point, when transported along the surface to neighboring points (as described previously), should agree with the measurements at those points. We now develop this intuition. At a given point $\mathbf{p}$ we would like to study how the position and surface normal change as we move in various directions in the tangent plane (Fig. 2(a)). $\mathbf{X}$ denotes the position vector field (thus $\mathbf{X}(\mathbf{p}) = \mathbf{p}$) and $\mathbf{N}$ the unit surface normal vector field. We require explicit formulas for their change as we move along $\mathbf{v}$ in the tangent plane $T_p(M)$ (i.e. $\nabla_v \mathbf{X}$ and $\nabla_v \mathbf{N}$).

Proposition 1. *Let $\mathbf{X}$ be the special vector field $\Sigma_{i=1}^{3} x_i \mathbf{E}_i$, where x_1, x_2, and x_3 are the Euclidian coordinate functions of $\mathbb{R}^3$. Then $\nabla_v \mathbf{X} = \mathbf{v}$ for every tangent vector $\mathbf{v}$.*

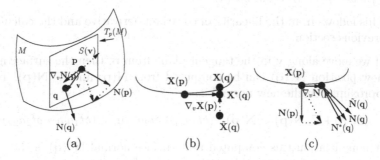

(a)   (b)   (c)

Fig. 2. (a) Shows the change of position vector field $\mathbf{X}$ and the unit surface normal vector field $\mathbf{N}$ by moving $\mathbf{v}$ in the tangent plane. (b) The predicted position $\mathbf{X}^*(\mathbf{q})$ in the neighborhood can be obtained from $\mathbf{X}(\mathbf{p})$ and $\nabla_v \mathbf{X}(\mathbf{p})$. Geometric consistency in position is determined by comparing $\mathbf{X}^*(\mathbf{q})$ with the true measurements $\mathbf{X}(\mathbf{q})$ in the neighborhood. Also shown is a less consistent one $\tilde{\mathbf{X}}(\mathbf{q})$. (c) The predicted surface normal $\mathbf{N}^*(\mathbf{q})$ in the neighborhood can be obtained from $\mathbf{N}(\mathbf{p})$ and $\nabla_v \mathbf{N}(\mathbf{p})$. Geometric consistency in orientation is determined by comparing $\mathbf{N}^*(\mathbf{q})$ with the true measurements $\mathbf{N}(\mathbf{q})$ in the neighborhood. Also shown is a less consistent one $\tilde{\mathbf{N}}(\mathbf{q})$.

Proof: Rewrite $\nabla_v \mathbf{X}$ according to its definition and express it as the sum of directional derivatives. We have $\nabla_v \mathbf{X} = \Sigma_{i=1}^3 \mathbf{v}[x_i]\mathbf{E}_i(\mathbf{p})$. Further expand the directional derivative part by $\mathbf{v}_p[f] = \Sigma_{j=1}^3 v_j \frac{\partial f}{\partial x_i}(\mathbf{p})$; we have $\Sigma_{i=1}^3 \mathbf{v}[x_i]\mathbf{E}_i(\mathbf{p}) = \Sigma_{i=1}^3 \Sigma_{j=1}^3 v_j \frac{\partial x_i}{\partial x_i}(\mathbf{p})\mathbf{E}_i = \Sigma_{i=1}^3 v_i \mathbf{E}_i = \mathbf{v}$. $\qquad\square$

From point $\mathbf{p}$ on M, if we move along $\mathbf{v}$ in the tangent plane, then to first order approximation the new position is:

$$\mathbf{X}^*(\mathbf{q}) = \mathbf{X}(\mathbf{p}) + \nabla_v \mathbf{X}(\mathbf{p}) = \mathbf{X}(\mathbf{p}) + \mathbf{v} \tag{5}$$

Interpret this computed position $\mathbf{X}^*(\mathbf{q})$ as the "transported" geometric information to a neighboring position $\mathbf{q}$ along the surface (from the measurements) at $\mathbf{p}$. Since direct measurements are also available at $\mathbf{q}$ (denoted $\mathbf{X}(\mathbf{q})$), the discrepancy between $\mathbf{X}^*(\mathbf{q})$ and $\mathbf{X}(\mathbf{q})$ can be used to measure the geometric consistency between nearby candidate matching points $\mathbf{p}$ and $\mathbf{q}$. Fig. 2(b) illustrates this point using two (possible) measured points $\mathbf{X}(\mathbf{q})$. Clearly the one on the same surface as $\mathbf{p}$ should be very close to the transported position, i.e. $\mathbf{X}^*(\mathbf{q})$.

And similarly for surface normal. Given the shape operator $S_p(\mathbf{v}) = -\nabla_v \mathbf{N}$ of M at $\mathbf{p}$, the change of surface normal $\mathbf{N}$ is characterized by the covariant derivative $\nabla_v \mathbf{N}$ for any $\mathbf{v}$ in the tangent plane $T_p(M)$. To emphasize its importance we show it as a proposition.

Proposition 2. *Let $\mathbf{N}$ be the unit normal vector field. Then for every tangent vector $\mathbf{v} = \delta t_1 \mathbf{r}_x + \delta t_2 \mathbf{r}_y$ in the tangent plane, $\nabla_v \mathbf{N}$ is given by:*

$$\begin{aligned}
\nabla_v \mathbf{N} = \nabla_{\delta t_1 \mathbf{r}. + \delta t_2 \mathbf{r}.} \mathbf{N} &= (\delta t_1 \nabla_r . \mathbf{N} + \delta t_2 \nabla_r . \mathbf{N}) \\
&= -(\delta t_1 a_{11} + \delta t_2 a_{12})\mathbf{r}_x - (\delta t_1 a_{21} + \delta t_2 a_{22})\mathbf{r}_y
\end{aligned} \tag{6}$$

where a_{ij}'s are given in equation (4).

Proof: This follows from the linearity of covariant derivative and the calculations in the previous section. $\qquad\square$

Again, if we move along $\mathbf{v}$ in the tangent plane from $\mathbf{p}$, then the surface normal at the new position $\mathbf{N}^*(\mathbf{q})$ can be computed from $\mathbf{N}(\mathbf{p})$ and $\nabla_v \mathbf{N}(\mathbf{p})$. To first order approximation the new normal is:

$$\mathbf{N}^*(\mathbf{q}) = \mathbf{N}(\mathbf{p}) + \nabla_v \mathbf{N}(\mathbf{p}) = \mathbf{N}(\mathbf{p}) - (\delta t_1 a_{11} + \delta t_2 a_{12})\mathbf{r}_x - (\delta t_1 a_{21} + \delta t_2 a_{22})\mathbf{r}_y \tag{7}$$

After nomalization this computed unit surface normal $\mathbf{N}^*(\mathbf{q})$ is the "transported" geometric information along the surface (from the measurements) at $\mathbf{p}$. Since direct measurements are also available at $\mathbf{q}$ to obtain $\mathbf{N}(\mathbf{q})$, the discrepancy between $\mathbf{N}^*(\mathbf{q})$ and $\mathbf{N}(\mathbf{q})$ can be used to measure the geometric consistency between nearby candidate matching points p and q. Fig. 2(c) illustrates this point by showing the transported normal $\mathbf{N}^*(\mathbf{q})$, which should agree with the geometrically consistent normal at $\mathbf{q}$. Observe that for planar surfaces (all zeros for matrix II) this implies constant surface normal (e.g. see Remark 2), which was discussed in [14].

The principle of *geometric consistency* between two neighboring points $\mathbf{p}$ and $\mathbf{q}$ holds that, based on the geometric information at $\mathbf{p}$ (i.e. $\mathbf{X}(\mathbf{p})$, $\mathbf{N}(\mathbf{p})$, $\nabla_v \mathbf{X}(\mathbf{p})$, and $\nabla_v \mathbf{N}(\mathbf{p})$), the transported (computed) geometric information at $\mathbf{q}$ (i.e. $\mathbf{X}^*(\mathbf{q})$ and $\mathbf{N}^*(\mathbf{q})$) should agree with the measurements at $\mathbf{q}$ (i.e. $\mathbf{X}(\mathbf{q})$ and $\mathbf{N}(\mathbf{q})$) if it is on the same surface as $\mathbf{p}$.

4.1 Geometric Contextual Information for Stereo

Our geometric way of using contextual information is in the Cartan moving frame model [6, 11]. It specifies how adpated frame fields change when they are transported along an object, and is concisely encoded in the connection equations. This model can be used to integrate local geometric information with geometric information in the neighborhood. Given candidate matches (obtained from initial local measurements), now we can impose the smoothness constraint in the neighborhood based on the geometric study just performed. Note that this is our unique construction in using contextual information geometrically. Both the position and the normal should be used in defining such geometric consistency.

Definition. The *geometric compatibility* between candidate match points $\mathbf{p}$ and $\mathbf{q}$ is:

$$r_{pq} = \frac{1}{2}\left(\left(1 - \frac{1}{m}\|\mathbf{X}^*(\mathbf{q}) - \mathbf{X}(\mathbf{q})\|\right) + |\mathbf{N}^*(\mathbf{q}) \cdot \mathbf{N}(\mathbf{q})|\right) \qquad (8)$$

where m is a normalization constant related to the neighborhood size.

Remark 4. $0 \le r_{pq} \le 1$, with $r_{pq} = 1$ for consistent $\mathbf{p}$ and $\mathbf{q}$, while $r_{pq} = 0$ for inconsistent $\mathbf{p}$ and $\mathbf{q}$. We use a mixed norm in defining such geometric consistency, but other formulas are also possible. $\square$

The geometric constraint (eqn. (8)) can be used in the cooperative framework. For a candidate match point $\mathbf{p}$ (hypothesis), we initialize its support s_p^0 according to its deformed window SSD (denoted by c_p) and iteratively update s_p by the geometric support it receives from its neighboring candidate matching point $\mathbf{q}$:

$$s_p^0 = 1 - \frac{c_p}{c} \qquad (9)$$

$$s_p^{t+1} = \frac{\sum_{q \in \mathcal{N}.} r_{pq} s_q^t}{\sum_{q \in \mathcal{N}.} s_q^t} \qquad (10)$$

with c a normalization factor, $\mathcal{N}_p$ denotes the neighbors of $\mathbf{p}$ (in our experiments we use a 21x21x7 (u, v, d) region). Note that here we use subscript to denote the measure with respect to candidate match point $\mathbf{p}$ (not the partial derivatives!). The true correspondence will be supported by its neighbors since their local surface geometry estimates are geometrically consistent. False matches are unlikely to get support from neighbors. We also experimented with a two label relaxation labeling algorithm [15, 13], and observed similar results. According to the taxonomy [22], such an iterative algorithm is neither a *local method* (e.g. SSD) nor a *global method* (e.g. graph cuts). It is in the spirit of a cooperative algorithm [17, 27], which iteratively performs local computations and uses nonlinear operations resulting in a final effect similar to global optimization.

Assuming the noise in the surface normals is roughly zero mean Gaussian i.i.d. (independent and identically distributed), the "best fit" (in a least-squares sense) unit normal at $\mathbf{p}$ is updated as [20]: $\mathbf{N}_p^{t+1} = (\sum \mathbf{N}_q^t)/\|\sum \mathbf{N}_q^t\|$, with $\mathbf{q}$ points in the neighborhood of $\mathbf{p}$ and within a normal threshold (e.g. $\pi/4$).

4.2   Stereo Algorithm

A simple algorithm illustrates how such geometric contextual information could be used.

(1) Use deformed window SSD to get the intial candidate matches. We first use a traditional SSD (15x15 window) to get integer disparity values at each (u, v) and only keep the top $\delta\%$ (we use 3 non-immediate neighboring ones) as the initial guesses. Then as explained in Section 2, for each disparity guess at every (u, v), we obtain $\{d, \frac{\partial d}{\partial u}, \frac{\partial d}{\partial v}\}$ (interpolated in the continuous domain) that minimizes deformed window SSD in equation (1). Several local minima could exist at each pixel (u, v). Geometric contextual information will be explored in the next few steps.

(2) Compute differential properties (e.g. surface normal $\mathbf{N}$, shape operator S) for every candidate match point $\mathbf{p}$ (Section 3).

(3) Compute the initial support s_p^0 for each candidate match point $\mathbf{p}$ by equation (9), which encodes the similarity measure based on deformed window SSD.

(4) Iteratively update the geometric support s_p at every $\mathbf{p}$ by equation (10) until it converges (in practice we run a preset number (e.g. 8) of iterations). To get the geometric compatibilities between nearby putative matches r_{pq} (eqn. (8)): first project $(\mathbf{q} - \mathbf{p})$ onto the tangent plane of $\mathbf{p}$, resulting in the displacement vector $\mathbf{v} \in T_p(M)$; then compute the predicted position and normal according to eqn. (5)(7); and finally use eqn. (8). Also update surface normal $\mathbf{N}_p$ at $\mathbf{p}$ based on the normals of neighbors, to reduce the effect of local noisy measurements.

(5) For each (u, v) select the the updated candidate match with the highest support s, output disparity (depth) and surface normal.

Observe that steps (2)-(5) are the unique geometric content of our algorithm.

5   Experimental Results

Fig. 3 provides a comparison between algorithms guided by the frontal parallel plane assumption for contextual interaction (e.g., graph cuts [3, 12], belief propagation [24, 26]) and those designed for more general surfaces (e.g., diffusion [21] and our algorithm). As expected, the first group yields "scalloped" surfaces broken into piecewise frontal parallel planar patches, even with subpixel interpolation (by parabola fitting of the costs of a 15x15 SSD window), while the second group follows the surface more robustly.

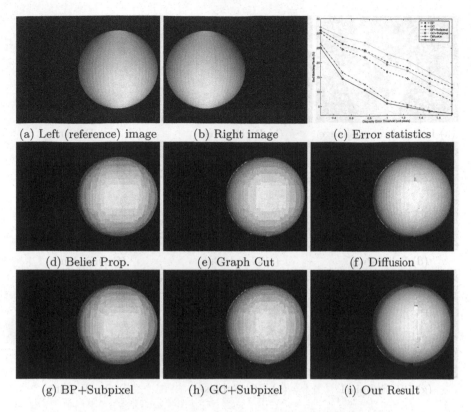

(a) Left (reference) image   (b) Right image   (c) Error statistics

(d) Belief Prop.   (e) Graph Cut   (f) Diffusion

(g) BP+Subpixel   (h) GC+Subpixel   (i) Our Result

Fig. 3. Synthetic sphere example separates the performance of algorithms with the frontal parallel plane assumption from those designed for smooth surfaces. (c) shows the percentage of bad matching pixels (occluded region not counted) using the taxonomy package [22] at 7 different thresholds ranging from 0.25–1.75 pixels. Performance for the diffusion algorithm and our approach were similar for this spherical surface. Other algorithms were obtained from the stereo package provided by Scharstein and Szeliski [22] for nonlinear diffustion (the membrane model) [21], and max-product ([26]) for belief propagation; The α-expansion algorithm [12] for graph cuts. The stereo pair was rendered with 152mm baseline and focal length 1303 pixels (obtained from real calibration data). Image size is 640x480 pixels, disparity range 41 pixels; Sphere has radius 100mm and center at 750mm distance.

Remark 5. To illustrate the numerical stability of our computation we pick a typical point $(u, v) = (526, 240)$, i.e. $(x, y) = (1.90, 0.0)$. From the ground truth we obtain $z = 687.29mm$, and $(z_x, z_y) = (1.242, 0.0)$. In our result we get $(z_x, z_y) = (1.239, 0.0)$ and $(z_{xx}, z_{xy}, z_{yy}) = (0.0406, 0, 0.0159)$, further computation shows matrix I is $\begin{bmatrix} 2.5432 & 0.0000 \\ 0.0000 & 1.0000 \end{bmatrix}$, matrix II is $\begin{bmatrix} 0.0254 & 0.0000 \\ 0.0000 & 0.0100 \end{bmatrix}$, and the matrix of the shape operator is: $\begin{bmatrix} 0.0100 & 0.0000 \\ 0.0000 & 0.0100 \end{bmatrix}$. These numbers are clearly meaningful numerically; however, by Remark 1, note that previous attempts

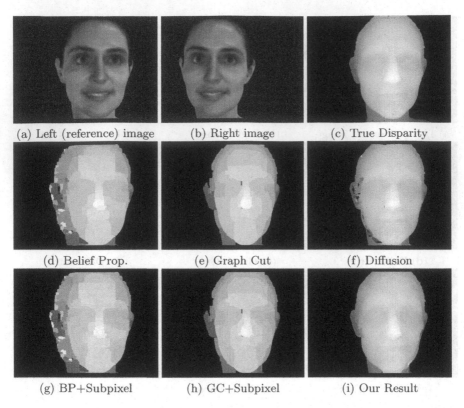

(a) Left (reference) image   (b) Right image   (c) True Disparity

(d) Belief Prop.   (e) Graph Cut   (f) Diffusion

(g) BP+Subpixel   (h) GC+Subpixel   (i) Our Result

Fig. 4. Human face example. Shown are results from other algorithms (as in previous caption), and our result. While the scalloping remains present in belief propagation and graph cuts, again diffusion and our algorithm appear smoothest. A detailed analysis of the statistical data reveals the difference (in the next Fig.). Ground truth data from $Cyberware^{TM}$ laser scanner dataset. Timing: Our algorithm takes 982.69 seconds on a Intel Xeon 2.4GHz CPU; accelerated belief propogation takes 1977.57 sec.; graph cuts takes 221.28 sec. and diffusion 59.82 sec.

(e.g.,[5]) at surface computations in (u, v)-space would have to multiply the above entries by (about) 10^{-4} for second order properties, thus placing them right at the limit of measurable quantities even for this idealized example.   □

The second set of examples illustrates the difference between our approach and diffusion. Faces have rich surface geometry needed to support graphical rendering and different types of recognition, and the 3D details matter. Ground truth data (3D geometry and texture map) were obtained from the $Cyberware^{TM}$ laser scanner dataset. The true disparity map is then computed. The stereo pair has a baseline of 6cm and focal length 1143 pixels. The human head ranges from 26.5cm to 53.5cm in front of the camera. The original image size is 1024x768 pixels but is then subsampled to 512x384 pixels with a disparity range 66 pixels. Results are in Fig. 4; once again, the diffusion algorithm is closest to ours but differences are emerging.

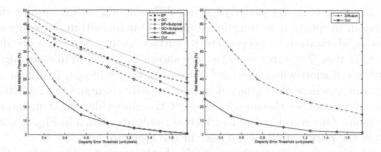

Fig. 5. Error statistics of bad matching pixels: (LEFT) Whole image. (RIGHT) A 30x30 pixel region around the side of the nose. Notice in particular how the statistics diverge for the nose region, where surface normal is changing rapidly. It is in places such as this that our algorithm noticeably outperforms diffusion.

Fig. 6. Reconstruction results. (LEFT) Reconstructed surface normal. (RIGHT) Zoom in of nose region. For display purpose surface normal and depth are subsampled to one in five pixels in both x and y directions.

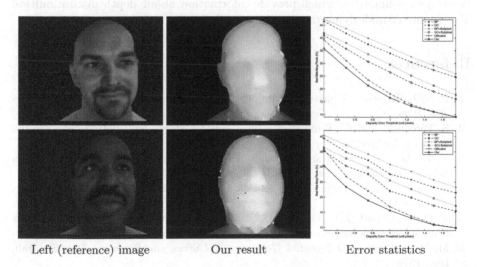

Left (reference) image   Our result   Error statistics

Fig. 7. More results on face stereo pair with ground truth

The membrane model underlying the diffusion algorithm applies uniform smoothing in proportion to iteration number. Our algorithm, by contrast, implements regularization in proportion to surface geometry, as a more detailed analysis indicates. The error statistics are shown in Fig. 5. While our algorithm differs from diffusion when averaged across the entire image, it differs *sharply* in those regions where the surface normal is rapidly changing (Fig. 5(RIGHT)). Diffusion oversmoothes these regions to get the smoothing right in larger, less varied regions. Our reconstructed surface normals are shown in Fig. 6; note how exquisitely the normal follows the nose in the blow-up.

Several other stereo face pairs are basically the same; see Fig. 7. Due to space limits we only report our result and error statistics of bad matching pixels; again, zooms on rapidly curving regions are informative.

6   Conclusion

We introduced the principle of geometric consistency to stereo, which holds that local observations of spatial disparity and surface shape should agree with neighboring observations; and that agreement between these neighboring observations can be implemented with a transport operation. In effect, nearby normals can be transported along (estimates of) the surface to be compared with directly measured normals. We provided direct calculations of these transport operations, and demonstrated their efficacy with a simple stereo algorithm. The geometric compatibility function could also be used in more powerful inference frameworks [26, 3], or developed into a richer probabilistic form.

Several limitations remain, though. Occlusion is not considered currently, nor the object boundaries, which provide information about depth discontinuities. The geometry underlying these will be studied in our next paper.

References

1. P. N. Belhumeur. A bayesian approach to binocular stereopsis. *IJCV*, 19(3):237–262, 1996.
2. S. Birchfield and C. Tomasi. Multiway cut for stereo and motion with slanted surfaces. In *Proc. ICCV*, 1999.
3. Y. Boykov, O. Veksler, and R. Zabih. Fast approximate energy minimization via graph cuts. *IEEE Trans. on PAMI*, 23(11):1222–1239, 2001.
4. R. Cipolla and P. Giblin. *Visual Motion of Curves and Surfaces*. Cambridge Univ. Press, 2000.
5. F. Devernay and O. D. Faugeras. Computing differential properties of 3-d shapes from stereoscopic images without 3-d models. In *Proc. CVPR*, 1994.
6. M. P. do Carmo. *Differential Geometry of Curves and Surfaces*. Prentice-Hall, Inc., 1976.
7. O. Faugeras. *Three-Dimensional Computer Vision*. The MIT Press, 1993.
8. R. Hartley and A. Zisserman. *Multiple View Geometry in Computer Vision*. Cambridge Univ. Press, 2000.

9. W. Hoff and N. Ahuja. Surfaces from stereo: Integrating feature matching, disparity estimation, and contour detection. *IEEE Trans. on PAMI*, 11(2):121–136, 1989.
10. T. Kanade and M. Okutomi. A stereo maching algorithm with an adaptive window: Theory and experiment. *IEEE Trans. on PAMI*, 16(9):920–932, 1994.
11. J. J. Koenderink. *Solid Shape*. The MIT Press, 1990.
12. V. Kolmogorov and R. Zabih. Computing visual correspondence with occlusions using graph cuts. In *Proc. ICCV*, 2001.
13. G. Li and S. W. Zucker. A differential geometrical model for contour-based stereo correspondence. In *Proc. IEEE Workshop on Variational, Geometric, and Level Set Methods in Computer Vision (at ICCV'03)*, 2003.
14. G. Li and S. W. Zucker. Stereo for slanted surfaces: First order disparities and normal consistency. In *Proc. EMMCVPR, LNCS 3757*, 2005.
15. G. Li and S. W. Zucker. Contextual inference in contour-based stereo correspondence. *IJCV, in press*, 2006.
16. M. H. Lin and C. Tomasi. Surfaces with occlusions from layered stereo. *IEEE Trans. on PAMI*, 26(8):1073–1078, 2004.
17. D. Marr and T. Poggio. Cooperative computation of stereo disparity. *Science*, 194:283–287, 1976.
18. B. O'Neill. *Elementary Differential Geometry*. Academic Press, 2nd edition, 1997.
19. W. H. Press, S. A. Teukolsky, W. T. Vetterling, and B. P. Flannery. *Numerical Reciples in C*. Cambridge University Press, second edition, 1992.
20. P. T. Sander and S. W. Zucker. Inferring surface trace and differential structure from 3-d images. *IEEE Trans. on PAMI*, 12(9):833–854, 1990.
21. D. Scharstein and R. Szeliski. Stereo matching with nonlinear diffusion. *IJCV*, 28(2):155–174, 1998.
22. D. Scharstein and R. Szeliski. A taxonomy and evaluation of dense two-frame stereo correspondence algorithms. *IJCV*, 47(1/2/3):7–42, 2002.
23. C. Strecha, T. Tuytelaars, and L. V. Gool. Dense matching of multiple wide-baseline views. In *Proc. ICCV*, 2003.
24. J. Sun, N.-N. Zheng, and H.-Y. Shum. Stereo matching using belief propagation. *IEEE Trans. on PAMI*, 25(7):787–800, 2003.
25. H. Tao, H. S. Sawhney, and R. Kumar. A global matching framework for stereo computation. In *Proc. ICCV*, 2001.
26. M. F. Tappen and W. T. Freeman. Comparison of graph cuts with belief propagation for stereo, using identical mrf parameters. In *Proc. ICCV*, 2003.
27. C. Zitnick and T. Kanade. A cooperative algorithm for stereo mathching and occlusion detection. *IEEE Trans. on PAMI*, 22(7):675–684, 2000.

Resolution-Enhanced Photometric Stereo

Ping Tan[1], Stephen Lin[2], and Long Quan[1]

[1] Computer Science Department,
Hong Kong University of Science and Technology
{ptan, quan}@cs.ust.hk
[2] Microsoft Research Asia
stevelin@microsoft.com

Abstract. Conventional photometric stereo has a fundamental limitation that the scale of recovered geometry is limited to the resolution of the input images. However, surfaces that contain sub-pixel geometric structures are not well modelled by a single normal direction per pixel. In this work, we propose a technique for resolution-enhanced photometric stereo, in which surface geometry is computed at a resolution higher than that of the input images. To achieve this goal, our method first utilizes a generalized reflectance model to recover the distribution of surface normals inside each pixel. This normal distribution is then used to infer sub-pixel structures on a surface of uniform material by spatially arranging the normals among pixels at a higher resolution according to a minimum description length criterion on 3D textons over the surface. With the presented method, high resolution geometry that is lost in conventional photometric stereo can be recovered from low resolution input images.

1 Introduction

From a given viewing direction, the appearance of surface points vary according to their orientation, reflectance, and illumination conditions. With an assumed reflectance, photometric stereo methods utilize this relationship to compute surface normals by examining transformations in image intensities that result from changes in lighting directions. Traditionally, reflectance is assumed to be Lambertian [1, 2], and with calibrated illumination directions, three images are sufficient to recover surface normals and albedos [3].

The reflectance of a surface, however, often does not adhere to the Lambertian model, and in such cases, conventional photometric stereo may yield poor results. To deal with this problem, methods based on non-Lambertian reflectance models have been proposed. Some techniques utilize a composite reflectance model that consists of Lambertian diffuse reflection plus specular reflection [4, 5, 6], while others employ physically-based models that account for the effects of fine-scale roughness in surface structure [7, 8]. In all of these approaches, reflectance is assumed to be a function of a single principal normal direction.

In many instances, the surface structure within a pixel exhibits greater complexity, and the resulting reflectance cannot be accurately expressed in terms of

A. Leonardis, H. Bischof, and A. Pinz (Eds.): ECCV 2006, Part III, LNCS 3953, pp. 58–71, 2006.
© Springer-Verlag Berlin Heidelberg 2006

a single normal. When a surface is imaged at a resolution coarser than its surface structure, multiple disparate principal normal directions may exist within each pixel. Since previous photometric stereo methods compute a normal map at the same resolution as the input images, they are unable to recover this sub-pixel geometric structure.

In this work, we present a technique for estimating the geometry of a uniform-material surface at a resolution higher than that of the input images. The proposed method recovers a general distribution of normals per pixel from an ample number of photometric stereo images, and then estimate a spatial arrangement of this normal distribution in a higher resolution image. For normal distribution recovery, we perform photometric stereo with a reflectance model that is based on a general representation of normal distributions. For robustness in the recovery of these complex distributions, we present an Expectation-Maximization approach to solve for the distribution parameters.

With the recovered normal distributions of each pixel, enhanced resolution of surface geometry is computed by dividing the distribution according to the level of enhancement, e.g., four sub-distributions in a 2x2 enhancement of photometric stereo. After partitioning the distribution, their arrangement in the higher resolution normal map is formulated from constraints that favor consistency of geometric structure over a surface. Consistency is evaluated in terms of surface integrability and simplicity of surface description with respect to 3D textons, which is motivated by the minimum description length principle [9] and the observation that a surface is generally composed of only a small number of perceptually distinct local structures [10]. To solve this complicated arrangement problem, we utilize the Belief Propagation algorithm [11, 12] to compute an initial solution from a graphical model that represents integrability constraints. Starting from this initial solution, simulated annealing [13] is used to find an optimal arrangement that accounts for complexity of surface description.

This approach enhances resolution differently from image super-resolution methods [14, 15] in that sub-pixel viewpoint displacements are not used to obtain variations in spatial sampling. In photometric stereo, all images are captured at a fixed viewpoint, and the proposed technique estimates higher spatial resolution based on super-resolution recovery of surface normals and constraints on surface structure. The described approach also differs from learning-based hallucination methods [16, 17] that utilize a training set of high resolution / low resolution image pairs to infer enhanced resolution. In contrast to image hallucination methods, our technique is able to recover partial information from the input for resolution enhancement, in the form of the actual normal distribution within a low resolution pixel. Therefore, our method need not fully conjecture on the high resolution data, which is difficult to do by hallucination since reliable training databases are challenging to construct for general geometric structure. Rather, it infers only the arrangement of known surface normal information. With this approach, fine-scale surface detail that is missed in conventional photometric stereo can be revealed.

2   Recovery of Normal Distributions

In the first stage of our technique, we use photometric stereo to recover a normal distribution for each pixel of the input images. To determine a distribution of normals, our method utilizes a generalized reflectance model, where a Gaussian mixture model (GMM) of normal distributions is used to account for reflectance effects of sub-pixel geometric structure. We briefly review this reflectance model and present a method for employing it in photometric stereo to recover a general normal distribution within each pixel.

2.1   Generalized Reflectance Model

In physically-based reflectance modeling [18, 19, 20], a surface is typically modelled as a collection of tiny flat faces, called microfacets. The overall reflectance of a surface area imaged within a pixel is therefore an aggregate effect of this microfacet collection, which is generally described by the distribution of their normal directions. For an arbitrary microfacet normal distribution $p(\mathbf{n})$, reflectance may be physically represented by a model proposed in [20]:

$$\rho(\mathbf{l}, \mathbf{v}) = \frac{p(\mathbf{h})F(\mathbf{l} \cdot \mathbf{h})}{4K_s(\mathbf{l})K_m(\mathbf{v})}$$

where $\mathbf{l}, \mathbf{v}$ are unit lighting and viewing directions, and $\mathbf{h}$ is their unit bisector. F denotes the Fresnel reflectance term, and K_s, K_m are factors that account for shadowing and masking among microfacets. Since microfacet-based models generally treat microfacets as mirror reflectors, recovery of $p(\mathbf{h})$ gives us $p(\mathbf{n})$.

Generally in reflectance modeling, the normal distribution is considered to be centered at a principal surface normal direction, around which the collection of microfacet normals is distributed. When the scale of geometric structure is smaller than the image resolution, as illustrated in Fig. 1, multiple principal surface normals may exist within a pixel. To more generally represent normal distributions, we utilize Gaussian mixture models, which have long been used

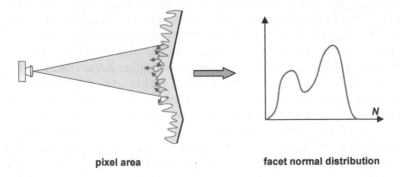

pixel area   facet normal distribution

Fig. 1. At low resolution, sub-pixel geometric structure can lead to a complex distribution of normals within a pixel

to represent general distributions. In this work, to facilitate parameter estimation the shadowing and masking terms K_s, K_m and the Fresnel term F are all
modelled as constant, as done in numerous reflectance modeling works (e.g.,
[5, 20, 21]). With this simplification and a normal distribution represented by
a Gaussian mixture model $G(\mathbf{n}) = \sum_{i=1}^{N} \alpha_i g(\mathbf{n}; \mu_i, \sigma_i)$, reflectance can be expressed as

$$\rho(\mathbf{l}, \mathbf{v}) = \frac{F}{4K_s K_m} \sum_{i=0}^{N} \alpha_i g(\mathbf{h}; \mu_i, \sigma_i) = A \cdot G(\mathbf{h}) \tag{1}$$

where A is a constant, and μ_i, σ_i denote the mean and variance of Gaussian i.
By incorporating this generalized reflectance model into photometric stereo, our
method more comprehensively acquires surface normal information in each pixel.

2.2   Reflectance Estimation

Due to the complexity of this reflectance model, it is non-trivial to determine
from photometric stereo images the parameters of a general normal distribution.
In photometric stereo, a set of K images containing reflectance data $\{O_k; 1 \leq
k \leq K\}$ is measured under different lighting conditions $\{\mathbf{l}_k; 1 \leq k \leq K\}$ and a
fixed viewing direction $\mathbf{v}$. From this data, parameters of the Gaussian mixture
normal distribution could in principle be estimated at each pixel by general
non-linear least squares fitting:

$$\Theta = \arg\min \sum_{k=1}^{K} ||\rho(\mathbf{l}_k, \mathbf{v}) - O_k||^2 = \arg\min \sum_{k=1}^{K} ||A \sum_{i=0}^{N} \alpha_i g(\mathbf{h}_k; \mu_i, \sigma_i) - O_k||^2,$$

where $\Theta = \{A, (\alpha_i, \mu_i, \sigma_i); 1 \leq i \leq N\}$ signifies the reflectance parameters with
an N-Gaussian GMM. However, as described in [21], due to the high nonlinearity
of reflectance functions, fitting a model with more than two lobes by general non-
linear least squares is rather unstable and gives unreliable results.

To deal with this issue, we can regard Eq. (1) as a probability distribution
function (pdf) defined on a hemisphere with respect to bisector direction $\mathbf{h}$ and
scaled by a factor A. We can furthermore consider measured intensities in the
photometric stereo images as samples from this distribution. Estimation of a pdf
in terms of a Gaussian mixture model from a set of samples is a well studied
problem and can be robustly computed by the Expectation-Maximization (EM)
algorithm [22, 23]. With a generalized reflectance model that represents normal
distributions with a GMM, we can conveniently utilize this method to recover
this detailed surface information.

According to the Law of Large Numbers, the value of a pdf at a given point
is the frequency that the point appears in random sampling. For each bisector
direction $\mathbf{h}_k$, the actual pdf function has the value O_k/A, which should lead to
O_k/A samples being observed at position $\mathbf{h}_k$. In other words, for each observation
O_k, we put a sample of weight O_k/A at direction $\mathbf{h}_k$. To estimate the actual pdf,
GMM parameters can be computed according to these weighted samples using
the EM algorithm, by iteratively computing the E-step:

$$Ez_{ik} = \alpha_i g(\mathbf{h}_k; \mu_i, \sigma_i) / \sum_{j=1}^{N} \alpha_j g(\mathbf{h}_k; \mu_j, \sigma_j)$$

and the M-step:

$$\alpha_i = \frac{\sum_{k=1}^{K} \frac{O_{\cdot}}{A} Ez_{ik}}{\sum_{k=1}^{K} \frac{O_{\cdot}}{A}} = \frac{\sum_{k=1}^{K} O_k Ez_{ik}}{\sum_{k=1}^{K} O_k}$$

$$\mu_i = \frac{\sum_{k=1}^{K} \frac{O_{\cdot}}{A} Ez_{ik}\mathbf{h}_k}{\sum_{k=1}^{K} \frac{O_{\cdot}}{A}} = \frac{\sum_{k=1}^{K} O_k Ez_{ik}\mathbf{h}_k}{\sum_{k=1}^{K} O_k}$$

$$\sigma_i^2 = \frac{\sum_{k=1}^{K} \frac{O_{\cdot}}{A} Ez_{ik}||\mathbf{h}_k - \mu_i||^2}{\sum_{k=1}^{K} \frac{O_{\cdot}}{A}} = \frac{\sum_{k=1}^{K} O_k Ez_{ik}||\mathbf{h}_k - \mu_i||^2}{\sum_{k=1}^{K} O_k}$$

where z_{ik} are hidden variables and Ez_{ik} is the probability that the k-th sample is generated by the i-th component. For purposes of resolution enhancement as later described in Sec. 3, we utilize GMMs with Gaussians of equal weight, such that we set $\alpha_i = \frac{1}{N}$ for an N-Gaussian GMM.

The scale factor A is seen to cancel out in the computation of the normal distribution parameters. Intuitively, these GMM parameters, which describe the geometric characteristics of a surface, are independent of A, which represent optical properties, and can be optimized separately. With the computed GMM parameters, A may be solved by linear least squares

$$A = \arg\min \sum_{k-1}^{K} ||O_k - AG(\mathbf{h}_k)||,$$

but need not be estimated in our application because only the normal distributions are used in surface reconstruction.

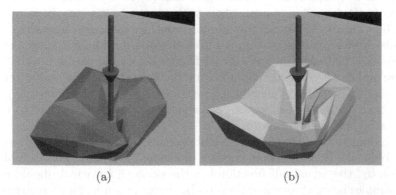

(a)   (b)

Fig. 2. (a) Visualization of observed data from 65 photometric stereo images. The radius of each sample point is set to the radiance intensity at the corresponding lighting direction. (b) Radiance distribution computed according to our fitted parameters.

The performance of this EM-based parameter estimation is exemplified in Fig. 2, which compares a radiance distribution computed with our generalized model and recovery technique to the observed data from photometric images with 65 sampled illumination directions. The intensity of a single pixel under different lighting directions is visualized as a function defined on a hemisphere, whose value is represented by the radius. While some deviation can be observed at grazing angles, the fitted radiance distribution approximately models the captured distribution using 4-Gaussian GMMs. With greater numbers of Gaussians, closer approximations can be obtained.

3   Resolution Enhancement

For resolution enhancement, our method divides the recovered distribution of normal directions among pixels at a higher resolution. For an $R \times R$ enhancement, with $M = R^2$, each higher resolution pixel covers $1/M$ of a pixel at the original resolution, such that $1/M$ of the recovered normal distribution should be assigned to each of the higher resolution pixels. Using a mixture of M uniform-weight Gaussians in the reflectance estimation of Sec. 2.2, we employ a simplified arrangement procedure where each component of the M-Gaussian GMM is assigned to one of the M higher resolution pixels. With this, the principal normal direction of each high resolution pixel is given by the mean vector of the assigned GMM component.

For determining the spatial organization of these GMM components among the high resolution pixels, we employ constraints based on geometric consistency. These constraints lead to a challenging optimization problem, which is solved using a combination of belief propagation and simulated annealing.

3.1   Constraints on Normal Arrangement

Since no direct information on sub-pixel spatial arrangements of principal normal directions can be derived from fixed-view photometric stereo images, our method relies upon common characteristics of surface structure to constrain the solution. One fundamental constraint in a normal map is that the curl of the normal map be equal to zero, which is known as the integrability constraint and is widely used in surface reconstruction (e.g., [24, 25, 26]). This constraint itself does not provide sufficient information for determining a reliable solution, so we additionally take advantage of the observation that at a local scale there generally exists only a small number of perceptually distinct structural features on a surface. This surface property is the basis for work on 3D textons [10], which represent the appearance of points on a surface by indexing to a small vocabulary of prototype surface patches.

In our method, we utilize a constraint on normal arrangements that is motivated by the work on 3D textons and the minimum description length principle [9]. Specifically, our formulation favors normal arrangements that minimize the number of local structural features, or 3D textons, needed to describe the imaged surface at the enhanced resolution. In [10], 3D texton primitives are represented

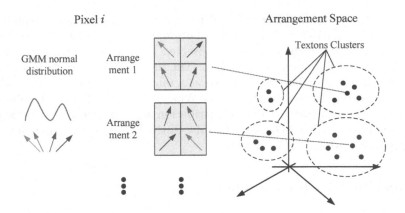

Fig. 3. Mapping of possible normal arrangements of all pixels into a high dimensional arrangement space. Each arrangement of a pixel is a point in this space. Similar arrangements form clusters that represent possible textons of the surface.

in terms of co-occurring responses to a bank of Gaussian derivative filters of different orientations and spatial frequencies, but for our context of photometric stereo, we instead describe these structural primitives simply as a concatenated vector of principal normal orientations. In our implementation, the size of the texton area is set to be the that of a pixel at the original, captured image resolution.

To minimize the number of distinct structural features (textons) in the surface description, we first cluster similar normal arrangements that may occur on the surface, and represent each cluster by a single representative arrangement, or texton. As illustrated in Fig. 3, every possible arrangement of the GMM components of all low resolution pixels on the surface are plotted as points in an arrangement space, and these normal arrangements are grouped into texton clusters that are each represented by its mean vector. Specifically, in clustering, each arrangement is represented by a concatenated vector of principal normal directions inside each pixel. For example, in the case of 2×2 resolution enhancement, a 12-D space is formed by concatenating four principal normals expressed as 3D vectors. In our implementation, the structure of this space is obtained by employing the EM algorithm to cluster arrangements as components of a GMM $\mathbb{G}$, referred to as the texton GMM. In this process, we fit a GMM with a large number of components and then eliminate components that have weights below a threshold.

Distinct textons may contain the same set of GMM components of a normal distribution and differ only in their arrangement, as is the case for multiple arrangements for a given pixel. To minimize the geometric description, we also group these textons into equivalence classes as shown in Fig. 4(a), and represent each class by a single texton. These equivalence classes can be determined by grouping texton clusters that are associated with the same pixels, since this indicates that the textons are rearrangements of each other. In real applications, this grouping is computed by a voting scheme in which the affinity of two textons

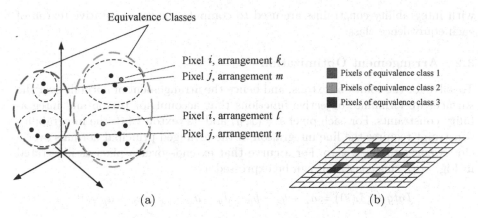

Fig. 4. Texton equivalence classes. (a) Textons that differ in high-resolution structure but have a similar low-resolution distribution of normals are grouped in an equivalence class. (b) Each pixel belongs to one of the equivalent classes. A single texton is computed for each class, and the pixels of the class are assigned the geometric structure of this representative texton.

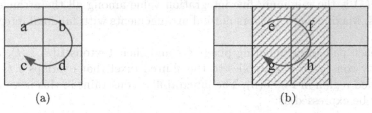

Fig. 5. Closed curves for evaluating integrability. (a) each pixel at the original resolution; (b) each shifted pixel (shaded area) that overlaps two pixels.

is measured by the number of common pixels among the two sets of clusters. Thresholding this affinity measure gives a partitioning of textons into equivalence classes. With this partitioning, each pixel is associated with the equivalence class that contains the largest number of its possible normal arrangements, as illustrated in Fig. 4(b). When a texton is later assigned to represent an equivalence class, the pixels associated with the class will then be assigned the normal arrangement of that texton.

To determine the set of textons that are used to represent the set of equivalence classes, which we refer to as *solution textons*, we solve for the set of textons that best models the surface. Since any integrable texton from an equivalence class can accurately represent the pixels associated with the class, we determine the solution textons that maximize the consistency with the resulting shifted pixels, where shifted pixels refer to pixel areas that overlap multiple pixels at low resolution as exemplified in Fig. 5(b). Based on our criterion for surface consistency, shifted pixels should also be represented by the solution textons. In the following section, we describe how a minimal texton description in conjunction with integrability constraints are used to compute the representative texton of each equivalence class.

3.2 Arrangement Optimization

To solve for the solution textons, and hence the arrangement of normals over the surface, we formulate objective functions that account for texton and integrability constraints. For each pixel $\bar{s} = (x, y)$ and its texton $\mathbb{L}(\bar{s})$, the integrability constraint requires the line integration of the arranged principal normals over a closed curve to equal zero. For a curve that extends over a pixel as illustrated in Fig. 5(a), this constraint can be expressed as

$$Intg_1(\bar{s}, \mathbb{L}(\bar{s})) = a_x + b_x - b_y - d_y - d_x - c_x + c_y + a_y = 0$$

where $\mathbf{a} = (a_x, a_y, 1), \mathbf{b} = (b_x, b_y, 1), \mathbf{c} = (c_x, c_y, 1)$ and $\mathbf{d} = (d_x, d_y, 1)$ are the principal normal directions of the pixel. An energy function with respect to integrability can therefore be defined on each pixel as

$$E_1(\bar{s}, \mathbb{L}(\bar{s})) = exp\left(-||Intg_1(\bar{s}, \mathbb{L}(\bar{s})) - c_1(\bar{s})||^2\right)$$

where $c_1(\bar{s})$ is the minimum line integration value among all the arrangements of pixel $\bar{s}$. Maximizing E_1 favors normal arrangements with minimal integration values.

For each pair of neighboring pixels $\bar{s}, \bar{t}$ and their textons $\mathbb{L}(\bar{s}), \mathbb{L}(\bar{t})$, the integrability constraint also applies to the shifted pixel that overlaps $\bar{s}, \bar{t}$, shown as a shaded region in Fig. 5(b). The integrability constraint in this instance can similarly be expressed as:

$$Intg_2(\bar{s}, \bar{t}, \mathbb{L}(\bar{s}), \mathbb{L}(\bar{t})) = e_x + f_x - f_y - h_y - h_x - g_x + g_y + e_y = 0.$$

A shifted pixel additionally should be associated to a solution texton. This condition can be quantified as $\max_{1 \leq j \leq T} \mathcal{P}_{i.}(\mathbf{efgh})$, where $\mathbf{efgh}$ is the concatenated vector of principal normals $\mathbf{e}, \mathbf{f}, \mathbf{g}, \mathbf{h}$, $\{\mathbb{L}_{i_1}, \mathbb{L}_{i_2}, \ldots \mathbb{L}_{i.}\}$ is the set of solution textons, $\mathcal{P}_{i.}(\cdot)$ is the pdf function of the i_j-th Gaussian component of the texton GMM model $\mathbb{G}$. Then an energy function can be defined on each pixel pair as:

$$E_2(\bar{s}, \bar{t}, \mathbb{L}(\bar{s}), \mathbb{L}(\bar{t})) = exp\left(-||Intg_2(\bar{s}, \bar{t}, \mathbb{L}(\bar{s}), \mathbb{L}(\bar{t})) - c_1(\bar{s}, \bar{t})||^2\right) \cdot \max_{1 \leq j \leq T} \mathcal{P}_{i.}(\mathbf{efgh})$$

Maximizing E_2 will favor the selection of textons for $\bar{s}$ and $\bar{t}$ for which the normal arrangement of their shifted pixel is integrable and consistent with the set of solution textons.

In principle, integrability and an association to solution textons should also exist for other pixel displacements, e.g., a shifted pixel that overlaps the corners of four pixels. In our current implementation, these cases are not considered because the added complexity to the energy formulation makes optimization quite challenging.

The solution textons $\{\mathbb{L}_{i_1}, \mathbb{L}_{i_2}, \ldots \mathbb{L}_{i.}\}$ can be computed by maximizing the product of E_1 and E_2 over the whole image as

$$\{\mathbb{L}_{i_1}, \mathbb{L}_{i_2}, \ldots \mathbb{L}_{i.}\} = \arg \max \prod_{\bar{s}} E_1(\bar{s}, \mathbb{L}(\bar{s})) \prod_{Neighbor(\bar{s}, \bar{t})} E_2(\bar{s}, \bar{t}, \mathbb{L}(\bar{s}), \mathbb{L}(\bar{t}))$$

where $\bar{s}$ indexes all the pixels in the image, and $Neighbor(\bar{s}, \bar{t})$ represent all pairs of neighboring pixels. Due to the complexity of this optimization problem, a solution is obtained using a two-step process. In the second step, we use simulated annealing to compute an arrangement solution that accounts for both texton and integrability constraints. To aid simulated annealing in reaching a good solution, the first step formulates the integrability constraints in a graphical network and employs belief propagation to compute a good initial solution for input into the annealing process.

In this first step, the problem is formulated as an undirected graph model, where each node v of the graph represents an equivalence class. Two nodes are connected if and only if they contain pixels that are 4-neighbors of each other in the image. Each node has a number of candidate textons that are indexed by labels. Integrability constraints are applied to the graphical model as energy functions defined on nodes and edges.

From the above discussion, we can define an energy term for each label $\mathbb{L}$ of a node as

$$E(\mathbb{L}; v) = \prod_{\bar{s} \in v} E_1(\bar{s}, \mathbb{L}(\bar{s})) = \prod_{\bar{s} \in v} E_1(\bar{s}, \mathbb{L})$$

where $\bar{s} \in v$ denotes pixels $\bar{s}$ in equivalence class v. For each pair of connected nodes v_1, v_2 in the graphical model and their labels $\mathbb{L}_1, \mathbb{L}_2$, we define an energy on the connecting edge as:

$$E(\mathbb{L}_1, \mathbb{L}_2; v_1, v_2) = \prod_{Neighbor(\bar{s}, \bar{t}); \bar{s} \in v_1; \bar{t} \in v_2} E_2'(\bar{s}, \bar{t}, \mathbb{L}(\bar{s}), \mathbb{L}(\bar{t}))$$

$$= \prod_{Neighbor(\bar{s}, \bar{t}); \bar{s} \in v_1; \bar{t} \in v_2} E_2'(\bar{s}, \bar{t}, \mathbb{L}_1, \mathbb{L}_2)$$

where E_2' denotes the energy E_2 without the texton constraint $\max_{1 \le j \le T} \mathcal{P}_i$. (**efgh**). The initial solution is determined by maximizing the energy over the entire graphical model using the belief propagation algorithm in [12].

The second step takes the solution of the first step as an initialization to the simulated annealing process for the energy function

$$E = \prod_{\bar{s}} E_1(\bar{s}, \mathbb{L}(\bar{s})) \prod_{Neighbor(\bar{s}, \bar{t})} \cdot E_2(\bar{s}, \bar{t}, \mathbb{L}(\bar{s}), \mathbb{L}(\bar{t})).$$

At each iteration of simulated annealing, an equivalence class is randomly selected and its texton label is randomly exchanged. This randomized modification is accepted according to its change in energy and a given temperature schedule.

With this approach, various degrees of resolution enhancement can be obtained, but greater amounts of enhancement lead to substantial increases in computation, due to the R^2! possible normal arrangements for an $R \times R$ enhancement. To alleviate this problem, an approximation can be employed where 2×2 enhancements are performed iteratively to reach higher levels of resolution.

4   Results

In our experiments, a surface is captured by a fixed camera with evenly sampled lighting directions given by seven bulbs attached to an arc that rotates around the surface. The seven bulbs are attached to the arc at equal angular intervals, and the arc rotates at intervals of 30 degrees. At two of the arc rotation angles, lighting is occluded by the capture device, and other occlusions of illumination occasionally occur. Generally, 60 – 70 photometric stereo images are captured for each surface.

We applied our method to several real surfaces, displayed in Fig. 6, Fig. 7, and Fig. 8. For each of the figures, an input image at the original, captured resolution is shown. For visualization purposes, normal maps are integrated into height fields according to the method in [25]. Height fields computed at the captured resolution lack the geometric detail. With 2×2 resolution enhancement, sub-pixel structures lost in conventional photometric stereo are recovered. 4×4 enhancement adds further detail. As greater enhancement is applied, some

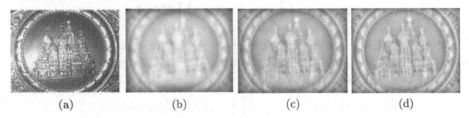

| (a) | (b) | (c) | (d) |

Fig. 6. Example of a shiny metal surface. Images are normalized in size for easier comparison. To view finer detail, please zoom in on the electronic version. (a) One of the photometric stereo images; (b) Height field recovered at original resolution; (c) Height field recovered at 2×2 enhanced resolution; (d) Height field recovered at 4×4 enhanced resolution.

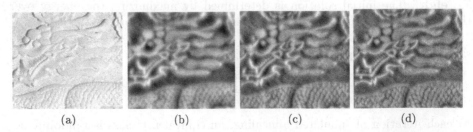

| (a) | (b) | (c) | (d) |

Fig. 7. Example of a stone carving. Images are normalized in size for easier comparison. To view finer detail, please zoom in on the electronic version. (a) One of the photometric stereo images; (b) Height field recovered at original resolution; (c) Height field recovered at 2×2 enhanced resolution; (d) Height field recovered at 4×4 enhanced resolution.

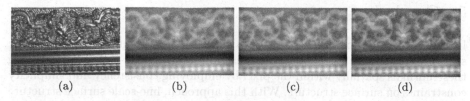

(a)   (b)   (c)   (d)

Fig. 8. Example of a wood flower frame with shiny paint. Images are normalized in size for easier comparison. To view finer detail, please zoom in on the electronic version. (a) One of the photometric stereo images; (b) Height field recovered at original resolution; (c) Height field recovered at 2×2 enhanced resolution; (d) Height field recovered at 4×4 enhanced resolution.

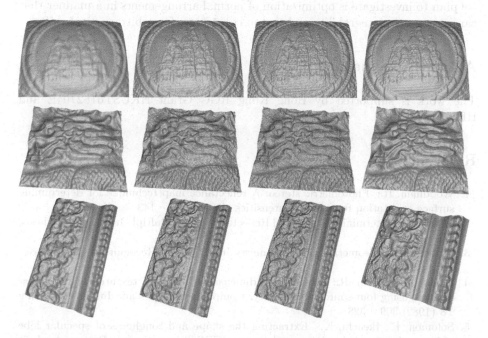

Fig. 9. Rendering of the recovered height fields from a novel viewpoint. Left to right: original resolution, 2×2 enhancement, 4×4 enhancement and ground truth computed from a close-up image sequence captured at around 3×3 enhancement.

increase in noise is evident, partially due to the greater complexity in determining proper normal arrangements. Noise may also arise from deviations of the actual reflectance from the mathematical model we used for normal recovery.

In Fig. 9, to provide another form of visualization and comparison to ground truth height field, we render the recovered height fields from a novel viewpoint for the original resolution, 2×2 enhancement, 4×4 enhancement and the ground truth computed from a close-up image sequence captured at around 3×3 enhancement. Geometric detail that is seen in the ground truth height field become increasing clearer with greater enhancement.

5   Conclusion

In this work, we proposed a method to enhance the resolution of photometric stereo by recovering a general normal distribution per pixel and then arranging these normals spatially within the pixel by employing consistency and simplicity constraints on surface structure. With this approach, fine-scale surface structure that is missing in conventional photometric stereo can be inferred from low resolution input.

There exist a number of interesting directions for future work. In our current technique, information from shadows in photometric stereo images is not utilized, but can provide useful constraints in the enhancement process. Another direction we plan to investigate is optimization of normal arrangements in a manner that can incorporate integrability and texton constraints for arbitrary pixel shifts.

Acknowledgement

The work is supported by Hong Kong RGC Grant HKUST6182/04E and HKUST6190/05E.

References

1. Woodham, R.: Photometric stereo: A reflectance map technique for determining surface orientation from image intensities. (1978) 136 – 143
2. Silver, W.: Determining Shape and Reflectance Using Multiple Images. PhD thesis, MIT (1980)
3. Shashua, A.: Geometry and Photometry in 3D Visual Recognition. PhD thesis, MIT (1992)
4. Coleman, E., Jain, R.: Obtaining 3-dimensional shape of textured and specular surfaces using four-source photometry. Computer Graphics and Image Processing **18** (1982) 309 – 328
5. Solomon, F., Ikeuchi, K.: Extracting the shape and roughness of specular lobe objects using four light photometric stereo. IEEE Transactions on Pattern Analysis and Machine Intelligence **18** (1996) 449 – 454
6. Drbohlav, O., Sara, R.: Specularities reduce ambiguity of uncalibrated photometric stereo. In: Proc. European Conference on Computer Vision (2). (2002) 46–62
7. Tagare, H., de Figueiredo, R.: A theory of photometric stereo for a class of diffuse non-lambertian surfaces. IEEE Transactions on Pattern Analysis and Machine Intelligence **13** (1991) 133 – 152
8. Georghiades, A.: Incorporating the torrance and sparrow model of reflectance in uncalibrated photometric stereo. In: Proceeding of IEEE International Conference on Computer Vision 2003. Volume 2., IEEE Computer Society (2003) 816– 823
9. Rissanen, J.: A universal prior for integers and estimation by minimum description length. The Annals of Statistics **11** (1983) 416 – 431
10. Leung, T., Malik, J.: Representing and recognizing the visual appearance of materials using three-dimensional textons. International Journal of Computer Vision **43** (2001) 29 – 44

11. Pearl, J.: Probabilistic Reasoning in Intelligent Systems: Networks of Plausible Inference. Morgan Kaufmann (1988)

12. Kolmogorov, V.: Convergent tree-reweighted message passing for energy minimization. Microsoft Technical Report MSR-TR-2005-38 (2005)

13. Geman, S., Geman, D.: Stochastic relaxation, gibbs distribution, and the bayesian restoration of images. IEEE Transactions on Pattern Analysis and Machine Intelligence **6** (1984) 721 – 741

14. Irani, M., Peleg, S.: Improving resolution by image registration. CVGIP: Graphical Models and Image Processing **53** (1991) 231 – 239

15. Ben-Ezra, M., Zomet, A., Nayar, S.K.: Video super-resolution using controlled subpixel detector shifts. IEEE Transactions on Pattern Analysis and Machine Intelligence **27** (2005) 977 – 987

16. Freeman, W., Pasztor, E., Carmichael, O.: Learning low-level vision. International Journal of Computer Vision **40** (2000) 24 – 57

17. Sun, J., Zheng, N.N., Tao, H., Shum, H.Y.: Image hallucination with primal sketch priors. (In: Proceedings of IEEE Computer Vision and Pattern Recognition 2003)

18. Cook, R.L., Torrance, K.E.: A reflectance model for computer graphics. In: Proceedings of SIGGRAPH 1981. (1981) 307–316

19. Westin, S.H., Arvo, J.R., Torrance, K.E.: Predicting reflectance functions from complex surfaces. In: Proceedings of SIGGRAPH 1992. (1992) 255–264

20. Ashikhmin, M., Premonze, S., Shirley, P.: A microfacet-based brdf generator. In: Proceedings of SIGGRAPH 2000. (2000) 65–74

21. Ngan, A., Durand, F., Matusik, W.: Experimental analysis of brdf models. In: Proceedings of 16th Eurographics Symposium on Rendering. (2005)

22. Dempster, A.P., Laird, N.M., Rubin, D.B.: Maximum-likelihood from incomplete data via the em algorithm. Journal of the Royal Statistical Society **39**(1) (1977) 1–38

23. Bilmes, J.: A gentle tutorial on the em algorithm and its application to parameter estimation for gaussian mixture and hidden markov models. Technical Report ICSI-TR-97-021, Univ. of California-Berkeley (1997)

24. Frankot, R., Chellappa, R.: A method for enforcing integrability in shape from shading algorithms. IEEE Transactions on Pattern Analysis and Machine Intelligence **10** (1988) 439 – 451

25. Kovesi, P.: Shapelets correlated with surface normals produce surfaces. (In: Proceedings of IEEE International Conference on Computer Vision 2005)

26. Agrawal, A., Chellappa, R., Raskar, R.: An algebraic approach to surface reconstruction from gradient fields. (In: Proceedings of IEEE International Conference on Computer Vision 2005)

The 4-Source Photometric Stereo Under General Unknown Lighting

Chia-Ping Chen[1,2] and Chu-Song Chen[1,3]

[1] Institute of Information Science,
Academia Sinica, Taipei, Taiwan
[2] Department of Computer Science and Information Engineering,
National Taiwan University, Taipei, Taiwan
[3] Graduate Institute of Networking and Multimedia,
National Taiwan University, Taipei, Taiwan
{cpchen, song}@iis.sinica.edu.tw

Abstract. Many previous works on photometric stereo have shown how to recover the shape and reflectance properties of an object using multiple images taken under a fixed viewpoint and variable lighting conditions. However, most of them only dealt with a single point light source in each image. In this paper, we show how to perform photometric stereo with four images which are taken under distant but general lighting conditions. Our method is based on the representation that uses low-order spherical harmonics for Lambertian objects. Attached shadows are considered in this representation. We show that the lighting conditions can be estimated regardless of object shape and reflectance properties. The estimated illumination conditions can then help to recover the shape and reflectance properties.

1 Introduction

Photometric stereo methods recover the shape and reflectance properties of an object using multiple images under varying lighting conditions but fixed viewpoint. Most works on this problem assumed that lighting comes from a single source, generally a point source or a controlled, diffused source of light. Woodham [1] first introduced photometric stereo for Lambertian surfaces assuming known albedos and known lighting directions. The method was based on the use of the so-called reflectance maps in the form of look-up tables. Three images were used to solve the reflectance equation for recovering surface gradients and albedos of a Lambertian surface. Coleman and Jain [2] used four images to detect and exclude highlight pixels. They used four combinations of three light sources to compute four albedo values at each pixel. Presence of specular highlight will make the computed albedos different, indicating that some measurement should be excluded. Barskey and Petrou [3] showed that the method in [2] is still problematic if shadows are present, and generalized it to handle color images.

Moses [4] and Shashua [5] have pointed out that one can only recover the scaled surface normals up to an unknown linear transformation when each image

A. Leonardis, H. Bischof, and A. Pinz (Eds.): ECCV 2006, Part III, LNCS 3953, pp. 72–83, 2006.
© Springer-Verlag Berlin Heidelberg 2006

of the target object is lit by a single point source with unknown intensity and direction. Hayakawa [6] used [4, 5]'s result in a factorization framework to handle many images. These results assumed there is no shadow. In [7, 8, 9], it has been shown that integrability reduces the ambiguity to a generalized bas-relief transformation, which allows the recovery of a surface up to a stretch and shear in the z-direction.

By considering non-Lambertian surfaces, Tagare and deFigueriredo [10] developed a theory of photometric stereo for the class of m-lobed reflectance map. Kay and Caelly [11] continued their work and investigated the problem from a practical point of view. They applied nonlinear regression to a larger number of input images. Solomon and Ikeuchi [12] extended the method in [2] by separating the object into different areas. The Torrance-Sparrow model was then used to compute the surface roughness. Nayar et al. [13] used a hybrid reflectance model, and recovered not only the surface gradients but also parameters of the reflectance model. In these approaches, the models used are usually somewhat complex, and more parameters need to be estimated.

Hertzmann and Seitz [14] used a reference object and presented an approach to compute surface orientations and reflectance properties. They made use of orientation consistency to establish correspondence between the unknown object and a known reference object. In many cases, however, obtaining a reference object for correspondence can be very difficult. Goldman et al. [15] further extended this method so that the reference object is no longer needed but assumed that objects are composed of a small number of fundamental materials.

Previous work on this problem shows a progression towards lighting conditions that are less constrained, but most of them still focused on recovering structure based on the assumption of a single point source in each image. For complicated lighting environments, Basri et al. [16] and Ramamoorthi et al. [17] have provided a new way to describe the effect of general lighting on a Lambertian object. Their results showed that only the low frequency components of lighting have a significant effect on the reflectance function of a Lambertian object. These components are represented as low-order spherical harmonics. They showed that the set of images produced by a convex Lambertian object under arbitrary lighting can be well approximated by a low dimensional linear set of images. This set is 4D for a first-order approximation, 9D for a second-order approximation.

Basri and Jacobs [18] used this representation to handle the photometric stereo problem under general lighting. They assumed that the zero- and first-order harmonics, which correspond to the albedos and surface normals scaled by albedos, will show up in the space spanned by the principal components obtained by performing SVD on input images. Their method can reconstruct object shape well when a large number of images are available.

In this paper, we also consider images produced by general lighting conditions that are not known ahead of time, and we require only four images of the target object. The starting point of our method is the spherical harmonic representation. We first estimate the lighting condition without knowing the object shape with the 4D approximation. Then we couple our refinement techniques for surface normal, albedo, and lighting condition into an iterative process, where improved shape results in improved lighting and albedo estimation and vice versa. We confirm experimentally that these optimization procedures produce good results in spite of the approximations made by the low-order spherical harmonic representations. Existing techniques can then be used to translate these normals into an integrable surface, if desired. We also present some experiments to illustrate the potential of our method.

We formulate our problem and show the spherical harmonic representation used by our method in Section 2. Lighting estimation method without knowing object shape is described in Section 3. The shape and reflectance reconstruction process is shown in Section 4, where we also propose an iterative optimization algorithm to obtain a more robust solution. Section 5 shows experimental results of both synthetic and real images, while conclusions and future work are made in Section 6.

2   Problem Formulation

The inputs of our method are four images of a static object taken at a fixed pose but under different illuminations. The lighting conditions, shape, and reflectance properties are all unknown. From these inputs, we seek to estimate the lighting conditions, and to reconstruct the shape and reflectance properties.

We assume that the surface of the target object has Lambertian reflectance. The only parameter of this model is the albedo of each point on the object, which describes the fraction of the light reflected. We also assume that this object is illuminated by distant light sources, so that the directions and intensities of light sources are the same for all points of this object. We do not model the effects of cast shadows and interreflections.

The output of our method are albedos, surface normals of each pixel, and the lighting conditions of four input images. We can then reconstruct the surface by integrating the normal field. We can also render novel images under new lighting conditions or new viewpoints.

2.1   Modeling Reflection

We use the symbol I_i to represent the intensity of a certain pixel in input image i, $i = 1 \ldots 4$. With distant light source assumption, the intensities of a Lambertian object under general lighting conditions can be represented as follows:

$$I_i = \rho \int L_i(l) \max(l \cdot N, 0) \, dl, \tag{1}$$

where ρ and N are the albedo and surface normal of this pixel, l is the unit vector indicating the direction of incoming light, and $L_i(l)$ is the radiance intensity from direction l in image i. The integral is over all possible lighting directions.

In [16, 17], the authors viewed this process of light reflection as a convolution, where the incident illumination signal is filtered by the reflective properties of the surface, which is the Lambertian kernel in our case. They also showed that the Lambertian kernel acts like a low-pass filter, preserving only the lowest frequency components of the lighting. According to their results, the effects of general lighting on a Lambertian object can be represented by spherical harmonics:

$$I_i = \rho \sum_{n=0}^{\infty} \sum_{m=-n}^{n} \sqrt{\frac{4\pi}{2n+1}} k_n l_{nm} Y_{nm}(N), \tag{2}$$

where Y_{nm} are the surface spherical harmonics, k_n and l_{nm} are the coefficients of harmonic expansions of the Lambertian kernel and lighting, respectively. It has been proved in [16] that for any distant and isotropic lighting, at least 98% of the resulting function can be captured by the second-order spherical harmonic approximation. A first-order approximation captures at least 75% of the reflectance. These bounds are not tight, and in fact many common lighting conditions yield significantly better approximations. For example, under a point source illumination the first- and second-order harmonics approximate the reflectance function to 87.5% and 99.22% respectively.

Then, we can relate the intensity quadruple of the same pixel in four input images to the spherical harmonics with the second-order approximation:

$$I = \begin{bmatrix} I_1 \\ I_2 \\ I_3 \\ I_4 \end{bmatrix} = \rho L_{4\times 9} H_{9\times 1} = \rho L_{4\times 9} \begin{bmatrix} 1 \\ N_x \\ N_y \\ N_z \\ 3N_z^2 - 1 \\ N_x N_y \\ N_x N_z \\ N_y N_z \\ N_x^2 - N_y^2 \end{bmatrix}, \tag{3}$$

where I is the stack of intensity quadruple, each row of $L_{4\times 9}$ is the lighting configuration of each image, and $H_{9\times 1}$ is the spherical harmonics which can be decided analytically when the surface normal $N = [N_x, N_y, N_z]^T$ is known. Note that we omit additional constant factors since they do not change the space spanned by these bases.

3   Lighting Estimation

In an uncalibrated photometric stereo problem, the lighting condition L, albedo ρ, and surface normal N are all unknown, making it highly unconstrained. However, with first-order approximation of spherical harmonics, we show in this section that, regardless of object shape and reflectance, the lighting conditions are constrained and can be estimated up to a subgroup of the 4×4 linear transformation, called *Lorentz* transformations (also in [18]).

When first-order approximation of spherical harmonics is adopted, the intensity quadruple can be rewritten from (3) as follows:

$$I = \rho L_{4 \times 4} H_{4 \times 1} = \rho L_{4 \times 4} \left[1 \ N_x \ N_y \ N_z \right]^T . \tag{4}$$

When L is known, the albedo and surface normal can be recovered simply by inverting this equation as:

$$\rho H = \left[\rho \ \rho N_x \ \rho N_y \ \rho N_z \right]^T = L^{-1} I . \tag{5}$$

However, in a photometric stereo problem under general lighting, L is usually unknown. In the following, we show how to estimate L with this first-order approximation.

Since N is the unit surface normal, $N^T N = 1$. Let $J = \text{diag}\{-1, 1, 1, 1\}$, it can be easily verified that

$$(\rho H)^T J (\rho H) = \left(I^T L^{-T} \right) J \left(L^{-1} I \right) = I^T B I = 0, \tag{6}$$

where $B = L^{-T} J L^{-1}$ is a 4×4 symmetric matrix. Equation (6) indicates that intensity quadruples are constrained to lie on a quadratic surface regardless of what the albedos and surface normals are:

$$\begin{aligned}
0 = & B_{11} I_1^2 + B_{22} I_2^2 + B_{33} I_3^2 + B_{44} I_4^2 + \\
& 2 B_{12} I_1 I_2 + 2 B_{13} I_1 I_3 + 2 B_{14} I_1 I_4 + \\
& 2 B_{23} I_2 I_3 + 2 B_{24} I_2 I_4 + 2 B_{34} I_3 I_4 .
\end{aligned} \tag{7}$$

This equation has only ten unknowns, which follows from the fact that the matrix B is symmetric, and we can list one equation per pixel.

The ten unknowns of B can be determined even when the lighting conditions L is unknown and even when there is no object point where the albedo ρ and surface normal N are given. All that is required is having sufficient measured intensity quadruples. A standard linear least-squares method can be used to estimate these ten unknowns. This least-squares estimation should be robust since the number of image pixels are usually large and each measured intensity quadruple contributes useful information. However, because this linear system is homogeneous, B can only be solved up to an unknown scale. This ambiguity comes from (4). For any scalar $s > 0$,

$$I = (\frac{\rho}{s})(sL)H, \tag{8}$$

which means that we cannot distinguish between brighter surfaces lit by a dimmer illumination or darker surfaces lit by a brighter illumination. In the remainder of this paper, we will therefore ignore this scale ambiguity.

Thus, empirical measurements determine the matrix B. The constraint that B imposes on the lighting condition L can be interpreted when expressed in terms of B^{-1}:

$$B^{-1} = (L^{-T} J L^{-1})^{-1} = L J L^T, \tag{9}$$

where $J^{-1} = J$. Because B^{-1} is also symmetric, B^{-1} can be factorized as follows by Symmetric Schur Decomposition:

$$B^{-1} = QJ\Lambda Q^T, \tag{10}$$

where Q contains the orthogonal eigenvectors and $\Lambda = \text{diag}\{|\lambda_1|, \lambda_2, \lambda_3, \lambda_4\}$ is the eigenvalue matrix. Without lost of generality, we order Λ and Q so that the negative eigenvalue λ_1 is the first, and we move the negative sign into J to ensure that every element of Λ is positive. Then we can decide that $L = \sqrt{\Lambda}Q$. If there is only one positive eigenvalue we reverse the sign of B^{-1}.

When there is significant noise, or when the assumptions do not strictly hold (Lambertian surfaces, distant light source, etc.), the eigenvalues of B may not have the proper signs. In that case we resort to an iterative optimization to find L that minimizes the Frobenous norm $\|B^{-1} - LJL^T\|$.

At this point we have recovered a valid L. However, there is still an unsolved ambiguity. For any matrix C that satisfies $CJC^T = J$, $B^{-1} = (LC)J(LC)^T = LJL^T$. This set of transformations forms the Lorentz group [19]. Because the symmetric quadratic form $CJC^T = J$ gives ten quadratic equations in the 16 unknown components of C, a Lorentz transformation has six degrees of freedom. We can resolve this ambiguity, for example, if we know the surface normals and albedos of two points, or we can remove this ambiguity by enforcing surface integrability as in [9].

In sum, the lighting condition can be estimated using the first-order approximation of spherical harmonics, regardless of the albedo and surface normal. Although not very accurate, this first-order approximation suffices for good initial lighting conditions. It helps us reconstruct shape and reflectance properties of the target object and can be refined afterwards.

4   Shape and Reflectance Reconstruction

In the previous section we show how to estimate the initial lighting conditions without knowing the albedos and surface normals of the target object. With this initial estimation $L_{4\times4}$, we can easily recover the albedo ρ and surface normal N by (5). However, the results could not be accurate enough because only first-order spherical harmonics are used. In this section, we apply the estimated lighting conditions and surface normals from the first-order approximation as initial, and iteratively refine lighting conditions, albedos, and surface normals by incorporating second-order spherical harmonics into an optimization process.

4.1   Refine Lighting Estimation

When the surface normals are reconstructed to some extent, they can really help the re-estimation of lighting conditions even if they are not very accurate. In the following, we show how to refine the lighting conditions with the second-order spherical harmonics when surface normals are available.

Given a surface normal N and two image intensities I_s and I_t, its albedo can be estimated using Equation 3 as:

$$\rho_s = \frac{I_s}{L_s H_{9\times 1}} \quad \text{or as} \quad \rho_t = \frac{I_t}{L_t H_{9\times 1}}, \tag{11}$$

where L_s and L_t are the sth and tth rows of $L_{4\times 9}$, respectively. By expanding $\rho_s = \rho_t$, we obtain:

$$\left[-I_s \ I_t \right]_{1\times 2} \begin{bmatrix} L_t \\ L_s \end{bmatrix}_{2\times 9} H_{9\times 1} = 0, \tag{12}$$

where $H_{9\times 1}$ can be derived analytically given surface normal N, and I_s, I_t are the observed intensities in two input images. This forms a linear equation where only the lighting conditions L_s and L_t are unknown. Four observed intensities in the four input images yield three independent equations for every pixel. With P pixels, we have $3P$ equations to solve the 36 unknown coefficients of $L_{4\times 9}$. Since usually $3P \gg 36$, we can solve $L_{4\times 9}$ effectively using least-squares methods with the help of known surface normals.

4.2 Refine Reflectance

Once we have a better estimation of the lighting conditions, we can improve the albedo estimation with known surface normals. This can be easily done with the following equation:

$$\rho L_{4\times 9} H_{9\times 1} = \rho \begin{bmatrix} L_1 H \\ L_2 H \\ L_3 H \\ L_4 H \end{bmatrix} = \begin{bmatrix} I_1 \\ I_2 \\ I_3 \\ I_4 \end{bmatrix}. \tag{13}$$

The optimal albedo which has the least square error can be derived as:

$$\rho = \sum_{i=1}^{4} (L_i H I_i) / \sum_{s=1}^{4} (L_i H)^2 . \tag{14}$$

4.3 Refine Surface Normals

With refined lighting conditions and albedos, we can further improve the estimation of surface normals. For each pixel, we seek to find the best unit surface normal N that minimizes the following energy function:

$$E(N) = \|\rho L_{4\times 9} H_{9\times 1} - I\|^2 = \sum_{i=1}^{4} (\rho L_i H_{9\times 1} - I_i)^2 . \tag{15}$$

Instead of using conventional convex minimization over the continuous surface normal field and enforcing unity constraint explicitly on N, we adopt discrete optimization over a fixed number of available unit normals. We seek an optimal labeling which minimizes (15)

$$v^* = \arg\min_{v} E(\hat{N}_v), \tag{16}$$

where $\{\hat{N}_v | v = 1, 2, \ldots V\}$ is the set of available unit directions. Then the surface normal N is refined as $\hat{N}_{v^*}$. To produce uniform sampling of normal directions, we start with an icosahedron, and perform subdivision on each face 5 times recursively [20]. Totally, 10168 points are uniformly sampled on the unit sphere.

One problem of the above estimation is that the surface normals are refined one by one independently. The generated normal field is not guaranteed to be consistent with a 3D surface, thus we enforce integrability by solving a Poisson equation to obtain a least-squares surface reconstruction, and subsequently the normals are recomputed by differentiate this surface. To compute a 3D surface from the estimated surface orientations, given the normal field $N(x, y)$, we solve the height field $z(x, y)$ that minimizes

$$\Psi(z) = \sum_{x,y} \left(\frac{\delta z(x,y)}{\delta x} + \frac{N_x(x,y)}{N_z(x,y)} \right)^2 + \left(\frac{\delta z(x,y)}{\delta y} + \frac{N_y(x,y)}{N_z(x,y)} \right)^2. \tag{17}$$

This amounts to integrating the normal field. The minimization gives rise to a large but sparse system of linear equations. The normals are then recomputed from this surface approximation. This step can be viewed as projecting the possibly non-integrable normal field into the subspace of feasible normal fields.

4.4 Iterative Algorithm

We couple our lighting, albedo, and shape estimation techniques described above into an iterative process, where improved shape estimation leads to improved lighting and albedo estimation and vice versa.

Initialization. Get an initial estimation of lighting condition $L_{4 \times 4}$ as described in Section 2, then recover the surface normal N by (5).
Step 1. Refine lighting conditions $L_{4 \times 9}$ with the help of the estimated surface normal N by solving (12).
Step 2. Refine albedos with currently estimated surface normals and lighting conditions according to (14).
Step 3. Search the optimal surface normal for each pixel by (16). Integrate the normal field to get an approximated surface according to (17) and then recompute the surface normals again.
Termination. Step 1-3 are iterated until the estimated components no longer change or the specified maximum iteration number is reached.

Each step in our iterative algorithm is guaranteed to monotonically decrease the reconstruction error $|\rho L H - I|$ between reconstructed images and input images, except the enforcement of integrability. However, this integration step only makes little changes to the surface in our experience and the reconstruction error does not change much after a few iterations. Therefore, our optimization algorithm is likely to find a solution near a local optimum.

5   Experiments

We now present experiments to evaluate our method. Because we use the second-order approximation of spherical harmonics, certain built-in errors persist even in the ideal case. So we first describe experiments on synthetic data to verify some basic properties of our method.

We generate four images of a diffuse unit sphere with uniform albedo under four different lighting conditions. We then use our method to recover the surface normals of this sphere. Since we have ground truth, we can resolve the Lorentz ambiguity by some known surface normals. Figure 1 shows the four input images of this unit sphere. The recovered surface normals are shown in Figure 2, where positive values are shown in green, and negative values are shown in red. The mean error between the recovered and real surface normals is 0.12 degrees. This experiment tells us that our method will produce good results in ideal situation, that is, in the absence of sensing error, cast shadow, specularity and any other source of noise.

We have also run our method on real images from Yale Face Database B [21]. To reduce the effect that may be caused by cast shadows, only frontally illuminated images are used. Each image is lit by a single point source; thus we average pairs of images to simulate complicated lighting conditions. This time we enforce the integrability constraint to resolve the Lorentz ambiguity. Figure 3(a) shows the four input images. The recovered albedos and surface normals are shown in Figure 4. Note that there are some cast shadows, noises, unreliable pixels that have been saturated in the four input images. But the results of our method are still quite satisfactory. Noticeable artifacts occur in the eyes which exhibit highly specular reflection, in the side of the nose where there are cast shadows that we do not model, as well as in the outline of eyebrow because of alignment error since this target object is not really static.

Fig. 1. Four input images of an unit sphere

Fig. 2. Recovered surface normals of the unit sphere. Positive values are shown in green, and negative values are shown in red.

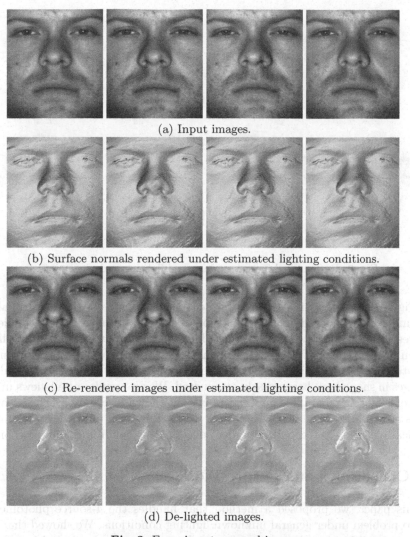

(a) Input images.

(b) Surface normals rendered under estimated lighting conditions.

(c) Re-rendered images under estimated lighting conditions.

(d) De-lighted images.

Fig. 3. Experiments on real images

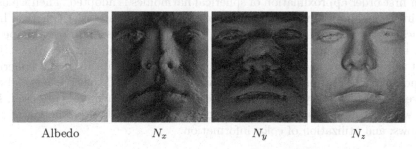

Albedo N_x N_y N_z

Fig. 4. Recovered albedo and surface normals. Positive values are shown in green, and negative values are shown in red.

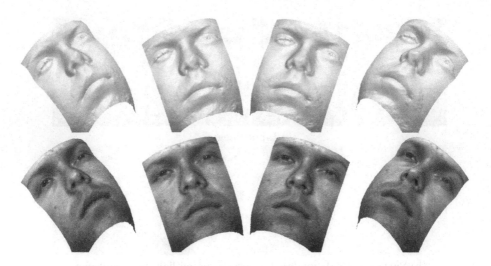

Fig. 5. Re-rendered images under novel lighting and viewpoints

Figure 3(b) shows the recovered surface normals rendered with uniform albe-dos under the estimated lighting condition of each input image. The re-rendered images with the estimated albedos reproduce the four input images quite well, as shown in Figure 3(c). The de-lighted images shown in Figure 3(d) exhibit much less structure than original ones, because shading effects that are accounted for changes in shape have been greatly attenuated. We also render novel views under different lighting conditions and viewpoints, as shown in Figure 5. These novels views are quite realistic, which indicates the usefulness of our method for many applications, such as recognition under novel lighting conditions and viewpoints.

6   Conclusions and Future Work

In this paper, we proposed a method that handles the 4-source photometric stereo problem under general unknown lighting conditions. We showed that the lighting conditions can be estimated regardless of the albedos and object shape when first-order approximation of spherical harmonics is adopted. Then we used this initial estimation in an iterative process, where second-order spherical harmonics were incorporated. During the optimization process, improved shape estimation leads to improved lighting and albedo estimation and vice versa. The effects of attached shadows are considered, which benefits from the spherical harmonic representation. The experimental results showed that our method can derive quite satisfactory results even when only four input images are used. Future work will be focused on introducing specularity models, prediction of cast shadows, and utilization of color information.

Acknowledgments. This work was supported in part under grants NSC 94-2213-E-001-002 and NSC 94-2752-E-002-007-PAE.

References

1. R.J. Woodham. Photometric Method for Determining Surface Orientation from Multiple Images. *Optical Engineering*, 19(1):139-144, 1980.
2. E.N. Coleman, Jr. and R. Jain. Obtaining 3-dimensional shape of textured and specular surfaces using four-source photometry. *CGIP*, 18(4):309-328, April 1982.
3. S. Barsky and M. Petrou. The 4-source photometric stereo technique for three-dimensional surfaces in the presence of highlights and shadows. *PAMI*, 25(10):1239-1252, October 2003.
4. Y. Moses. Face recognition: generalization to novel images. Ph.D. Thesis, Weizmann Institute of Science, 1993.
5. A. Shashua, On Photometric Issues in 3D Visual Recognition from a Single 2D Image. *IJCV* 21(1-2):99-122, 1997.
6. H. Hayakawa. Photometric stereo under a light source with arbitrary motion. *JOSA*, 11(11):3079-3089, 1994.
7. P.N. Belhumeur, D.J. Kriegman, A.L. Yuille. The Bas-Relief Ambiguity. *IJCV*, 35(1):33-44, 1999.
8. J. Fan, L.B. Wolff. Surface Curvature and Shape Reconstruction from Unknown Multiple Illumination and Integrability. *CVIU* 65(2):347-359, 1997.
9. A. Yuille, D. Snow, R. Epstein, P. Belhumeur. Determining Generative Models of Objects Under Varying Illumination: Shape and Albedo from Multiple Images Using SVD and Integrability. *IJCV*, 35(3):203-222, 1999.
10. H.D. Tagare and R.J.P. deFigueiredo. A theory of photometric stereo for a class of diffuse non-lambertian surfaces. *PAMI*, 13(2):133-152, February 1991.
11. G. Kay and T. Caelly. Estimating the parameters of an illumination model using photometric stereo. *GMIP*, 57(5):365-388, 1995.
12. F. Solomon and K. Ikeuchi. Extracting the shape and roughness of specular lobe objects using four light photometric stereo. *PAMI*, 18(4):449-454, April 1996.
13. S.K. Nayar, K. Ikeuchi, and T. Kanade. Determining shape and reflectance of hybrid surfaces by photometric sampling. *IEEE Trans. on Robotics and Automation*, 6(4):418-431, 1990.
14. A. Hertzmann and S.M. Seitz. Shape and materials by example: a photometric stereo approach. *CVPR*, 2003.
15. D.B. Goldman, B. Curless, A. Hertzmann, and S.M. Seitz. Shape and Spatially-Varying BRDFs From Photometric Stereo. *ICCV*, 2005.
16. R. Basri and D. Jacobs. Lambertian reflectance and linear subspaces. *PAMI*, 25(2):218-233, 2003.
17. R. Ramamoorthi and P. Hanrahan, On the relationship between radiance and irradiance: determining the illumination from images of a convex Lambertian object. *Journal of the Optical Society of America A*, 18(10):2448-2459, 2001.
18. R. Basri, D. Jacobs. Photometric Stereo with General Unknown Lighting. *CVPR*, 2001.
19. K. Kanatani. Geometric Computation for Machine Vision. *Oxford University Press*, 1993.
20. D.H. Ballard and C.M. Brown. Computer Vision. In *Prentice Hall*, 1982.
21. A.S. Georghiades and P.N. Belhumeur. From Few to many: Illumination cone models for face recognition under variable lighting and pose. *PAMI*, 23(6):643-660, 2001.

Incorporating Non-motion Cues into 3D Motion Segmentation

Amit Gruber and Yair Weiss

School of Computer Science and Engineering,
The Hebrew University of Jerusalem,
Jerusalem 91904, Israel
{amitg, yweiss}@cs.huji.ac.il

Abstract. We address the problem of segmenting an image sequence into rigidly moving 3D objects. An elegant solution to this problem is the multibody factorization approach in which the measurement matrix is factored into lower rank matrices. Despite progress in factorization algorithms, the performance is still far from satisfactory and in scenes with missing data and noise, most existing algorithms fail.

In this paper we propose a method for incorporating 2D non-motion cues (such as spatial coherence) into multibody factorization. We formulate the problem in terms of constrained factor analysis and use the EM algorithm to find the segmentation. We show that adding these cues improves performance in real and synthetic sequences.

1 Introduction

The task of segmenting an image or an image sequence into objects is a basic step towards the understanding of image contents. Despite vast research in this area, performance of automatic systems still falls far behind human perception.

Motion segmentation provides a powerful cue for separating scenes consisting of multiple independently moving objects. Multibody factorization algorithms [1, 2, 3, 4, 5] provide an elegant framework for segmentation based on the 3D motion of the object. These methods get as input a matrix that contains the location of a number of points in many frames, and use algebraic factorization techniques to calculate the segmentation of the points into objects, as well as the 3D structure and motion of each object. A major advantage of these approaches is that they explicitly use the full temporal trajectory of every point, and therefore they are capable of segmenting objects whose motions cannot be distinguished using only two frames [4].

Despite recent progress in multibody factorization algorithms, their performance is still far from satisfactory. In many sequences, for which the correct segmentation is easily apparent from a single frame, current algorithms often fail to reach it.

Given the power of single frame cues and the poor performance of 3D motion segmentation algorithms, it seems natural to search for a common framework that could incorporate *both cues*. In this paper we provide such a framework. We use a latent variable approach to 3D motion segmentation and show how to modify the M step in an EM algorithm to take advantage of 2D affinities. We show that these cues improve performance in real and synthetic image sequences.

A. Leonardis, H. Bischof, and A. Pinz (Eds.): ECCV 2006, Part III, LNCS 3953, pp. 84–97, 2006.

1.1 Previous Work

The factorization approach to 3D segmentation has been suggested by Costeira and Kanade [1] who suggested to search for a block structure in the 3D structure matrix by computing a $P \times P$ affinity matrix Q from the SVD of the measurements matrix. It can be shown that in the absence of noise, $Q(i,j) = 0$ for points belonging to different segments. In noisy situations the inter block elements $Q(i,j)$ are not zero, and in general they cannot be separated from the intra block elements by thresholding. Sorting the matrix Q to find the segments is an NP-complete problem. Instead, Costeira and Kanade, suggested a greedy suboptimal clustering heuristic which turns out to be very sensitive to noise. In addition, the rank of the noise free measurements matrix should be found from the noisy measurements matrix as an initial step. This is a difficult problem which is discussed extensively in [2].

Gear [2] suggested a similar method that use the reduced row echelon form of the measurements matrix as an affinity matrix. Again, in noisy situations the algorithm does not guarantee correct segmentation. Some assumptions regarding the rank of the motion matrix are needed. Zelnik et al. [3] incorporate directional uncertainty by applying Gear's method on a matrix defined by measurable image quantities (spatial and temporal derivatives). Kanatani [6] proposed an algorithm that takes advantage of the affine subspace constraint. Recent works by [5, 4] have addressed the problem of motion segmentation with missing data. Both methods do not make any assumptions nor require prior information regarding the rank of the motion matrix. In addition [4] handles correlated non-uniform noise in the measurements and utilizes probabilistic prior knowledge on camera motion and scene structure.

Several authors have addressed the related, but different problem of 3D rigid body segmentation based on two frames or instantaneous motion [7, 8, 9, 10]. While these methods show encouraging results, they lack the attractive property of factorization methods in which information from the full temporal sequence is used simultaneously.

A different approach for image segmentation is to use single image cues such as color, intensity, texture and spatial proximity. A common approach is to present segmentation problems as problems of partitioning a weighted graph where the nodes of the graph represent pixels and the weights represent similarity or dissimilarity between them. Then some cost function of the partition should be minimized to find the desired segmentation. In many cases this optimization problem is NP-complete. Shi and Malik [11] introduced the Normalized Cut criterion and suggested an approximation algorithm based on the spectral properties of a weighted graph describing the affinities between pixels. Shi and Malik extend their work to 2D motion segmentation [12].

Single image cues have been used to improve the performance of various segmentation algorithms. An EM framework for incorporating spatial coherence and 2D image motion was presented in [13]. Kolmogorov and Zabih [14] have discussed incorporating spatial coherence into various segmentation algorithms. In this work we show how to incorporate spatial coherence (as well as other 2D non-motion cues) into 3D motion segmentation, as an extension of [15, 4].

1.2 Main Contribution of This Work

In this paper we present a unified framework for segmentation using information emerging from a diversity of cues. While previous segmentation methods can utilize either 3D motion information or 2D affinities but not both, we combine both sources of information.

We follow the constrained factorization approach for motion segmentation [4] based on the factorization formulation introduced by Costeira-Kanade [1]. We use 2D affinities to place priors on the desired semgnetation similar to [11] and show how the priors on the segmentation induce priors directly on the desired matrix factors. Then *constrained factorization with priors* is performed using the EM algorithm.

In contrast, previous approaches ([1, 2, 3, 5]) are based on algorithms (svd, reduced row echelon form, powerfactorization) which do not provide any apparent way to use priors on the segmentation.

Using the constrained factorization approach, we avoid the combinatorial search required by previous factorization approaches (e.g. [1, 2, 3]) in noisy scenarios. In our approach it is guaranteed to find a factorization where the interaction between points that belong to different motions is strictly 0 even in the presence of noise. In addition, with this formulation it is easy to deal with *missing data* and *directional uncertainty* (correlated non-uniform noise in the coordinates of tracked points such as the aperture problem). Another benefit of our formulation is that *no assumptions are made regarding the rank of the motion matrix* M (all affine motions are dealt with), and no prior knowledge about it is needed, unlike most previous methods for $3D$ motion segmentation that require some knowledge or assumptions regarding the rank of the motion matrix M (see [2] for discussion).

The EM algorithm is guaranteed to find a local maximum of the likelihood of S. Our experiments show that the additional information in the form of 2D affinities reduces the dependency in the initialization of the algorithm. Compared to the previous motion-only EM algorithm [4], the number of initializations required for success has diminished (details are given in the experiments section).

2 Model

2.1 3D Motion Segmentation – Problem Formulation

A set of P feature points in F images are tracked along an image sequence. Let (u_{fp}, v_{fp}) denote image coordinates of feature point p in frame f. Let $U = (u_{fp})$, $V = (v_{fp})$ and $W = (w_{ij})$ where $w_{2i-1,j} = u_{ij}$ and $w_{2i,j} = v_{ij}$ for $1 \leq i \leq F$, i.e. W is an interleaving of the rows of U and V. Let K be the number of different motion components in the sequence. Let $\{G_k\}_{k=1}^{K}$ be a partition of the tracked feature points into K disjoint sets, each consists of all the points that conform to the kth motion, and let P_k be the number of feature points in G_k ($\sum P_k = P$). Let M_i^j be a 2×4 matrix describing the jth camera parameters at time i, and let S_j be a $4 \times P_j$ matrix describing the $3D$ homogeneous coordinates of the P_j points in G_j moving according to the jth motion component.

Let

$$\left[M_i^j\right]_{2\times 4} = \left[\begin{array}{cc} m_i^{jT} & d_i^j \\ n_i^{jT} & e_i^j \end{array}\right] \quad \text{and} \quad S_j = \left[\begin{array}{ccc} X_{j1} & \cdots & X_{jP} \\ Y_{j1} & \cdots & Y_{jP} \\ Z_{j1} & \cdots & Z_{jP} \\ 1 & \cdots & 1 \end{array}\right]_{4\times P} \tag{1}$$

m_i^j and n_i^j are 3×1 vectors that describe the rotation of the jth camera; d_i^j and e_i^j are scalars describing camera translation[1], and S_j describes points location in $3D$. Let $\tilde{W}$ be a matrix of observations ordered according to the grouping $\{G_k\}_{k=1}^K$, i.e. the first P_1 columns of $\tilde{W}$ correspond to the points in G_1 and so on. Under affine projection, and in the absence of noise, Costeira and Kanade [1] formulated this problem in the form:

$$\left[\tilde{W}\right]_{2F\times P} = [M]_{2F\times 4K} \left[\tilde{S}\right]_{4K\times P} \tag{2}$$

where

$$M = \left[\begin{array}{ccc} M_1^1 & \cdots & M_1^K \\ \vdots & & \\ M_F^1 & \cdots & M_F^K \end{array}\right]_{2F\times 4K} \quad \text{and} \quad \tilde{S} = \left[\begin{array}{cccc} S_1 & 0 & \cdots & 0 \\ 0 & S_2 & \cdots & 0 \\ \vdots & & & \\ 0 & 0 & \cdots & S_K \end{array}\right]_{4K\times P} \tag{3}$$

If the segmentation $\{G_k\}_{k=1}^K$ were known, then we could have separated the point tracks (columns of the observations matrix) into K disjoint submatrices according to $\{G_k\}$, and run a single structure from motion algorithm (for example [16]) on each submatrix. In real sequences, where segmentation is unknown, the observation matrix, W, is a column permutation of the ordered matrix $\tilde{W}$:

$$W = \tilde{W}\Pi = MS \Rightarrow S = \tilde{S}\Pi \tag{4}$$

where S is a $4K \times P$ matrix describing scene structure (with unordered columns) and $\Pi_{P\times P}$ is a column permutation matrix. Hence, the structure matrix S is in general not block diagonal, but rather a column permutation of a block diagonal matrix. The motion matrix, M, remains unchanged.

For noisy observations, the model is:

$$[W]_{2F\times P} = [M]_{2F\times 4K} [S]_{4K\times P} + [\eta]_{2F\times P} \tag{5}$$

where η is Gaussian noise. We seek a factorization of W to M and S under the constraint that S is a permuted block diagonal matrix $\tilde{S}$, that minimizes the weighted squared error $\sum_t[(W_t - M_tS)^T \Psi_t^{-1}(W_t - M_tS)]$, where Ψ_t^{-1} is the inverse covariance matrix of the $2D$ tracked feature points in frame t.

Let π be a labeling of all points, i.e. $\pi = (\pi_1, \ldots, \pi_P)$, where $\pi_p = k$ stands for point p is moving according to the kth motion ($p \in G_k$). Let s_p denote the $3D$

---

[1] We do not subtract the mean of each row from it, since in case of missing data the centroid of points visible in a certain frame does not coincide with the centroid of all points.

coordinates of point p, and let $\hat{S}$ denote $[s_1, \ldots, s_P]$ the $3D$ coordinates of all points (S contains both segmentation and geometry information, $\hat{S}$ contains only geometry information). Taking the negative log of the complete likelihood (which will be needed for the EM algorithm presented in section 3), the energy function due to 3D motion is:

$$E_{\text{3D-Motion}}(\hat{S}, \pi, M) = \sum_p E_{\text{3D-Motion}}(s_p, \pi_p, M) = \tag{6}$$

$$\sum_p \sum_t ((W_{t,p} - M_t^{\pi} s_p)^T \Psi_{t,p}^{-1} (W_{t,p} - M_t^{\pi} s_p))$$

Notice that if the motion M is given, $E_{\text{3D-Motion}}(\hat{S}, \pi, M)$ is a sum of functions of variables related to a single point independent of the others.

2.2 2D Affinities

We define affinity between pixels along a sequence similar to [11]. Shi et al. [11] define similarity weights in an image as the product of a feature similarity term and a spatial proximity term:

$$w_{i,j} = e^{\frac{-\| \cdot (\cdot) - \cdot (\cdot) \|_2^2}{\cdot \cdot^2}} \cdot \begin{cases} e^{\frac{-\| \cdot (\cdot) - \cdot (\cdot) \|_2^2}{\cdot \cdot^2}} & \text{if } \|X(i) - X(j)\|_2^2 < r \\ 0 & \text{otherwise} \end{cases} \tag{7}$$

where $X(i)$ is the 2D coordinates of point i in the image and F is the vector of features used for segmentation. For example, if segmentation is performed according to spatial proximity, $F(i) = 1$ for all points.

The weights w_{ij} were defined in [11] for a single image. We adapt them to a sequence of images:

1. In order to use the information from all given frames rather than only one, we sum the energy terms $\frac{-\|X.(i)-X.(j)\|_2^2}{\sigma_\cdot^2}$, $\frac{-\|F.(i)-F.(j)\|_2^2}{\sigma_\cdot^2}$, over the entire sequence. In the summation, if one of the points is unobserved at a certain frame, this frame is omitted.

2. Since point locations along the sequence are the output of a tracking algorithm, they are given up to some uncertainty. We give weights to these locations according to $R_t^{-1}(i, j)$, the inverse covariance matrix of $(X_t(i) - X_t(j))$ in frame t (it can be shown that the posterior inverse covariance matrix of a 2D point location is $\begin{bmatrix} \sum I_x^2 & \sum I_x I_y \\ \sum I_x I_y & \sum I_y^2 \end{bmatrix}$. see [15, 4, 17]), thereby replacing $\|X_t(i) - X_t(j)\|_2^2$ with $(X_t(i) - X_t(j))^T R_t^{-1}(i, j)(X_t(i) - X_t(j))$. For frames where either point i or j is missing, $R_t^{-1}(i, j) = 0$. In other words, frame t is omitted from the summation.

The energy of an assignment due to spatial coherence is then:

$$E_{\text{2D-coherence}}(\pi) = \sum_{p,q} w_{p,q} \cdot (1 - \delta(\pi_p - \pi_q)) \tag{8}$$

Notice that $E_{\text{2D-coherence}}(\pi)$ is a sum of functions of two variables at a time.

3   An EM Algorithm for Multibody Factorization

Our goal is to find the best segmentation and 3D structure. We are looking for

$$\hat{S}, \pi = \arg\max_{\hat{S},\pi} \Pr(\hat{S}, \pi | W) = \arg\max_{\hat{S},\pi} < \Pr(\hat{S}, \pi | M, W) >_M \qquad (9)$$

Maximizing the likelihood of W given $\hat{S}, \pi, M$ is equivalent to minimizing the energy $E(\hat{S}, \pi, M)$, i.e. the negative log of the likelihood function. This energy consists of two terms: a term of 3D motion information and a term of 2D coherence. These are the terms $E_{\text{3D-Motion}}(s_p, \pi_p, M)$ and $E_{\text{2D-coherence}}(\pi)$ introduced before.

$$E(\hat{S}, \pi, M) = E_{\text{3D-Motion}}(\hat{S}, \pi, M) + \lambda E_{\text{2D-coherence}}(\pi) \qquad (10)$$

In order to find the optimal $\hat{S}$ and π, we minimize the energy with respect to $\hat{S}$ and π while averaging over M using the EM algorithm. The EM algorithm works with the expected complete log likelihood which is the expectation of the energy (taken with respect to the motion, M).

$$E(\hat{S}, \pi) = < E(\hat{S}, \pi, M) >_M =$$
$$< E_{\text{3D-Motion}}(\hat{S}, \pi, M) + \lambda E_{\text{2D-coherence}}(\pi) >_M = \qquad (11)$$
$$< E_{\text{3D-Motion}}(\hat{S}, \pi, M) >_M + \lambda E_{\text{2D-coherence}}(\pi)$$

In the E step, sufficient statistics of the motion distribution are computed, such that $< E(\hat{S}, \pi, M) >_M$ can be computed for every $\hat{S}, \pi$. In the M-step, $< E(\hat{S}, \pi, M) >_M$ is minimized with respect to $\hat{S}$ and π.

3.1   Optimization with Respect to π

In this section, we focus on the optimization of $< E(\hat{S}, \pi, M) >_M$ with respect to π which is a part of the M-step. The missing details regarding the E step and optimization with respect to $\hat{S}$ in the M step are given in the next subsection.

The motion energy term (averaged over M) can be written as a sum of functions, D_p, each of which is a function of variables (s_p, π_p) related to a single pixel:

$$< E_{\text{3D-Motion}}(\hat{S}, \pi, M) >_M = \sum_p < E_{\text{3D-Motion}}(s_p, \pi_p, M) >_M = \qquad (12)$$
$$\sum_p D_p(s_p, \pi_p)$$

The 2D coherence energy function is a sum of terms of pairwise energy $V_{p,q}(\pi_p, \pi_q)$ for each pair of pixels p, q:

$$E_{\text{2D-coherence}}(\pi) = \sum_{p,q} E_{\text{2D-coherence}}(\pi_p, \pi_q) = \qquad (13)$$
$$\sum_{p,q} V_{p,q}(\pi_p, \pi_q)$$

Therefore $< E(\hat{S}, \pi, M) >_M$ can be represented as a sum of terms D_p involving a single point and terms $V_{p,q}$ involving pairs of points.

$$< E(\hat{S}, \pi, M) >_M = \sum_p D_p(s_p, \pi_p) + \sum_{p,q} V_{p,q}(\pi_p, \pi_q) \tag{14}$$

With this representation, if s_p is known for all p, then π_p can be found for all p by solving a standard energy minimization problem in a Potts model. In the binary case (i.e. $K = 2$), the optimal minimum of the energy function can be found efficiently using graph cuts [18]. If there are more than two objects, an approximation can be found using either graph cuts [18] or loopy belief propagation [19].

Since s_p is not known, we define

$$D_p(\pi_p) = \min_{s.} D_p(s_p, \pi_p) \tag{15}$$

and then

$$\min_{\hat{S}, \pi} < E(\hat{S}, \pi, M) >_M = \tag{16}$$

$$\min_{\pi} \left[\sum_p \min_{s.} D_p(s_p, \pi_p) + \sum_{p,q} V_{p,q}(\pi_p, \pi_q) \right] =$$

$$\min_{\pi} \left[\sum_p D_p(\pi_p) + \sum_{p,q} V_{p,q}(\pi_p, \pi_q) \right]$$

In the next section we show how $D_p(\pi_p)$ is computed for each possible value of π_p. The pairwise terms, $V_{p,q}(\pi_p, \pi_q)$ are computed directly from the images. Given $D_p(\pi_p)$, $V_{p,q}(\pi_p, \pi_q)$ for all possible values of π_p, π_q, then one of the standard minimization algorithms for Potts model can be applied to find the optimal π.

3.2 Complete Description of the EM Algorithm

In the E-step, sufficient statistics of $< E(\hat{S}, \pi) >_M$ are computed. Recall that only the 3D motion energy term of $< E(\hat{S}, \pi) >_M$ depends on M, therefore only calculation of the expectation $< E_{\text{3D-Motion}}(s_p, \pi_p, M_p) >_M$ is required ($E_{\text{2D-coherence}}(\pi)$ is constant with respect to M). We compute these sufficient statistics by representing the factorization problem of equation 5 as a problem of factor analysis [15, 4].

In standard factor analysis we have a set of observations $\{y(t)\}$ that are linear combinations of a latent variable $x(t)$:

$$y(t) = Ax(t) + \eta(t) \tag{17}$$

with $x(t) \sim N(0, \sigma_x^2 I)$ and $\eta(t) \sim N(0, \Psi_t)$. We now show how to rewrite the multibody factorization problem in this form.

In equation 5 the horizontal and vertical coordinates of the same point appear in different rows. To get an equation with all the measurements taken from the same frame in the same line of the measurements matrix, It can be rewritten as:

$$[U \ V]_{F \times 2P} = [M_U \ M_V]_{F \times 8K} \begin{bmatrix} S & 0 \\ 0 & S \end{bmatrix}_{8K \times 2P} + [\eta]_{F \times 2P} \tag{18}$$

where M_U is the submatrix of M consisting of rows corresponding to U (odd rows), and M_V is the submatrix of M consisting of rows corresponding to V (even rows).

Let $A = \begin{bmatrix} S^T & 0 \\ 0 & S^T \end{bmatrix}$. Identifying $y(t)$ with the tth row of the matrix $[U \ V]$ and $x(t)$ with the tth row of $[M_U \ M_V]$, then equation 18 is equivalent (transposed) to equation 17. For diagonal covariance matrices Ψ_t (the case where Ψ_t is not diagonal is discussed in [15, 4]) the standard algorithm [20] gives:

E step:

$$E(x(t)|y(t)) = \left(\sigma_x^{-2}I + A^T \Psi_t^{-1} A\right)^{-1} A^T \Psi_t^{-1} y(t) \tag{19}$$

$$V(x(t)|y(t)) = \left(\sigma_x^{-2}I + A^T \Psi_t^{-1} A\right)^{-1} \tag{20}$$

$$< x(t) > \; = E(x(t)|y(t)) \tag{21}$$

$$< x(t)x(t)^T > \; = V(x(t)|y(t)) + < x(t) >< x(t) >^T \tag{22}$$

Although in our setting the matrix A must satisfy certain constraints, the E-step (in which the matrix A is assumed to be given from the M-step) remains the same as in standard factor analysis. In [15], priors regarding the motion are incorporated into the E-step.

M step:
In the M-step, $< E(\hat{S}, \pi) >_M$ is minimized with respect to $\hat{S}$ and π. Section 3 describes how π is found provided that $D_p(k)$ is known. Here we describe how to compute $D_p(k)$ for all p and k before the algorithm from section 3 can be applied. We also describe how the optimal $\hat{S}$ is found.

Denote by s_p^k a vector of length 3 that contains the optimal $3D$ coordinates of point p assuming it belongs to motion model k. In other words,

$$s_p^k \overset{\triangle}{=} \arg\min_{s_\cdot} D_p(s_p, k) \tag{23}$$

For a diagonal noise covariance matrix Ψ_t (for a non-diagonal Ψ_t see [15, 4]), by taking the derivative of $< E(\hat{S}, \pi) >_M$, we get:

$$s_p^k = B_{pk} C_{pk}^{-1} \tag{24}$$

where

$$B_{pk} = \sum_t \left[\Psi_t^{-1}(p, p)(u_{tp} - < d_t^k >) < m_k(t)^T > \right. \tag{25}$$

$$+ \Psi_t^{-1}(p + P, p + P)(v_{tp} - < e_t^k >) < n_k(t) >^T\right]$$

$$C_{pk} = \sum_t \left[\Psi_t^{-1}(p, p) < m_k(t)m_k(t)^T > \right.$$

$$+ \Psi_t^{-1}(p + P, p + P) < n_k(t)n_k(t)^T >\right]$$

The expectations required in the M step are the appropriate subvectors and submatrices of $< x(t) >$ and $< x(t)x(t)^T >$ (recall equation 1 and the definition of $x(t)$). Notice that s_p^k depends only on the motion distribution, the observations of point p and k. It is independent on the other points and their assignments, given the motion distribution. $D_p(k)$ is therefore

$$D_p(k) = \min_{s.} D_p(s_p, k) = D_p(s_p^k, k) = \tag{26}$$

$$< \sum_t (W_{t,p} - M_t^k s_p^k)^T \Psi_{t,p}^{-1}(W_{t,p} - M_t^k s_p^k) >_M =$$

$$\sum_t < (W_{t,p} - M_t^k s_p^k)^T \Psi_{t,p}^{-1}(W_{t,p} - M_t^k s_p^k) >_M =$$

$$\sum_t [W_{t,p}^T \Psi_{t,p}^{-1} W_{t,p} - 2 < x_{t,k} >^T a_{p,k}^T \Psi_{t,p}^{-1} W_{t,p} +$$

$$\text{trace}(a_{p,k}^T \Psi_{t,p}^{-1} a_{p,k} < x_{t,k} x_{t,k}^T >)]$$

where $a_{p,k}$ is a 2×8 matrix $a_{p,k} = \begin{bmatrix} (s_p^k)^T & 0 \\ 0 & (s_p^k)^T \end{bmatrix}$, $x_{t,k}$ is the subvector of $x(t)$ corresponding to the k-th motion (entries $4(k-1)+1, \ldots, 4k$ and $4K+4(k-1)+1, \ldots, 4K+4k$) and the required expectations $< x_{t,k} >_M$ and $< x_{t,k} x_{t,k}^T >_M$ were computed in the E-step.

Now that $D_p(k)$ is known for all p for every k, π is found as described in section 3. After finding π, then $s_p = s_p^{\pi.}$. An outline of the algorithm is given in Algorithm 1.

Algorithm 1. An outline of the EM algorithm for segmentation

Iterate until convergence:

1. E-step:
   (a) for $t = 1, \ldots, T$,
       – Compute $< x(t) >, < x(t)x(t)^T >$ using equations 19 - 22.
2. M-step:
   (a) for $p = 1, \ldots, P$,
       – for $k = 1, \ldots, K$,
           i. Compute s_p^k using equation 24.
           ii. Compute $D_p(k)$ using equation 26.
   (b) find π using a standard energy minimization algorithm (for example, graph cuts or BP).
   (c) for $p = 1, \ldots, P$,
       – assign $s_p = s_p^{\pi.}$
   (d) Update A

The proposed segmentation algorithm can handle correlated non-uniform noise and can be applied even when there is missing data (these are just points for which $\Psi_t^{-1}(i,i) = 0$). See [15, 4] for further details. Even in the presence of noise and missing data, it is guaranteed to find a factorization where the structure matrix has at most 4 nonzero elements per column, resulting in increased robustness.

4   Experiments

In this section we test our algorithm and compare it to previous algorithms on synthetic and real sequences.

EM guarantees convergence to a local maximum which is dependent on the initialization. In these experiments, we start with several (random) initializations for each input, and choose the output that achieves maximal likelihood to be the final result. Empirical results show that for (synthetic) noise free scenes, the global maximum is usually found with a single initialization. As the amount of noise increases, the number of initializations needed for success also increases. For the experiments reported here, the maximal number of initializations is 10 (for both EM versions).

The global minimum of equation 16 was found using graph cuts in the experiments with two objects. Loopy belief propagation was used for minimization in experiments with more than two objects.

4.1   Experiments with Synthetic Data

We begin with a series of synthetic examples that demonstrate our approach vs. previous approaches of: [2] [1, 11, 4] and normalized cut with affinities that are a linear combination of 2D affinities and the Costeira-Kanade motion interaction matrix (referred as NCut Motion+2D in table 1). The following scenarios are tested (see figure 1):

1. A scene containing two objects with different 3D motions that are located far away from each other,
2. A scene with two coaxial objects (and thus cannot be separated spatially) rotating with different angular velocities,
3. And a scene containing two objects that are close to each other and have similar (yet different) motions.

We test each of these scenes in the presence and absence of mild amount of noise ($\sigma = 0.5$) and significant amount of noise ($\sigma = 10$, that was selected to show the difference in the performance of the two versions of EM).

In the first scenario, both 3D motion and spatial proximity provide a good separation between the objects. All algorithms have shown perfect results when there was no noise, as expected. Once mild amount of noise was added, the performance of CK (Costeira-Kanade, [1]) deteriorated while the segmentation results of the 3 other algorithms remained unchanged.

In the second scenario, the objects cannot be separated spatially in each individual image, but in the overall sequence some spatial information exists as the objects have different angular velocities. Despite of the existence of some spatial information, both versions of Normalized Cut failed to segment the objects in both the clean and noisy scenes. The other 3 algorithms have separated the objects perfectly in the noise free scenario due to their different motions (which were chosen to create a full rank motion matrix, M). Once mild amount of noise was added, again CK failed while the results of

---
[2] For the experiments with Normalized Cut we used the code available at http://www.seas.upenn.edu/~timothee/software_ncut/software.html

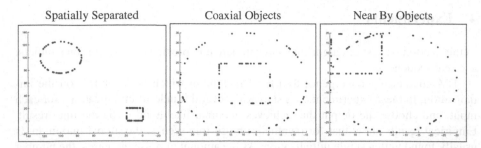

Fig. 1. Three scenarios we use to demonstrate the power of combining 3D motion information and 2D affinities. We compare the EM algorithm proposed in this paper with [1],[11] and [4] on clean and noisy ($\sigma = 0.5$ and $\sigma = 10$) input for scenes where (a) objects are spatially separable (and have different motions), (b) motion is the only cue for separation and (c) information from both sources is available, and in the noisy case required for separation. results are reported in table 1.

Table 1. Numbers of points that were misclassified by each of the algorithms for scenes from figure 1. These examples demonstrate the additional power of combining motion and non-motion information and the robustness of EM.

Scene Properties	Costeira-Kanade [1]	NCut [11]	NCut Motion+2D	Motion-Only EM [4]	Spatially-Coherent EM
Clean, Spatially separated	0	0	0	0	0
Noisy ($\sigma = 0.5$), Spatially separated	26	0	0	0	0
Noisy ($\sigma = 10$), Spatially separated	34	0	0	9	0
Clean, Coaxial	0	22	23	0	0
Noisy ($\sigma = 0.5$), Coaxial	14	22	25	1	0
Noisy ($\sigma = 10$), Coaxial	46	29	28	33	31
Clean, Near by	0	25	24	0	0
Noisy ($\sigma = 0.5$), Near by	8	25	24	3	1
Noisy ($\sigma = 10$), Near by	48	35	27	27	1

Fig. 2. The first image from the sequences: Can Book, Tea Tins and 3-Cars used for comparing the proposed EM algorithm and [5]. Results of this comparison are summarized in table 2.

both versions of the EM algorithm did not change. When a significant amount of noise was added, all algorithms failed because there was not enough information neither in the 3D motion nor in the spatial proximity.

Table 2. Misclassification error of segmentation using PowerFactorization and GPCA ([5]) and the algorithm proposed in this paper (EM) for the inputs from [5]

Sequence	Points	Frames	Motions	GPCA [5]	EM
Can Book	170	3	2	1.18%	0.00%
Tea Tins	84	3	2	1.19%	0.00%
3-Cars	173	15	3	4.62%	0.00%
Puma	64	16	2	0.00%	0.00%
Castle	56	11	2	0.00%	0.00%

In the last scenario we tested what do we gain from the combination of 2D spatial coherence information and 3D motion information. Although objects were not coaxial as in the previous scenario, they were not separated spatially well enough and both versions of Normalized Cut failed in both the noise free and noisy scenarios. As in previous cases CK found perfect segmentation when there was no noise, but failed in the noisy case. In the presence of significant amount of noise, we see that spatially coherent EM utilizes spatial information if it exists, and outperforms motion-only based EM.

4.2 Experiments with Real Data

We compared our algorithm to GPCA [5] by using 5 sequences that appeared in [5]. These sequences contain degenerate and non-degenerate motions, some contain only 3 frames. In this experiment, the maximal number of initializations of EM was 5, and the results of GPCA were taken from [5]. The results are presented in table 2: EM shows perfect results on all these input sequences, even when the number of frames is small (3) or when the motions matrix, M, is rank deficient.

Next, we checked the performance of spatially coherent EM on the sequence used in [4] and compared it to the motion based only EM algorithm from [4]. The input sequence consists of two cans rotating horizontally around parallel different axes in different angular velocities. 149 feature points were tracked along 20 frames, from which 93 are from one can, and 56 are from the other. Some of the feature points were occluded in part of the sequence, due to the rotation. Using motion-only based

(a)   (b)

Fig. 3. (a) A sequence of two cans rotating around different parallel axes. Spatial coherent EM succeeds to find correct segmentation and 3D structure up to 2 segmentation errors, comparing to 8 of motion-only EM and a failure of other methods. (b) First out of 13 frames taken from "Matrix Reloaded". 6 points were misclassified comparing to 14 by motion-only EM.

EM 8 points were misclassified. With the addition of spatial coherence, only 2 points were misclassified and the 3D was correctly reconstructed. Figure 3(a) shows the first frame of the sequence and the tracks superimposed. For comparison, Costeira-Kanade (using the maximal full submatrix of the measurements matrix) resulted in 30 misclassified points and a failure in $3D$ structure reconstruction.

Our last input sequence is taken from the film "Matrix Reloaded". In this experiment 69 points were tracked along 13 frames: 28 on the car rotating in the air and 41 points were tracked on the front car approaching on the left (see figure 3(b)). On each object, points were selected from to be roughly in the same depth to avoid projective effects. Spatially coherent EM misclassified 6 points comparing to 14 points that were misclassified by motion-only EM and 19 points that were misclassified by Ncut.

5   Discussion

In this paper we presented an algorithm for incorporating 2D non-motion affinities into 3D motion segmentation using the EM algorithm. We showed that using a coherence prior on the segmentation is easily implemented and gives rise to better segmentation results. In the E step, the mean and covariance of the 3D motions are calculated using matrix operations, and in the M step the structure and the segmentation are calculated by performing energy minimization.

With the EM framework, missing data and directional uncertainty are easily handled. Placing meaningful priors and imposing constraints on the desired factorization greatly increase the robustness of the algorithm.

Future work includes incorporation of other sources of information, for examples other principles of perceptual organization suggested by the Gestalt psychologists. Another direction for future work is to place the spatial coherence prior directly on the 3D of the points: solving together for structure and segmentation, where the prior on the segmentation depends directly on the reconstructed 3D structure.

Acknowledgements. Supported by EC Contract 027787 DIRAC. The authors would like to thank V. Kolmogorov for the graph cut code and T. Meltzer for the BP code.

References

1. Costeira, J., Kanade, T.: A multi-body factorization method for motion analysis. In: ICCV. (1995)
2. Gear, C.: Multibody grouping from motion images. IJCV (1998) 133–150
3. Zelnik-Manor, L., Machline, M., Irani, M.: Multi-body segmentation: Revisiting motion consistency (2002)
4. Gruber, A., Weiss, Y.: Multibody factorization with uncertainty and missing data using the EM algorithm. In: Computer Vision and Pattern Recognition (CVPR). (2004)
5. Vidal, R., Hartely, R.: Motion segmentation with missing data using powerfactorization and gpca. In: Computer Vision and Pattern Recognition (CVPR). (2004)
6. Kanatani, K.: Evaluation and selection of models for motion segmentation. In: ECCV. (2002) (3) 335–349

7. Vidal, R., Soatto, S., Ma, Y., Sastry, S.: Segmentation of dynamic scenes from the multibody fundamental matrix (2002)
8. Wolf, L., Shashua, A.: Two-body segmentation from two perspective views. In: IEEE Conf. on Computer Vision and Pattern Recognition (CVPR). (2001) 263–270
9. Feng, X., Perona, P.: Scene segmentation from 3D motion. CVPR (1998) 225–231
10. MacLean, W.J., Jepson, A.D., Frecker, R.C.: Recovery of egomotion and segmentation of independent object motion using the em algorithm. In: BMVC. (1994)
11. Shi, J., Malik, J.: Normalized cuts and image segmentation. IEEE Transactions on Pattern Analysis and Machine Intelligence **22** (2000) 888–905
12. Shi, J., Malik, J.: Motion segmentation and tracking using normalized cuts. In: ICCV. (1998) 1154–1160
13. Weiss, Y., Adelson, E.: A unified mixture framework for motion segmentation: incorporating spatial coherence and estimating the number of models. In: Proceedings of IEEE conference on Computer Vision and Pattern Recognition. (1996) 321–326
14. Zabih, R., Kolmogorov, V.: Spatially coherent clustering with graph cuts. In: Computer Vision and Pattern Recognition (CVPR). (2004)
15. Gruber, A., Weiss, Y.: Factorization with uncertainty and missing data: Exploiting temporal coherence. In: Neural Information Processing Systems (NIPS). (2003)
16. Tomasi, C., Kanade, T.: Shape and motion from image streams under orthography: A factorization method. Int. J. of Computer Vision **9** (1992) 137–154
17. Irani, M., Anandan, P.: Factorization with uncertainty. In: ECCV (1). (2000) 539–553
18. Kolmogorov, V., Zabih, R.: What energy functions can be minimized via graph cuts ? Transactions on Pattern Analysis and Machine Intelligence (PAMI) (2004)
19. Weiss, Y., Freeman, W.T.: On the optimality of solutions of the max-product belief propagation algorithm in arbitrary graphs. IEEE Transactions on Information Theory **47** (2001) 723–735
20. Rubin, D., Thayer, D.: EM algorithms for ML factor analysis. Psychometrika 47(1) (1982) 69–76

Multi-camera Tracking and Segmentation of Occluded People on Ground Plane Using Search-Guided Particle Filtering

Kyungnam Kim[1,2] and Larry S. Davis[1]

[1] Computer Vision Lab, University of Maryland, College Park, MD 20742
{knkim, lsd}@umiacs.umd.edu
http://www.umiacs.umd.edu/~knkim
[2] IPIX Corporation, Sunset Hills Rd. Suite 410, Reston, VA, 20190

Abstract. A multi-view multi-hypothesis approach to segmenting and tracking multiple (possibly occluded) persons on a ground plane is proposed. During tracking, several iterations of segmentation are performed using information from human appearance models and ground plane homography. To more precisely locate the ground location of a person, all center vertical axes of the person across views are mapped to the top-view plane and their intersection point on the ground is estimated. To tackle the explosive state space due to multiple targets and views, iterative segmentation-searching is incorporated into a particle filtering framework. By searching for people's ground point locations from segmentations, a set of a few good particles can be identified, resulting in low computational cost. In addition, even if all the particles are away from the true ground point, some of them move towards the true one through the iterated process as long as they are located nearby. We demonstrate the performance of the approach on several video sequences.

1 Introduction

Tracking and segmenting people in cluttered or complex situations is a challenging visual surveillance problem since the high density of objects results in occlusion. Elgammal and Davis [20] presented a general framework which uses maximum likelihood estimation and occlusion reasoning to obtain the best arrangement for people. To handle more people in a crowded scene, Zhao and Nevatia [9] described a model-based segmentation approach to segment individual humans in a high-density scene using a Markov chain Monte Carlo method.

When a single camera is not sufficient to detect and track objects due to limited visibility or occlusion, multiple cameras can be employed. There are a number of papers which address detection and tracking using overlapping or non-overlapping multiple views, for example, [6, 7, 19]. M_2Tracker [19], which is similar to our work, used a region-based stereo algorithm to find 3D points inside an object, and Bayesian pixel classification with occlusion analysis to segment people occluded in different levels of crowd density. Unlike M_2Tracker's requirement of having calibrated stereo pairs of cameras, we do not require strong

A. Leonardis, H. Bischof, and A. Pinz (Eds.): ECCV 2006, Part III, LNCS 3953, pp. 98–109, 2006.

calibration, but only a ground plane homography. For outdoor cameras, it is practically very challenging to accurately calibrate them, so 3D points at a large distance from a camera are difficult to measure accurately.

Our goal is to 'segment' and 'track' people on a ground plane viewed from multiple overlapping views. To make tracking robust, multiple hypothesis trackers, such as *particle filter* [12], are widely used [17, 16]. However, as the numbers of targets and views increase, the state space of combination of targets' states increases exponentially. Additionally, the observation processes for visual tracking are typically computationally expensive. Previous research has tried to solve this state space explosion issue as in [13, 1, 14, 8, 15]. We also designed our tracker to solve this issue. Each hypothesis is refined by iterative mean-shift-like multi-view segmentation to maintain mostly "good" samples, resulting in lower computational cost.

This paper is organized as follows. Sec.2 presents a human appearance model. A framework for segmenting and tracking occluded people moving on a ground plane is presented in Sec.3. In Sec.4, the multi-view tracker is extended to a multi-hypothesis framework using particle filtering. We demonstrate the experimental results of the proposed approach on video sequences in Sec.5. Conclusion and discussion are given in the final section.

2   Human Appearance Model

First, we describe an appearance color model as a function of height that assumes that people are standing upright and are dressed, generally, so that consistently colored or textured color regions are aligned vertically. Each body part has its own color model represented by a color distribution. To allow multimodal densities inside each part, we use kernel density estimation.

Let $M = \{c_i\}_{i=1...N}$. be a set of pixels from a body part with colors c_i. Using Gaussian kernels and an independence assumption between d color channels, the probability that an input pixel $c = \{c_1, ..., c_d\}$ is from the model M is estimated as

$$p_M(c) = \frac{1}{N_M} \sum_{i=1}^{N.} \prod_{j=1}^{d} \frac{1}{\sqrt{2\pi}\sigma_j} e^{-\frac{1}{2}\left(\frac{\cdot\cdot - \cdot \cdots}{\cdot\cdot}\right)^2} \qquad (1)$$

In order to handle illumination changes, we use normalized color ($r = \frac{R}{R+G+B}$, $g = \frac{G}{R+G+B}$, $s = \frac{R+G+B}{3}$) or Hue-Saturation-Value (HSV) color space with a wider kernel for 's' and 'V' to cope with the higher variability of these lightness variables. We used both the normalized color and HSV spaces in our experiments and observed similar performances.

Viewpoint-independent models can be obtained by viewing people from different perspectives using multiple cameras. A related calibration issue was addressed in [2, 5] since each camera output of the same scene point taken at the same time or different time may vary slightly depending on camera types and parameters. We used the same type of cameras and observed there is almost no difference between camera outputs except for different illumination levels (due to shadow and orientation effects) depending on the side of person's body. This level of variability is accounted for by our color model.

3   Multi-camera Multi-person Segmentation and Tracking

3.1   Foreground Segmentation

Given image sequences from multiple overlapping views including people to track, we start by performing detection using background subtraction to obtain the foreground maps in each view. The codebook-based background subtraction algorithm [18] is used. Its shadow removal capability increases the performance of segmentation and tracking.

Each foreground pixel in each view is labelled as the best matching person (i.e., the most likely class) by Bayesian pixel classification as in [19]. The posterior probability that an observed pixel $\mathbf{x}$ (containing both color $\mathbf{c}$ and image position (x, y) information) comes from person k is given by

$$P(k|\mathbf{x}) = \frac{P(k)P(\mathbf{x}|k)}{P(\mathbf{x})} \qquad (2)$$

We use the color model in Eq.1 for the conditional probability $P(\mathbf{x}|k)$. The color model of the person's body part to be evaluated is determined by the information of $\mathbf{x}$'s position as well as the person's ground point and full-body height in the camera view (See Fig.1(a)). The ground point and height are determined initially by the method defined subsequently in Sec.3.2.

The prior reflects the probability that person k occupies pixel $\mathbf{x}$. Given the ground point and full-body height of the person, we can measure $\mathbf{x}$'s height from the ground and its distance to the person's center vertical axis. The occupancy probability is then defined by

$$O_k(h_k(\mathbf{x}), w_k(\mathbf{x})) = P[w_k(\mathbf{x}) < W(h_k(\mathbf{x}))] = 1 - \mathrm{cdf}_{W(h.\,(\mathbf{x}))}(w_k(\mathbf{x})) \qquad (3)$$

where $h_k(\mathbf{x})$ and $w_k(\mathbf{x})$ are the height and width of $\mathbf{x}$ relative to the person k. h_k and w_k are measured relative to the full height of the person. $W(h_k(\mathbf{x}))$ is the person's height-dependent width and $\mathrm{cdf}_W(.)$ is the cumulative density function for W. If $\mathbf{x}$ is located at distance $W(h_k(\mathbf{x}))$ from the person's center at a distance W, the occupancy probability is designed so that it will be exactly 0.5 (while it increases or decreases as $\mathbf{x}$ move towards or move away from the center).

The prior must also incorporate possible occlusion. Suppose that some person l has a lower ground point than a person k in some view. Then the probability that l occludes k depends on their relative positions and l's (probabilistic) width. Hence, the prior probability $P(k)$ that a pixel $\mathbf{x}$ is the image of person k, based on this occlusion model, is

$$P(k) = O_k(h_k, w_k) \prod_{g.\,(k)<g.\,(l)} (1 - O_l(h_l, w_l)) \qquad (4)$$

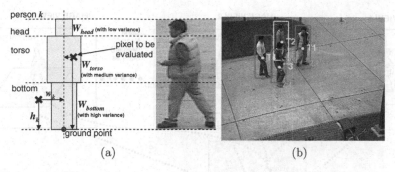

(a)   (b)

Fig. 1. (a) Illustration of appearance model, (b) Bounding box detection

where $g_y(k)$ is the y-location of the ground point of k and $\mathbf{x}$ is omitted for simplicity (i.e., $h_k = h_k(\mathbf{x})$ and $w_k = w_k(\mathbf{x})$). The best class k^* is determined by maximum a posteriori (MAP) estimation: $k^* = \arg\max_k P(k)P(\mathbf{x}|k)$. Finally, the foreground maps are segmented into the best matching persons based on their appearance models and occlusion information.

3.2 Model Initialization and Update

Full automatic tracking is enabled by initializing the human appearance model when a person is detected in a view by searching for isolated foreground blobs (See Fig.1(b)). In order to get a bounding box of a person from the foreground map, we used the object detection technique in [3]. The bounding boxes in the figure were created when the blobs are isolated before. For the case when a person does not constitute an isolated blob, a manual selection is employed.

The full-body height of a person is initialized upon model creation and is updated during segmentation. In some cases, fixing the average height scaled by the y-location of the ground point provides a robust height measurement when the segmentation is unreliable. When the unclassified pixels (those having a probability in Eq.1 lower than a given threshold) constitute a connected component of non-negligible size, a new appearance model should be created.

3.3 Multi-view Integration

Ground Plane Homography. The segmented blobs across views are integrated to obtain the ground plane locations of people. The correspondence of a human across multiple cameras is established by the geometric constraints of planar homographies. For N_V camera views, $N_V(N_V - 1)$ homography matrices can possibly be calculated for correspondence; but in order to reduce the computational complexity we instead reconstruct the top-view of the ground plane on which the hypotheses of peoples' locations are generated.

Integration by Vertical Axes. Given the pixel classification results from Sec.3.1, a ground point of a person could be simply obtained by detecting the lowest point of the person's blob. However those ground points are not reliable due to the errors from background subtraction and segmentation.

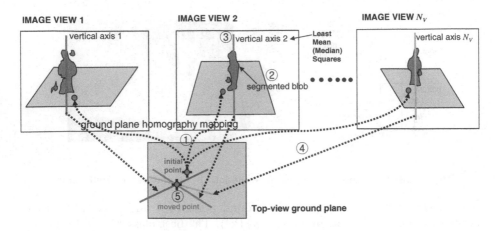

Fig. 2. All vertical axes of a person across views intersect at (or are very close to) a single point when mapped to the top-view

We, instead, develop a localization algorithm that employs the center vertical axis of a human body, which can be estimated more robustly even with poor background subtraction [11]. Ideally, a person's body pixels are arranged more of less symmetrically about a person's central vertical axis. An estimate of this axis can be obtained by Least Mean Squares of the perpendicular distance between the body pixel and the axis as in ③ in Fig.2. Alternatively, the Least *Median* Squares could be used since it is more robust to outliers.

The homographic images of all the vertical axes of a person across different views intersect at (or are very close to) a single point (the location of that person on the ground) when mapped to the top-view (See [11]). In fact, even when the ground point of a person from some view is occluded, the top-view ground point integrated from all the views is obtainable if the vertical axis is estimated correctly. This intersection point can be calculated by minimizing the perpendicular distances to the axes. Fig.2 depicts an example of reliable detection of the ground point from the segmented blobs of a person. The N_v vertical axes are mapped to the top-view and transferred back to each image view. Let each axis L_i be parameterized by two points $\{(x_{i,1}, y_{i,1}), (x_{i,2}, y_{i,2})\}_{i=1...N}$. When mapped to the top-view by homography as in ④ in Fig.2, we obtain $\{(\hat{x}_{i,1}, \hat{y}_{i,1}), (\hat{x}_{i,2}, \hat{y}_{i,2})\}_{i=1...N}$. The distance of a ground point (x, y) to the axis is written as $d((x,y), L_i) = \frac{|a_i \cdot x + b_i \cdot y + c_i|}{\sqrt{a_i^2 + b_i^2}}$ where $a_i = \hat{y}_{i,1} - \hat{y}_{i,2}$, $b_i = \hat{x}_{i,2} - \hat{x}_{i,1}$, and $c_i = \hat{x}_{i,1}\hat{y}_{i,2} - \hat{x}_{i,2}\hat{y}_{i,1}$. The solution is the point that minimizes a weighted sum of square distances:

$$(x^*, y^*) = \arg\min_{(x,y)} \sum_{i=1}^{N} w_i^2 d^2((x,y), L_i) \tag{5}$$

The weight w_i is determined by the segmentation quality (confidence level) of the body blob of L_i (We used the pixel classification score in Eq.2).

If a person is occluded severely by others in a view (i.e., the axis information is unreliable), the corresponding body axis from that view will not contribute heavily to the calculation in Eq.5. When only one axis is found reliably, then the lowest body point along the axis is chosen.

To obtain a better ground point and segmentation result, we can iterate the segmentation and ground-point integration process until the ground point converges to a fixed location within a certain bound ϵ. That is, given a set of initial ground-point hypotheses of people as in ① in Fig.2, segmentation in Sec.3.1 is performed (②), and then newly moved ground points are obtained based on multi-view integration (④ and ⑤). These new ground points are an input to the next iteration. 2-3 iterations gave satisfactory results for our data sets.

There are several advantages of our approach. Even though a person's ground point is invisible or there are segmentation and background subtraction errors, the robust final ground point is obtainable once at least two vertical axes are correctly detected. When total occlusion occurs from one view, robust tracking is possible using the other views' information if available; visibility of a person can be maximized if cameras are placed at proper angles. Since the good views for each tracked person are changing over time, our algorithm maximizes the effective usage of all available information across views. By iterating the multi-view integration process, a ground point moves to the optimal position that explains the segmentation results of all views. This nice property is used, in the next section, for a small number of hypotheses to explore in a large state space that incorporates multiple persons and multiple views.

4   Extension to Multi-hypothesis Tracker

Next, we extend our single-hypothesis tracker to one with multiple hypotheses. A single hypothesis tracker, while computationally efficient, can be easily distracted by occlusion or nearby similarly colored objects.

As the number of targets and views increase, the state space of combination of targets' states increases exponentially. Additionally, the observation processes for visual tracking are typically very expensive. We would, therefore, choose to employ techniques that require small numbers of particles.

The iterative segmentation-searching presented in Sec.3 is naturally incorporated with a particle filtering framework. There are two advantages - (1) By searching for a person's ground point from a segmentation, a set of a few good particles can be identified, resulting in low computational costs, (2) Even if all the particles are away from the true ground point, some of them will move towards the true one as long as they are initially located nearby. This does not happen generally with particle filters, which need to wait until the target "comes to" the particles.

Our final algorithm of segmentation and tracking is presented with a particle filter overview and our state space, dynamics, and observation model.

4.1 Overview of Particle Filter, State Space, and Dynamics

The key idea of particle filtering is to approximate a probability distribution by a weighted sample set $S = \{(\mathbf{s}^{(n)}, \pi^{(n)}) | n = 1...N\}$. Each sample, $\mathbf{s}$, represents one hypothetical state of the object, with a corresponding discrete sampling probability π, where $\sum_{n=1}^{N} \pi^{(n)} = 1$. Each element of the set is then weighted in terms of the observations and N samples are drawn with replacement, by choosing a particular sample with probability $\pi_t^{(n)} = P(\mathbf{z}_t | \mathbf{x}_t = \mathbf{s}_t^{(n)})$.

In our particle filtering framework, each sample of the distribution is simply given as $s = (x, y)$ where x, y specify the ground location of the object in the *top-view*. For multi-person tracking, a state $\mathbf{s}_t = (\mathbf{s}_{1,t}, ..., \mathbf{s}_{N.,t})$ is defined as a combination of N_p single-person states. Our state transition dynamic model is a random walk where a new predicted single-person state is acquired by adding a zero mean Gaussian with a covariance Σ to the previous state. Alternatively, the velocity $\dot{x}, \dot{y}$ or the size variable *height* and *width* can be added to the state space and then a more complex dynamic model can be applied if relevant.

4.2 Observation

Each person is associated with a reference color model $\mathbf{q}^\star$ which is obtained by histogram techniques [16]. The histograms are produced using a function $b(\mathbf{c}_i) \in \{1, ..., N_b\}$ that assigns the color vector $\mathbf{c}_i$ to its corresponding bin. We used the color model defined in Sec.2 to construct the histogram of the reference model in the normalized color or HSV space using N_b (e.g., $10 \times 10 \times 5$) bins to make the observation less sensitive to lighting conditions.

The histogram $\mathbf{q}(C) = \{q(u; C)\}_{u=1...N.}$ of the color distribution of the sample set C is given by

$$q(u; C) = \eta \sum_{i=1}^{N.} \delta[b(\mathbf{c}_i) - u] \tag{6}$$

where u is the bin index, δ is the Kronecker delta function, and η is a normalizing constant ensuring $\sum_{u=1}^{N.} q(u; C) = 1$. This model associates a probability to each of the N_b color bins.

If we denote $\mathbf{q}^\star$ as the reference color model and $\mathbf{q}$ as a candidate color model, $\mathbf{q}^\star$ is obtained from the stored samples of person k's appearance model as mentioned before while $\mathbf{q}$ is specified by a particle $\mathbf{s}_{k,t} = (x, y)$. The sample set C in Eq.6 is replaced with the sample set specified by $\mathbf{s}_{k,t}$. The top-view point (x, y) is transformed to an image ground point for a certain camera view v, $H_v(\mathbf{s}_{k,t})$, where H_v is a homography mapping the top-view to the view v. Based on the ground point, a region to be compared with the reference model is determined. The pixel values inside the region are drawn to construct $\mathbf{q}$. Note that the region can be constrained from the prior probability in Eq.4, including the occupancy and occlusion information (i.e., by picking pixels such that $P(k) > Threshold$, typically 0.5). In addition, as done in pixel classification, the color histograms are separately defined for each body part to incorporate the spatial layout of the color distribution. Therefore, we apply the likelihood as the sum of the histograms associated with each body part.

Then, we need to measure the data likelihood between $\mathbf{q}^\star$ and $\mathbf{q}$. The Bhattacharyya similarity coefficient is used to define a distance d on color histograms:
$d[\mathbf{q}\star, \mathbf{q}(\mathbf{s})] = \left[1 - \sum_{u=1}^{N_c} \sqrt{q \star (u) q(u; \mathbf{s})}\right]^{\frac{1}{2}}$. Thus, the likelihood $(\pi_{v,k,t})$ of person k consisting of N_r body parts at view v, the actual view-integrated likelihood $(\pi_{k,t})$ of a person $\mathbf{s}_{k,t}$, and the final weight of the particle $(\pi_{k,t})$ of a concatenation of N_p person states are respectively given by:

$$\pi_{v,k,t} \propto e^{\sum_{i=1}^{N_r} -\lambda d^2[\mathbf{q}_i^\star, \mathbf{q}_i \cdot (H \cdot (\mathbf{s} \cdots))]}, \quad \pi_{k,t} = \Pi_{v=1}^{N_r} \pi_{v,k,t}, \quad \pi_t = \Pi_{k=1}^{N_p} \pi_{k,t} \qquad (7)$$

where λ is a constant which can be experimentally determined.

4.3   The Final Algorithm

The algorithm below combines the particle filtering framework described before and the iterated segmentation-and-search in Sec.3 into a final multi-view multi-target multi-hypothesis tracking algorithm. Iteration of segmentation and multi-view integration moves a predicted particle to a better position on which all the segmentation results of the person agree. The transformed particle is re-sampled for processing of the next frames.

Algorithm for Multi-view Multi-target Multi-hypothesis tracking

---

I. From the "old" sample set $S_{t-1} = \{\mathbf{s}_{t-1}^{(n)}, \pi_{t-1}^{(n)}\}_{n=1,...,N}$ at time $t - 1$, construct the new samples as follows:

II. **Prediction:** for $n = 1, ..., N$, draw $\tilde{\mathbf{s}}_t^{(n)}$ from the dynamics. **Iterate** Step III to IV for each particle $\tilde{\mathbf{s}}_t^{(n)}$.

III. **Segmentation & Search**
$\tilde{\mathbf{s}}_t = \{\tilde{\mathbf{s}}_{k,t}\}_{k=1...N}$. contains all persons' states. The superscript (n) is omitted through the Observation step.
  i. **for** $v \leftarrow 1$ to N_V **do**
    (a) For each person k, $(k = 1...N_p)$, transform the top-view point $\tilde{\mathbf{s}}_{k,t}$ into the ground point in view v by homography, $H_v(\tilde{\mathbf{s}}_{k,t})$
    (b) perform segmentation on the foreground map in view v with the occlusion information according to Sec2.
  end for
  ii. For each person k, obtain the center vertical axes of the person across views, then integrate them on the top-view to obtain a newly moved point $\tilde{\mathbf{s}}_{k,t}^*$ as in Sec3.
  iii. For all persons, if $\|\tilde{\mathbf{s}}_{k,t} - \tilde{\mathbf{s}}_{k,t}^*\| < \varepsilon$, then go to the next step. Otherwise, set $\tilde{\mathbf{s}}_{k,t} \leftarrow \tilde{\mathbf{s}}_{k,t}^*$ and go to Step III-i.

IV. **Observation**
> i. **for** $v \leftarrow 1$ to N_V **do**
>> For each person k, estimate the likelihood $\pi_{v,k,t}$ in view v according to Eq.7. $\tilde{s}_{k,t}$ needs to be transferred to view v by mapping through H_v for evaluation. Note that $q_r(H_v(\tilde{s}_{k,t}))$ is constructed only from the non-occluded body region.
>
> **end for**
>
> ii. For each person k, obtain the person likelihood $\pi_{k,t}$ by Eq.7.
>
> iii. Set $\pi_t \leftarrow \Pi_{k=1}^{N.} \pi_{k,t}$ as the final weight for the multi-person state $\tilde{s}_t$.

V. **Selection:** Normalize $\{\pi_t^{(n)}\}_i$ so that $\sum_{n=1}^{N} \pi_t^{(n)} = 1$.
> For $i = n...N$, sample index $a(n)$ from discrete probability $\{\pi_t^{(n)}\}_i$ over $\{1...N\}$, and set $s_t^{(n)} \leftarrow \tilde{s}_t^{a(n)}$.

VI. **Estimation:** the mean top-view position of person k is $\sum_{n=1}^{N} \pi_t^{(n)} s_{k,t}^{(n)}$.

---

5   Experiments

We now present experimental results obtained on outdoor and indoor multi-view sequences to illustrate the performance of our algorithm.

The results on the indoor sequences are depicted in Fig.3. The bottom-most row shows how the persons' vertical axes are intersecting on the top-view to obtain their ground points. Small orange box markers are overlaid on the images of frame 198 for determination of the camera orientations. Note that, in the figures of 'vertical axes', the axis of a severely occluded person does not contribute to localization of the ground point. When occlusion occurs, the ground points being tracked are displaced a little from their correct positions but are restored to the correct positions quickly. Only 5 particles (one particle is a combination of 4 single-person states) was used for robust tracking. Those indoor cameras could be easily placed properly in order to maximize the effectiveness of our multi-view integration and the visibility of the people.

Fig.4(a) depicts the graph of the total distance error of people's tracked ground points to the ground truth points. It shows the advantage of multiple views for tracking of people under severe occlusion.

Fig.4(b) visualizes the homographic top-view images of possible vertical axes. A vertical axis in each indoor image view can range from 1 to each maximum image width. 7 transformed vertical axes for each view are depicted for visualization. It helps to understand how the vertical axis location obtained from segmentation affects ground point (intersection) errors on the top-view. When angular separation is close to 180 degrees (although visibility is maximized), the intersection point of two vertical axes transformed to top-view may not be reliable because a small amount of angular perturbation make the intersection point move dramatically.

The outdoor sequences (3 views, 4 persons) are challenging in that three people are wearing similarly-colored clothes and the illumination conditions change

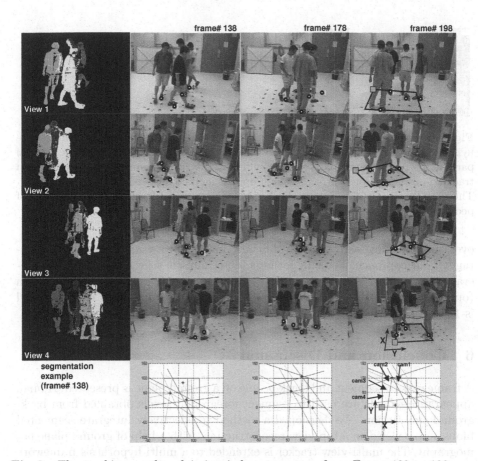

Fig. 3. The tracking results of 4-view indoor sequences from Frame 138 to 198 are shown with the segmentation result of Frame 138

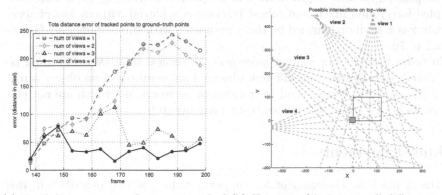

(a) Total distance error of persons' tracked ground points to the ground truth points

(b) Homographic images all different vertical axes

Fig. 4. Graphs for indoor 4 camera views

Fig. 5. Comparison on three methods: While the deterministic search with a single hypothesis (persons 2 and 4 are good, cannot recover lost tracks) and the general particle filter (only person 3 is good, insufficient observations during occlusion) fail in tracking all the persons correctly, our proposed method succeeds with a minor error. The view 2 was only shown here. The proposed system tracks the ground positions of people afterwards over nearly 1000 frames.

over time, making segmentation difficult. In order to demonstrate the advantage of our approach, single hypothesis (deterministic search only) tracker, general particle filter, and particle filter with deterministic search by segmentation (our proposed method) are compared in Fig.5. The number of particles used is 15.

6   Conclusion and Discussion

A framework to segment and track people on a ground plane is presented. Human appearance models are used to segment foreground pixels obtained from background subtraction. We developed a method to effectively integrate segmented blobs across views on a top-view reconstruction, with a help of ground plane homography. The multi-view tracker is extended to a multi-hypothesis framework using particle filtering.

We have illustrated results on challenging videos to show the usefulness of the proposed approach. Segmentation of people is expedited by processing sub-sampled foreground pixels and robust tracking is achieved without loss of accuracy; it was actually confirmed by the experiments with sub-sampling by factors from 2 to 70.

In order to make our system more general, several improvements could be considered, such as handling different observed appearances of an object across views [2], extending the method to tracking in environments which are not planar, or including automatic homography mapping [10].

Acknowledgements

We thank the U.S. Government for supporting the research described in this paper. We are also grateful to Bohyung Han for very helpful suggestions about the particle filtering framework.

References

1. Zhuowen Tu, Song-Chun Zhu, "Image segmentation by data-driven Markov chain Monte Carlo," *IEEE Transactions on PAMI*, Volume 24, Issue 5, May 2002.
2. Omar Javed, Khurram Shafique and Mubarak Shah, "Appearance Modeling for Tracking in Multiple Non-overlapping Cameras," *IEEE CVPR 2005*.
3. A. W. Senior, "Tracking with Probabilistic Appearance Models," in *ECCV workshop on Performance Evaluation of Tracking and Surveillance Systems*, 2002, pp 48-55.
4. I. Haritaoglu, D. Harwood, L.S. Davis, "W^4: real-time surveillance of people and their activities" *IEEE Transactions on PAMI*, Volume: 22, Issue: 8, Aug 2000.
5. Chang, T.H., Gong, S., Ong, E.J., "Tracking Multiple People Under Occlusion Using Multiple Cameras," BMVC 2000.
6. J. Kang, I. Cohen, G. Medioni, "Multi-Views Tracking Within and Across Uncalibrated Camera Streams", *ACM SIGMM 2003 Workshop on Video Surveillance*, 2003.
7. Javed O, Rasheed Z, Shafique K and Shah M, "Tracking Across Multiple Cameras With Disjoint Views," *The Ninth IEEE ICCV*, 2003.
8. D. Comaniciu, P. Meer, "Mean Shift: A Robust Approach toward Feature Space Analysis," *IEEE Trans. on PAMI*, Vol. 24, No. 5, 603-619, 2002.
9. T. Zhao, R. Nevatia, "Bayesian human segmentation in crowded situations," *CVPR*, June 2003.
10. Chris Stauffer, Kinh Tieu. "Automated multi-camera planar tracking correspondence modeling," *CVPR*, vol. 01, no. 1, p. 259, 2003.
11. Min Hu, Jianguang Lou, Weiming Hu, Tieniu Tan, "Multicamera correspondence based on principal axis of human body," *IEEE ICIP*, 2004.
12. S. Arulampalam, S. Maskell, N. J. Gordon, and T. Clapp, "A Tutorial on Particle Filters for On-line Non-linear/Non-Gaussian Bayesian Tracking", *IEEE Transactions of Signal Processing*, Vol. 50(2), pages 174-188, February 2002.
13. J. Deutscher, A. Blake and Ian Reid, "Articulated Body Motion Capture by Annealed Particle Filtering," *CVPR* 2000.
14. J. Sullivan and J. Rittscher, "Guiding random particles by. deterministic search," *ICCV*, 2001.
15. C. Shan, Y. Wei, T. Tan, F. Ojardias, "Real Time Hand Tracking by Combining Particle Filtering and Mean Shift," *IEEE International Conference on Automatic Face and Gesture Recognition*, 2004.
16. P. Perez, C. Hue, J. Vermaak, and M. Gangnet, "Color-based probabilistic tracking," *ECCV* 2002.
17. Michael Isard and Andrew Blake, "CONDENSATION – conditional density propagation for visual tracking," *Int. J. Computer Vision*, 29, 1, 5–28, 1998.
18. K. Kim, T.H. Chalidabhongse, D. Harwood, L. Davis, "Real-time foreground-background segmentation using codebook model,", *Real-Time Imaging*, June 2005.
19. Anurag Mittal and Larry S. Davis, "M_2Tracker: A Multi-View Approach to Segmenting and Tracking People in a Cluttered Scene," *IJCV*, Vol. 51 (3), 2003.
20. A. Elgammal and L. S. Davis, "Probabilistic Framework for Segmenting People Under Occlusion", *ICCV*, Vancouver, Canada July 9-12, 2001.

Learning Semantic Scene Models by Trajectory Analysis

Xiaogang Wang, Kinh Tieu, and Eric Grimson

Computer Science and Artificial Intelligence Laboratory,
Massachusetts Institute of Technology,
Cambridge, MA 02139, USA
{xgwang, tieu, welg}@csail.mit.edu

Abstract. In this paper, we describe an unsupervised learning framework to segment a scene into semantic regions and to build semantic scene models from long-term observations of moving objects in the scene. First, we introduce two novel similarity measures for comparing trajectories in far-field visual surveillance. The measures simultaneously compare the spatial distribution of trajectories and other attributes, such as velocity and object size, along the trajectories. They also provide a comparison confidence measure which indicates how well the measured image-based similarity approximates true physical similarity. We also introduce novel clustering algorithms which use both similarity and comparison confidence. Based on the proposed similarity measures and clustering methods, a framework to learn semantic scene models by trajectory analysis is developed. Trajectories are first clustered into vehicles and pedestrians, and then further grouped based on spatial and velocity distributions. Different trajectory clusters represent different activities. The geometric and statistical models of structures in the scene, such as roads, walk paths, sources and sinks, are automatically learned from the trajectory clusters. Abnormal activities are detected using the semantic scene models. The system is robust to low-level tracking errors.

1 Introduction

The visual surveillance task is to monitor the activity of objects in a scene. In far-field settings (*i.e.*, wide outdoor areas), the majority of visible activities are objects moving from one location to another. Monitoring activity requires low-level detection, tracking, and classification of moving objects. Both high-level activity analysis and low-level vision can be improved with knowledge of scene structure (*e.g.*, roads, paths, and entry and exit points). Scene knowledge supports activity descriptions with spatial context, such as "car moving off *road*," and "person waiting at *bus stop*." Scene information can also improve low-level tracking and classification [1]. For example, if an object disappears, but not at an exit point, then it is likely a tracking failure instead of a true exit. In classification, we can leverage the fact that vehicles are much more likely than pedestrians to move on the road.

Complementary to the geometric description are the statistics of the scene. A statistical scene model provides an *a priori* probability distributions on where, when, and what types of activities occur. It also places priors on the attributes of moving objects, such as velocity and size. Figure 1(d), shows distributions of location and direction of vehicles on three paths.

A. Leonardis, H. Bischof, and A. Pinz (Eds.): ECCV 2006, Part III, LNCS 3953, pp. 110–123, 2006.

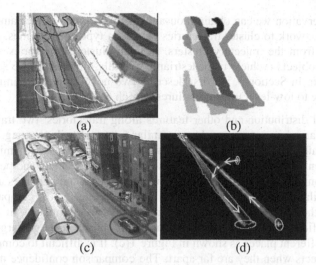

Fig. 1. Examples of far-field scene structures. (a): Far-field scene S1; (b): Semantic regions automatically learned in S1. (c): Far-field scene S2. Images of objects undergo substantial projective distortion so that nearby pedestrians appear larger than far vehicles. (d): Automatically learned spatial layout of three vehicle paths showing distributions of location and moving direction, sources marked by cyan cross and sinks marked by magenta cross in S2.

One way to formally model a scene is to represent it as an attributed graph. Vertices as regions and edges as paths represent the coarse structure and topology of the scene. Attributes on vertices and edges further describe the geometry and statistics of the scene. For example, a source (entry) vertex can be attributed with a mean location and covariance, along with a birth probability. An edge joining a source and sink (exit) can be attributed with the spatial extent of the path and its velocity distribution. In far-field settings, we primarily deal with sources, sinks, and paths between them.

A scene model may be manually input, or possibly automatically extracted from the static scene appearance. However, manual input is tedious if many scenes require labeling, and static scene appearance has large variation and ambiguity. In addition, it is difficult to handcraft the statistics of a scene, or to estimate them from static appearance alone. An example is shown in Figure 1(a)(b). From the image of scene S1, we see one road. However, the road is composed of two lanes of opposing traffic (cyan and red paths). The black path is a one-way u-turn lane. There are two entrances on the left. Vehicles from these entrances wait in the orange region in Figure 1(b) and cross the yellow region on the cyan lane in order to enter the red lane. Pedestrians cross the road via the gray region. In this paper we show how this information can be automatically learned by passive observation of the scene. Our method is based on the idea that because scene structure affects the behavior of moving objects, the structure of the scene can be learned from observing the behavior of moving objects.

1.1 Our Algorithm

Gross positions and sizes of moving objects can be obtained from a blob tracker. A moving object traces out a trajectory of locations and sizes from entry to exit. From long-term observation we can obtain thousands of trajectories in the same scene. We propose a framework to cluster trajectories based on types of activities, and to learn scene models from the trajectory clusters. In each cluster, trajectories are from the same class of objects (vehicle or pedestrian), spatially close and have similar directions of motion. In Section 3, we first describe two novel trajectory similarity measures insensitive to low-level tracking failures, which compare:

(I) both spatial distribution and other features along trajectories: two trajectories are similar if they are close in space and have similar feature distribution, e.g. velocity.

(II) only particular features along trajectories, and augment trajectory similarity with a comparison confidence measure. This is used to separate vehicle and pedestrian trajectories by comparing object size. Under this measure, two trajectories are similar if they have similar features, but need not be close in space. A low comparison confidence means the observed similarity may not reflect true similarity in the physical world. In far-field visual surveillance, images of objects undergo large projective distortion in different places as shown in Figure 1(c). It is difficult to compare the size of the two objects when they are far apart. The comparison confidence measure captures this uncertainty.

In Section 4, we propose novel clustering methods which use both similarity and confidence measures, whereas traditional clustering algorithms assume certainty in the similarities. Based on the novel trajectory similarity measures and clustering methods, we propose a framework to learn semantic scene models summarized in Figure 2. The method is robust to tracking errors and noise.

Input: a set of trajectories obtained by the Stauffer-Grimson tracker [2] from raw video (trajectories may be fragmented because of tracking errors).

1. Cluster trajectories into vehicles and pedestrians based on size using trajectory similarity measure II and clustering methods in Section 4.

2. Detect and remove outlier trajectories which are anomalous or noisy.

3. Further subdivide vehicle and pedestrian trajectories into different clusters based on spatial and velocity distribution using trajectory similarity I.

4. Learn semantic scene models from trajectory clusters. In particular, sources and sinks are estimated using local density-velocity maps from each cluster, which is robust to fragmented trajectories.

5. Real-time detection of anomalous activity using the learned semantic scene models.

Fig. 2. Summary of the scene model learning process

2 Related Work

Two path detection approaches can be found in [3][4]. Both iteratively merge trajectories into an expanded path. In many settings where observed trajectories are noisy and there are objects roaming between paths, the path regions will become increasingly broader, finally merging into a single large path after long observation. In our framework, trajectories can be well clustered even with the existence of noisy and outlier trajectories. [3][4] ignored attributes along the trajectories.

A straightforward way to learn sources and sinks is to build Gaussian mixture models from the start and end points of the trajectories [5][6]. However, tracking sequences are often fragmented because of object interaction, occlusion, and scene clutter. False entry/exit points caused by broken trajectories will bias the estimation of sources and sinks. We solve this problem utilizing the fact that sources and sinks can only appear at the two ends of a path. False entry/exit points inside the path region are detected and removed by inspecting the local density-velocity distribution in a small neighborhood.

There is a large literature on vehicle vs. pedestrian classification. Our work is related to [7][8] which used object positions in the scene to normalize object features with projective distortion. In both previous approaches, spatial location was treated as extra features for similarity, while in out method spatial location is used to calculate the comparison confidence.

3 Trajectory Similarity

A trajectory is a sequence of observations $A = \{\vec{a}_i\}$, where $\vec{a}_i = \, < x_i^a, y_i^a, \beta_i^a >, (x_i^a, y_i^a)$ are the spatial coordinates of the ith observation, and β_i^a is its feature vector, such as object size and velocity.

3.1 Trajectory Similarity I

Considering two trajectories $A = \{\vec{a}_i\}$ and $B = \{\vec{b}_i\}$, for a observation $\vec{a}_i$ on A, its nearest observation on B is

$$\psi(i) = \arg\min_{j \in B} \left\| \left(x_i^a - x_j^b, y_i^a - y_j^b \right) \right\|.$$

The directed spatial distance between A and B is

$$h(A,B) = \frac{1}{N_A} \sum_{\vec{a}_i \in A} \left\| \left(x_i^a - x_{\psi(i)}^b, y_i^a - y_{\psi(i)}^b \right) \right\|, \tag{1}$$

where N_A is the observation number in A. This is similar to the modified Hausdorff distance [9]. It is small when A is close to B in space. However, in some cases, we want to distinguish two trajectories even though they are close in space. For example, to separate a road and a walkway beside it, we need to distinguish vehicles and pedestrians by their size difference. If we want to separate two lanes in opposite moving directions, we have to distinguish trajectories with different velocities. Therefore, we further compare other features along the trajectories, and the directed distance is,

$$f(A,B) = \frac{1}{N_A} \sum_{a_i \in A} \left(\left\| x_i^a - x_{\psi(i)}^b, y_i^a - y_{\psi(i)}^b \right\| + \gamma d\left(\beta_i^a, \beta_{\psi(i)}^b \right) \right),$$ (2)

where $d(\beta_i^a, \beta_{\psi(i)}^b)$ is the dissimilarity measure between features β_i^a and $\beta_{\psi(i)}^b$, and γ is a weighting parameter. The symmetric distance between A and B is

$$F(A,B) = \begin{cases} f(A,B) & if \quad h(A,B) < h(B,A) \\ f(B,A) & if \quad h(A,B) > h(B,A) \end{cases}.$$ (3)

It is transformed to a similarity measure

$$S_f(A,B) = \exp(-F(A,B)/\sigma).$$ (4)

Under this measure, two trajectories are similar only if they are close in space and their observations in nearby locations have similar attributes. In (3), we use a minimum instead of the maximum used in the Hausdorff distance. Thus this measure can handle broken trajectories caused by tracking errors. If A is a short broken trajectory beside a long trajectory B, $h(A, B)$ is small while $h(B, A)$ is large. Under (3), the dissimilarity between A and B could be small. It satisfies our expectation that all broken trajectories on the same path should be grouped into the same cluster.

3.2 Trajectory Similarity II

The above similarity measure is inadequate for clustering all trajectories into two classes, vehicles and pedestrians, by comparing size differences. Trajectories of the same class are not necessarily close in space. Furthermore, features on the trajectories cannot be directly compared because of different geometric and photometric transformations in the scene. For example, vehicles are much larger than pedestrians, and thus should be easily distinguished by size. However, as shown in Figure 1(c), because of projective distortion, some pedestrians close to the camera appear larger than vehicles far away in the scene. Without knowledge of camera geometric parameters, we only have the sense that if two objects are close in space, their observed image size similarity reflects their true size similarity, since both objects undergo the same geometric transform in the same place.

If two pedestrian trajectories are far apart or they are only close at some points, such as A and C in Figure 3, their similarity will be small using the measure in Section 3.1. In the former case, it is difficult to ascertain the true similarity because of projective distortion. In the latter case, we can obtain similarity by comparing the trajectories at intersection points, and ignoring other points which are far apart. This leads us to augment the trajectory similarity measure with a comparison confidence.

We first define the comparison confidence between two observations as

$$c(\vec{a}_i, \vec{b}_i) = \exp\left(-\left\| x_i^a - x_j^b, y_i^a - y_j^b \right\| / \sigma_1 \right).$$ (5)

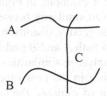

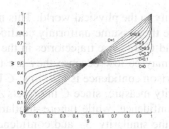

Fig. 3. A, B, C are three trajectories in the same class. Because of projective distortion, A and B has low similarity, while C has high similarity with both A and B.

Fig. 4. Transform functions from S to W, setting $C = 0, 0.1, 0.2, \ldots, 0.9, 1$

To compare trajectories A and B, the directed similarity $S_{A \to B}$ and comparison confidence $C_{A \to B}$ are:

$$S_{A \to B} = \sum_{\bar{a}_i \in A} c(\bar{a}_i, \bar{b}_{\psi(i)}) s(\bar{a}_i, \bar{b}_{\psi(i)}) \Big/ \sum_{\bar{a}_i \in A} c(\bar{a}_i, \bar{b}_{\psi(i)}). \tag{6}$$

$$C_{A \to B} = \sum_{\bar{a}_i \in A} c(\bar{a}_i, \bar{b}_{\psi(i)})^2 \Big/ \sum_{\bar{a}_i \in A} c(\bar{a}_i, \bar{b}_{\psi(i)}) \tag{7}$$

Here, $s(\bar{a}_i, \bar{b}_{\psi(i)}) = \exp(-d(\bar{\beta}_i^a, \bar{\beta}_{\psi(i)}^b) / \sigma_2)$ is the feature similarity between observations $\bar{a}_i$ and $\bar{b}_{\psi(i)}$. For each observation $\bar{a}_i$ on trajectory A, we find its spatially nearest observation $\bar{b}_{\psi(i)}$ on B, and compute the feature similarity $s(\bar{a}_i, \bar{b}_{\psi(i)})$ and comparison confidence $c(\bar{a}_i, \bar{b}_{\psi(i)})$. Along trajectory A, feature similarities of observations are averaged, weighted by the comparison confidences to get $S_{A \to B}$. The similarity of observations close in space has larger weight for computing trajectory similarity. $C_{A \to B}$ indicates how far apart A is from B. The symmetric similarity $S(A, B)$ and comparison confidence $C(A, B)$ for trajectories are,

$$S(A, B) = \begin{cases} S_{A \to B} & if \quad C_{A \to B} > C_{B \to A} \\ S_{B \to A} & if \quad C_{A \to B} < C_{B \to A} \end{cases}, \tag{8}$$

$$C(A, B) = \begin{cases} C_{A \to B} & if \quad C_{A \to B} > C_{B \to A} \\ C_{B \to A} & if \quad C_{A \to B} < C_{B \to A} \end{cases}. \tag{9}$$

The behavior of the comparison confidence measure in several typical cases is analyzed in [11].

4 Clustering with Confidences

Our clustering method is based on pairwise similarity. As mentioned in Section 3.2, some measured similarities between samples may not well approximate the true similarity in the physical world. This makes traditional clustering methods inadequate because they assume uniformly confident similarity values. For example, in Figure 3, A, B and C are three trajectories in the same class. The observed similarity between A and B may be low because they are far apart and there is projective distortion, and comparison confidence is also low. C has high similarity with both A and B under our similarity measure, since C intersects A and B. We should emphasize similarities with high confidence, while ignore similarities with low confidence in the cost function. Given the similarity S_{ij} and confidence C_{ij} between any pair of samples, the task is to partition the sample set V into two subsets V_1 and V_2. There are two ways to augment clustering methods using both similarity and comparison confidence measures: (a) map similarity and confidence measures to a new weight measure, and then apply traditional clustering methods, such as spectral clustering, to the new weight; (b) modify the clustering cost function.

4.1 Remapping Weights

Let g be a function mapping S_{ij} and C_{ij} to a new weight, $W_{ij} = g(S_{ij}, C_{ij})$. The key is to preserve similarities with high confidence and leave low confidence similarities uncertain. If the confidence is small, the weight should be set to a median value. We compute W_{ij} as

$$W_{ij} = \frac{S_{ij}^{C_{ij}}}{\left(1 - S_{ij}\right)^{C_{ij}} + S_{ij}^{C_{ij}}}. \tag{10}$$

The transform functions from similarity to weight given different confidence values from 0 to 1 are shown in Figure 4. When we have no confidence in the similarity ($C = 0$), the weight is 0.5, providing little information for clustering. When we have full confidence ($C = 1$), the weight is exactly the similarity measure. When C changes from 0 to 1, the transform function has a gradual change between the two extremes. Before doing the transform, we first perform histogram equalization on the distribution of similarity values of all the samples in the data set, so that similarities have a uniform distribution from 0 to 1. This normalization makes 0.5 a reasonable value for zero confidence in similarity. Then we apply spectral clustering using the new weights.

4.2 Modify the Clustering Criterion

Traditional clustering methods also can be augmented by including the comparison confidence measure in the cost function. In this work we modify the *average cut*. Let z be an $N = |V|$ dimensional indicator vector, $z_i = 1$ if sample i is in V_1, and $z_i = 0$ if sample i is in V_2. We propose the cost function as the average similarity of the edges connecting V_1 and V_2, weighted by the confidence measures:

$$ave\_cut(V_1, V_2) = \frac{\sum_{i \in V_1, j \in V_2} C_{ij} S_{ij}}{\sum_{i \in V_1, j \in V_2} C_{ij}} = \frac{z^T (D - Q) z}{z^T (T - C) z} \tag{11}$$

The goal is to find the optimal z minimizing $ave\_cut(V_1,V_2)$. Here, $Q = [Q_{ij}]_{N \times N}$, $Q_{ij} = C_{ij}S_{ij}$, $C = [C_{ij}]_{N \times N}$. D and T are two $N \times N$ diagonal matrix with d and t on their diagonal, $d(i) = \sum_j Q_{ij}$, $t(i) = \sum_j C_{ij}$. Similar to the spectral clustering methods, (11) can be minimized by solving the generalized eigenvalue system. Because of the space limit, we omit the proof. A detailed description can be found in [11].

5 Trajectory Clustering

5.1 Clustering Different Types of Trajectories (Vehicles vs. Pedestrians)

Scene structures and activities are often related to the class of objects, we first cluster trajectories into vehicles and pedestrians using the similarity and confidence measure proposed in Section 3.2 and the clustering methods in Section 4. The feature similarity between observations in (6), is defined as

$$ s(\vec{a}_i,\vec{b}_j) = \exp\left(-\left(\frac{(r_i^a - r_j^b)^2}{r_i^a r_j^b}\right)/\sigma_2\right), \tag{12} $$

where r_i^a and r_j^b are the sizes of observations $\vec{a}_i$ and $\vec{b}_j$. We set parameter $\sigma_1 = \sigma_2 = 0.01$ in (5) and (12).

5.2 Clustering Activity Group

Each class of trajectories, vehicles or pedestrians, is further clustered according to different spatial and velocity distributions. We define the trajectory similarity as described in Section 3.1, considering velocity direction along the trajectories. Dissimilarity between observation features in (2) is

$$ d(\beta_i^a, \beta_{\psi(i)}^b) = 1 - \frac{\vec{v}_i^a \cdot \vec{v}_{\psi(i)}^b}{\|\vec{v}_i^a\| \cdot \|\vec{v}_{\psi(i)}^b\|} \tag{13} $$

$\vec{v}_i^a$ and $\vec{v}_{\psi(j)}^b$ are the velocities of $\vec{a}_i$ and $\vec{b}_{\psi(i)}$. The width and the height of the scene is normalized to 1 and parameter γ in (2) is set to 0.25. Spectral clustering is applied using the defined trajectory similarity.

Before clustering, we first remove outlier trajectories. Usually these are noisy trajectories caused by tracking errors, anomalous trajectories, e.g., a car drives out of the way, or some pedestrians roaming between different paths. In visual surveillance, they may be of particular interest, and it is nice that our algorithm can detect them by comparing trajectories. Because they are not strongly constrained by scene structures, the scene structure models will be learnt more accurately by removing them. For each trajectory A, we find its N nearest trajectories B_i $(i = 1,...,N)$, and compute the average distance. We reject trajectories with large average distance to neighbors as outliers.

118   X. Wang, K. Tieu, and E. Grimson

Table 1. Results of clustering trajectories into vehicles and pedestrians. I: compare average observation size along the trajectory and use spectral clustering; II: compare more observation features, (size, speed, size variation, aspect ratio and percentage occupancy of silhouette), also averaged along the trajectory; III: size similarity defined in (2)(3)(4) without considering comparison confidence; IV: compare trajectory distance in space as define in (1); V: combine size similarity and comparison confidence as described in Section 3.2 and 4.

Method	Scene	Cluster	Vehicle	Pedestrian
I	S1	Cluster 1	127	0
		Cluster 2	42	368
	S2	Cluster 1	55	2
		Cluster 2	14	16
II	S1	Cluster 1	162	154
		Cluster 2	7	214
	S2	Cluster 1	65	0
		Cluster 2	4	18
III	S1	Cluster 1	152	0
		Cluster 2	17	368
	S2	Cluster 1	61	0
		Cluster 2	8	18
IV	S1	Cluster 1	166	242
		Cluster 2	3	126
	S2	Cluster 1	40	8
		Cluster 2	29	10
V	S1	Cluster 1	167	0
		Cluster 2	2	368
	S2	Cluster 1	69	0
		Cluster 2	0	18

5.3 Experiments

In Table 1, we report the results of clustering trajectories into vehicles and pedestrians using different clustering methods and similarity measures. There are two data sets from the two scenes shown in Figure 1. We show the numbers of vehicle and pedestrian trajectories in each cluster. The average observation size along the trajectory cannot separate vehicles and pedestrians, since there is overlap between the size distributions of the two classes. In method II, we add more features, such as speed, size variation, aspect ratio and percentage occupancy of silhouette, which proved effective in vehicle/pedestrian classification [8], to compute the similarity. Although these discriminative features work well in supervised classification using some complex classifiers, they are not effective in clustering. Our two clustering approaches in Section 4.1 and 4.2 using both similarity and confidence measures give the same result on this data set. They perfectly separate vehicle and pedestrian trajectories in Scene S2, and incorrectly cluster only two among 537 trajectories in Scene S1. If we only use the size similarity measure as define in (2)(3)(4), or only compare spatial distance as defined in (1), the result is worse. Note that our method is essentially unsupervised and only requires labeling a cluster as vehicle or pedestrian.

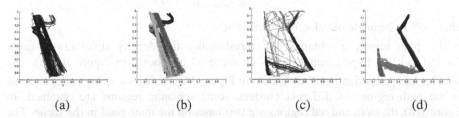

| (a) | (b) | (c) | (d) |

Fig. 5. Clustering vehicle and pedestrian trajectories in Scene S1. (a): outlier vehicle trajectories in red; (b): six vehicle trajectory clusters (c): outlier pedestrian trajectories in red; (d): five pedestrian clusters.

The separated vehicle trajectories and pedestrian trajectories are further clustered into different activity groups. Some results from scene S1 are shown in Figure 5. The vehicle trajectories are clustered into six clusters. Because the road has two opposite driving directions, the trajectories on the two lanes are separated into cyan and red clusters. The vehicles from the two entrances on the left of the scene enter the road along three different paths. The black clusters detect the one-way road and u-turn in the upper center of the scene. Most of the pedestrian trajectories crossing the road and roaming between the two walk paths are first removed as outlier trajectories. The remaining pedestrian trajectories are well clustered into five clusters on the two walk paths aside the road and one path crossing the road, because there are two opposite moving directions on each walk path aside the road.

6   Learning Semantic Scene Models

6.1   Road and Walk Path Models

For each cluster Ω, we detect its spatial extent in the scene, and estimate the density and velocity direction distributions in the region. The density at position (x, y) is estimated as,

$$p_\Omega(x, y) = \sum_{\bar{a} \in A} \sum_{A \in \Omega} \phi_{(x_i^a, y_i^a)}^{(x, y)}, \qquad (14)$$

where $\phi_{(x_i^a, y_i^a)}^{(x,y)} = \exp\left(-\left\|x - x_i^a, y - y_i^a\right\|^2 / \sigma_3\right)$. The velocity direction distribution at (x, y) is modeled as a circular normal (von Mises) distribution [12],

$$p(\theta) = \frac{e^{\cos\theta - \alpha_\Omega(x,y)}}{2\pi I_0(\kappa)} \quad (15)$$

with mean $\alpha_\Omega(x, y)$ computed by

$$\alpha_\Omega(x, y) = \arctan \frac{\sum_{\bar{a}_i \in A} \sum_{A \in \Omega} \phi_{(x_i^a, y_i^a)}^{(x,y)} \sin\theta_i^a}{\sum_{\bar{a}_i \in A} \sum_{A \in \Omega} \phi_{(x_i^a, y_i^a)}^{(x,y)} \cos\theta_i^a} \quad (16)$$

where θ_i^a is the angle of velocity direction at $\bar{a}_i$.

The path region is obtained by thresholding the density distribution, using $\max P_\Omega(x, y)/10$. Experimental results on scene S1 are shown in Figure 1(a)(b). The vehicles and pedestrian paths are shown in Figure 1(a). Using some logical operations on the path regions of different clusters, some semantic regions are obtained. In Figure 1(b), the cyan and red regions are two lanes on the main road in the scene. The black color marks a u-turn. When the vehicles merge from two entrances on the left of the scene, they wait in the orange region before entering the road, and cross the yellow region on the cyan road in order to be on the red road. The purple region has a similar semantic explanation. Pedestrians cross the road via the gray region.

6.2 Sources and Sinks

Two interesting scene structures are locations where vehicles or pedestrians enter or exit the scene. They are called sources and sinks. Trajectories are often broken because of inevitable tracking failures. There are false entry/exit points biasing the estimation of sources and sinks as shown in Figure 7(a). We remove them using the local density-velocity map. Sources and sinks should be on the two ends of the path regions. A false entry/exit point inside the path region has high density around its neighborhood, since there are many other trajectories passing through this point. In

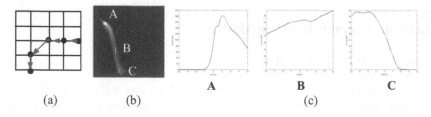

(a)   (b)   (c)

Fig. 6. Removing break points in trajectory clusters. (a): Find local path of the red point based on velocity distribution; (b): Examples of entry point (**A**), exit point (**C**), false entry/exit point (**B**) on cluster density map; (c): Density distributions along local paths of **A**, **B**, **C**.

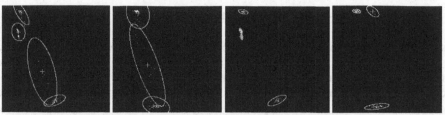

(a) Gaussian mixture models of sources and sinks directly learnt from the start and end points of trajectories.

(b) Gaussian mixture models of sources and sinks learnt from the trajectory clusters after removing break points.

Fig 7. Learning vehicle sources and sinks models in Scene S1

each trajectory cluster, starting from a start/end point of the trajectory, we find its local path by searching forward and backward L steps. On the local path, the next point is decided by the average velocity direction at the current position as shown in Figure 6 (a). In Figure 6 (b), we sample an entry point (A), an exit point (C), and a false entry/exit point (B) on the density map of one trajectory cluster. We can clearly see their difference on density distribution along the local path. The entry point has a very low density along the path behind it. The exit point has a very low density along the local path ahead of it. A false entry/exit point has little change on density along the whole local path, since trajectories in the same cluster have similar moving directions and they do not diverge. We distinguish them comparing the average densities of the two halves of the local path. Results are shown in Figure 7.

6.3 More Experimental Results

More experimental results of learning semantic scene models in scene S2 and S3 are shown in Figure 1(c)(d) and Figure 8. In S3, there is a red pedestrian path crossing the road, however, it is not the crosswalk beside it. People tend to take a short cut instead of using the crosswalk. This is one illustration of how our learnt scene models can provide additional information unavailable from the static image.

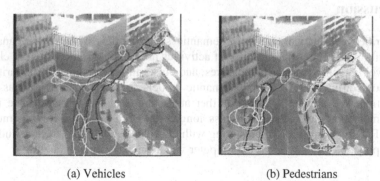

(a) Vehicles

(b) Pedestrians

Fig. 8. Extract paths, sources and sinks of vehicles and pedestrians in Scene S3. Path boundaries are marked by different color, the source and sink centers are marked by cyan and magenta crosses. The yellow ellipses indicate the estimated extent of sources/sinks.

7 Abnormal Trajectory Detection

As mentioned in Section 5, anomalous trajectories can be detected as outlier samples. In Figure 9 (a), outlier vehicle trajectories in S3 are marked by different colors. The green trajectory is a car backing up in the middle of the road. The car on the red trajectory first drives along the purple path in Figure 9(a), then it turns left, crosses the red path on its left side, and has opposite moving direction with the trajectories in the cyan cluster. So it is detected as an anomalous trajectory.

We further develop the system to real-time detect anomalous activity. When an object enters the scene, we classify it into vehicle or pedestrian. For each vehicle/pedestrian class, we model the density and velocity direction distributions in the scene as mixture models, since we have built the statistical model for each cluster in Section 7. When the object passes a location, a likelihood is computed, so we can monitor the object at each position without requiring the whole trajectory data. In Figure 9 (b) we plot the log likelihood of the red trajectory in Figure 9(a) at different locations. The probability is very low when it turns left crossing the red path.

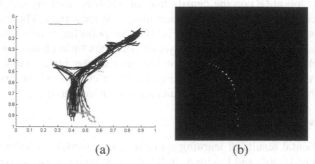

(a)   (b)

Fig. 9. Detect anomalous trajectories in S3. (a): outlier trajectories; (b): transform the log-likelihood into density map. The white color indicates low probabilities (highly anomalous).

8 Discussion

We described a framework to learn semantic scene models by trajectory analysis. Trajectories related to different kinds of activities are separated into different clusters using novel trajectory similarity measures, and clustering methods with similarity and comparison confidences. The scene semantic models are applied to anomalous activity detection. We believe there are further applications of our learned scene model such as more complex activities across longer time scales and involving multiple objects. Finally, our notion of clustering with confidences deserves further study and may be applicable to other areas of computer vision and statistical modeling.

Acknowledgement

The research described in this paper was supported in part by funding from DARPA.

References

[1] R. Kaucic, A. Perera, G. Brooksby, J. Kaufhold, and A. Hoogs, "A Unified Framework for Tracking through Occlusions and across Sensor Gaps," in Proceedings of CVPR 2005.

[2] C. Stauffer and E. Grimson, "Learning Patterns of Activity Using Real-Time Tracking," IEEE Trans. on PAMI, Vol. 22, No. 8, pp. 747-757, 2000.

[3] D. Makris and T. Ellis, "Path Detection in Video Surveillance," Image and Vision Computing, Vol. 20, pp. 859-903, 2002.

[4] J. H. Fernyhough, A. G. Cohn, and D. C. Hogg, "Generation of Semantic Regions from Image Sequences," in Proc. of ECCV, 1996.

[5] D. Makris and T. Ellis, "Automatic Learning of an Activity-Based Semantic Scene Model," in Proc. of IEEE Conference on Advanced Video and Signal Based Surveillance 2003.

[6] S. J. Mckenna and H. Nait-Charif, "Learning Spatial Context from Tracking Using Penalized Likelihood," in Proc. of ICPR, 2004.

[7] B. Bose and E. Grimson, "Improving Object Classification in Far-Field Video," in Proc. CVPR, 2004.

[8] C. Stauffer, "Minimally-Supervised Classification using Multiple Observation Sets," ICCV 2003.

[9] M. P. Dubuisson and A. K. Jain, "A Modified Hausdorff distance for Object Matching," in Proc. of ICPR, 1994.

[10] M. Meila and J. Shi, "A Random Walk View of Spectral Segmentation," in Proc. of AISTATS, 2001.

[11] X. Wang, K. Tieu, and E. Grimson, "Learning Semantic Scene Models by Trajectory Analysis," Tech. Rep. MIT-CSAIL-TR-2006-08, http://hdl.handle.net/1721.1/31208.

[12] E. J. Gumbel and J. A. Greenwood "The Circular Normal Distribution: Theory and Tables," J. Amer. Stat. Soc., Vol. 48, No. 261,, pp. 131-152, 1953.

Multivariate Relevance Vector Machines for Tracking

Arasanathan Thayananthan[1], Ramanan Navaratnam[1], Björn Stenger[2],
Philip H.S. Torr[3], and Roberto Cipolla[1]

[1] University of Cambridge, UK
{at315, rn246, cipolla}@eng.cam.ac.uk
[2] Toshiba Corporate R&D Center, Kawasaki, Japan
bjorn@cantab.net
[3] Oxford Brookes University, UK
philiptorr@brookes.ac.uk

Abstract. This paper presents a learning based approach to tracking articulated human body motion from a single camera. In order to address the problem of pose ambiguity, a one-to-many mapping from image features to state space is learned using a set of relevance vector machines, extended to handle multivariate outputs. The image features are Hausdorff matching scores obtained by matching different shape templates to the image, where the multivariate relevance vector machines (MVRVM) select a sparse set of these templates. We demonstrate that these Hausdorff features reduce the estimation error in clutter compared to shape-context histograms. The method is applied to the pose estimation problem from a single input frame, and is embedded within a probabilistic tracking framework to include temporal information. We apply the algorithm to 3D hand tracking and full human body tracking.

1 Introduction

This paper considers the problem of estimating the 3D pose of an articulated object such as the human body from a single view. This problem is difficult due to the large number of degrees of freedom and the inherent ambiguities that arise when projecting a 3D structure into the 2D image [5, 9]. In generative methods for tracking, the pose is estimated using a 3D geometric model and a likelihood function that evaluates different pose estimates. For example, various algorithms based on particle filtering have been proposed for human body or hand tracking [7, 15, 17, 26]. However, in order to track the motion of the full body or the hand, a large number of particles and a strong dynamic model are required.

More importantly, in order to build a practical system, the initialization task needs to be solved. This can be seen as an multi-object recognition problem, where recognizing a single object corresponds to recognizing the articulated object in a particular pose. Once this problem is solved, temporal information can be used to smooth motion and resolve potential pose ambiguities. This divides

A. Leonardis, H. Bischof, and A. Pinz (Eds.): ECCV 2006, Part III, LNCS 3953, pp. 124–138, 2006.

the continuous pose estimation task into two distinct problems: (1) estimate a distribution of possible configurations from a single frame, (2) combine frame-by-frame estimates to obtain smooth trajectories.

One approach to pose estimation is to generate a large database of examples from a 3D model and use efficient techniques to classify the current input image, e.g. using hierarchical search [18] or hashing techniques [14]. The main problem in this approach, however, is the very large number of templates required to represent the pose space. The number of templates depends on the range of possible motion and required accuracy, and can be in the order of hundreds of thousands of templates [14]. Only a fraction of the templates is searched for each query image, however all templates need to be stored.

The method for hand pose estimation from a single image by Rosales et al. addressed some of these issues [13]. Image features were directly mapped to likely hand poses using a set of *specialized mappings*. A 3D model was projected into the image in these hypothesized poses and evaluated using an image based cost function. The features used were low-dimensional vectors of silhouette shape moments, which are often not discriminative enough for precise pose estimation.

Agarwal and Triggs proposed a method for selecting relevant features using RVM regression [1]. The used image features were shape-contexts [4] of silhouette points. Pose estimation was formulated as a one-to-one mapping from the feature space to pose space. This mapping required about 10% of the training examples. The method was further extended to include dynamic information by joint regression with respect to two variables, the feature vector and a predicted state obtained with a dynamic model [2]. There are two concerns with this approach. Firstly, features from a single view, such as silhouettes, are

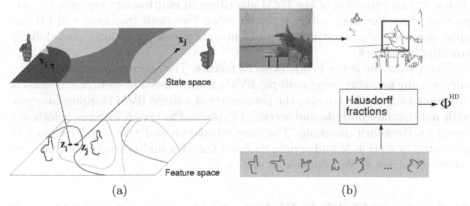

(a)   (b)

Fig. 1. **(a) Multiple mapping functions.** Given a single view, the mapping from image features to pose is inherently one-to-many. Mutually exclusive regions in state space can correspond to overlapping regions in feature space. This ambiguity can be resolved by learning several mapping functions from the feature space to different regions of the state space. **(b) Feature extraction.** The features are obtained from matching costs (Hausdorff fractions) of shape templates to the edge map. These costs are used for creating the basis function vector ϕ^{HD}.

often not powerful enough to solve the pose ambiguity problem. The mapping from silhouette features to state space is inherently one-to-many, as similar features can be generated by regions in the parameter space that are far apart, see figure 1(a). Hence it is important to maintain multiple hypotheses over time. The second concern is that shape-context features have been shown to be sensitive to background clutter [20] and hence a relatively clean silhouette is needed as input. In this paper we propose the use of robust measures that are based on edge-based template matching. Edge-based matching has been used in a number of pose estimation and tracking algorithms [8, 12, 18, 23].

In this paper the pose estimation problem from template matching is formulated as learning one-to-many mapping functions that map from the feature space to the state space. The features are Hausdorff matching scores, which are obtained by matching a set of shape templates to the edge map of the input image, see figure 1(b). A set of RVM mapping functions is then learned to map these scores to different state-space regions to handle pose ambiguity, see figure 1(a). Each mapping function achieves sparsity by selecting only a small fraction of the total number of templates. However, each RVM function will select a different set of templates. This work is closely related to the work of Sminchisescu et al. [16] and Agarwal et al. [3]. Both follow a mixture of experts [11] approach to learn a number of mapping functions (or experts). A gating function is learned for each mapping function during training, and these gating functions are then used to assign the input to one or many mapping functions during the inference stage. In contrast, we use likelihood estimation from projecting the 3D-model to verify the output of each mapping function.

The main contributions of this paper are (1) an EM type algorithm for learning a one-to-many mapping using a set of RVMs, resulting in a sparse set of templates, (2) an extension of the RVM algorithm to multivariate outputs, (3) improving the robustness to image clutter using Hausdorff fractions, and (4) the application to the pose estimation problem and embedding within a probabilistic tracking framework.

The rest of the paper is organized as follows: The algorithm for learning the one-to-many mapping using multiple RVMs is introduced in section 2. Section 3 describes a scheme for training the parameters of a single RVM mapping function with multivariate outputs and section 4 explains the image features, which are based on Hausdorff matching. The pose estimation and tracking framework is presented in section 5, and results on hand tracking and full body tracking are shown in section 6. We conclude in section 7.

2   Learning Multiple RVMs

The pose of an articulated object, in our case a hand or a full human body, is represented by a parameter vector $\mathbf{x} \in \mathbb{R}^M$. The features $\mathbf{z}$ are Canny edges extracted from the image. Given a set of training examples or templates $\mathcal{V} = \{v^{(n)}\}_{n=1}^N$ consisting of pairs $v^{(n)} = \{(\mathbf{x}^{(n)}, \mathbf{z}^{(n)})\}$ of state vector and feature vector, we want to learn a one-to-many mapping from feature space to state

---

Algorithm 1. EM for learning multiple mapping functions $\mathbf{W}_k$

---

1. Initialize

Partition the training set $\mathcal{V}$ into K subsets by applying the K-means algorithm on the state variable $\mathbf{x}_n$ of each data point v_n. Initialize probability matrix $\mathbf{C}$.

2. Iterate

(i) Estimate regression parameters

Given the matrix $\mathbf{C} \in \mathbb{R}^{N \times K}$, where element $c_{nk} = c_k^{(n)}$ is the probability that sample point n belongs to mapping function k, learn the parameters $\{\mathbf{W}^k, \mathbf{S}^k\}$ of each mapping function, by multivariate RVM regression minimizing the following cost function

$$L^k = \sum_{n=1}^{N} c_k^{(n)} \left(\mathbf{y}_k^{(n)}\right)^T \mathbf{S}^k \left(\mathbf{y}_k^{(n)}\right), \text{ where } \mathbf{y}_k^{(n)} = x^{(n)} - \mathbf{W}^k \phi(\mathbf{z}^{(n)}). \quad (1)$$

Note: for speed up, samples with low probabilities may be ignored.

(ii) Estimate probability matrix C

Estimate the probability of each example belonging to each of the mapping function:

$$p(\mathbf{x}^{(n)}|\mathbf{z}^{(n)}, \mathbf{W}^k, \mathbf{S}^k) = \frac{1}{2\pi|\mathbf{S}|^{1/2}} \exp\left\{-0.5 \left(\mathbf{y}_k^{(n)}\right)^T \mathbf{S}^k \left(\mathbf{y}_k^{(n)}\right)\right\}, \quad (2)$$

$$c_k^{(n)} = \frac{p(\mathbf{x}^{(n)}|\mathbf{z}^{(n)}, \mathbf{W}^k, \mathbf{S}^k)}{\sum_{j=1}^{K} p(\mathbf{x}^{(n)}|\mathbf{z}^{(n)}, \mathbf{W}^j, \mathbf{S}^j)}. \quad (3)$$

---

space. We do this by learning K different regression functions, which map the input $\mathbf{z}$ to different regions in state space. We choose the following model for the regression functions

$$\mathbf{x} = \mathbf{W}^k \phi(\mathbf{z}) + \xi^k, \quad (4)$$

where ξ^k is a Gaussian noise vector with $\mathbf{0}$ mean and diagonal covariance matrix $\mathbf{S}^k = diag\left\{(\sigma_1^k)^2, \ldots, (\sigma_M^k)^2\right\}$. Here $\phi(\mathbf{z})$ is a vector of basis functions of the form $\phi(\mathbf{z}) = [1, G(\mathbf{z}, \mathbf{z}^{(1)}), G(\mathbf{z}, \mathbf{z}^{(2)}), \ldots, G(\mathbf{z}, \mathbf{z}^{(N)})]^T$, where G can be any function that compares two sets of image features. The weights of the basis functions are written in matrix form $\mathbf{W}^k \in \mathbb{R}^{M \times P}$ and $P = N + 1$. We use an EM type algorithm, outlined in Algorithm 1, to learn the parameters $\{\mathbf{W}^k, \mathbf{S}^k\}_{k=1}^K$ of the mapping functions. The regression results on a toy dataset are shown in figure 2.

The case of ambiguous poses means that the training set contains examples that are close or the same in feature space but are far apart in state space, see figure 1(a). When a single RVM is trained with this data, the output states tend to average different plausible poses [1]. We therefore experimentally evaluated the effect of learning mapping functions with different numbers of RVMs (with Hausdorff fractions as the input to the mapping functions, see section 4). The data was generated by random sampling from a region in the 4-dimensional state space of global rotation and scale, and projecting a 3D hand model into the image. The size of the training set was 7000 and the size of the test set was 5000. Different numbers of mapping functions were trained to obtain a one-to-many mapping from the features to the state space. The results are shown in figure 3(a). Training multiple mapping functions reduces the estimation error

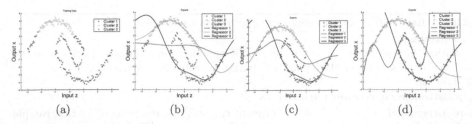

(a)   (b)   (c)   (d)

Fig. 2. RVM regression on a toy dataset. The data set consists of 200 samples from three polynomial functions with added Gaussian noise. (a) Initial clustering using K-means. (b), (c),(d) Learned RVM regressors after the 1st, 4th and 10th iteration, respectively. Each sample data is shown with the colour of the regressor with the highest probability. A Gaussian kernel with a kernel width of 1.0 was used to create the basis functions. Only 14 samples were retained after convergence.

# RVMs	relevant templates	approx. total training time	mean RMS error
1	13.48 %	360 min	15.82°
5	13.04 %	150 min	7.68°
10	10.76 %	90 min	5.23°
15	9.52 %	40 min	4.69°
20	7.78 %	25 min	3.89°

(a)   (b)

Fig. 3. (a) Single vs. multiple RVMs. Results of training different numbers of RVMs on the same dataset. Multiple RVMs learn sparser models, require less training time and yield a smaller estimation error. **(b) Robustness analysis.** Pose estimation error when using two different types of features: histograms of shape contexts (SC) and Hausdorff matching costs (HD). Plotted is the mean and standard deviation of the RMS error of three estimated pose parameters as a function of image noise level. Hausdorff features are more robust to edge noise.

and creates sparser template sets. Additionally, the total training time is reduced because the RVM training time increases quadratically with the number of data points and the samples are divided among the different RVMs.

3   Training an RVM with Multivariate Outputs

During the regression stage, each mapping function is learned using an extension of the RVM regression algorithm [21]. The attraction of the RVM is that it has good generalization performance, while achieving sparsity in the representation. For our case this means that the matrices $\mathbf{W}^k$ only have few non-zero columns. Each column corresponds to the Hausdorff scores obtained by matching a specific shape template to the examples edge maps. Hence, only a fraction of the total number of shape templates needs to be stored. The RVM is a Bayesian regression framework, in which the weights of each input example are governed by a set of hyperparameters. These hyperparameters describe the posterior distribution of the weights and are estimated iteratively during training. Most hyperparameters approach infinity, causing the posterior distributions of the effectively setting the corresponding weights to zero. The remaining examples with non-zero weights are called *relevance vectors*.

Tipping's formulation in [21] only allows regression from multivariate input to a univariate output variable. One solution is to use a single RVM for each output dimension. For example, Williams *et al.* used separate RVMs to track the four parameters of a 2D similarity transform of an image region [25]. This solution has the drawback that one needs to keep separate sets of selected examples for each RVM. We introduce the multivariate RVM (MVRVM) which extends the RVM framework to multivariate outputs, making it a general regression tool.[1] This formulation allows us to choose the same set of templates for all output dimensions.

A ridge regression scheme is used in [1, 2], which also allows selecting the same templates for all output dimensions. However, ridge regression directly optimizes over the weights without the use of hyperparameters. In contrast, we extend the framework in [21] to handle multivariate outputs. A data likelihood is obtained as a function of weight variables and hyperparameters. The weight variables are then analytically integrated out to a obtain marginal likelihood as function of the hyperparameters. An optimal set of hyperparameters is obtained by maximizing the marginal likelihood over the hyperparameters using a version of the fast marginal likelihood maximization algorithm [22]. The optimal weight matrix is obtained using the optimal set of hyperparameters.

The rest of this section details our proposed extension of the RVM framework to handle multivariate outputs and how this is used to minimize the cost function described in eqn (1) and learn the parameters of a mapping function, $\mathbf{W}^k$ and $\mathbf{S}^k$. We can rewrite eqn (1) in the following form

$$L^k = \sum_{n-1}^{N} \log \mathcal{N}(\hat{\mathbf{x}}_k^{(n)} | \mathbf{W}^k \hat{\boldsymbol{\phi}}_k(\mathbf{z}^{(n)}), \mathbf{S}^k), \qquad (5)$$

$$\text{where,} \quad \hat{\mathbf{x}}_k^{(n)} = \sqrt{c_k^{(n)}} \mathbf{x}^{(n)} \quad \text{and} \quad \hat{\boldsymbol{\phi}}_k(\mathbf{z}^{(n)}) = \sqrt{c_k^{(n)}} \boldsymbol{\phi}(\mathbf{z}^{(n)}) \qquad (6)$$

We need to specify a prior on the weight matrix to avoid overfitting. We follow Tipping's relevance vector approach [21] and assume a Gaussian prior for the weights of each basis function. Let $\mathbf{A} = diag(\alpha_1^{-2}, \ldots, \alpha_P^{-2})$, where each element α_j is a hyperparameter that determines the *relevance* of the associated basis function. The prior distribution over the weights is then

$$p(\mathbf{W}^k | \mathbf{A}^k) = \prod_{r=1}^{M} \prod_{j=1}^{P} \mathcal{N}(w_{rj}^k | 0, \alpha_j^{-2}), \qquad (7)$$

---

[1] Code is available from *http://mi.eng.cam.ac.uk/~at315/MVRVM.htm*

where w_{rj}^k is the element at (r, j) of the weight matrix $\mathbf{W}^k$. We can now completely specify the parameters of the kth mapping function as $\{\mathbf{W}^k, \mathbf{S}^k, \mathbf{A}^k\}$. As the form and the learning routines of parameters of each expert are the same, we drop the index k for clarity in the rest of the section. A likelihood distribution of the weight matrix $\mathbf{W}$ can be written as

$$p(\{\hat{\mathbf{x}}^{(n)}\}_{n=1}^N | \mathbf{W}, \mathbf{S}) = \prod_{n=1}^N \mathcal{N}(\hat{\mathbf{x}}^{(n)} | \mathbf{W}\hat{\phi}(\mathbf{z}^{(n)}), \mathbf{S}) \,. \tag{8}$$

Let $\mathbf{w}_r$ be the weight vector for the rth component of the output vector $\mathbf{x}$, such that $\mathbf{W} = [\mathbf{w}_1, \ldots, \mathbf{w}_r, \ldots, \mathbf{w}_M]^T$ and let τ_r be the vector with the rth component of all the example output vectors. Exploiting the diagonal form of $\mathbf{S}$, the likelihood can be written as a product of separate Gaussians of the weight vectors of each output dimension:

$$p(\{\hat{\mathbf{x}}^{(n)}\}_{n=1}^N | \mathbf{W}, \mathbf{S}) = \prod_{r=1}^M \mathcal{N}(\tau_r | \mathbf{w}_r \hat{\boldsymbol{\Phi}}, \sigma_r^2) \,, \tag{9}$$

where $\hat{\boldsymbol{\Phi}} = [\mathbf{1}, \hat{\phi}(\mathbf{z}_1), \hat{\phi}(\mathbf{z}_2), \ldots, \hat{\phi}(\mathbf{z}_N)]$ is the *design matrix*. The prior distribution over the weights is rewritten in the following form

$$p(\mathbf{W}|\mathbf{A}) = \prod_{r=1}^M \prod_{j=1}^P \mathcal{N}(w_{rj}|0, \alpha_j^{-2}) = \prod_{r=1}^M \mathcal{N}(\mathbf{w}_r|\mathbf{0}, \mathbf{A}). \tag{10}$$

Now the posterior on $\mathbf{W}$ can be written as the product of separate Gaussians for the weight vectors of each output dimension:

$$p(\mathbf{W}|\{\hat{\mathbf{x}}\}_{n=1}^N, \mathbf{S}, \mathbf{A}) \propto p(\{\hat{\mathbf{x}}\}_{n=1}^N | \mathbf{W}, \mathbf{S}) \, p(\mathbf{W}|\mathbf{A}) \tag{11}$$

$$\propto \prod_{r=1}^M \mathcal{N}(\mathbf{w}_r | \mu_r, \boldsymbol{\Sigma}_r) \,, \tag{12}$$

where $\mu_r = \sigma_r^{-2} \boldsymbol{\Sigma}_r \boldsymbol{\Phi}^T \tau_r$ and $\boldsymbol{\Sigma}_r = (\sigma_r^{-2} \boldsymbol{\Phi}^T \boldsymbol{\Phi} + \mathbf{A})^{-1}$ are the mean and the covariance of the distribution of $\mathbf{w}_r$. Given the posterior for the weights, we can choose an optimal weight matrix if we obtain a set of hyperparameters that maximise the data likelihood in eqn (12). The Gaussian form of the distribution allows us to the remove the weight variables by analytically integrating them out. Exploiting the diagonal form of $\mathbf{S}$ and $\mathbf{A}$ once more, we marginalize the data likelihood over the weights:

$$p(\{\hat{\mathbf{x}}\}_{n=1}^N | \mathbf{A}, \mathbf{S}) = \int p(\{\hat{\mathbf{x}}\}_{n=1}^N | \mathbf{W}, \mathbf{S}) \, p(\mathbf{W}|\mathbf{A}) \, d\mathbf{W} \tag{13}$$

$$= \prod_{r=1}^M \int \mathcal{N}(\tau_r | \mathbf{w}_r \hat{\boldsymbol{\Phi}}, \sigma_r^2) \, \mathcal{N}(\mathbf{w}_r | \mathbf{0}, \mathbf{A}) \tag{14}$$

$$= \prod_{r=1}^M |\mathbf{H}_r|^{-\frac{1}{2}} \exp(-\frac{1}{2} \tau_r^T \mathbf{H}_r^{-1} \tau_r) \,, \tag{15}$$

where $\mathbf{H}_r = \sigma_r^2 \mathbf{I} + \hat{\boldsymbol{\Phi}} \mathbf{A}^{-1} \hat{\boldsymbol{\Phi}}^T$. An optimal set of hyperparameters $\{\alpha_j^{opt}\}_{j=1}^P$ and noise parameters $\{\sigma_r^{opt}\}_{r=1}^M$ is obtained by maximising the marginal likelihood using bottom-up basis function selection as described by Tipping et al. in [22]. Again, the method was extended to handle the multivariate outputs. Details of this extension can be found in [19]. The optimal hyperparameters are then used to obtain the optimal weight matrix:

$$\mathbf{A}^{opt} = diag(\alpha_1^{opt}, \ldots, \alpha_P^{opt}) \qquad \boldsymbol{\Sigma}_r^{opt} = ((\sigma_r^{opt})^{-2} \hat{\boldsymbol{\Phi}}^T \hat{\boldsymbol{\Phi}} + \mathbf{A}^{opt})^{-1}$$

$$\boldsymbol{\mu}_r^{opt} = (\sigma_r^{opt})^{-2} \boldsymbol{\Sigma}_r^{opt} \boldsymbol{\Phi}^T \, \tau_r \qquad \mathbf{W}^{opt} = [\boldsymbol{\mu}_1^{opt}, \ldots, \boldsymbol{\mu}_M^{opt}]^T$$

4 Robust Representation of Image Features

In this paper, we use Hausdorff fractions [10] in the feature comparison function G. Given two shapes represented by edge point sets $\mathbf{z}^{(i)}$ and $\mathbf{z}^{(j)}$, the Hausdorff fraction f^{HD} is defined as the ratio of points of the first shape that are within a certain distance δ from the points of the second shape:

$$f^{HD}(\mathbf{z}^{(i)}, \mathbf{z}^{(j)}) = \frac{|\mathbf{z}_\delta^{(i)}|}{|\mathbf{z}^{(i)}|}, \text{ where } \mathbf{z}_\delta^{(i)} = \{a \in \mathbf{z}^{(i)} : \min_{b \in \mathbf{z}^{(\cdot)}} ||a - b|| < \delta\}. \quad (16)$$

$$G^{HD}(\mathbf{z}^{(i)}, \mathbf{z}^{(j)}) = \exp\{-f^{HD}\}. \quad (17)$$

The use of edge gradient information increases the discriminative power of these matching methods [12], thus we compute the matching cost with eight discrete orientation channels [8, 18].

We performed experiments comparing the robustness of Hausdorff fraction based features G^{HD} and features based on 100-dimensional shape-context histograms G^{SC}, described in [1, 2]. For this, a training image set is created by sampling a region in state space, in this case three rotation angles over a limited range, and using the sampled pose vectors to project a 3D hand model into the image. Because the Hausdorff features are neither translation nor scale invariant, additional training images of scaled and locally shifted examples are generated. After RVM training, a set of around 30 templates out of 200 are chosen for both, shape context and Hausdorff features. However note that the templates chosen by the RVM for each methods may differ. For testing, 200 poses are generated by randomly sampling the same region in parameter space and introducing different amounts of noise by introducing edges of varying length and curvature. Figure 3(b) shows the dependency of the RMS estimation error (mean and standard deviation) on the noise level. Hausdorff features are significantly more robust to edge noise than shape context features.

5 Pose Estimation and Tracking

Given a candidate object location in the image we obtain K possible poses from the mapping functions, see figure 4(a). For each mapping function $\mathbf{W}_k$

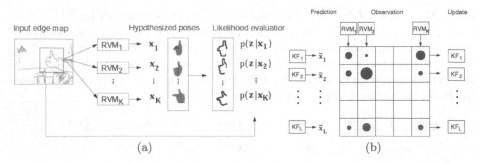

(a)   (b)

Fig. 4. (a) Pose estimation. At each candidate location the features are obtained by Hausdorff matching and the RVMs yield pose estimates. These are used to project the 3D model and evaluate likelihoods. **(b) Probabilistic tracking.** The modes of likelihood distribution, obtained through the RVM mapping functions, are propagated through a bank of Kalman filters [6]. The posterior distributions are represented with an L-mode piecewise Gaussian model. At each frame, the L Kalman filter predictions and K RVM observations are combined to generate possible $L \times K$ Gaussian distributions. Out of these, L Gaussians are chosen to represent the posterior probability and propagated to the next level. The circles in the figure represent the covariance of Gaussians.

the templates selected by the RVM are matched to the input and the resulting Hausdorff fractions form the basis function vector ϕ^{HD}. We then use regression to obtain K pose estimates via $\mathbf{x}_k = \mathbf{W}^k \phi^{HD}$. A set of candidate object locations is obtained by skin colour detection for hands and background estimation for full human body motion. Given M candidate positions we thus obtain $K \times M$ pose hypotheses, which are used to project the 3D object model into the image and obtain image likelihoods.

The observation model for the likelihood computation is based on edge and silhouette cues. As a likelihood model for hand tracking we use the function proposed in [18], which combines chamfer matching with foreground silhouette matching, where the foreground is found by skin colour segmentation. The same likelihood function is used in the full body tracking experiments, with the difference that in this case the foreground silhouette is estimated by background subtraction.

Temporal information is needed to resolve the ambiguous poses and to obtain a smooth trajectory through the state-space after the pose estimation is done at every frame. We embed pose estimation with multiple RVMs within a probabilistic tracking framework, which involves representing and maintaining distributions of the state $\mathbf{x}$ over time.

The distributions are represented using a piecewise Gaussian model [6] with L components. The evaluation of the distribution at one time instant t involves the following steps (see figure 4(b)):

(1) Predict each of the L components,
(2) perform RVM regression to obtain K hypotheses,
(3) evaluate likelihood computation for each hypothesis,

(4) compute the posterior distribution for each of $L \times K$ components,
(5) select L components to propagate to next time step.

The dynamics are modeled using a constant velocity model with large process noise [6], where the noise variance is set to the variance of the mapping error estimated at the RVM learning stage. At step (5) k-means clustering is used to identify the main components of the posterior distribution in the state space, similar to [24]. Components with the largest posterior probability are chosen from each cluster in turn, ensuring that not all components represent only one region of the state-space.

For a given frame the correct pose does not always have the largest posterior probability. Additionally, the uncertainty of pose estimation is larger in some regions in state space than in others, and a certain number of frames may be needed before the pose ambiguity can be resolved. The largest peak of the posterior fluctuates among different trajectories as the distribution is propagated. Hence a history of the peaks of the posterior probability needs to be considered before a consistent trajectory is found that links the peaks over time. In our experiments a batch Viterbi algorithm is used to find such a path.

6   Results and Evaluation

Global pose: In our first experiment, we estimate the three rotation angles and the scale of a pointing hand. We use 10 RVMs to learn the mapping. First 5000 templates are created from a 3D model by random sampling from the state-space. The task is to choose the relevant templates for pose estimation from these templates. Even though we do not estimate image plane translation using the mapping functions, we allow random translation within 7 pixels range in the generated images to achieve translation invariance within a short range. After training the RVMs, a total of 325 relevant templates out of 5000 were selected. For comparison, Stenger *et al.* used approximately 12 000 templates to estimate a similar type of motion [18]. The learned RVM mapping functions are used to estimate the rotation angles and the scale of a pointing hand in a sequence of 1100 frames. Skin colour detection is used to find candidate locations

Fig. 5. Tracking a pointing hand. Example frames from tracking a pointing hand sequence with 1100 frames using a single camera are shown. The model contours corresponding to the optimal path through the state distribution are superimposed, and the 3D model is shown below. A total of 389 relevant templates, divided between 10 RVM mapping functions, were used to estimate the hand pose. For comparison, Stenger et al. [18] used 12 000 templates to estimate a similar type of motion.

for applying the mapping functions. However, the mapping functions themselves only receive an edge map as their input. The tracking framework described in section 5 is then applied to the detection results at every frame. Figure (5) shows some example frames from this sequence.

Hand articulation : The method is applied to the hand open-close sequence with 88 frames from [18], where approximately 30 000 templates were required for tracking. To capture typical hand motion data, we use a large set of 10 dimensional joint angle data obtained from a data glove. The pose data was approximated by the first four principal components. We then projected original hand glove data into those 4 dimensions. The global motion of the hand in that sequence was limited to a certain region of the global space (80°, 60°and 40° in rotation angles and 0.6 to 0.8 in scale). The eight-dimensional state space is defined by the four global and four articulation parameters. A set of 10 000 templates is generated by random sampling in this state space. After training 10 RVMs, 455 templates out of 10 000 are retained. Due to the large amount of background clutter in the sequence, skin colour detection is used in this sequence to remove some of the background edges for this sequence. Tracking results are shown in figure (6).

Full body articulation: In order to track full body motion, we use a data set from the CMU motion capture database of walking persons ($\sim$ 9000 data points). In order to reduce the RVM training time, the data is projected onto the first six principal components.

The first input sequence is a person walking fronto parallel to the camera. The global motion is mainly limited to translation. The eight-dimensional state-space is defined by two global and six articulation parameters. A set of 13,000 training samples were created by sampling the region. We use 4 RVM mapping functions to approximate the one-to-many mapping. A set of 118 relevant templates is retained after training. Background subtraction is used to remove some of the background edges. The tracking results are shown in figure (7). The second input sequence is a video of a person walking in a circle from [15]. The range of global motion is set to 360° around axis normal to the ground plane and 20°

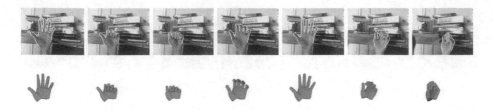

Fig. 6. Tracking an opening and closing hand. This sequence shows tracking of opening and closing hand motion together with global motion on a sequence from [18]. A total of 537 relevant templates were used with 20 RVM mapping functions for pose estimation. As a comparison [18] used about 30 000 templates to track the same sequence.

Fig. 7. Tracking a person walking fronto parallel to the camera. The first and second rows shows the frames from [15], overlaid with the body pose corresponding to the optimal path through the posterior distribution and the corresponding the 3D model, respectively. Similarly, second and third rows show the second best path. Notice that the second path describes the walk equally well except for the right-left leg flip which is one of the common ambiguity that arises in human pose estimation from monocular view. A total of 118 templates with 4 RVM mapping functions were used.

Fig. 8. Tracking a person walking in a circle. This figure shows the results of the tracking algorithm on a sequence from [15]. Overlaid is the body pose corresponding to the optimal path through the posterior distribution, the 3D model is shown below. A total of 1429 templates with 50 RVM mapping functions were used.

in the tilt angle. The range of scales is 0.3 to 0.7. The nine-dimensional state-space region is defined by these three global and six articulation parameters. A set of 50 000 templates is generated by sampling this region. We use 50 RVM mapping functions to approximate the one-to-many mapping. A set of 984 relevant templates is retained after training. Background subtraction is used to remove some of the background edges. The tracking results are shown in figure (8).

Computation time: The execution time in the experiments varies from 5 to 20 seconds per frame (on a Pentium IV, 2.1 GHz PC), depending on the number of candidate locations in each frame. The computational bottleneck is the model projection in order to compute the likelihoods (approximately 100 per second). For example, for 30 search locations and 50 RVM mapping functions result in 1500 model projections, requiring 15 seconds. It can be observed that most mapping functions do not yield high likelihoods, thus identifying them early will help to reduce the computation time.

7   Summary and Conclusion

This paper has introduced an EM type algorithm to learn a one-to-many mapping using multiple relevance vector machines. To this end the original RVM formulation was extended to allow for multivariate outputs. The method was applied to the problem of pose estimation from a single frame, where the RVMs were used to select relevant templates from a large set of candidate templates.

Pose estimation was embedded within a tracking framework, combining both discriminative and generative methods: At each frame the set of mappings from feature to parameter space generates a set of pose hypotheses, which are then used to project a 3D model and compute an image likelihood. The state posterior distribution, represented by a piecewise Gaussian distribution, is propagated over time, and dynamic information is included using a bank of Kalman filters. A batch Viterbi algorithm is used to find a path through the peaks of this distribution in order to resolve ambiguous poses.

Template-based pose estimation schemes solve the problem of initialisation and pose-recovery and maintain multiple hypothesis in tracking articulated objects. Furthermore edge-based schemes are resistant to background clutter and image deformations to a certain degree. However, a major problem is the large number of templates that are needed for the pose estimation of articulated objects [18]. We have presented a scheme where we achieve reduction of two to three orders of magnitude in the number of templates.

Acknowledgments. This work was supported by the Gates Cambridge Trust, the ORS Programme, and Toshiba Research.

References

1. A. Agarwal and B. Triggs. 3D human pose from silhouettes by relevance vector regression. In *Proc. Conf. Computer Vision and Pattern Recognition*, volume II, pages 882–888, Washington, DC, July 2004.
2. A. Agarwal and B. Triggs. Learning to track 3D human motion from silhouettes. In *In Proceedings of the 21st International Conference on Machine Learning*, pages 9–16, Banff, Canada, 2004.
3. A. Agarwal and B. Triggs. Monocular human motion capture with a mixture of regressors. In *In IEEE Workshop on Vision for Human Computer Interaction*, 2005.
4. S. Belongie, J. Malik, and J. Puzicha. Shape matching and object recognition using shape contexts. *IEEE Trans. Pattern Analysis and Machine Intell.*, 24(4):509–522, April 2002.

5. M. Brand. Shadow puppetry. In *Proc. 7th Int. Conf. on Computer Vision*, volume II, pages 1237–1244, Corfu, Greece, September 1999.

6. T. J. Cham and J. M. Rehg. A multiple hypothesis approach to figure tracking. In *Proc. Conf. Computer Vision and Pattern Recognition*, volume II, pages 239–245, Fort Collins, CO, June 1999.

7. J. Deutscher, A. Blake, and I. Reid. Articulated body motion capture by annealed particle filtering. In *Proc. Conf. Computer Vision and Pattern Recognition*, volume II, pages 126–133, Hilton Head, SC, June 2000.

8. D. M. Gavrila. Pedestrian detection from a moving vehicle. In *Proc. 6th European Conf. on Computer Vision*, volume II, pages 37–49, Dublin, Ireland, June/July 2000.

9. N. R. Howe, M. E. Leventon, and W. T. Freeman. Bayesian reconstruction of 3D human motion from single-camera video. In *Adv. Neural Information Processing Systems*, pages 820–826, Denver, CO, November 1999.

10. D. P. Huttenlocher, J. J. Noh, and W. J. Rucklidge. Tracking non-rigid objects in complex scenes. In *Proc. 4th Int. Conf. on Computer Vision*, pages 93–101, Berlin, May 1993.

11. M. Jordan and R. Jacobs. Hierarchical mixtures of experts and the em algorithm. *Neural Computation*, 6:181–214, 1994.

12. C. F. Olson and D. P. Huttenlocher. Automatic target recognition by matching oriented edge pixels. *Transactions on Image Processing*, 6(1):103–113, January 1997.

13. R. Rosales, V. Athitsos, L. Sigal, and S. Scarloff. 3D hand pose reconstruction using specialized mappings. In *Proc. 8th Int. Conf. on Computer Vision*, volume I, pages 378–385, Vancouver, Canada, July 2001.

14. G. Shakhnarovich, P. Viola, and T. Darrell. Fast pose estimation with parameter-sensitive hashing. In *Proc. 9th Int. Conf. on Computer Vision*, volume II, pages 750–757, 2003.

15. H. Sidenbladh, F.D.L Torre, and M. J. Black. A framework for modeling the appearance of 3d articulated figures. In *IEEE International Conference on Automatic Face and Gesture Recognition*, pages 368–375, Grenoble, France, 2000.

16. C. Sminchisescu, A. Kanaujia, Z. Li, and D. Metaxas. Discriminative density propagation for 3d human motion estimation. In *Proc. Conf. Computer Vision and Pattern Recognition*, pages 217–323, June 2005.

17. C. Sminchisescu and B. Triggs. Estimating articulated human motion with covariance scaled sampling. *Int. Journal of Robotics Research*, 22(6):371–393, 2003.

18. B. Stenger, A. Thayananthan, P. H. S. Torr, and R. Cipolla. Filtering using a tree-based estimator. In *Proc. 9th Int. Conf. on Computer Vision*, volume II, pages 1063–1070, 2003.

19. A. Thayananthan. *Template-based pose estimation and tracking of 3D hand motion*. PhD thesis, University of Cambridge, UK, 2005.

20. A. Thayananthan, B. Stenger, P. H. S. Torr, and R. Cipolla. Shape context and chamfer matching in cluttered scenes. In *Proc. Conf. Computer Vision and Pattern Recognition*, volume I, pages 127–133, 2003.

21. M. E. Tipping. Sparse Bayesian learning and the relevance vector machine. *J. Machine Learning Research*, pages 211–244, 2001.

22. M. E. Tipping and A. Faul. Fast marginal likelihood maximisation for sparse bayesian models. In *Proc. Ninth Intl. Workshop on Artificial Intelligence and Statistics*, Key West, FL, January 2003.

23. K. Toyama and A. Blake. Probabilistic tracking with exemplars in a metric space. *Int. Journal of Computer Vision*, 48(1):9–19, June 2002.

24. J. Vermaak, A. Doucet, and P. Pérez. Maintaining multi-modality through mixture tracking. In *Proc. 9th Int. Conf. on Computer Vision*, 2003.
25. O. Williams, A. Blake, and R. Cipolla. A sparse probabilistic learning algorithm for real-time tracking. In *Proc. 9th Int. Conf. on Computer Vision*, volume I, pages 353–360, Nice, France, October 2003.
26. Y. Wu, J. Y. Lin, and T. S. Huang. Capturing natural hand articulation. In *Proc. 8th Int. Conf. on Computer Vision*, volume II, pages 426–432, Vancouver, Canada, July 2001.

Real-Time Upper Body Detection and 3D Pose Estimation in Monoscopic Images

Antonio S. Micilotta, Eng-Jon Ong, and Richard Bowden

Centre for Vision, Speech and Signal Processing,
University of Surrey,
Guildford GU2 7XH, Surrey, United Kingdom
{e.ong, r.bowden}@surrey.ac.uk

Abstract. This paper presents a novel solution to the difficult task of both detecting and estimating the 3D pose of humans in monoscopic images. The approach consists of two parts. Firstly the location of a human is identified by a probabalistic assembly of detected body parts. Detectors for the face, torso and hands are learnt using adaBoost. A pose likliehood is then obtained using an a priori mixture model on body configuration and possible configurations assembled from available evidence using RANSAC. Once a human has been detected, the location is used to initialise a matching algorithm which matches the silhouette and edge map of a subject with a 3D model. This is done efficiently using chamfer matching, integral images and pose estimation from the initial detection stage. We demonstrate the application of the approach to large, cluttered natural images and at near framerate operation (16fps) on lower resolution video streams.

1 Introduction

Our objective is to automatically locate the presence of human figures in natural images, and to estimate the 3D skeletal pose of that figure. Fitting a 3D model to a monocular image of a person requires a reliable estimate of the position of that person. Our first objective is therefore to robustly estimate the location and approximate 2D pose of a user in a real world cluttered scene. This is a challenging task as the shape and appearance of the human figure is highly variable. We have extended AdaBoost [15] to create body part detectors for the face, torso and hands. Detections are then assembled into an upper body pose via RANSAC [4] in real-time. Once an upper body 2D pose is selected, the second objective, is to reconstruct the 3D upper body pose making use of a prior dataset of human motion capture.

Human detection is often facilitated by detecting individual body parts, and assembling them into a human figure. Ioffe and Forsyth [6] make use of a parallel edge segment detector to locate body parts, and assemble them into a 'body plan' using a pre-defined top level classifier. Similarly, Felzenszwalb and Huttenlocher [3] use rectangular colour-based part detectors, and assemble detected parts into a body plan using pictorial structures. Ronfard et al.[10] use detectors trained

A. Leonardis, H. Bischof, and A. Pinz (Eds.): ECCV 2006, Part III, LNCS 3953, pp. 139–150, 2006.
© Springer-Verlag Berlin Heidelberg 2006

by dedicated Support Vector Machines (SVM) where a feature set consists of a Gaussian filter image and 1st and 2nd derivatives. Haar wavelets are used by Mohan et al. [9] to represent candidate regions and SVMs to classify the patterns. Roberts et al. [11] have created probabilistic region templates for the head, torso and limbs where likelihood ratios for individual parts are learned from the dissimilarity of the foreground and adjacent background distributions. Mikolajczyk et al. [8] model humans as flexible combinations of boosted face, torso and leg detectors. Parts are represented by the co-occurrence of orientation features based on 1st and 2nd derivatives. The procedure is computationally expensive, and 'robust part detection is the key to the approach' [8].

Our approach is novel in that it uses RANSAC to combine appearance, colour and structural cues with a strong prior on pose configuration to detect human structures. 3D reconstruction from a single camera has also recieved considerable attention. Howe [5] et al. tracked 20 body points from a monocular sequence, and adopted a bayesian framework to compute prior probabilities of 3D motions with the aid of training data. An alternative is proposed by Sigal et al. [13] where the human body is represented as a graphical model where relationships between body parts are represented by conditional probability distributions. The pose estimation problem becomes one of probabilistic inference over a graphical model with random variables modelling individual limb parameters. Fitting a 3D model to a single image of an object is achieved by comparing shape and edge templates of an example database to the object of interest. This has been applied to hand pose estimation [14] where shape matching follows a cascaded approach to reduce the number of edge template comparisons. Most 3D reconstruction approaches rely upon tracking assuming an initial pose is already known. Here, we combine robust detection with 3D estimation allowing the visually accurate reconstruction of pose within a single image. We also extend this approach to tracking in a video stream.

This paper is set out as follows: A basic discussion of AdaBoost applied to object detection is presented in Section 2. Our first contribution offers a method of assembling body part detections using RANSAC, a heuristic, and an a priori mixture model of upper-body configurations (Section 3). The chosen assembly is then used to assist in reconstructing the corresponding upper body 3D pose (Section 5). Section 5.1 describes the acquisition of the database of 2D upper body frontal poses from the 3D animated avatar, which is then subdivided into subsidiary databases. Matching the silhouette and edge templates of the user to those of example databases is discussed in Section 5.4.Finally, results are shown, and conclusions drawn.

2 Boosted Body Parts Detectors

Boosting is a general method that can be used for improving the accuracy of a given learning algorithm.More specifically, it is based on the principle that a highly accurate or 'strong' classifier can be produced through the linear combination of many inaccurate or 'weak' classifiers. The efficiency of the final classifier is increased further by organising the weak classifiers into a collection of cascaded layers. This design consists of a set of layers with an increasing number of weak classifiers, where each layer acts as a non-body-part rejector with increasing complexity. An input image is first passed to the simplest top layer for consideration, and is only moved to the next layer if it is classified as true by the current layer. The reader is directed to [15] for a detailed discussion of AdaBoost cascades.

Using AdaBoost, we separately trained four different body part detectors using their respective image databases. In order to detect a specific body part in a bounding box, we offset all the weak classifiers belonging to that detector to that location. A positive or negative detection is then computed by combining weak classifier outputs in strong-classifier layers. Each detector returns a score for part detection, which is then normalised to produce a likelihood, defined as L_F, L_T, and L_H respectively.

Since detections are performed in gray scale, it would be advantageous to exploit colour cues to contribute to a detection's legitimacy. Here, the face and hands benefit from this constraint. Initially, a weak skin colour model in the Hue-Saturation colour space built from a large selection of natural images containing skin regions. Using this generic skin model, we determine the median skin likelihood for the face (L_{FS}) and from this face detection we obtain a refined user specific skin model for use in hand detection (L_{HS}).

3   Human Body Assembly

The methods described in the previous sections provide the detected body parts needed to construct a human model. To ensure that most of the body parts are detected, fewer layers in the cascade are selected, resulting in a larger number of false detections. In order to determine likliey body configuration from the numerous detected body parts, a three step process is followed: 1) RANSAC is used to assemble random body configurations, each consisting of a head, a torso, and a pair of hands. A weak heuristic is then applied to each configuration to eliminate obvious outliers (3.1). 2) Each remaining configuration is compared to an a priori mixture model of upper-body configurations, yielding a likelihood for the upper body pose (3.2). 3) A resultant likelihood for each configuration

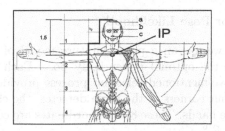

Fig. 1. Virtuvian Man

is obtained by combining the likelihood determined by the prior model with those of the body part detectors and corresponding skin colour (if applicable). Configurations with a high likelihood are determined and the support assessed via RANSAC (3.3).

3.1 Building a Coarse Heuristic

An image with several human figures and dense background clutter can produce multiple part detections in addition to false detections. RANSAC selects subsets of detections that represent body configurations, however testing all these configurations would be computationally expensive; a coarse heuristic is therefore employed to discard unlikely configurations.

Rules of the heuristic are designed according to a generic human model, and include a reference length measurement. Referring to Da Vinci's Virtuvian Man (Figure 1) the human figure is subdivided into eight lengths, each equal to the "head length (the top of the skull to the chin). For the purpose of this paper, this length is referred to as a *skeletal unit length*. The head can be further subdivided into 3 lengths, a,b and c – a typical face detection occupies b and c, thereby allowing us to approximate the skeletal unit length.

Comparing the ROC curves of Figure 6a it is evident that the face detector is the most robust. For this reason, the face detector forms the base for every body configuration. The skeletal unit length and centre position of a selected face is determined, and form the parameters that assist in solving a body configuration.

The rules of the heuristic are set out in the following order, with x and y referring to horizontal and vertical directions: 1) A torso is added to the model only if: its centre x position lies within the face width; the torso scale is approximately $3 \times$ face scale ($\pm$ 0.5); the face centre lies within the detected torso region. 2) A pair of hands are added only if: both hands are less that $4 \times$ skeletal unit lengths from the face; the hand scale $\approx$ face scale ($\pm$ 0.2). False hand detections form the bottleneck in the system as a large number are accepted by the heuristic. The configurations that are passed by the heuristic are then compared to an a priori mixture model of upper-body configurations to obtain a likelihood for the upper body pose (see equation 1), which plays an important role in eliminating false hand detections as awkward hand poses yield a low likelihood.

3.2 Prior Data for Pose Likelihood

In this second step, we use an a priori mixture model of upper-body configurations to estimate the optimal upper body pose. Each body configuration obtained by the above-mentioned selection process provides the position of 8 points, namely the four corners of the torso detector, the chin and brow of the face detector, and the hands. These 8 x, y coordinates are concatenated to form a feature vector $\mathbf{Y} \in \Re^{16}$.

An a priori model ϕ of upper-body configurations was built from approximately 4500 hand labelled representative examples ($\in \Re^{16}$ as above) from image sequences of subjects performing various articulated motions. A Gaussian Mixture Model (GMM) is then used to represent this non-linear training set. The number of components k is chosen through analysis of the cost function, constructed from k-means. Here, $k = 100$. k 16x16 covariance matrices $Cov_{\phi,k}$ are formed from data set ϕ, where $Cov_{\phi,k} = \frac{1}{N.-1}(\phi_i - \mu_{\phi,k})(\phi_i - \mu_{\phi,k})^T$, and $\mu_{\phi,k}$ is the mean of each component of the GMM. A measure of how well each newly assembled body configuration fits the prior data set can now be determined.

The Mahalanobis distance between the configuration and the prior is determined and a final pose likelihood L_P is obtained from the weighted sum of the likelihoods for each component:

$$L_P = \sum_{i=1}^{k} \frac{N_i}{N} \left[\left(2\pi^{\frac{1}{2}} |Cov_{\phi,i}|^{\frac{1}{2}} \right)^{-1} exp(-\frac{1}{2}md_{\phi,i}^2) \right] \qquad (1)$$

3.3 Final Configuration Selection

The eight determined likelihoods, namely the mixture model (L_P), face (L_F), face skin (L_{FS}), torso (L_T), left hand (L_{LH}), left hand skin (L_{LHS}), right hand (L_{RH}) and right hand skin (L_{RHS}) are combined to provide an overall body configuration likelihood, L_{BC}.

$$L_{BCi} = L_{Pi}.L_{Fi}.L_{FSi}.L_{Ti}.L_{LHi}.L_{LHSi}.L_{RHi}.L_{RHSi} \qquad (2)$$

To determine the most likely pose consensus for a specific pose is accumulated by RANSAC. This is possible as objects tend to produce multiple overlapping detections.

4 Detection in Sequences

Extending this work to video sequences allows us to take advantage of background segmentation and to apply the detectors in a tracking framework.

Our background removal algorithm was originally developed for exterior visual surveillance and relies upon modelling the colour distribution with a Gaussian mixture model on a per pixel basis [7]. This allows each pixel to be assigned a foreground likelihood which increases according to sudden intensity variation. We apply the detectors on the full natural frame, and include the mean foreground likelihood L_{FG} of a detection's bounding box. The body configuration likelihood of Equation 2 is therefore updated as follows:

$$L_{BC.} = (L_{Pi}) \times (L_{Fi}.L_{FSi}.L_{FG}..) \times (L_{Ti}.L_{FG}..)$$
$$\times (L_{LHi}.L_{LHSi}.L_{FG}...) \times (L_{RHi}.L_{RHSi}.L_{FG}...) \qquad (3)$$

The chief advantage of detection in a video sequence lies in the tracking framework where the search space is localised in subsequent frames, thereby reducing the number of false detections, the number of hypotheses assessed by

RANSAC, and therefore improving speed performance. An initial face detection is conducted as before, with consequent body part detections limited by the heuristic proximity rules as defined in section 3.1. Subsequent position and scale variations of each detector are governed by prior detections. Should a body part fail to be detected, the search region for the corresponding detector is increased linearly and the scale is adjusted by a Gaussian drift term until the detector recovers.

5   Estimating the 3D Pose

Once an upper body assembly is selected, we estimate the corresponding 3D pose by matching the silhouette and edge map of the user to those of the animated 3D avatar.

5.1   Data Acquisition

Using a 3D graphics package, a skeleton is skinned with a generic human mesh to resemble a person wearing loose fitting clothing and rendered using cell shading. A rendered model with one colour level resembles a simple silhouette. We therefore colour the respective body parts independently to preserve edges between different limbs and the body. The left and right hands are coloured blue and yellow respectively to provide independent labelling. Only the upper body is rendered by assigning the lower body a transparent material.

A single target camera (a camera whereby the camera-to-target distance remains fixed) is then attached to the chest bone of the skeleton, and is allowed to roll in accordance with it. The skeleton is then animated and rendered with a variety of movements using motion capture data (5000 frames), yielding a database of 2D frontal view images (Frontal View Database) of an upright upper body that has a fixed scale, and is centred at position P (Figure 2 (a)).

Subsidiary Datasets. The images of the Frontal View Database are then used to produce a hierarchy of three subsidiary databases. These are computed offline, and are loaded in when the application is executed. All examples in these databases are indexed according to the original frontal image database and the

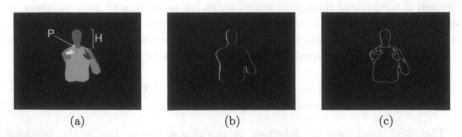

(a)   (b)   (c)

Fig. 2. (a) Frontal 2D representation of 3D model (b) Boundary image (c) Edge map

corresponding pose configuration data that generated it. From parent down: **1)** **Hand Position Database.** This consists of the 2D positions of the left and right hands that are obtained by determining the centroid of the blue and yellow (hand) regions of each frame. **2) Silhouette Database.** This is easy to create as the background of each example is black. The boundary of silhouette images are efficiently stored as entry and exit pairs for each row of the silhouette. This representation also offers a fast and efficient method of comparison to the input silhouette, which is represented as an integral image (see Section 5.4). **3) Edge Map Database.** Conducting an edge detection on the cell shaded and multi-coloured model provides clean edge images (Figure 2 (c)). Again, to conserve memory, only the edge locations are stored.

5.2 Input Image Adjustment

The sections below discuss the processes that occur at run-time, after the subsidiary databases have been loaded. Referring to an example of the Frontal View Database (Figure 2 (a)), the length from the top of the head to the neckline H, is constant across all examples, and is used as the reference point with which to scale the input image. Position P and length H are pre-computed.

Comparing the Frontal View Database and its subsidiaries to the input image requires that the input image foreground exists in same spatial domain (see Figure 3 (b)). To do this, the input image neck centre IP and head length IH must be determined. The assembled body determined in Section 4 provides the dimensions of the face, from which the skeletal unit length is approximated (Section 3.1).

The scale factor is determined by $S = IH/H$, and the offset from P to IP is determined by $offset = P - IP/S$. The input image is scaled and translated in a single pass, creating the *adjusted input image* (*AdjIm*) of Figure 3 (b). We then extract an input silhouette IS and edge map from this adjusted input image.

5.3 Extracting Subsidiary Database Examples

Before conducting silhouette matching, we initially extract a subset of the Silhouette Database by considering the user's hand positions. Using the left and right hand bounding boxes provided by the tracking algorithm as reference, we

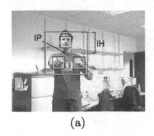 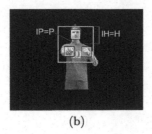 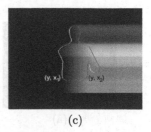

(a)   (b)   (c)

Fig. 3. Input Image: (a) Original (b) Adjusted (c) Integral image / boundary overlap

search through the Hand Position Database for hand positions that are simultaneously contained by these bounding boxes, and extract the corresponding examples from the Silhouette Database. This too can be precomputed by indexing examples in the database to the gaussian components of the GMM used in the pose likliehood. From the possible examples identified; a matching score is therefore calculated for each example as per Section 5.4.

5.4 Silhoutte Matching Using Integral Images and Chamfer Matching

We determine a set of matching scores for the Slihouette Database subset by computing the percentage pixel overlap between the input silhouette and each example. The matching procedure is made more efficient by using an integral image II as an intermediate representation of the input silhouette IS.

The II encodes the shape of the object by computing the summation of pixels on a row by row basis. The value of the $II(x, y)$ equals the sum of all the non-zero pixels to the left of, and including $IS(x, y)$:$II(x, y) = \int_{i=0}^{x} IS(i, y)\mathrm{d}i$.

The entire II can be computed in this manner for all (x, y), however for efficiency we compute this incrementally: $\forall x, y\ II(x, y) = IS(x, y) + II(x - 1, y)$ Figure 3 (c) offers a visualisation of the integral image of the input silhouette (extracted from Figure 3 (b)), with a silhouette boundary example of the Silhouette Database superimposed. Referring to Figure 3 (c), the number of pixels between boundary pair (y, x_1) to (y, x_2) is computed as $N_B(y) = x_2 - x_1 + 1$. The number of pixels of the input silhouette for the corresponding range is therefore computed as $N_{IS}(y) = II(y, x_2) - II(y, x_1) + 1$,where $\sum N_B$ and $\sum N_{IS}$ are computed for all boundary pairs, and the matching score is therefore computed as $S = \sum N_{IS} / \sum N_B$. This score is computed in a few hundred operations; considerably less than tens of thousands of pixel-pixel comparisons.

A matching score is computed for each example of the Silhouette Database subset, the top 10% of which are compared to the corresponding edge maps from the Edge Map Database using Chamfer Matching [1]. To achieve this, the distance transform [2] of the input edge image (Figure 4 (a)) is obtained to 'blur' the edges (Figure 4 (b)), where the intensity of a distance transform pixel is proportional to its distance to an edge. We then superimpose the example

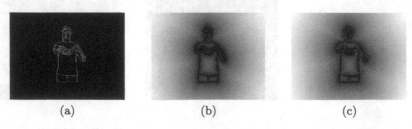

(a)   (b)   (c)

Fig. 4. (a) Edge image   (b) Distance image   (c) Chamfer match

edge map on the distance image, and determine the *edge distance* – the mean of the distance image pixel values that co-occur with example edge maps. The example that yields the shortest distance represents the best match, and is used to access the 3D data from the original database.

6 Results

Comparison of the different part detectors is a difficult task. The most obvious problem is that each part is of different scale, and we would therefore expect a larger number of false hand detections than false torso detections for example. Our in-house face database consists of colour images containing 500 faces, and is similar in size to the MIT-CMU face database (507 faces). The torso were tested on 460 (of 900) images of the MIT pedestrian database, while the hand detector was tested on a colour image database containing 400 hands. Figure 6a shows the detection performance of the detectors applied to their respective test datasets, where layers from the classifier are removed to increase the detection rate. In this research, detection is considered true if at least 75% of its bounding box encloses the groundtruthed body part. In addition, we do not merge overlapping false detections as in [12]. We have plotted two curves for the face detector to

Fig. 5. Top row (from left): All detections, Reduced detections and Final Assembly. Middle Row: Body part assembly from a video sequence. Bottom row (from left): synthesised leg positions due to leg detection failure, synthesised hand positions due to hand occlusions, detections for non-frontal body and face poses.

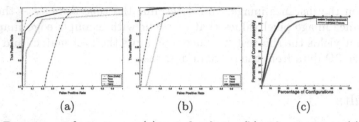

(a)   (b)   (c)

Fig. 6. Detector performance on (a) test databases (b) video sequence (c) simulated occlusions of body parts

show the advantage of including colour. The face detector proves to be the most robust of the detectors, since the face is a self contained region. Other body parts are affected by background clutter and have a greater variability in appearance. Due to the high variability of hand shape, we expect the hand detector to offer the poorest performance.

Making use of the ROC curves plotted for each detector, the desired number of layers was chosen such that the probability of detecting all objects was no less than 80%, with the trade-off of an increased number of false detections. The initial detections from the body part detectors are rapidly eliminated using RANSAC and the heuristic, before being narrowed down to the body configuration with the largest likelihood as determined by the joint-likelihood model as shown in Figure 5 (top row). The entire process from detection to assembly takes approximately 5 seconds on a P4, an improvement over [8], which takes 10 seconds and does not include hand detection.

The middle row of Figure 5 illustrates the body part assembly of a subject walking into an office and performing hand gestures using background segmentation as described in Section 4. The scene is particularly complex with wooden furniture and cream walls, thereby yielding poor background segmentation. Our assembly system overcomes these difficulties and operates at 8 frames/sec (frames sized at 640x480), a considerable improvement from the static image case. For completeness, elbow positions that have been determined by statistical inference [7] are given. A corresponding performance curve for this sequence is given (Figure 6b). To maintain consistency with the performance curves of Figure 6a, each frame of this sequence was treated as a discrete image, with the search space encompassing the entire image. However, to illustrate the benefit of background suppression, the hand detector includes the foreground fitness, and offers similar performance to the torso detector. In using a sequence the performance of the assembly method on a full subject could be evaluated. As expected, the assembly curve supersedes the others, illustrating the robust false part elimination of the assembly methodology.

To test our method for tolerance to occlusions, an increasing number of body parts detections were deliberately removed randomly at each frame. The number of correct assembly body configurations found across the entire video sequence was calculated, repeated 5 times and the mean result of correct assembly vs percentage of removed body parts obtained (Figure 6c). The black plot is the output

Fig. 7. Frontal pose with corresponding 3D model

from using a tracking framework where the detection window for each part is limited. The red plot treats each frame independently and has lower performance due to increased ambiguities. Also illustrated is how other cases of occlusions and non-frontal body poses through synthesis of missing parts are handled (Figure 5(bottom row)). Figure 7 shows the selected body assembly of subjects from various sequences and its representative CG model. The frames are captured at 320x240, and runs at 16 frames/sec. Comparison of the various scenes shows the matching method to be invariant to the user's scale and position.

7 Conclusions

We have extended an existing boosting technique for face detection to build two additional body part detectors. Due to the variability of these body parts, their detection performance is lower, and a technique was developed to eliminate false detections. By combining a coarse body configuration heuristic with RANSAC and an a priori mixture model of upper-body configurations, we are able to assemble detections into accurate configurations to estimate the upper body pose. When this approach is applied to a video sequence, exploitation of temporal data reduces the false detection rate of all the detectors, and improves speed performance dramatically. We have also been successful in matching a corresponding 3D model to the selected body part assembly. Matching by example does however require a large example dataset, and we have therefore stored our datasets in their simplest forms. These simple representations Examples from the large example dataset, were stored in their simplest forms, for fast access, contributing efficiency to the fast matching methods employed. Furthermore, the hierarchical structure restricts analysis to subsets of the subsidiary databases, thereby contributing to the real-time aspect of the approach.

Acknowledgements

This work is partly funded under the EU FP6 Project "COSPAL", IST-2003-2.3.2.4.

References

1. H. Barrow, J. Tenenbaum, R. Bolles, and H. Wolf. Parametric correspondence and chamfer matching: Two new techniques for image matching. In *Proc. of Joint Conf. Artificial Intelligence*, pages 659–663, 1977.
2. P. Felzenszwalb and D. Hurrenlocher. Distance transforms of sampled functions. Technical Report TR2004-1963, Cornell Computing and Information Science, 2004.
3. P. F. Felzenszwalb and D. P. Huttenlocher. Efficient matching of pictorial structures. In *Proc. of CVPR*, volume 2, pages 66 – 73, 2000.
4. M. A. Fischler and R. C. Bolles. Random sample consensus: A paradigm for model fitting with applications to image analysis and automated cartography. In *Comm. of the ACM*, volume 24, pages 381–395, 1981.
5. N. Howe, M. Leventon, and W. Freeman. Bayesian reconstruction of 3d human motion from single camera video. In *Advances in Neural Information Processing Systems*, volume 12, pages 820–826, 2000.
6. S. Ioffe and D. Forsyth. Probabilistic methods for finding people. *International Journal of Computer Vision*, 43(1):45–68, 2001.
7. A.S. Micilotta and R. Bowden. View-based location and tracking of body parts for visual interaction. In *Proc. of British Machine Vision Conference*, volume 2, pages 849–858, September 2004.
8. K. Mikolajczyk, C. Schmid, and A. Zisserman. Human detection based on a probabilistic assembly of robust body part detectors. In *Proc. of ECCV*, volume 1, pages 69–82, 2004.
9. A. Mohan, C. Papageorgiou, and T. Poggio. Example-based object detection in images by components. *IEEE Transactions on PAMI*, 23(4):349–361, April 2001.
10. B. Triggs R. Ronfard, C. Schmid. Learning to parse pictures of people. In *Proc. of ECCV*, volume 4, pages 700–707, 2002.
11. T. Roberts, S. McKenna, and I. Ricketts. Human pose estimation using learnt probabilistic region similarities and partial configurations. In *Proc. of ECCV*, pages 291–303, 2004.
12. H.A. Rowley, S. Baluja, and T.Kanade. Neural network-based face detection. *IEEE Transactions on PAMI*, 20(1):23–38, January 1998.
13. L. Sigal, M. Isard, B. Sigelman, and M. Black. Attractive people: Assembling loose-limbed models using non-parametric belief propagation. In *Proc. of Advances in Neural Information Processing Systems*, volume 16, pages 1539–1546, 2003.
14. B. Stenger, A. Thayananthan, P. Torr, and R. Cipolla. Hand pose estimation using hierarchical detection. In *Workshop on Human Computer Interaction*, pages 105–116, 2004.
15. P. Viola and M. Jones. Robust real-time object detection. In *Proc. of IEEE Workshop on Statistical and Computational Theories of Vision*, 2001.

Gait Recognition Using a View Transformation Model in the Frequency Domain

Yasushi Makihara, Ryusuke Sagawa, Yasuhiro Mukaigawa,
Tomio Echigo, and Yasushi Yagi

Department of Intelligent Media, The Institute of Scientific and Industrial Research,
Osaka University, 567-0047, 8-1 Mihogaoka, Ibaraki, Osaka, Japan
{makihara, sagawa, mukaigaw, echigo, yagi}@am.sanken.osaka-u.ac.jp
http://www.am.sanken.osaka-u.ac.jp/index.html

Abstract. Gait analyses have recently gained attention as methods of
identification of individuals at a distance from a camera. However, appearance changes due to view direction changes cause difficulties for
gait recognition systems. Here, we propose a method of gait recognition
from various view directions using frequency-domain features and a view
transformation model. We first construct a spatio-temporal silhouette
volume of a walking person and then extract frequency-domain features
of the volume by Fourier analysis based on gait periodicity. Next, our
view transformation model is obtained with a training set of multiple
persons from multiple view directions. In a recognition phase, the model
transforms gallery features into the same view direction as that of an input feature, and so the features match each other. Experiments involving
gait recognition from 24 view directions demonstrate the effectiveness of
the proposed method.

1 Introduction

There is a growing necessity in modern society for identification of individuals
in many situations, such as from surveillance systems and for access control.
For personal identification, many biometrics-based authentication methods are
proposed using a wide variety of cues; fingerprint, finger or hand vein, voiceprint,
iris, face, handwriting, and gait. Among these, gait recognition has recently
gained considerable attention because gait is a promising cue for surveillance
systems to ascertain identity at a distance from a camera.

Current approaches of gait recognition are mainly divided into model-based
and appearance-based ones.

The model-based approaches extract gait features such as shape and motion
by fitting the model to input images. Some methods [1][2] extracted periodical
features of leg motion by Fourier analysis. Bobick et al. [3] extracted parameters
of shape and stride. Wagg et al. [4] extracted static shape parameters and gait
period with an articulated body model, and Urtasun et al. [5] extracted joint
angles with an articulated body model. Those model-based approaches often
face difficulties with model fitting or feature extraction.

A. Leonardis, H. Bischof, and A. Pinz (Eds.): ECCV 2006, Part III, LNCS 3953, pp. 151–163, 2006.
© Springer-Verlag Berlin Heidelberg 2006

Appearance-based approaches directly analyze images and extract features without body models. Sarkar et al. [6] proposed direct matching of silhouette image sequences as a baseline algorithm. Murase et al. [7] represented a gait image sequence as a trajectory in an eigen space and matched the trajectories. Ohara et al. [8] and Niyogi et al. [9] constructed a spatio-temporal volume (x-y-t volume) by combining gait images and matched features extracted from the volume. Indeed, many gait features are proposed as being useful [10][11][12][13][14][15][16].

One of the difficulties facing appearance-based approaches is that appearance changes due to a change of the viewing or walking directions. In fact, BenAbdelkader [17] and Yu et al. [18] reported that view changes caused a drop in gait recognition performance.

To cope with the view changes, Shakhnarovich et al. [19] and Lee [20] proposed methods to synthesize an image for a virtual view direction using a visual hull. However, this method needs images taken synchronously from multiple view directions for all subjects and then necessitates the use of a multi-camera system or for there to be a solution to the troublesome problem of frame synchronization. Kale et al. [21] proposed a method to synthesize arbitrary-view images from a single-view image with perspective projection by assuming gait motion occurs in a sagittal plane. This method, however, does not work well because self occlusion occurs when an angle formed by an image plane and the sagittal plane is large.

To overcome these defects, we exploit a view transformation model (VTM) for appearance-based gait recognition. In the proposed method, once we obtain a VTM using a training set, made up of images of multiple subjects from multiple views, we can make images of a new subject taken from the multiple view directions by transforming a single-view image of the new subject.

In other computer vision areas, many methods have achieved adaptation to view direction changes with VTM. Mukaigawa et al. [22] applied the model to face image synthesis with pose and expression changes, and Utsumi et al. [23] applied it to transform images with pose and view changes.

However, these approaches just transform a static image into another static image; gait analysis, on the other hand, treats not a static image but a spatio-temporal volume. View transformation from a volume into another volume, though, causes troublesome problems such as frame synchronization. To overcome this, we first extract frequency-domain features from a spatio-temporal gait silhouette volume (GSV), and then we apply the VTM for frequency-domain features. Note that the use of the frequency-domain features releases us from the need for frame synchronization when view transformation and matching are performed.

The outline of this paper is as follows. We describe the construction of a GSV in section 2, and the matching of a GSV in section 3. Then, adaptation to view direction changes is addressed with the formulation of our VTM in section 4, and experiments of gait recognition from various view directions are shown in section 5. In section 6, we present our conclusions and indicate future works.

2   Construction of a GSV

2.1   Extraction of Gait Silhouette Images

The first step in constructing a GSV is to extract gait silhouette images; to do this, background subtraction is exploited. Background subtraction, however, sometimes fails because of cast shadows and illumination condition changes (see Fig. 1 (a) (b)). To avoid such difficulties, we execute a temperature-based background subtraction using an infrared-ray camera (NEC TH1702MX) instead of a conventional color camera. The infrared-ray camera captures 30 frames per second sized at 320 × 240 pixels. Figure 1(c) is an input image taken by the infrared-ray camera. In it we can see that the temperatures of a person are higher than those of the background; therefore we can extract clear regions as a gait silhouette image (see Fig. 1(d)). Here, for simplicity we assume only one person exists in the image, thus we keep only the largest connected region as the person.

2.2   Scaling and Registration of Silhouette Images

The next step is scaling and registration of the extracted silhouette images. First, the top, the bottom, and horizontal center of the regions for each frame are

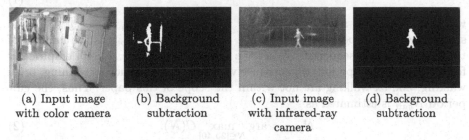

| (a) Input image with color camera | (b) Background subtraction | (c) Input image with infrared-ray camera | (d) Background subtraction |

Fig. 1. Comparison of background subtraction between color camera and infrared-ray camera (In (c), brighter colors indicate higher temperature))

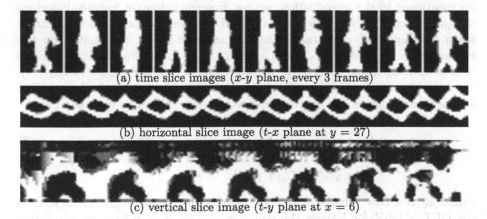

(a) time slice images (x-y plane, every 3 frames)

(b) horizontal slice image (t-x plane at $y = 27$)

(c) vertical slice image (t-y plane at $x = 6$)

Fig. 2. An example of GSV

obtained. The horizontal center is chosen as the median of horizontal positions belonging to the region. Second, a moving average filter of 30 frames is applied to those positions. Third, we scale the silhouette images so that the height can be just 30 pixels based on the averaged positions, and so that the aspect ratio of each region can be kept. Finally, we produce a 20 × 30 pixel-sized image in which the averaged horizontal median corresponds to the horizontal center of the image.

We show an example of a constructed GSV in Fig. 2 as time slice (x-y plane), horizontal slice (t-x plane), and vertical slice (t-y plane) images. We can confirm gait periodicity from Fig. 2(b), (c).

3   Matching of a GSV

3.1   Gait Period Detection

The first step for matching is gait period detection. We calculate the normalized autocorrelation of a GSV for the temporal axis as

$$C(N) = \frac{\sum_{x,y} \sum_{n=0}^{N.....-N-1} g_{gsv}(x,y,n) g_{gsv}(x,y,n+N)}{\sqrt{\sum_{x,y} \sum_{n=0}^{N.....-N-1} g_{gsv}(x,y,n)^2} \sqrt{\sum_{x,y} \sum_{n=0}^{N.....-N-1} g_{gsv}(x,y,n+N)^2}},$$

(1)

where $C(N)$ is the autocorrelation for the N frame shift, $g_{gsv}(x,y,n)$ is the silhouette value at position (x,y) at the nth frame, and N_{total} is the number of total frames in the sequence. We set the domain of N to be [20, 40] empirically for the natural gait period; this because various gait types such as running, brisk walking, and ox walking are not within the scope of this paper. Thus, the gait period N_{gait} is estimated as

$$N_{gait} = \arg \max_{N \in [20,40]} C(N).$$

(2)

3.2   Extraction of Frequency-Domain Features

As mentioned in the introduction, we use frequency-domain features based on the gait period N_{gait} as gait features to avoid troublesome frame synchronization when matching and view transformations are executed. First we pick up the subsequences $\{S_i\}(i = 1, 2, ..., N_{sub})$ for every N_{gait} frames from a total sequence S. Note that the frame range of the ith subsequence S_i is $[iN_{gait}, (i+1)N_{gait} - 1]$. Then the Discrete Fourier Transformation (DFT) for the temporal axis is applied for each subsequence, and amplitude spectra are subsequently calculated as

$$G_i(x,y,k) = \sum_{n=iN.....}^{(i+1)N.....-1} g_{gsv}(x,y,n) e^{-j\omega_0 kn}$$

(3)

$$A_i(x,y,k) = |G_i(x,y,k)|,$$

(4)

where ω_0 is a base angular frequency for the gait period N_{gait}, $G_i(x,y,k)$ is the DFT of GSV for k-times the gait period, and $A_i(x,y,k)$ is an amplitude spectrum for $G_i(x,y,k)$.

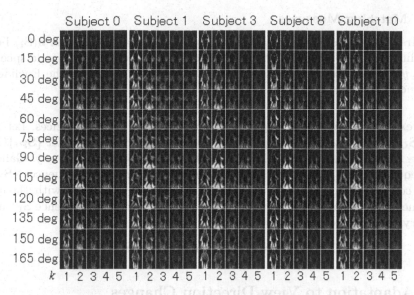

Fig. 3. Extracted features for every 15 degree view direction for some subjects

Direct-current elements ($k = 0$) of the DFT do not represent gait periodicity; therefore, they should be removed from the features. Moreover, high frequency elements ($k > k_{thresh}$) have less intensity than lower-frequency ones and mainly consist of noise, thus they also should be removed. In this paper, we decide $k_{thresh} = 5$ experimentally. As a result, $A_i(x, y, k)(k = 1, \cdots, 5)$ is used as the gait feature and its dimension N_A sums up to $20 \times 30 \times 5 = 3000$.

Figure 3 shows extracted amplitude spectra for various view directions. The view direction is defined as the angle formed by an optical axis and a walking direction, as shown in Fig. 4, and in this paper the unit of the view direction is a degree. Amplitude spectra vary widely among view directions for each subject, and to some extent they also have individual variations for each view direction. Moreover, we can see that all the subjects have similar common tendencies for amplitude spectra variations across view direction changes. This fact indicates a real possibility that the variations across view direction changes are expressed with the VTM independently of individual variations.

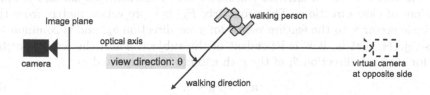

Fig. 4. Definition of view direction θ at top view

3.3   Matching Measures

We first define a matching measure between two subsequences. Let $\mathbf{a}(\mathbf{S}_i)$ be a N_A dimensional feature vector composed of elements of the amplitude spectra $A_i(x, y, k)$. The matching measure $d(\mathbf{S}_i, \mathbf{S}_j)$ is simply chosen as the Euclidean distance:

$$d(\mathbf{S}_i, \mathbf{S}_j) = \|\mathbf{a}(\mathbf{S}_i) - \mathbf{a}(\mathbf{S}_j)\|. \tag{5}$$

Next, we define a matching measure between two total sequences. Let $\mathbf{S_P}$ and $\mathbf{S_G}$ be total sequences for probe and gallery, respectively, and let $\{\mathbf{S_P}_i\}(i = 1, 2, \ldots)$ and $\{\mathbf{S_G}_j\}(j = 1, 2, \ldots)$ be their subsequences, respectively. Gallery subsequences $\{\mathbf{S_G}_j\}$ have variations in general and probe subsequences $\{\mathbf{S_P}_i\}$ may contain outliers. A measure candidate $D(\mathbf{S_P}, \mathbf{S_G})$ to cope with them is the median value of the minimum distances of each probe subsequence $\mathbf{S_P}_i$ and gallery subsequences $\{\mathbf{S_G}_j\}(j = 1, 2, \ldots)$:

$$D(\mathbf{S_P}, \mathbf{S_G}) = \mathrm{Median}_i[\min_j\{d(\mathbf{S_P}_i, \mathbf{S_G}_j)\}]. \tag{6}$$

4   Adaptation to View Direction Changes

We briefly describe the formulation of a VTM in a way similar to that in [23]. Note that we apply the model to the frequency-domain feature extracted from gait image sequences while that in [23] directly applied it to a static image.

We first quantize view directions into K directions. Let $\mathbf{a}_\theta^m$ be a N_A dimensional feature vector for the kth view direction of the mth subject. Supposing that the feature vectors for K view directions of M subjects are obtained as a training set, we can construct a matrix whose row indicates view direction changes and whose column indicates each subject; and so can decompose it by Singular Value Decomposition (SVD) as

$$\begin{bmatrix} \mathbf{a}_{\theta_1}^1 & \cdots & \mathbf{a}_{\theta_1}^M \\ \vdots & \ddots & \vdots \\ \mathbf{a}_{\theta.}^1 & \cdots & \mathbf{a}_{\theta.}^M \end{bmatrix} = USV^T = \begin{bmatrix} P_{\theta_1} \\ \vdots \\ P_{\theta.} \end{bmatrix} \begin{bmatrix} \mathbf{v}^1 \cdots \mathbf{v}^M \end{bmatrix}, \tag{7}$$

where U is the $KN_A \times M$ orthogonal matrix, V is the $M \times M$ orthogonal matrix, S is the $M \times M$ diagonal matrix composed of singular values, $P_{\theta.}$ is the $N_A \times M$ submatrix of US, and $\mathbf{v}^m$ is the M dimensional column vector.

The vector $\mathbf{v}^m$ is an intrinsic feature vector of the mth subject and is independent of view directions. The submatrix $P_{\theta.}$ is a projection matrix from the intrinsic vector $\mathbf{v}$ to the feature vector for view direction θ_k, and is common for all subjects, that is, it is independent of the subject. Thus, the feature vector $\mathbf{a}_{\theta.}^m$ for the view direction θ_i of the mth subject is represented as

$$\mathbf{a}_{\theta.}^m = P_{\theta.}\mathbf{v}^m. \tag{8}$$

Then, feature vector transformation from view direction θ_j to θ_i is easily obtained as

$$\mathbf{a}_{\theta.}^m = P_{\theta.}P_{\theta.}^+\mathbf{a}_{\theta.}^m, \tag{9}$$

where $P_{\theta.}^{+}$ is the pseudo inverse matrix of $P_{\theta.}$. In practical use, transformation from one view direction may be insufficient because motions orthogonal to the image plane are degenerated in the silhouette image. For example, it is difficult for even us humans to estimate a feature $\mathbf{a}_{90}^{m}$ from $\mathbf{a}_{0}^{m}$ (see Fig. 3 for example). Therefore, when features for more than one view direction (let them be $\theta_j(1), \ldots, \theta_j(k)$) are obtained, we can more precisely transform a feature for the view direction θ_i as

$$\mathbf{a}_{\theta.}^{m} = P_{\theta.} \begin{bmatrix} P_{\theta.(1)} \\ \vdots \\ P_{\theta.(k)} \end{bmatrix}^{+} \begin{bmatrix} \mathbf{a}_{\theta.(1)}^{m} \\ \vdots \\ \mathbf{a}_{\theta.(k)}^{m} \end{bmatrix}. \tag{10}$$

In the above formulation, there are no constraints for view transformation, but each body point such as head, hands, and knees appears at the same height, respectively, for all view directions because of the height scaling as described in sec. 2. Therefore, we constrain transformation from a height y_i to another height $y_j (\neq y_i)$ and define the above transformation separately at each height y_i.

Moreover, we introduce a simple opposite view transformation. Let the range of a view direction $[\theta_i, \theta_j]$ be $R_{[\theta., \theta.]}$. When a target subject is observed at a distance from a camera and weak perspective projection is assumed, the silhouette image observed with a virtual camera at the opposite side from the view direction[1] θ as shown in Fig. 4 (let the image be $I_{opp}(\theta)$), becomes a mirror image of the original silhouette image from view direction θ (let it be $I(\theta)$). In addition, it is clear that $I_{opp}(\theta)$ is the same as $I(\theta + 180)$. Hence, $I(\theta + 180)$ is transformed as a mirror image of $I(\theta)$. In the same way, once the amplitude spectra for $R_{[0,180)}$ are obtained, the remaining features for $R_{[180,360)}$ are obtained by transformation. Thus, a training set for VTM is only composed of features for $R_{[0,180)}$.

5 Experiments

5.1 Datasets

We use a total of 719 gait sequences from 20 subjects for the experiments. The sequences include 24 view directions at every 15 degrees. The training set for the VTM is composed of 120 sequences of 10 subjects from 12 view directions: $\theta =$ 0, 15, 30, 45, 60, 75, 90, 105, 120, 135, 150, and 165. Then, we prepare 5 gallery sets: $G_0, G_{45}, G_{90}, G_{135}, G_{0-90}$, where G_θ has 20 sequences from 20 subjects with view direction θ, and $G_{\theta. -\theta.}$ is a compound gallery of $G_{\theta.}$ and $G_{\theta.}$; that is, it has 40 sequences from 20 subjects with 2 views, θ_i and θ_j. A probe set (test set) is composed of the other sequences except for those of subjects included in the training set, and each sequence is indexed in advance with the view direction because view direction estimation is easily done using a walking person's velocity in the image or by view direction classification with averaged

---

[1] Note that the view direction θ is defined for the actual camera and that it is used in common for both the actual and the virtual cameras.

features for each view direction. In the following subsections, for convenience, we represent a gallery transformed by eq. (9) or eq. (10), and probe with view direction θ as Gs_θ and Pr_θ, respectively.

5.2   Feature Transformation

For comparison, we first briefly describe image transformation by perspective projection (PP) [21]. This method approximates that gait motion is represented in the sagittal plane when the person is observed at a distance from a camera. This method cannot transform images if G_0 is given, thus we substitute a longitudinal plane orthogonal to the sagittal plane in such case. Moreover, in the case of G_{0-90}, we use the sagittal plane for $R_{[45,135]}$ and $R_{[225,315]}$ and use the orthogonal plane for the other directions.

We show transformed features using PP in Fig. 5. We can see that the transformed features whose view directions are near those of the original galleries are relative fine (especially Gs_{75} and Gs_{105} for G_{90}) and that the other features differ a lot from the original features.

We show transformed features with our VTM in Fig. 6. Because G_0 contains relatively few features, the transformed features from G_0 are very poor (Fig. 6(b)). On the other hand, the other view directions contain relatively many features, and the transformed features (Fig. 6(c)-(f)) seem to be similar to the original ones (Fig. 6(a)).

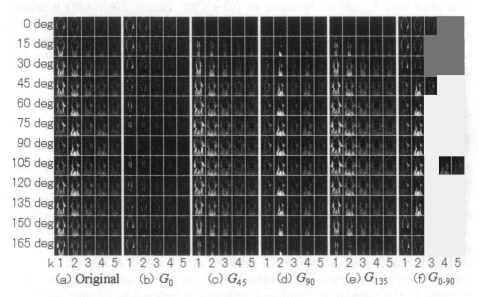

(a): original feature, (b)-(f): transformed features from G_0, G_{45}, G_{90}, G_{135}, and G_{0-90} respectively.

Fig. 5. Transformed features with PP

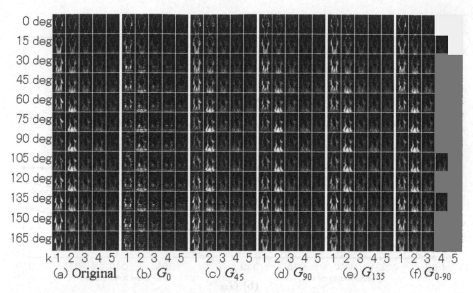

0 deg
15 deg
30 deg
45 deg
60 deg
75 deg
90 deg
105 deg
120 deg
135 deg
150 deg
165 deg

k 1 2 3 4 5   1 2 3 4 5   1 2 3 4 5   1 2 3 4 5   1 2 3 4 5   1 2 3 4 5

(a) Original   (b) G_0 (c) G_{45} (d) G_{90} (e) G_{135} (f) G_{0-90}

(a): original feature, (b)-(f): transformed features from G_0, G_{45}, G_{90}, G_{135}, and G_{0-90} respectively.

Fig. 6. Transformed features with VTM

5.3   Performance of Gait Recognition

We constructed a matching test using the transformed features by both PP and VTM from the 5 above gallery sets. A probe is assigned verification when eq. (6) is above a certain threshold value, and a Receiver Operating Characteristics (ROC) [24] curve is obtained by plotting pairs of verification rate and false alarm rate for various threshold values. The tests are repeated for different 20 training sets and the averaged performance evaluated by the ROC curve shown in Fig. 7. In this graph, probes are limited to Pr_0, Pr_{45}, Pr_{90}, and Pr_{135} for visibility.

It is clear that the probes with the same view direction as the gallery have very high performances for all galleries. Then, as seen from the transformed features in the previous subsection, the performances for G_0 are very poor for both PP and VTM. In the other galleries, Pr_{135} for G_{45} and Pr_{45} for G_{135} in PP have relatively high performances; which is why the transformed features for the view directions θ and $(180 - \theta)$ become the same in the case that gait motion is completely symmetric with a phase shift of a half of the gait period. Except for this point, the performances of the VTM are better than those of PP, especially in G_{0-90} (Fig. 7(e)).

Figure 8 shows that the verification rate at a false positive rate (P_F) is 10 % in the ROC curves and the averaged verification rate. For view directions $R_{[180,360)}$, the mirror (horizontally reversed) features are transformed as described in sec. 4.

As shown in Fig. 7, performances for G_0 are very poor in both PP and VTM. As for PP, probes whose view directions are near to those of the gallery

%begincenter

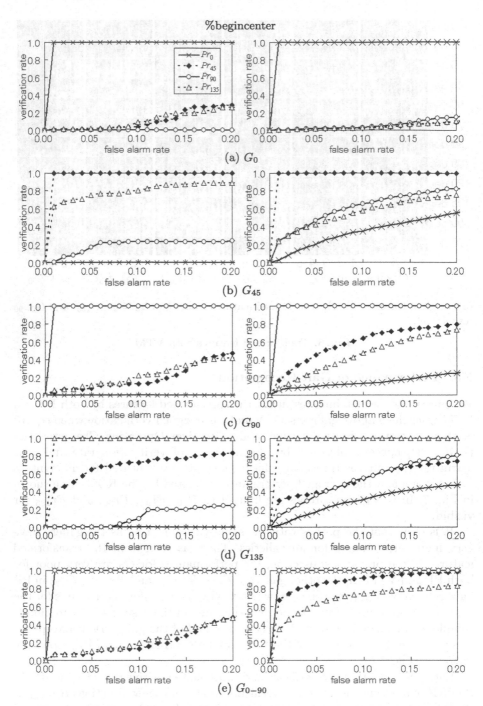

Fig. 7. ROC curves of gait recognition performance for PP (left side) and VTM (right side). Legend marks are common in all graphs.

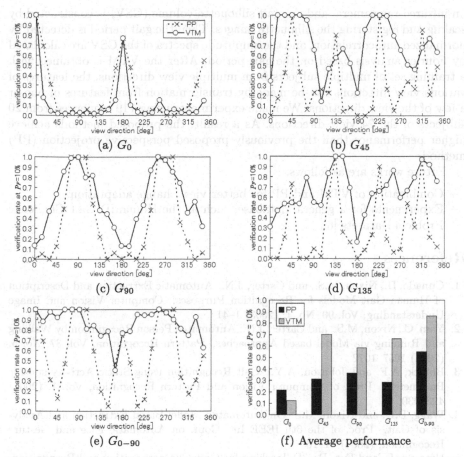

(a) G_0
(b) G_{45}
(c) G_{90}
(d) G_{135}
(e) G_{0-90}
(f) Average performance

Fig. 8. Performance comparison of PP and VTM with verification rate at $P_F = 10\%$. Legend marks are common in (a)-(e).

have relatively high performances (e.g. Pr_{75} and Pr_{105} for G_{90}) because the weak perspective projection to the sagittal plane works well. In addition, probes with advantages of symmetry (e.g. Pr_{135} for G_{45} and Pr_{45} for G_{135}) also have relatively high performances.

On the other hand, almost all of the other VTM performances except for the above probes are superior to those of PP, especially Pr_{45}, Pr_{135}, Pr_{225}, and Pr_{315} in G_{0-90} achieve fairly good performances compared with PP. As a result, the averaged performance of the VTM is superior to that of PP, except for G_0.

6   Conclusion and Future Works

In this paper, we proposed a gait recognition method using amplitude spectra for the temporal axis and our view transformation model (VTM). First, a walking person is extracted utilizing temperature-based background subtraction using an infrared-ray camera, and the gait silhouette volume (GSV) is constructed by scaling and registering the silhouette images. Then the gait period is detected by normalized autocorrelation, and the amplitude spectra of the GSV are calculated by Fourier analysis based on the gait period. After the VTM is obtained with a training set of multiple subjects from multiple view directions, the features of various view directions can be made by transformation from features of one or a few of the view directions. We made experiments using 719 sequences from 20 subjects of the 24 view directions. As a result, the proposed methods achieve higher performance than the previously proposed perspective projection (PP) method.

Future works are as follows.

− Combination of VTM and PP for better view change adaptation.
− Experiments for a general database, such as the HumanID Gait Challenge Problem Datasets [6].

References

1. Cunado, D., Nixon, M.S., and Carter, J.N.: Automatic Extraction and Description of Human Gait Models for Recognition Purposes, Computer Vision and Image Understanding, Vol. 90, No. 1, (2003) 1–41
2. Yam, C., Nixon, M.S., and Carter, J.N.: Automated Person Recognition by Walking and Running via Model-based Approaches, Pattern Recognition, Vol. 37, No. 5, (2004) 1057–1072
3. Bobick, A.F. and Johnson, A.Y.: Gait Recognition using Static Activity-specific Parameters, Proc. of Computer Vision and Pattern Recognition, Vol. 1, (2001) 423–430
4. Wagg, D.K. and Nixon, M.S: On Automated Model-Based Extraction and Analysis of Gait, Proc. of the 6th IEEE Int. Conf. on Automatic Face and Gesture Recognition, (2004) 11–16
5. Urtasun, R. and Fua, P.: 3D Tracking for Gait Characterization and Recognition, Proc. of the 6th IEEE Int. Conf. on Automatic Face and Gesture Recognition, (2004) 17–22
6. Sarkar, S., Phillips, J.P., Liu, Z., Vega, I.R., Grother, P., and Bowyer, K.W.: The HumanID Gait Challenge Problem: Data Sets, Performance, and Analysis, Trans. of Pattern Analysis and Machine Intelligence, Vol. 27, No. 2, (2005) 162–177
7. Murase, H. and Sakai, R.: Moving Object Recognition in Eigenspace Representation: Gait Analysis and Lip Reading, Pattern Recognition Letters, Vol. 17, (1996) 155–162
8. Ohara, Y., Sagawa, R., Echigo, T., and Yagi., Y.: Gait volume: Spatio-temporal analysis of walking, Proc. of the 5th Workshop on Omnidirectional Vision, Camera Networks and Non-classical cameras, (2004) 79–90
9. Niyogi, S and Adelson, E.: Analyzing and recognizing walking figures in xyt, Proc. of IEEE Conf. on Computer Vision and Pattern Recognition, (1994) 469–474
10. Liu, Z and Sarkar, S.: Simplest Representation Yet for Gait Recognition: Averaged Silhouette, Proc. of the 17th Int. Conf. on Pattern Recognition, Vol. 1, (2004) 211–214
11. BenAbdelkader, C., Culter, R., Nanda, H., and Davis, L.: Eigengait: Motion-based recognition people using image self-similarity, Proc. of Int. Conf. on Audio and Video-based Person Authentication, (2001) 284–294

12. Cuntoor, N, Kale, A, and Chellappa, R: Combining Multiple Evidences for Gait Recognition, Proc. of IEEE Int. Cont. Acoustics, Speech, and Signal Processing, Vol. 3, (2003) 33–36
13. Liu, Y., Collins, R.T., and Tsin, Y.: Gait sequence analysis using frieze patterns, Proc. of the 7th European Conf. on Computer Vision, Vol. 2, (2002) 657–671
14. Kobayashi, T. and Otsu, N.: Action and Simultaneous Multiple-Person Identification Using Cubic Higher-Order Local Auto-Correlation, Proc. of the 17th Int. Conf. on Pattern Recognition, Vol. 3, (2004) 741–744
15. Mowbray, S.D and Nixon, M.S.: Automatic Gait Recognition via Fourier Descriptors of Deformable Objects, Proc. of IEEE Conf. on Advanced Video and Signal Based Surveillance, (2003) 566–573
16. Zhao, G., Chen, R., Liu, G., and Li, H.: Amplitude Spectrum-based Gait Recognition, Proc. of the 6th IEEE Int. Conf. on Automatic Face and Gesture Recognition, (2004) 23–30
17. BenAbdelkader, C.: Gait as a Biometric For Person Identification in Video, Ph.D. thesis in Maryland Univ., (2002)
18. Yu, S., Tan, D., and Tan, T.: Modelling the Effect of View Angle Variation on Appearance-Based Gait Recognition, Proc. of the 7th Asian Conf. on Computer Vision, (2006), 807–816
19. Shakhnarovich, G., Lee, L, and Darrell, T.: Integrated Face and Gait Recognition from Multiple Views, Proc. of IEEE Conf. on Computer Vision and Pattern Recognition, Vol. 1, (2001) 439–446
20. Lee, L.: Gait Analysis for Classification, Ph.D. thesis in Massachusetts Institute of Technology, (2002)
21. Kale, A., Chowdhury, K.R., and Chellappa, R.: Towards a View Invariant Gait Recognition Algorithm, Proc. of IEEE Conf. on Advanced Video and Signal Based Surveillance, (2003) 143–150
22. Mukaigawa, Y., Nakamura, Y, and Ohta, Y.: Face Synthesis with Arbitrary Pose and Expression from Several Images - An integration of Image-based and Model-based Approach - Proc. of the 3rd Asian Conf. on Computer Vision, Vol. 1, (1998), 680–687.
23. Utsumi, A., Tetsutani, N.: Adaptation of appearance model for human tracking using geometrical pixel value distributions, Proc. of the 6th Asian Conf. on Computer Vision, (2004)
24. Phillips, P.J., Moon, H., Rizvi, S, and Rauss, P: The FERET Evaluation Methodology for Face-Recognition Algorithms, Trans. of Pattern Analysis and Machine Intelligence, Vol. 22, No. 10, (2000), 1090–1104

Video Mensuration Using a Stationary Camera

Feng Guo[1] and Rama Chellappa[2]

[1] Computer Science & Center for Automation Research,
University of Maryland, College Park, MD 20742, USA
fguo@cfar.umd.edu
[2] Electrical and Computer Engineering & Center for Automation Research,
University of Maryland, College Park,
MD 20742, USA
rama@cfar.umd.edu

Abstract. This paper presents a method for video mensuration using a single stationary camera. The problem we address is simple, i.e., the mensuration of any arbitrary line segment on the reference plane using multiple frames with minimal calibration. Unlike previous solutions that are based on planar rectification, our approach is based on fitting the image of multiple concentric circles on the plane. Further, the proposed method aims to minimize the error in mensuration. Hence we can calculate the mensuration of the line segments not lying on the reference plane. Using an algorithm for detecting and tracking wheels of an automobile, we have implemented a fully automatic system for wheel base mensuration. The mensuration results are accurate enough that they can be used to determine the vehicle classes. Furthermore, we measure the line segment between any two points on the vehicle and plot them in top and side views.

1 Introduction

Mensuration in image and videos has been studied as an interesting problem with many applications. It has two stages: spatial localization and estimation of dimension. The spatial localization stage estimates an object's position relative to the environment, e.g., the ball's position with respect to the goal post can be used to determine whether a goal has been scored in a soccer game [1]. Since the object's location changes with time, generally multiple concurrent views are needed. Determining the dimension involves the estimation of the distance between two points on the same rigid object [2]. It has received more attention since the results can be used to recognize or identify the object itself. As the two points are invariant relative to the object in the world system, evidences accumulated using multiple frames always improve the mensuration result.

Mensuration requires less calibration information compared to 3D reconstruction problems. A common setup includes one or more parallel reference planes. In stationary surveillance scenarios, the reference plane generally refers to the ground. Minimal calibration [3], defined as the combination of the vanishing line of the reference plane and vertical vanishing point, is assumed to be available.

A. Leonardis, H. Bischof, and A. Pinz (Eds.): ECCV 2006, Part III, LNCS 3953, pp. 164–176, 2006.

The objective is to estimate the ratio of lengths between two parallel line segments in the world system. If one of them has a known length, the length of other can be calculated.

Unlike existing approaches, we consider the lengths of line segments that are *nonparallel* in multiple frames under minimal calibration. Our method can be briefly described in three steps: (1) moving the line segments in parallel to share a common point; (2) fitting ellipses through the other end points under concentric constraints; and (3) calculating the ratio of lengths from the fitting parameters. We then extend the method to measure any line segments that do not lie on the reference plane.

Surveillance applications require the recognition of vehicles as well as human beings. Since different types of vehicles appear similar (e.g., BMW 3 and BMW 5), distinguishing among vehicle classes is very important. We have built a mensuration system for vehicles using the result of a wheel detection and tracking algorithm. Based on the color difference between the black tire and the silver wheel cover, wheels are extracted using an intensity threshold. An algorithm for measuring the wheel base, the distance between two wheel centers on the same side, is implemented and the result is used for mensuration of other parts of the vehicle.

The rest of the paper is organized as follows: Section 2 discusses related work. Section 3 introduces the basic idea of mensuration, the algorithm and error analysis. Section 4 describes the mensuration system for determining the wheel base of vehicles. Section 5 presents real video experiments results.

2   Related Work

Mensuration and related problems have been studied for more than ten years. It is well known that the ratio of two line segments can be recovered when the camera's parameters (intrinsic and extrinsic) are known. To simplify the problem, many assumptions have been made, such as: unit aspect ratio, zero skew and coincidence of principal point and the image center. Caprile and Torre, in their classical work, developed an algorithm to compute the focal length and projection matrix using the properties of vanishing points from a single view [4]. Liebowitz and Zisserman presented a two-step algorithm to rectify the perspective images of planes [5]. The first step estimates the vanishing line by detecting vanishing points, and transforms the image from projective to affine. The second step transforms the image from affine to metric using three constrains. Triggs presented a systematic error analysis [6] for autocalibration from planar scenes. Criminisi, *et al.* considered the estimation of height from an uncalibrated image [3] using projective geometry and cross-ratio, which have become popular in height estimation. In their subsequent work [2], the idea is extended to multiple reference planes. Kim, *et al.* calibrated a camera using a pattern of concentric circles [7]. Chen rectified a planar metric by obtaining the absolute conic from a projected circle and the vanishing line. [8]. Given two sets of perpendicular lines, Wang *et al.* measured the line segments on the reference plane without rectification [9]. Moons *et al.* presented an algorithm for recovering the 3D affine structure from two perspective views taken by a camera undergoing pure translation [10]. Assuming that the focal lengths are constant, Hartley developed an algorithm based on matrix factorizations for self calibration [11]. In the context of video mensuration, Lv *et al.* proposed an algorithm for calibrating a stationary camera from a video using walking humans [12]. Stauffer *et al.* built a linear model to normalize objects size in a video [13]. Bose and Grimson rectified the plane by tracking objects moving on a straight line with constant speed [14].

Existing mensuration approaches rely on parallel line segments, which is not practical in video. Although sometimes mensuration can be solved by other methods such as rectification, those algorithms estimate global parameters, which may not be optimal to a specific object. The simplest problem of video mensuration can be stated as:

Problem 1. Given a reference length on the reference plane in multiple frames, estimate the length of any line segment on the reference plane (in multiple frames).

This problem cannot be solved using a single frame. It can be proved that at least three reference lengths are needed. First, we present the solution based on three frames and then show how more frames can be used. Combining the probe and reference lengths together, we obtain the ratio between the two lengths by fitting two concentric ellipses; our solution is computationally efficient and optimal. Using the results of wheel centers detection and tracking algorithm, mensuration results are provided for measuring the wheel base of cars.

3   Algorithm

In the rest of the paper, we use upper case letters to indicate points in the world system and the corresponding lower case letters for their images. A line segment with endpoints $\mathbf{P}$ and $\mathbf{Q}$ is denoted as $\mathbf{PQ}$ and its length is denoted as $\|\mathbf{PQ}\|$. The reference plane is labelled as $\mathcal{R}$, its vanishing line as $\mathcal{L}$. The vertical vanishing point is denoted as $\mathbf{z}$.

3.1   Lemmas on Projective Geometry

We present two lemmas:

Lemma 1. *Given four collinear points* $\mathbf{m}$, $\mathbf{n}$, $\mathbf{p}$ *and* $\mathbf{q}$ *in the image plane and the vanishing point* $\mathbf{v}$ *along this direction. Let* $d_{\mathbf{k}}$ *stand for* $\|\mathbf{vk}\|$ *for* $\mathbf{k} = \mathbf{m}$, $\mathbf{n}$, $\mathbf{p}$ *and* $\mathbf{q}$. *The ratio between two line segments* $\|\mathbf{MN}\|$ *and* $\|\mathbf{PQ}\|$ *can be written as:*

$$r = \frac{\|\mathbf{MN}\|}{\|\mathbf{PQ}\|} = \frac{d_{\mathbf{p}}}{d_{\mathbf{m}}} \frac{d_{\mathbf{q}}}{d_{\mathbf{n}}} \frac{(d_{\mathbf{m}} - d_{\mathbf{n}})}{(d_{\mathbf{p}} - d_{\mathbf{q}})} \tag{1}$$

Lemma 1 can be easily proved using the property of cross-ratio.

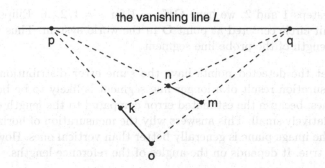

the vanishing line L

Fig. 1. An illustration of Lemma 2. **mn** is parallel moved to **ok**, where **o** is given and **k** is unknown. **p** and **q** are two points on the vanishing line.

Lemma 2. *Given a line segment* **mn** *and a point* **o**, *let* **mn** *and* **mo** *intersect the vanishing line* $\mathcal{L}$ *at points* **p**, **q** *respectively. Denote the intersecting point of lines* **nq** *and* **op** *as* **k** *(see Fig. 1). In the world system,* **OK** *is parallel to* **MN** *and* $\|OK\| = \|MN\|$.

Proof. Because **p** and **q** are vanishing points, **OP** and **MN** are parallel, and **NQ** and **MN** are parallel. **MNKO** forms a parallelogram, so $\|OK\| = \|MN\|$ □

k can be represented using the dot product as:

$$k = \frac{(n \bullet \mathcal{L})(o \bullet \mathcal{L})m - (m \bullet \mathcal{L})(n \bullet \mathcal{L})o - (o \bullet \mathcal{L})(m \bullet \mathcal{L})n}{(n \bullet \mathcal{L})(o \bullet \mathcal{L}) - (m \bullet \mathcal{L})(n \bullet \mathcal{L}) - (o \bullet \mathcal{L})(m \bullet \mathcal{L})} \qquad (2)$$

Lemma 2 enables the parallel move of a line segment **MN** in the world system so that **M** maps to a given point **O** and **N** to an unknown point **K**. The image of **K** can be localized in the image plane using the image of other three points.

3.2   Reference Length in Three Frames

We consider a simplified problem

Problem 2. Given the reference length $\|MN\| = 1$ on the reference plane in three frames as $m_i n_i$ $(i = 1, 2, 3)$, estimate the length of any line segment **OP** on the reference plane using one frame.

$\|OP\|$ can be acquired using the following steps:

1. Localize k_i on the image plane using the method in Lemma 2, such that OK_i is a parallel move of $M_i N_i$ in the world system.
2. Estimate the point k_{i+3} on the line $k_i o$ so that $\|K_i O\| = \|OK_{i+3}\|$.
3. Fit an ellipse E passing through all the points k_i $(i = 1, 2, ..., 6)$. Denote the intersection between line **op** and E as k_0.
4. Calculate $r = \|OP\| : \|OK_0\|$ using the cross-ratio as the mensuration result.

Proof. Using steps 1 and 2, we have $\mathbf{OK}_i = 1$ for $i = 1, 2, ..6$. Ellipse E is the image of a unit circle centered at point $\mathbf{O}$ in the world system. Thus $\mathbf{OK}_0 = 1$, and r is the length of the probe line segment.   □

Assuming that the detected points have the same error distribution, we note that the mensuration result of a longer line segment is likely to be better than for shorter lines, because the estimated error compared to the length of the line segment is relatively small. This answers why the mensuration of horizontal line segments in the image plane is generally better than vertical ones. However, this is not always true. It depends on the angles of the reference lengths.

3.3   Reference and Probe Lengths in Multiple Frames

Now consider the mensuration of a probe length using multiple frames while the reference length also appears in multiple frames. This can be expressed as

Problem 3. Given a reference length $\|\mathbf{MN}\| = 1$ in multiple frames $\mathbf{m}_i\mathbf{n}_i$ ($i = 1, 2, ...f$) and and a probe line segment $\mathbf{ST}$ also in multiple frames $\mathbf{s}_j\mathbf{t}_j$ ($j = 1, 2, ...g$), measure $\|\mathbf{ST}\|$.

Arbitrarily select a point on the image plane as $\mathbf{o}$. Parallel move $\mathbf{m}_i\mathbf{n}_i$ to $\mathbf{op}_i$ and $\mathbf{s}_j\mathbf{t}_j$ to $\mathbf{oq}_j$; localize $\mathbf{p}_{i+f}$ on $\mathbf{op}_i$ so that $\|\mathbf{OP}_i\| = \|\mathbf{OP}_{i+f}\|$, same for $\mathbf{q}_{j+g}$.

Consider the relationship between points in the world system: $\|\mathbf{OP}_i\| = 1$ ($i = 1, 2, ...2f$), $\|\mathbf{OQ}_j\| = r$ ($j = 1, 2, ...2g$), and all points on the reference plane. Denote $\mathbf{O}$'s coordinate as (x_0, y_0), then $\mathbf{P}_i$ and $\mathbf{Q}_i$ are on two concentric circles $C_p : (x - x_0)^2 + (y - y_0)^2 - 1 = 0$ and $C_q : (x - x_0)^2 + (y - y_0)^2 - r^2 = 0$ respectively. Define a trivial circular conic as

$$C_0 = \begin{pmatrix} 1 & 0 & -x_0 \\ 0 & 1 & -y_0 \\ -x_0 & -y_0 & x_0^2 + y_0^2 \end{pmatrix} \tag{3}$$

which represents the single point $\mathbf{O}$. We have

$$C_p = C_0 - \begin{pmatrix} 0 & 0 & 0 \\ 0 & 0 & 0 \\ 0 & 0 & 1 \end{pmatrix}, \qquad C_q = C_0 - r^2 \begin{pmatrix} 0 & 0 & 0 \\ 0 & 0 & 0 \\ 0 & 0 & 1 \end{pmatrix} \tag{4}$$

The 3×3 matrix from the world reference plane to the image plane is denoted as H. Then the conic in the image plane is known as $E = H^{-\top}CH^{-1}$. Define $L = H^{-\top}diag(0, 0, 1)H^{-1}$. The image of concentric circles is of the form

$$E_p = E_0 - L \qquad E_q = E_0 - r^2 L \tag{5}$$

Let the vanishing line be denoted as $\mathcal{L} = (\mathcal{L}(1) \ \mathcal{L}(2) \ \mathcal{L}(3))$. H^{-1} can be written as

$$H^{-1} = \alpha \begin{pmatrix} h_{11} & h_{12} & h_{13} \\ h_{21} & h_{22} & h_{23} \\ \mathcal{L}(1) & \mathcal{L}(2) & \mathcal{L}(3) \end{pmatrix} \tag{6}$$

Since E_0 stands for a single point $o = (x_o, y_o)$, it can be written as $a_0(x - x_o)^2 + b_0(x - x_o)(y - y_o)^2 + c_0(y - y_o)^2 = 0$ (we ignore the restriction $b^2 < 4ac$). Ellipse E_p and E_q then can be written as

$$a_0(x - x_o)^2 + b_0(x - x_o)(y - y_o) + c_0(y - y_o)^2 - \alpha v1 = 0 \qquad (7)$$
$$a_0(x - x_o)^2 + b_0(x - x_o)(y - y_o) + c_0(y - y_o)^2 - \beta v1 = 0 \qquad (8)$$

where $\beta = \alpha r^2$ and $v = (x^2 \ xy \ y^2 \ x \ y \ 1)$

$$1 = (\mathcal{L}(1)^2 \ 2\mathcal{L}(1)\mathcal{L}(2) \ \mathcal{L}(2)^2 \ 2\mathcal{L}(1)\mathcal{L}(3) \ 2\mathcal{L}(2)\mathcal{L}(3) \ \mathcal{L}(3)^2)^\top$$

Define $e = (a \ b \ c \ \alpha \ \beta)^\top$, a vector with components

$$u_p = ((x - x_o)^2 \ (x - x_o)(y - y_o) \ (y - y_o)^2 \ v(p)1 \quad 0 \ )$$

$$u_q = ((x - x_o)^2 \ (x - x_o)(y - y_o) \ (y - y_o)^2 \quad 0 \quad v(q)1)$$

The coefficient matrix is $M = (u_{p1} \ u_{p1} \dots u_{pf} \ u_{q1} \dots u_{qg})^\top$, and it becomes a linear fitting problem:

$$Me = 0 \qquad (9)$$

The nontrivial least square solution is:

$$e = argmin\|Me\| \quad \text{subject to } \|e\| = 1$$

It can be solved by performing a Singular Value Decomposition (SVD), $M = USV^\top$ where e is the singular vector corresponding to the smallest singular value of M [15].

After determining α and β, the length of the probe line segment can be calculated directly from

$$r = \sqrt{\beta/\alpha} \qquad (10)$$

This method also works for mensuration of multiple line segments by estimating α, β, and γ, etc.

Algorithm in noisy environments. The above algorithm assumes that reference (probe) lengths are equally important during the fitting process. The real case is that the noise from each detected endpoint is independent identically distributed. The perturbation of k_i due to the noise can be derived using (2), which is decomposed into two parts: the one tangent to the ellipse, t_i, the one normal to the ellipse, n_i. Since t_i does not affect the fitting result, only n_i is considered. The mensuration algorithm can then be modified as follows:

1. Fit the two ellipses using M as described before.
2. Calculate the perturbation of the reference and probe lengths along with the normal direction of the fitted ellipses.
3. Estimate the total errors of each probe, denoted as n_i
4. Refit the two ellipse using a new matrix M'. Each row of M' is constructed by the row of M times a factor $f_i \sim 1/n_i$.

The algorithm actually gives a weight to each point during fitting, which is inversely proportional to the perturbation. The Expectation-Maximization (EM) algorithm may be applied: the E-step is for estimating the errors from the ellipses; and the M-step for fitting the ellipses to minimize the errors. However, experiments have shown that the EM algorithm may not be necessary as one iteration often produces acceptable results.

3.4 Arbitrary Line Segment Mensuration

We briefly discuss the mensuration of line segments not lying on the reference plane, given a line segment on the reference plane as a reference. Since the reference lengths can be freely parallel moved on the reference plane, the problem can be restated as:

Problem 4. Given a reference line segment $\mathbf{m}_i\mathbf{n}_i$, estimate the length of $\mathbf{m}_i\mathbf{p}_i$.

Let $\mathbf{Q}$ be the projective point of $\mathbf{P}$ onto $\mathcal{R}$. From the results of last section, $\mathbf{mq}$ can be measured using $\mathbf{mn}$. The mensuration of $\mathbf{pq}$ can be obtained using Criminisi's method [3]. $\|\mathbf{MP}\|$ can be achieved using the Pythagoras's rule: $\|\mathbf{MP}\| = \sqrt{\|\mathbf{MQ}\|^2 + \|\mathbf{PQ}\|^2}$. This problem reduces to localizing the projective point $\mathbf{q}$ on the image plane.

Simplified Case. We first study a simplified version of the problem by adding a constraint to point $\mathbf{P}$:

Problem 5. Given a reference line segment $\mathbf{mn}$, estimate the length of $\mathbf{mp}$, under the constraint that the plane formed by $\mathbf{M}, \mathbf{N}$, and $\mathbf{P}$ is perpendicular to the reference plane $\mathcal{R}$.

Let the lines $\mathbf{mn}$ and $\mathbf{pz}$ interest at $\mathbf{q}$, where $\mathbf{z}$ is the vertical vanishing point. Point $\mathbf{q}$ is the projective point because (1) the line $\mathbf{PQ}$ is perpendicular to $\mathcal{R}$ as it passes through the vertical vanishing point and (2) $\mathbf{Q}$ lies at the intersection of plane $\mathbf{MNP}$ and plane $\mathcal{R}$.

General Case. To solve problem 4 at least two frames are required.

Theorem 1. *Given reference lengths* $\mathbf{m}_i\mathbf{n}_i$ *(*$\|\mathbf{M}_1\mathbf{N}_1\| = \|\mathbf{M}_2\mathbf{N}_2\|$*) and a point* $\mathbf{q}_1$ *on the reference plane* $\mathcal{R}$*, a point* $\mathbf{q}_2$ *can be localized so that* $\|\mathbf{Q}_2\mathbf{M}_2\| = \|\mathbf{Q}_1\mathbf{M}_1\|$ *and* $\angle\mathbf{Q}_2\mathbf{M}_2\mathbf{N}_2 = \mathbf{Q}_1\mathbf{M}_1\mathbf{N}_1$.

Proof. Draw an ellipse $\mathbf{E_m}$ so that for any point $\mathbf{x}$ on $\mathbf{E_m}$, $\|\mathbf{XM}_2\| = \|\mathbf{Q}_1\mathbf{M}_1\|$; ellipse $\mathbf{E_n}$ so that for any point $\mathbf{x}$ on $\mathbf{E_n}$, $\|\mathbf{XN}_2\| = \|\mathbf{Q}_1\mathbf{N}_1\|$. Denote the intersection point of the two ellipses as $\mathbf{q}_2$. We have $\triangle\mathbf{M}_2\mathbf{N}_2\mathbf{Q}_2 \simeq \triangle\mathbf{M}_1\mathbf{N}_1\mathbf{Q}_1$, thus $\mathbf{q}_2$ satisfies the requirement.   □

Theorem 1 actually suggests a rotation operation on the reference plane. We can then obtain $\mathbf{q}$ from two frames by: rotating frame 1 to 1' so that $\mathbf{m}_1' = \mathbf{m}_2$ and $\mathbf{n}_1' = \mathbf{n}_2$. The vertical point $\mathbf{z}$ then becomes $\mathbf{z}'$. The intersection point of $\mathbf{z}'\mathbf{p}_1'$ and $\mathbf{z}\mathbf{p}_2$ is $\mathbf{q}_2 = \mathbf{q}_1'$ (see Fig. 2), since during the rotation, $\mathbf{q}$ is always on the line $\mathbf{pz}$. A mensuration method from multiple frames can then be described as:

1. Denote **MN**'s midpoint as **K**, find **K**$_i$ in each frame.
2. Properly rotate each frame, so that $\mathbf{k}'_i = \mathbf{k}_0$ and $\mathbf{m}'_i\mathbf{n}'_i$ is parallel to x-axis. Here $\mathbf{k}_0$ is any fixed point.
3. Localize the point $\mathbf{q}_0$ which minimizes the distance to $\mathbf{z}'_i\mathbf{p}'_i$:

$$\mathbf{q}_0 = argmin_{\mathbf{q}} \; dist^2(\mathbf{q}, \mathbf{z}'_i\mathbf{p}'_i).$$

4. Project $\mathbf{q}_0$ to $\mathbf{z}'_i\mathbf{p}'_i$ as $\mathbf{q}'_i$.
5. Estimate $\|\mathbf{M}'_i\mathbf{P}'_i\|$ through $\mathbf{q}'_i$ and combine the result.

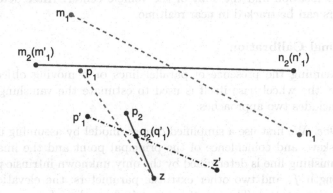

Fig. 2. Illustration of Theorem 1. Red dashed and blue solid indicate frames 1 and 2 separatively. The black dash dot line is the transformed frame 1.

4 System Implementation

In this section we discuss the implementation details for a wheel base mensuration system.

4.1 Wheels Detection and Tracking

After background subtraction [16], we estimate the vehicle's direction of motion using optical flow. We attach a system of skew coordinates to the moving vehicle (x', y'). x' is along the direction of motion, as shown in Fig. 3. Since the tire of a vehicle is always black and the wheel cover is silver or gray, even a simple

Fig. 3. Skew coordinate using vehicle's moving direction

intensity filter can separate the wheel cover from the tire. We gradually raise the threshold and remove pixels whose intensity is lower than the threshold from the foreground vehicle mask. The whole mask breaks into pieces step by step. The threshold stops increasing when two similar blobs appear at the bottom (with low y'). These two blobs are treated as the mask of wheel covers. The centers of the blobs are used as the detected wheel centers.

The algorithm to track wheels uses the same idea. To speed up the procedure, the initial threshold of the current frame is set as the threshold from the previous frame after subtracting a small value. The detected region focuses on the previous wheel center location and the shift of the vehicle center. After detection, the wheel centers can be tracked in near realtime.

4.2   Minimal Calibration

Without assuming the presence of parallel lines or a moving object along a straight line, the wheel base itself is used to estimate the vanishing line. Our algorithm includes two approaches.

Approach One. We first use a simplified camera model by assuming unit aspect ratio, zero skew, and coincidence of the principal point and the image center. Then the vanishing line is determined by the only unknown intrinsic parameter: the focal length f, and two other extrinsic parameters: the elevation angle θ and the rotation angle ϕ. The transform matrix from the reference plane to the image plane can be written as:

$$\mathbf{H} = \begin{pmatrix} \cos(\phi) & -\sin(\phi)\cos(\theta) & 0 \\ \sin(\phi) & \cos(\phi)\cos(\theta) & 0 \\ 0 & \sin(\theta) & 1 \end{pmatrix} \tag{11}$$

The vanishing line is

$$\mathcal{L} = (-\sin(\phi)\sin(\theta) \quad \cos(\phi)\sin(\theta) \quad -f\cos(\theta)) \tag{12}$$

Since the inverse transform can be written as $\mathbf{H}^{-1} = \mathbf{SAP}$, where $\mathbf{S}$, $\mathbf{A}$ and $\mathbf{P}$ are similarity, affine, and perspective transform matrices respectively, with structure as [5]

$$\mathbf{A} = \begin{pmatrix} \frac{1}{\beta} & -\frac{\alpha}{\beta} & 0 \\ 0 & 1 & 0 \\ 0 & 0 & 1 \end{pmatrix}, \quad \mathbf{P} = \begin{pmatrix} 1 & 0 & 0 \\ 0 & 1 & 0 \\ \mathcal{L}(1) & \mathcal{L}(2) & \mathcal{L}(3) \end{pmatrix} \tag{13}$$

By comparison, (α, β) can be solved as

$$\alpha = \frac{\cos(\phi)\sin(\phi)\sin(\theta)}{\cos^2(\theta)\cos^2(\phi) + \sin^2(\phi)}, \quad \beta = \frac{\cos(\theta)}{\cos^2(\theta)\cos^2(\phi) + \sin^2(\phi)} \tag{14}$$

If the vanishing line $\mathcal{L}$ is known, ϕ can be obtained from $\tan(\phi) = -\mathcal{L}(1)/\mathcal{L}(2)$. $\mathbf{P}$ can be applied to the end points of the wheel base. Assume that the resulting wheel bases in two different frames are joined by (x_{i1}, y_{i1}) and (x_{i2}, y_{i2}) $(i = 1, 2$

is the frame number). Using the constraint that the two wheel bases are of the same length in the world system, Liebowitz proved the following condition [5]: In 2D complex space with α and β as real and imaginary axes respectively, the point (α, β) lies on a circle with center $(c_\alpha, 0)$ and radius r.

$$c_\alpha = \frac{\delta x_1 \delta y_1 - \delta x_2 \delta y_2}{\delta y_1^2 - \delta y_2^2}, \quad r = \left| \frac{\delta x_2 \delta y_1 - \delta x_1 \delta y_2}{\delta x_1^2 - \delta t_2^2} \right| \qquad (15)$$

where $\delta x_i = x_{i1} - x_{i2}$, $\delta y_i = y_{i1} - y_{i2}$. Using (14), θ can be solved by

$$\cos^2 \theta = -\frac{\cos^2 \phi - r^2 \sin \phi - 2c_\alpha \cos \phi \sin \phi + c_\alpha^2 \sin \phi}{\sin^2 \phi - r^2 \cos^2 \phi + c_\alpha \cos \phi \sin \phi + c_\alpha^2 \cos \phi}. \qquad (16)$$

Since the wheel base appears in multiple frames, each pair of two (if they are not parallel) can be used to solve for $\cos^2 \theta$. If the vanishing line is correct, all the estimated results of $\cos^2 \theta$ should be same or very close to each other; otherwise, the result should be different from each other. We use the variance to indicate how close the results are. The vanishing line can then be coarsely estimated using the following steps:

1. Select those wheel base pairs, which are unlikely to be parallel in the world system
2. Guess the vanishing line $\mathcal{L}$. Note that in a video sequence, as ϕ normally is close to 0, only the small slope of the vanishing line is considered.
3. Estimate $\cos^2 \theta$ from each pair, and calculate its variance $var(\cos^2 \theta)$
4. Choose the best vanishing line with minimized $var(\cos^2 \theta)$ from all of them. Denote the vanishing line as $\mathcal{L}$

Although step 2 requires a lot of examples, this algorithm is very fast and obtains a good estimate of the vanishing line.

Approach Two. This does not require the simplified camera model assumption. First, we prove that the vanishing line can be obtained from the image of a circle and its center on the reference plane:

Lemma 3. *Given the image of a circle on the reference plane as* E *with parameter vector* $e = (a\ b\ c\ d\ e\ f)^\top$ *and the image of the circle center as* $o = (0, 0)$, *the vanishing line can be written as* $\mathcal{L} = (d\ e\ 2f)$.

Proof. As explained in the last section, the parameter vector of the ellipse can be written as $e = e_0 - \alpha 1$. By comparing the elements in each vector, we have

$$d = 2\alpha \mathcal{L}(1)\mathcal{L}(3), \quad e = 2\alpha \mathcal{L}(2)\mathcal{L}(3), \quad f = \alpha \mathcal{L}(3)^2 \qquad (17)$$

which leads to $\mathcal{L} = (d\ e\ 2f)$.   □

Using the above Lemma, we can refine the estimate of the vanishing line from a start point $\mathcal{L}_0$ using the following steps:

1. Let the iteration number $p = 0$
2. Parallel move the wheel base in frames $\mathbf{m}_i \mathbf{n}_i$ using $\mathcal{L}_p$ so that one of their end point shares the common point $\mathbf{o}$ and the other becomes $\mathbf{k}_i$.
3. Fit an ellipse E though $\mathbf{k}_i$.
4. Estimate the vanishing line, denoted as $\mathcal{L}_{p+1}$. If $\mathcal{L}_{p+1} \simeq \mathcal{L}_p$, output $\mathcal{L}_{p+1}$ and exit; otherwise, $p = p + 1$ and repeat from 2.

5   Experiment Results

The video sequences were captured using cameras located above 25 meters from the ground. Four type of vehicles: 2004 Toyota Camry, 2001 Honda Civic, 2004 Huyndai Elantra and 2004 Ford Explorer were imaged. The frame rate is 20 frame/second and each frame has 480×720 pixels. The sample frames are shown in Fig. 4. Samples of detected wheels are shown in Fig. 4 (e).

The probability of the mensuration result is shown in Fig. 5. From Table 1, although Civic and Elantra are not distinguishable, the Camry vehicle can be separated from them. The Explorer is different from Camry also. Thus the result can be used to determine the vehicles class.

Side View and Top View. By tracking feature points on the object using the KLT [17][18] tracker, the geometric properties of an object can be derived. We track the window corners and rack crossing points of the Ford Explorer and then measure their spacial locations using our method. The window corners are assumed to form a vertical plane passing through the two wheel centers (thus we can use the simplified method) and the rack points have no such constraint. The initial points are manually selected.

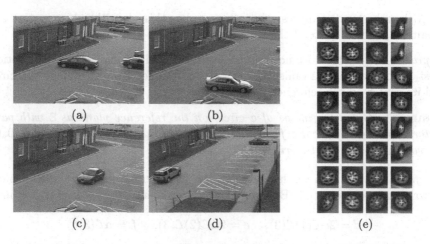

(a)   (b)

(c)   (d)   (e)

Fig. 4. Sample frames from outdoor sequences. (a) Toyota Camry (b) Honda Civic (c) Hyundai Elantra (d) Ford Explorer and (e) Sample of detected wheels. The detected wheel centers are indicated bye white crosses.

Table 1. Wheel base mensuration results

Year/Make/Model	Size/Category	Ground Truth(In.)	Mensuration result(In.)
2004 Hyundai Elantra	compact sedan	102.7	102.83 ± 1.75
2001 Honda Civic	compact sedan	103.1	103.47 ± 2.77
2004 Toyota Camry	midsize sedan	107.1	108.02 ± 2.45
2004 Ford Explorer	Large SUV	113.8	115.04 ± 2.32

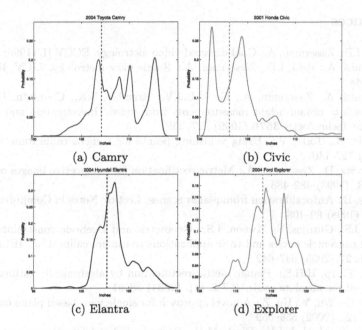

(a) Camry   (b) Civic

(c) Elantra   (d) Explorer

Fig. 5. Wheelbase mensuration probability plots

(a) side view   (b) top view

Fig. 6. Mensuration of the tracked points from reference wheel base

Fig. 6 compares our result with the ground truth images from side and top views. Major errors occur when the tracking points drift away as frames are processed.

6   Summary

We have presented a method for video mensuration. It measures any arbitrary line segments, including those with an angle to the reference plane. A fully automatic system has been developed for vehicle mensuration. We recover the minimal calibration of the scene by tracking the wheel centers. Further, the line segments joined by any two points on the vehicle is measured using the reference wheel base in single or multiple frames. The wheel base mensuration is very accurate and can be applied to classify the size of vehicles. Other mensuration steps generate side and top views of a vehicle with decent accuracies.

References

1. Reid, I.D., Zisserman, A.: Goal-directed video metrology. ECCV II. (1996) 647–658
2. Criminisi, A., Reid, I.D., Zisserman, A.: Single view metrology. IJCV **40** (2000) 123–148
3. Criminisi, A., Zisserman, A., Gool, L.J.V., Bramble, S.K., Compton, D.: New approach to obtain height measurements from video. Investigation and Forensic Science Technologies **3576** (1999) 227–238
4. Caprile, B., Torre, V.: Using vanishing points for camera calibration. IJCV **4** (1990) 127–140
5. Liebowitz, D., Zisserman, A.: Metric rectification for perspective images of planes. CVPR. (1998) 482–488
6. Triggs, B.: Autocalibration from planar scenes. Lecture Notes in Computer Science **1406** (1998) 89–108
7. Kim, J.S., Gurdjos, P., Kweon, I.S.: Geometric and algebraic constraints of projected concentric circles and their applications to camera calibration. IEEE Trans. PAMI. **27** (2005) 637–642
8. Chen, Y., Ip, H.H.S.: Planar metric rectification by algebraically estimating the image of the absolute conic. ICPR (4). (2004) 88–91
9. Wang, G., Wu, Y., Hu, Z.: A novel approach for single view based plane metrology. ICPR (2). (2002) 556–559
10. Moons, T., Gool, L.J.V., Diest, M.V., Pauwels, E.J.: Affine reconstruction from perspective image pairs obtained by a translating camera. Applications of Invariance in Computer Vision. (1993) 297–316
11. Hartley, R.I.: Estimation of relative camera positions for uncalibrated cameras. ECCV. (1992) 579–587
12. Lv, F., Zhao, T., Nevatia, R.: Self-calibration of a camera from video of a walking human. ICPR (1). (2002) 562–567
13. Stauffer, C., e Kinh, Lily, T.: Robust automated planar normalization of tracking data. VS-PETS. (2003)
14. Bose, B., Grimson, E.: Ground plane rectification by tracking moving objects. VS-PETS. (2003)
15. Hartley, R.I., Zisserman, A.: Multiple View Geometry in Computer Vision. Second edn. Cambridge University Press (2004)
16. Wren, C.R., Azarbayejani, A., Darrell, T., Pentland, A.: Pfinder: Real-time tracking of the human body. IEEE Trans. PAMI **19** (1997) 780–785
17. Lucas, B.D., Kanade, T.: An iterative image registration technique with an application to stereo vision. IJCAI. (1981) 674–679
18. Tomasi, C., Kanade, T.: Detection and tracking of point features. Technical Report CMU-CS-91-132, Carnegie Mellon University (1991)

Revisiting the Brightness Constraint: Probabilistic Formulation and Algorithms

Venu Madhav Govindu*

HIG-25, Simhapuri Layout,
Visakhapatnam, AP 530047, India
venu@narmada.org

Abstract. In this paper we introduce a principled approach to modeling the image brightness constraint for optical flow algorithms. Using a simple noise model, we derive a probabilistic representation for optical flow. This representation subsumes existing approaches to flow modeling, provides insights into the behaviour and limitations of existing methods and leads to modified algorithms that outperform other approaches that use the brightness constraint. Based on this representation we develop algorithms for flow estimation using different smoothness assumptions, namely constant and affine flow. Experiments on standard data sets demonstrate the superiority of our approach.

1 Introduction

Computing the optical flow field between images has been a central problem in computer vision. Thanks to numerous investigations over the past two decades, both our understanding of the problem and its algorithmic implementation have become increasing sophisticated (see [1, 2, 3, 4, 5, 6] and references therein). Most flow algorithms are based on the brightness constraint that is derived from an intensity conservation principle. Given two images taken at time-instants t and $t+1$ and denoting the flow at pixel (x, y) by (u, v), by conservation of intensity we have the relationship, $I(x, y, t) = I(x + u, y + v, t + 1)$. By expanding this function as a Taylor series we have a first-order approximation $I(x + u, y + v, t + 1) \approx I(x, y, t) + \frac{\partial I}{\partial x}u + \frac{\partial I}{\partial y}v + \frac{\partial I}{\partial t} \cdot 1$ which simplifies to $I_x u + I_y v + I_t = 0$ where I_x, I_y and I_t are the derivatives in the x, y and t dimensions respectively. This relationship is known as the brightness constraint and can be interpreted as a line in the (u, v) flow space. Since the flow at a point consists of two values, a single brightness constraint is insufficient, i.e. flow estimation is *ill-posed*. Therefore, flow is estimated by imposing additional assumptions of smoothness on the flow field.

There are three significant issues with using the brightness constraint that need to be addressed *simultaneously* in any representation. Firstly, the brightness constraint is derived using a first-order Taylor approximation implying that the flow magnitude is assumed to be small. However many algorithms violate this underlying assumption and

---

* The work in this paper was partially supported by NSF Grant IIS-03-25715 during the author's visit to the University of Maryland, College Park, USA.

A. Leonardis, H. Bischof, and A. Pinz (Eds.): ECCV 2006, Part III, LNCS 3953, pp. 177–188, 2006.

treat the brightness constraint as an *algebraic* line with infinite extent[1]. Secondly, the interpretation of the brightness constraint as a single line in the $u - v$ space is based on the assumption that the image derivatives observed are 'true' values. Thus the existence of noise in the observed image data is not explicitly accounted for, leading to unprincipled algorithms. Thirdly and most importantly, the derivation of the brightness constraint itself is based on an incorrect model where the temporal dimension is treated differently from the spatial dimensions which introduces undesirable biases. Perhaps this derives from the early methods which assumed that only two images were available, i.e. with a time-step of 1. We shall demonstrate in this paper that the correct approach is to *model* the spatio-temporal volume in a uniform and continuous manner and introduce the specific discretisation of the spatio-temporal image data only as an *algorithmic* detail. This approach immediately allows us to explain the behaviour of well-known flow algorithms and also recast their assumptions into more accurate versions.

In this paper we simultaneously address all the three limitations mentioned above. We systematically account for the data noise and also naturally allow for incorporation of priors that agree with the small flow assumption. By treating the spatio-temporal dimensions in a uniform framework, a key insight that arises is that the correct *representation* for estimating image flow is not the two-dimensional vector field, but rather its homogeneous counterpart, i.e. *normalised volume-flow*[2]. We will also show that the popular least-squares (i.e. Lucas-Kanade) and Total Least Squares (henceforth referred to as TLS) methods for constant flow in a patch can both be seen as specific instances of our model. We also emphasise that an optic flow estimator consists of two components, namely the choice of data representation (brightness constraint in our case) and the computational model used to solve the estimation problem. Recent advances in flow estimation have been based on increasingly sophisticated computational approaches, eg. [4, 5, 6, 7]. In contrast this paper focuses on the choice of data representation and *not* on the computational model. The representation proposed here can be incorporated into any computational framework that uses the brightness constraint. We also point out that important issues like robustness to data outliers and motion segmentation are outside the scope of this paper.

2   Probabilistic Brightness Constraint

In this section we derive a probabilistic model for the image brightness constraint. We develop our solution assuming a continuous space-time image volume. We re-emphasise that a time-step of 1 is an artifact of image acquisition and should not influence our problem formulation. Thus, although the spatial and temporal resolutions are different, we make an essential distinction between the model and its algorithmic

---

[1] While multi-scale techniques exist they are designed to reduce the magnitude of the true flow in an image. This, in principle, does not impose any constraint on the magnitude of the *estimated* flow.

[2] Volume-flow measures the flow field in the spatio-temporal volume and optical flow is its projection onto the image plane. The unit-norm vector, normalised volume-flow is projectively equivalent to optic flow and should not be confused with 'normal flow' which represents the projection of optical flow in a direction orthogonal to the brightness constraint line.

utilisation. We develop our method for continuous data and at the appropriate juncture replace the image derivatives involved by those calculated on discrete image data. This model is at the heart of the subsequent algorithms that we shall develop using different smoothness assumptions.

The estimated image derivatives are represented by $I_d = [I_x, I_y, I_t]^T$. We represent the error in the image derivatives using an additive Gaussian noise model, i.e. $I_d = I_{d0} + n$, where $I_{d0} = [I_{x0}, I_{y0}, I_{t0}]^T$ is the true value of the derivatives and $n = [n_x, n_y, n_t]^T$ is the noise term. For the sake of simplicity of presentation, we shall in the following assume that the noise is zero-mean, independent and identically distributed, i.e. $n \sim N(0, \sigma^2 I_3)$ where I_3 is the 3×3 identity matrix. However this does not preclude the use of more general forms of noise covariance matrices since the measurements can be whitened before applying our analysis. In general, it is realistic to assume that the spatial and temporal derivatives have different covariances due to the nature of sampling in space and time. We denote the three-dimensional volume-flow at a point as $F = [U, V, W]^T$ where U, V and W are the displacements in the x, y and t dimensions respectively. The two-dimensional optical flow is the projection of the volume-flow vector F onto the $x - y$ image plane and is denoted as (u, v) where $u = \frac{U}{W}$ and $v = \frac{V}{W}$. It will be noted that normalised volume-flow f is given by $f = \frac{F}{\|F\|}$ and is also projectively equivalent to the optical flow (u, v), i.e. $f \propto [u, v, 1]^T$. Using the principle of image brightness conservation, we have $I(x + U, y + V, t + W) = I(x, y, t)$. By a Taylor series expansion around the point (x, y, t) we have $I(x, y, t) + \frac{\partial I}{\partial x} U + \frac{\partial I}{\partial y} V + \frac{\partial I}{\partial t} W = I(x, y, t)$ leading to

$$\frac{\partial I}{\partial x} U + \frac{\partial I}{\partial y} V + \frac{\partial I}{\partial t} W = 0 \tag{1}$$

which is a brightness constraint equation in three-dimensions and can be simply expressed as $I_d^T F = 0$. It will be immediately observed here that we have an unknown scale factor for F, i.e. $I_d^T F = I_d^T(\alpha F) = 0$, implying that we can only derive F upto a scale factor. Hence we fix the scale by using the normalised volume-flow vector, $f = \frac{F}{\|F\|}$. However, Eqn. 1 applies to the true image derivatives, whereas we can only observe the estimated derivatives. Thus to define the conditional distribution of the flow given the observed image derivatives I_d using the relationship, $I_{d0}^T F = (I_d - n)^T F = 0$, we apply the chain rule for conditional probabilities resulting in

$$P(F|I_d) = \int P(F|I_{d0}) P(I_{d0}|I_d) \, dI_{d0} \tag{2}$$

From Eqn. 1, for the true image derivatives we note that the linear constraint implies that only flow values that satisfy this equation are admissible. Thus the conditional probability $P(F|I_{d0})$ is described by our brightness constraint and is equal to $\delta(I_{d0}^T F)$ where $\delta(.)$ is the Delta Function. Also since the true derivatives are perturbed by Gaussian noise to give the observed derivative estimates, we can represent the conditional probability $P(I_{d0}|I_d)$ by using the Gaussian noise prior. This is true since we can equivalently write $I_{d0} = I_d - n$. Thus $P(I_{d0}|I_d) = e^{-\frac{n \cdot n}{2 \cdot \sigma^2}}$ where $n = [n_x, n_y, n_t]^T$ represent the noise in the image derivatives. Consequently

$$P(F|I_d) = \int \underbrace{\delta(I_{d0}{}^T F)}_{P(F|I._0)} \underbrace{e^{-\frac{1}{2\cdot 2}(n.^2 + n.^2 + n.^2)}}_{P(I._0|I.)} dn_x dn_y dn_t$$

For, simplicity of presentation we ignore the normalisation required here to ensure that the integral measure on the delta-function is equal to one. Expanding the constraint into its respective terms we have $I_{d0}{}^T F = I_d{}^T F - (n_x U + n_y V + n_t W)$. To solve for the integral, we integrate out one variable (n_t in this case) to derive the following

$$P(F|I_d) = \frac{1}{|W|} \int e^{-\frac{1}{2\cdot 2}(n.^2 + n.^2 + \frac{(\cdots + \cdots - \cdot)^2}{\cdot^2})} dn_x dn_y \qquad (3)$$

where $c = I_d{}^T F$. This is obtained by integrating out the constraint and substituting for n_t. After some simple algebra, we can rewrite the exponential term of Eqn. 3 as the form

$$(n - \mu)^T R(n - \mu) + \mu_0 \qquad (4)$$

with $R = \frac{1}{W^2} \begin{bmatrix} U^2 + W^2 & UV \\ UV & V^2 + W^2 \end{bmatrix}$, $\mu_0 = \frac{(I.U + I.V + I.W)^2}{U^2 + V^2 + W^2}$. Therefore ,

$$P(F|I_d) = \frac{e^{-\frac{\cdot_0}{2\cdot 2}}}{|W|} \int e^{-\frac{1}{2\cdot 2}(n-\mu)^\cdot R(n-\mu)} dn \qquad (5)$$

The integral can be seen to be that of a Gaussian with a covariance of R^{-1} implying that the integral is equal to $|R|^{-\frac{1}{2}}$ and is independent of the value of μ. Now $|R| = \frac{U^2 + V^2 + W^2}{W^2}$, implying that

$$P(F|I_d) \propto \frac{e^{-\frac{1}{2\cdot 2}\frac{(\cdot\cdot + \cdot\cdot + \cdot\cdot)^2}{(\cdot^2 + \cdot^2 + \cdot^2)}}}{\sqrt{U^2 + V^2 + W^2}}$$

As observed earlier, the optical flow (u, v) is independent of the magnitude of the volume-flow vector F, hence we can set $\|F\| = 1$. This implies that for the homogeneous image flow f (or normalised volume-flow) we have

$$P(f|I_d) \propto e^{-\frac{1}{2\cdot 2}\frac{\cdot\cdot\cdot}{\cdots}} \qquad (6)$$

where the 3×3 matrix M is given by

$$M = \begin{bmatrix} I_x \\ I_y \\ I_t \end{bmatrix} \times \begin{bmatrix} I_x & I_y & I_t \end{bmatrix} = \begin{bmatrix} I_x I_x & I_x I_y & I_x I_t \\ I_x I_y & I_y I_y & I_y I_t \\ I_x I_t & I_y I_t & I_t I_t \end{bmatrix} \qquad (7)$$

An analysis of this distribution is instructive. If we consider a single pixel, we will note that the probability value in Eqn. 6 is maximised when f is orthogonal to I_d, i.e. $I_d{}^T f_{max} = 0$. Thus f_{max} lies in the plane that is normal to I_d. However since $\|f\| = 1$, we have f_{max} confined to the surface of a unit-sphere. Therefore, the locus of f_{max} is a great circle on the unit-sphere, see Fig. 1(a). As f deviates from the great circle f_{max},

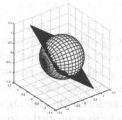 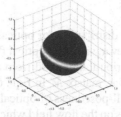 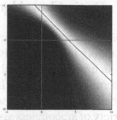

(a) Single pixel constraint   (b) Probability form of   (c) Projection of distribution
                          constraint   on image plane

Fig. 1. Representations of a brightness constraint. (a) the brightness constraint plane intersects with the unit-sphere resulting in a great circle which is equivalent to the conventional brightness constraint line; (b) shows the probability distribution of normalised volume-flow for a single pixel. (c) shows the projection of the distribution in (b) on the $x - y$ image plane. Note the 'fuzzy bow-tie' form of the flow distribution. The maxima of this distribution is the conventional brightness constraint line.

the magnitude of the probability distribution decreases according to Eqn. 6. Thus the probability distribution of the normalised volume-flow vector for a single pixel is a Gaussian-like distribution on the unit-sphere centered on the great circle f_{max} as seen in Fig. 1(b). The great circle and distribution in Fig. 1(b) can be seen to be the unit-sphere equivalents of the brightness constraint line and a Gaussian distribution centered on the line respectively.

However instead of considering a representation of f on the unit-sphere, the conventional approach has been to use $F = [u, v, 1]$. If we substitute this form in Eqn. 6, we see that the exponential term is equal to $\frac{(I.\,u+I.\,v+I.)^2}{(u^2+v^2+1)}$ which is identical to the TLS form used in [8, 9, 10]. In turn the equivalent probability distribution for (u, v) is shown in Fig. 1(c) and can be seen to have the so-called 'fuzzy bow-tie' form [11]. As is obvious from the above analysis and the distributions of f in Fig. 1, we note that the fuzzy bow-tie form of the flow distribution is nothing but an *artifact* of using a reduced representational space for the flow information. This arises from projecting a Gaussian-like form on the unit-sphere onto the image plane, i.e. the fuzzy bow-tie form in Fig. 1(c) is the projection of the distribution of Fig. 1(b) onto the image plane. Thus the fuzzy bow-tie distribution is not very illuminating and the probability form of Eqn. 6 is desirable as it leads to more accurate flow estimates. We also point out that our probability model is fundamentally different from that of [12] where a Gaussian noise model is applied to the flow (instead of the image derivatives) and a Gaussian distribution of flow on the image plane is derived. In our case the flow distribution in Eqn. 6 is the *natural representation* of the information in the image derivatives and as will be seen in the rest of the paper, this is a powerful, general representation that can be applied to various smoothness assumptions. It is also germane to point out that in this paper we are modeling the *optic flow field* based on image derivatives which should not be confused with modeling the *motion field* which would depend on a taxonomy of camera motions, zooming, rotating, translating etc. which results in specific types of motion fields.

3 Optic Flow Algorithms

In Sec. 2 we derived a probability distribution for optical flow at a pixel given its corresponding image derivatives. However, since the optical flow field consists of two values at each pixel, the probability distribution derived from a single pixel is insufficient to determine optical flow. In particular, matrix M in Eqn. 6 for a single pixel can be seen to be of rank one. In general, the ill-posedness of optical flow is addressed by making a variety of smoothness assumptions on the flow field which allows us to estimate the flow field using fewer parameters than the number of constraints available. The smoothness assumptions can be broadly characterised as being implicitly due to a parametric model or explicitly due to the use of a regularising smoothness term. Examples of the former are the constant flow assumption of Lucas and Kanade [3], affine flow [13, 14, 15], whereas [2, 6] are examples of an explicit smoothing strategy. In all of these methods, the estimation process is considerable affected by the assumption of a time-step of 1 in the corresponding formulations resulting in bias or a greater error. By explicitly applying our probabilistic formulation to these smoothness assumptions we derive modified algorithms that both clarify the behaviour of the conventional methods and significantly improve their performance. In the remainder of this section we consider constant and affine models and examine their implications for estimating optical flow.

3.1 Constant Flow

The simplest assumption for flow estimation is that of constant flow for an image patch which is the basis for the famous Lucas-Kanade algorithm [3]. Here the brightness constraint is represented by $I_x u + I_y v + I_t = 0$ and for a patch, the residual error is $\mathbf{E} = \sum_k (I_x{}^k u + I_y{}^k v + I_t{}^k)^2$ where k denotes the index of individual pixels in the patch. The minimiser of $\mathbf{E}$ is the Lucas-Kanade solution and is identical to the Ordinary Least Squares (henceforth OLS) solution:

$$\begin{bmatrix} u \\ v \end{bmatrix} = \begin{bmatrix} \overline{I_x I_x} & \overline{I_x I_y} \\ \overline{I_x I_y} & \overline{I_y I_y} \end{bmatrix}^{-1} \begin{bmatrix} -\overline{I_x I_t} \\ -\overline{I_y I_t} \end{bmatrix} \tag{8}$$

where $\overline{I_x I_x} = \sum_k I_x{}^k I_x{}^k$ etc. As had been noted in [16] this yields a linear, biased estimate of the flow. The bias appears due to the implicit assumption that the temporal derivatives are noise-free and the use of the TLS method has been suggested to overcome this bias [8, 9]. This can also be explained using our probability distribution for optical flow. For constant flow over a patch, using the conditional probability distribution of Eqn. 6 we have $P(f|patch) = \prod_k P(f|I_d{}^k)$. The flow can be estimated by maximising the conditional probability distribution

$$\max_f \prod_k P(f|I_d{}^k) \Rightarrow \min_f e^{-\frac{1}{2 \cdot 2} f^{\cdot} (\sum \cdot M \cdot) f} \tag{9}$$

The estimated flow is the smallest eigen-vector for matrix

$$\overline{M} = \frac{1}{N} \sum_{k=1}^{N} M_k = \frac{1}{N} \begin{bmatrix} \overline{I_x I_x} & \overline{I_x I_y} & \overline{I_x I_t} \\ \overline{I_x I_y} & \overline{I_y I_y} & \overline{I_y I_t} \\ \overline{I_x I_t} & \overline{I_y I_t} & \overline{I_t I_t} \end{bmatrix} \tag{10}$$

where N is the number of pixels in the patch. This is identical to the TLS solution. However, it must be pointed out that the above derivation of the Maximum Likelihood Estimate (MLE) of flow does not incorporate a prior distribution for the flow values. As has been noted in Sec. 1, the brightness constraint is valid only for a small deviation from the point around which the Taylor series expansion is made, i.e. flow cannot be large. This implicit assumption cannot be captured by treating the brightness constraint as an algebraic equation and is often ignored. In our case, since we represent the information at a pixel as a conditional probability distribution we can incorporate the small flow assumption as a prior on the flow field. For the flow values to be small, we note that since $(u, v) = (\frac{U}{W}, \frac{V}{W})$, we require the contribution of U and V to the magnitude of the volume-flow $||F|| = ||(U, V, W)||$ to be small. This notion can be captured by using a Gaussian distribution on the relative magnitudes of U and V, i.e. $\frac{U}{||F||}$ and $\frac{V}{||F||}$. This leads to a distribution of the form

$$P(.) = e^{-\frac{1}{2 \cdot \sigma^2} \cdot \frac{\cdot U^2 + \cdot V^2}{\cdot U^2 + \cdot V^2 + \cdot W^2}} = e^{-\frac{1}{2 \cdot \sigma^2} \cdot \frac{\cdot D \cdot}{\cdot \cdot \cdot}}$$

where D is a diagonal matrix $D = diag([1, 1, 0])$ and the variable σ_f controls the influence of the prior on the estimator. If we reintroduce this prior into Eqn. 2 to weight the δ-function appropriately, our measurement matrix for flow estimation is modified into a Maximum A Posteriori (MAP) Estimate. Thus instead of averaged matrix $\overline{M}$ of Eqn. 10, the flow is seen to be the smallest eigen-vector of matrix $\overline{M}_{map}$ for

$$\overline{M}_{map} = \frac{1}{\sigma_n^2} N \overline{M} + \frac{1}{\sigma_f^2} D \qquad (11)$$

where N is the number of pixels in the patch and σ_n and σ_f are the priors for the image derivative noise and flow magnitude respectively. It will be noted that the observation matrix in Eqn. 11 represents a regularised solution for the TLS problem [17]. For the sake of simplicity we reparametrise this matrix as $\overline{M} + \lambda D$ where λ represents the weight (influence) of the regularising term D. For a given value of λ, the estimated

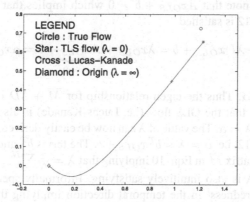

Fig. 2. Flow as a function of the regularisation term λ. The least-squares solution (Lucas-Kanade) lies on this curve. True flow and the TLS solution are also indicated. See Sec. 3.1 for details.

optical flow value is given by the smallest eigen-vector associated with the matrix $\overline{M} + \lambda D$. The behaviour of this parametrised form is particularly illuminating as illustrated in Fig. 2. In the case when $\lambda = 0$, the regulariser has no influence on the estimate and we get the TLS solution. When $\lambda = \infty$, the solution is determined solely by the null-space of the regularising matrix D, i.e. $[0, 0, 1]^T$ equivalent to a flow of $(0, 0)$. This is intuitively correct since here the flow is determined only by the prior which is a Gaussian centered at the origin. As λ varies from 0 to ∞ the estimated optic flow traces a curve from the TLS solution to the origin. Of particular significance is the fact that the Lucas-Kanade (or OLS) solution lies *exactly* on this parametrised curve, i.e. it is identical to a regularised TLS solution of optical flow for a particular value of λ! This relationship is formally described by the following lemma.

Lemma 1. *The Lucas-Kanade estimate of flow (i.e. OLS solution) is identical to the TLS solution for the regularised observation matrix $\overline{M} + \lambda D$ where $\lambda = \frac{1}{N} \sum_{k=1}^{N} I_t{}^k$ $(I_x{}^k u + I_y{}^k v + I_t{}^k)$, N is the number of pixels in the patch and (u, v) is the Lucas-Kanade (or OLS) solution.*

Proof: We represent the three-dimension homogeneous co-ordinates of the flow vector as $[x, 1]^T = [u, v, 1]^T$. Further we partition the 3×3 observation matrix as $\overline{M} = \begin{bmatrix} A & b \\ b^T & c \end{bmatrix}$. Since the regularising matrix D=diag([1,1,0]) we have $\overline{M} + \lambda D = \begin{bmatrix} A + \lambda I & b \\ b^T & c \end{bmatrix}$ where I is the 2×2 identity matrix. For the TLS solution of the regularised observation matrix, we have

$$(\overline{M} + \lambda D) \begin{bmatrix} x \\ 1 \end{bmatrix} = \begin{bmatrix} A + \lambda I & b \\ b^T & c \end{bmatrix} \begin{bmatrix} x \\ 1 \end{bmatrix} = \alpha \begin{bmatrix} x \\ 1 \end{bmatrix}$$

$$\Rightarrow (A + \lambda I)x + b = \alpha x \qquad (12)$$

Here α is the eigen-value associated with the TLS solution for a given λ. The lemma can now be proved by examination. Let us assume that the flow estimate x is the OLS solution x_{OLS}. By examining the observation matrix $\overline{M}$ of Eqn. 10 and the solution for x_{OLS} in Eqn. 8 we note that $Ax_{OLS} + b = 0$ which implies that for $x = x_{OLS}$ the relationship in Eqn. 12 is satisfied

$$(A + \lambda I)x_{OLS} + b = \lambda x_{OLS} + \underbrace{Ax_{OLS} + b}_{=0} = \alpha x_{OLS}$$

implying that $\lambda = \alpha$. Thus the eigen-relationship for $\overline{M} + \lambda D$ is satisfied for $x = x_{OLS}$ which proves that the OLS flow (i.e. Lucas-Kanade) is also a solution for the regularised TLS for $\lambda = \alpha$. The value of λ can now be easily derived by noting the lower relationship in Eqn. 12, i.e. $\alpha = \lambda = b^T x_{OLS} + c$. The terms b^T and c are the third row of the observation matrix $\overline{M}$ in Eqn. 10 implying that $\lambda = \frac{1}{N} \sum_{k=1}^{N} I_t{}^k (I_x{}^k u + I_y{}^k v + I_t{}^k)$. The form of λ is also intuitively satisfying. Informally speaking, it represents a measure of 'texturedness' in the temporal direction implying that as the temporal derivatives grow in magnitude, the Lucas-Kanade method introduces a greater amount of bias. It is well known that while the TLS solution is unbiased, compared to the OLS solution, the TLS has greater variance. In this context, the influence of the patch size on λ is informative. When the patch size (N) is small, λ is large implying that our solution introduces a bias to reduce the variance of the solution. Conversely, when the patch size is large, λ is small implying that our solution is closer to the TLS estimate as desired. Thus our formulation can naturally capture the correct representation required for accurate flow estimation and also explains the behaviour of Lucas-Kanade and TLS algorithms.

3.2 Affine Flow

While the constant flow model is simple to implement, its accuracy is inherently limited as flow fields are seldom close to a piece-wise constant model. A more appropriate assumption is that of an affine model. An affine flow field is described by $\begin{bmatrix} u \; v \end{bmatrix}^T = A \begin{bmatrix} x \; y \end{bmatrix}^T + \begin{bmatrix} t_x \; t_y \end{bmatrix}^T$ where (u, v) is the flow at position (x, y) and A is a 2×2 matrix. The affine model has been used to estimate optical flow in [13, 14, 15]. While the TLS estimator is unbiased it has a higher variance than the OLS solution. This implies that for small image patches, with few equations the Lucas-Kanade solution is preferable to the TLS solution. However as we noted in the previous subsection, when we have many equations the TLS solution is preferable to the biased OLS estimate. In general, the affine flow model is estimated for patches larger than those for constant flow since we need many more equations to reliably estimate the six parameters of the affine model. This implies that in our probabilistic model, the prior has little influence on affine estimation and can be neglected in our analysis here. By re-writing the optical flow in homogeneous co-ordinates we have $\mathbf{f} = \mathbf{P}\mathbf{a}$, where $\mathbf{P}$ represents terms relating to pixel position (x, y) and $\mathbf{a}$ is the vectorised representation for the affine parameters. Using this form in the probability model of Eqn. 6 we have

$$P(flow|patch) = \max_{model} \prod_k e^{-\frac{1}{2 \cdot 2} \frac{\mathbf{f} \cdot \cdot \mathbf{f}}{\mathbf{f}' \; \mathbf{f}}}$$

$$\Rightarrow P(\mathbf{a}|patch) = \max_{\mathbf{a}} \prod_k e^{-\frac{1}{2 \cdot 2} \frac{(\mathbf{P} \cdot \mathbf{a})' \cdot \cdot \mathbf{P} \cdot \mathbf{a}}{(\mathbf{P} \cdot \mathbf{a})' \; \mathbf{P} \cdot \mathbf{a}}}$$

$$\Rightarrow \mathbf{a} = \arg\min_{\mathbf{a}} \sum_k \frac{\mathbf{a}^T \mathbf{P}_k{}^T M_k \mathbf{P}_k \mathbf{a}}{\mathbf{a}^T \mathbf{P}_k{}^T \mathbf{P}_k \mathbf{a}} \qquad (10)$$

Thus the problem of estimating the affine parameters is reduced to the minimisation of a sum of Rayleigh quotients[3]. This particular quotient form occurs frequently in computer vision problems like ellipse fitting etc. and a significant body of work has been devoted to its minimisation. In our solution for the affine parameters we use the First-Order Renormalisation of [19].

3.3 Performance of Affine Flow Estimation

In this subsection we evaluate our affine flow estimation scheme using the standard image sequences of Barron et al [1]. All experiments are performed with a fixed set of

---

[3] In [18], the authors use algebraic arguments to approximate the above objective function as a single ratio of quadratic forms where the numerator is an average over the patch for the terms $\mathbf{P}^T M \mathbf{P}$ and the denominator is held to be $\mathbf{P}^T \mathbf{P}$ for a given pixel co-ordinates (x, y).

parameters. Each image sequence is smoothed using a separable Gaussian kernel with uniform spatial and temporal standard deviation of 1.4 pixels. The derivative filter is the series-design filter used in [18]. Apart from the image derivative filter the patch size is an important parameter that influences performance by determining the trade-off between estimation accuracy (requiring large patches) and resolution (requiring small patches). Throughout our experiments we use a constant patch size of 31×31 pixels and estimate the affine flow for such patches with a shift of 5 pixels in each direction. Thus each pixel is present in multiple patches and the flow estimate is the average over all patch estimates. We tabulate our results in Tables 1- 4. The error measure is identical to that of [1] and can be seen to measure the angle between the normalised volume-flow representations of the ground truth and the estimate. The error values for the first four methods are taken from [1]. As can be easily observed, our algorithm performs very well with respect to the other procedures. In particular, we point out that our accuracy is achieved without the use of any adaptive schemes. Also the standard deviation of our error values are *significantly* smaller compared to other methods. For the Yosemite sequence, we note that in comparison with the adaptive scheme of [4], our estimator has almost the same performance (error of $1.16°$ compared to $1.14°$) whereas our standard deviation is significantly smaller ($1.17°$ compared to $2.14°$). While, the results of [5] on the Yosemite sequence are superior to ours, we reiterate that our performance

Table 1. Sinusoid Sequence Results

Method	Error (in °)		Density
	μ	σ	
Lucas-Kanade	2.47	0.16	100 %
Horn-Schunck	2.55	0.59	100 %
Fleet-Jepson	0.03	0.01	100 %
Uras *et al.*	2.59	0.71	100 %
Farneback [20]	0.74	0.03	100 %
Liu *et al.* [18]	0.31	0.05	100 %
Our method	**0.09**	**0.03**	**100 %**

Table 2. Translating Tree Results

Method	Error (in °)		Density
	μ	σ	
Lucas-Kanade	0.66	0.67	39.8 %
Horn-Schunck	2.02	2.27	100 %
Fleet-Jepson	0.32	0.38	74.5 %
Uras *et al.*	0.62	0.52	100 %
Farneback [20]	0.62	1.99	100 %
Liu *et al.* [18]	0.20	0.62	100 %
Our method	**0.15**	**0.10**	**100 %**

Table 3. Diverging Tree Results

Method	Error (in °)		Density
	μ	σ	
Lucas-Kanade	1.94	2.06	48.2 %
Horn-Schunck	2.55	3.67	100 %
Fleet-Jepson	0.99	0.78	61.0 %
Uras *et al.*	4.64	3.48	100 %
Farneback [20]	0.75	0.69	100 %
Liu *et al.* [18]	0.65	1.73	100 %
Our method	**0.51**	**0.21**	**100 %**

Table 4. Yosemite Results (without clouds)

Method	Error (in °)		Density
	μ	σ	
Lucas-Kanade ($\lambda_2 \geq 1.0$)	3.21	5.34	39.5 %
Horn-Schunck	3.68	4.90	100 %
Uras *et al.*	6.47	9.48	84.6 %
Memin-Perez [7]	1.58	1.21	100 %
Weickert *et al.* [6]	1.46	*	100 %
Liu *et al.* [18]	1.39	2.83	100 %
Farneback [20]	1.40	2.57	100 %
Farneback [4]	1.14	2.14	100 %
Papenberg *et al.* [5]	0.99	1.17	100 %
Our method	**1.16**	**1.17**	**100 %**

is achieved by focusing on the *representation* of the brightness constraint and not on sophisticated numerical minimisers. In summary, we note that our probability representation is powerful and even a straight-forward application of this model outperforms almost all other flow estimators. Other refinements like robustness, adaptive patches, and more accurate minimisers can be expected to further improve our results.

4 Conclusions

In this paper we have introduced a principled approach to modeling the brightness constraint. The resultant probabilistic model is shown to be powerful and can both explain the behaviour of existing flow algorithms and significantly improve their performance. Future work will address more sophisticated minimisation approaches and also the utilisation of our probabilistic model to solve for volume-flow in the spatio-temporal volume of images and for direct motion estimation and segmentation.

Acknowledgments

Thanks are due to Rama Chellappa for his continuous support and encouragement. Yonathan Wexler, David Jacobs and Sameer Agarwal provided useful comments on various drafts of this paper.

References

1. Barron, J., Fleet, D., Beauchemin, S.: Performance of optical flow techniques. International Journal of Computer Vision **12** (1994) 43–77
2. Horn, B., Schunck, B.: Determining optical flow. Artificial Intelligence **17** (1981) 185–203
3. Lucas, B., Kanade, T.: An iterative image registration technique with an application to stereo vision. In: Proc. of DARPA Workshop. (1981) 121–130
4. Farneback, G.: Very high accuracy velocity estimation using orientation tensors, parametric motion, and simultaneous segmentation of the motion field. In: Proc. International Conf. on Computer Vision. Volume 1. (2001) 77–80
5. Papenberg, N., Bruhn, A., Brox, T., Didas, S., Weickert, J.: Highly accurate optic flow computation with theoretically justified warping. International Journal of Computer Vision (to appear)
6. Bruhn, A., Weickert, J., Schnorr, C.: Lucas/kanade meets horn/schunck: Combining local and global optic flow methods. International Journal of Computer Vision **61** (2005) 211–231
7. Memin, E., Perez, P.: Hierarchical estimation and segmentation of dense motion fields. International Journal of Computer Vision **46** (2002) 129–155
8. Weber, J., Malik, J.: Robust computation of optical-flow in a multiscale differential framework. International Journal of Computer Vision **14** (1995) 67–81
9. Nestares, O., Fleet, D., Heeger, D.: Likelihood functions and confidence bounds for total-least-squares problems. In: Proc. of IEEE Conf. on Computer Vision and Pattern Recognition. (2000) I: 523–530
10. Wang S., Markandey V., R.A.: Total least squares fitting spatiotemporal derivatives to smooth optical flow field. In: Proc. of the SPIE: Signal and Data processing of Small Targets. Volume 1698. (1992) 42–55

11. Weiss, Y., Fleet, D.J.: Velocity likelihoods in biological and machine vision. In: Probabilistic Models of the Brain: Perception and Neural Function. MIT Press (2002) 77–96
12. Simoncelli, E.P., Adelson, E.H., Heeger, D.J.: Probability distributions of optical flow. In: Proc. IEEE Conf. Computer Vision and Pattern Recognition. (1991) 310–315
13. Bergen, J., Anandan, P., Hanna, K., Hingorani, R.: Hierarchical model-based motion estimation. In: Proc. of European Conference on Computer Vision. (1992) 237–252
14. Wang, J., Adelson, E.: Representing moving images with layers. IEEE Transactions on Image Processing 3 (1994) 625–638
15. Ju, S., Black, M., Jepson, A.: Skin and bones: Multi-layer, locally affine, optical flow and regularization with transparency. In: IEEE Conf. on Computer Vision and Pattern Recognition. (1996) 307–314
16. Van Huffel, S., Vandewalle, J.: The Total Least Squares Problem : Computational Aspects and Analysis. SIAM (1991)
17. Golub, G.H., Hansen, P.C., O'Leary, D.P.: Tikhonov regularization and total least squares. SIAM Journal on Matrix Analysis and Applications 21 (1999) 185–194
18. Liu, H., Chellappa, R., Rosenfeld, A.: Accurate dense optical flow estimation using adaptive structure tensors and a parametric model. IEEE Transactions on Image Processing 12 (2003) 1170–1180
19. Chojnacki, W., Brooks, M., van den Hengel, A.: Rationalising the renormalisation method of kanatani. Journal of Mathematical Imaging and Vision 14 (2001) 21–38
20. Farneback, G.: Fast and accurate motion estimation using orientation tensors and parametric motion models. In: Proc. of 15th International Conference on Pattern Recognition. Volume 1. (2000) 135–139

Triangulation for Points on Lines

Adrien Bartoli and Jean-Thierry Lapresté

LASMEA – CNRS, Université Blaise Pascal,
Clermont-Ferrand, France
Adrien.Bartoli@gmail.com

Abstract. Triangulation consists in finding a 3D point reprojecting the best as possible onto corresponding image points. It is classical to minimize the reprojection error, which, in the pinhole camera model case, is nonlinear in the 3D point coordinates. We study the triangulation of points lying on a 3D line, which is a typical problem for Structure-From-Motion in man-made environments. We show that the reprojection error can be minimized by finding the real roots of a polynomial in a single variable, which degree depends on the number of images. We use a set of transformations in 3D and in the images to make the degree of this polynomial as low as possible, and derive a practical reconstruction algorithm. Experimental comparisons with an algebraic approximation algorithm and minimization of the reprojection error using Gauss-Newton are reported for simulated and real data. Our algorithm finds the optimal solution with high accuracy in all cases, showing that the polynomial equation is very stable. It only computes the roots corresponding to feasible points, and can thus deal with a very large number of views – triangulation from hundreds of views is performed in a few seconds. Reconstruction accuracy is shown to be greatly improved compared to standard triangulation methods that do not take the line constraint into account.

1 Introduction

Triangulation is one of the main building blocks of Structure-From-Motion algorithms. Given image feature correspondences and camera matrices, it consists in finding the position of the underlying 3D feature, by minimizing some error criterion. This criterion is often chosen as the reprojection error – the Maximum Likelihood criterion for a Gaussian, centred and *i.i.d.* noise model on the image point positions - though other criteria are possible [5, 9, 10].

Traditionally, triangulation is carried out by some sub-optimal procedure and is then refined by local optimization, see *e.g.* [7]. A drawback of this is that convergence to the optimal solution is not guaranteed. Optimal procedures for triangulating points from two and three views were proposed in [6, 13].

We address the problem of triangulating points lying on a line, that is, given image point correspondences, camera matrices and a 3D line, finding the 3D point lying on the 3D line, such that the reprojection error is minimized.

A. Leonardis, H. Bischof, and A. Pinz (Eds.): ECCV 2006, Part III, LNCS 3953, pp. 189–200, 2006.
© Springer-Verlag Berlin Heidelberg 2006

Our main contribution is to show that the problem can be solved by computing the real roots of a degree-$(3n-2)$ polynomial, where n is the number of views. Extensive experiments on simulated data show that the polynomial is very well balanced since large number of views and large level of noise are handled. The method is valid whatever the calibration level of the cameras is – projective, affine, metric or Euclidean.

One may argue that triangulating points on a line only has a theoretical interest since in practice, triangulating a line from multiple views is done by minimizing the reprojection error over its supporting points which 3D positions are hence reconstructed along with the 3D line. Indeed, most work consider the case where the supporting points do *not* match accross the images, see *e.g.* [3]. When one identifies correspondences of supporting points accross the images, it is fruitful to incorporate these constraints into the bundle adjustment, as is demonstrated by our experiments. This is typically the case in man-made environments, where one identifies *e.g.* matching corners at the meet of planar facades or around windows. Bartoli *et al.* [2] dubbed Pencil-of-Points or 'POP' this type of features. In order to find an initial 3D reconstruction, a natural way is to compute the 3D line by some means (*e.g.* by ignoring the matching constraints of the supporting points, from 3D primitives such as the intersection of two planes, or from a registered wireframe CAD model) and then to triangulate the supporting point correspondences using point on line triangulation. The result can then be plugged into a bundle adjustment incorporating the constraints.

Our triangulation method is derived in §2. A linear least squares method minimizing an algebraic distance is provided in §3. Gauss-Newton refinement is summarized in §4. Experimental results are reported in §5 and our conclusions in §6.

Notation. Vectors are written using bold fonts, *e.g.* $\mathbf{q}$, and matrices using sans-serif fonts, *e.g.* P. Almost everything is homogeneous, *i.e.* defined up to scale. Equality up to scale is denoted $\sim$. The inhomogenous part of a vector is denoted using a bar, *e.g.* $\mathbf{q}^\mathsf{T} \sim (\bar{\mathbf{q}}^\mathsf{T} \ 1)$ where $^\mathsf{T}$ is transposition. Index $i = 1, \ldots, n$, and sometime j are used for the images. The point in the i-th image is $\mathbf{q}_i$. Its elements are $\mathbf{q}_i^\mathsf{T} \sim (q_{i,1} \ q_{i,2} \ 1)$. The 3D line joining points $\mathbf{M}$ and $\mathbf{N}$ is denoted $(\mathbf{M}, \mathbf{N})$. The $\mathcal{L}_2$-norm of a vector is denoted as in $\|\mathbf{x}\|^2 = \mathbf{x}^\mathsf{T}\mathbf{x}$. The Euclidean distance measure d_e is defined by:

$$d_e^2(\mathbf{x}, \mathbf{y}) = \left\| \frac{\mathbf{x}}{x_3} - \frac{\mathbf{y}}{y_3} \right\|^2 = \left(\frac{x_1}{x_3} - \frac{y_1}{y_3} \right)^2 + \left(\frac{x_2}{x_3} - \frac{y_2}{y_3} \right)^2. \tag{1}$$

Related work. Optimal procedures for triangulating points in 3D space, and points lying on a plane were previously studied. Hartley and Sturm [6] showed that triangulating points in 3D space from two views, in other words finding a pair of points satisfying the epipolar geometry and lying as close as possible to the measured points, can be solved by finding the real roots of a degree-6 polynomial. The optimal solution is then selected by straightforward evaluation of the reprojection error. Stewénius *et al.* [13] extended the method to three views. The optimal solution is one of the real roots of a system of 3 degree-6 polynomials in the 3 coordinates of the point. Chum *et al.* [4] show that triangulating points lying on a plane, in other words finding a pair of points satisfying an homography and lying as close as possible to the measured points, can be solved by finding the real roots of a degree-8 polynomial.

2 Minimizing the Reprojection Error

We derive our optimal triangulation algorithm for point on line, dubbed 'POLY'.

2.1 Problem Statement and Parameterization

We want to compute a 3D point $\mathbf{Q}$, lying on a 3D line $(\mathbf{M}, \mathbf{N})$, represented by two 3D points $\mathbf{M}$ and $\mathbf{N}$. The (3×4) perspective camera matrices are denoted P_i with $i = 1, \ldots, n$ the image index. The problem is to find the point $\hat{\mathbf{Q}}$ such that:

$$\hat{\mathbf{Q}} \sim \arg \min_{\mathbf{Q} \in (\mathbf{M}, \mathbf{N})} \mathcal{C}_n^2(\mathbf{Q}),$$

where $\mathcal{C}_n$ is the n-view *reprojection error*:

$$\mathcal{C}_n^2(\mathbf{Q}) = \sum_{i=1}^{n} d_e^2(\mathbf{q}_i, \mathsf{P}_i \mathbf{Q}). \tag{2}$$

We parameterize the point $\mathbf{Q} \in (\mathbf{M}, \mathbf{N})$ using a single parameter $\lambda \in \mathbb{R}$ as:

$$\mathbf{Q} \sim \lambda \mathbf{M} + (1 - \lambda)\mathbf{N} \sim \lambda(\mathbf{M} - \mathbf{N}) + \mathbf{N}. \tag{3}$$

Introducing this parameterization into the reprojection error (2) yields:

$$\mathcal{C}_n^2(\lambda) = \sum_{i=1}^{n} d_e^2(\mathbf{q}_i, \mathsf{P}_i(\lambda(\mathbf{M} - \mathbf{N}) + \mathbf{N})).$$

Defining $\mathbf{b}_i = \mathsf{P}_i(\mathbf{M} - \mathbf{N})$ and $\mathbf{d}_i = \mathsf{P}_i \mathbf{N}$, we get:

$$\mathcal{C}_n^2(\lambda) = \sum_{i=1}^{n} d_e^2(\mathbf{q}_i, \lambda \mathbf{b}_i + \mathbf{d}_i). \tag{4}$$

Note that a similar parameterization can be derived by considering the inter-image homographies induced by the 3D line [12].

2.2 Simplification

We simplify the expression (4) of the reprojection error by changing the 3D coordinate frame and the image coordinate frames. This is intended to lower the degree of the polynomial equation that will ultimately have to be solved. Since the reprojection error is based on Euclidean distances measured in the images, only rigid image transformations are allowed to keep invariant the error function, while full projective homographies can be used in 3D. We thus setup a standard canonical 3D coordinate frame, see *e.g.* [8], such that the first camera matrix becomes $P_1 \sim (\ I \ \ 0)$. Note that using a projective basis does not harm Euclidean triangulation since the normalization is undone once the point is triangulated. The canonical basis is setup by the following simple operations:

$$H \leftarrow \begin{pmatrix} P_1 \\ 0\,0\,0\,1 \end{pmatrix} \quad P_i \leftarrow P_i H^{-1} \quad M \leftarrow HM \quad N \leftarrow HN.$$

Within this coordinate frame, we can write $M^T = (\bullet \ \ \bullet \ \ 1 \ \ \bullet)$ and $N^T = (\bullet \ \ \bullet \ \ 1 \ \ \bullet)$ without loss of generality, as pointed out in [7, §A6], from which we get:

$$b_1 = P_1(M - N) = (b_{1,1} \ \ b_{1,2} \ \ 0)^T$$
$$d_1 = P_1 N = (d_{1,1} \ \ d_{1,2} \ \ 1)^T.$$

We then apply a rigid transformation T_i in each image defined such that $T_i b_i$ lies on the y-axis and such that $T_i d_i = T_i P_i N$ lies at the origin. This requires that the point N does not project at infinity is any of the images. We ensure this by constraining N to project as close as possible to one of the image points[1], say q_1. The reprojection error (4) for the first view is $C_1^2(\lambda) = d_e^2(q_1, \lambda b_1 + d_1) = \|\lambda \bar{b}_1 + \bar{d}_1 - \bar{q}_1\|^2$. We compute λ as the solution of $\frac{\partial C_1^2}{\partial \lambda} = 0$, which gives, after some minor calculations, $\lambda = (\bar{q}_1 - \bar{d}_1)^T \bar{b}_1 / \|\bar{b}_1\|^2$. Substituting in equation (3) yields the following operations:

$$N \leftarrow \frac{(P_1 N - q_1)^T P_1(M - N)}{\|P_1(M - N)\|^2}(M - N) + N.$$

Obviously, the $d_i = P_i N$ must be recomputed. These simplifications lead to:

$$b_1 = (0 \ \ b_{1,2} \ \ 0)^T \quad d_1 = (0 \ \ 0 \ \ 1)^T \quad b_{i>1} = (0 \ \ b_{i,2} \ \ b_{i,3})^T \quad d_{i>1} = (0 \ \ 0 \ \ d_{i,3})^T.$$

The rigid transformations T_i are quickly derived below. For each image i, we look for T_i mapping d_i to the origin, and b_i to a point on the y-axis. We decompose T_i as a rotation around the origin and a translation:

$$T_i = \begin{pmatrix} R_i & 0 \\ 0^T & 1 \end{pmatrix} \begin{pmatrix} I & -t_i \\ 0^T & 1 \end{pmatrix}.$$

The translation is directly given from $T_i d_i \sim (0 \ \ 0 \ \ 1)^T$ as $t_i = \bar{d}_i / d_{i,3}$. For the rotation, we consider $T_i b_i \sim (0 \ \ \bullet \ \ \bullet)^T$, from which, setting $r_i = \bar{b}_i - b_{i,3} t_i$, we obtain $R_i = \begin{pmatrix} r_{i,2} & -r_{i,1} \\ r_{i,1} & r_{i,2} \end{pmatrix} / \|\bar{r}_i\|$.

---

[1] Note that this is equivalent to solving the single view triangulation problem.

This leads to the following expression for the reprojection error (4) where we separated the leading term:

$$C_n^2(\lambda) = q_{1,1}^2 + (\lambda b_{1,2} - q_{1,2})^2 + \sum_{i=2}^{n} \left(q_{i,1}^2 + \left(\frac{\lambda b_{i,2}}{\lambda b_{i,3} - d_{i,3}} - q_{i,2} \right)^2 \right).$$

The constant terms $q_{1,1}^2$ and $q_{i,1}^2$ represent the vertical counterparts of the point to line distance in the images. This means that only the errors along the lines are to be minimized.

2.3   Solving the Polynomial Equation

Looking for the minima of the reprojection error C_n^2 is equivalent to finding the roots of its derivative, i.e. solving $\frac{\partial C_n^2}{\partial \lambda} = 0$. Define $\mathcal{D}_n = \frac{1}{2} \frac{\partial C_n^2}{\partial \lambda}$:

$$\mathcal{D}_n(\lambda) = (\lambda b_{1,2} - q_{1,2}) b_{1,2} + \sum_{i=2}^{n} \left(\frac{\lambda b_{i,2}}{\lambda b_{i,3} + d_{i,3}} - q_{i,2} \right) \left(\frac{b_{i,2} d_{i,3}}{(\lambda b_{i,3} + d_{i,3})^2} \right).$$

This is a nonlinear function. Directly solving $\mathcal{D}_n(\lambda) = 0$ is therefore very difficult in general. We thus define $\tilde{\mathcal{D}}_n(\lambda) = \mathcal{D}_n(\lambda) \mathcal{K}_n(\lambda)$, where we choose $\mathcal{K}_n$ in order to cancel out the denominators including λ in $\mathcal{D}_n$. Finding the zeros of $\tilde{\mathcal{D}}_n$ is thus equivalent to finding the zeros of $\mathcal{D}_n$. Inspecting the expression of $\mathcal{D}_n$ reveals that $\mathcal{K}_n(\lambda) = \prod_{i=2}^{n} (\lambda b_{i,3} + d_{i,3})^3$ does the trick:

$$
\begin{aligned}
\tilde{\mathcal{D}}_n(\lambda) = {} & (\lambda b_{1,2} - q_{1,2}) b_{1,2} \prod_{i=2}^{n} (\lambda b_{i,3} + d_{i,3})^3 \\
& + \sum_{i=2}^{n} \left(b_{i,2} d_{i,3} (\lambda b_{i,2} - q_{i,2}(\lambda b_{i,3} + d_{i,3})) \prod_{j=2, j \neq i}^{n} (\lambda b_{j,3} + d_{j,3})^3 \right).
\end{aligned}
\tag{5}
$$

As expected, $\tilde{\mathcal{D}}_n$ is a polynomial function, whose degree depends on the number of images n. We observe that cancelling the denominator out for the contribution of each $(i > 1)$-image requires to multiply $\mathcal{D}_n$ by a cubic, namely $(\lambda b_{i,3} + d_{i,3})^3$. Since the polynomial required for image $i = 1$ is linear, the degree of the polynomial to solve is $3(n-1) + 1 = 3n - 2$.

Given the real roots λ_k of $\tilde{\mathcal{D}}_n(\lambda)$, that we compute as detailled below for different number of images, we simply select the one for which the reprojection error is minimized, i.e. $\hat{\lambda} = \arg\min_k C_n^2(\lambda_k)$, substitute it in equation (3) and transfer the recovered point back to the original coordinate frame:

$$\hat{\mathbf{Q}} \sim \mathsf{H}^{-1} \left(\hat{\lambda} \mathbf{M} + \left(1 - \hat{\lambda} \right) \mathbf{N} \right).$$

A single image. For $n = 1$ image, the point is triangulated by projecting its image onto the image projection of the line. The intersection of the associated viewing ray with the 3D line gives the 3D point. In our framework, equation (5) is indeed linear in λ for $n = 1$: $\tilde{\mathcal{D}}_1(\lambda) = (\lambda b_{1,2} - q_{1,2}) b_{1,2} = b_{1,2}^2 \lambda - q_{1,2} b_{1,2}$.

A pair of images. For $n = 2$ images, equation (5) gives:

$$\tilde{\mathcal{D}}_2(\lambda) = (\lambda b_{1,2} - q_{1,2})b_{1,2}(\lambda b_{2,3} + d_{2,3})^3 + b_{2,2}d_{2,3}(\lambda b_{2,2} - q_{2,2}(\lambda b_{2,3} + d_{2,3})),$$

which is a quartic in λ that can be solved in closed-form using Cardano's formulas: $\tilde{\mathcal{D}}_2(\lambda) \sim \sum_{d=1}^{4} c_d \lambda^d$, with:

$$\begin{cases} c_0 = -q_{2,2}d_{2,3}^2 b_{2,2} - b_{1,2}q_{1,2}d_{2,3}^3 \\ c_1 = d_{2,3}(b_{2,2}^2 - 3b_{1,2}q_{1,2}b_{2,3}d_{2,3} + b_{1,2}^2 d_{2,3}^2 - q_{2,2}b_{2,3}b_{2,2}) \\ c_2 = 3b_{1,2}b_{2,3}d_{2,3}(b_{1,2}d_{2,3} - q_{1,2}b_{2,3}) \\ c_3 = b_{1,2}b_{2,3}^2(3b_{1,2}d_{2,3} - q_{1,2}b_{2,3}) \\ c_4 = b_{1,2}^2 b_{2,3}^3. \end{cases}$$

Multiple images. Solving the $n \geq 3$ view case is done in two steps. The first step is to compute the coefficients c_j, $j = 0, \ldots, 3n\text{-}2$ of a polynomial. The second step is to compute its real roots. Computing the coefficients in closed-form from equation (5), as is done above for the single- and the two-view cases, lead to very large, awkward formulas, which may lead to roundoff errors. We thus perform a numerical computation.

A standard root-finding technique is to compute the eigenvalues of the $((3n\text{-}2) \times (3n\text{-}2))$ companion matrix of the polynomial, see *e.g.* [1]. Computing all the roots ensures the optimal solution to be found. This can be done if the number of images is not too large, *i.e.* lower than 100, and if computation time is not an issue. However, for large numbers of images, or if real-time computation must be achieved, it is not possible to compute and try all roots. In that case, we propose to compute only the roots corresponding to feasible points.

Let λ_0 be an approximation of the sought-after root. For example, one can take the result of the algebraic method of §3, or even $\lambda_0 = 0$ since our parameterization takes the sought-after root very close to 0. Obviously, we could launch an iterative root-finding procedure such as Newton-Raphson from λ_0 but this would not guarantee that the optimal solution is found.

One solution to efficiently compute only the feasible roots is to reparameterize the polynomial such that those lie close to 0, and use an iterative algorithm for computing the eigenvalues of the companion matrix on turn. For example, Arnoldi or Lanczos' methods, compute the eigenvalues with increasing magnitude starting from the smallest one. Let λ_c be the last computed eigenvalue, and $\mathbf{Q}_1$ and $\mathbf{Q}_2$ the reconstructed points corresponding to λ_c and $-\lambda_c$. If both $\mathbf{Q}_1$ and $\mathbf{Q}_2$ reproject outside the images, the computation is stopped. Indeed, the next root that would be computed would have greater magnitude than λ_c, and would obviously lead to a point reprojecting further away than the previous one outside the images.

The reparameterization is done by computing a polynomial $\mathcal{P}_n(\lambda) = \tilde{\mathcal{D}}_n(\lambda + \lambda_0)$. A simple way to achieve this reparameterization is to estimate the coefficients c_j, $j = 1, \ldots, 3n\text{-}1$, of $\mathcal{P}_n$, as follows. We evaluate $z \geq 3n\text{-}1$ values $v_k = \tilde{\mathcal{D}}_n(\lambda_k + \lambda_0)$ from equation (5) for $\lambda_k \in [-\delta, \delta]$, and solve the associated Vandermonde system: $\sum_{j=0}^{3n-2} c_j \lambda_k^j = v_k$ for $k = 1, \ldots, z$. We typically use

$z = 10(3n\text{-}1)$. The parameter $\delta \in \mathbb{R}^{*+}$ reflects the size of the sampling interval around λ_0. We noticed that this parameter does not influence the results, and typically chose $\delta = 1$. Obviously, in theory, using $z = 3n\text{-}1$, *i.e.* the minimum number of samples, at distinct points, is equivalent for finding the coefficients. However we experimentally found that using extra samples evenly spread around the expected root λ_0 has the benefit of 'averaging' the roundoff error, and stabilizes the computation.

One could argue that with this method for estimating the coefficients, the simplifying transformations of §2.2 are not necessary. A short calculation shows that this is partly true since if the canonical 3D projective basis were not used along with the normalization of the third entries of $\mathbf{M}$ and $\mathbf{N}$ to unity, then the degree of the polynomial would be $3n$ instead of $3n\text{-}2$.

3 An Algebraic Criterion

We give a linear algorithm, dubbed 'ALGEBRAIC', based on approximating the reprojection error (2) by replacing the Euclidean distance measure d_e by the algebraic distance measure d_a defined by $d_a^2(\mathbf{x}, \mathbf{y}) = \mathsf{S}[\mathbf{x}]_\times \mathbf{y}$ with $\mathsf{S} = \left(\begin{smallmatrix} 1 & 0 & 0 \\ 0 & 1 & 0 \end{smallmatrix}\right)$, and where $[\mathbf{x}]_\times$ is the (3×3) skew-symmetric matrix associated to cross-product, *i.e.* $[\mathbf{x}]_\times \mathbf{y} = \mathbf{x} \times \mathbf{y}$. This gives an algebraic error function:

$$\mathcal{E}_n^2(\lambda) = \sum_{i=1}^{n} d_a^2(\lambda \mathbf{b}_i + \mathbf{d}_i, \mathbf{q}_i) = \sum_{i=1}^{n} \|\lambda \mathsf{S}[\mathbf{q}_i]_\times \mathbf{b}_i + \mathsf{S}[\mathbf{q}_i]_\times \mathbf{d}_i\|^2.$$

A closed-form solution is obtained, giving λ_a in the least squares sense:

$$\lambda_a = -\frac{\sum_{i=1}^{n} \mathbf{b}_i^\mathsf{T}[\mathbf{q}_i]_\times \tilde{\mathsf{I}}[\mathbf{q}_i]_\times \mathbf{d}_i}{\sum_{i=1}^{n} \mathbf{b}_i^\mathsf{T}[\mathbf{q}_i]_\times \tilde{\mathsf{I}}[\mathbf{q}_i]_\times \mathbf{b}_i} \quad \text{with} \quad \tilde{\mathsf{I}} \sim \mathsf{S}^\mathsf{T}\mathsf{S} \sim \left(\begin{smallmatrix} 1 & 0 & 0 \\ 0 & 1 & 0 \\ 0 & 0 & 0 \end{smallmatrix}\right).$$

4 Gauss-Newton Refinement

As is usual for triangulation and bundle adjustment [7], we use the Gauss-Newton algorithm for refining an estimate of $\hat{\lambda}$ by minimizing the nonlinear least squares reprojection error (2). The algorithm, that we do not derived in details, is dubbed 'GAUSS-NEWTON'. We use the best solution amongst POLY and ALGEBRAIC as the initial solution.

5 Experimental Results

5.1 Simulated Data

We simulated a 3D line observed by n cameras P_i. In order to simulate realistic data, we reconstructed the 3D line as follows. We projected the line onto the images, and regularly sampled points on it, that were offset orthogonally to the image line with a Gaussian centred noise with variance σ_l. The 3D line

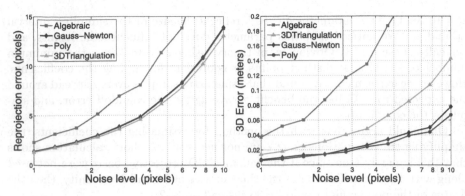

Fig. 1. Reprojection error (left) and 3D error (right) versus the level of noise

was then reconstructed from the noisy points using the Maximum Likelihood triangulation method in [3], which provided $\mathbf{M}$ and $\mathbf{N}$. Finally, a point lying on the true 3D line was projected onto the images, and corrupted with a Gaussian centred noise with variance σ_p, which gave the $\mathbf{q}_i$. We varied some parameters of this setup, namely n and σ_p, and the spatial configuration of the cameras, in order to compare the algorithms under different conditions. We compared two cases for the cameras: a stable one, in which they were evenly spread around the 3D line, and an unstable one, in which they were very close to each other. The default parameters of the setup are $\sigma_l = 0.1$ pixels, $\sigma_p = 3$ pixels, $n = 10$ views and stable cameras.

We had two main goals in these experiments. First, we wanted to determine what in practice is the maximum number of views and noise that the proposed triangulation method can deal with, for stable and unstable camera configurations. Second, we wanted to determine to which extent the line constraint improves the accuracy of the reconstructed 3D point, compared to standard unconstrained triangulation. We measured two kinds of error: the reprojection error, quantifying the ability of the methods to fit the measurements, and a 3D error, quantifying the accuracy of the reconstruction.

We compared the three algorithms, described in the paper (POLY, §2 ; ALGE-BRAIC, §3 ; GAUSS-NEWTON, §4) and 3DTRIANGULATION, which is a standard Maximum Likelihood triangulation, ignoring the line constraint, e.g. [7].

Figure 1 shows the results for varying noise level on the image points ($\sigma_p = 1, \ldots, 10$ pixels), and figure 2 for varying number of views ($n = 2, \ldots, 200$). Note the logarithmic scaling on the abscissa. General comments can be made about these results:

– 3DTRIANGULATION always gives the lowest reprojection error.
– ALGEBRAIC always gives the highest reprojection error and 3D error.
– POLY and GAUSS-NEWTON always give the lowest 3D error.

Small differences in the reprojection error may lead to large discrepancies in the 3D error. For example, POLY and GAUSS-NEWTON are undistinguisable on figures 1 (left) and 2 (left), showing the reprojection error, while they can clearly

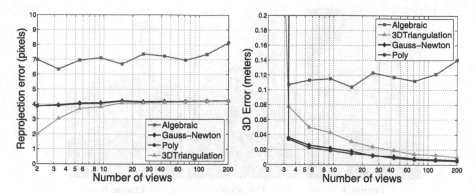

Fig. 2. Reprojection error (left) and 3D error (right) versus the number of views

be distinguished on figures 1 (right) and 2 (right), showing the 3D error. This is due to the fact that GAUSS-NEWTON converges when some standard precision is reached on the reprojection error. Increasing the precision may improve the results, but would make convergence slower.

For $n = 10$ views, figure 1 shows that the accuracy of the 3D reconstruction is clearly better for the optimal methods POLY and GAUSS-NEWTON using the line constraint, compared to 3DTRIANGULATION that does not use this constraint. The difference in 3D accuracy is getting larger as the noise level increases. For a $\sigma_p = 1$ pixel noise, which is what one can expect in practice, the difference in accuracy is 1 cm, corresponding to 1% of the simulated scene scale. This is an important difference.

However, for $\sigma_p = 3$ pixels, beyond 20 views, figure 2 (left) shows that the reprojection error for 3DTRIANGULATION and POLY/GAUSS-NEWTON are hardly distinguishable, while we expect from figure 2 (right) the difference in 3D error to be negligible beyond 200 views.

The results presented above concern the stable camera setup. For the unstable case, we obtained slightly lower reprojection errors, which is due to the fact that the 3D model is less constrained, making the observations easier to "explain". However, as was expected, the 3D errors are higher by a factor of around 2. The order of the different methods remains the same as in the stable case. We noticed that incorporating the line constraint improves the accuracy compared to 3DTRIANGULATION to a much higher extent than in the stable case.

5.2 Real Data

We tested the four reconstruction algorithms on several real data sets. For two of them, we show results. We used a Canny detector to retrieve salient edgels in the images, and adjusted segments using robust least squares. Finally, we matched the segments by hand between the images, except for the 387 frame 'building' sequence where automatic traking was used. The point on line correspondences were manually given, again besides for the 'building' sequence for which

Frame 1   Frame 3   Frame 6

Fig. 3. 3 out of the 6 images taken from the 'Valbonne church' sequence, overlaid with 6 matching segments and 13 corresponding points

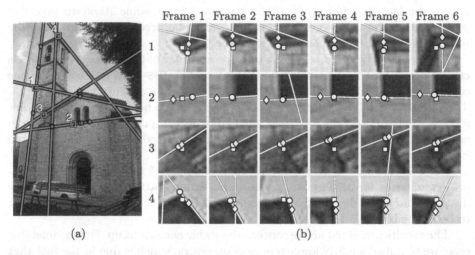

(a)   (b)

Fig. 4. Reprojected 3D lines and 3D points. (a) shows 4 different numbered points, for which (b) shows a close up for all the 6 images. The squares are the original points, the diamonds are the points reconstructed by ALGEBRAIC, and the circles are the points reconstructed from POLY and GAUSS-NEWTON (they are undistinguishable).

correlation based tracking was used. We reconstructed the 3D lines from the edgels by the Maximum Likelihood method in [3].

The 'Valbonne church' sequence. We used 6 views from the popular 'Valbonne church' image set. Some of them are shown on figure 3, together with the 6 input segments and 13 inputs points. The cameras were obtained by Euclidean bundle adjustment over a set of points [11]. The reprojection errors we obtained were: ALGEBRAIC → 1.37 pixels ; POLY → 0.77 pixels ; GAUSS-NEWTON → 0.77 pixels. Figure 4 (a) shows lines and points reprojected from the 3D reconstruction. The reprojection errors we obtained for the points shown on figure 4 (b) were:

Point	ALGEBRAIC	POLY	GAUSS-NEWTON
1	4.03 pixels	2.14 pixels	2.14 pixels
2	6.97 pixels	1.95 pixels	1.95 pixels
3	2.84 pixels	2.21 pixels	2.21 pixels
4	4.65 pixels	2.14 pixels	2.14 pixels

The 'Building' sequence. This sequence is a continuous video stream consisting of 387 frames, showing a building imaged by a hand-held camera, see figure 5. We reconstructed calibrated cameras by bundle adjustment from interest points that were tracked using a correlation based tracker.

The segment we tracked is almost the only one that is visible throughout the sequence, and thus allows to test our triangulation methods for a very large number of views, namely 387. For the 7 points we selected, we obtained a mean reprojection error of 4.57 pixels for ALGEBRAIC, of 3.45 pixels for POLY and GAUSS-NEWTON. Unconstrained triangulation gave a 2.90 pixels reprojection error. These errors which are higher than for the two previous data sets, are explained by the fact that there is non negligible radial distortion in the images, as can be seen on figure 5.

Frame 1   Frame 387

Fig. 5. 2 out of the 387 images of the 'building' sequence, overlaid with the matching segments and 7 corresponding points

6 Conclusions

We proposed an algorithm for the optimal triangulation, in the Maximum Likelihood sense, of a point lying on a given 3D line. Several transformations of 3D space and in the images lead to a degree-$(3n-2)$ polynomial equation. An efficient algorithm computes the real roots leading to feasible points only. Experimental evaluation on simulated and real data show that the method can be applied to large numbers of images, up to 387 in our experiments. The experiments were done for many different real data sets, indoor and outdoor, small, medium and large number of images, calibrated and uncalibrated reconstructions. Comparison of triangulated points with ground truth for the case of simulated data show that using the line constraint greatly improves the accuracy of the reconstruction.

200   A. Bartoli and J.-T. Lapresté

Acknowledgements. The first author thanks F. Schaffalitzky and A. Zisserman
for having provided the projection matrices of the 'Valbonne church' sequence.

References

1. F. S. Acton. *Numerical Methods That Work.* Washington: Mathematical Association of America, 1990. Corrected edition.
2. A. Bartoli, M. Coquerelle, and P. Sturm. A framework for pencil-of-points
   structure-from-motion. *European Conference on Computer Vision,* 2004.
3. A. Bartoli and P. Sturm. Multiple-view structure and motion from line correspondences. *International Conference on Computer Vision,* 2003.
4. O. Chum, T. Pajdla, and P. Sturm. The geometric error for homographies. *Computer Vision and Image Understanding,* 97(1):86–102, January 2005.
5. R. Hartley and F. Schaffalitzky. L_∞ minimization in geometric reconstruction
   problems. *Conference on Computer Vision and Pattern Recognition,* 2004.
6. R. Hartley and P. Sturm. Triangulation. *Computer Vision and Image Understanding,* 68(2):146–157, 1997.
7. R. I. Hartley and A. Zisserman. *Multiple View Geometry in Computer Vision.*
   Cambridge University Press, 2003. Second Edition.
8. Q.T. Luong and T. Vieville. Canonic representations for the geometries of multiple
   projective views. *Computer Vision and Image Understanding,* 64(2):193–229, 1996.
9. D. Nistèr. *Automatic Dense Reconstruction From Uncalibrated Video Sequences.*
   PhD thesis, Royal Institute of Technology, KTH, March 2001.
10. J. Oliensis. Exact two-image structure from motion. IEEE *Transactions on Pattern
    Analysis and Machine Intelligence,* 24(12):1618–1633, 2002.
11. F. Schaffalitzky and A. Zisserman. Multi-view matching for unordered image sets.
    In *Proceedings of the European Conference on Computer Vision,* 2002.
12. C. Schmid and A. Zisserman. The geometry and matching of lines and curves over
    multiple views. *International Journal of Computer Vision,* 40(3):199–234, 2000.
13. H. Stewénius, F. Schaffalitzky, and D. Nistér. How hard is 3-view triangulation
    really? In *Proceedings of the International Conference on Computer Vision,* 2005.

A Fast Line Segment Based Dense Stereo Algorithm Using Tree Dynamic Programming

Yi Deng and Xueyin Lin

Department of Computer Science,
Intitute of HCI and Media Integration, Key Lab of Pervasive Computing(MOE),
3-524, Fit building, Tsinghua University, Beijing 100084, P.R. China
dengyi00@mails.tsinghua.edu.cn,
lxy-dcs@mail.tsinghua.edu.cn

Abstract. Many traditional stereo correspondence methods emphasized on utilizing epipolar constraint and ignored the information embedded in inter-epipolar lines. Actually some researchers have already proposed several grid-based algorithms for fully utilizing information embodied in both intra- and inter-epipolar lines. Though their performances are greatly improved, they are very time-consuming. The new graph-cut and believe-propagation methods have made the grid-based algorithms more efficient, but time-consuming still remains a hard problem for many applications. Recently, a tree dynamic programming algorithm is proposed. Though the computation speed is much higher than that of grid-based methods, the performance is degraded apparently. We think that the problem stems from the pixel-based tree construction. Many edges in the original grid are forced to be cut out, and much information embedded in these edges is thus lost. In this paper, a novel line segment based stereo correspondence algorithm using tree dynamic programming (LSTDP) is presented. Each epipolar line of the reference image is segmented into segments first, and a tree is then constructed with these line segments as its vertexes. The tree dynamic programming is adopted to compute the correspondence of each line segment. By using line segments as the vertexes instead of pixels, the connection between neighboring pixels within the same region can be reserved as completely as possible. Experimental results show that our algorithm can obtain comparable performance with state-of-the-art algorithms but is much more time-efficient.

1 Introduction

Stereo correspondence has been one of the most important problems in computer vision, and still remains a hard problem that needs more efforts. It is used in many areas like robot navigation, 3D reconstruction, tracking and so on. Introduction of different stereo correspondence algorithms can be found in the survey by Scharstern and Szeliski [1] and the one by Brown *et al.* [2].

Because of the noise and ambiguity, stereo correspondence problem is considered to be greatly ill-posed. To achieve a reasonable result, people use some

A. Leonardis, H. Bischof, and A. Pinz (Eds.): ECCV 2006, Part III, LNCS 3953, pp. 201–212, 2006.

assumptions on the scene, one of which is the *smoothness assumption*. This assumption supposes that the disparity map is almost smooth everywhere except at the borders of the objects, or equivalently that the scene is composed of several smooth structures. We formulate stereo algorithms as an energy minimization framework, and impose the smoothness assumption in a smoothness energy function. The optimal disparity map f will minimize the energy function as follow:

$$E(f) = \sum_p E_{data}^p(f_p) + \sum_{\langle p,q \rangle \in \mathcal{N}} E_{smooth}^{p,q}(f_p, f_q) , \qquad (1)$$

where p and q are some points in the image, f_p and f_q are the disparities assigned to them, $E_{data}^p(f_p)$ is the matching energy (error) for point p if assigned with disparity f_p, and $E_{smooth}^{p,q}(f_p, f_q)$ is the smoothness energy that imposes punishment if disparities of two neighboring points are not *smooth*. $\mathcal{N}$ is a neighboring system that contains the pairs of points which need to be imposed with smoothness assumption. The choice of $\mathcal{N}$ is essential because it will affect both the accuracy and efficiency of the algorithm.

In traditional algorithms, e.g. classic dynamic programming methods [3] [4], $\mathcal{N}$ is often chosen within the same scanline (without lost of generality, from now on we use scanline as rectified epipolar line) for imposing the disparity inconsistency punishment. The inter-scanline smoothness is usually ignored or considered in the post-processing procedure. The equivalent neighboring system graph is shown in Fig. 1.b. It is obvious that such asymmetric manner is unnatural and can not receive good performance. Based on this observation, graph-based *global* method (we use the terminology of [1]) has been proposed. In a global method, $\mathcal{N}$ is chosen as a four-connected grid in the image (shown in Fig. 1.a). Except the points on the image borders and corners, each point is connected with its four neighbors. This structure fully uses the correlation between neighboring points, and leads to the state-of-the-art performance [1] [5] [6]. But except for some special cases [7], the four-connected grid structure makes the minimization of the energy function generally NP-hard, and even using approximation methods are still very time-consuming. The traditional simulated annealing [8] algorithm usually takes hours to run, and the recent fast minimization methods, e.g. graph-cuts [6] and belief propagation[5], still need several minutes. They are still far from being in real-time.

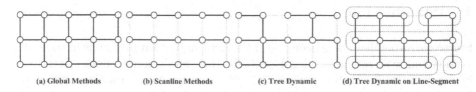

(a) Global Methods   (b) Scanline Methods   (c) Tree Dynamic   (d) Tree Dynamic on Line-Segment

Fig. 1. Effective edges (marked by solid lines) for difference algorithms. In (d), points of each line segment are encircled by a dashed line.

Recently, Veksler [9] proposed a novel approach that connected all the pixels with a tree, and performed the dynamic programming on that tree (see Fig. 1.c). Since more edges are remained, and more importantly, horizontal and vertical edges are chosen in a symmetric style, better performance than classic dynamic programming methods is obtained. When using some special smoothness functin, the complexity of dynamic programming becomes as low as $O(hn)$ [9], supposing h is the number of possible disparities and n is the number of points.

Nevertheless, the performance of dynamic programming methods is still not comparable with that of global methods. We consider this problem by analyzing how much information has been lost in dynamic programming compared with global methods. Suppose the image is in the size of $N \times N$. We can see that the number of edges in Fig. 1.a is about $2N^2$, and in Fig. 1.b and Fig. 1.c the number of *effective*[1] edges has been reduced to about N^2. That is to say, half of the edges are discarded in dynamic programming methods, and much information embodied in these edges is lost. This is the main reason why their performance is apparently worse than global methods. Then our new approach is motivated by how to remain as many effective edges as possible while still utilizing the time efficiency of dynamic programming. This is achieved with the help of color segmentation.

Color segmentation is used in recent years to improve the performance of stereo correspondence in several publications [10] [11] [12] [13], called segment-based approaches. In the surfaces in the scene can be approximated by several slanted planes, better performance is achieved especially on textureless and discontinuity areas. The main assumption they use is that discontinuity may happen at the boundary of a segmented area. All the pixels within a segment are assigned with the same label, which means they must belong to the same plane in the scene. At the same time, we only need one vertex for all the pixels in one segment, which means the scale of the graph is decreased. Besides, segment-based methods commonly use a 3-parameter linear transform label space which can well model slanted planes in the scene.

In our approach, we segment each scanline into several line segments according to the colors of pixels. Pixels in one line segment are assigned with the same label, or we use the line segment as the matching unit. A tree is constructed to connect all segments, and smoothness is imposed in a line segment level. In this way, when the edge connecting two line segments in different scanlines are remained, it is equivalent to remain a number of edges in pixel level. The number of effective edges removed is greatly reduced, as shown in Fig. 1.d. Therefor our algorithm gives a much better approximation to the four-connected grid, and better correspondence result can be achieved. Our experimental results also show that the accuracy of our algorithm is comparable to the global methods, while the algorithm is still very time-efficient. Besides, using the 3-parameter linear transform space, we can well model the slanted plane and give a sub-pixel disparity map as the results. Disparities of the half-occluded area are given a good guess which will be shown in our experimental results in Sect. 4.1.

---

[1] The effective edges mentioned here means the information embodied in those edges are used.

The rest of the paper is organized as follow: Section 2 introduces our formulation of the stereo correspondence problem and how to compose a tree on line segments that can mostly estimate the grid structure. In Sect. 3, we discuss some implementation issues which are also essential to the performance of our algorithm. Experimental results and analysis are given in Sect. 4 and Sect. 5 is the conclusion.

2 Tree Dynamic Programming on Line Segments

In this section, we firstly formulate the stereo correspondence problem into a labelling problem in the line segment level. Then the construction of the tree for dynamic programming, which is the key of our algorithm, is introduced.

2.1 Problem Formulation

We denote the left and right images as I_L and I_R, and choose the left image as the reference image. The color segmentation algorithm, (described in Sect. 3.1 in detail), will segment the scanlines of the image into a set of line segments, denoted as S. Our goal is to assign each line segment $s \in S$ a label $f_s \in \mathcal{L}$, where $\mathcal{L}$ is the set of all possible labels (the label space). Each label in $\mathcal{L}$ represents a correspondence between points in left and right image respectively.

In order to model the slanted plane in the scene, the label space $\mathcal{L}$ is chosen to be a 3-parameter linear transform space:

$$f_s = \langle c_1, c_2, c_3 \rangle \Leftrightarrow$$

$$\forall p \in s, p \overset{\langle c_1, c_2, c_3 \rangle}{\leftrightarrow} p', \text{ with } p'_x = c_1 p_x + c_2 p_y + c_3, \ p'_y = p_y \ ,$$

where p' is a point in the right image, and $p \overset{\langle c_1, c_2, c_3 \rangle}{\leftrightarrow} p'$ means p and p' are corresponding points if assigned by a label $\langle c_1, c_2, c_3 \rangle$.

We formulate the correspondence problem in an energy minimization framework, and the optimal label configuration f_{opt} for line segments S is:

$$f_{opt}(S) = \underset{D(S)}{\arg\min} \sum_s E^s_{data}(f_s) + \sum_{\langle s,t \rangle \in \mathcal{N}} E^{s,t}_{smooth}(f_s, f_t) \ , \qquad (2)$$

where $f(S)$ is the disparity map represented in the line segment level, and $\mathcal{N}$ is the neighboring system in the line segment level. $E^s_{data}(f_s)$ is the data term that measures how well the label f_s agrees with the input image pairs. One simple choice (which is used in our experiment in this paper) is to use the summation of the matching costs of all the points in the segment, i.e.:

$$E^s_{data}(f_s) = \sum_{p \in s} C(p, p'), \ p \overset{f_s}{\leftrightarrow} p', \ p \in I_L, p' \in I_R \ . \qquad (3)$$

We use the combination of trimmed linear function and Potts model as our smoothness energy function $E_{smooth}^{s,t}$:

$$E_{smooth}^{s,t}(f_s, f_t) = v_{st}L_c(s,t) \cdot \begin{cases} s_T^{\lambda,\tau}(f_s, f_t) & FRNT(f_s) \text{ and } FRNT(f_t) \\ s_P(f_s, f_t) & otherwise \end{cases}, \quad (4)$$

where v_{st} is a coefficient which is a descending function of the color difference between s and t, and $L_c(s,t)$ is the length of the boundary shared by s and t. $FRNT(f_s)$ returns whether f_s represents a fronto plane, i.e.:

$$FRNT(\langle c_1, c_2, c_3 \rangle) = \begin{cases} true & c_1 = c_2 = 0 \\ false & otherwise \end{cases}.$$

s_T is the trimmed linear function defined as:

$$s_T^{\lambda,\tau}(\langle 0, 0, c_3^s \rangle, \langle 0, 0, c_3^t \rangle) = \min\{\lambda|c_3^s - c_3^t|, \tau\} .$$

s_P is the Potts smoothness function:

$$s_P(f_s, f_t) = \begin{cases} 0 & f_s = f_t \\ 1 & otherwise \end{cases}.$$

2.2 Constructing the Tree

Selecting the neighboring system $\mathcal{N}$ or constructing the tree is the key of our algorithm.

Let $G(V, E)$ be a graph with vertices V and edges E. Each vertex in V represents a line segment in S. All possible edges in E reflects the connection between two neighboring line segments. In general, G is a graph with many loops inside. Our goal is to find a spanning tree of G, denoted as G^T, to best estimate the full grid graph.

Two criteria for the selection of the optimal tree among all possible ones are used:

1. The line segments connected by a remained edge in the G^T are likely with similar disparities, they are probably belonging to the same region in the image, and
2. The connected line segment pair should have as many neighboring pixels as possible from each other.

The first criterion is similar to the strategy used in [9], which means the neighboring segments with similar color attribution values more likely share the same disparity. The second one assures that the edge that connects line segment pair sharing the longer boundary are preferred to remain in G^T.

Combining above two criteria, we define a weight function w_{st} between two neighboring line segments $\langle s, t \rangle$ as follows:

$$w_{st} = L_{max} - \sigma(\bar{I}_s, \bar{I}_t)L_c(s,t) ,$$

where L_{max} is the length of the longest segment of S in pixels, $\bar{I}_s$ and $\bar{I}_t$ are average colors of the segments s and t respectively, σ is a similarity function which returns a real value between 0 and 1 representing how similar the two colors are. For consecutive segments within the same scanline, $L_c(s,t)$ is 1, and for segments in neighboring scanlines $L_c(s,t) = \min\{s_{max}, t_{max}\} - \max\{s_{min}, t_{min}\}$, where s_{min} and t_{min} are horizontal coordinates of the left ends of segment s and t, and s_{max} and t_{max} are those of the right ends.

After defining the weights for each neighboring line segment pair, we use standard minimum-spanning tree (MST) algorithm, which can be found in any data-structure book, to choose the optimal tree. The complexity is almost linear to the number of segments $|S|$. It can be seen that the MID tree construction algorithm in [9] can be considered as a special case of ours, in which line segments have degenerated to individual points. In their situation, L_{max} and L_c are always 1, and then $w_{pq} = 1 - \sigma(I_p, I_q)$ is proportional to the intensity (or color) difference between two neighboring pixels.

3   Implementation

The flowchart of our algorithm is shown in Fig. 2. Each part is described in detail in the sub-sections.

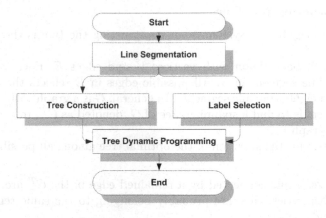

Fig. 2. The flowchart of our LSTDP algorithm

3.1   Line Segmentation

The line segmentation algorithm segments each scanline into several small parts, each of which contains pixels with similar colors. We do not choose some complicated segmentation algorithms, such as mean-shift [14] or normalized cuts [15], because they are not efficient and may become the bottleneck of the whole algorithm. Instead, we design a simple and fast scanline segmentation algorithm.

Our algorithm contains 3 steps as follows:

1. Computing Initialization Marks

   For each image line, we scan the pixels from left to right. Two registers stores the minimum and maximum intensities of the current segment. For color images, the registers are both vectors with three channels. If the difference between the minimum and maximum intensities are greater than a threshold T_{seg}, a mark is put at the current position and two registers are reset. After processing, the points between two marks are considered as one line segment. The maximum intensity difference between pixels within a segment is no more than T_{seg}.

2. Repositioning Marks

   The marks made in the first step may not lay at the accurate edge. So a repositioning procedure is performed. Each mark is moved to the near local maximum of intensity gradients without changing their orders.

3. Removing Isolated Marks

   The image noise often leads to some isolated marks in the image, and makes the image being wrongly segmented. We check each mark and remove those who do not have enough close neighbors in 2D area.

This segmentation method works fast and produces good segmentation in our algorithm. We show the results of segmentation results in Fig. 3.

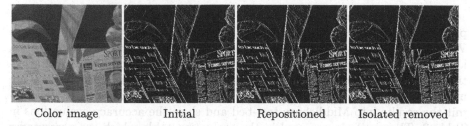

Color image   Initial   Repositioned   Isolated removed

Fig. 3. Results of different steps of the segmentation on the "Venus" image

3.2 Label Selection

The label set $\mathcal{L}$ is first initialized with all possible fronto linear transforms, i.e. $\{\langle 0, 0, -d\rangle | d = 0, \dots, D_{max}\}$.

Then we need to estimate some possible 3-parameter linear transform labels. To do this, we first segment both left and right images. Line segments on two images are matched locally according to their average colors. For each matched line segment pair, whose colors are similar enough, we obtain two matched point pairs(the corresponding ends). This matching is rough and may contains many errors. A robust estimation method, like M-estimators [16], is then used to extract the linear planes by fitting on the sparse correspondences robustly.

3.3 Tree Construction

The algorithm described in Sect. 2.2 is used to construct a tree on the reference image.

3.4 Dynamic Programming

Dynamic programming is performed on the constructed tree to minimize the energy function defined in (2). Readers can find more details in [9]. Using the technology introduced in [17] and [9], our energy function with smoothness energy defined in (4) can be minimized with the complexity of $O(hn)$.

4 Experiments

Our experiments include two parts. First, we perform our algorithm on the testbed of Middlebury University [1], and performance is compared with other algorithms submitted to that testbed. To further test the accuracy and efficiency on the real-time system, we embed our algorithm into a realtime automatic navigation system, in which outdoor image series are processed.

4.1 Experiments on Middlebury dataset

We adopted Birchfield and Tomasi's matching cost [18] which is insensitive to image sampling as $C(p, p')$ in (3). v_{st} in (4) is defined as

$$v_{st} = C_1 + \sigma(\bar{I}_s, \bar{I}_t)C_2$$

All parameters are listed in Table 1, and are used for all image pairs. Computed disparity maps are shown in Fig. 4 accompany with the results from [9]. We also listed the time (in milliseconds) of the different parts of our algorithm, i.e. DSI (Disparity Space Image[1]) computing, line segmentation, label selection, and tree dynamic programming, and the total time in Table 3. They are measured on a computer with an Intel Pentium IV 2.4 GHz processor. We submit the results into Middlebury test-bed and show the accuracy evaluations in Table 2. Three criteria are used in the evaluation table which are percentages of: bad points in *non-occluded* area, in *all* area, and *near discontinuities*. A *bad* point is a point whose absolute disparity error is greater than one [1].

From the evaluation table we can see that our algorithm can achieve overall accuracy comparable with the state-of-the-art global methods (4 out of 13). The result of "venus" is almost equal to the best one. For all the four images, the rank of "all" column of our algorithm, which includes the guessing for half-occluded areas, is better than the other two. That is because we use the line segment as the matching unit, and the disparities of some occluded pixels can be inferred by the disparity of the segment where the occluded pixels belong to. Besides the good performance, our algorithm runs very fast. Processing time for "tsukuba" is only about 160ms, and the other three can be processed within one

Table 1. Parameter values set for experiments for Middlebury image pairs

Parameter	C_1	C_2	λ	τ	T_{seg}
Value	5	75	0.5	1.0	20

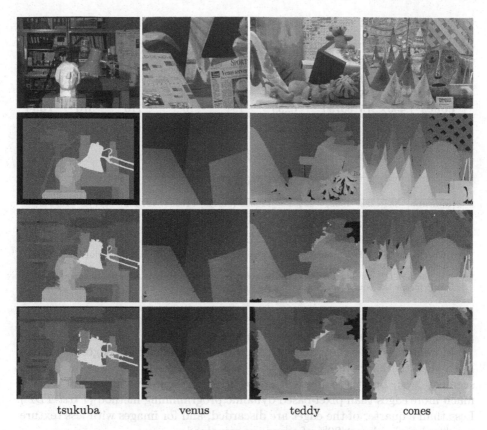

tsukuba   venus   teddy   cones

Fig. 4. Experimental results for Middlebury database. The first row is left images, the second row is ground truth of disparity map, the third row is results by our LSTDP algorithm, and the last row is the results of pixel-based Tree DP method from [9].

Table 2. Accuracy Evaluation Results on Middlebury Stereo Test-bed

Algorithm	Tsukuba			Venus			Teddy			Cones		
	nonocc	all	disc	nonocc	all	disc	nonocc	all	disc	nonocc	all	disc
Sym.BP+occ	0.07_1	1.75_2	$\mathbf{5.09}_1$	$\mathbf{0.10}_1$	0.33_2	$\mathbf{2.19}_1$	6.47_3	10.7_2	17.0_3	4.79_4	10.7_3	10.9_3
Segm+visb	1.30_4	$\mathbf{1.57}_1$	6.92_4	0.79_3	1.06_3	6.76_5	$\mathbf{5.00}_1$	$\mathbf{6.54}_1$	$\mathbf{12.3}_1$	3.72_2	$\mathbf{8.62}_1$	10.2_2
SemiGlob	3.26_9	3.96_8	12.8_{12}	1.00_4	1.57_4	11.3_9	6.02_2	12.2_3	16.3_2	$\mathbf{3.06}_1$	9.75_2	$\mathbf{8.90}_1$
LSTDP	*1.93_6*	*2.59_6*	*9.70_8*	*0.19_2*	*0.26_1*	*2.49_2*	*11.1_6*	*16.4_5*	*23.4_8*	*6.39_7*	*11.8_5*	*13.5_7*
Layered	1.57_5	1.87_3	8.28_5	1.34_6	1.85_5	6.85_6	8.64_4	14.3_4	18.5_4	6.59_8	14.7_8	14.4_8
GC+occ	1.19_2	2.01_5	6.24_2	1.64_8	2.19_8	6.75_4	11.2_7	17.4_7	19.8_5	5.36_6	12.4_7	13.0_6
MultiCamGC	1.27_3	1.99_4	6.48_3	2.79_{10}	3.13_9	3.60_3	12.0_8	17.6_8	22.0_7	4.89_5	11.8_6	12.1_4
TensorVoting	3.79_{10}	4.79_{10}	8.86_6	1.23_5	1.88_6	11.5_{10}	9.76_5	17.0_6	24.0_9	4.38_3	11.4_4	12.2_5
TreeDP	1.99_8	2.84_7	9.96_9	1.41_7	2.10_7	7.74_7	15.9_{10}	23.9_{10}	27.1_{12}	10.0_{10}	18.3_{10}	18.9_{10}
⋮												
SO[1c]	5.08_{12}	7.22_{13}	12.2_{11}	9.44_{12}	10.9_{12}	21.9_{13}	19.9_{13}	28.2_{13}	26.3_{11}	13.0_{13}	22.8_{13}	22.3_{12}

second. From Table 3, we can see that besides the dynamic programming modula, half of the processing time is spent on preprocessing modules, and they can be greatly accelerated with special hardware if necessary. Like other segment-based methods, some artifacts caused by segmentation can be found in the disparity

Table 3. Time Analysis of Our Algorithm on Middlebury Dataset

	Size	$|S|$	Disp. Range	DSI	Line-Segm.	Lab-Sel	Tree-DP	Total
tsukuba	384×288	19621	0..15	30	8	37	88	**163**
venus	434×384	29664	0..19	76	12	89	143	**320**
teddy	450×375	37435	0..59	195	10	359	299	**863**
cones	450×375	50780	0..59	194	16	170	370	**750**

† Unit for all the time (the last 5 columns) in this table is millisecond.

Table 4. Effective edges of three kinds of algorithms

	Size	$|S|$	Global	Pixel-TDP	LSTDP		
					Total	Hard	Soft
tsukuba	384×288	19621	220512	110591 (50.1%)	192517 (87.3%)	90971	101546
venus	434×384	29664	332494	166655 (50.1%)	283241 (85.2%)	136558	146683
teddy	450×375	37435	336675	168749 (50.1%)	274557 (81.6%)	131315	143242
cones	450×375	50780	336675	168749 (50.1%)	259205 (77.0%)	117970	141235

† The percentages of equivalent edges of *Pixel-TDP* and *LSTDP* over full grid(*Global*) are
listed in brackets.
‡ In the *LSTDP* columns, *Hard* means edges connecting pixels within a line segment, and
Soft means the equivalent edges crossing line segments.

map. But this only happens along the scanline direction, because we do not
perform a hard constraint on inter-scanlines.

Moreover, we give the statistics on the numbers of effective edges in Table 4.
Note that the effective edges here are not the edges in the tree on the line
segment level, but the equivalent edges in pixel level. Our algorithm remains
much more edges than pixel-based dynamic programming method (*Pixel-TDP*).
Less than a quarter of the edges are discarded, and for images with less texture,
e.g. "tsukuba", almost 90% of edges are remained.

Left Image   Disparity Map

Fig. 5. Disparity and elevation results in a real-time outdoor automatic navigation
system. The upper row is one of the frame captured on an avenue, and the lower row
is from a country road.

4.2   Results on a Real-Time System

Our algorithm is used in a real-time outdoor stereo system. Because the outdoor images are of relatively higher contrast and for obtaining higher efficiency, the input images are first converted into gray-level images. The dynamic histogram warping algorithm by Cox *et al.* [19] is used to rectify the difference of image capturing. We only use fronto labels and hence label selection is not performed. The size of the input images is 320 × 240, and disparity ranges from 0 to 40. No acceleration hardware is used. Two frames of results are shown in Fig. 5. One is from an avenue environment and the other is from a country road. We can see that our matching results are rather accurate. The system is running on a Dual Intel Xeron 2.4 GHz processor, and the processing time for each frame is only 60–70ms.

5   Conclusion

In this paper, we proposed a fast stereo correspondence algorithm based on line segments using tree dynamic programming. From our preliminary experimental results on both standard image pairs and real image sequences, it can be seen that the performance of our algorithm is comparable to those of state-of-the-art algorithms while our algorithm runs much faster. It can be used in different real-time systems providing high accuracy disparity map.

We will continue our work on this proposed method to further improve the performance of our method. Our future work includes occlusion modelling, new construction rules for the tree, and parallel algorithm for the tree dynamic programming.

References

1. Scharstein, D., Szeliski, R.: A taxonomy and evaluation of dense two-frame stereo correspondence algorithms. Int'l J. Comput. Vision **47**(1) (2002) 7–42 http://cat.middlebury.edu/stereo/.
2. Brown, M.Z., Burschka, D., Hager, G.D.: Advances in computational stereo. IEEE Trans. Pattern Anal. Machine Intell. **25**(8) (2003) 993–1008
3. Baker, H., Binford, T.: Depth from edge and intensity based stereo. In: Int'l Joint Conf. on Artificial Intell. Volume 2 of 20-26. (1981) 384–390
4. Cox, I., Hingorani, S., Rao, S., Maggs, B.: A maximum likelyhood stereo algorithm. Computer Vision, Graphics and Image Processing **25**(8) (2003) 993–1008
5. Sun, J., Li, Y., Kang, S.B., Shum, H.Y.: Symmetric stereo matching for occlusion handling. In: Proc. IEEE Int'l Conf. on Computer Vision and Pattern Recognition. Volume 2. (2005) 399–406
6. Kolmogorov, V., Zabih, R.: Computing visual correspondence with occlusions using graph cuts. In: Proc. IEEE Int'l Conf. on Computer Vision. Volume 2. (2001) 508–515
7. Roy, S.: Stereo without epipolar lines: A maximum-flow formulation. Int'l J. Comput. Vision **24**(2/3) (1999) 147–161

8. Geman, S., Geman, D.: Gibbs distributions, and the baysian restoration of images. IEEE Trans. Pattern Anal. Machine Intell. **6** (1984) 721–741

9. Veksler, O.: Stereo correspondenc by dynamic programming on a tree. In: Proc. IEEE Int'l Conf. on Computer Vision and Pattern Recognition. Volume 2 of 20-26. (2005) 384–390

10. Tao, H., Sawhney, H.S., Kumar, R.: A global matching framework for stereo computation. In: Proc. IEEE Int'l Conf. on Computer Vision. Volume 1. (2001) 532–539

11. Wei, Y., Quan, L.: Region-based progressive stereo matching. In: Proc. IEEE Int'l Conf. on Computer Vision and Pattern Recognition. Volume 1. (2004) 106–113

12. Hong, L., Chen, G.: Segment-based stereo matching using graph cuts. In: Proc. IEEE Int'l Conf. on Computer Vision and Pattern Recognition. Volume 1. (2004) 74–81

13. Deng, Y., Yang, Q., Lin, X., Tang, X.: A symmetric patch-based correspondence model for occlusion handling. In: Proc. IEEE Int'l Conf. on Computer Vision. Volume II., Beijing, China, 2005 (2005) 1316–1322

14. Comaniciu, D., Meer, P.: Robust analysis of feature spaces: Color image segmentation. In: Proc. IEEE Int'l Conf. on Computer Vision and Pattern Recognition, Puerto Rico (1997) 750–755

15. Shi, J., Malik, J.: Normalized cuts and image segmentation. IEEE Trans. Pattern Anal. Machine Intell. **22**(8) (2000) 888–905

16. Stewart, C.V.: Robust parameter estimation in computer vision. SIAM Reviews **41**(3) (1999) 513–537

17. Felzenszwalb, P.F., Huttenlocher, D.P.: Efficient belief propagation for early vision. In: Proc. IEEE Int'l Conf. on Computer Vision and Pattern Recognition. Volume 1. (2004) 261–268

18. Birchfield, S., Tomasi, C.: A pixel dissimilarity measure that is insensitive to image sampling. IEEE Trans. Pattern Anal. Machine Intell. **20**(4) (1998) 401–406

19. Cox, I.J., Roy, S., Hingorani, S.L.: Dynamic histogram warping of image pairs for constant image brightness. In: Proc. Int'l Conf. on Image Processing. Volume II. (1995) 366–369

Describing and Matching 2D Shapes by Their Points of Mutual Symmetry*

Arjan Kuijper[1] and Ole Fogh Olsen[2]

[1] RICAM, Linz, Austria
arjan.kuijper@oeaw.ac.at
[2] IT-University of Copenhagen, Denmark
fogh@itu.dk

Abstract. A novel shape descriptor is introduced. It groups pairs of points that share a geometrical property that is based on their mutual symmetry. The descriptor is visualized as a diagonally symmetric diagram with binary valued regions. This diagram is a fingerprint of global symmetry between pairs of points along the shape. The descriptive power of the method is tested on a well-known shape data base containing several classes of shapes and partially occluded shapes. First tests with simple, elementary matching algorithms show good results.

1 Introduction

One method to describe 2D objects is by their outlines, or shapes. The complicated task of comparing objects then changes to comparing shapes. With a suitable representation, this task can be simplified. Several representations of shapes have been investigated in order to be able to perform this comparison efficiently and effectively. One of the earliest representations is Blum's biologically motivated skeleton [1]. As Kimia points out [2], there is evidence that humans use this type of representation.

Research on skeleton-based methods has been carried out in enormous extent ever since, see e.g. [3, 4]. The Shock Graph approach [5] has lead to a shape descriptor that can perform the comparison task very well [4, 6, 7]. This method depends on results obtained from the so-called Symmetry Set [8, 9], a super set of the Medial Axis. In these cases, the shape is probed with circles tangent to it at at least two places. The Symmetry Set is obtained as the centres of all these circles, while the Medial Axis is the sub set containing only maximal circles.

From the field of robotics, probing shapes is also of interest. Blake et al. [10, 11] describe a grasping method by the set of points that are pair wise parallel. At such a pair a parallel jaw gripper can grasp the object. These points form

---

* This work was supported by the European Union project DSSCV (IST-2001-35443).
A.K. acknowledges for funding the Johann Radon Institute (RICAM) of the ÖAW, the Austrian Science Funding Agencies FWF, through the Wittgenstein Award (2000) of Peter Markowich, and FFG, through the Research & Development Project 'Analyse Digitaler Bilder mit Methoden der Differenzialgleichungen'.

A. Leonardis, H. Bischof, and A. Pinz (Eds.): ECCV 2006, Part III, LNCS 3953, pp. 213–225, 2006.

the union of the Symmetry Set and a set they called anti-Symmetry Set, as it is closely related to the symmetry set [12].

In this work, we combine the ideas of these two fields of shape analysis by investigating the set of pairs of points at which a circle is tangent to the shape. We do not consider the centre of the circle, but the combination of the two points. A geometric method is given to derive the pairs of points, based on a zero crossing argument. Therefore, to each pair of points a signed value can be assigned, yielding a matrix of values $(-1, 0, 1)$.

This matrix is then used as a shape descriptor. Its properties and allowed changes follow directly from the Symmetry Set, just as in the Shock Graph method. Next, a simple comparison algorithm is introduced to perform the task of object comparison. For this purpose, the two matrices for each pair of objects are set to equal dimensions and the normalised inner product is taken as equivalence measure. This procedure is tested on two data bases containing objects in different classes, where some objects are occluded or noisy. Given the simplicity of the algorithm, results are promising and main erroneous results are due to the algorithm, showing the potential power of the representation.

2   Problem Framework and Definitions

The Medial Axis can be defined as the closure of the loci of the maximal circles tangent to a shape (see e.g. [9]). This somewhat abstract formulation can be made clear by investigation of Figure 1a. A circle with radius r is tangent to a shape at two points. The unit length normal vectors (N_1 and N_2) of the circle and the shape coincide. The centre of the circle is a Medial Axis point, that is found by multiplying each normal vector with $-r$ and taking the tangency point as tail of the vector $-rN_i$. As there are for each point several combinations satisfying this tangency argument[1], the set is taken for with $-r$ is maximal, i.e. the set with the smallest radius.

The two points can be found using geometrical arguments [8], see Fig. 1b. Take an arbitrary origin point and let p_1 and p_2 be vectors pointing to the two locations of tangency. Then $p_1 - p_2$ is a vector pointing from one tangency point to the other. From the construction of the circle as described before, the vector $-rN_1 + rN_2$ (and when normal vectors are pointing inward and outward $-rN_1 - rN_2$) is parallel to $p_1 - p_2$. Consequently $(p_1 - p_2).(N_1 \pm N_2) = 0$ for these two points. Let a shape be continuously parameterised then for each point p several points q_j can be found for which

$$(p - q_j).(N(p) \pm N(q_j)) = 0 \tag{1}$$

where $N(.)$ denotes the normal vector. Note that if the normal vectors are parallel, the inner product is zero as well. Such points are the anti-Symmetry Set points described by Blake et al. [10, 11] for the parallel jaw gripper. If the shape

---

[1] It can be shown that for each point there are at least two other points [8]. Constellations with tangency normal vectors pointing inside and outside can occur [9].

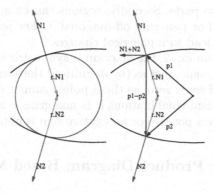

Fig. 1. a) A pair of tangency points that gives rise to a Medial Axis point. b) The constellation of position and normal vectors is special at such points.

is parameterised by N points $(p_1, p_2, \ldots, p_N)$, then the tangency pairs are found as the zero crossings of Eq. 1. To find these zero crossings, it suffices to look at the square sign of inner product diagram $P(i, j)$ of the signed values of Eq.1:

$$P(i, j) = \text{sign} \left[(p_i - p_j).(N_i \pm N_j) \right] \qquad (2)$$

In Figure 2 a fish shape is shown, together with its sign of inner product diagram. When actual zero crossings are computed, i.e. when the boundaries of the regions in such a diagram are taken, one obtains a so-called pre-Symmetry Set that is used to derive the distinct branches of the Symmetry Set [8, 13]. The possible changes of these boundaries when the shape changes, are known [14] and relate to the possible changes of the Medial Axis [9].

Changes in the shape lead to movement of the boundaries and therefore to changes of areas. Topological changes fall apart into two classes: Firstly, boundaries can meet and establish a different connection when a white (or black) region

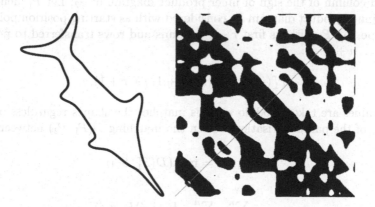

Fig. 2. a) A fish shape. b) Sign of inner product diagram for the fish shape.

is locally split into two parts. Secondly, regions can be annihilated or created, either on the diagonal or pair-wise off-diagonal. Other possible changes of the Symmetry Set do not lead to topological changes.

As may be clear from Eq. 2, the diagram is symmetric in the diagonal. It can be identified with the shape, just as (by definition) the axes of the diagram. The values on the diagonal equal zero, as these points cannot be evaluated in Eq. 1. Second, on all other point combinations it is non-generic to encounter exactly a zero-crossing, so either a positive or a negative sign is obtained.

3   Sign of Inner Product Diagram Based Matching

The task of comparing objects has now become the task of comparing diagrams. If the parameterisations of two shapes consist of the same amount of points n, the corresponding sign of inner product diagrams can be multiplied element wise with each other. If the shapes are identical and the parameterisations are equal, this inner product equals $n(n-1)$, since the diagonal consists of n points.

If the parameterisations are taken at a different starting position, so that $p_i = q_{i+\alpha}$, rotated version of the sign of inner product diagram should be taken into account. This rotation takes place in horizontal and vertical directions simultaneously, as $P(i,j) = Q(i+\alpha, j+\alpha)$, values taken modulo n. So to validate each possible starting position, n instances need to be compared.

Finally, the number of points for both shapes need not be equal. If the difference is m rows (and columns), a method must be chosen that removes m rows and columns. One choice is to remove them equally spread over the largest sign of inner product diagram. This relates to removing a set of equidistant points along shape with the largest number of points. It can be regarded as a re-parameterisation of the shape with the largest number of points.

Now let two shapes S_1, S_2 be parameterised with n_1 and n_2 points. Assume without loss of generality $n_1 \leq n_2$. The sign of inner product diagram of S_2 is denoted by P_1. Let $n = n_1$ and $m = n_2 - n_1$. Build P_2 by removing each $(\frac{m}{n_2})^{th}$ row and column of the sign of inner product diagram of S_2. Let P_1^r denote the sign of inner product diagram P_1 considered with as starting position point r on the shape, i.e. P_1 with its first $r-1$ columns and rows transferred to positions $n+1, \ldots, n+r-1$:

$$P_1^r(i,j) = P_1(i-r+1, j-r+1),$$

where values are taken modulo n. This matches the shapes regardless of begin position of the parameterisations. Then the matching $D(P_1, P_2)$ between S_1, S_2 is set as

$$D(S_1, S_2) = \max_r (D(S_1^r, S_2)) \tag{3}$$

with

$$D(S_1^r, S_2) = \frac{\sum_{i=1}^{n} \sum_{j=1}^{n} P_1^r(i,j) P_2(i,j)}{n(n-1)} - \frac{m}{2n_2} \tag{4}$$

The first term in Eq. 4 denotes the weighted equality of the two sign of inner product diagram P_1^r, P_2. Perfect match is given by 1, while a complete mismatch equals -1 and a random match 0. The second term penalises the difference in number of points in a parameterisation, as this difference is ignored in the first term by construction. Adding this penalty is motivated by the way the shapes are obtained, viz. as the outlines of standardised binary images. Therefore, the number of points relates to the complexity of the shape.

4 Data Base Matching

As first test set 41 shapes from an online data base are taken[2]. They form three classes: fishes, planes, and tools. Some fishes and planes are artificially drawn, and form inter class instances. The results of matching all shapes with each

Fig. 3. Matching of fishes, tools, and planes

---

[2] http://www.lems.brown.edu/vision/researchAreas/SIID/

other can be seen in Figure 3. For each shape, the best eight matches are shown:
The first column has score zero, as each shape matches to itself without difference. The second column gives the second best match, etc.

The matching is consistent with [15], where this database is introduced. One
can see, for instance, that tools match to tools, and that the wrenches and double
wrenches match to the correct set. The erroneous matches – the appearances of
shapes of a different class – occur at a match $D = .5$ or less. These errors can

Table 1. Score of inter-class matches

class	score
1	11,11,11,11,11,11,11,8,6,7,1
2	11,11,9,10,8,6,8,5,4,5,2
3	11,10,10,10,10,10,9,8,9,7,2
4	11,11,11,10,10,8,9,10,7,6,3
5	11,10,9,9,7,8,1,2,0,3,6
6	11,11,11,11,11,11,11,11,11,11,11
7	11,11,11,10,10,8,6,8,2,3,3
8	11,10,10,11,9,9,9,8,7,3,2
9	11,11,11,11,11,11,11,11,11,11,11

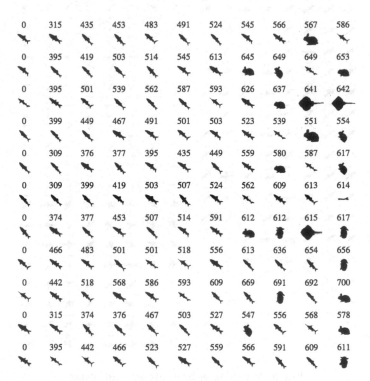

Fig. 4. Class 1

Fig. 5. Classes 2 and 3

visually be explained: A coarse plane "looks" more like a fish with two big fins than a very detailed plane.

Next, this approach is used on the data base used by Sebastian et al. [16]. This data base contains 9 classes with 11 shapes each. Some of the shapes are occluded or deformed versions of another shape in the class. Just as in [16], a score $D^*(S_1, S_2)$ is set to be a non-negative number, ranging towards 1000. This is achieved by taking (recall Eq. 3)

$$D^*(S_1, S_2) = 1000(1 - D(S_1, S_2)) \tag{5}$$

Now 0 denotes a perfect match and values towards 1000 a random match. The results per class are shown in Figs. 4-8. We have chosen to show all results, as this better reveals the potential of matching methodology.

In each of the figures, the first column resembles the shape matched with itself, resulting in a score of 0. The next 10 columns give the second to eleventh best match. Ideally, this would be shapes from the same class. The score of each shape is taken as an eleven dimensional vector with each value being zero or one. A one at position i denotes a shape at the ith position that belongs to the same class, while a zero denotes a shape of a different class. The total class score is then given as the sum of the eleven vectors in the class, ideally being a vector containing 11 elevens. Table 1 gives these results.

5   Discussion of Results

Table 1 shows that some classes (6 and 9) yield a perfect score. Other classes contain matchings to objects of other classes. For some this occurs at higher positions, but in three cases already the second best match is wrong.

All these cases are caused by the choice of the matching algorithm, the removal of equidistant points. This is strongest visible in the third class, bottom of Fig. 5. The 9th row introduces a shape that has a large occlusion. This relates to removing a set of neighbouring points along the shape instead of the taken approach. An indication that "something is wrong" is given by the high cost for the second best match (620), compared to the other second best matches in this class (≤ 269). Is introduces a complete row of wrong matches.

A similar effect, albeit in the opposite way, occurs in the fifth class, bottom of Fig. 6. The third row shows an occluded hand, which relates to a local addition of a set of neighbouring points along the shape. Again a high cost for the second best match is obtained. Assuming only equidistant removal of points, however, the second best match is visually correct. The fingers correspond to the four legs of the cow, while the blown-up thumb relates to the cow's head and body. The same thing can be said about the occluded rabbit in class 8, top of Fig. 8.

Obviously, the human classification is not perfectly mimicked by the algorithm. The total amount of errors compared to the human observer classification is given by $(0, 3, 6, 6, 12, 17, 24, 28, 42, 43, 58)$. If the three most clear occlusion-caused outliers are left out, this is $(0, 0, 3, 5, 9, 15, 22, 25, 39, 41, 56)$.

As a way to avoid the removal of points in one of the sign of inner product diagram, one can obtain a parameterisation of exactly n points. This results in more or less the same outcome, since it still does not take into account the effects of occlusion. Secondly, forcing a standard number of points along the

Fig. 6. Classes 4 and 5

Fig. 7. Classes 6 and 7

shape wipes out the complexity of shape, so the matching actually yields worse results.

First attempts have been made in order to remove a set of $\frac{m}{n_2}$ locally neighbouring points. For the occluded human figure, this yielded a better matching to other human shapes. It is, however, computationally very expensive implemented. To compare two shapes takes approximately tens of minutes, compared

0	124	318	353	358	404	441	446	556	578	585
0	537	556	575	580	583	584	592	637	642	649
0	490	505	549	577	600	602	635	671	685	689
0	124	338	362	379	430	448	520	537	547	554
0	505	561	587	591	615	632	642	686	689	700
0	310	318	338	362	379	449	491	505	592	613
0	338	338	358	439	469	494	567	587	601	606
0	446	449	494	498	520	561	561	590	614	615
0	425	430	441	491	514	549	551	560	575	590
0	353	366	379	379	425	469	561	583	589	629
0	310	366	404	439	448	498	514	584	591	608
0	189	193	219	330	417	456	515	533	573	578
0	189	225	262	320	373	406	438	489	493	502
0	219	225	228	337	339	395	438	457	459	471
0	255	393	406	413	427	438	453	455	456	484
0	193	228	262	278	393	445	519	549	577	592
0	160	230	243	266	455	471	502	505	577	578
0	160	230	259	293	453	459	493	497	573	592
0	216	228	259	266	337	373	413	417	445	478
0	255	278	320	330	339	478	497	505	520	535
0	216	243	287	293	395	438	484	515	519	520
0	228	230	230	287	427	457	489	533	535	549

Fig. 8. Classes 8 and 9

to several seconds in the equidistant case. However, as the optimal match is a summation of a set of multiplications, a fast dynamic program may be available. In this case the task would be to find a shortest manifold in 4D.

6   Summary and Conclusions

A new shape descriptor is introduced. It is based on pairs of points on the shape that lie on a circle that is tangent to the shape at these points. It is therefore closely related to both Medial Axis and Symmetry Set methods. Each point on the shape is compared to all other points on the shape regarding a geometrical relation. Based on this, to each pair of points a value +1 or −1 is assigned. This yields an efficient data structure.

Secondly, shapes can be compared using this data structure. As test, a general data base [16] was used, containing shapes in different classes. Some of the shapes are severely occluded. To compare two data structures, the used approach removed a set of equidistant points along the shape, thus enforcing two shapes parameterised with the same number of points. This allows simple comparison of two data structures.

Although this matching assumption is very general and a priori not suited for occluded shapes, results were relatively good. The comparison of two shapes can be done in few seconds, using non-optimised Mathematica code. Some shape classes were completely correct classified, while other had a correct score for most of the shapes. The shapes that significantly scored bad were shapes with a large blocked occlusion, or with a locally removed part. These parts cannot be matched correctly by definition with the used method. We note that these deformed shapes give a relatively simple different Medial Axis. Secondly, we only matched one shape to another, allowing the changes to appear in only one shape. In general, the matching involves changes to both shapes, for example in matching the hands of class 5 (see Fig. 6, bottom) with different occluded fingers.

An obvious amendment of the matching algorithm is the possibility of removing a set of neighbouring points. This will solve the problem of occluded parts, both where a part of the shape is removed, and where a part (a block) is added. Second, the method is to be designed to find the optimal solution allowing both data structures to be changed. As the optimal match is a summation of a series of multiplications, a fast shortest-path based dynamic program may be available to incorporate these two amendments simultaneously.

References

1. Blum, H.: Biological shape and visual science (part i). Journal of Theoretical Biology **38** (1973) 205–287
2. Kimia, B.: On the role of medial geometry in human vision. Journal of Physiology - Paris **97** (2003) 155–190
3. Ogniewicz, R.L., Kübler, O.: Hierarchic voronoi skeletons. Pattern Recognition **28** (1995) 343–359

4. Sebastian, T., Kimia, B.B.: Curves vs. skeletons in object recognition. Signal Processing **85** (2005) 247–263
5. Siddiqi, K., Kimia, B.: A shock grammar for recognition. Proceedings CVPR '96 (1996) 507–513
6. Sebastian, T., Klein, P., Kimia, B.B.: Recognition of shapes by editing shock graphs. IEEE Transactions on Pattern Analysis and Machine Intelligence **26** (2004) 550–571
7. Pelillo, M., Siddiqi, K., Zucker, S.: Matching hierarchical structures using association graphs. IEEE Transactions on Pattern Analysis and Machine Intelligence **21** (1999) 1105–1120
8. Bruce, J.W., Giblin, P.J., Gibson, C.: Symmetry sets. Proceedings of the Royal Society of Edinburgh **101** (1985) 163–186
9. Giblin, P.J., Kimia, B.B.: On the local form and transitions of symmetry sets, medial axes, and shocks. International Journal of Computer Vision **54** (2003) 143–156
10. Blake, A., Taylor, M., Cox, A.: Grasping visual symmetry. Proceedings Fourth International Conference on Computer Vision (1993) 724–733
11. Blake, A., Taylor, M.: Planning planar grasps of smooth contours. Proceedings IEEE International Conference on Robotics and Automation (1993) 834–839 vol.2
12. Kuijper, A., Olsen, O.: On extending symmetry sets for 2D shapes. In: Proceedings of S+SSPR. (2004) 512–520 LNCS 3138.
13. Kuijper, A., Olsen, O., Giblin, P., Bille, P., Nielsen, M.: From a 2D shape to a string structure using the symmetry set. In: Proceedings of the 8th European Conference on Computer Vision. Volume II. (2004) 313–326 LNCS 3022.
14. Kuijper, A., Olsen, O.: Transitions of the pre-symmetry set. In: Proceedings of the 17th International Conference on on Pattern Recognition. Volume III. (2004) 190–193
15. Sharvit, D., Chan, J., Tek, H., Kimia, B.: Symmetry-based indexing of image databases. Journal of Visual Communication and Image Representation **9** (1998) 366–380
16. Sebastian, T., Klein, P., Kimia, B.B.: Recognition of shapes by editing shock graphs. In: Proceedings of the 8th ICCV. (2001) 755–762

Oriented Visibility for Multiview Reconstruction

V. Lempitsky[1], Y. Boykov[2], and D. Ivanov[1]

[1] Department of Mathematics,
Moscow State University,
Moscow, Russia
{vitya, dvi}@fit.com.ru
[2] Department of Computer Science,
The University of Western Ontario,
London, ON, Canada
yuri@csd.uwo.ca

Abstract. Visibility estimation is arguably the most difficult problem in dense 3D reconstruction from multiple arbitrary views. In this paper, we propose a simple new approach to estimating visibility based on position and orientation of local surface patches. Using our concept of *oriented visibility*, we present a new algorithm for multiview reconstruction based on exact global optimization of surface photoconsistency using graph cuts on a CW-complex. In contrast to many previous methods for 3D reconstruction from arbitrary views, our method does not depend on initialization and is robust to photometrically difficult situations.

Keywords: multiview reconstruction, image-based modeling, visibility, dense stereo, graph cuts, directed graphs, CW-complex, global optimization.

1 Introduction

A multiview reconstruction is a problem of inferring a 3D shape of a scene from a set of its 2D views. In a sequel, we assume that these views are registered within the global world coordinate system, i.e. for each point in the world space, it is possible to determine the coordinates of its projection onto each view.

Recent advances in multiview reconstruction are by far concerned with discrete optimization methods. Such methods (graph cuts [5], belief propagation[12], tree-reweighted message passing [19]) allow efficient minimization of a specific class of energies that can be associated with Markov random fields (MRF). These methods do not require initialization and converge to strong minima of the energy functionals; in particular, graph cuts are able to find a globally optimal labelling for a wide class of binary-labelled MRFs [10]. Due to all these benefits, approaches based on discrete optimization methods are now considered as state-of-the-art for several special cases of multiview reconstruction, namely, reconstruction from a stereo pair [8], from a set of views with similar viewing directions [9, 11], and from a set of views with controlled background [16].

A. Leonardis, H. Bischof, and A. Pinz (Eds.): ECCV 2006, Part III, LNCS 3953, pp. 226–238, 2006.

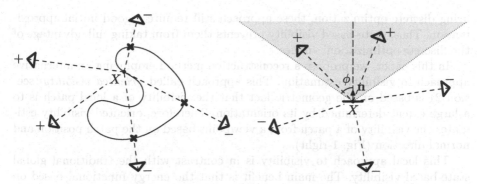

Fig. 1. Two approaches to visibility approximation. Left — *state-based visibility*: a current global scene configuration is used to estimate the visibility for a point X on its surface. Right — *oriented visibility*: a local patch (X, n) is considered visible from the viewpoints within the predefined angle from the normal direction n.

In this paper, we consider the most general case of multiview reconstruction, i.e. reconstruction from the views observing the scene from the arbitrarily distributed viewpoints. Only this case allows to infer the complete shape of an object and therefore is the most interesting for many applications. Unfortunately, this case is the most difficult, as any matching process between views has to reason explicitly about *visibility* of different scene parts in different views.

To estimate the true visibility of some surface element one needs to know the true scene geometry and vice versa. To solve this chicken-and-egg problem, it is necessary to use some approximation of visibility. Current approaches (space carving [7], level sets stereo [4]) reconstruct the scene geometry during iterative process, and at each moment of time, a point is considered visible from a viewpoint if it is not occluded with current scene configuration (Fig. 1-left). We call this approach *state-based visibility*, as the visibility is determined by the current state of the scene.

Using iterative optimization results in a significant problem: iterative updates are not guaranteed to converge to the globally optimal configuration. This convergence essentially depends on the initialization and/or on the threshold values. The problem with convergence is worsened by the fact that if the current scene state is far from the true state, state-based visibility approximates the true visibility with significant errors.

The convergence problem could be solved by the application of discrete optimization. Unfortunately, state-based visibility results in an energy function that models interaction between distant scene parts, and discrete optimization methods become really inefficient for such energies with long-range dependence. One possible way to get rid of long-range dependence and to apply discrete optimization is proposed in [15, 17, 18]. There, the reconstruction is initialized with some given-from-aside approximation, and the state-based visibility is calculated based on this approximation. As the true surface is assumed to be close to the initialization, the energy function ignores the visibility changes and is, therefore, short-range dependent and suitable for discrete optimization. Though using discrete optimization, these approach still require a good initial approximation. Thus, state-based visibility prevents them from taking full advantage of the discrete optimization' virtues.

In this paper, we propose a reconstruction method employing an alternative approach to visibility estimation. This approach called *oriented visibility* (section 2) is based on the geometric fact that the visibility of a local patch is to a large extent determined by its orientation. Therefore, oriented visibility estimates the visibility of a patch from a viewpoint based on the patch position and normal direction (Fig. 1-right).

This local approach to visibility is in contrast with the traditional global state-based visibility. The main benefit is that the energy functional based on this visibility estimate (formulated in section 3) is amenable for efficient discrete minimization with graph cuts (section 4), which yield its global minimum. From the application standpoint, the key advantage of our method is its ability to find the globally optimal (with respect to the reconstruction functional) scene configuration within given bounding volume without any initialization.

Both state-based visibility (global) and oriented visibility (local) are not exact. We argue, however, that in the situation when no good initialization is given, our reconstruction method based on oriented visibility is a good choice. At the very least, it can be used to supply an initial guess to any of the reconstruction methods relying on state-based visibility; due to their dependency on initialization, this would greatly promote their convergence to the correct scene state. We also briefly discuss an alternative iterative reconstruction method, which fuses state-based and oriented visibilities (section 5). The results of our approach on real and synthetic imagery are demonstrated in section 6, and the discussion of its perspectives in section 7 concludes the paper.

2   Oriented Visibility

To formalize the idea of oriented visibility, we need to introduce some notations. We assume, that the whole scene (or its part we are interested in) is located within some bounding volume $\mathcal{B}$. Each allowed scene configuration is characterized by some occupied subvolume $M \subset \mathcal{B}$ with the piecewise-smooth oriented boundary ∂M (the *scene surface*).

Let us assume that the scene is observed by N views, taken with pinhole cameras with viewpoints $p_1, p_2, \ldots p_N$. The positions, orientations, and intrinsic parameters of the cameras are assumed known. Consequently, each point $X \in \mathcal{B}$ can be projected onto each view. Then, let $c_1(X), c_2(X), \ldots c_N(X)$ be the colors of the projections (either grayscale intensities or RGB triples). Let also $v_1(X), v_2(X), \ldots v_N(X)$ be the vectors representing normalized viewing directions from X to p_i:

$$v_i(X) = \frac{p_i - X}{\|p_i - X\|} . \tag{1}$$

Let (X, n) denote an infinitesimal *patch* located at point X and having outward looking normal n. Then the scene surface ∂M can be regarded as a union

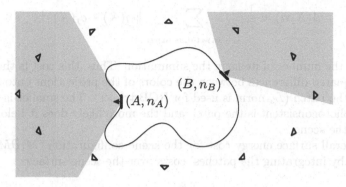

Fig. 2. Oriented visibility in action. Note, that the shown oriented visibility corresponding to the value $\phi = 60°$ is correct for patch (A, n_A) but underestimates visibility for patch (B, n_B).

of patches $(X, n_{\partial M})$, where X lies on ∂M and $n_{\partial M}$ is an outward normal to ∂M at X.

Let $\alpha_1(X, n), \alpha_2(X, n), \ldots \alpha_M(X, n)$ be the binary variables indicating the visibility of a patch (X, n) in the corresponding view. Then, orientation-based α_i is calculated as

$$\alpha_i(X, n) = \begin{cases} 1, & \text{if } \angle\Big(v_i(X), n\Big) < \phi \\ 0, & \text{otherwise} \end{cases}, \quad (2)$$

where ϕ is some acute angle (Fig. 1-right).

Thus, our approximation of visibility reflects the fact that the surface element will be always self-occluded for the viewpoints behind it and frequently self-occluded for the viewpoints observing it from oblique angles. The angle ϕ, therefore, determines the threshold of obliqueness, below which the observation from the viewpoint is considered unreliable. Setting ϕ small allows to estimate visibility correctly for concave parts of a scene, while setting it large allows to involve more cameras and hence to increase the discriminative power of our photoconsistency measure (Fig. 2). In our experiments, we found $\phi \approx 60°$ to suit a large variety of scenes and adhered to this value.

3 Energetic Formulation

The goal of this section is to render a multiview reconstruction as an energy minimization problem by assigning an energy cost based on oriented visibility to each scene configuration. As do most other approaches, we assume that the surface of the unknown scene is nearly lambertian, i.e. the color of some small patch on its surface is independent on the viewpoint it is observed from.

Under this assumption, patches belonging to the true surface should have similar colors in the viewpoints observing them (be *photoconsistent*). Therefore, the energy cost $A(X, n)$ of a patch can be defined as:

$$A(X, n) = \frac{1}{T} \sum_{\cdots \cdot (\cdot \, \cdot n)=1 \cdots \cdot (\cdot \, \cdot n)=1} \|c_i(X) - c_j(X)\|^2 , \qquad (3)$$

where T is the number of items in the summation. Thus, this cost is the mean of pairwise squared differences between the colors of the projections onto the views observing the patch (L_2-norm is used for RGB triples). The smaller is this cost, the more photoconsistent is the patch and the more likely does it belong to the surface of the scene.

The overall surface energy cost for the scene configuration $(M, \partial M)$ is then calculated by integrating the patches' costs over the scene surface:

$$\mathbf{E_I}(\partial M) = \iint_{\partial M} A(X, n_{\partial M}) \, dS . \qquad (4)$$

Now, we have expressed the surface photoconsistency with an energy term $\mathbf{E_I}(\partial M)$. Minimizing $\mathbf{E_I}(\partial M)$ solely is, however, uninteresting as it has an obvious global minimum $(M, \partial M) = \emptyset$ that equals zero. In fact, it has been demonstrated in [7] that in the absence of noise, the scene configuration consistent with a given set of views is not unique, and there is a continuous family of such configurations. Therefore, reconstruction based solely on photoconsistency is an ill-posed problem.

To regularize it, we propose to augment the energy functional with a regularization term $\mathbf{E_R}(M) = \iiint_M B(X) \, dV$. Here, $B(X)$ is some volume potential corresponding to the prior tendency for point X to belong or not to the reconstruction. E.g., constant negative $B(X)$ produces monotonic ballooning effect biasing the reconstruction process towards larger reconstructions. This simple potential can be used if no prior knowledge is available. It is also possible to introduce boundary conditions in the problem by setting $B(X)$ to large positive or negative values near the boundary. In our experiments, we used the combination of the ballooning potential and the potential encoding the boundary conditions (more details are given in Section 6). An interesting option is to construct $B(X)$ based on the information about background in a way analogous to [16]. Finally, $B(X)$ can encode some prior domain-specific knowledge about the scene geometry.

In conclusion of this section, let us write down the full energy functional guiding the reconstruction:

$$\mathbf{E}(M, \partial M) = \mathbf{E_I}(\partial M) + \mathbf{E_R}(M) = \iint_{\partial M} A(X, n_{\partial M}) \, dS + \iiint_M B(X) \, dV . \qquad (5)$$

4   Energy Minimization

4.1   Problem Discretization

To make the minimization of functional (5) tractable, we discretize our problem. The bounding volume $\mathcal{B}$ is subdivided into polyhedral cells $R_1, R_2, \dots R_K$

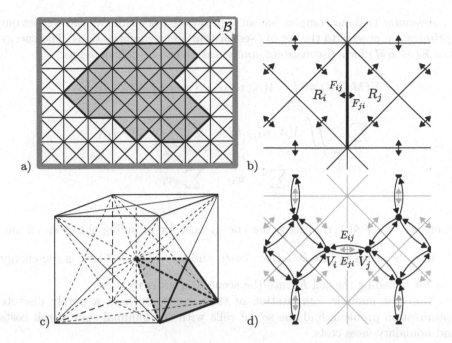

Fig. 3. Discrete optimization of our energy. **a)** A bounding volume $\mathcal{B}$ is discretized into a complex $\mathcal{C}$. One of the $\mathcal{C}$-consistent configurations is shaded. **b)** The local structure of our complex. Two adjacent cells R_i and R_j are separated with a pair of oriented faces F_{ij} and F_{ji}. **c)** The cells of our three-dimensional complex produced by voxel subdivision. One of the cells is emphasized. **d)** Local structure of the graph $\mathcal{G}$ dual to the complex from b). The vertices V_i and V_j dual to the cells R_i and R_j are connected with two directed n-links E_{ij} and E_{ji} dual to the faces F_{ij} and F_{ji} (t-links are not shown).

(Fig. 3a). Each pair of neighboring cells R_i and R_j is considered to be separated with a pair of oriented polygonal faces – F_{ij} separating R_j from R_i and F_{ji} separating R_i from R_j (Fig. 3b). We denote an outward looking normal to F_{ij} directed towards R_j as n_{ij}. We will refer to our discretization structure $\{R_i, F_{ij}\}$ as *complex* (borrowing this term from algebraic geometry where similar structures are called 'CW-complexes').

Given a particular complex $\mathcal{C}$, we may introduce the notion of $\mathcal{C}$-consistent scene configuration (Fig. 3a). We call the scene configuration $(M, \partial M)$ *consistent with complex $\mathcal{C}$* (or, simply, $\mathcal{C}$-consistent) if M is composed from the cells of the complex:

$$M = \bigsqcup_{k=1..Q} R_i. \tag{6}$$

Then, the boundary ∂M consists of oriented faces, separating a cell not belonging to M from a cell within M:

$$\partial M = \bigsqcup_{..\mathcal{C}^+..\mathcal{C}^-} F_{ij}. \tag{7}$$

Assuming that our complex has an appropriate resolution, we can restrict our optimization process to the set of C-consistent scene configurations. The energy cost $\mathbf{E}(M, \partial M)$ for a C-consistent configuration can be calculated as:

$$\mathbf{E}(M, \partial M) = \iint_{\partial M} A(X, \boldsymbol{n}_{\partial M})\, dS + \iiint_{M} B(X)\, dV =$$

$$\sum_{\cdots\, C^{\cdot}\, \cdots\, . C^{\overline{\cdot}}\, F_{\cdot\cdot}} \iint_{F_{\cdot\cdot}} A(X, \boldsymbol{n}_{ij})\, dS + \sum_{A.\, C M} \iiint_{R_{\cdot}} B(X)\, dV =$$

$$\sum_{\cdots\, C^{\cdot}\, \cdots\, . C^{\overline{\cdot}}} w_{ij} + \sum_{A.\, C M} w_i ,$$

where $w_{ij} = \iint_{F_{\cdot\cdot}} A(X, \boldsymbol{n}_{ij})\, dS$ is the energy cost for including the oriented face F_{ij} into the scene surface ∂M (*face cost*), and $w_i = \iiint_{R_{\cdot}} B(X)\, dV$ is the energy cost for including the cell R_i into the scene M (*cell cost*).

After the numeric computation of these costs, we have a purely discrete optimization problem: find the set of cells with the minimal sum of cell costs and boundary faces costs.

4.2   Graph Cuts Minimization

Although there are so many (2^K) possible C-consistent configurations, the best C-consistent configuration can be found in a low order polynomial on K time using graph cuts, recently employed for the optimization of energies in many vision problems (e.g. [1, 14, 2]; the last one having the most similar optimization scheme to ours). Under graph cuts, they usually mean the mincut/maxflow algorithm solving the following problem.

Consider a directed graph with two distinguished vertices (*terminals*) S and T. To each edge between non-terminal vertices (*n-link*), a nonnegative scalar weight is assigned. Edges going to and from terminal vertices (*t-links*) are attributed with arbitrary real weights. A *cut* is a partition of all vertices into two non-intersecting sets called S-*set* and T-*set*, such that the former contains terminal S and the latter contains terminal T. A weight of a cut is by definition the sum of the weights of all edges going from a vertex in S-set to a vertex in T-set (*cut edges*). Mincut algorithms are able to find the cut with the minimal possible weight (the *minimal cut*) in the time that is low order polynomial on the graph complexity.

To render our problem as a mincut/maxflow problem, we embed a dual graph $\mathcal{G}$ into our complex $\mathcal{C}$ (Fig. 3d). For each cell R_i from $\mathcal{C}$, $\mathcal{G}$ contains a vertex V_i located in the center of a cell. For each oriented face F_{ij} from $\mathcal{C}$, $\mathcal{G}$ contains an n-link E_{ij} going from V_i to V_j with the weight w_{ij}. Thus, the direction of this n-link is in accordance with the direction of an outward looking normal $\boldsymbol{n}_{ij}$. We also augment $\mathcal{G}$ with two terminal vertices S and T and add t-links E_i^T going from V_i to T having weights w_i.

To any C-consistent scene configuration $(M, \partial M)$, there corresponds the cut on $\mathcal{G}$ with S-set including the vertices corresponding to the cells within M plus the terminal S.

$$M = \bigsqcup_{k=1..Q} R_i. \qquad \longleftrightarrow \qquad S\text{-set} = \{V_i. \,|k = 1..Q\} \cup \{S\}. \qquad (8)$$

With such correspondence, any n-link is cut iff the corresponding oriented face is included in the boundary ∂M, and any t-link is cut iff the corresponding cell is included in the scene. Consequently, the weight of a cut always equals the energy cost of a corresponding C-consistent configuration.

Due to this equality, the minimal cut corresponds to the C-consistent scene configuration with the minimal energy. The multiview reconstruction is therefore performed as follows. First, construct a complex C. Second, calculate face costs and cell costs. Third, embed a dual graph $\mathcal{G}$; find a minimal cut on $\mathcal{G}$ and the corresponding scene configuration.

4.3   Complex Construction

Let us now consider the choice of an exact structure of the complex C. Assume that our bounding volume $\mathcal{B}$ is a box, and let us qualitatively analyze the factors that should be taken into consideration while choosing the complex.

The choice of C determines how "densely" C-consistent configurations sample the set of all configurations and how close would be the minimal C-consistent scene configuration to the global minimum over the whole set of scene configurations. Obviously, the smaller is the size of cells and faces, and the larger are their numbers, the richer is the set of C-consistent configurations. The fineness of resolution is not, however, the only factor to be considered. Due to the dependence of $A(x, n)$ on the orientation, another important matter is how densely the orientations of complex faces sample the set of all possible orientations. Thus, a straightforward but not a proper choice for C would be a commonly-used rectangular voxel grid. The deficiency of such grid is that it has the oriented faces of only six orientations irrespective of the resolution.

There can be several strategies in constructing complex better than rectangular grid. In our experiments, we first subdivide our bounding box into voxel cubes and then subdivide each cube with six planes, each passing through a pair of opposite cube edges (Fig. 3c). As a result, the voxel in split into 24 tetrahedral cells. This complex has an advantage of having oriented faces with as much as 18 different orientations.

Apart from the tripled number of orientations, another pleasant property of our complex is that the surfaces of scene configurations consistent with it are triangular meshes suitable for immediate storage and rendering. More than that, with such complex, typical reconstructed surfaces are not so jaggy as those composed from voxels and do not require additional smoothening quality-degrading postprocessing like marching cubes.

5   Semi-local Optimization

Oriented visibility gives incorrect visibility estimate in a situations when a part of a scene has an orientation visible from a viewpoint but is occluded by another distant part of a scene (*distant occlusion*). In many cases, however, such distantly occluded areas constitute a relatively small part of the scene surface.

When the accurate reconstruction of distantly occluded parts is required, the result obtained with our method can be used as a starting point for any other reconstruction method relying on iterative optimization and state-based visibility. Alternatively, we developed our own algorithm for a (semi-)local optimization, which searches for a globally optimal configuration within a band around the previous configuration.

Making use of the current state of the scene, this algorithm combines both state-based and oriented approaches to visibility, yielding the following visibility estimate for a patch (X, n) from the ith viewpoint:

$$\alpha_i(X, n) = \alpha_i^{or}(X, n) \cdot \alpha_i^{state}(X) , \qquad (9)$$

where $\alpha_i^{or}(X, n)$ is the oriented visibility indicator defined in (2), and $\alpha_i^{state}(X)$ is a visibility computed based on the current state of the scene. Thus, the role of $\alpha_i^{state}(X)$ is to detect distant occlusions. In all other aspects, our semi-local optimization procedure is similar to the initial global optimization step.

With such visibility updates, the semi-local optimization can be reapplied several times, each time considering the band around a previous configuration as a novel bounding volume. Changing the thickness of a band allows to trade between the accuracy of distant occlusion estimate on one side and the speed of convergence and the robustness to trapping in local minima on the other. Typically, a few (< 10) iterations is enough to converge.

As the computations are restricted to a narrow band around current configuration, it is also possible to use finer resolution of the complex within the same amount of memory and computation time, thus obtaining more accurate results.

6   Experimental Results

In this section, we present the results of our method on three image sets (Fig. 4). The artificial *solids* setup contains virtual objects "hanging" in the air. Its main challenges are fine texture details paired with a uniform background. For many photoconsistency-based algorithms such combination results in numerous "floating" artifacts. The real *camel* and *matreshkas* setups contain objects placed on the ground table/plane. The position of this plane as well as camera parameters using structure-and-motion methods. The *matreshkas* setup is particularly difficult for reconstruction, as the varnished surfaces are highly non-lambertian.

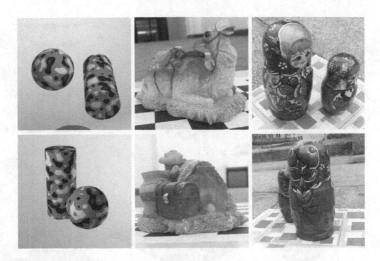

Fig. 4. Samples of the source imagery in our experiments. Image sets comprised 16–20 views surrounding the scene from all accessible positions. Left — *solids* setup was rendered artificially using POV-Ray^{tm} [13]. Middle and right — *camel* and *matreshkas* setups were taken using consumer digital camera.

The following volume potentials expressing the prior geometric knowledge were used for reconstruction (B_1 for *solids*, B_2 for *camel* and *matreshkas*):

$$B_1(X) = \begin{cases} +\infty & \text{near the bounding box boundary ,} \\ \beta & \text{inside bounding box .} \end{cases}$$

$$B_2(X) = \begin{cases} -\infty & \text{below ground plane ,} \\ +\infty & \text{near the bounding box boundary above ground plane ,} \\ \beta & \text{inside bounding box .} \end{cases}$$

Here, β is some small negative value introducing a slight ballooning effect, which was kept constant throughout our experiments. Infinities in the volume potential ensure the closeness of the recovered scene for *solids* and the "object on the ground" topology for *camel* and *matreshkas*.

For the evaluation purposes, we implemented an improved version [3] of the popular space carving approach [7]. Since space carving is very sensitive to the selection of photoconsistency threshold, we did our best while selecting the optimal threshold for each setup. However, as demonstrates Fig. 5a, our setups were too photometrically difficult for space carving.

The results of our method are presented on the rest of Fig. 5. Note, that despite significant distant occlusions, global optimization based on the oriented visibility solely (Fig. 5-middle) produced generally correct reconstructions for *solids* and *camel* setups. This suggests that the ability to find a global minimum often justifies the use of inexact visibility estimate.

In our experiments, the complex $\mathcal{C}$ comprised upto 20 million of cells resulting in the same number of vertices in the dual graph $\mathcal{G}$. Therefore the

Fig. 5. The reconstruction results. **a)** The results of space carving algorithm. **b)** The results of the proposed algorithm after global optimization. **c)** The results after three steps of subsequent semi-local optimization. **d)** Renderings of image based textured models created from real imagery with our method.

mincut/maxflow algorithm was the computational bottleneck for our approach. Performing global reconstruction for such resolution demanded upto 20 minutes on a P4-2.6GHz computer. Subsequent semi-local updates took few minutes.

7   Discussion

In this paper, we have proposed a novel orientation-based approach to visibility estimation. Such purely local visibility estimate allows us to cast a multiview reconstruction problem as an optimization of a novel energy functional amenable for minimization with graph cuts.

Our main advantage over other methods, which rely on state-based visibility and on iterative updates, is the independence from the initialization due to the ability of our optimization to yield a global minimum of the energy functional. The result produced with our global optimization can be improved with our semi-local optimization combining oriented and state-based approaches to visibility. Alternatively, it can be used as a good starting point for any of the other reconstruction methods.

The main limitation of our method in its current implementation is its computational demands. To deal with this problem, one can consider complexes based on spatially non-uniform sampling of the reconstruction space. Non-uniform sampling can be driven by some domain-specific knowledge or the cues resulting from another reconstruction algorithm. In both cases, uncertain knowledge about position and orientation of the surface may be used to include faces in the complex at some positions and with some orientations more frequently then others. An interesting option for implementing this are random grids arranged in BSP-trees proposed for discrete minimal surface search in [6].

The second deficiency of our method is the difficulties it faces while recovering the protruding parts of objects (e.g. camel ears). This problem is, however, inherent to all minimal surface methods, since they minimize the integral of non-negative energy function over a scene surface.

Another prospect for future investigation is concerned with the fact that our patch energy cost $A(X, n)$ accounts for both position and orientation of a patch. This can allow to use different shading models in our method. Thus, we can consider the reconstruction based on non-lambertian reflectivity models (e.g. Phong model) or shape-from-shading reconstruction.

References

1. Y. Boykov and V. Kolmogorov. An Experimental Comparison of Min-Cut/Max-Flow Algorithms for Energy Minimization in Vision. PAMI, vol. 26, no. 9, pp. 1124-1137, Sept. 2004.
2. C. Buehler, S. J. Gortler, M. Cohen, and L. McMmillan. Minimal Surfaces for Stereo Vision. Proc. ECCV 2002, vol. 3, pp. 885-899.
3. W. Culbertson, T. Malzbender, and G. Slabaugh. Generalized Voxel Coloring. Workshop on Vision Algorithms'1999, pp. 100-115
4. O. Faugeras and R. Keriven. Complete Dense Stereovision Using Level Set Methods. Proc. ECCV 1998, vol. 1, pp. 379–393.
5. D. Greig, B. Porteous, and A. Seheult. Exact maximum a posteriori estimation for binary images. Journal of the Royal Statistical Society, 51(2):271-279, 1989.
6. D. Kirsanov and S. J. Gortler. A Discrete Global Minimization Algorithm for Continuous Variational Problems. Harvard CS Technical Report TR-14-04, 2004.

7. K. N. Kutulakos and S. M. Seitz. A Theory of Shape by Space Carving. IJCV, 2000, 38(3), pp. 199–218.
8. Middlebury Stereo Vision Page. http://cat.middlebury.edu/stereo/
9. V. Kolmogorov and R. Zabih. Multi-camera Scene Reconstruction via Graph Cuts. Proc. ECCV 2002.
10. Vladimir Kolmogorov, Ramin Zabih. What Energy Functions Can Be Minimized via Graph Cuts? Proc. ECCV'2002, vol. 3, pp. 65-81
11. S. Paris, F. Sillion, and L. Quan. A Surface Reconstruction Method Using Global Graph Cut Optimization. IJCV (to appear).
12. J. Pearl. Probabilistic Reasoning in Intelligent Systems: Networks of plausible Inference. San Francisco, CA: Morgan Kaufmann, 1988.
13. POV-Ray^{tm} raytracer. http://www.povray.org
14. S. Roy and I. Cox. A maximum-flow formulation of the n-camera stereo correspondence problem. Proc. ICCV 1998, pp. 492-499.
15. S. Sinha and M. Pollefeys. Multi-View Reconstruction Using Photo-consistency and Exact Silhouette Constraints: A Maximum-Flow Formulation. Proc. ICCV 2005, pp. 349-356.
16. D. Snow, P. Viola, and R. Zabih. Exact voxel occupancy with graph cuts. Proc. CVPR 2000, vol. 1, pp. 345–352.
17. G. Vogiatzis, P. H. S. Torr, S. Seitz, and R. Cipolla. Reconstructing Relief Surfaces. Proc. BMVC 2004, pp. 117-126.
18. G. Vogiatzis, P. H. S. Torr, and R. Cipolla. Multi-view stereo via Volumetric Graph-cuts. Proc. CVPR 2005, pp. 391–398.
19. M. J. Wainwright, T. S. Jaakkola, A S. Willsky. MAP estimation via agreement on trees: Message-passing and linear programming. IEEE Trans. on Information Theory, vol. 51, no. 11, 2005.

Integrating Surface Normal Vectors Using Fast Marching Method

Jeffrey Ho[1], Jongwoo Lim[2], Ming-Hsuan Yang[2],
and David Kriegman[3]

[1] Department of CISE, University of Florida,
Gainesville, FL, USA
jho@cise.ufl.edu
[2] Honda Research Institute,
Mountain View, CA, USA
{jlim, myang}@honda-ri.com
[3] Department of Computer Science and Engineering,
University of California, San Diego, CA, USA
kriegman@cs.ucsd.edu

Abstract. Integration of surface normal vectors is a vital component in many shape reconstruction algorithms that require integrating surface normals to produce their final outputs, the depth values. In this paper, we introduce a fast and efficient method for computing the depth values from surface normal vectors. The method is based on solving the Eikonal equation using Fast Marching Method. We introduce two ideas. First, while it is not possible to solve for the depths Z directly using Fast Marching Method, we solve the Eikonal equation for a function W of the form $W = Z + \lambda f$. With appropriately chosen values for λ, we can ensure that the Eikonal equation for W can be solved using Fast Marching Method. Second, we solve for W in two stages with two different λ values, first in a small neighborhood of the given initial point with large λ, and then for the rest of the domain with a smaller λ. This step is needed because of the finite machine precision and rounding-off errors. The proposed method is very easy to implement, and we demonstrate experimentally that, with insignificant loss in precision, our method is considerably faster than the usual optimization method that uses conjugate gradient to minimize an error function.

1 Introduction

Many shape reconstruction algorithms in computer vision require integrating surface normal vectors. Reconstruction algorithms that use multi-view correspondences, such as structure from motion, generally recover the depth values directly from the pixel correspondences. However, algorithms that depend on exploiting illumination effects, such as photometric stereo and shape from shading, the depth values in general cannot be computed directly. Instead, under the usual Lambertian assumption, the normal vectors of the object's surface are recovered, and the depth values are obtained by integrating the surface normals. Successes

A. Leonardis, H. Bischof, and A. Pinz (Eds.): ECCV 2006, Part III, LNCS 3953, pp. 239–250, 2006.

abound in applying these techniques to important reconstruction problems in computer vision, ranging from the human face reconstruction [1] to the more recent optical-flow based object reconstruction from video sequences [2]. And in all these successes, integration of normal vectors is an important part of the story. This paper proposes a new method for integrating surface normals, which, with insignificant loss in precision, is about two order of magnitude faster than the traditional algorithm that uses conjugate descent to minimize some error function. This improvement in performance is particularly noticeable on large-scale problems, with images containing up to two million pixels.

The normal integration problem can be stated very simply as follows. For an usual XY grid, we are given a normal vector $\mathbf{N} = \mathbf{N}(x, y)$ at each grid point (x, y). The task is then to recover a surface S, represented by the height function $Z(x, y)$, such that $\mathbf{N}$ is a normal vector field of S. A simple calculation shows that a normal vector of S at a point (x, y) is given by the formula,

$$\mathbf{N}(x, y) = (\frac{\partial Z}{\partial x}, \frac{\partial Z}{\partial x}, -1). \tag{1}$$

In the following discussion, we will adhere to the convention and denote quotients $\frac{N.}{N.}$ and $\frac{N.}{N.}$ by P and Q, respectively. Since the normal vector is only defined up to multiplication by a constant, for any normal vector $\mathbf{N}$, the ratios of its x and y components with its z-component are the partial derivatives of Z with respect to x and y, respectively. Namely,

$$\frac{\partial Z}{\partial x} = -\frac{N_x}{N_z} = -P, \tag{2}$$

$$\frac{\partial Z}{\partial y} = -\frac{N_y}{N_z} = -Q, \tag{3}$$

where N_x, N_y and N_z are the x, y and z components of $\mathbf{N}$. A straightforward way of solving this system of PDEs is then to minimize the following error function over the entire grid [3]:

$$\mathcal{E}(Z) = \sum_{i,j}(\frac{\partial Z}{\partial x} + \frac{N_x}{N_z})^2 + (\frac{\partial Z}{\partial y} + \frac{N_y}{N_z})^2. \tag{4}$$

The error function $\mathcal{E}$ is a quadratic function of its variables, $z_{i,j}$, the values of the function Z at the grid point (i, j). In principle, its global minimum can be determined by solving the K-by-K^1 linear system $Ax = b$ derived from the condition,

$$\nabla \mathcal{E} = 0. \tag{5}$$

While this is perfectly doable, it is definitely not recommended for a large system. For example, on an image of size 1401-by-1401, the dimension of the linear system above is roughly two millions. While A is sparse, it is still a daunting

---

[1] K is the number of grid points.

task to solve the linear system $Ax = b$ directly using, e.g. LU factorization, which has the complexity of $O(K^3)$. Therefore, conjugate gradient is often used to find a minimum of $\mathcal{E}$. The main problem with this approach is the speed of convergence. As is well-known, it depends on the initial point (some given height function Z) that starts the iteration as well as the conditioning of the matrix A. Of course, it also depends on the size of the problem. Not surprisingly, for large scale problems, the convergence of the conjugate gradient optimization of Equation 4 is often excruciatingly slow.

The other commonly used method for solving the normal integration problem is to transform the problem to the frequency domain [4]. Suppose P and Q have the following Fourier expansions:

$$P = \sum c_P(\omega_x, \omega_y)e^{i(\omega \cdot x + \omega \cdot y)},$$

$$Q = \sum c_Q(\omega_x, \omega_y)e^{i(\omega \cdot x + \omega \cdot y)},$$

where ω_x, ω_y are the fundamental frequencies. Then, a best surface (in the least square sense) is then given by the formula

$$Z = \sum c(\omega_x, \omega_y)e^{i(\omega \cdot x + \omega \cdot y)},$$

where

$$c(\omega_x, \omega_y) = \frac{i\omega_x c_P(\omega_x, \omega_y) + i\omega_y c_Q(\omega_x, \omega_y)}{\omega_x^2 + \omega_y^2}$$

Fast Fourier Transform can be applied to efficiently solve the problem. However, as is well-known, FFT works well only with grids whose sizes are powers of 2, and there are also other problems associated with this approach.

In this paper, we propose a fast method for solving the normal integration problem. The algorithm is based on solving the Eikonal equation, and it uses the Fast Marching Method developed by Sethian and others for solving the Eikonal equation [5]. Our idea is as follows. While Fast Marching Method cannot be applied directly to solve for the height values Z, we can nevertheless try to solve for a function W of the form $W = Z + \lambda f$, where λ is a parameter and f is some known function. The idea is to find a pair of λ and f so that we can use Fast Marching Method to solve for the Eikonal equation for W. Even though the idea is simple, to the best of our knowledge, nothing similar has been reported in the computer vision literature before.

This paper is structured as follows. In the next section, we describe the proposed method of integration. In Section 3, we briefly review some related work, and we describe the similarities as well as disparities between the problem we solve here and the shape from shading problem. Experimental results comparing our method with the direct optimization of Equation 4 using conjugate gradient is reported in Section 4. The paper ends with a short summary and conclusion.

2   Integrating Surface Normals by Solving Eikonal Equation

It is well-known that the problem of integrating surface normals is intimately related to the solution of the Eikonal equation (e.g. [5]). Starting with the pair of equations in Equations 2 and 3, we have the following Eikonal equation:

$$\|\nabla Z\| = \sqrt{P^2 + Q^2}. \tag{6}$$

Therefore, a solution of the above equation is the desired height function Z. The Eikonal equation has appeared in various places in computer vision literature. For example, in many algorithms that use the level-set technique, Eikonal equation is often solved to produce a signed-distance function from the level set, and this re-initialization of the level-set function is a crucial step. Lately, there has been a considerable amount of interests in studying a modified Eikonal equation for solving the shape from shading problems [6]. Our approach here is also about solving the Eikonal equation.

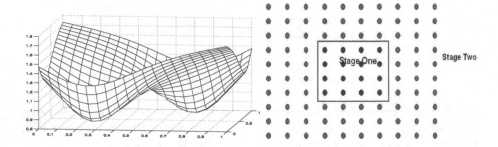

Fig. 1. Left: A function with two local minimums that cannot be recovered using Fast Marching Method. **Right**: We solve for W with two different λ values in two complementary regions.

The Fast Marching Method [5] provides a very efficient method to solve the Eikonal equation. Starting with an initial value at some given point u, it determines the Z value at every point by computing the time of arrival of an expanding wavefront. This method is very efficient, and it has the time complexity of roughly $O(K \log K)$ with K the number of grid points, using an auxiliary heap structure for keeping track of the wavefront. In addition, it is also very easy to implement. Unfortunately, Fast Marching Method cannot be applied directly here. For one thing, the initial point u has to be the global minimum of Z and in general, this information is not available. Furthermore, it will also have a difficulty dealing with functions that have local minimums. For example, the simple function depicted in Figure 1(**Left**) with two local minimums cannot be recovered by a straightforward application of Fast Marching Method. A modified Fast Marching approach [5][7] is to determine the local minimums first, and starting from these local minimums, every step extends reconstruction to higher depths and the entire reconstruction is then accomplished in one single pass. However, in our problem, we do not assume that we know the locations of these local minimums. In principle, one can detect the local minimums by determining the locations where $\partial Z/\partial x = \partial Z/\partial y = 0$, **and** the Hessian

$$H(x,y) = \begin{pmatrix} \frac{\partial^2 Z}{\partial^2 x} & \frac{\partial^2 Z}{\partial y \partial x} \\ \frac{\partial^2 Z}{\partial x \partial y} & \frac{\partial^2 Z}{\partial^2 y} \end{pmatrix} \tag{7}$$

is positive definite. However, with the noise present in the data as well as quantization effect, there is no guarantee on how accurately these local minimums can be located.

Instead, we propose to solve the Eikonal equation for a function W of the form

$$W = Z + \lambda f, \tag{8}$$

where λ is a constant and f is some function such that W is a function with one single global minimum at the initial point u and without any other critical points. In a way, the function f is here to cancel off any critical point of Z so that W is critical point free except at u. In particular, the level-set $W^{-1}(c)$ is always topologically the same for any value of c such that $W^{-1}(c)$ contains more than one point. Clearly, W can be solved using Fast Marching Method, and hence Z can be recovered from W if f and λ are known.

Since we are solving the height function Z over a finite domain, we can assume that both Z as well as its derivatives are bounded, $|Z| < c_1$ and $\|\nabla Z\| < c_2$. In practice, this is not a restrictive assumption since the surfaces been recovered by most shape reconstruction algorithms are often assumed to be smooth, and in many variational approaches [8], there is usually a smoothing term that minimizes the norm of ∇Z anyway. With this assumption in mind, we take f to be the squared-distance function (from the point $u = (u_x, u_y)$):

$$f = (x - u_x)^2 + (x - u_y)^2.$$

Without loss of generality, we assume that the initial point u is the origin in the following discussion. The derivatives of f vanish at the origin; therefore, u is not a critical point of $W = Z + \lambda f$ unless it is a critical point of Z. However, with sufficiently large λ, one can show that the critical points of $W = Z + \lambda f$ are all confined to a disk centered at origin with radius $r = q/2$, where q is the grid spacing, the distance between two neighboring grid points:

Lemma 1. *Suppose* $\|\nabla Z\| < c_2$. *If* $\lambda > \frac{c_2}{2R}$ *for some real number* R, *then* $W = Z + \lambda f$ *has no critical point outside of a disk* $\mathcal{D}_r$ *centered at the origin with radius* R.

The proof is trivial since in the region outside $\mathcal{D}_r$, $\|\nabla f\| > 2R$ and $\|\lambda \nabla f\| > 2R\lambda > c_2 > \|\nabla Z\|$. That is, $\nabla W = \nabla Z + \lambda \nabla f$ can never be zero outside of $\mathcal{D}_r$ since ∇Z and $\lambda \nabla f$ can never be the same. Therefore, in principle, we can choose a sufficiently large λ such that W only has critical points in the disk of radius $q/2$. Since we are computing everything on the grid, these critical points will be invisible, and we can treat the origin as the only critical point of W. The constant c_2 can be determined in a single pass over the input datum P and Q. Note that since we know the derivatives of Z as well as those of f, the Eikonal equation for W is simply

$$\|\nabla W\| = \sqrt{(P + 2x)^2 + (Q + 2y)^2}. \tag{9}$$

Once W is computed, Z can be easily recovered.

While the approach above is mathematically valid, because of finite machine precision, large λ would have incurred large rounding-off errors for the Z values. The situation is particularly urgent for points far away from the origin, where the term λf would have been considerably larger than Z. In this region, we prefer a small λ, while in the region close to the origin, we can accommodate a larger value for λ. Our second idea is then to solve the problem in two stages. In the first stage, we solve for Z in a small neighborhood of the origin, e.g., in a disk of radius $R = 1$. In this region, we can use larger values for λ because the term $\lambda(x^2 + y^2)$ will in general still be manageable. In the second stage, we solve Z for the rest of the domain using the result from the first stage as the initial values. By the Lemma above, we can take λ to be $\frac{c_2}{2} + 1$. See Figure 1(**Right**). In our implementation, we choose the neighborhood $\mathcal{D}_r$ beforehand, and we fix it to be a window $\mathcal{W}$ of size, say 15-by-15, centered at the given point u. We take λ to be

$$\lambda = \max_{p=(x,y)\notin\mathcal{W}} \frac{\|\nabla Z\|}{2\|p\|} + 1 = \max_{p=(x,y)\notin\mathcal{W}} \frac{\sqrt{P^2 + Q^2}}{2\sqrt{x^2 + y^2}} + 1. \tag{10}$$

Again, λ can be determined in a single pass over the input datum P and Q.

The other way to solve for the Z values in a small neighborhood of the origin is to explicitly invert the linear system $Ax = b$. Since the neighborhood is supposed to be small, it makes sense to solve the system directly, and the inversion process is relatively cheap. In particularly, if we fix the size of this neighborhood $\mathcal{W}$, and because A depends only on the connectivity of $\mathcal{W}$, the LU factorization of A can be computed off-line and the online inversion of the linear system is then fast and effortless.

3   Comparison with Shaping from Shading Literature

One common method for solving the shape from shading problem is to solve an Eikonal equation of the form [5]:

$$\|Z\| = \sqrt{\frac{1}{I^2} - 1}. \tag{11}$$

Here we assume that the single light source is from the direction $(0, 0, 1)$, and the Lambertian object has uniform albedo of value 1. I above denotes the image intensity value. Many papers have been devoted to solving this equation (e.g. [6]).

We point out, however, that the major distinction between our problem of integrating surface normal vectors and the shape from shading problem formulated above is that in our case, we have the values for the x and y components of ∇Z, while in the shape from shading problem, only the magnitude of ∇Z is known, and it is related to the intensity value through the equation above.

It is precisely because we know the x and y components of ∇Z, we can solve the Eikonal equation for W in Equation 9 since the right hand side can be computed. An equation analogous Equation 9 is not available for the shape from shading problem. Therefore, more elaborated scheme has to be designed in order to solve the Eikonal equation efficiently.

Finally, we also mention one important fact about the comparison between using the proposed method and the direct minimization of Equation 4 using conjugate gradient descent. While Fast Marching Method is unquestionably efficient in solving the Eikonal equation, it is not an iterative process and therefore, there is no way to further improve the quality of the solution. Typically, as in the experiments reported in the next section, there will always be errors between the reconstructed depths and the true depths. In our experiment, the error is usually at most 1% of the true depth value. The point we try to make in this paper is that to reach the precision obtained via our method would usually require conjugate gradient to run as much as 200 times longer. However, being an iterative scheme, conjugate gradient can keep running until it reaches a global minimum (or within the given tolerance set by the machine precision and the user). Therefore, there are two ways to apply our proposed method in a normal integration problem. If the precision requirement is stringent (with relative error $< 10^{-3}$), one can use the proposed method to quickly obtain an initial surface estimate, and feed this result into an efficient optimization method to yield a more precise result. On the other hand, if the precision requirement is not too demanding, the output of our method will usually be sufficient.

4   Experiments and Results

In this section, we report our experimental results. All experiments reported below were run on a 3.19 GHz DELL Pentium desktop computer with 2.00 GB of RAM running Windows XP. We implemented the proposed method using a simple C++ implementation without any optimization except a heap structure for keeping track of the front points and their neighbors. We compare the performance of the proposed method with the standard conjugate gradient minimization of Equation 4[2]. The implementation of the conjugate gradient descent is taken straight out of [9]. Except for the Brent line minimization, no further optimization of the code has been implemented.

Below, we provide two types of experiments. In the second group of experiments, we work with the (noisy) normal vectors of a human face estimated using

---

[2] The standard conjugate gradient without line search usually fails to converge to the precision we required. Therefore, we include the line minimization to ensure that the iterative process will converge to the required precision.

the photometric stereo algorithm [1]. In the first group of experiments, which is our main focus, we work with surfaces with known depths and normal vectors. The goal is to compare the speed of our method and that of the conjugate gradient descent under the same precision requirement. For each of the four functions $Z = Z(x, y)$ given below, we compute the normals of the surface represented by Z using Equation 1. The estimated depth value Z' is computed using both methods at each point, and also the relative error

$$\epsilon = \frac{|Z - Z'|}{|Z|}.$$

The mean, median and also the standard deviation of the relative errors are computed for each function, and they serve as the measurements used to compare both methods.

4.1   Experiment with Simulated Data

In this group of experiments, we study the performance of our method for surfaces with known depths and normals. We run the experiments on a grid of size 1401×1401, and there are roughly two million grid points. In all experiments, it takes less than three seconds (2.677 to be exact) for our method to finish. Note that the speed of our method is independent of the value of λ as well as the chosen initial starting point. We compute the mean, median and standard deviation of the relative errors of the reconstruction result given by our method. We then run the conjugate gradient (CG) with sufficiently many iterations in order to reach the same precision requirement. In the experiments reported below, CG usually takes about 250 to 350 iterations to converge to the required precision, and this translates into roughly from 475 to 700 seconds. Averagely, our method is about 200 times faster than the conjugate gradient method.

Sphere. For the first experiment, we look at the simplest case of a sphere,

$$Z = \sqrt{1.5^2 - x^2 - y^2}$$

over the domain $\mathcal{D} \equiv \{(x, y)| - 0.7 \leq x, y \leq 0.7\}$. In this example, we take the domain $\mathcal{D}_r$ to be the disk with radius $r = 7$ grid points. For the first experiment, the initial starting point is chosen at the center of the grid, the apex of the sphere over the domain $\mathcal{D}$. We pick the optimal value of $\lambda = 6$ determined by Equation 9. The mean, median and the standard deviation of the relative errors with this λ setting are 0.0046, 0.0045, and 0.0015, respectively, which is sufficiently accurate for many applications.

Next, we vary the value of λ from 0 to 100. The mean, median and the stand derivation for these values of λ are plotted in Figure 2. The optimal λ value of 6 is very close to the empirical optimal value of $\lambda = 4$, which gives the mean, median, standard deviation of 0.0042, 0.0042, and 0.0015, respectively. Note that with $\lambda = 0$, which corresponds to a direct application of Fast Marching Method to solve the Eikonal equation, the result is, as expected, completely incorrect. Also

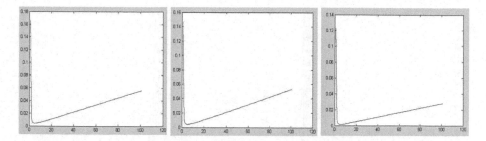

Fig. 2. From Left to Right: Plots of the mean, median and standard deviation of the relative errors of the reconstruction results for the sphere with λ ranging from 0 to 100

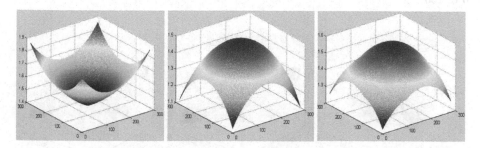

Fig. 3. From Left to Right: Reconstruction results for the sphere using $\lambda = 0, 6$ and 100, respectively. The images are colored-coded according to depth values.

as expected, as the value of λ increases, the rounding-off errors start creeping in and accumulating, the reconstruction result begins to deteriorate. However, even with the relatively large value of $\lambda = 60$, the median and mean of the relative error is still below 3% with standard deviation less than 2%.

In Figure 3, we show the reconstruction results using $\lambda = 0, 6, 100$. Clearly, the reconstruction result for $\lambda = 0$ is completely incorrect.

Monkey Saddle. While we have passed the rudimentary test using sphere, the next example, which is a little more challenging, uses the function

$$Z = x(x^2 - 3y^2) + 3.$$

Instead of the global maximum in the example above, the origin is now a saddle point of the function Z. We run the experiment over the same range of λ, from 0 to 100. The mean, median and the stand derivation of the relative errors for these values of λ are plotted in Figure 4. Again, we observe the similar pattern as above that when $\lambda = 0$, the reconstruction result is completely incorrect. Furthermore, the quality of the reconstruction, as measured by the mean, median and standard deviation of the relative errors, deteriorates as λ increases. In this example, we have used $\lambda = 12$ and it is close to the empirical optimal value of $\lambda = 18$.

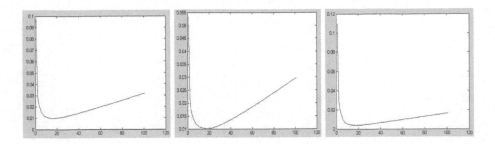

Fig. 4. From Left to Right: Plots of the mean, median and standard deviation of the relative errors of the reconstruction results for the Monkey Saddle with λ ranging from 0 to 100

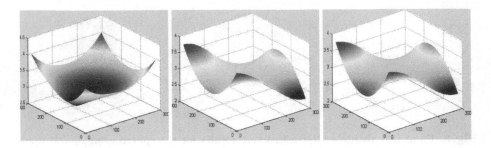

Fig. 5. From Left to Right: Reconstruction results for the Monkey Saddle using $\lambda = 0, 12$ and 100, respectively

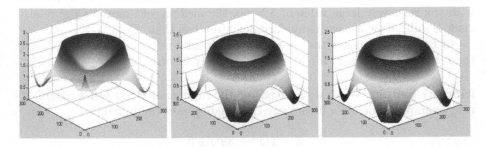

Fig. 6. From Left to Right: Reconstruction results for the function $Z = \sin(2\pi(x^2 + y^2)) + 3$ using $\lambda = 4, 30$ and 100, respectively

Sinusoidal Function and Gaussian. Figures 6 and 7 display the reconstruction results for the following two functions:

$$Z = \sin(2\pi(x^2 + y^2)) + 3 \tag{12}$$
$$Z = e^{-x^2 - y^2} + 10 \tag{13}$$

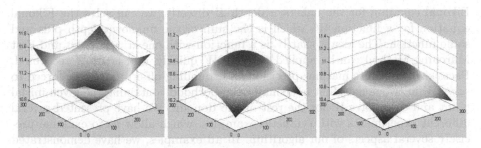

Fig. 7. From Left to Right: Reconstruction results for $Z = e^{-x^2 - y^2} + 10$ using $\lambda = 0, 8$ and 100, respectively

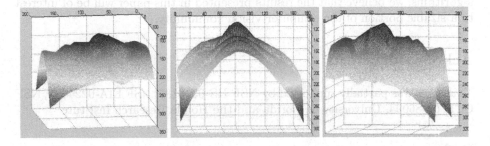

Fig. 8. From Left to Right: Three views of the reconstruction result of one individual in the Yale Face Database B

For the gaussian exponential function, again, we see that the reconstruction result for $\lambda = 0$ is incorrect. For the function $Z = \sin(2\pi(x^2 + y^2)) + 3$, instead of displaying the reconstruction result for $\lambda = 0$, we show the result with $\lambda = 4$, which is clearly incorrect and incomplete.

4.2   Experiment with Real Data

In this experiment, we work with the normal vectors provided in the Yale Face Database B [1]. Images of each of the ten individuals in the database were taken under different illumination conditions. The normal vectors are estimated using the photometric stereo algorithm of [10]. Figure 8 shows the reconstruction result using our method for one individual in the database. Since the image here is of size 168×192, which is considerably smaller than the ones we used above, it takes less then 0.02 second for our method to complete the integration.

5   Conclusion

In this paper, we have presented a method for computing depth values from surface normal vectors. The proposed method is based on the Fast Marching Method for solving the Eikonal equation. Our main contribution is the observation that while we cannot apply Fast Marching Method directly to solve the

Eikonal equation for the unknown depth Z directly, we can solve the Eikonal equation for a function W, which is the sum of the unknown depth plus and some function. The idea is that W is a function with one critical point and Fast Marching Method can be applied to solve W quickly, and hence Z recovered. Because of the finite machine precision and rounding-off errors, we are forced to solve W in two stages, first in a small neighborhood containing the given initial point and then solve W for the rest of the domain. We have presented several different experiments with synthetic examples, which allow us to examine precisely several aspects of our algorithm. In all examples, we have demonstrated that given the same precision requirement, the proposed method is considerably faster than the old method based on conjugate gradient descent. Since surface normal integration is an important component in many shape reconstruction algorithms, we believe that the results presented in this paper will be of interest to a sizable portion of the computer vision community.

Acknowledgements

This work was partially supported by NSF IIS-0308185, NSF EIA-0224431, NSF CCR 00-86094, University of Florida and the Honda Research Institute.

References

1. Georghiades, A., Kriegman, D., Belhumeur, P.: From few to many: Generative models for recognition under variable pose and illumination. IEEE Transactions on Pattern Analysis and Machine Intelligence **23** (2001) 643–660
2. L. Zhang, B. Curless, A.H., Seitz, S.: Shape and motion under varying illumination: Unifying structure from motion, photometric stereo, and multi-view stereo. In: Proc. Int. Conf. on Computer Vision. (2003) 618–625
3. Horn, B.K.P., Brook, M.J.: Shape from Shading. MIT Press (1997)
4. Frankot, R., Chellappa, R.: A method of enforcing integrability in shape from shading algorithms. IEEE Transactions on Pattern Analysis and Machine Intelligence **10** (1988) 439–451
5. Sethian, J.A.: Level Set Methods and Fast Marching Methods. Cambridge Press (1996)
6. Prado, E., Faugeras, O.: Shape from shading: A well-posed problem ? In: Proc. IEEE Conf. on Comp. Vision and Patt. Recog. (2005) 158–164
7. A. Tankus, N.S., Yeshurun, H.: Perspective shape from shading by fast marching. In: Proc. IEEE Conf. on Comp. Vision and Patt. Recog. (2004) 618–625
8. Trucco, E., Verri, A.: Introductory Techniques for 3D Computer Vision. Prentice Hall (1998)
9. W. H. Press, S. A. Teukolsky, W.T.V., Flannery, B.P.: Numerical Recipes in C, Second Edition. Cambridge Press (1992)
10. Yuille, A., Snow, D.: Shape and albedo from multiple images using integrability. In: Proc. IEEE Conf. on Comp. Vision and Patt. Recog. (1997) 158–164

Learning Discriminative Canonical Correlations
for Object Recognition with Image Sets

Tae-Kyun Kim[1], Josef Kittler[2], and Roberto Cipolla[1]

[1] Department of Engineering, University of Cambridge,
Cambridge, CB2 1PZ, UK
{tkk22, cipolla}@eng.cam.ac.uk
[2] Centre for Vision, Speech and Signal Processing, University of Surrey,
Guildford, GU2 7XH, UK
J.Kittler@surrey.ac.uk

Abstract. We address the problem of comparing sets of images for object recognition, where the sets may represent arbitrary variations in an object's appearance due to changing camera pose and lighting conditions. The concept of Canonical Correlations (also known as principal angles) can be viewed as the angles between two subspaces. As a way of comparing sets of vectors or images, canonical correlations offer many benefits in accuracy, efficiency, and robustness compared to the classical parametric distribution-based and non-parametric sample-based methods. Here, this is demonstrated experimentally for reasonably sized data sets using existing methods exploiting canonical correlations. Motivated by their proven effectiveness, a novel discriminative learning over sets is proposed for object recognition. Specifically, inspired by classical Linear Discriminant Analysis (LDA), we develop a linear discriminant function that maximizes the canonical correlations of within-class sets and minimizes the canonical correlations of between-class sets. The proposed method significantly outperforms the state-of-the-art methods on two different object recognition problems using face image sets with arbitrary motion captured under different illuminations and image sets of five hundred general object categories taken at different views.

1 Introduction

Whereas most previous works for object recognition have focused on the problems of *single-to-single* or *single-to-many* vector matching, many tasks can be cast as matching problems of vector sets (i.e. *many-to-many*) for robust object recognition. In object recognition, e.g., a set of vectors may represent a variation in an object's appearance – be it due to camera pose changes, non-rigid deformations or variation in illumination conditions. The objective of this work is to efficiently classify a novel set of vectors to one of the training classes, each also represented by one or several vector sets. In this study, sets may be derived from sparse and unordered observations acquired by e.g. multiple still shots of a three dimensional object or a long term surveillance systems, where a subject would not face the camera all the time. Without temporal coherence,

A. Leonardis, H. Bischof, and A. Pinz (Eds.): ECCV 2006, Part III, LNCS 3953, pp. 251–262, 2006.
© Springer-Verlag Berlin Heidelberg 2006

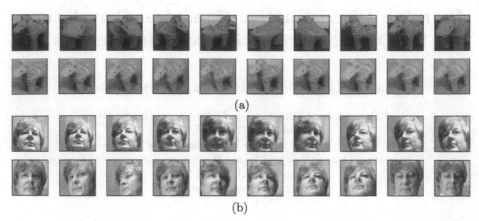

(a)

(b)

Fig. 1. Examples of image sets. (a) Two sets (top and bottom) contain images of an 3D object taken from different views but with a certain overlap in their views. (b) Face image sets collected from videos taken under different illumination settings. Face patterns of the two sets (top and bottom) vary in both lighting and pose.

training sets can be conveniently augmented. See Figure 1 for examples of pattern sets of objects. The previous works exploiting temporal coherence between consecutive images [1, 2] are irrelevant to this study. Furthermore, this work does not explicitly exploit any data-semantics in images, but is purely based on automatic learning of given labelled image sets. Therefore, we expect that the proposed method can be applied to many other problems requiring a set comparison.

Relevant previous approaches for set matching can be broadly partitioned into **model-based** and **sample-based** methods. In the parametric model-based approaches [3, 4], each set is represented by a parametric distribution function, typically Gaussian. The closeness of the two distributions is then measured by the Kullback-Leibler Divergence (KLD) [3]. Due to the difficulty of parameter estimation under limited training data, these methods easily fail when the training and test sets do not have strong statistical correlations.

More suitable methods for comparing sets are based on the matching of pairwise samples of sets, e.g. Nearest Neighbour (NN) or Hausdorff distance matching [5]. The methods are based on the premise that similarity of a pair of sets is reflected by the similarity of the modes (or NNs) of the two respective sets. This is useful in many computer vision applications, where the data acquisition conditions and the semantics of sets may change dramatically over time. However, they do not take into account the effect of outliers as well as the natural variability of the sensory data due to the 3D nature of the observed objects. Note also that such methods are very computationally expensive as they require a comparison of every pairwise samples of any two sets.

Another model-based approaches are based on the concept of **canonical correlations**, which has attracted increasing attention for image set matching in [8]-[11], following the early works [12, 13]. Each set is represented by a linear subspace and the angles between two subspaces are exploited as a similarity measure of two sets. As a method of comparing sets, the benefits of canonical correlations, as compared with both, distribution based and sample based matching, have been noted in [4, 10]. A nonlinear extension of canonical correlation has been proposed in [9, 10]. The previous work called Constrained Mutual Subspace Method (CMSM) [11] is the most related with this paper. In CMSM, a constrained subspace is defined as the subspace in which the entire class population exhibits small variance. The authors showed that the sets of different classes in the constrained subspace had small canonical correlations. However, the principle of CMSM is rather heuristic, especially the process of selecting the dimensionality of the constrained subspace. If the dimensionality is too low, the subspace will be a null space. In the opposite case, the subspace simply passes all the energy of the original data and thus could not play a role as a discriminant function.

Given a similarity function of two sets, an important problem in set classification is how to learn discriminative information (or a discriminant function) from data associated with the given similarity function. To our knowledge, the topic of discriminative learning over sets has not been given a proper attention in literature. This paper presents a novel method for an optimal linear discriminant function of image sets based on canonical correlations. A linear discriminant function that maximizes the canonical correlations of within-class sets and minimizes the canonical correlations of between-class sets is devised, by analogy to the optimization concept of Linear Discriminant Analysis (LDA) [6]. The linear mapping is found by a novel iterative optimization algorithm. The discriminative capability of the proposed method is shown to be significantly better than the method [8] that simply aggregates canonical correlations and the k-NN methods in LDA subspace [5]. Compared with CMSM [11], the proposed method is more practical by easiness of feature selection as well as it is more theoretically appealing.

2   Discriminative Canonical Correlations (DCC)

2.1   Canonical Correlations

Canonical correlations, which are cosines of principal angles $0 \leq \theta_1 \leq \ldots \leq \theta_d \leq (\pi/2)$ between any two d-dimensional linear subspaces $\mathcal{L}_1$ and $\mathcal{L}_2$ are uniquely defined as:

$$\cos \theta_i = \max_{\mathbf{u}_i \in \mathcal{L}_1} \max_{\mathbf{v}_i \in \mathcal{L}_2} \mathbf{u}_i^T \mathbf{v}_i \qquad (1)$$

subject to $\mathbf{u}_i^T \mathbf{u}_i = \mathbf{v}_i^T \mathbf{v}_i = 1$, $\mathbf{u}_i^T \mathbf{u}_j = \mathbf{v}_i^T \mathbf{v}_j = 0$, for $i \neq j$. Of the various ways to solve this problem, the Singular Value Decomposition (SVD) solution [13] is more numerically stable. The SVD solution is as follows: Assume that $\mathbf{P}_1 \in \mathbf{R}^{n \times d}$ and $\mathbf{P}_2 \in \mathbf{R}^{n \times d}$ form unitary orthogonal basis matrices for two linear subspaces, $\mathcal{L}_1$ and $\mathcal{L}_2$. Let the SVD of $\mathbf{P}_1^T \mathbf{P}_2$ be

$$\mathbf{P}_1^T \mathbf{P}_2 = \mathbf{Q}_{12} \mathbf{\Lambda} \mathbf{Q}_{21}^T \quad s.t. \quad \mathbf{\Lambda} = diag(\sigma_1, ..., \sigma_d) \qquad (2)$$

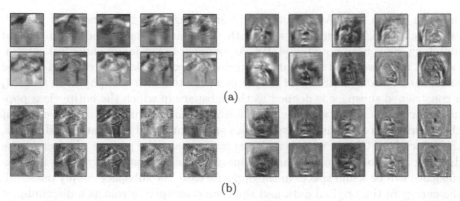

Fig. 2. Principal components vs. canonical vectors. (a) The first 5 principal components computed from the four image sets shown in Figure 1. The principal components of the different image sets (see each column) show significantly different variations even for the same objects. (b) The first 5 canonical vectors of the four image sets. Every pair of canonical vectors (each column) well captures the common modes (views and illuminations) of the two sets, i.e. the pairwise canonical vectors are almost similar. The canonical vectors of different dimensions represent different pattern variations e.g. in pose or lighting.

where $\mathbf{Q}_{12}, \mathbf{Q}_{21}$ are orthogonal matrices, i.e. $\mathbf{Q}_{ij}^T \mathbf{Q}_{ij} = \mathbf{Q}_{ij}\mathbf{Q}_{ij}^T = \mathbf{I}_d$. Canonical correlations are $\{\sigma_1, ..., \sigma_d\}$ and the associated canonical vectors are $\mathbf{U} = \mathbf{P}_1 \mathbf{Q}_{12} = [\mathbf{u}_1, ..., \mathbf{u}_d]$, $\mathbf{V} = \mathbf{P}_2 \mathbf{Q}_{21} = [\mathbf{v}_1, ..., \mathbf{v}_d]$. The canonical correlations tell us how close are the closest vectors of two subspaces. Different canonical correlations tell about the proximity of vectors in other dimensions (perpendicular to the previous ones) of the two subspaces. See Figure 2 for the canonical vectors computed from the sample image sets given in Figure 1. Whereas the principal components vary for different imaging conditions of the sets, the canonical vectors well capture the common modes of the two different sets.

Compared with the parametric distribution-based matching, this concept is much more flexible as it effectively places a uniform prior over the subspace of possible pattern variations. Compared with the NN matching of samples, this approach is much more stable as patterns are confined to certain subspaces. The low computational complexity of matching by canonical correlations is also much favorable.

3   Learning a Discriminant Function of Canonical Correlations

3.1   Problem Formulation

Assume m sets of vectors are given as $\{\mathbf{X}_1, ..., \mathbf{X}_m\}$, where $\mathbf{X}_i$ describes a data matrix of the i th set containing observation vectors (or images) in its columns. Each set belongs to one of object classes denoted by C_i. A d-dimensional linear subspace of the i th set is represented by an orthonormal basis matrix $\mathbf{P}_i \in \mathbf{R}^{n \times d}$ s.t. $\mathbf{X}_i \mathbf{X}_i^T \simeq \mathbf{P}_i \mathbf{\Lambda}_i \mathbf{P}_i^T$, where $\mathbf{\Lambda}_i, \mathbf{P}_i$ are the eigenvalue and eigenvector matrices of the d largest eigenvalues respectively and n denotes the vector dimension. We define a transformation matrix $\mathbf{T}$ s.t. $\mathbf{T} : \mathbf{X}_i \rightarrow \mathbf{Y}_i = \mathbf{T}^T \mathbf{X}_i$. The matrix $\mathbf{T}$ is to transform images so that the transformed image sets are more class-wise discriminative using canonical correlations.

Representation. Orthonormal basis matrices of the subspaces for the transformed data are obtained from the previous matrix factorization of $\mathbf{X}_i \mathbf{X}_i^T$:

$$\mathbf{Y}_i \mathbf{Y}_i^T = (\mathbf{T}^T \mathbf{X}_i)(\mathbf{T}^T \mathbf{X}_i)^T \simeq (\mathbf{T}^T \mathbf{P}_i) \mathbf{\Lambda}_i (\mathbf{T}^T \mathbf{P}_i)^T \qquad (3)$$

Except when $\mathbf{T}$ is an orthogonal matrix, $\mathbf{T}^T \mathbf{P}_i$ is not generally an orthonormal basis matrix. Note that canonical correlations are only defined for orthonormal basis matrices of subspaces. Any orthonormal components of $\mathbf{T}^T \mathbf{P}_i$ now defined by $\mathbf{T}^T \mathbf{P}'_i$ can represent an orthonormal basis matrix of the transformed data. See Section 3.2 for details.

Set Similarity. The similarity of any two transformed data sets are defined as the sum of canonical correlations by

$$F_{ij} = \max_{\mathbf{Q}_{..}, \mathbf{Q}_{..}} \mathrm{tr}(M_{ij}), \qquad (4)$$

$$M_{ij} = \mathbf{Q}_{ij}^T \mathbf{P}'_i^T \mathbf{T} \mathbf{T}^T \mathbf{P}'_j \mathbf{Q}_{ji} \quad \text{or} \quad \mathbf{T}^T \mathbf{P}'_j \mathbf{Q}_{ji} \mathbf{Q}_{ij}^T \mathbf{P}'_i^T \mathbf{T}, \qquad (5)$$

as $\mathrm{tr}(AB) = \mathrm{tr}(BA)$ for any matrix A, B. $\mathbf{Q}_{ij}, \mathbf{Q}_{ji}$ are the rotation matrices defined in the solution of canonical correlations (2).

Discriminant Function. The discriminative function $\mathbf{T}$ is found to maximize the similarities of any pairs of sets of within-classes while minimizing the similarities of pairwise sets of between-classes. Matrix $\mathbf{T}$ is defined by

$$\mathbf{T} = \arg \max_{\mathbf{T}} \frac{\sum_{i=1}^m \sum_{k \in W_.} F_{ik}}{\sum_{i=1}^m \sum_{l \in B_.} F_{il}} \qquad (6)$$

where $W_i = \{j \,|\mathbf{X}_j \in C_i\}$ and $B_i = \{j \,|\mathbf{X}_j \notin C_i\}$. That is, the two sets W_i, B_i denote the within-class and between-class sets of a given set class i respectively, which are similarly defined with [7].

3.2 Iterative Optimization

The optimization problem of $\mathbf{T}$ involves the variables of $\mathbf{Q}, \mathbf{P}'$ as well as $\mathbf{T}$. As the other variables are not explicitly represented by $\mathbf{T}$, a closed form solution for $\mathbf{T}$ is hard to find. We propose an iterative optimization algorithm. Specifically, we compute an optimal solution for one of the three variables at a time by fixing the other two and repeating this for a certain number of iterations.

Algorithm 1. Discriminative Canonical Correlations (DCC)

Input: All $\mathbf{P}_i \in \mathcal{R}^{n \times d}$ **Output:** $\mathbf{T} \in \mathcal{R}^{n \times n}$

---

1. $\mathbf{T} \leftarrow \mathbf{I}_n$
2. Do iterate the followings:
3.   For all i, do QR-decomposition: $\mathbf{T}^T \mathbf{P}_i = \mathbf{\Phi}_i \mathbf{\Delta}_i \rightarrow \mathbf{P}'_i = \mathbf{P}_i \mathbf{\Delta}_i^{-1}$
4.   For every pair i, j, do SVD: $\mathbf{P}'_i^T \mathbf{T} \mathbf{T}^T \mathbf{P}'_j = \mathbf{Q}_{ij} \mathbf{\Lambda} \mathbf{Q}_{ji}^T$
5.   Compute $\mathbf{S}'_b = \sum_{i=1}^m \sum_{l \in B.} (\mathbf{P}'_l \mathbf{Q}_{li} - \mathbf{P}'_i \mathbf{Q}_{il})(\mathbf{P}'_l \mathbf{Q}_{li} - \mathbf{P}'_i \mathbf{Q}_{il})^T$,
     $\mathbf{S}'_w = \sum_{i=1}^m \sum_{k \in W.} (\mathbf{P}'_k \mathbf{Q}_{ki} - \mathbf{P}'_i \mathbf{Q}_{ik})(\mathbf{P}'_k \mathbf{Q}_{ki} - \mathbf{P}'_i \mathbf{Q}_{ik})^T$.
6.   Compute eigenvectors $\{\mathbf{t}_i\}_{i=1}^n$ of $(\mathbf{S}'_w)^{-1} \mathbf{S}'_b$, $\mathbf{T} \leftarrow [\mathbf{t}_1, ..., \mathbf{t}_n]$
7. End

Thus, the proposed iterative optimization is comprised of the three main steps: normalization of $\mathbf{P}$, optimization of matrices $\mathbf{Q}$, and $\mathbf{T}$. Each step is explained below:

Normalization. The matrix $\mathbf{P}_i$ is normalized to $\mathbf{P}'_i$ for a fixed $\mathbf{T}$ so that the columns of $\mathbf{T}^T \mathbf{P}'_i$ are orthonormal. QR-decomposition of $\mathbf{T}^T \mathbf{P}_i$ is performed s.t. $\mathbf{T}^T \mathbf{P}_i = \mathbf{\Phi}_i \mathbf{\Delta}_i$, where $\mathbf{\Phi}_i \in \mathbf{R}^{n \times d}$ is the orthonormal matrix with the first d columns and $\mathbf{\Delta}_i \in \mathbf{R}^{d \times d}$ is the invertible upper-triangular matrix with the first d rows. From (3), $\mathbf{Y}_i = \mathbf{T}^T \mathbf{P}_i \sqrt{\mathbf{\Lambda}_i} = \mathbf{\Phi}_i \mathbf{\Delta}_i \sqrt{\mathbf{\Lambda}_i}$. As $\mathbf{\Delta}_i \sqrt{\mathbf{\Lambda}_i}$ is still an upper-triangular matrix, $\mathbf{\Phi}_i$ can represent an orthonormal basis matrix of the transformed data $\mathbf{Y}_i$. As $\mathbf{\Delta}_i$ is invertible,

$$\mathbf{\Phi}_i = \mathbf{T}^T (\mathbf{P}_i \mathbf{\Delta}_i^{-1}) \quad \rightarrow \quad \mathbf{P}'_i = \mathbf{P}_i \mathbf{\Delta}_i^{-1}. \tag{7}$$

Computation of Rotation Matrices Q. Rotation matrices $\mathbf{Q}_{ij}$ for every i, j are obtained for a fixed $\mathbf{T}$ and $\mathbf{P}'_i$. The correlation matrix M_{ij} in the left of (5) can be conveniently used for the optimization of $\mathbf{Q}_{ij}$, as it has $\mathbf{Q}_{ij}$ outside of the matrix product. Let the SVD of $\mathbf{P}'_i^T \mathbf{T} \mathbf{T}^T \mathbf{P}'_j$ be

$$\mathbf{P}'_i^T \mathbf{T} \mathbf{T}^T \mathbf{P}'_j = \mathbf{Q}_{ij} \mathbf{\Lambda} \mathbf{Q}_{ji}^T \tag{8}$$

where $\mathbf{\Lambda}$ is a singular matrix and $\mathbf{Q}_{ij}, \mathbf{Q}_{ji}$ are orthogonal rotation matrices.

Computation of T. The optimal discriminant transformation $\mathbf{T}$ is computed for given $\mathbf{P}'_i$ and $\mathbf{Q}_{ij}$ by using the definition of M_{ij} in the right of (5) and (6). With $\mathbf{T}$ being on the outside of the matrix product, it is convenient to solve for. The discriminative function is found by

$$\mathbf{T} = \max_{arg \mathbf{T}} \ \mathrm{tr}(\mathbf{T}^T \mathbf{S}_w \mathbf{T}) / \mathrm{tr}(\mathbf{T}^T \mathbf{S}_b \mathbf{T}) \tag{9}$$

$$\mathbf{S}_w = \sum_{i=1}^m \sum_{k \in W.} \mathbf{P}'_k \mathbf{Q}_{ki} \mathbf{Q}_{ik}^T \mathbf{P}'_i^T, \quad \mathbf{S}_b = \sum_{i=1}^m \sum_{l \in B.} \mathbf{P}'_l \mathbf{Q}_{li} \mathbf{Q}_{il}^T \mathbf{P}'_i^T \tag{10}$$

where $W_i = \{j \mid \mathbf{X}_j \in C_i\}$ and $B_i = \{j \mid \mathbf{X}_j \notin C_i\}$. For a more stable solution, an alternative optimization is finally proposed by

$$\mathbf{T} = \max_{arg \mathbf{T}} \ \mathrm{tr}(\mathbf{T}^T \mathbf{S}'_b \mathbf{T}) / \mathrm{tr}(\mathbf{T}^T \mathbf{S}'_w \mathbf{T}) \tag{11}$$

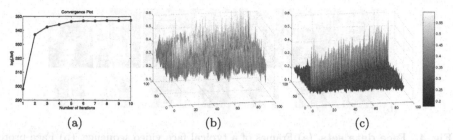

(a)   (b)   (c)

Fig. 3. Example of learning. (a) The cost function for the number of iterations. Confusion matrices of the training set (b) before the learning ($\mathbf{T} = \mathbf{I}$) and (c) after the learning. The discriminability of canonical correlations was significantly improved by the proposed learning.

$$\mathbf{S}'_b = \sum_{i=1}^{m} \sum_{l \in B.} (\mathbf{P}'_l \mathbf{Q}_{li} - \mathbf{P}'_i \mathbf{Q}_{il})(\mathbf{P}'_l \mathbf{Q}_{li} - \mathbf{P}'_i \mathbf{Q}_{il})^T, \qquad (12)$$

$$\mathbf{S}'_w = \sum_{i=1}^{m} \sum_{k \in W.} (\mathbf{P}'_k \mathbf{Q}_{ki} - \mathbf{P}'_i \mathbf{Q}_{ik})(\mathbf{P}'_k \mathbf{Q}_{ki} - \mathbf{P}'_i \mathbf{Q}_{ik})^T. \qquad (13)$$

Note that no loss of generality is incurred by this modification of the objective function as
$$A^T B = \mathbf{I} - 1/2 \cdot (A - B)^T (A - B),$$

where $A = \mathbf{T}^T \mathbf{P}'_i \mathbf{Q}_{ij}, B = \mathbf{T}^T \mathbf{P}'_j \mathbf{Q}_{ji}$. The solution $\{\mathbf{t}_i\}_{i=1}^{n}$ is obtained by solving the following generalized eigenvalue problem: $\mathbf{S}'_b \mathbf{t} = \lambda \mathbf{S}'_w \mathbf{t}$. When $\mathbf{S}'_w$ is non singular, the optimal $\mathbf{T}$ is computed by eigen-decomposition on $(\mathbf{S}'_w)^{-1} \mathbf{S}'_b$. Note also that the proposed learning can avoid a singular case of $\mathbf{S}'_w$ by pre-applying PCA to data similarly with the Fisherface method [6] and speed up by using a small number of nearest neighboring sets for B_i, W_i in (6) like [7].

With the identity matrix $\mathbf{I} \in \mathbf{R}^{n \times n}$ as the initial value of $\mathbf{T}$, the algorithm is iterated until it converges to a stable point. A Pseudo-code for the learning is given in **Algorithm 1**. See Figure 3 for an example of learning. It converges fast and stably and dramatically improves the discriminability of the simple aggregation method of canonical correlations (i.e. $\mathbf{T} = \mathbf{I}$). After $\mathbf{T}$ is found to maximize the canonical correlations of within-class sets and minimize those of between-class sets, a comparisons of any two sets is achieved using the similarity value defined in (4).

4   Experimental Results and Discussion

4.1   Experimental Setting for Face Recognition

Database and Protocol. We have acquired a database called the *Cambridge-Toshiba Face Video Database* with 100 individuals of varying age and ethnicity, and equally represented genders. For each person, 7 video sequences of the person in arbitrary motion were collected. Each sequence was recorded in a different illumination setting for 10s at 10fps and 320×240 pixel resolution (see Figure 4). Following automatic localization using a cascaded face detector [14]

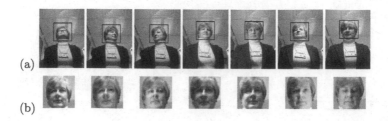

(a)

(b)

Fig. 4. Face data sets. (a) Frames of a typical face video sequence. (b) Face proto-types of 7 different lighting sequences.

and cropping to the uniform scale of 20×20 pixels, images of faces were histogram equalized. Training of all the algorithms was performed with data acquired in a single illumination setting and testing with a single other setting. We used 18 randomly selected training/test combinations for reporting identification rates.

Comparative Methods. We compared the performance of our learning algo-rithm (DCC) to that of:

- K-L Divergence algorithm (KLD) [3],
- k-Nearest Neighbours (k-NN) and Hausdorff distance[1] in (i) PCA, and (ii) LDA [6] subspaces estimated from training data [5],
- Mutual Subspace Method (MSM) [8], which is equivalent to the simple ag-gregation of canonical correlations,
- Constrained MSM (CMSM) [11] used in a state-of-the-art commercial system FacePass [16].

Dimensionality Selection. In KLD, 96% of data energy was explained by the principal subspace of training data used. In NN-PCA, the optimal number of principal components was 150 without the first three. In NN-LDA, PCA with 150 dimensions (removal of the first 3 principal components did not improve the LDA performance) was applied first to avoid singularity problems and the best dimension of LDA subspace was 150 again. In both MSM and CMSM, the PCA dimension of each image set was fixed to 10, which represents more than 98% of data energy of the set. All 10 canonical correlations were exploited. In CMSM, the best dimension of the constrained subspace was found to be 360 in terms of the test identification rates as shown in Figure 5. The CMSM exhibits a peaking and does not have a principled way of choosing dimensionality of the constrained subspace in practice. By contrast, the proposed method provided constant identification rates regardless of dimensionality of **T** beyond a certain point, as shown in Figure 5. Thus we could fix the dimensionality at 400 for all experiments. This behaviour is highly beneficial from the practical point of view. The PCA dimension of image sets was also fixed to 10 for the proposed method.

Construction of Within-Class Sets for the Proposed Method. In the face image set experiment, the images drawn from a single video sequence of arbitrary

---

[1] $d(X_1, X_2) = \min_{x_1 \in X_1} \max_{x_2 \in X_2} d(x_1, x_2)$

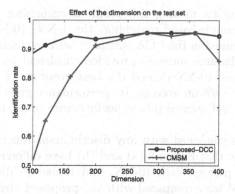

Fig. 5. Dimensionality selection for the proposed method and CMSM. The proposed method is more favorable than CMSM in dimensionality selection. CMSM shows a high peaking. The accuracy of CMSM at 400 is just equivalent to that of simple aggregation of canonical correlations.

head movement were randomly divided into the two within-class sets. The test recognition rates changed by less than 1-2 % for the different trials of random partitioning. In the experiment of general object recognition in Section 4.3, the two sets defined according to different viewing scopes comprised the within class sets.

4.2 Accuracy Comparison for Face Experiments

The 18 experiments were arranged in the order of increasing K-L Divergence between the training and test data. Lower K-L Divergence indicates more similar conditions. The identification rates of the evaluated algorithms is shown in Figure 6.

First, different methods of measuring set similarity were compared in Figure 6 (a). Most of the methods generally had lower recognition rates for experiments having larger KL-Divergence. The KLD method achieved by far the worst recognition rate. Seeing that the illumination conditions varied across data and that the face motion was largely unconstrained, the distribution of within-class face

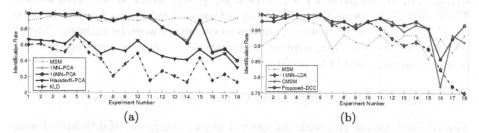

Fig. 6. Identification rates for the 18 experiments. (a) Methods of set matching. (b) Methods of set matching combined with discriminative transformations. (The variation between the training and test data of the experiments increases along the horizontal axis. Note that (a) and (b) have different scales for vertical axis.)

patterns was very broad, making this result unsurprising. As representatives of non-parametric sample-based matching, the 1-NN, 10-NN, and Hausdorff-distance methods defined in the PCA subspace were evaluated. It was observed that the Hausdorff-distance measure provided consistent but far poorer results than the NN methods. 10-NN yielded the best accuracy of the three, which is worse than MSM by 8.6% on average. Its performance greatly varied across the experiments while MSM showed robust performance under the different experimental conditions.

Second, methods combined with any discriminant function were compared in Figure 6 (b). Note that Figure 6 (a) and (b) have different scales. By taking MSM as a gauging proxy, 1-NN, 10-NN, and Hausdorff distance in the LDA subspace and CMSM were compared with the proposed algorithm. Here again, 10-NN was the best of the three LDA methods. For better visualization of comparative results, the performance of 1-NN and Hausdorff in LDA was removed from the figure. 10-NN-LDA yielded a big improvement over 10-NN-PCA but the accuracy of the method again greatly varied across the experiments. Note that 10-NN-LDA outperformed MSM for similar conditions between the training and test sets, but it became noticeably inferior as the conditions changed. The recognition rate of NN-LDA was considerably inferior to our method for the more difficult experiments (experiments 11 to 18 in Figure 6 (b)). NN-LDA yielded just 75% recognition rate for exp.18 where two very different illumination settings (see last two of Figure 4 (b)) were used for the training and test data. The accuracy of our method remained high at 97%. Note that the experiments 11 to 18 in Figure 6 are more realistic than the first half because they have greater variation in lighting conditions between training and testing. The proposed method also constantly provided a significant improvement over MSM. Just one exception for the proposed method due to overfitting were noted. Except this single case, the proposed method improved MSM by 5-10 % reaching almost more than 97% recognition rate.

Although the proposed method achieved a comparable accuracy with CMSM in the face recognition experiment, the latter had to be optimised aposteriori by dimensionality selection. By contrast, DCC does not need any feature selection. The underlying concept of CMSM is to orthogonalize different class subspaces [17], i.e. to make $\mathbf{P}_i^T\mathbf{P}_j = \mathbf{O}$ if $C_i \neq C_j$, where $\mathbf{O}$ is a zero matrix. Then, canonical correlations (2) of the orthogonal subspaces become zeros as $\mathrm{tr}(\mathbf{Q}_{ij}^T\mathbf{P}_i^T\mathbf{P}_j\mathbf{Q}_{ji}) = 0$. However, subspaces can not always be orthogonal to all the other subspaces. Then, a direct optimization of canonical correlations in the proposed method would be preferred.

4.3   Experiment on Large Scale General Object Classes

The ALOI database [15] with 500 general object categories of different viewing angles provides another experimental data set for the comparison. Object images were segmented from the simple background and scaled to 20×20 pixel size. The training and five test sets were set up with different viewing angles of the objects as shown in Figure 7 (a) and (b). All images in the test sets had at least

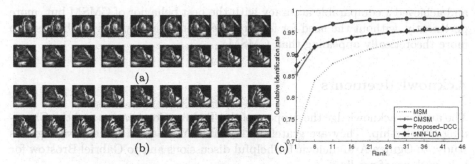

Fig. 7. ALOI experiment. (a) The training set consists of 18 images taken at every 10 degree. (b) Two test sets are shown. Each test set contains 9 images at 10 degree intervals, different from the training set. (c) Cumulative identification plots of several methods.

5 degree pose difference from every sample of the training set. The methods of MSM, NN-LDA and CMSM were compared with the proposed method in terms of identification rate. The PCA dimensionality of each set was fixed to 5 and thus 5 canonical correlations were exploited for MSM, CMSM and the proposed method. Similarly, 5 nearest neighbours were used in LDA. See Figure 7 (c) for the cumulative identification rates. Unlike the face experiment, NN-LDA yielded better accuracy than MSM. This might be due to the nearest neighbours of the training and test set differed only slightly by the five degree pose difference (The two sets had no changes in lighting and they had accurate localization of the objects.). Here again, the proposed method were substantially superior to both MSM and NN-LDA. The proposed method outperformed even the best behaviour of CMSM in this scenario.

4.4 Computational Complexity

The matching complexity of the methods using canonical correlations, $O(d^3)$, is far lower than that of the sample-based matching methods such as k-NN, $O(c^2 n)$, where d is the subspace dimension of each set, c is the number of samples of each set and n is the dimensionality of feature space, since $d \ll c, n$.

5 Conclusions

A novel discriminative learning framework has been proposed for object recognition using canonical correlations of image sets. The proposed method has been evaluated on both face image sets obtained from videos and image sets of five hundred general object categories. The new technique facilitates effective discriminative learning over sets, thus providing an impressive set classification accuracy. It significantly outperformed the KLD method representing a parametric distribution-based matching and NN in both PCA/LDA subspaces as examples of non-parametric sample-based matching. It also largely outperformed MSM and achieved a comparable accuracy with the best behavior of CMSM but, more pertinently, without the need for feature selection. The proposed method is also more theoretically appealing than CMSM.

Acknowledgements

The authors acknowledge the support of the Toshiba Corporation and the Chevening Scholarship. They are grateful to Osamu Yamaguchi for motivating this study; to Ognjen Arandjelović for helpful discussions and to Gabriel Brostow for help with proof-reading.

References

1. K. Lee, M. Yang, and D. Kriegman. Video-based face recognition using probabilistic appearance manifolds. *CVPR*, pages 313–320, 2003.
2. S. Zhou, V. Krueger, and R.Chellappa. Probabilistic recognition of human faces from video. *Computer Vision and Image Understanding*, 91(1):214–245, 2003.
3. G. Shakhnarovich, J. W. Fisher, and T. Darrel. Face recognition from long-term observations. *ECCV*, pages 851–868, 2002.
4. O. Arandjelović, G. Shakhnarovich, J. Fisher, R. Cipolla, and T. Darrell. Face recognition with image sets using manifold density divergence. *CVPR*, 2005.
5. S. Satoh. Comparative Evaluation of Face Sequence Matching for Content-based Video Access. *Int'l Conf. on Automatic Face and Gesture Recognition*, 2000.
6. P.N.Belhumeur, J.P.Hespanha, and D.J.Kriegman. Eigenfaces vs. Fisherfaces: Recognition Using Class Specific Linear Projection. *PAMI*, 19(7):711–720, 1997.
7. M. Bressan, J. Vitria Nonparametric discriminant analysis and nearest neighbor classification. *Pattern Recognition Letters*, 24(2003):2743–2749, 2003.
8. O. Yamaguchi, K. Fukui, and K. Maeda. Face recognition using temporal image sequence. *AFG*, (10):318–323, 1998.
9. L. Wolf and A. Shashua. Learning over sets using kernel principal angles. *JMLR*, 4(10):913–931, 2003.
10. T.K. Kim, O. Arandjelović and R. Cipolla, Learning over Sets using Boosted Manifold Principal Angles (BoMPA). *BMVC*, 2005.
11. K. Fukui and O. Yamaguchi. Face recognition using multi-viewpoint patterns for robot vision. *Int'l Symp. of Robotics Research*, 2003.
12. H. Hotelling. Relations between two sets of variates. *Biometrika*, 28:321–372, 1936.
13. Å. Björck and G. H. Golub. Numerical methods for computing angles between linear subspaces. *Mathematics of Computation*, 27(123):579–594, 1973.
14. P. Viola and M. Jones. Robust real-time face detection. *IJCV*, 57(2):137–154, 2004.
15. J.M. Geusebroek, G.J. Burghouts, and A.W.M. Smeulders. The Amsterdam library of object images. *IJCV*, 61(1):103–112, January, 2005.
16. Toshiba. Facepass. http://www.toshiba.co.jp/rdc/mmlab/tech/w31e.htm.
17. E.Oja, Subspace Methods of Pattern Recognition. Research Studies Press, 1983.

Statistical Priors for Efficient Combinatorial Optimization Via Graph Cuts

Daniel Cremers[1] and Leo Grady[2]

[1] Department of Computer Science, University of Bonn, Germany
[2] Department of Imaging and Visualization,
Siemens Corporate Research, Princeton, NJ

Abstract. Bayesian inference provides a powerful framework to optimally integrate statistically learned prior knowledge into numerous computer vision algorithms. While the Bayesian approach has been successfully applied in the Markov random field literature, the resulting combinatorial optimization problems have been commonly treated with rather inefficient and inexact general purpose optimization methods such as Simulated Annealing. An efficient method to compute the global optima of certain classes of cost functions defined on binary-valued variables is given by graph min-cuts. In this paper, we propose to reconsider the problem of statistical learning for Bayesian inference in the context of efficient optimization schemes. Specifically, we address the question: Which prior information may be learned while retaining the ability to apply Graph Cut optimization? We provide a framework to learn and impose prior knowledge on the distribution of pairs and triplets of labels. As an illustration, we demonstrate that one can optimally restore binary textures from very noisy images with runtimes on the order of a second while imposing hundreds of statistically learned constraints per pixel.

1 Introduction

In his 1948 paper, Shannon considered the formation of text as a stochastic process. He suggested to learn the probabilities governing this process by computing the histograms of occurrences and co-occurrences of letters from a sample text. Subsequently he validated the accuracy of the generated model by sampling new texts from the estimated stochastic model. Not surprisingly, the successive integration of higher order terms (occurrence of letter triplets rather than pairs etc.) provides for the emergence of increasingly familiar or meaningful structures in the synthesized text.

In the context of images, similar approaches have been proposed in the Markov random field literature. We refer to [24] for an excellent introduction. Going back at least as far as Abend's work [1], Markov random fields have endured a sustained interest in the vision community. Besag [3] applied them in the context of binary image restoration and Derin [8] and Gimelfarb and coworkers [12] analyzed texture in the context of a Markov random field using learned priors based on gray level co-occurrences. Work has continued through new applications such as texture segmentation [20] or through extension of the basic model, for example by considering higher-order cliques [23].

There are two major computational challenges arising in the application of Markov random fields for Bayesian inference. Firstly, one needs to devise methods to efficiently

A. Leonardis, H. Bischof, and A. Pinz (Eds.): ECCV 2006, Part III, LNCS 3953, pp. 263–274, 2006.

learn priors given a set of representative sample data. Secondly, upon imposing the learned prior, the inference problem requires global optimization of a given cost function. In this work, we will focus on binary-valued cost functions

$$E : \{0,1\}^n \rightarrow \mathbb{R} \tag{1}$$

over a large set of variables $\{x_1, \ldots, x_n\}$. The optimization of such functions has a long tradition, going back to the work of Ising on ferromagnetism [15]. Numerous methods have been proposed to tackle these combinatorial optimization problems. Geman and Geman [11] showed that the method of Simulated Annealing [16, 21] is guaranteed to find the global optimum of a given function. Alternative continuation methods such as Graduated Non-Convexity [4] have been proposed as well. Unfortunately, general purpose optimization methods such as Simulated Annealing require exponential runtime and can be quite slow for the number of nodes considered in most realistic applications.[1] In contrast, deterministic or approximation algorithms are not guaranteed to find a global optimum. The key challenge addressed in the present paper is therefore to devise methods to *efficiently* impose statistically learned knowledge in such combinatorial optimization problems.

The optimization of cost functions of the form (1) is in general an NP-hard combinatorial problem. The pioneering works of Picard and Ratliff [22] and of Greig *et al.* [13] showed that certain functions E of binary-valued variables can be represented by a directed graph $\mathcal{G}(\mathcal{V}, \mathcal{E})$ with nonnegative edge weights and two nodes s and t, called source and sink, such that the optimum of the function E corresponds to the minimal s-t-cut of the respective graph. According to the theorem of Ford and Fulkerson [9], the computation of the minimal cut is equivalent to computing the maximum flow from the source to the sink. Several algorithms exist to compute this flow in polynomial time (see e.g. [5]). For applications of Graph Cuts to non-binary cases, we refer to [6, 14]. To restate, for certain combinatorial optimization problems, max-flow/min-cut algorithms provide both a fast and an exact solution.

Recently, theoretical efforts have been made to determine which classes of functions can be optimized by Graph Cuts. Ishikawa [14] provided constructive results showing how Graph Cuts may be applied to optimize Markov random fields for convex expressions. Kolmogorov and Zabih [17] pointed out that a class of energies satisfying certain submodularity constraints are *graph representable*, i.e. they can be efficiently minimized by computing the cut of an appropriate graph.

One should mention that Belief Propagation (BP) has become popular to efficiently perform Bayesian inference on graphs (see [10]). While BP is not limited by the above submodularity constraints, to the best of our knowledge there are no optimality guarantees for graphs with loops, such as the ones considered here.

The goal of the present paper is to provide a framework for learning empirical distributions of labels from sample graphs, to impose these as statistical priors in the framework of Bayesian inference on graphs and to specify which kinds of priors are consistent with graph-representable energy terms. The interpretation of submodularity in the context of statistical learning allows us to specify a class of priors which can be

---

[1] In practice, increased speed of Markov Chain Monte Carlo methods can be obtained by using bottom-up proposals and flipping entire patches of label values [2].

learned from samples and efficiently imposed within the framework of Bayesian inference. By restricting ourselves to graph-representable priors, we can guarantee global optima in polynomial time. In practice, we find the optimization times to be extremely fast.

As an illustration of our approach, we consider the problem of Bayesian restoration of binary images. In particular, we will show that one can impose previously learned information on correlation of the labels of pairs and triplets of vertices, as long as vertex labels are positively correlated. Numerical experiments demonstrate that fairly complex textural information can be learned, compactly represented and used for the efficient and optimal restoration from noisy images. While the restoration of binary textures may be considered a toy example, it shows that our method allows to impose statistically learned shape information in large-scale combinatorial optimization problems, providing global optima in polynomial runtime.

The outline of the paper is as follows. In Section 2, we will briefly review two lines of work which form the backbone of our method, namely the concept of Bayesian inference on graphs, and the submodularity conditions discussed in [17]. In Section 3, we introduce the key contribution of this paper, namely a characterization of a class of translation-invariant statistical priors on vertex labels which can be learned from sample graphs and which can be efficiently imposed in Bayesian inference via Graph Cuts. We define a measure of relevance of coupling terms which allows one to impose only the most relevant of learned priors. In Section 4, we provide numerical results on the restoration of binary images that illuminate different aspects of our method: highly accurate restorations despite large amounts of noise, optimal restorations of fairly complex textures in runtimes below one second, drastic speed-up through the use of sparse priors, and improved restoration by using higher-order priors.

2 Bayesian Inference on Graphs

Let $x = (x_1, \ldots, x_n) \in \{0, 1\}^n$ be a vector of binary variables. Assume we are given a noisy version $I = (I_1, \ldots, I_n) \in \mathbb{R}^n$ of this binary-valued vector. Then we can make use of the framework of Bayesian inference in order to reconstruct the vector x by maximizing the posterior probability

$$\mathcal{P}(x \mid I) = \frac{\mathcal{P}(I \mid x) \, \mathcal{P}(x)}{\mathcal{P}(I)}. \qquad (2)$$

The Bayesian reasoning has become increasingly popular in the computer vision community [24], mainly for two reasons. Firstly, the conditional probability $\mathcal{P}(I \mid x)$ is often easier to model, since it represents the likelihood of a certain observation I given a state of the model x. Secondly, the Bayesian inference allows one to optimally integrate prior knowledge by the term $\mathcal{P}(x)$, specifying which interpretations of the data are *a priori* more or less likely.

In this paper, we will consider the specific case that the measurements I_i are mutually independent and that moreover they only depend on the value x_i at the node i. Under these assumptions, the data term in (2) can be written as: $\mathcal{P}(I \mid x) = \prod_i \mathcal{P}(I_i \mid x_i)$.

In this paper, we consider the data term:

$$P(I_i \mid x_i) \propto \exp\left(\frac{\lambda}{1 + |I_i - x_i|}\right). \tag{3}$$

While alternative choices are conceivable, this is not the focus of this work. The free parameter λ is currently chosen manually. Future research is focused on identifying an automatic estimate. The application of Bayesian inference amounts to a combinatorial optimization problem.

Kolmogorov and Zabih [17] recently discussed a class of cost functions which are able to be optimized efficiently by Graph Cuts. To this end, one considers two classes of cost functions denoted by $\mathcal{F}^2$ (and $\mathcal{F}^3$), representing functions E which can be written as a sum of functions of up to two variables at a time:

$$E(x_1, \ldots, x_n) = \sum_{i<j} E_{ij}(x_i, x_j), \tag{4}$$

and up to three variables for $\mathcal{F}_3$. In this way, one can consider nested classes of progressively more complex functions $\mathcal{F}^1 \subset \mathcal{F}^2 \subset \ldots \subset \mathcal{F}^n$, where the latter class corresponds to the full class of binary-valued functions.

In [17], Kolmogorov and Zabih pointed out that functions in $\mathcal{F}^1$, $\mathcal{F}^2$ and $\mathcal{F}^3$ can be optimized in polynomial time with the Graph Cuts algorithm if they fulfill certain *submodularity constraints* [18]. Namely, all functions in $\mathcal{F}^1$ are submodular, while functions in $\mathcal{F}^2$ and $\mathcal{F}^3$ are submodular if, for all terms $E_{ij}(x_i, x_j)$ of two arguments

$$E_{ij}(0,0) + E_{ij}(1,1) \leq E_{ij}(0,1) + E_{ij}(1,0), \tag{5}$$

and, for all terms $E_{ijk}(x_i, x_j, x_k)$ of three arguments, the same inequality must hold in the remaining two arguments once any one of them is fixed.

3 Statistical Priors for Bayesian Inference

In the context of restoration of binary images, researchers have successfully exploited generic priors $\mathcal{P}(x)$ on the space of label configurations x — such as the one used in the well-known Ising model [15] — which favor neighboring nodes to have the same label. Such priors lead to smooth restorations and are well suited for the removal of noise. Yet they also lead to a blurring of (possibly relevant) small-scale structures. Moreover, given sample images of the structures of interest, one may ask whether it is possible to *learn* more appropriate object-specific priors $\mathcal{P}(x)$ and impose these within the framework of Bayesian inference.

In this work, we are interested in priors which can be easily computed from the histograms of joint co-occurrence of label pairs or triplets, along the lines pioneered in [7, 12]. For a more sophisticated alternative to directly learn posterior distributions using MCMC sampling, we refer to [19]. To link statistical priors to co-occurrence frequencies, we rewrite the generic prior on a set of n variables as follows:

$$\begin{aligned}
\mathcal{P}(x_1, \ldots, x_n) &= \mathcal{P}(x_1, x_2 \mid x_3, \ldots, x_n)\mathcal{P}(x_3, \ldots, x_n) \\
&= \mathcal{P}(x_1, x_2 \mid x_3, \ldots, x_n)\mathcal{P}(x_3, x_4 \mid x_5, \ldots, x_n)\mathcal{P}(x_5, \ldots, x_n) \\
&= \ldots = \prod_{i \text{ odd}} \mathcal{P}(x_i, x_{i+1} \mid x_{i+2}, \ldots, x_n).
\end{aligned} \tag{6}$$

Let us now assume that the co-occurrence probability for any two variables does not depend on a third variable. Under this assumption, (6) then simplifies to

$$\mathcal{P}(x_1, \ldots, x_n) = \prod_{i \text{ odd}} \mathcal{P}(x_i, x_{i+1}). \tag{7}$$

Obviously, we can carry out the same rearrangement using arbitrary pairings of the n variables x_i. Upon multiplying all these equations, each pair (x_i, x_j) obviously appears the same number of times as a factor in the right-hand side. We get:

$$(\mathcal{P}(x_1, \ldots, x_n))^\Gamma = \prod_{i \neq j} \mathcal{P}(x_i, x_j), \tag{8}$$

where the constant Γ denotes the number of ways to generate such pairings divided by the number of times each pair appears in the overall product. In the case of label pairs, we have $\Gamma = \binom{n}{2}$. We obtain the *prior energy*:

$$E(x_1, \ldots, x_n) = -\log \mathcal{P}(x_1, \ldots, x_n) = -\frac{1}{\Gamma} \sum_{i \neq j} \log \mathcal{P}(x_i, x_j). \tag{9}$$

Similarly, the relaxed assumption that the co-occurrence of labels for any triplet (x_i, x_j, x_k) does not depend on a fourth node, leads to an energy of the form

$$E(x_1, \ldots, x_n) = -\frac{1}{\tilde{\Gamma}} \sum_{ijk} \log \mathcal{P}(x_i, x_j, x_k), \tag{10}$$

where the sum extends over all pairwise distinct triplets of nodes and $\tilde{\Gamma} = \binom{n}{3}$. While the above independency assumptions will generally not be fulfilled, let us make two remarks: Firstly, the expressions for the priors (9) and (10) also hold if higher-order effects do not contribute *on the average*. Secondly, the independency assumption can be gradually relaxed by considering terms of increasing order of interaction. We will refer to priors with an energy $E \in \mathcal{F}^k$ as priors of order k. In the following, we will focus on the spaces $\mathcal{F}^2$ and $\mathcal{F}^3$. To circumvent the approximation in (7), the Markov random field community has developed more sophisticated techniques to approximate the prior in terms of local characteristics (see e.g. [24]).

For a second-order prior $\mathcal{P}$, the energy E in (6) is of the form (4). Since we are dealing with binary-valued variables, the each term E_{ij} in (4) is of the form

$$E_{ij}(x_i, x_j) = \alpha_{ij}^{11} x_i x_j + \alpha_{ij}^{10} x_i(1-x_j) + \alpha_{ij}^{01}(1-x_i)x_j + \alpha_{ij}^{00}(1-x_i)(1-x_j), \tag{11}$$

with four parameters associated with each vertex pair. According to (6), we can relate these parameters to the probability of co-occurrence of label values:

$$\alpha_{ij}^{11} = -\log \mathcal{P}\left(x_i = 1 \cap x_j = 1\right), \quad \alpha_{ij}^{10} = -\log \mathcal{P}\left(x_i = 1 \cap x_j = 0\right), \ldots \tag{12}$$

In the case of a third-order prior on binary-valued variables, the energy E in (6) is given by a sum of energies E_{ijk} taking on the form

$$E_{ijk}(x_i, x_j, x_k) = \alpha_{ijk}^{111} x_i x_j x_k + \alpha_{ijk}^{110} x_i x_j (1-x_k) + \alpha_{ijk}^{101} x_i (1-x_j) x_k + \ldots$$

with eight parameters associated with each vertex triplet and

$$\alpha_{ijk}^{111} = -\log \mathcal{P}(x_i=1 \cap x_j=1 \cap x_k=1), \quad \alpha_{ijk}^{110} = \ldots \tag{13}$$

The central idea of learning priors is to determine the parameters of the probabilistic model (6) from samples of labeled graphs. According to (13), the parameter α_{ijk}^{111}, for example, corresponds to the negative logarithm of the relative frequency of label configuration $(1, 1, 1)$ at the three nodes i, j and k.

In most relevant restoration algorithms one does not know the location of structures of interest. Therefore it is meaningful to focus on the subclass of *translation-invariant priors*, i.e. priors which treat all nodes identically. These are also referred to as *spatially homogeneous priors* [24]. For priors of second order, the model parameters in expression (11) can only depend on the *relative* location of node i and node j. In other words $\alpha_{ij} = \alpha_{(j-i)}$ etc., where $(j-i)$ denotes the vector connecting node i to node j. Given a training image, one can estimate the parameters $\alpha_{(j-i)}^{11}, \alpha_{(j-i)}^{01}, \alpha_{(j-i)}^{10}$, and $\alpha_{(j-i)}^{00}$ defining the translation-invariant prior distributions of second order, because the probabilities of co-occurrence of label pairs in (12) can be approximated by their histogram values. Similarly, in the case of third-order priors, the eight parameters α_{ijk} in (3) associated with each triplet of nodes only depend on the relative location of nodes i, j and k. These parameters can be estimated from joint histograms of triplets computed on a sample image.

Along the lines sketched above, it is possible to learn priors on the set of binary variables from the empirical histograms computed on sample images. Such statistical priors can be used in various ways. For example, as suggested by Shannon, one could generate synthetic label configurations (binary images if the nodes correspond to image pixels) by randomly sampling from the estimated distributions — see for example [7]. In the following, we will instead employ the empirically learned priors for the purpose of reconstructing a labeling $x = \{x_1, \ldots, x_n\} \in \{0, 1\}^n$ of a graph given a noisy version $I = \{I_1, \ldots, I_n\} \in \mathbb{R}^n$ of it and given the knowledge that the labeling is statistically similar to previously observed label configurations. The optimal restoration is given by the maximum *a posteriori* estimate in (2). Equivalently, we can minimize the negative logarithm of (2). With (3) and a translation-invariant prior of second order obtained from equations (9), (4) and (11) this leads to an energy of the form:

$$E(x_1, .., x_n) = \sum_i \frac{-\lambda}{1+|I_i - x_i|} + \sum_{i<j} \left(\alpha_{(j-i)}^{11} x_i x_j + \alpha_{(j-i)}^{10} x_i (1-x_j) \right. \tag{14}$$

$$\left. + \alpha_{(j-i)}^{01} (1-x_i) x_j + \alpha_{(j-i)}^{00} (1-x_i)(1-x_j) \right).$$

Similarly binary restoration with a translation-invariant prior of third order is done by minimizing an energy of the form:

$$E(\{x_i\}) = \sum_i \frac{-\lambda}{1 + |I_i - x_i|} + \sum_{i<j<k} \left(\alpha^{111}_{(j-i,k-i)} x_i x_j x_k + \alpha^{110}_{(j-i,k-i)} x_i x_j (1-x_k) + ... \right),$$
(15)

with eight terms imposing learned correlations of the label at node i with labels at nodes j and k. Due to the translation invariance, the parameters $\alpha_{ijk} = \alpha_{(j-i,k-i)}$ merely depend on the vectors from i to j and from i to k.

Minimizing energies of the forms (14) or (15) over the space of binary variables $x \in \{0,1\}^n$ is in general a hard combinatorial problem.[2] In the context of images with relevant size, the number of nodes is on the order of $n \sim 256^2$ or larger, therefore an exhaustive search or stochastic optimization methods such as simulated annealing are not well-suited for this task.

While the Graph Cuts algorithm allows an efficient global optimization in polynomial time, it only applies to a certain class of energies. The submodularity constraints reviewed in Section 2, however, allow us to make a precise statement about which priors *can* be efficiently imposed in the Bayesian restoration using Graph Cuts. Using the relation between energies and prior distributions given in (9), we can express the submodularity constraint (5) in terms of probabilities:

$$-\log \mathcal{P}_{00} - \log \mathcal{P}_{11} \leq -\log \mathcal{P}_{01} - \log \mathcal{P}_{10},$$
(16)

where $\mathcal{P}_{00} = \mathcal{P}(x_i = 0 \cap x_j = 0)$ stands for the probability that both labels are 0 etc. The above inequality is equivalent to the requirement that:

$$\mathcal{P}_{00} \, \mathcal{P}_{11} \geq \mathcal{P}_{01} \, \mathcal{P}_{10}.$$
(17)

If the joint probability of label values at nodes i and j fulfills the above inequality, then it can be efficiently imposed in the Bayesian restoration by solving the respective max-flow/min-cut problem. In particular, this implies that for any two nodes which are positively correlated (i.e. $\mathcal{P}_{00} \geq \max\{\mathcal{P}_{01}, \mathcal{P}_{10}\}$ and $\mathcal{P}_{11} \geq \max\{\mathcal{P}_{01}, \mathcal{P}_{10}\}$), one can impose their joint probability within the Graph Cuts framework. Beyond this, one can also integrate priors stating that, for example, the label configuration (01) dominates all other configurations while the configuration (10) is sufficiently unlikely for inequality (17) to be fulfilled. On the other hand, joint priors modeling negative correlation, where opposite labels (01) and (10) dominate, are not consistent with inequality (17).

Similarly, the submodularity constraints in [17] impose conditions for which the distributions of triplets can be imposed within the Graph Cuts optimization. Namely, the inequalities have to hold with respect to the remaining two arguments once any one of them is fixed, i.e. if $x_i = 0$ is fixed then the inequality in nodes j and k states:

$$\mathcal{P}_{000} \, \mathcal{P}_{011} \geq \mathcal{P}_{001} \, \mathcal{P}_{010},$$
(18)

where $\mathcal{P}_{000} = \mathcal{P}(x_i = 0 \cap x_j = 0 \cap x_k = 0)$ represents the joint occurrence of three labels of 0, etc. There are eight such constraints for each triplet.

In practice, we compute these joint histograms from sample images and retain only those priors which are consistent with the submodularity constraints (17) or (18). The

---

[2] For an example of an NP-hard problem in the class $\mathcal{F}^2$ see [17].

resulting cost function can be efficiently optimized by the Graph Cuts algorithm. In other words: once we have selected an appropriate set of statistically learned priors, we can perform the Bayesian inference in polynomial runtime. For details on how to convert energy terms into respective edge weights of a graph, we refer to [17].

While the global optimum of the resulting restoration problem is guaranteed to be computable in polynomial time, experimental evidence shows that increasing the number of constraints (and thereby the number of edges in the graph) will typically increase the computation time: While the computation time for $n = 256^2$ nodes with four constraints per node was on the order of 0.03 seconds, increasing the number of constraints per node to 716 leads to a computation time of more than one minute. A simple remedy to this problem is to only impose the most *relevant* constraints. The submodularity constraint in (5) guarantees that the edges of the corresponding graph have non-negative weights [17]. Moreover, if the left side of inequality (5) is much smaller than the right side, then the respective edges will have very large positive weights, hence they will be very relevant to the computation of the minimal cut. Therefore, we can heuristically define the relevance of a coupling term (11) between nodes i and j as the weight of introduced edges:

$$\text{rel}_{ij} = \alpha_{ij}^{10} + \alpha_{ij}^{01} - \alpha_{ij}^{11} - \alpha_{ij}^{00}. \tag{19}$$

In the context of priors of third order, there are six submodularity constraints associated with each node triplet. As a measure of the relevance of a given triplet of nodes, we simply compute the mean of the associated six relevance measures in (19). Qualitatively, this relevance measure states that the co-occurrence of identical label values should dominate the histogram for a prior to be relevant.

4   Experimental Results

Figure 1 shows a binary pattern of vertical stripes of width two pixels, corrupted by various amounts of salt-and-pepper noise.[3] The second image shows the restoration (with $\lambda = 1$) obtained using a second order prior coupling each pixel to the two nodes directly above and to the right. The priors estimated from empirical histograms of stripe patterns simply state that vertically neighboring pixels are very likely to be of the same color. There is no preference in the horizontal direction: since the stripes are two pixels wide, all pair combinations are equally likely. As a consequence, the restoration of the noisier version is suboptimal in that the vertical stripes in the restoration are no longer equidistantly spaced.[4] With increasing noise level, the Bayesian restoration requires increasingly sophisticated priors. The above prior on neighboring pairs of labels can be extended in two ways: by increasing the neighborhood size and by generalizing to higher-order interactions.

By increasing the neighborhood window in which priors are learned and imposed, the resulting prior is still of second order, but it integrates correlations of a given node with more distant nodes. In the case of the stripe pattern in Figure 1, we learned the joint probabilities for a pixel and its neighbors in 9×9 window. This provides coupling

---

[3] "80% noise" means 80% of the pixels are replaced by a random value.
[4] The restoration error gives the percentage of incorrectly labeled pixels.

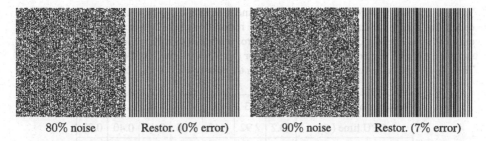

| 80% noise | Restor. (0% error) | 90% noise | Restor. (7% error) |

Fig. 1. Fast restoration of simple patterns: Optimal restorations of noisy stripe patterns using statistical priors learned from the joint histograms of a pixel with the neighbor above and the neighbor to the right. While the left image was perfectly restored in 0.02 seconds, the right one has a restoration error[6] of 7% in 0.03 seconds (on a 200×200 image). Including couplings in larger neighborhoods improves the restoration.

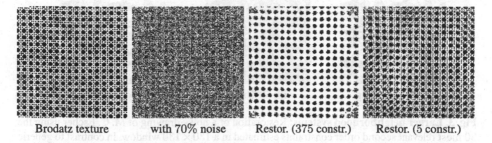

| Brodatz texture | with 70% noise | Restor. (375 constr.) | Restor. (5 constr.) |

Fig. 2. Efficient restoration of complex textures: The images on the left show a binarized Brodatz texture with 70% of noise. Using only relevant constraints (right image), the algorithm is not only faster, but it also provides a better restoration. See Table 1 for a numerical comparison.

to 40 neighbors, 22 of which are submodular. This prior allows to identify horizontal correlations. In the case of the stripe pattern in Figure 1, bottom, it provides a perfect restoration in 1.6 seconds for an image of size 200×200, with $\lambda = 1$.[5]

In order to restore more complex patterns, it is necessary to consider joint distributions of labels in increasingly large neighborhoods. This will lead to an increasing number of edges in the respective graph, coupling each pixel to a larger and larger number of surrounding pixels. In order to keep the computation time low, we impose only the most relevant constraints according to the measure defined in (19). Figure 2 shows a binarized Brodatz texture (256×256 pixels) and the same texture with 70% salt-and-pepper noise. On a sample texture image, we estimated the pairwise joint distributions for pixel couplings in a neighborhood of 35×35 pixels. Among these 612 possible neighbor nodes, 375 provided submodular constraints fulfilling the inequality (17). Using all 375 constraints, the computation of the optimal restoration took 23.2 seconds, giving a restoration error of 23.6%. Using only the five most relevant constraints allowed an optimal restoration in 0.4 seconds. Surprisingly, the restoration error was only 20%. Respective restorations are shown in Figure 2, third and fourth image.

---

[5] Imposing pair priors on a neighborhood size of 9×9, we found that one obtains perfect restorations of the stripe pattern in Figure 1 even with 99% noise.

Table 1. Efficiency with sparse priors: Run time, restoration error and appropriate λ values for decreasing number of constraints imposed in the restoration of the Brodatz texture (Fig. 2). Using only the most relevant constraints leads to improvements both with respect to the run time and, surprisingly, with respect to the restoration error (up to a minimal set of constraints) — see text. The highlighted error values are associated with the restorations in Fig. 2.

Number of constraints	375	53	21	13	7	5	3
CPU time (s)	23.2	2.92	1.45	0.86	0.47	0.40	0.33
Restoration error (%)	**23.6**	23.6	22.2	21.2	20.0	**20.0**	23.3
λ	38	38	33	20	13	8	4

Escher drawing   with 50% noise   Restoration (19.6% error)

Fig. 3. Larger neighborhood systems: Restoration of a noisy drawing of M. C. Escher using the 20 most relevant second order constraints estimated in a 130×130 window. In contrast to generic smoothness priors, the statistically learned priors do not lead to a blurring of image structures.

Table 1 shows respective run-times, restoration errors and appropriate values of λ for imposing varying numbers of relevant constraints which were selected by thresholding the relevance (19) computed for each node pair. The computation time decreases with fewer constraints used. Moreover, the restoration error decreases when using only the most relevant constraints (up to a certain minimal set of constraints). We believe that this property is due to the fact that less relevant constraints may impose spurious correlations, especially when computed from not perfectly periodic textures such as the Brodatz texture. Using only the relevant constraints will assure that the algorithm makes use of only those couplings that are persistent throughout the entire texture.

The selection of relevant terms becomes more crucial when learning priors for larger-scale structures, as these require to consider larger neighborhoods. Figure 3 shows the restoration of a noisy version of a drawing by M. C. Escher.

As suggested in Section 2, one can learn and impose priors on the joint distribution of triplets of labels — provided that the submodularity conditions (18) are fulfilled. In practice, the key difficulty of learning third-order priors is that the consideration of all possible node triplets is infeasible for graphs of meaningful size: For a graph of 256×256 nodes, there exist $\binom{256^2}{3} \approx 5 \cdot 10^{13}$ possible triplets. To consider all possible triplets within a certain neighborhood of each node (without counting some more often than others) turns out to be a challenging problem as well. In order to count all triplets in

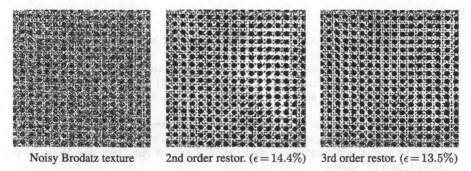

Noisy Brodatz texture   2nd order restor. ($\epsilon = 14.4\%$)   3rd order restor. ($\epsilon = 13.5\%$)

Fig. 4. Triplets versus pairs: Restoration using priors of second and third order on a Brodatz texture with 50% noise. Both priors impose the eleven most relevant constraints in a neighborhood of 15 pixels. Including terms of third order reduces the reconstruction error ϵ from 14.4% (computed in 0.5 seconds) to 13.5% (computed in 2.8 seconds). Exploiting knowledge about the joint probability of triplets (rather than pairs) provides additional submodularity of the reconstruction.

a certain "vicinity" of a node, we revert to the following solution: For each node of the graph, we consider all triangles of a fixed maximal circumference δ (measured in the Manhattan distance) with one vertex at the node of interest. The parameter δ provides a measure of the "vicinity" analogous to the window size in the case of pairs. Figure 4 shows restorations of a noisy Brodatz texture obtained with second and third order priors, respectively. In the specified neighborhood, we identified 215760 triplets per node, 7873 of which provided submodular constraints. We used a threshold $\theta = 2.1$ on the respective relevance of pairs (or triplets) — see (19) — leaving eleven constraints for each node in the graph. Imposing constraints on the joint distribution of triplets (rather than pairs) reduced the restoration error ϵ from 14.4% to 13.5%.

5 Conclusion

We proposed to introduce statistically learned priors into an efficient method for Bayesian inference on graphs. Building up on submodularity constraints for graph-representability, we specified a class of spatially homogeneous priors of second and third order which can be learned from co-occurrence histograms and which can be efficiently imposed by computing Graph Cuts. In particular, we showed that priors favoring labels to be similar are part of this class. To the best of our knowledge, this is the first time that statistically learned priors of second and third order were introduced into an efficient and exact combinatorial optimization algorithm. We believe that our contribution will help to bridge the gap between statistical learning for Bayesian inference and efficient combinatorial optimization. As an illustration of our method, we demonstrated that one can compute optimal restorations of rather complex binary textures from images which are heavily corrupted by noise in runtimes on the order of seconds. Future work aims at answering several open questions: Are there graph-representable priors beyond the class considered here? Are there ways of generalizing the invariance group from translation to rotation and scale invariance?

References

1. K. Abend, T. Harley, and L. N. Kanal. Classification of binary random patterns. *IEEE Transactions on Information Theory*, 11:538–544, 1965.
2. A. Barbu and S.-C. Zhu. Generalizing Swendsen-Wang to sampling arbitrary posterior probabilities. *IEEE Trans. on Patt. Anal. and Mach. Intell.*, 27(8):1239–1253, 2005.
3. J. Besag. On the statistical analysis of dirty pictures. *J. Roy. Statist. Soc., Ser. B.*, 48(3):259–302, 1986.
4. A. Blake and A. Zisserman. *Visual Reconstruction*. MIT Press, 1987.
5. Y. Boykov and V. Kolmogorov. An experimental comparison of min-cut/max-flow algorithms for energy minimization in vision. *IEEE Trans. on Patt. Anal. and Mach. Intell.*, 26(9):1124–1137, 2004.
6. Y. Boykov, O. Veksler, and R. Zabih. Fast approximate energy minimization via graph cuts. *IEEE Trans. on Patt. Anal. and Mach. Intell.*, 23(11):1222–1239, 2001.
7. G.R. Cross and A.K. Jain. Markov random fields texture models. *IEEE Trans. on Patt. Anal. and Mach. Intell.*, 5(1):25–39, 1983.
8. H. Derin and H. Elliott. Modeling and segmentation of noisy and textured images using Gibbs random fields. *IEEE Trans. on Patt. Anal. and Mach. Intell.*, 9(1):39–55, Jan. 1987.
9. L. Ford and D. Fulkerson. *Flows in Networks*. Princeton University Press, Princeton, New Jersey, 1962.
10. W.T. Freeman, E. C. Pasztor, and O. T. Carmichael. Learning low-level vision. *Int. J. of Computer Vision*, 40(1):24–57, 2000.
11. S. Geman and D. Geman. Stochastic relaxation, Gibbs distributions, and the Bayesian restoration of images. *IEEE Trans. on Patt. Anal. and Mach. Intell.*, 6(6):721–741, 1984.
12. G. Gimelfarb. Texture modeling by multiple pairwise pixel interaction. *IEEE Trans. on Patt. Anal. and Mach. Intell.*, 18(11):1110–1114, 1993.
13. D. M. Greig, B. T. Porteous, and A. H. Seheult. Exact maximum *a posteriori* estimation for binary images. *J. Roy. Statist. Soc., Ser. B.*, 51(2):271–279, 1989.
14. H. Ishikawa. Exact optimization for Markov random fields with convex priors. *IEEE Trans. on Patt. Anal. and Mach. Intell.*, 25(10):1333–1336, Oct. 2003.
15. E. Ising. Beitrag zur Theorie des Ferromagnetismus. *Zeitschrift für Physik*, 23:253–258, 1925.
16. S. Kirkpatrick, C. D. Gelatt Jr., and M. P. Vecchi. Optimization by simulated annealing. *Science*, 220(4598):671–680, 1983.
17. V. Kolmogorov and R. Zabih. What energy functions can be minimized via graph cuts? *IEEE Trans. on Patt. Anal. and Mach. Intell.*, 24(5):657–673, 2004.
18. B. Korte and J. Vygen. *Combinatorial Optimization: Theory and Algorithms*. Springer, 3rd edition, 2006.
19. S. Kumar and M. Hebert. Approximate parameter learning in discriminative fields. In *Snowbird Learning Workshop*, Utah, 2004.
20. B. S. Manjunath and R. Chellappa. Unsupervised texture segmentation using Markov random field models. *IEEE Trans. on Patt. Anal. and Mach. Intell.*, 13(5):478–482, May 1991.
21. N. Metropolis, A. Rosenbluth, M. Rosenbluth, A. Teller, and E. Teller. Equation of state calculations by fast computing machines. *J. Chem. Physics*, 21:1087–1092, 1953.
22. J. C. Picard and H. D. Ratliff. Minimum cuts and related problems. *Networks*, 5:357–370, 1975.
23. W. Pieczynski, D. Benboudjema, and P. Lanchantin. Statistical image segmentation using triplet Markov fields. In Sebastiano B. Serpico, editor, *SPIE Int. Symposium on Image and Signal Processing for Remote Sensing VIII*, volume 4885, pages 92–101. SPIE, March 2003.
24. G. Winkler. *Image Analysis, Random Fields and Markov Chain Monte Carlo Methods*, volume 27 of *Appl. of Mathematics*. Springer, Heidelberg, 2003.

Sampling Representative Examples for Dimensionality Reduction and Recognition – Bootstrap Bumping LDA

Hui Gao and James W. Davis

Dept. of Computer Science and Engineering
The Ohio State University, 2015 Neil Ave,
Columbus, OH 43220, USA
{gaoh, jwdavis}@cse.ohio-state.edu

Abstract. We present a novel method for dimensionality reduction and recognition based on Linear Discriminant Analysis (LDA), which specifically deals with the Small Sample Size (SSS) problem in Computer Vision applications. Unlike the traditional methods, which impose specific assumptions to address the SSS problem, our approach introduces a variant of bootstrap bumping technique, which is a general framework in statistics for model search and inference. An intermediate linear representation is first hypothesized from each bootstrap sample. Then LDA is performed in the reduced subspace. Lastly, the final model is selected among all hypotheses for the best classification. Experiments on synthetic and real datasets demonstrate the advantages of our Bootstrap Bumping LDA (BB-LDA) approach over the traditional LDA based methods.

1 Introduction

As a statistical method for dimensionality reduction and classification [1], Linear Discriminant Analysis (LDA) has been widely employed in Computer Vision research (e.g., face and gait recognition [2, 3, 4, 5]). Since LDA assumes multiple Gaussians with equal covariance, its success largely depends on accurate estimates of the model parameters (class means and common covariance). However in most Computer Vision applications, the sample size N is relatively small in comparison to the input dimension D. The traditional Maximum Likelihood (ML) estimates show poor convergence to the true parameters due to the curse of the dimensionality. Furthermore, when $N < D$, the ML estimate of the common covariance $\hat{\Sigma}$ is even singular (the LDA solution is underconstrained due to the non-existence of $\hat{\Sigma}^{-1}$). These two issues together constitute the so-called Small Sample Size (SSS) problem in LDA.

The traditional LDA methods [6, 2, 3, 7, 8] focus only on the second issue of a singular $\hat{\Sigma}$, but ignore the accurate estimate of the true model parameters. Even if $N > D$, as long as N is not much larger than D, the SSS problem persists. From this point of view, the dual impact of the SSS problem is crucial to the success of LDA in Computer Vision applications.

In this work, we propose to deal with the SSS problem from a more general aspect with the goal of accurately estimating the model parameters. Instead of imposing explicit assumptions to simply invert the singular $\hat{\Sigma}$, we introduce a variant of a general

A. Leonardis, H. Bischof, and A. Pinz (Eds.): ECCV 2006, Part III, LNCS 3953, pp. 275–287, 2006.

statistical framework, bootstrap bumping, which creates a hypothesis from each bootstrap sample (a subset of examples) and selects the best model according to a target criteria. The original bumping technique was developed in [9] for finding better local minima, resistant fitting, and optimization under constraints. We develop the idea to deal with the SSS problem by hypothesizing an intermediate linear representation from each bootstrap sample and choosing the final model (representation) with the best recognition performance. This extension not only has the same asymptotical property as the original bumping procedure, but now improves the estimation accuracy and implicitly handles the singularity problem of $\hat{\Sigma}$ in the SSS problem. We present experiments on synthetic and real datasets to clearly show the advantages of our approach over the traditional LDA methods.

In the remainder of this paper, we first discuss the background and related work of LDA and bootstrap bumping in Sect. 2. Then we describe our proposed approach in Sect. 3, which specifically deals with the SSS problem in LDA. Lastly, experimental results are presented in Sect. 4, followed by conclusions in Sect. 5.

2   Background and Related Work

There are two different perspectives looking at LDA. Fisher's LDA is defined by maximizing the ratio of the between-class and within-class scatter matrices (S_b and S_w) in a linear feature space [10, 11]. In Bayesian decision theory, LDA is defined for the case of multiple Gaussians with equal covariance. The two approaches were shown to be equivalent in [12] with S_w being the ML estimate $\hat{\Sigma}$ and S_b being derived from the ML estimates of the class means. The mathematical description of both approaches can be found in detail in [13], which we omit here due to space constraints.

2.1   LDA and the SSS Problem

Although well-grounded in theory, LDA faces the challenge of the SSS problem in real applications. Traditional methods only aim to solve the singularity problem of $\hat{\Sigma}$ by imposing specific assumptions to simply invert $\hat{\Sigma}$.

The simple approach PINV-LDA [6] substitutes the inverse operation with pseudoinverse. The two-stage method PCA+LDA [2] projects the data in the nearly complete PCA subspace to make the $\hat{\Sigma}$ projection just full rank. However, with a small number of examples, $\hat{\Sigma}$ is unstable especially in those components with small eigenvalues which are mostly emphasized in the inverse operation. Both methods of PINV-LDA and PCA+LDA are sensitive to noise and small perturbations.

As one improvement, Enhanced Fisher's Linear Discriminant (EFLD) [3] varies the number of PCA components to regulate the projection of $\hat{\Sigma}$. This assumes that the small components are not informative for classification, which may impose a performance limitation. Another approach Direct LDA (D-LDA) [7] assumes the null space of S_b contains no useful information for recognition. However, as shown in our prior work [14], D-LDA is equivalent to directly taking the linear space of class means as the LDA solution. It has severe limitations by ignoring the common covariance estimate $\hat{\Sigma}$ (or S_w). Lastly, $\hat{\Sigma}$ can be modified to avoid the singularity problem, such as $\hat{\Sigma} + \sigma I$

in Regularized LDA (R-LDA) [8][1]. With σ usually being a small scalar, R-LDA heavily relies on the small components and even null components for recognition, which is neither stable nor supported by the existing examples. For $\sigma = inf$, R-LDA is equivalent to D-LDA by ignoring $\hat{\Sigma}$. Furthermore, R-LDA is computationally inefficient for a large input dimension D since the full-rank matrix $\hat{\Sigma} + \sigma I$ is of size $D \times D$ and is to be inverted in LDA.

Traditional LDA methods only focus on the singularity problem of $\hat{\Sigma}$. Systematic attempts to reduce the variance of the ML estimates (for both class means and common covariance) in the general SSS problem have not yet been reported. We address this issue in our proposed framework of Bootstrap Bumping LDA.

Additionally there are approaches to address the model limitations of LDA, such as methods to extract non-linear features in Quadratic Discriminant Analysis (QDA) [13] for multiple Gaussians with non-equal covariance, kernel-based Generalized LDA (GLDA) [15], and Locally Linear Discriminant Analysis (LLDA) [16]. Since more examples are usually required to constrain more complex solutions, these methods are even more sensitive to the SSS problem. As a hybrid model of LDA and QDA, Oriented Discriminant Analysis (ODA) [17] assumes the same as QDA of multiple Gaussians with non-equal covariance, but extracts linear features by maximizing the Kullback-Liebler divergence between classes. However its explicit explanation remains unclear in Bayesian decision theory since quadratic features are inherently required under the model assumption. As another modification, Optimal Linear Representation [18] allows classifiers (e.g., k-Nearest Neighbor) other than thresholding (assumed by LDA) by searching the solution space (a set of linear subspaces, or Grassmann manifold) with regard to a searching strategy. But this heuristic approach lacks theoretical support from Bayesian decision theory. It is computationally expensive, as Markov Chain Monte Carlo (MCMC) simulation is often employed, and it is even doubtful whether such a search is bounded or stable in a high dimensional space with few examples.

2.2 Bootstrap Methods

The general bumping procedure was proposed in [9] as a method for model search and inference. It is based on bootstrap resampling theory [19], which was originally used for assessing the statistical accuracy of an estimator. A "bootstrap sample" is a "subset of examples" randomly drawn *with replacement* from the original set of training examples. It was shown that the empirical distribution of bootstrap samples can be used to approximate the sampling distribution of random variables (e.g., variance of an estimator) to be estimated from the observed data. Additionally, recent research demonstrated that the bootstrap technique can be employed to improve the accuracy of an estimator, such as *bagging* [20], *boosting* [21, 22] (with an enhanced version called AdaBoosting [23, 24] which employs adaptive sampling and weighted voting), and *bumping* [9]. By averaging the estimates from multiple bootstrap samples, *bagging* produces a new estimator, which often has a smaller variance. In comparison, the *boosting* method improves the classification performance by combining multiple weak learners, individually trained

---

[1] The original idea was to smoothly blend LDA with Quadratic Discriminant Analysis (QDA) by adding the common covariance (scaled by σ) to the individual covariance of each class. Although not explicitly described in [8], R-LDA is often referred to $\hat{\Sigma} + \sigma I$ in the literature.

from a subset of examples. However, if we desire a single LDA classifier or a set of LDA linear features for dimensionality reduction, the bagged (averaged) linear classifier from subsets may not perform well, and the boosted classifier results in complex decision boundaries, which is non-linear and is not applicable for dimensionality reduction. In this sense, both bagged and boosted LDA [25, 26] are no longer true "LDA".

However, in our proposed approach, the *bumping* procedure [9] follows the paradigm of hypothesis and test. Bootstrap samples are used to provide candidate models. The procedure then selects the model which best explains the observed data according to a target criteria. The method reduces the variance of the original estimates, while preserving the same structure and interpretation. This ideally suites our need to address the SSS problem in LDA.

3 Bootstrap Bumping LDA (BB-LDA)

The original bumping procedure [9] directly hypothesizes a model from each bootstrap sample and selects the best model for a target criteria. However, this approach is not directly applicable to the SSS problem in LDA. Because each bootstrap sample contains even fewer examples, the SSS problem is more problematic for the LDA model directly trained/estimated from bootstrap samples. Furthermore, the singularity problem of $\hat{\Sigma}$ in LDA is not yet addressed in the original bumping procedure.

Instead we propose a *new* bumping procedure called Bootstrap Bumping LDA (BB-LDA). The approach first hypothesizes an intermediate linear representation from each bootstrap sample. Then all of the training examples are projected into the representation space and analyzed by the classic LDA. The new procedure not only has the same asymptotic property of convergence as original bumping, but now avoids the singularity problem of $\hat{\Sigma}$ and improves the estimation accuracy of model parameters in the SSS problem. Our approach is significant in that it addresses the dual aspects of the SSS problem in a general statistical framework without imposing specific assumptions (as the traditional methods). It also preserves LDA interpretation by avoiding averaging (bagging) or voting (boosting). We begin with a description of the general bumping procedure in Sect. 3.1 and present our extension in Sect. 3.2.

3.1 Bootstrap Bumping

Let $\mathbf{z} = (z_1, z_2, \cdots, z_N)$ be the set of all labeled training examples. Assume a data model depends on a set of parameters θ, which is to be estimated by minimizing a *target* criteria R as

$$\hat{\theta} = \text{argmin}_\theta \ R(\mathbf{z}, \theta). \tag{1}$$

The criteria R can be of any general form, such as median squared error for linear regression, or the Maximum Likelihood (ML) estimates of the model parameters, which have closed-form solutions. Ultimately, minimizing R obtains the target estimation $\hat{\theta}$ from the input data $\mathbf{z}$

Suppose there is another *working* criteria R_0, which may be more convenient for minimization (e.g., replacing least median square with least mean square). At a particular sampling rate/ratio α, each bootstrap sample $\mathbf{z}^{*1}, \mathbf{z}^{*2}, \cdots, \mathbf{z}^{*B}$ is randomly drawn from $\mathbf{z}$ with replacement (each sample has αN training examples). The estimate of θ via R_0 from each bootstrap sample is

$$\hat{\theta}^{*b} = \text{argmin}_\theta \ R_0(\mathbf{z}^{*b}, \theta). \tag{2}$$

The original bumping procedure [9] chooses $\hat{\theta}^{BB}$ as the value among the $\hat{\theta}^{*b}$ which has the smallest value in the target criteria $R(\mathbf{z}, \theta)$ for the entire dataset $\mathbf{z}$:

$$\hat{\theta}^{BB} = \hat{\theta}^{*\hat{b}}, \text{ where } \hat{b} = \text{argmin}_b \ R(\mathbf{z}, \hat{\theta}^{*b}) \tag{3}$$

The working criteria R_0 may be the same as the target criteria R, in which case the bumping procedure simply estimates suboptimal parameters $\hat{\theta}^{*b}$ from each bootstrap sample (a subset of training examples) and selects the best $\hat{\theta}^{*b}$ over all hypothesized candidates. This has been shown in [9] to be useful for finding a better local minima. For different working and target criteria [9], the bumping procedure can also be used for robust fitting (with R_0 as the outlier-free version of R) and constrained optimization (R_0 as the unconstrained version of R).

Furthermore, the working criteria R_0 needs to be "compatible" with the target criteria R in order for the bumping estimate $\hat{\theta}^{BB}$ to asymptotically converge to the true model parameters θ. For the same criteria R_0 and R, it has been proven in [9] that the bumping procedure preserves the property of asymptotic convergence. For different criteria R_0 and R, compatibility should be carefully examined by considering the asymptotic behavior of the procedure. Otherwise, the bumping procedure only provides an approximation of R with a simple form R_0 largely for the ease of computation.

3.2 Proposed Approach – Bootstrap Bumping LDA

The original bumping procedure was not designed to handle the SSS problem. With regards to LDA, we choose the target criteria R as the ML solution, which measures the misclassification rate on $\mathbf{z}$ for linear decision boundaries θ. The minimization of R has a closed-form solution by first obtaining the ML estimates of LDA from $\mathbf{z}$ and then calculating the corresponding decision boundaries $\hat{\theta}$ (the linear projections and thresholds). If we employ the same working criteria $R_0 = R$, the original bumping procedure hypothesizes linear decision boundaries $\hat{\theta}^{*b}$ from each bootstrap sample $\mathbf{z}^{*b}$. However, since each bootstrap sample $\mathbf{z}^{*b}$ has fewer examples than $\mathbf{z}$, when there are not enough examples, the estimate $\hat{\theta}^{*b}$ is even more unstable than the original $\hat{\theta}$. The impact of the SSS problem is magnified, not suppressed.

To deal with this issue, instead of directly estimating θ, we propose to first hypothesize an intermediate representation space $\hat{L}^{*b}$ from each bootstrap sample $\mathbf{z}^{*b}$ as

$$\hat{L}^{*b} = \text{argmin}_L \ R_{rep}(\mathbf{z}^{*b}, L). \tag{4}$$

Here the new *working* criteria R_{rep} measures the capacity of a given representation L (e.g., linear, quadratic, etc.) for the bootstrap sample $\mathbf{z}^{*b}$, which we call the *representation* criteria. We want to choose the representation with minimum capacity (the simplest representation), which still faithfully reconstructs the bootstrap sample and is compatible with the model assumption. With regards to LDA, a linear subspace defined by $\mathbf{z}^{*b}$

is minimum in terms of capacity among all compatible representations. Therefore we can directly replace Eqn. 4 with

$$\hat{L}^{*b} = LinearSpace(\mathbf{z}^{*b}).\tag{5}$$

For other models, the representation should be chosen accordingly. For example, for QDA a quadratic representation should be hypothesized from each bootstrap sample.

Then we follow the similar bumping procedure. we evaluate the discrimination performance of the hypothesized representation $\hat{L}^{*b}$ over the entire dataset $\mathbf{z}$ and choose the representation with the minimum misclassification rate as in

$$\hat{L}^{\mathcal{BB}-\mathcal{LDA}} = \hat{L}^{*\hat{b}}, \text{ where } \hat{b} = \text{argmin}_b \, R_{dis}(\mathbf{z}, \hat{L}^{*b})\tag{6}$$

The new *target* criteria R_{dis} measures the misclassification rate of $\mathbf{z}$ with regard to the representation space $\hat{L}^{*b}$, which we call the *discrimination* criteria. The target criteria R_{dis} can be easily evaluated using the best estimated model parameters $\hat{\theta}^{*b}$ based on the representation $\hat{L}^{*b}$

$$R_{dis}(\mathbf{z}, \hat{L}^{*b}) = R(\mathbf{z}, \hat{\theta}^{*b}), \text{ where}\tag{7}$$

$$\hat{\theta}^{*b} = \text{argmin}_\theta \, \tilde{R}(\mathbf{z}, \theta; \hat{L}^{*b}).\tag{8}$$

As a constrained version of the original bumping criteria R in the representation space $\hat{L}^{*b}$, the modified criteria $\tilde{R}$ is equivalent to first projecting $\mathbf{z}$ into $\hat{L}^{*b}$ (e.g., correlating with a linear basis in LDA), estimating the model parameters (e.g., ML), and lastly reconstructing the parameters back to the original D-dimensional space (e.g., multiplying the feature vectors with the basis).

Lastly, we obtain the LDA solution of BB-LDA as the corresponding model estimates for the selected representation space

$$\hat{\theta}^{\mathcal{BB}-\mathcal{LDA}} = \hat{\theta}^{*\hat{b}}.\tag{9}$$

In essence, the approach seeks out the key prototype examples that best represent the space of $\mathbf{z}$ for the purpose of discrimination. The BB-LDA algorithm is summarized in Alg. 1. For any new example z_{new}, it can then be classified by projecting it onto the reconstructed feature space and thresholding.

Our proposed approach addresses the SSS problem in a general statistical framework. At a particular sampling ratio α, only a portion of examples are used to hypothesize a representation, which can ensure $\hat{\Sigma}$ being full rank in the projection space $\hat{L}^{*b}$ for the entire dataset $\mathbf{z}$. Since duplicate examples do not affect the representation, bootstrap samples are drawn at a fixed size αN from $\mathbf{z}$ *without replacement* in BB-LDA for the ease of analysis and implementation. The prior probability of each class is also maintained in sampling to ensure a fair representation. Furthermore because LDA is invariant to the basis selection, a non-orthonormal basis T_b is used for simplicity, which is equivalent to linearly correlating the entire dataset with examples in each bootstrap sample. The smaller the sampling ratio α, the more compact the representation, and the more examples left to generalize the model for discrimination. However, too few examples negatively affect the representation power, which may in turn limit the upper bound for

---

Algorithm 1. BB-LDA Algorithm

1: Randomly draw B bootstrap samples $\mathbf{z}^{*1}, \mathbf{z}^{*2}, \cdots, \mathbf{z}^{*B}$ from $\mathbf{z}$ at the sampling ratio α.
2: **for** $b = 1$ to B **do**
3:    Let $A_b = [z_1^{*b}, z_2^{*b}, \cdots, z_k^{*b}]$ be one basis of the linear subspace $\hat{L}^{*b}$.
4:    Project $\mathbf{z}$ in A_b as $y_b = A_b^T \mathbf{z}$. Run LDA with ML estimates on y_b to obtain the model parameters, including the feature vector(s) w_b and the threshold(s) t_b.
5:    Calculate the misclassification rate on y_b based on the estimated model parameters.
6: **end for**
7: Choose the representation A_b which has the minimum misclassification rate. Obtain the BB-LDA solution $\hat{\theta}^{BB-\mathcal{LDA}}$ by reconstructing the feature vectors $A_b w_b$ and keeping the same threshold t_b.

---

discrimination. The application-dependent sampling ratio α can be determined through cross-validation to properly balance the representation and discrimination.

With regards to the the number of bootstrap samples B, the percentage of training examples p covered by all bootstrap samples is $p = 1 - (1 - \alpha)^B$. At a given sampling ratio α, B can be calculated for a specific coverage (e.g., $p = 99.9\%$) with

$$B = log(1 - p)/log(1 - \alpha). \tag{10}$$

While the traditional subspace LDA approaches (e.g., PINV-LDA, PCA+LDA) have the time complexity of $O(N^2 D)$ in the SSS problem, BB-LDA has the time complexity of $O(B\alpha N^2 D)$. From Eqn. 10, the worse case time complexity of BB-LDA occurs at $O(-log(1 - p)N^2 D)$ when $\alpha \to 0$, which is on the same order as the traditional subspace LDA [6, 2, 3]. Additionally, it is possible to reduce the computational cost of BB-LDA with a smaller coverage p, which may be useful for extremely large datasets.

Since different *working* (R_{rep}) and *target* (R_{dis}) criteria are used for representation and discrimination, according to the bumping theory [9], R_{rep} needs to be "compatible" with R_{dis} in order for our new procedure to asymptotically converge to the true parameters. This can be proved by considering the compatibility between a linear representation and LDA. At a fixed sampling ratio α, when the number of representative examples $\alpha N > D$ (as in BB-LDA), the representation space is even larger than the original input space (assuming linear independence among examples in each bootstrap sample). Estimating an LDA model in each hypothesized representation in Eqn. 8 is equivalent to directly applying ML in the original input space. Thus the bumping procedure is equivalent to LDA with ML estimates when $N > D/\alpha$. Because of the asymptotic convergence property of the ML estimates, this proves the compatibility of our *working* criteria R_{rep} and *target* criteria R_{dis}.

Lastly, the bootstrap sampling process is not limited to be uniform. Parameterized bootstrapping [27] can be utilized to accommodate the underlying structure of the data. Other extensions, such as employing clustering or domain knowledge for bootstrap resampling, are possible.

4   Experiments

We evaluated the performance of BB-LDA with both synthetic and real datasets in comparison to traditional LDA methods in dealing with the SSS problem.

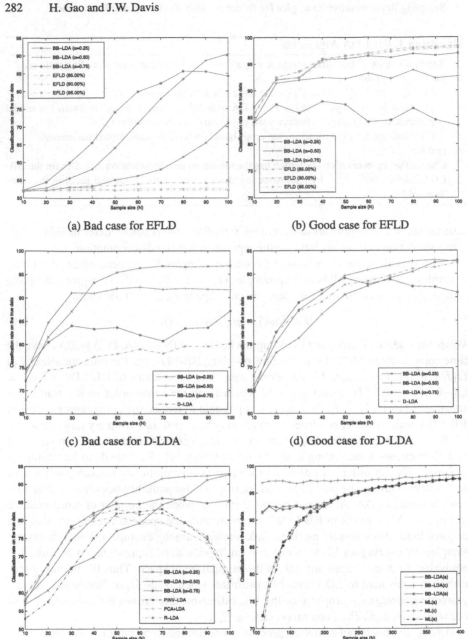

(a) Bad case for EFLD

(b) Good case for EFLD

(c) Bad case for D-LDA

(d) Good case for D-LDA

(e) Sensitivity to noise

(f) Larger sample sizes

Fig. 1. Results of synthetic experiments. With the best $\alpha \in [0.25, 0.5, 0.75]$, BB-LDA outperformed traditional LDA methods when their assumptions were intentionally violated in (a), (c), and (e), and yielded comparable performance when the assumptions were satisfied in (b) and (d). As shown in (f), BB-LDA converges to the ML estimate with a large enough sample size.

4.1 Results on Synthetic Data

In our synthetic experiments, two Gaussians with equal covariance were simulated with equal priors in a $D = 100$ dimensional space for a range of sample sizes $N = [10 : 10 : 400]$. The difficulty of the classification was controlled using a fixed Fisher ratio of 4, which corresponds to a 97.7% Bayesian classification rate. Each configuration (class means and common covariance) was simulated 25 times to report the average recognition rate of the model with regards to the ground-truth data. We chose the percentage coverage $p = 99.9\%$ to determine the number of bootstrap samples, which achieves good utilization of training examples and reasonable computational efficiency.

We first looked at the case of $N \leq 100$ (singular $\hat{\Sigma}$), which was previously focused on by the traditional methods (PINV-LDA, PCA+LDA, EFLD, R-LDA, and D-LDA). As shown in Fig. 1a, the EFLD recognition rates were hardly better than 50% for 3 selected percentage fits (85%, 90%, and 95%) of the simulated data, when the true feature vector lies outside the major PCA components (90% fit of the true data variance). This is because EFLD assumes no information in the small components and discards them to constrain the LDA solution. Similarly, D-LDA showed low performance in Fig. 1c when a large portion of the true feature vector resides in the null space of S_b (class means). For the remaining methods, PINV-LDA, PCA+LDA, and R-LDA also performed poorly for a large N as they are sensitive to noise and small perturbations due to the over-emphasis of small components in their solutions (Fig. 1e).

As a comparison, at an appropriate sampling ratio α, BB-LDA outperformed the traditional methods in all the above cases (see Fig. 1a,c,e). Furthermore, when the model assumptions of EFLD and D-LDA *were* satisfied as shown in Fig. 1b and 1d, BB-LDA still yielded comparable performance to the two methods. The valid case of PINV-LDA, PCA+LDA, and R-LDA is not available due to their unstable nature.

Then we studied the performance of BB-LDA in handling the SSS estimation problem for the case (a), (c), and (d) with $100 < N \leq 400$, which has enough examples to avoid a singular $\hat{\Sigma}$. The sampling ratio was selected for the best average recognition rate in the previous range of $N \leq 100$ with α at 0.5, 0.25, and 0.5. As shown in Fig. 1f, BB-LDA outperformed classic LDA in the lower end of the range of N, due to relatively few examples for the ML estimates to converge. In the higher end with enough examples, BB-LDA showed the trend of convergence to ML. The results demonstrate BB-LDA as a general method to deal with the SSS problem in various cases.

4.2 Results on Real Data

In our real experiments, we explored 3 datasets frequently used in Computer Vision research for face and gait recognition: Yale face database [2], ORL face dataset [28], and the CMU gait database [29]. For each dataset, images were first aligned to control position and scaling. Then they were down-sampled and tightly cropped to the region of interest as shown in Fig. 2. For the gait database, two different types of MHI (overlay of silhouette images with timestamps represented in pixel intensity) [30] templates were created, which correspond the stride opening and closing phase of a walking cycle (Fig. 2c and 2d). All traditional methods used in Sect. 4.1 were evaluated except R-LDA due to its inherit high computational complexity for a large input dimension (e.g., $D = 1600$ for images in the Yale face database). Cross-validation was employed to determine the

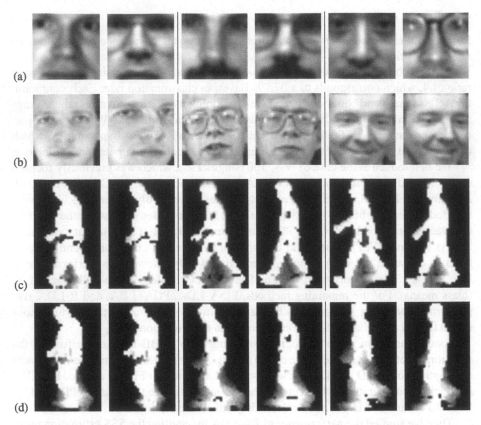

Fig. 2. Sample images of 3 datasets. (a) Yale face database (15 subjects, glasses vs. no glasses). (b) ORL face dataset (40 subjects). (c) CMU Gait database (25 subjects, fast vs. slow walk) in Type-1 MHI representation. (d) Corresponding Type-2 MHI Gait representation.

optimal model parameters of BB-LDA (the sampling ratio $\alpha \in [0.1 : 0.1 : 0.9]$ and the best representation/classifier) and EFLD (the number of PCA components) with each time 10% of examples drawn for testing. The same bootstrap coverage $p = 99.9\%$ was chosen as in Sect. 4.1.

The Yale face dataset includes 15 subjects and 11 images of each person across various conditions (e.g., lighting, expressions, etc.). In addition to face recognition, we examined the task of distinguishing people with glasses from people without glasses (36 with and 129 without), a much larger set than the case of 36 images studied in [2]. We then examined face recognition using the ORL face dataset with 40 subjects and 10 images per person. Lastly, we looked at the CMU gait database of 25 subjects with 16 cycles extracted for each person (8 slow and 8 fast). Both identity and walking speed recognition were performed over two types of MHI representation.

The comparative results of those experiments are summarized in Table 1. Since PINV-LDA and PCA+LDA mostly emphasize the small components, they are sensitive to noise and yielded lower recognition rates. By adjusting the number of PCA components, EFLD improved the performance of PCA+LDA and is the best among

Table 1. Classification results of different LDA-based algorithms. Our proposed BB-LDA approach outperformed the other traditional LDA methods.

	Yale - ID (11 sets)	Yale - Glasses (36 sets)	ORL - ID (10 sets)	CMU - ID (24 sets)		CMU - Speed (30 sets)	
				Type-1	Type-2	Type-1	Type-2
PINV-LDA	82.7	83.6	88.8	99.7	99.1	92.6	89.5
PCA+LDA	45.5	85.2	27.3	54.6	62.7	93.6	90.7
EFLD	90.6 (57 PCs)	89.7 (85 PCs)	92.3 (95 PCs)	100.0 (90 PCs)	99.7 (132 PCs)	97.0 (318 PCs)	95.3 (321 PCs)
D-LDA	70.3	72.0	79.8	77.8	76.3	77.4	65.8
BB-LDA	93.9 ($\alpha = 0.3$)	95.1 ($\alpha = 0.3$)	95.5 ($\alpha = 0.2$)	100.0 ($\alpha = 0.2$)	100.0 ($\alpha = 0.2$)	97.8 ($\alpha = 0.6$)	97.1 ($\alpha = 0.4$)

all the traditional methods. But this assumes the small components contain no information for classification. Lastly, D-LDA imposes a significant performance limitation by constraining the feature vectors to be in the linear space of S_b (class means). As a comparison, our proposed BB-LDA approach gave the best classification rate in all test cases. Only in CMU-ID (Type-1), EFLD yielded the same classification of 100%, which is high due to the simplicity of the task (MHI images of multiple cycles for one subject are highly similar).

The performance advantages of BB-LDA come from the employment of a general statistical framework of bootstrap bumping in dealing with the SSS problem. This avoids the explicit assumptions in the traditional methods. By sampling a subset of training examples to hypothesize a representation and selecting the best model for discrimination over the entire dataset, our approach is capable of improving the estimation accuracy in the SSS problem. The sampling ratio α provides a balance of examples for representation and discrimination. In our real experiments, a small α value was used in most cases, which suggests that only a few prototype examples were needed for representation, while the rest can be used for discrimination. Both synthetic and real experiments illustrated the advantages of BB-LDA in dealing with the SSS problem.

5   Conclusion

We presented a novel method of Bootstrap Bumping LDA (BB-LDA) to deal with the SSS problem in Computer Vision applications. The method hypothesizes candidate representations from each subset of examples (bootstrap sample) and tests over the entire dataset for the best classification. As a general statistical framework, our approach is capable of improving the estimation accuracy without imposing explicit assumptions. The method asymptotically converges to the true LDA solution given enough examples and outperforms the traditional LDA methods in dealing with the SSS problem. Both synthetic and real experiments on several popular datasets showed the advantages of our BB-LDA approach. In future work, we plan to address the model limitations of LDA with more complex representations (e.g., non-linear) and investigate other applications of BB-LDA (e.g., person detection).

Acknowledgments

This research was supported in part by the National Science Foundation under grant No. 0236653.

References

1. Jain, A., Duin, R., Mao, J.: Statistical pattern recognition: a review. IEEE Trans. Patt. Analy. and Mach. Intell. **22**(1) (2000) 4–37
2. Belhumeur, P., Hespanha, J., Kriegman, D.: Eigenfaces vs. Fisherfaces: Recognition using class specific linear projection. IEEE Trans. Patt. Analy. and Mach. Intell. **19**(7) (1997) 711–720
3. Liu, C., Wechsler, H.: Enhanced Fisher linear discriminant models for face recognition. In: Proc. Int. Conf. Pat. Rec., IEEE (1998) 1368–1372
4. Cui, Y., Swets, D., Weng, J.: Learning-based hand sign recognition using SHOSLIF-M. In: Proc. Int. Conf. Comp. Vis., IEEE (1995) 631–636
5. Huang, P., Harris, C., Nixon, M.: Human gait recognition in canonical space using temporal templates. In: Proc. Vision Image Signal Process. Volume 146., IEE (1999) 93–100
6. Krzanowski, W., Jonathan, P., McCarthy, W., Thomas, M.: Discriminant analysis with singular covariance matrices:methods and applications to spectroscopic data. Applied Statistics **44** (1995) 101–115
7. Yu, H., Yang, J.: A direct LDA algorithm for high-dimensional data - with application to face recognition. Pattern Recognition **34** (2001) 2067–2070
8. Friedman, J.: Regularized discriminant analysis. J. Am. Statistical Assoc. **84**(405) (1989) 165–175
9. Tibshirani, R., Knight, K.: Model search by bootstrap "bumping". J. of Computational and Graphical Statistics **8**(4) (1999) 671–686
10. Fisher, R.: The use of multiple measurements in taxonomic problems. Annals of Eugenics **7 Part II** (1936) 179–188
11. Rao, C.: The utilization of multiple measurements in problems of biological classification. J. Royal Statistical Soc., B **10** (1948) 159–203
12. Campbell, N.: Canonical variate analysis - a general model formulation. Australian J. Statistics **26** (1984) 86–96
13. Duda, R., Hart, P., Stork, D.: Pattern Classification. John Wiley & Sons, New York (2001)
14. Gao, H., Davis, J.: Why Direct LDA is not equivalent to LDA. to appear in Pattern Recognition (2006)
15. Baudat, G., Anouar, F.: Generalized discriminant analysis using a kernel approach. Neural Computation **12**(10) (2000) 2385–2404
16. Kim, T., Kittler, J.: Locally linear discriminant analysis for multimodally distributed classes for face recognition with a single model image. IEEE Trans. Patt. Analy. and Mach. Intell. **27**(3) (2005) 318–327
17. Torre, F., Kanade, T.: Oriented discriminant analysis (ODA). In: Brit. Mach. Vis. Conf. (2004) 132–141
18. Liu, X., Srivastava, A., Gallivan, K.: Optimal linear representations of images for object recognition. IEEE Trans. Patt. Analy. and Mach. Intell. **26**(5) (2004) 662–666
19. Efron, B.: Bootstrap methods: another look at the jackknife. Annals of Statistics **7** (1979) 1–26
20. Breiman, L.: Bagging predictors. Machine Learning Journal **24**(2) (1996) 123–140
21. Schapire, R.: The strength of weak learnability. Machine Learning **5**(2) (1990) 197–227

22. Freund, Y.: Boosting a weak learning algorithm by majority. Information and Computation **121**(2) (1995) 256–285
23. Freund, Y., Schapire, R.: Experiments with a new boosting algorithm. In: Machine Learning: Proc. of the 13th Int. Conf. (1996) 148–156
24. Viola, P., Jones, M., Snow, D.: Detecting pedestrians using patterns of motion and appearance. In: Proc. Int. Conf. Comp. Vis. (2003) 734–741
25. Skurichina, M., Duin, R.: Bagging, boosting and the random subspace method for linear classifiers. Pattern Analysis & Applications **5** (2002) 121–135
26. Lu, X., Jain, A.K.: Resampling for face recognition. In: Int. Conf. on Audio and Video Based Biometric Person Auth. (2003) 869–877
27. Efron, B., Tibshirani, R.: An Introduction to the Bootstrap. Chapman and Hall, New York (1993)
28. Samaria, F., Harter, A.: Parameterisation of a stochastic model for human face identification. In: 2nd IEEE Workshop on Applications of Computer Vision. (1994)
29. R.Gross, Shi, J.: The CMU motion of body (MoBo) database. Technical Report CMU-RI-TR-01-18, Robotics Institute, Carnegie Mellon University, Pittsburgh, PA (2001)
30. Davis, J., Bobick, A.: The representation and recognition of action using temporal templates. In: Proc. Comp. Vis. and Pattern Rec., IEEE (1997) 928–934

Studying Aesthetics in Photographic Images Using a Computational Approach

Ritendra Datta*, Dhiraj Joshi, Jia Li, and James Z. Wang**

The Pennsylvania State University, University Park, PA 16802, USA

Abstract. Aesthetics, in the world of art and photography, refers to the principles of the nature and appreciation of beauty. Judging beauty and other aesthetic qualities of photographs is a highly subjective task. Hence, there is no unanimously agreed standard for measuring aesthetic value. In spite of the lack of firm rules, certain features in photographic images are believed, by many, to please humans more than certain others. In this paper, we treat the challenge of automatically inferring aesthetic quality of pictures using their visual content as a machine learning problem, with a peer-rated online photo sharing Website as data source. We extract certain visual features based on the intuition that they can discriminate between aesthetically pleasing and displeasing images. Automated classifiers are built using support vector machines and classification trees. Linear regression on polynomial terms of the features is also applied to infer numerical aesthetics ratings. The work attempts to explore the relationship between emotions which pictures arouse in people, and their low-level content. Potential applications include content-based image retrieval and digital photography.

1 Introduction

Photography is defined as the art or practice of taking and processing photographs. Aesthetics in photography is how people usually characterize beauty in this form of art. There are various ways in which aesthetics is defined by different people. There exists no single consensus on what it exactly pertains to. The broad idea is that photographic images that are pleasing to the eyes are considered to be higher in terms of their aesthetic beauty. While the average individual may simply be interested in how soothing a picture is to the eyes, a photographic artist may be looking at the composition of the picture, the use of colors and light, and any additional meanings conveyed by the picture. A professional photographer, on the other hand, may be wondering how difficult it may have been to take or to process a particular shot, the sharpness and the color contrast of the picture, or whether the "rules of thumb" in photography have been maintained. All these issues make the measurement of aesthetics in pictures or photographs extremely subjective.

---

* Corresponding author: R. Datta, datta@cse.psu.edu. More information: http://riemann.ist.psu.edu.
** This work is supported in part by the US National Science Foundation, the PNC Foundation, and SUN Microsystems.

A. Leonardis, H. Bischof, and A. Pinz (Eds.): ECCV 2006, Part III, LNCS 3953, pp. 288–301, 2006.

In spite of the ambiguous definition of aesthetics, we show in this paper that there exist certain visual properties which make photographs, *in general*, more aesthetically beautiful. We tackle the problem computationally and experimentally through a statistical learning approach. This allows us to reduce the influence of exceptions and to identify certain features which are statistically significant in good quality photographs.

Content analysis in photographic images has been studied by the multimedia and vision research community in the past decade. Today, several efficient region-based image retrieval engines are in use [13, 6, 21, 18]. Statistical modeling approaches have been proposed for automatic image annotation [4, 12]. Culturally significant pictures are being archived in digital libraries [7]. Online photo sharing communities are becoming more and more common [1, 3, 11, 15]. In this age of digital picture explosion, it is critical to continuously develop intelligent systems for automatic image content analysis.

1.1 Community-Based Photo Ratings as Data Source

One good data source is a large online photo sharing community, *Photo.net*, possibly the first of its kind, started in 1997 by Philip Greenspun, then a researcher on online communities at MIT [15]. Primarily intended for photography enthusiasts, the Website attracts more than 400, 000 registered members. Many amateur and professional photographers visit the site frequently, share photos, and rate and comment on photos taken by peers. There are more than one million photographs uploaded by these users for perusal by the community. Of interest to us is the fact that many of these photographs are peer-rated in terms of two qualities, namely *aesthetics* and *originality*. The scores are given in the range of one to seven, with a higher number indicating better rating. This site acts as the main source of data for our computational aesthetics work. The reason we chose such an online community is that it provides photos which are rated by a relatively diverse group. This ensures generality in the ratings, averaged out over the entire spectrum of amateurs to serious professionals. While amateurs represent the general population, the professionals tend to spend more time on the technical details before rating the photographs. *One caveat:* The nature of any peer-rated community is such that it leads to unfair judgments under certain circumstances, and *Photo.net* is no exception, making our acquired data fairly noisy. Ideally, the data should have been collected from a random sample of human subjects under controlled setup, but resource constraints prevented us from doing so.

We downloaded those pictures and their associated metadata which were rated by at least two members of the community. For each image downloaded, we parsed the pages and gathered the following information: (1) average aesthetics score between 1.0 and 7.0, (2) average originality score between 1.0 and 7.0, (3) number of times viewed by members, and (4) number of peer ratings.

1.2 Aesthetics and Originality

According to the Oxford Advanced Learner's Dictionary, *Aesthetics* means (1) *"concerned with beauty and art and the understanding of beautiful things"*, and

(2) *"made in an artistic way and beautiful to look at"*. A more specific discussion on the definition of aesthetics can be found in [16]. As can be observed, no consensus was reached on the topic among the users, many of whom are professional photographers. *Originality* has a more specific definition of being something that is unique and rarely observed. The originality score given to some photographs can also be hard to interpret, because what seems original to some viewers may not be so for others. Depending on the experiences of the viewers, the originality scores for the same photo can vary considerably. Thus the originality score is subjective to a large extent as well.

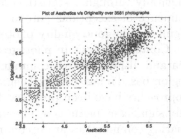

Fig. 1. Correlation between the aesthetics and originality ratings for 3581 photographs

One of the first observations made on the gathered data was the strong correlation between the aesthetics and originality ratings for a given image. A plot of 3581 unique photograph ratings can be seen in Fig. 1. As can be seen, aesthetics and originality ratings have approximately linear correlation with each other. This can be due to a number of factors. Many users quickly rate a batch of photos in a given day. They tend not to spend too much time trying to distinguish between these two parameters when judging a photo. They more often than not rate photographs based on a general impression. Typically, a very original concept leads to good aesthetic value, while beauty can often be characterized by originality in view angle, color, lighting, or composition. Also, because the ratings are averages over a number of people, disparity by individuals may not be reflected as high in the averages. Hence there is generally not much disparity in the average ratings. In fact, out of the 3581 randomly chosen photos, only about 1.1% have a disparity of more than 1.0 between average aesthetics and average originality, with a peak of 2.0.

Fig. 2. Aesthetics scores can be significantly influenced by the semantics. Loneliness is depicted using a person in this frame, though the area occupied by the person is very small. Avg. aesthetics: 6.0/7.0.

As a result of this observation, we chose to limit the rest of our study to aesthetics ratings only, since the value of one can be approximated to the value of the other, and among the two, aesthetics has a rough definition that in principle depends somewhat less on the content or the semantics of the photograph, something that is very hard for present day machine intelligence to interpret accurately. Nonetheless, the strong dependence on originality ratings means that aesthetics ratings are also largely influenced by the semantics. As a result, some visually similar photographs are rated very differently. For example in Fig. 2, loneliness is depicted using a man in the frame, increasing its appeal, while the lack of the person makes the photograph uninteresting and is likely to cause poorer ratings from peers. This makes the task of automatically determining aesthetics of photographs highly challenging.

1.3 Our Computational Aesthetics Approach

A classic treatise on psychological theories for understanding human perception can be found in [2]. Here, we take the first step in using a computational approach to understand what aspects of a photograph appeal to people, from a population and statistical standpoint. For this purpose, we aim to build (1) a classifier that can qualitatively distinguish between pictures of *high* and *low* aesthetic value, or (2) a regression model that can quantitatively predict the aesthetics score, both approaches relying on low-level visual features only. We define *high* or *low* in terms of predefined ranges of aesthetics scores.

There are reasons to believe that classification may be a more appropriate model than regression in tackling this problem. For one, the measures are highly subjective, and there are no agreed standards for rating. This may render absolute scores less meaningful. Again, ratings above or below certain thresholds on an average by a set of unique users generally reflect on the photograph's quality. This way we also get around the problem of consistency where two identical photographs can be scored differently by different groups of people. However, it is more likely that both the group averages are within the same range and hence are treated fairly when posed as a classification problem.

On the other hand, the 'ideal' case is when a machine can replicate the task of robustly giving images aesthetics scores in the range of (1.0-7.0) the humans do. This is the regression formulation of the problem. The possible benefits of building a *computational aesthetics* model can be summarized as follows: If the low-level image features alone can tell what range aesthetics ratings the image deserves, this can potentially be used by photographers to get a rough estimate of their shot composition quality, leading to adjustment in camera parameters or shot positioning for improved aesthetics. Camera manufacturers can incorporate a 'suggested composition' feature into their products. Alternatively, a content-based image retrieval (CBIR) system can use the aesthetics score to discriminate between visually similar images, giving greater priority to more pleasing query results. Biologically speaking, a reasonable solution to this problem may lead to a better understanding of the human vision.

2 Visual Feature Extraction

Experiences with photography lead us to believe in certain aspects as being critical to quality. This entire study is on such beliefs or hypotheses and their validation through numerical results. We treat each downloaded image separately and extract features from them. We use the following notation: The RGB data of each image is converted to HSV color space, producing two-dimensional matrices I_H, I_S, and I_V, each of dimension $X \times Y$.

Our motivation for the choice of features was principled, based on (1) rules of thumb in photography, (2) common intuition, and (3) observed trends in ratings. In photography and color psychology, color tones and saturation play important roles, and hence working in the HSV color space makes computation more convenient. For some features we extract information from objects within the photographs. An approximate way to find objects within images is segmentation, under the assumption that homogeneous regions correspond to objects. We use a fast segmentation method based on clustering. For this purpose the image is transformed into the LUV space, since in this space locally Euclidean distances model the perceived color change well. Using a fixed threshold for all the photographs, we use the K-Center algorithm to compute cluster centroids, treating the image pixels as a bag of vectors in LUV space. With these centroids as seeds, a K-means algorithm computes clusters. Following a connected component analysis, color-based segments are obtained. The 5 largest segments formed are retained and denoted as $\{s_1, ..., s_5\}$. These clusters are used to compute *region-based features* as we shall discuss in Sec. 2.7.

We extracted 56 visual features for each image. The feature set was carefully chosen but limited because our goal was mainly to study the trends or patterns, if any, that lead to higher or lower aesthetics ratings. If the goal was to only build a strong classifier or regression model, it would have made sense to generate exhaustive features and apply typical machine-learning techniques such as boosting. Without meaningful features it is difficult to make meaningful conclusions from the results. We refer to our features as *candidate features* and denote them as $\mathcal{F} = \{f_i | 1 \leq i \leq 56\}$ which are described as follows.

2.1 Exposure of Light and Colorfulness

Measuring the brightness using a light meter and a gray card, controlling the exposure using the aperture and shutter speed settings, and darkroom printing with dodging and burning are basic skills for any professional photographer. Too much exposure (leading to brighter shots) often yields lower quality pictures. Those that are too dark are often also not appealing. Thus light exposure can often be a good discriminant between high and low quality photographs. Note that there are always exceptions to any 'rules of thumb'. An over-exposed or under-exposed photograph under certain scenarios may yield very original and beautiful shots. Ideally, the use of light should be characterized as normal daylight, shooting into the sun, backlighting, shadow, night etc. We use the average pixel intensity $f_1 = \frac{1}{XY} \sum_{x=0}^{X-1} \sum_{y=0}^{Y-1} I_V(x, y)$ to characterize the use of light.

We propose a fast and robust method to compute relative color distribution, distinguishing multi-colored images from monochromatic, *sepia* or simply low contrast images. We use the Earth Mover's Distance (EMD) [17], which is a measure of similarity between any two weighted distributions. We divide the RGB color space into 64 cubic blocks with four equal partitions along each dimension, taking each such cube as a sample point. Distribution D_1 is generated as the color distribution of a hypothetical image such that for each of 64 sample points, the frequency is 1/64. Distribution D_2 is computed from the given image by finding the frequency of occurrence of color within each of the 64 cubes. The EMD measure requires that the pairwise distance between sampling points in the two distributions be supplied. Since the sampling points in both of them are identical, we compute the pairwise Euclidean distances between the geometric centers c_i of each cube i, after conversion to LUV space. Thus the *colorfulness* measure f_2 is computed as follows: $f_2 = emd(D_1, D_2, \{d(a,b) \mid 0 \le a, b \le 63\})$, where $d(a,b) = ||\text{rgb2luv}(c_a) - \text{rgb2luv}(c_b)||$.

Fig. 3. The proposed *colorfulness* measure. The two photographs on the *left* have high values while the two on the *right* have low values.

The distribution D_1 can be interpreted as the *ideal* color distribution of a 'colorful' image. How similar the color distribution of an arbitrary image is to this one is a rough measure of how colorful that image is. Examples of images producing high and low values of f_2 are shown in Fig. 3.

2.2 Saturation and Hue

Saturation indicates chromatic purity. Pure colors in a photo tend to be more appealing than dull or impure ones. In natural out-door landscape photography, professionals use specialized film such as the *Fuji Velvia* to enhance the saturation to result in deeper blue sky, greener grass, more vivid flowers, etc. We compute the average saturation $f_3 = \frac{1}{XY} \sum_{x=0}^{X-1} \sum_{y=0}^{Y-1} I_S(x,y)$ as the saturation indicator. Hue is similarly computed averaged over I_H to get feature f_4, though the interpretation of such a feature is not as clear as the former. This is because hue as defined in the HSV space corresponds to angles in a color wheel.

2.3 The Rule of Thirds

A very popular rule of thumb in photography is the *Rule of Thirds*. The rule can be considered as a sloppy approximation to the 'golden ratio' (about 0.618). It specifies that the main element, or the center of interest, in a photograph should lie at one of the four intersections as shown in Fig. 4 (a). We observed that most professional photographs that follow this rule have the main object stretch from an intersection up to the center of the image. Also noticed was the fact that centers of interest, e.g., the eye of a man, were often placed aligned to one of the edges, on the inside. This implies that a large part of the main object often lies on the periphery or inside of the inner rectangle. Based on these observations, we computed the average hue as $f_5 = \frac{9}{XY} \sum_{x=X/3}^{2X/3} \sum_{y=Y/3}^{2Y/3} I_H(x,y)$, with f_6 and f_7 being similarly computed for I_S and I_V respectively.

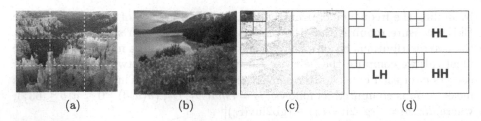

Fig. 4. (a) The *rule of thirds* in photography: Imaginary lines cut the image horizontally and vertically each into three parts. Intersection points are chosen to place important parts of the composition instead of the center. (b)-(d) Daubechies wavelet transform. *Left:* Original image. *Middle:* Three-level transform, levels separated by borders. *Right:* Arrangement of three bands LH, HL and HH of the coefficients.

2.4 Familiarity Measure

We humans learn to rate the aesthetics of pictures from the experience gathered by seeing other pictures. Our opinions are often governed by what we have seen in the past. Because of our curiosity, when we see something unusual or rare we perceive it in a way different from what we get to see on a regular basis. In order to capture this factor in human judgment of photography, we define a new measure of *familiarity* based on the integrated region matching (IRM) image distance [21]. The IRM distance computes image similarity by using color, texture and shape information from automatically segmented regions, and performing a robust region-based matching with other images. Primarily meant for image retrieval applications, we use it here to quantify familiarity. Given a pre-determined *anchor* database of images with a well-spread distribution of aesthetics scores, we retrieve the top K closest matches in it with the candidate image as query. Denoting IRM distances of the top matches for each image in decreasing order of rank as $\{q(i)|1 \leq i \leq K\}$. We compute f_8 and f_9 as $f_8 = \frac{1}{20} \sum_{i=1}^{20} q(i)$, $f_9 = \frac{1}{100} \sum_{i=1}^{100} q(i)$.

In effect, these measures should yield higher values for uncommon images. Two different scales of 20 and 100 top matches are used since they may potentially tell different stories about the uniqueness of the picture. While the former measures average similarity in a local neighborhood, the latter does so on a more global basis. Because of the strong correlation between aesthetics and originality, it is intuitive that a higher value of f_8 or f_9 corresponds to greater originality and hence we expect greater aesthetics score.

2.5 Wavelet-Based Texture

Graininess or smoothness in a photograph can be interpreted in different ways. If as a whole it is grainy, one possibility is that the picture was taken with a grainy film or under high ISO settings. If as a whole it is smooth, the picture can be out-of-focus, in which case it is in general not pleasing to the eye. Graininess can also indicate the presence/absence and nature of *texture* within the image.

The use of texture is a composition skill in photography. One way to measure spatial smoothness in the image is to use Daubechies wavelet transform [10], which has often been used in the literature to characterize texture. We perform a *three-level* wavelet transform on all three color bands I_H, I_S and I_V. An example of such a transform on the intensity band is shown in Fig. 4 (b)-(c). The three levels of wavelet bands are arranged from top left to bottom right in the transformed image, and the four coefficients per level, LL, LH, HL, and HH are arranged as shown in Fig. 4 (d). Denoting the coefficients (except LL) in level i for the wavelet transform on hue image I_H as w_i^{hh}, w_i^{hl} and w_i^{lh}, $i = \{1, 2, 3\}$, we define features f_{10}, f_{11} and f_{12} as follows:

$$f_{i+9} = \frac{1}{S_i}\left\{ \sum_x \sum_y w_i^{hh}(x,y) + \sum_x \sum_y w_i^{hl}(x,y) + \sum_x \sum_y w_i^{lh}(x,y) \right\}$$

where $S_k = |w_i^{hh}| + |w_i^{hl}| + |w_i^{hh}|$ and $i = 1, 2, 3$. The corresponding wavelet features for saturation (I_S) and intensity (I_V) images are computed similarly to get f_{13} through f_{15} and f_{16} through f_{18} respectively. Three more wavelet features are derived. The sum of the average wavelet coefficients over all three frequency levels for each of H, S and V are taken to form three additional features: $f_{19} = \sum_{i=10}^{12} f_i$, $f_{20} = \sum_{i=13}^{15} f_i$, and $f_{21} = \sum_{i=16}^{18} f_i$.

2.6   Size and Aspect Ratio

The size of an image has a good chance of affecting the photo ratings. Although scaling is possible in digital and print media, the size presented initially must be agreeable to the content of the photograph. A more crucial parameter is the aspect ratio. It is well-known that $4 : 3$ and $16 : 9$ aspect ratios, which approximate the 'golden ratio,' are chosen as standards for television screens or $70mm$ movies, for reasons related to viewing pleasure. The 35mm film used by most photographers has a ratio of $3 : 2$ while larger formats include ratios like $7 : 6$ and $5 : 4$. While size feature is $f_{22} = X + Y$, the aspect ratio feature is $f_{23} = \frac{X}{Y}$.

2.7   Region Composition

Segmentation results in rough grouping of similar pixels, which often correspond to objects in the scene. We denote the set of pixels in the largest five connected components or *patches* formed by the segmentation process described before as $\{s_1, ...s_5\}$. The number of patches $t \leq 5$ which satisfy $|s_i| \geq \frac{XY}{100}$ denotes feature f_{24}. The number of color-based clusters formed by K-Means in the LUV space is feature f_{25}. This number is image dependent and dynamically chosen, based on the complexity of the image. These

Fig. 5. The HSV Color Wheel

two features combine to measure how many distinct color *blobs* and how many disconnected significantly large regions are present.

We then compute the average H, S and V values for each of the top 5 patches as features f_{26} through f_{30}, f_{31} through f_{35} and f_{36} through f_{40} respectively. Features f_{41} through f_{45} store the relative size of each segment with respect to the image, and are computed as $f_{i+40} = |s_i|/(XY)$ where $i = 1, ..., 5$.

The hue component of HSV is such that the colors that are 180° apart in the color circle (Fig. 5) are complimentary to each other, which means that they add up to 'white' color. These colors tend to look pleasing together. Based on this idea, we define two new features, f_{46} and f_{47} in the following manner, corresponding to *average color spread* around the wheel and *average complimentary colors* among the top 5 patch hues. These features are defined as

$$f_{46} = \sum_{i=1}^{5}\sum_{j=1}^{5}|h_i - h_j|, \quad f_{47} = \sum_{i=1}^{5}\sum_{j=1}^{5}l(|h_i - h_j|), \quad h_i = \sum_{(x,y)\in s.} I_H(x,y),$$

where $l(k) = k$ if $k \leq 180°$, $360° - k$ if $k > 180°$. Finally, the rough positions of each segment are stored as features f_{48} through f_{52}. We divide the image into 3 equal parts along horizontal and vertical directions, locate the block containing the centroid of each patch s_i, and set $f_{47+i} = (10r + c)$ where $(r, c) \in \{(1, 1), ..., (3, 3)\}$ indicates the corresponding block starting with top-left.

2.8 Low Depth of Field Indicators

Pictures with a simplistic composition and a well-focused center of interest are sometimes more pleasing than pictures with many different objects. Professional photographers often reduce the depth of field (DOF) for shooting single objects by using larger aperture settings, macro lenses, or telephoto lenses. DOF is the range of distance from a camera that is acceptably sharp in the photograph. On the photo, areas in the DOF are noticeably sharper.

We noticed that a large number of low DOF photographs, e.g., insects, other small creatures, animals in motion, were given high ratings. One reason may be that these shots are difficult to take, since it is hard to focus steadily on small and/or fast moving objects like insects and birds. A common feature is that they are taken either by *macro* or by telephoto lenses. We propose a novel method to detect low DOF and macro images. We divide the image into 16 equal rectangular blocks $\{M_1, ...M_{16}\}$, numbered in row-major order. Let $w_3 = \{w_3^{lh}, w_3^{hl}, w_3^{hh}\}$ denote the set of wavelet coefficients in the high-frequency (level 3 by the notation in Sec. 2.5) of the hue image I_H. The *low depth of field indicator* feature f_{53} for hue is computed as follows, with f_{54} and f_{55} being computed similarly for I_S and I_V respectively:

$$f_{53} = \frac{\sum_{(x,y)\in M_6 \cup M_7 \cup M_{10} \cup M_{11}} w_3(x,y)}{\sum_{i=1}^{16} \sum_{(x,y)\in M.} w_3(x,y)}$$

The object of interest in a macro shot is usually in sharp focus near the center, while the surrounding is usually out of focus. This essentially means that a large value of the low DOF indicator features tend to occur for macro shots.

2.9 Shape Convexity

It is believed that shapes in a picture also influence the degree of aesthetic beauty perceived by humans. The challenge in designing a shape feature lies in the understanding of what kind of shape pleases humans, and whether any such

Fig. 6. Demonstrating the *shape convexity* feature. *Left*: Original photograph. *Middle*: Three largest non-background segments shown in original color. *Right*: Exclusive regions of the *convex hull* generated for each segment are shown in white. The proportion of white regions determine the convexity value.

measure generalizes well enough or not. As always, we hypothesize that convex shapes like perfect moon, well-shaped fruits, boxes, or windows have an appeal, positive or negative, which is different from concave or highly irregular shapes. Let the image be segmented, as described before, and R patches $\{p_1, ..., p_R\}$ are obtained such that $|p_k| \geq \frac{XY}{200}$. For each p_k, we compute its convex hull, denoted by $g(p_k)$. For a perfectly convex shape, $p_k \cap g(p_k) = p_k$, i.e. $\frac{|p.|}{|g(p.)|} = 1$. We define the *shape convexity* feature as $f_{56} = \frac{1}{XY}\{\sum_{k=1}^{R} I(\frac{|p.|}{|g(p.)|} \geq 0.8)|p_k|\}$, allowing some room for irregularities of edge and error due to digitization. Here $I(\cdot)$ is the indicator function. This feature can be interpreted as the fraction of the image covered by approximately convex-shaped homogeneous regions, ignoring the insignificant image regions. This feature is demonstrated in Fig. 6. Note that a critical factor here is the segmentation process, since we are characterizing shape by segments. Often, a perfectly convex object is split into concave or irregular parts, considerably reducing the reliability of this measure.

3   Feature Selection, Classification, and Regression

A contribution of our work is the feature extraction process itself, since each feature represents an interesting aspects of photography. We now perform selection in order to (1) discover features that show correlation with community-based aesthetics scores, and (2) build a classification/regression model using a subset of strongly/weakly relevant features such that generalization performance is near optimal. Instead of using any regression model, we use a one-dimensional support vector machine (SVM) [20]. SVMs are essentially powerful binary classifiers that project the data space into higher dimensions where the two classes of points are linearly separable. Naturally, for one-dimensional data, they can be more flexible than a single threshold classifier.

For the 3581 images downloaded, all 56 features in $\mathcal{F}$ were extracted and normalized to the $[0, 1]$ range to form the experimental data. Two classes of data are chosen, *high* containing samples with aesthetics scores greater than 5.8, and *low* with scores less than 4.2. Only images that were rated by at least two unique members were used. The reason for choosing classes with a gap is that pictures with close lying aesthetic scores, e.g., 5.0 and 5.1 are not likely to have any distinguishing feature, and may merely be representing the noise in the whole peer-rating process. For all experiments we ensure equal priors by replicating data to generate equal number of samples per class. A total of 1664 samples is thus obtained, forming the basis for our classification experiments. We perform classification using the standard RBF Kernel ($\gamma = 3.7$, $cost = 1.0$) using the LibSVM package [9]. SVM is run 20 times per feature, randomly permuting the data-set each time, and using a 5-fold cross-validation (5-CV). The top 15 among the 56 features in terms of model accuracy are obtained. The stability of these single features as classifiers is also tested. We proceed to build a classifier that can separate *low* from *high*. For this, we use SVM as well as the classification and regression trees (CART) algorithm [8]. While SVM is a powerful classifier, a limitation is that when there are too many irrelevant features in the data, the *generalization performance* tends to suffer. Feature selection for classification purposes is a well-studied topic [5], with some recent work related specifically to feature selection for SVMs. *Filter-based methods* and *wrapper-based methods* are two broad techniques for feature selection. While the former eliminates irrelevant features before training the classifier, the latter chooses features using the classifier itself as an integral part of the selection process. In this work, we combine these two methods to reduce computational complexity while obtaining features that yield good generalization performance: (1) The top 30 features in terms of their one-dimensional SVM performance are retained while the rest of the features are *filtered* out. (2) We use *forward selection*, a wrapper-based approach in which we start with an empty set of features and iteratively add one feature at a time that increases the 5-fold CV accuracy the most. We stop at 15 iterations (i.e. 15 features) and use this set to build the SVM-based classifier.

Classifiers that help understand the influence of different features directly are tree-based approaches such as CART. We used the recursive partitioning (RPART) implementation [19], to build a two-class classification tree model for the same set of 1664 data samples. Finally, we perform linear regression on polynomial terms of the features values to see if it is possible to directly predict the aesthetics scores in the 1 to 7 range from the feature vector. The quality of regression is usually measured in terms of the *residual sum-of-squares error* $R^2_{res} = \frac{1}{N-1} \sum_{i=1}^{N} (Y_i - \hat{Y}_i)^2$ where $\hat{Y}_i$ is the predicted value of Y_i. Here Y being the aesthetics scores, in the worst case $\bar{Y}$ is chosen every time without using the regression model, yielding $R^2_{res} = \sigma^2$ (variance of Y). Hence, if the independent variables explain something about Y, it must be that $R_{res} \leq \sigma^2$. For this part, all 3581 samples are used, and for each feature f_i, the polynomials (f_i, f_i^2, f_i^3, $f_i^{\frac{1}{3}}$, and $f_i^{\frac{2}{3}}$) are used as independent variables.

4   Experimental Results

For the one-dimensional SVM performed on individual features, the top 15 results obtained in decreasing order of 5-CV accuracy are as follows: $\{f_{31}, f_1, f_6, f_{15}, f_9, f_8, f_{32}, f_{10}, f_{55}, f_3, f_{36}, f_{16}, f_{54}, f_{48}, f_{22}\}$. The maximum classification rate achieved by any single feature was f_{31} with 59.3%. With accuracy over 54%, they act as weak classifiers and hence show some correlation with the aesthetics.

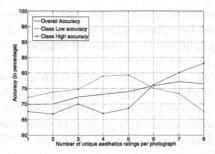 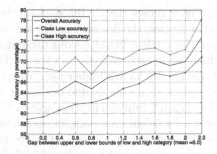

Fig. 7. *Left*: Variation of $5 - CV$ SVM accuracy with the minimum number of unique ratings per picture. *Right*: Variation of $5 - CV$ SVM accuracy with inter-class gap δ.

The combined filter and wrapper method for feature selection yielded the following set of 15 features:$\{f_{31}, f_1, f_{54}, f_{28}, f_{43}, f_{25}, f_{22}, f_{17}, f_{15}, f_{20}, f_2, f_9, f_{21}, f_{23}, f_6\}$. The accuracy achieved with 15 features is 70.12%, with precision of detecting *high* class being 68.08%, and *low* class being 72.31%. Considering the nature of this problem, these classification results are indeed promising.

The stability of these classification results in terms of number of ratings is considered next. Samples are chosen in such a way that each photo is rated by at least K unique users, K varying from 1 to 8, and the 5-CV accuracy and precision plotted, as shown in Fig. 7. It is observed that accuracy values show an upward trend with increasing number of unique ratings per sample, and stabilize somewhat when this value touches 5. This reflects on the peer-rating process - the inherent

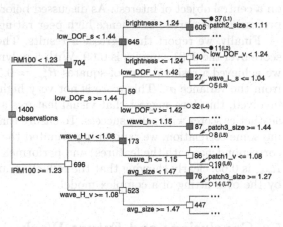

Fig. 8. Decision tree obtained using CART and the 56 visual features (partial view)

noise in this data gets averaged out as the number of ratings increase, converging toward a somewhat 'fair' score. We then experimented with how accuracy and precision varied with the gap in aesthetics ratings between the two classes *high* and *low*. So far we have considered ratings ≥ 5.8 as *high* and ≤ 4.2 as *low*. In general, considering that $ratings \geq 5.0 + \frac{\delta}{2}$, be (*high*) and $ratings \leq 5.0 - \frac{\delta}{2}$ be (*low*), we have based all classification experiments on $\delta = 1.6$. The value 5.0 is chosen as it is the *median* aesthetics rating over the 3581 samples. We now vary δ while keeping all other factors constant, and compute SVM accuracy and precision for each value. These results are plotted in Fig. 7. Not surprisingly, the accuracy increases as δ increases. This is accounted by the fact that as δ increases, so does the distinction between the two classes.

Fig. 8 shows the CART decision tree obtained using the 56 visual features. In the figures, the decision nodes are denoted by squares while leaf nodes are denoted by circles. The decisions used at each split and the number of observations which fall in each node during the decision process, are also shown in the figures. Shaded nodes have a higher percentage of *low* class pictures, hence making them *low nodes*, while un-shaded nodes are those where the dominating class is *high*. The RPART implementation uses 5-CV to prune the tree to yield lowest risk. We used a 5-fold cross validation scheme. With *complexity parameter* governing the tree complexity set to 0.0036, the tree generated 61 splits, yielding an 85.9% model accuracy and a modest 62.3% 5-CV accuracy. More important than the accuracy, the tree provides us with a lot of information on how aesthetics can be related to individual features. We do not have the space to include and discuss the entire tree. Let us discuss some interesting decision paths, in each tree, which support our choice of features. The features denoted by $IRM100$, i.e. f_9, and the low DOF indicators for S and V components, respectively (denoted by low_DOF_s, i.e. f_{54} and low_DOF_v, i.e. f_{55}), appear to play crucial roles in the decision process. The expected loss at L_3 and L_4 are 0% and 9%, respectively. A large numeric value of the low DOF indicators shows that the picture is focused on a central object of interest. As discussed before, taking such pictures requires professional expertise and hence high peer rating is not unexpected.

Finally, we report the regression results. The variance σ^2 of the aesthetics score over the 3581 samples is 0.69. With 5 polynomial terms for each of the 56, we achieved a residual sum-of-squares $R^2_{res} = 0.5020$, which is a 28% reduction from the variance σ^2. This score is not very high, but considering the challenge involved, this does suggest that visual features are able to predict human-rated aesthetics scores with some success. To ensure that this was actually demonstrating some correlation, we randomly permuted the aesthetics scores (breaking the correspondence with the features) and performed the same regression. This time, R_{res} is 0.65, clearly showing that the reduction in expected error was not merely by the over-fitting of a complex model.

5   Conclusions and Future Work

We have established significant correlation between various visual properties of photographic images and their aesthetics ratings. We have shown, through using a community-based database and ratings, that certain visual properties tend to yield better discrimination of aesthetic quality than some others. Despite the inherent noise in data, our SVM-based classifier is robust enough to produce good accuracy using only 15 visual features in separating *high* and *low* rated photographs. In the process of designing the classifier, we have developed a number of new features relevant to photographic quality, including a low depth-of-field indicator, a colorfulness measure, a shape convexity score and a familiarity measure. Even though certain extracted features did not show a significant correlation with aesthetics, they may have applications in other photographic image analysis work as they are sound formulations of basic principles in photographic art. In summary, our work is a significant step toward the highly challenging task of understanding the correlation of human emotions and pictures they see by a computational approach. There are yet a lot of open avenues in this direction. The accuracy can potentially be improved by incorporating new features like dominant lines, converging lines, light source classification, and subject-background relationships.

References

1. Airlines.Net, http://www.airliners.net.
2. R. Arnheim, *Art and Visual Perception: A Psychology of the Creative Eye*, University of California Press, Berkeley, 1974.
3. ARTStor.org, http://www.artstor.org.
4. K. Barnard, P. Duygulu, D. Forsyth, N. -de. Freitas, D. M. Blei, and M. I. Jordan, "Matching Words and Pictures," *J. Machine Learning Research*, 3:1107–1135, 2003.
5. A. L. Blum and P. Langley, "Selection of Relevant Features and Examples in Machine Learning," *Artificial Intelligence*, 97(1-2):245–271, 1997.
6. C. Carson, S. Belongie, H. Greenspan, and J. Malik, "Blobworld: Color and Texture-Based Image Segmentation using EM and its Application to Image Querying and Classification," *IEEE Trans. on Pattern Analysis and Machine Intelli.*, 24(8):1026–1038, 2002.
7. C-c. Chen, H. Wactlar, J. Z. Wang, and K. Kiernan, "Digital Imagery for Significant Cultural and Historical Materials - An Emerging Research Field Bridging People, Culture, and Technologies," *Int'l J. on Digital Libraries*, 5(4):275–286, 2005.
8. L. Breiman, J.H. Friedman, R.A. Olshen, and C.J. Stone, *Classification and Regression Trees*, Wadsworth, Belmont, CA, 1983.
9. C.-c. Chang, C.-j. Lin, "LIBSVM : A Library for SVM", http://www.csie.ntu.edu.tw/~cjlin/libsvm, 2001.
10. I. Daubechies, *Ten Lectures on Wavelets*, Philadelphia, SIAM, 1992.
11. Flickr, http://www.flickr.com.
12. J. Li and J. Z. Wang, "Automatic Linguistic Indexing of Pictures by a Statistical Modeling Approach," *IEEE Trans. on Pattern Analysis and Machine Intelli.*, 25(9):1075–1088, 2003.
13. W. Y. Ma and B. S. Manjunath, "NeTra: A Toolbox for Navigating Large Image Databases," *Multimedia Systems*, 7(3):184–198, 1999.
14. B.S. Manjunath, W.Y. Ma, "Texture Features for Browsing and Retrieval of Image Data", *IEEE Trans. on Pattern Analysis and Machine Intelli.*, 18(8):837–842, 1996.
15. Photo.Net, http://www.photo.net.
16. Photo.NetRatingSystem,http://photo.net/gallery/photocritique/standards.
17. Y. Rubner, C. Tomasi, L.J. Guibas, "The Earth Mover's Distance as a Metric for Image Retrieval," *Int'l. J. Computer Vision*, 4(2):99–121, 2000.
18. A. W. Smeulders, M. Worring, S. Santini, A. Gupta, and R. Jain, "Content-Based Image Retrieval at the End of the Early Years," *IEEE Trans. on Pattern Analysis and Machine Intelli.*, 22(12):1349–1380, 2000.
19. T. M. Therneau and E. J. Atkinson, "An Introduction to Recursive Partitioning Using RPART Routines," *Technical Report, Mayo Foundation*, 1997.
20. V. Vapnik, *The Nature of Statistical Learning Theory*, Springer, 1995.
21. J. Z. Wang, J. Li, and G. Wiederhold, "SIMPLIcity: Semantics-Sensitive Integrated Matching for Picture Libraries," *IEEE Trans. on Pattern Analysis and Machine Intelli.*, 23(9):947–963, 2001.

Located Hidden Random Fields: Learning Discriminative Parts for Object Detection

Ashish Kapoor[1] and John Winn[2]

[1] MIT Media Laboratory, Cambridge, MA 02139, USA
kapoor@media.mit.edu
[2] Microsoft Research, Cambridge, UK
jwinn@microsoft.com

Abstract. This paper introduces the Located Hidden Random Field (LHRF), a conditional model for simultaneous part-based detection and segmentation of objects of a given class. Given a training set of images with segmentation masks for the object of interest, the LHRF automatically learns a set of parts that are both discriminative in terms of appearance and informative about the location of the object. By introducing the global position of the object as a latent variable, the LHRF models the long-range spatial configuration of these parts, as well as their local interactions. Experiments on benchmark datasets show that the use of discriminative parts leads to state-of-the-art detection and segmentation performance, with the additional benefit of obtaining a labeling of the object's component parts.

1 Introduction

This paper addresses the problem of simultaneous detection and segmentation of objects belonging to a particular class. Our approach is to use a conditional model which is capable of learning discriminative parts of an object. A part is considered discriminative if it can be reliably detected by its local appearance in the image and if it is well localized on the object and hence informative as to the object's location.

The use of parts has several advantages. First, there are local spatial interactions between parts that can help with detection, for example, we expect to find the nose right above the mouth on a face. Hence, we can exploit local part interactions to exclude invalid hypotheses at a local level. Second, knowing the location of one part highly constrains the locations of other parts. For example, knowing the locations of wheels of a car constrains the positions where rest of the car can be detected. Thus, we can improve object detection by incorporating long range spatial constraints on the parts. Third, by inferring a part labeling for the training data, we can accurately assess the variability in the appearance of each part, giving better part detection and hence better object detection. Finally, the use of parts gives the potential for detecting objects even if they are partially occluded.

A. Leonardis, H. Bischof, and A. Pinz (Eds.): ECCV 2006, Part III, LNCS 3953, pp. 302–315, 2006.
© Springer-Verlag Berlin Heidelberg 2006

One possibility for training a parts-based system is to use supervised training with hand-labeled parts. The disadvantage of this approach is that it is very expensive to get training data annotated for parts, plus it is unclear which parts should be selected. Existing generative approaches try to address these problems by clustering visually similar image patches to build a codebook in the hope that clusters correspond to different parts of the object. However, this codebook has to allow for all sources of variability in appearance – we provide a discriminative alternative where irrelevant sources of variability do not need to be modeled.

This paper introduces Located Hidden Random Field, a novel extension to the Conditional Random Field [1] that can learn parts discriminatively. We introduce a latent part label for each pixel which is learned simultaneously with model parameters, given the segmentation mask for the object. Further, the object's position is explicitly represented in the model, allowing long-range spatial interactions between different object parts to be learned.

2   Related Work

There have been a number of parts-based approaches to segmentation or detection. It is possible to pre-select which parts are used as in [2] – however, this requires significant human effort for each new object class. Alternatively, parts can be learned by clustering visually similar image patches [3, 4] but this approach does not exploit the spatial layout of the parts in the training images. There has been work with generative models that do learn spatially coherent parts in an unsupervised manner. For example, the constellation models of Fergus et al. [5, 6] learn parts which occur in a particular spatial arrangement. However, the parts correspond to sparsely detected interest points and so parts are limited in size, cannot represent untextured regions and do not provide a segmentation of the image. More recently, Winn and Jojic [7] used a dense generative model to learn a partitioning of the object into parts, along with an unsupervised segmentation of the object. Their method does not learn a model of object appearance (only of object shape) and so cannot be used for object detection in cluttered images.

As well as unsupervised methods, there are a range of supervised methods for segmentation and detection. Ullman and Borenstein [8] use a fragment-based method for segmentation, but do not provide detection results. Shotton et al. [9] use a boosting method based on image contours for detection, but this does not lead to a segmentation. There are a number of methods using Conditional Random Fields (CRFs) to achieve segmentation [10] or sparse part-based detection [11]. The OBJ CUT work of Kumar et al. [12] uses a discriminative model for detection and a separate generative model for segmentation but requires that the parts are learned in advance from video. Unlike the work presented in this paper, none of these approaches achieves part-learning, segmentation and detection in a single probabilistic framework.

Our choice of model has been motivated by Szummer's [13] Hidden Random Field (HRF) for classifying handwritten ink. The HRF automatically learns parts of diagram elements (boxes, arrows etc.) and models the local interaction between them. However, the parts learned using an HRF are not spatially localized as the relative location of the part on the object is not modeled. In this paper we introduce the Located HRF, which models the spatial organization of parts and hence learns part which are spatially localized.

3 Discriminative Models for Object Detection

Our aim is to take an $n \times m$ image $\mathbf{x}$ and infer a label for each pixel indicating the class of object that pixel belongs to. We denote the set of all image pixels as V and for each pixel $i \in V$ define a label $y_i \in \{0, 1\}$ where the background class is indicated by $y_i = 0$ and the foreground by $y_i = 1$. The simplest approach is to classify each pixel independently of other pixels based upon some local features, corresponding to the graphical model of Fig. 1a. However, as we would like to model the dependencies between pixels, a conditional random field can be used.

Conditional Random Field (CRF): this consists of a network of classifiers that interact with one another such that the decision of each classifier is influenced by the decision of its neighbors. In the graphical model for a CRF, the class label corresponding to every pixel is connected to its neighbors in a 4-connected grid, as shown in Fig. 1b. We denote this new set of edges as E.

Given an image $\mathbf{x}$, a CRF induces a conditional probability distribution $p(\mathbf{y} \mid \mathbf{x}, \boldsymbol{\theta})$ using the potential functions ψ_i^1 and ψ_{ij}^2. Here, ψ_i^1 encodes compatibility of the label given to the ith pixel with the observed image $\mathbf{x}$ and ψ_{ij}^2 encodes

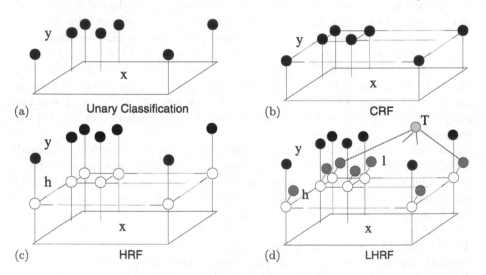

Fig. 1. Graphical models for different discriminative models of images. The image $\mathbf{x}$ and the shaded vertices are observed during training time. The parts $\mathbf{h}$, denoted by unfilled circles, are not observed and are learnt during the training. In the LHRF model, the node corresponding to T is connected to all the locations l_i, depicted using thick dotted lines.

the pairwise label compatibilities for all $(i, j) \in E$ conditioned on $\mathbf{x}$. Thus, the conditional distribution $p(\mathbf{y} \,|\, \mathbf{x})$ induced by a CRF can be written as:

$$p(\mathbf{y} \,|\, \mathbf{x}; \boldsymbol{\theta}) = \frac{1}{Z(\boldsymbol{\theta}, \mathbf{x})} \prod_{i \in V} \psi_i^1(y_i, \mathbf{x}; \boldsymbol{\theta}) \prod_{(i,j) \in E} \psi_{ij}^2(y_i, y_j, \mathbf{x}; \boldsymbol{\theta}) \tag{1}$$

where the partition function $Z(\boldsymbol{\theta}, \mathbf{x})$ depends upon the observed image $\mathbf{x}$ as well as the parameters $\boldsymbol{\theta}$ of the model. We assume that the potentials ψ_i^1 and ψ_{ij}^2 take the following form:

$$\psi_i^1(y_i, \mathbf{x}; \boldsymbol{\theta}_1) = \exp[\boldsymbol{\theta}_1(y_i)^{\mathrm{T}} \mathbf{g}_i(\mathbf{x})]$$
$$\psi_{ij}^2(y_i, y_j, \mathbf{x}; \boldsymbol{\theta}_2) = \exp[\boldsymbol{\theta}_2(y_i, y_j)^{\mathrm{T}} \mathbf{f}_{ij}(\mathbf{x})]$$

Here, $\mathbf{g}_i : \mathcal{R}^{n \times m} \to \mathcal{R}^d$ is a function that computes a d-dimensional feature vector at pixel i, given the image $\mathbf{x}$. Similarly, the function $\mathbf{f}_{ij} : \mathcal{R}^{n \times m} \to \mathcal{R}^d$ computes the d-dimensional feature vector for edge ij.

Hidden Random Field: a Hidden Random Field (HRF) [13] is an extension to a CRF which introduces a number of *parts* for each object class. Each pixel has an additional hidden variable $h_i \in \{1 \ldots H\}$ where H is the total number of parts across all classes. These hidden variables represent the assignment of pixels to parts and are not observed during training. Rather than modeling the interaction between foreground and background labels, an HRF instead models the local interaction between the parts. Fig. 1c shows the graphical model corresponding to an HRF showing that the local dependencies captured are now between parts rather than between class labels. There is also an additional edge from a part label h_i to the corresponding class label y_i. Similar to [13], we assume that every part is uniquely allocated to an object class and so parts are not shared. Specifically, there is deterministic mapping from parts to object-class and we can denote it using $y(h_i)$.

Similarly to the CRF, we can define a conditional model for the label image $\mathbf{y}$ and part image $\mathbf{h}$:

$$p(\mathbf{y}, \mathbf{h} \,|\, \mathbf{x}; \boldsymbol{\theta}) = \frac{1}{Z(\boldsymbol{\theta}, \mathbf{x})} \prod_{i \in V} \psi_i^1(h_i, \mathbf{x}; \boldsymbol{\theta}_1) \, \phi(y_i, h_i) \prod_{(i,j) \in E} \psi_{ij}^2(h_i, h_j, \mathbf{x}; \boldsymbol{\theta}_2) \tag{2}$$

where the potentials are defined as:

$$\psi_i^1(h_i, \mathbf{x}; \boldsymbol{\theta}_1) = \exp[\boldsymbol{\theta}_1(h_i)^{\mathrm{T}} \mathbf{g}_i(\mathbf{x})]$$
$$\psi_{ij}^2(h_i, h_j, \mathbf{x}; \boldsymbol{\theta}_2) = \exp[\boldsymbol{\theta}_2(h_i, h_j)^{\mathrm{T}} \mathbf{f}_{ij}(\mathbf{x})]$$
$$\phi(y_i, h_i) = \delta(y(h_i) = y_i)$$

where δ is an indicator function. The hidden variables in the HRF can be used to model parts and interaction between those parts, providing a more flexible model which in turn can improve detection performance. However, there is no guarantee that the learnt parts are spatially localized. Also, as the model only contains local connections, it does not exploit the long-range dependencies between all the parts of the object.

3.1   Located Hidden Random Field

The Located Hidden Random Field (LHRF) is an extension to the HRF, where the parts are used to infer not only the background/foreground labels but also a position label in a coordinate system defined relative to the object. We augment the model to include the position of the object T, encoded as a discrete latent variable indexing all possible locations. We assume a fixed object size so a particular object position defines a rectangular reference frame enclosing the object. This reference frame is coarsely discretized into bins, representing different discrete locations within the reference frame. Fig. 2 shows an example image, the object mask and the reference frame divided into bins (shown color-coded).

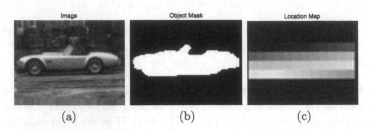

(a)   (b)   (c)

Fig. 2. Instantiation of different nodes in an LHRF. (a) image $\mathbf{x}$, (b) class labels $\mathbf{y}$ showing ground truth segmentation (c) color-coded location map l. The darkest color corresponds to the background.

We also introduce a set of location variables $l_i \in \{0, .., L\}$, where l_i takes the non-zero index of the corresponding bin, or 0 if the pixel lies outside the reference frame. Given a location T the location labels are uniquely defined according to the corresponding reference frame. Hence, when T is unobserved, the location variables are all tied together via their connections to T. These connections allow the long-range spatial dependencies between parts to be learned. As there is only a single location variable T, this model makes the assumption that there is a single object in the image (although it can be used recursively for detecting multiple objects – see Section 4).

We define a conditional model for the label image $\mathbf{y}$, the position T, the part image $\mathbf{h}$ and the locations l as:

$$p(\mathbf{y}, \mathbf{h}, \mathbf{l}, T \mid \mathbf{x}; \boldsymbol{\theta}) = \prod_{i \in V} \psi_i^1(h_i, \mathbf{x}; \boldsymbol{\theta}_1) \, \phi(y_i, h_i) \, \psi^3(h_i, l_i; \boldsymbol{\theta}_3) \, \delta(l_i = \mathrm{loc}(i, T))$$

$$\times \prod_{(i,j) \in E} \psi_{ij}^2(h_i, h_j, \mathbf{x}; \boldsymbol{\theta}_2) \times \frac{1}{Z(\boldsymbol{\theta}, \mathbf{x})} \tag{3}$$

where the potentials ψ^1, ψ^2, ϕ are defined as in the HRF, and $\mathrm{loc}(i, T)$ is the location label of the ith pixel when the reference frame is in position T. The potential encoding the compatibility between parts and locations is given by:

$$\psi^3(h_i, l_i; \boldsymbol{\theta}_3) = \exp[\boldsymbol{\theta}_3(h_i, l_i)] \tag{4}$$

where $\boldsymbol{\theta}_3(h_i, l_i)$ is a look-up table with an entry for each part and location index.

Table 1. Comparison of Different Discriminative Models

	Parts-Based	Spatially Informative Parts	Models Local Spatial Coherence	Models Long Range Spatial Configuration
Unary Classifier	No	–	No	No
CRF	No	–	Yes	No
HRF	Yes	No	Yes	No
LHRF	Yes	Yes	Yes	Yes

In the LHRF, the parts need to be compatible with the location index as well as the class label, which means that the part needs to be informative about the spatial location of the object as well as its class. Hence, unlike the HRF, the LHRF learns spatially coherent parts which occur in a consistent location on the object. The spatial layout of these parts is captured in the parameter vector θ_3, which encodes where each part lies in the co-ordinate system of the object.

Table 1 gives a summary of the properties of the four discriminative models which have been described in this section.

4 Inference and Learning

There are two key tasks that need to be solved when using the LHRF model: learning the model parameters θ and inferring the labels for an input image $\mathbf{x}$.

Inference: Given a novel image $\mathbf{x}$ and parameters θ, we can classify an ith pixel as background or foreground by first computing the marginal $p(y_i \mid \mathbf{x}; \theta)$ and assigning the label that maximizes this marginal. The required marginal is computed by marginalizing out the part variables $\mathbf{h}$, the location variables $\mathbf{l}$, the position variable T and all the labels $\mathbf{y}$ except y_i.

$$p(y_i \mid \mathbf{x}; \theta) = \sum_{\mathbf{y}/y_i} \sum_{\mathbf{h},\mathbf{l},T} p(\mathbf{y}, \mathbf{h}, \mathbf{l}, T \mid \mathbf{x}; \theta)$$

If the graph had small tree width, this marginalization could be performed exactly using the junction tree algorithm. However, even ignoring the long range connections to T, the tree width of a grid is the length of its shortest side and so exact inference is computationally prohibitive. The earlier described models, CRF and HRF, all have such a grid-like structure, which is of the same size as the input image; thus, we resort to approximate inference techniques. In particular, we considered both loopy belief propagation (LBP) and sequential tree-reweighted message passing (TRWS) [14]. Specifically, we compared the accuracy of max-product and the sum-product variants of LBP and the max-product form of TRWS (an efficient implementation of sum-product TRWS was not available – we intend to develop one for future work). The max-product algorithms have the advantage that we can exploit distance transforms [15] to reduce the running time of the algorithm to be linear in terms of number of states. We found that both max-product algorithms performed best on the CRF with TRWS outperforming LBP. However, on the HRF and LHRF models, the sum-product LBP gave significantly better performance than either max-product method. This is probably because the max-product assumption that the posterior mass is concentrated at the mode is inaccurate due to the uncertainty in the latent part variables. Hence, we used sum-product LBP for all LHRF experiments.

When applying LBP in the graph, we need to send messages from each h_i to T and update the approximate posterior $p(T)$ as the product of these; hence,

$$\log p(T) = \sum_{i \in V} \log \sum_{h.} b(h_i)\, \psi^3(h_i, \mathrm{loc}(i, T)) \tag{5}$$

where $b(h_i)$ is the product of messages into the ith node, excluding the message from T. To speed up the computation of $p(T)$, we make the following approximation:

$$\log p(T) \approx \sum_{i \in V} \sum_{h.} b(h_i) \log \psi^3(h_i, \mathrm{loc}(i, T)). \tag{6}$$

This posterior can now be computed very efficiently using convolutions.

Parameter Learning: Given an image $\mathbf{x}$ with labels $\mathbf{y}$ and location map $\mathbf{l}$, the parameters $\boldsymbol{\theta}$ are learnt by maximizing the conditional likelihood $p(\mathbf{y}, \mathbf{l}|\mathbf{x}, \boldsymbol{\theta})$ multiplied by the Gaussian prior $p(\boldsymbol{\theta}) = \mathcal{N}(\boldsymbol{\theta}|0, \sigma^2 \mathbf{I})$. Hence, we seek to maximize the objective function $\mathcal{F}(\boldsymbol{\theta}) = \mathcal{L}(\boldsymbol{\theta}) + \log p(\boldsymbol{\theta})$, where $\mathcal{L}(\boldsymbol{\theta})$ is the log of the conditional likelihood.

$$\mathcal{F}(\boldsymbol{\theta}) = \log p(\mathbf{y}, \mathbf{l}|\mathbf{x}; \boldsymbol{\theta}) + \log p(\boldsymbol{\theta}) = \log \sum_{\mathbf{h}} p(\mathbf{y}, \mathbf{h}, \mathbf{l}|\mathbf{x}; \boldsymbol{\theta}) + \log p(\boldsymbol{\theta})$$

$$= -\log Z(\boldsymbol{\theta}, \mathbf{x}) + \log \sum_{\mathbf{h}} \tilde{p}(\mathbf{y}, \mathbf{h}, \mathbf{l}, \mathbf{x}; \boldsymbol{\theta}) + \log p(\boldsymbol{\theta}) \tag{7}$$

where:

$$\tilde{p}(\mathbf{y}, \mathbf{h}, \mathbf{l}, \mathbf{x}; \boldsymbol{\theta}) = \prod_i \psi_i^1(h_i, \mathbf{x}; \boldsymbol{\theta}_1) \phi(y_i, h_i) \psi^3(h_i, l_i; \boldsymbol{\theta}_3) \prod_{(i,j) \in E} \psi_{ij}^2(h_i, h_j, \mathbf{x}; \boldsymbol{\theta}_2).$$

We use gradient ascent to maximize the objective with respect to the parameters $\boldsymbol{\theta}$. The derivative of the log likelihood $\mathcal{L}(\boldsymbol{\theta})$ with respect to the model parameters $\boldsymbol{\theta} = \{\boldsymbol{\theta}_1, \boldsymbol{\theta}_2, \boldsymbol{\theta}_3\}$ can be written in terms of the features, single node marginals and pairwise marginals:

$$\frac{\delta \mathcal{L}(\boldsymbol{\theta})}{\delta \boldsymbol{\theta}_1(h')} = \sum_{i \in V} \mathbf{g}_i(\mathbf{x}) \cdot (p(h_i = h'|\mathbf{x}, \mathbf{y}, \mathbf{l}; \boldsymbol{\theta}) - p(h_i = h'|\mathbf{x}; \boldsymbol{\theta}))$$

$$\frac{\delta \mathcal{L}(\boldsymbol{\theta})}{\delta \boldsymbol{\theta}_2(h', h'')} = \sum_{(i,j) \in E} \mathbf{f}_{ij}(\mathbf{x}) \cdot (p(h_i = h', h_j = h''|\mathbf{x}, \mathbf{y}, \mathbf{l}; \boldsymbol{\theta}) - p(h_i = h', h_j = h''|\mathbf{x}; \boldsymbol{\theta}))$$

$$\frac{\delta \mathcal{L}(\boldsymbol{\theta})}{\delta \boldsymbol{\theta}_3(h', l')} = \sum_{i \in V} p(h_i = h', l_i = l'|\mathbf{x}, \mathbf{y}, \mathbf{l}; \boldsymbol{\theta}) - p(h_i = h', l_i = l'|\mathbf{x}; \boldsymbol{\theta})$$

It is intractable to compute the partition function $Z(\boldsymbol{\theta}, \mathbf{x})$ and hence the objective function (7) cannot be computed exactly. Instead, we use the approximation to the partition function given by the LBP or TRWS inference algorithm, which is also used to provide approximations to the marginals required to compute the derivative of the objective. Notice that the location variable T comes into effect only when computing marginals for the unclamped model (where $\mathbf{y}$ and $\mathbf{l}$ are not observed), as the sum over $\mathbf{l}$ should be restricted to those configurations consistent with a value of T. We have trained the model both with and without this restriction. Better detection results are achieved without it. This is for two reasons: including this restriction makes the model very sensitive to changes in image size and secondly, when used for detecting multiple objects, the restriction of a single object instance does not apply, and hence should not be included when training part detectors.

Image Features: We aim to use image features which are informative about the part label but invariant to changes in illumination and small changes in pose. The features used in this work for both unary and pairwise potentials are SIFT descriptors [16], except that we compute these descriptors at only one scale and do not rotate the descriptor, due to the assumption of fixed object scale and rotation. For efficiency of learning, we apply the model at a coarser resolution than the pixel resolution – the results given in this paper use a grid whose nodes correspond 2×2 pixel squares. For the unary potentials, SIFT descriptors are computed at the center of the each grid square. For the edge potentials, the SIFT descriptors are computed at the location half-way between two neighboring squares. To allow parameter sharing between horizontal and vertical edge potentials, the features corresponding to the vertical edges in the graphs are rotated by 90 degrees.

Detecting Multiple Objects: Our model assumes that a single object is present in the image. We can reject images with no objects by comparing the evidence for this model with the evidence for a background-only model. Specifically, for each given image we compute the approximation of $p(\text{model} \,|\, \mathbf{x}, \boldsymbol{\theta})$, which is the normalization constant $Z(\boldsymbol{\theta}, \mathbf{x})$ in (3). This model evidence is compared with the evidence for a model which labels the entire image as background $p(\text{noobject} \,|\, \mathbf{x}, \boldsymbol{\theta})$. By defining a prior on these two models, we define the threshold on the ratio of the model evidences used to determine if an object is present or absent. By varying this prior, we can obtain precision-recall curves for detection.

We can use this methodology to detect multiple objects in a single image, by applying the model recursively. Given an image, we detect whether it contains an object instance. If we detect an object, the unary potentials are set to uniform for all pixels labeled as foreground. The model is then reapplied to detect further object instances. This process is repeated until no further objects are detected.

5   Experiments and Results

We performed experiments to (i) demonstrate the different parts learnt by the LHRF, (ii) compare different discriminative models on the task of pixelwise segmentation and (iii) demonstrate simultaneous detection and segmentation of objects in test images.

Training the Models: We trained each discriminative model on two different datasets: the TU Darmstadt car dataset [4] and the Weizmann horse dataset [8]. From the TU Darmstadt dataset, we extracted 50 images of different cars viewed from the side, of which 35 were used for training. The cars were all facing left and were at the same scale in all the images. To gain comparable results for horses, we used 50 images of horses taken from the Weizmann horse dataset, similarly partitioned into training and test sets. All images were resized to 75×100 pixels. Ground truth segmentations are available for both of these data sets, which were used either for training or for assessing segmentation accuracy. For the car images, the ground truth segmentations were modified to label car windows as foreground rather than background.

Training the LHRF on 35 images of size 75×100 took about 2.5 hours on a 3.2 GHz machine. Our implementation is in MATLAB except the loopy belief propagation, which is implemented in C. Once trained, the model can be applied to detect and segment an object in a 75×100 test image in around three seconds.

Learning Discriminative Parts: Fig. 3 illustrates the learned conditional probability of location given parts $p(l \mid h)$ for two, three and four parts for cars and a four part model for horses. The results show that spatially localized parts have been learned. For cars, the model discovers the top and the bottom parts of the cars and these parts get split into wheels, middle body and the top-part of the car as we increase the number of parts in the model. For horses, the parts are less semantically meaningful, although the learned parts are still localized within the object reference frame. One reason for this is that the images contain horses in varying poses and so semantically meaningful parts (e.g. head, tail) do not occur in the same location within a rigid reference frame.

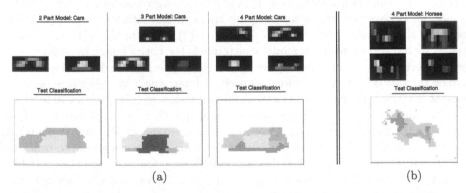

Fig. 3. The learned discriminative parts for (a) Cars (side-view) and (b) Horses. The first row shows, for each model, the conditional probability $p(l|h)$, indicating where the parts occur within the object reference frame. Dark regions correspond to a low probability. The second row shows the part labeling of an example test image for each model.

Test Image	Unary	CRF	HRF	LHRF

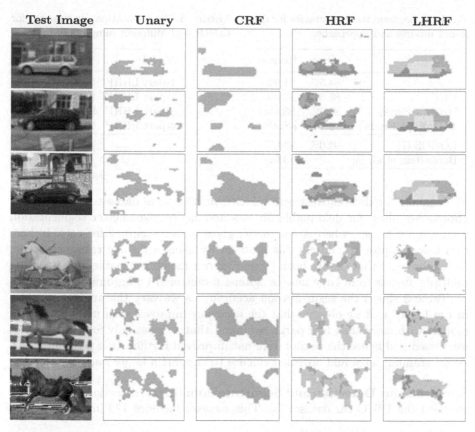

Fig. 4. Segmentation results for car and horse images. The first column shows the test image and the second, third, fourth and fifth column correspond to different classifications obtained using unary, CRF, HRF and LHRF respectively. The colored pixels correspond to the pixels classified as foreground. The different colors for HRF and LHRF classification correspond to pixels classified as different parts.

Segmentation Accuracy: We evaluated the segmentation accuracy for the car and horse training sets for the four different models of Fig. 1. As mentioned above, we selected the first 35 out of 50 images for training and used the remaining 15 to test. Segmentations for test images from the car and horse data sets are shown in Fig. 4. Unsurprisingly, using the unary model leads to many disconnected regions. The results using CRF and HRF have spatially coherent regions but local ambiguity in appearance means that background regions are frequently classified as foreground. Note that the parts learned by the HRF are not spatially coherent. Table 2 gives the relative accuracies of the four models where accuracy is given by the percentage of pixels classified correctly as foreground or background. We observe that LHRF gives a large improvement for cars and a smaller, but significant improvement for horses. Horses are deformable objects and parts occur varying positions in the location frame, reducing the advantage of the LHRF. For comparison, Table 2 also gives accuracies from [7] and

312   A. Kapoor and J. Winn

Table 2. Segmentation accuracies for different models and approaches

	Cars	Horses
Unary	84.5%	81.9%
CRF	85.3%	83.0%
HRF (4-Parts)	87.6%	85.1%
LHRF (4-Parts)	**95.0%**	**88.1%**
LOCUS [7]	94.0%	93.0%
Borenstein et al. [8]	-	93.6%

Table 3. Segmentation accuracies for LHRF with different numbers of parts

Model	Cars
1-part LHRF	89.8%
2-part LHRF	92.5%
3-part LHRF	93.4%
4-part LHRF	95.0%

[8] obtained for different test sets taken from the same dataset. Both of these approaches allow for deformable objects and hence gives better segmentation accuracy for horses, whereas our model gives better accuracy for cars. In Section 6 we propose to address this problem by using a flexible reference frame. Notice however that, unlike both [7] and [8] our model is capable of segmenting multiple objects from large images against a cluttered background.

Table 3 shows the segmentation accuracy as we vary the number of parts in the LHRF and we observe that the accuracy improves with more parts. For models with more than four parts, we found that at most only four of the parts were used and hence the results were not improved further. It is possible that a larger training set would provide evidence to support a larger number of parts.

Simultaneous Detection and Segmentation: To test detection performance, we used the UIUC car dataset [3]. This dataset includes 170 images provided

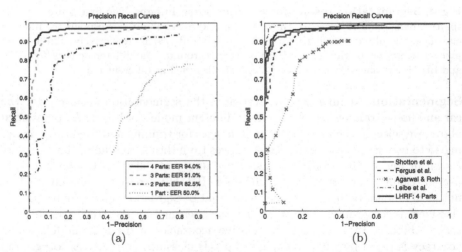

Fig. 5. Precision-recalls curves for detection on the UIUC dataset. (a) performance for different numbers of parts. Note that the performance improves as the number of parts increases. (b) relative performance for our approach against existing methods.

Table 4. Comparison of detection performance

	Number of Training Images	Equal Error Rate
Leibe et al.(MDL) [4]	50	97.5%
Our method	**35**	**94.0%**
Shotton et al. [9]	100	92.1%
Leibe et al. [4]	50	91.0%
Garg et al. [17]	1000	~88.5%
Agarwal & Roth [3]	1000	~79.0%

Fig. 6. Examples of detection and segmentation on the UIUC dataset. The top four rows show correct detections (green boxes) and the corresponding segmentations. The bottom row shows example false positives (red boxes) and false negatives.

for testing, containing a total of 200 cars, with some images containing multiple cars. Again, all the cars in this test set are at the same scale.

Detection performance was evaluated for models trained on 35 images from the TU Darmstadt dataset. Fig. 5(a) shows detection accuracy for varying numbers of foreground parts in the LHRF model. From the figure, we can see that increasing the number of parts increases the detection performance, by exploiting both local and long-range part interactions. Fig. 5(b) compares the detection performance with other existing approaches, with the results summarized in Table 4. Our method is exceeded in accuracy only by the Liebe et al. method and then only when an additional validation step is used, based on an MDL criterion. This validation step could equally be applied in our case – without it, our method gives a 3.0% improvement in accuracy over Liebe et al. Note, that the number of examples used to train the model is less than used by all of the existing methods. Fig. 6 shows example detections and segmentations achieved using the 4-part LHRF.

6 Conclusions and Future Work

We have presented a novel discriminative method for learning object parts to achieve very competitive results for both the detection and segmentation tasks simultaneously, despite using fewer training images than competing approaches. The Located HRF has been shown to give improved performance over both the HRF and the CRF by learning parts which are informative about the location of the object, along with their spatial layout. We have also shown that increasing the number of parts leads to improved accuracy on both the segmentation and detections tasks. Additionally, once the model parameters are learned, our method is efficient to apply to new images.

One extension of this model that we plan to investigate is to introduce edges between the location labels. These edges would have asymmetric potentials encouraging the location labels to form into (partial) regular grids of the form of Fig. 2c. By avoiding the use of a rigid global template, such a model would be robust to significant partial occlusion of the object, to object deformation and would also be able to detect multiple object instances in one pass. We also plan to extend the model to multiple object classes and learn parts that can be shared between these classes.

References

1. Lafferty, J., McCallum, A., Pereira, F.: Conditional random fields: Probabilistic models for segmenting and labeling sequence data. In: International Conference on Machine Learning. (2001)
2. Crandall, D., Felzenszwalb, P., Huttenlocher, D.: Spatial priors for part-based recognition using statistical models. In: CVPR. (2005)
3. Agarwal, S., Roth, D.: Learning a sparse representation for object detection. In: European Conference on Computer Vision. (2002)
4. Leibe, B., Leonardis, A., Schiele, B.: Combined object categorization and segmentation with an implicit shape model. In: Workshop on Statistical Learning in Computer Vision. (2004)
5. Fergus, R., Perona, P., Zisserman, A.: Object class recognition by unsupervised scale-invariant learning. In: Computer Vision and Pattern Recognition. (2003)
6. Fergus, R., Perona, P., Zisserman, A.: A sparse object category model for efficient learning and exhaustive recognition. In: Proceedings of the IEEE Conference on Computer Vision and Pattern Recognition, San Diego. (2005)
7. Winn, J., Jojic, N.: LOCUS: Learning Object Classes with Unsupervised Segmentation. In: International Conference on Computer Vision. (2005)
8. Borenstein, E., Sharon, E., Ullman, S.: Combining top-down and bottom-up segmentation. In: Proceedings IEEE workshop on Perceptual Organization in Computer Vision, CVPR 2004. (2004)
9. Shotton, J., Blake, A., Cipolla, R.: Contour-based learning for object detection. In: International Conference on Computer Vision. (2005)

10. Kumar, S., Hebert, M.: Discriminative random fields: A discriminative framework for contextual interaction in classification. In: ICCV. (2003)
11. Quattoni, A., Collins, M., Darrell, T.: Conditional random fields for object recognition. In: Neural Information Processing Systems. (2004)
12. Kumar, M.P., Torr, P.H.S., Zisserman, A.: OBJ CUT. In: Proceedings of the IEEE Conference on Computer Vision and Pattern Recognition, San Diego. (2005)
13. Szummer, M.: Learning diagram parts with hidden random fields. In: International Conference on Document Analysis and Recognition. (2005)
14. Kolmogorov, V.: Convergent tree-reweighted message passing for energy minimization. In: Workshop on Artificial Intelligence and Statistics. (2005)
15. Felzenszwalb, P., Huttenlocher, D.: Efficient belief propagation for early vision. In: Computer Vision and Pattern Recognition. (2004)
16. Lowe, D.: Object recognition from local scale-invariant features. In: International Conference on Computer Vision. (1999)
17. Garg, A., Agarwal, S., Huang., T.S.: Fusion of global and local information for object detection. In: International Conference on Pattern Recognition. (2002)

Learning Compositional Categorization Models

Björn Ommer and Joachim M. Buhmann*

Institute of Computational Science, ETH Zurich
8092 Zurich, Switzerland
{bjoern.ommer, jbuhmann}@inf.ethz.ch

Abstract. This contribution proposes a compositional approach to visual object categorization of scenes. Compositions are learned from the Caltech 101 database[1] and form intermediate abstractions of images that are semantically situated between low-level representations and the high-level categorization. Salient regions, which are described by localized feature histograms, are detected as image parts. Subsequently compositions are formed as bags of parts with a locality constraint. After performing a spatial binding of compositions by means of a shape model, coupled probabilistic kernel classifiers are applied thereupon to establish the final image categorization. In contrast to the discriminative training of the categorizer, intermediate compositions are learned in a generative manner yielding relevant part agglomerations, i.e. groupings which are frequently appearing in the dataset while simultaneously supporting the discrimination between sets of categories. Consequently, compositionality simplifies the learning of a complex categorization model for complete scenes by splitting it up into simpler, sharable compositions. The architecture is evaluated on the highly challenging Caltech 101 database which exhibits large intra-category variations. Our compositional approach shows competitive retrieval rates in the range of $53.6 \pm 0.88\%$ or, with a multi-scale feature set, rates of $57.8 \pm 0.79\%$.

1 Introduction

Automatically detecting and recognizing objects in images has been one of the major goals in computer vision for several decades. Recently, there has been significant interest in the subfield of object categorization, which aims at recognizing visual objects of some general class in scenes. The large intra-category variations which are observed in this setting turn learning and representing category models into a key challenge. Therefore, common characteristics of a category have to be captured while simultaneously offering invariance with respect to variabilities or absence of these features. Typically, this problem has been tackled by representing a scene with local descriptors and modeling their configuration in a more or less rigid way, e.g. [1, 2, 3, 4, 5, 6, 7, 8].

---

* This work was supported in part by the Swiss national fund under contract no. 200021-107636.

[1] www.vision.caltech.edu/feifeili/101_ObjectCategories

A. Leonardis, H. Bischof, and A. Pinz (Eds.): ECCV 2006, Part III, LNCS 3953, pp. 316–329, 2006.
© Springer-Verlag Berlin Heidelberg 2006

Overview over the Compositional Approach to Categorization: This contribution proposes a system that learns category-dependent agglomerations of local features, i.e. localized histograms, and binds them together using a shape model to categorize scenes. It is evaluated on the challenging Caltech 101 image database and shows competitive performance compared to the current state of the art. Our approach has its foundation in the principle of *compositionality* [9]: It can be observed that in cognition in general and especially in human vision (see [10]) complex entities are perceived as compositions of comparably few, simple, and widely usable parts. Objects are then represented based on their components and the relations between them. In contrast to modeling the constellation of parts directly (as [4]), the compositionality approach learns intermediate groupings of parts—possibly even forming a hierarchy of recursive compositions [11]. As a result compositions are establishing hidden layers between image features and scene categorization [7]. We do however restrict our system to a single layer of compositions as this already proves to be complex enough. The fundamental concept is then to find a trade-off between two extremes: On the one hand objects have high intra-category variations so that learning representations for whole objects directly becomes infeasible. On the other hand local part descriptors fail to capture reliable information on the overall object category. Therefore compositions represent category-distinctive subregions of an object, which show minor intra-category variations compared to the whole object and turn learning them into a feasible problem. As a result the description length of the intermediate compositional representation is reduced. Therefore we propose methods for both, learning a set of compositions and establishing image categorization based on compositions detected in an image. The underlying training is conducted in a weakly supervised manner using only category labels for whole images.

Learning compositions is then guided by three modeling decisions: (i) Firstly, it has to be determined which parts to group to form potential candidate compositions. Here we follow the principles of *perceptual organization* [12]. (ii) Secondly, we aim at learning a fairly small set of compositions (currently 250) so that estimating category statistics on the training data becomes feasible. Therefore, the system cannot afford to learn compositions that are observed only rarely in the visual world. As an approximation on the training set we cluster potential composition candidates and estimate the priors of the different composition prototypes. (iii) Thirdly, each composition should be valuable for the task of discriminating sets of categories from another—not necessarily one category from all others. Compositions representing background that is present in many different categories or compositions that are only present in individual instances of a category are to be discarded. This discriminative relevance of a composition is estimated by the entropy of the category posterior distributions given the composition. Finally, the priors of composition prototypes and the entropy of the category posterior are combined in a single cost function. Based on this function relevant compositions are selected from the set of all prototypical compositions.

Crucial Modeling Decisions and Related Work: Methods in this field differ in the way they are approaching crucial modeling decisions: Firstly, various local descriptors have been used. A classical way to capture image region information are *appearance patches* (e.g. [6, 4, 5, 3]). This method extracts image patches, converts them to grayscale, and subsamples them. As a result limited invariance with respect to minor variations in such patches is obtained. The resulting features are clustered to acquire a codebook of typically some thousand local patch representatives that are category specific. Another popular choice are *SIFT* features [13]. These are complex edge histogram features that have been proposed to distinguish different instances of an object class from another. Nevertheless they have also shown to perform reasonably well in the field of categorization. The high dimensionality and the specificity of these features with respect to individual visual realizations of an object require to cluster them into a large codebook representation. On the other end of the modeling spectrum are methods that compute histograms over complete images (cf. [14]). Such an approach offers utmost invariance with respect to changes of individual pixels at the cost of limited specificity. An approach which formulates a trade-off between these two classical extremes has been proposed in [7]. Here local edge and color histograms of subpatches are combined to obtain a low dimensional representation of an image patch. The lack of specificity is made up for by capturing relations between the local descriptors. We use these *localized histograms* in this contribution. Another approach that has shown to perform reasonably well is that of *geometric blur* [8]. This descriptor weights edge orientations around a feature point using a spatially varying kernel.

A second choice concerns the combination of all local features into a single model that captures the overall statistics of a scene. On the one hand individual local descriptors in a test image are to be matched against those from a learned model. On the other hand the co-occurence and spatial relation between individual features has to be taken into account. Here the simplest approach is to histogram over all local descriptors found in an image (e.g. [15]) and categorize the image directly based on the overall feature frequencies. On the one hand such *bag of features* methods offer robustness with respect to alteration of individual parts of an object (e.g. due to occlusion) at low computational costs. On the other hand they fail to capture any spatial relations between local image patches and have a high chance to adapt to background features. At the other end of the modeling spectrum are *constellation models*. Originally, Fischler and Elschlager [1] have proposed a spring model for coupling local features. Inspired by the *Dynamic Link Architecture* for cognitive processes, Lades et al. [2] followed the same fundamental idea when proposing their face recognizer. Lately increasingly complex models for capturing part constellations have been proposed, e.g. [16, 4, 5, 17]. Finally Fergus et al. [4] estimate the joint Gaussian spatial, scale, appearance, and edge curve distributions of all detected patches. However the complexity of the joint model causes only small numbers of parts to be feasible. In contrast to this [6, 3] build a comparably large codebook of distinctive parts for a single category. Leibe and Schiele [3] estimate the mean of all shifts between the positions of codebook patches in training and test images. A probabilistic Hough voting strategy is then used to distinguish one category from the background. [7] further refines this approach and groups parts prior to spatially coupling the resulting compositions in a graphical model. Conflicting categorization hypotheses proposed by compositions and the spatial model are then reconciled using belief propagation. In this contribution we extend the shape model underlying [7] using probabilistic kernel classifiers. Finally, Berg et al. [8] describe and regularize the spatial distortion resulting from matching an image to a training sample using thin plate splines.

The approaches mentioned above are weekly supervised, that is they only need training images (showing objects and probably even background clutter) and the overall category label of an image. The restriction of user assistance is a desirable property for scaling methods up to large numbers of categories with huge training sets. In contrast to this a supervised approach to finding an object of a certain class in images is taken by Felzenszwalb and Huttenlocher in [18]. Given example images and the object configurations present in each image they explicitly model the appearance of a small number of parts separately and capture their spatial configuration with spring-like connections. Similarly, Heisele et al. [19] learn characteristic regions of faces and their spatial constellation. They create training faces from a textured 3-D head model by rendering and determine rectangular components by manually selecting specific points of a face (e.g. nose). Component sizes are estimated by reducing the error of a SVM.

Finally there are two broad categories of learning methods to choose from, generative and discriminative models. While the former aims at estimating the joint probability of category labels and features, the latter one calculates the category posterior directly from the data. Although discriminative approaches have, in principle, superior performance generative models have been very popular in the vision community, e.g. [3, 4, 20, 6, 7, 8]. One reason is that they naturally establish correspondence between model components and image features. Thereby the missing of features can be modeled intuitively. In contrast to this [15, 21] pursue a discriminative approach to object class recognition. To recognize faces in real-time Viola and Jones [21] use boosting to learn simple features in a fixed configuration that measure the intensity difference between small image regions. Holub et al. [17] propose a hybrid approach using Fisher kernels, thereby trying to get the best of both worlds.

The next section summarizes our compositional approach to categorization. Section 3 evaluates our architecture on the challenging Caltech 101 database and shows competitive performance compared to other current approaches. We conclude this presentation with a final discussion.

2   Categorization Using Compositional Models

The model can be best explained by considering recognition, see Figure 1(a). Given a novel image, salient image regions are detected in a first stage using a scale invariant Harris interest point detector [22]. Each region is then described by localized histograms [7]. In a next step a perceptual grouping of these local part descriptors is conducted to obtain a set of possible candidate compositions.

320   B. Ommer and J.M. Buhmann

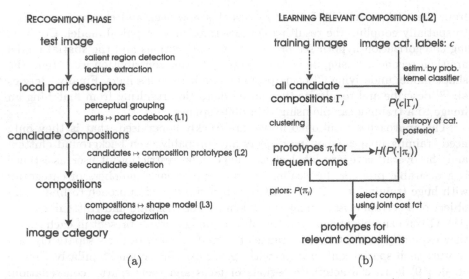

Fig. 1. (a) Recognition based on compositions. The three learning stages (L1–L3) which are involved are presented in Section 2.1, Section 2.3, and Section 2.4, respectively. (b) Learning relevant compositions (learning stage L2 from (a)), see text for details.

This grouping leads to a sparse image representation based on (probably over-lapping) subregions, where each candidate represents an agglomeration of local parts. Consecutively, composition candidates have to be encoded. Therefore all detected local part descriptors are represented as probability distributions over a codebook which is obtained using histogram quantization in the learning stage. This codebook models locally typical configurations of the categories under consideration. A composition is then represented as a mixture distribution of all its part distributions, i.e. a *bag of parts*.

In a next stage relevant compositions have to be selected, discarding irrelevant candidates that represent background clutter. The set of relevant compositions has to be computed in the learning phase from the training data in a weakly supervised manner (see Figure 1(b)). As intermediate compositional representations should have limited description length, this learning obeys the following rationale: (i) Firstly, we aim at a set of compositions that occur frequently in the visual world of the categories under consideration. For that purpose all composition candidates found in all the training images are clustered and the prior assignment probabilities of candidates to these prototypes are estimated. (ii) Secondly, relevant compositions have to support the discrimination of sets of categories from another. Clutter that is present in many different categories or configurations that are only observed in few instances of a category are to be discarded to reduce the model complexity. In order to find a relevance measure the category posteriors of compositions are learned from the training data. The relevance of a composition for discriminating categories is then estimated by the entropy of its category posterior. By combining both the priors of the prototypes and the entropy, a single cost function is obtained that guides the selection of relevant compositions.

After discarding the irrelevant compositions from a new test image, the image category has to be inferred based on all the remaining relevant compositions. These compositions are spatially coupled by using a shape model similar to the one presented in [7].

2.1 Codebook Representation of Local Part Descriptors

In order to render the learning of compositions robust and feasible, low dimensional representations of local descriptors extracted from an image are sought. We choose a slight variation of *localized histograms* presented in [7]. At each interest point detected in an image a quadratic patch is extracted with a side length of 10 to 20 pixel, depending on the local scale estimate. Each patch is then divided up into four subpatches with locations fixed relative to the patch center. For each of these subwindows marginal histograms of edge orientation and edge strength are computed (allocating four bins to each of them). Moreover, an eight bin color histogram over all subpatches is extracted. All these histograms are then combined in a common feature vector $\mathbf{e}_i$.

By performing a k-means clustering on all feature vectors detected in the training data a codebook (of currently $k = 100$ prototypes) is obtained. To robustify the representation each feature is not merely described by its nearest prototype but by a Gibbs distribution [23] over the codebook: Let $d_\nu(\mathbf{e}_i)$ denote the squared euclidean distance of a measured feature $\mathbf{e}_i$ to a centroid $\mathbf{a}_\nu$. The local descriptor is then represented by the following distribution of its cluster assignment random variable F_i,

$$P(F_i = \nu|\mathbf{e}_i) := Z(\mathbf{e}_i)^{-1} \exp\left(-d_\nu(\mathbf{e}_i)\right), \tag{1}$$

$$Z(\mathbf{e}_i) := \sum_\nu \exp\left(-d_\nu(\mathbf{e}_i)\right). \tag{2}$$

2.2 Forming Candidate Compositions

Given all detected local part descriptors in an image, our categorization algorithm follows the principles of perceptual organization, i.e. *Gestalt laws*, to search for possible candidates for compositions. For the sake of simplicity, the current approach uses only the grouping principle of *proximity* although other agglomeration strategies could be invoked: From the set of all parts detected in an image, a subset (currently 30) is randomly selected. Each of these parts is then grouped with neighboring parts that are not farther away than 60-100 pixel (depending on the local scale estimate of the part mentioned in Section 2.1). Consequently compositions sparsely cover salient image regions.

The resulting candidate compositions are then represented as mixtures of the part distributions in (1). Let $\Gamma_j = \{\mathbf{e}_1, \ldots, \mathbf{e}_m\}$ denote the grouping of parts represented by features $\mathbf{e}_1, \ldots, \mathbf{e}_m$. The candidate composition is then represented by the vector valued random variable G_j which is a bag of parts, i.e. its value $\mathbf{g}_j$ is a distribution over the k-dimensional codebook from Section 2.1

$$\mathbf{g}_j \propto \sum_{i=1}^{m} \left(P(F_i = 1|\mathbf{e}_i), \ldots, P(F_i = k|\mathbf{e}_i)\right)^T. \tag{3}$$

This mixture model has the favorable property of robustness with respect to variations in the individual parts.

2.3 Learning Relevant Compositions

Given all candidate compositions a selection has to be performed, retaining only the discriminative ones and discarding clutter. Learning such compositions is divided up into two stages, see Figure 1(b). First those groupings have to be retrieved which are representative for a large majority of objects observed among the considered categories. Thereby, the system avoids to memorize compositions that capture details of only specific instances of a category. Moreover, compositions should be shared among different categories. These concepts limit the description length of a compositional image representation and, thereby, reduce the risk of overfitting to specific object instances. In the learning phase the candidate compositions of all training images are therefore clustered (using k-means) into a comparably large set Π of prototypes $\pi_i \in \Pi$—currently 1000. Moreover, the prior assignment probabilities of candidates to clusters, $P(\pi_i)$, are computed.

In a second stage those prototypes have to be selected that help in distinguishing sets of categories from another. As the system combines multiple compositions found in one image, we do not have to solve the harder problem of finding groupings that are characteristic for a single category. In contrast to such an approach we pursue the robust setting of sharing compositions for multiple categories (cf. [24]). To begin with, the category posterior of compositions has to be estimated, i.e. the posterior of a categorization with label $c \in \mathcal{L}$ ($\mathcal{L}$ denotes the set of all category labels) given a composition Γ_j,

$$P_{\Gamma_j}(c) := P(C = c|\Gamma_j). \tag{4}$$

This distribution is learned by training probabilistic two-class kernel classifiers on all composition candidates found in the labeled training images. For the two-class classification we choose *nonlinear kernel discriminant analysis* (NKDA)[25] and perform a pairwise coupling to solve the multi-class problem (see [26, 25]). The rationale behind our choice is that a joint optimization over all classes (one vs. all classifiers) is unnecessarily hard and computationally much more costly than solving the simpler pairwise subproblems. The combined probabilistic classifier yields an estimate of the posterior (4) for the respective image category.

Subsequently the category posterior is used to calculate the relevance of a composition for discriminating categories. Groupings that are present in all categories are penalized by this idea, whereas combinations which are typical for only a few classes are fostered. The discriminative relevance measure is then modeled as the entropy of (4),

$$H(P_{\Gamma_j}) = -\sum_{c \in \mathcal{L}} P(C = c|\Gamma_j) \log P(C = c|\Gamma_j), \tag{5}$$

which should be minimized.

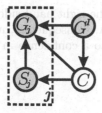

Fig. 2. Bayesian network that couples compositions G_j using their relative location S_j, a bag of features G^I, and image categorization C. Shaded nodes denote evidence variables. See text for details.

Finally a cost function can be formulated that measures the total relevance of a prototype π_i. It combines the prior assignment probabilities of clusters, $P(\pi_i)$, with the entropy (5),

$$\mathcal{S}(\pi_i) \propto -P(\pi_i) + \lambda H(P_\pi). \tag{6}$$

Both constituents of the cost function should be normalized to the same dynamic range, giving rise to an additional additive constant that can be discarded and to the parameter $\lambda > 0$. The latter trades the occurrence frequencies of compositions against their discriminative usefulness.

A set of 250 relevant composition prototypes that is shared by all categories can then be obtained by selecting the prototypes π_i with minimal cost $\mathcal{S}(\pi_i)$. An image is then represented by retaining only those composition candidates formed in Section 2.2 which are closer to one of the relevant prototypes than to any irrelevant one. However, at least the best 5 candidates are retained, thereby ensuring that images from the background category always yield a non-empty representation.

2.4 Binding Compositions Using a Shape Model

Subsequently, all relevant compositions which have been detected in an image are to be coupled with another using a shape model similar to that in [7]. First we have to estimate the object location $\mathbf{x}$. Therefore the positions $\mathbf{x}_j$ of all compositions $\mathbf{g}_j$ are considered. Moreover, we include a composition $\mathbf{g}^I$ of all parts $\mathbf{e}_i$ in the image, i.e. a bag of features descriptor for the whole image.

$$\mathbf{x} = \sum_j \mathbf{x}_j \sum_{c \in \mathcal{L}} p(\mathbf{g}_j | c, \mathbf{g}^I) \, P(c | \mathbf{g}^I). \tag{7}$$

The first distribution is estimated using Parzen windows and the second one using NKDA. For training images, for which the true category is available, the second sum collapses to only the true category c and the distribution over categories is dropped. Following [7] the composition locations $\mathbf{x}_j$ are transformed into shifts, $\mathbf{s}_j := \mathbf{x} - \mathbf{x}_j$. Finally, the bag of features descriptor $\mathbf{g}^I$, the relative positions $\mathbf{s}_j$, and the image categorization c couple the compositions $\mathbf{g}_j$ with another as depicted in the graphical model in Figure 2. Using this model, the categorization posterior can be written as

$$P(c | \mathbf{g}^I, \{\mathbf{g}_j, \mathbf{s}_j\}_{j=1:n}) \propto \exp\left[(1-n) \log P(c | \mathbf{g}^I) + \sum_j \log P(c | \mathbf{g}_j, \mathbf{s}_j, \mathbf{g}^I) \right]. \tag{8}$$

As already mentioned previously, both distributions on the right hand side are estimated separately from the training data using NKDA. Consequently, novel images cannot only be assigned a category label, but also a confidence in this categorization.

3   Experiments

We evaluate our approach on the challenging Caltech 101 database consisting of 101 object categories and a background category with varying numbers of samples (between about 30 and 800). The dataset contains the full spectrum of images ranging from photos with clutter to line drawings. However, there are only limited variations in pose. Subsequently, the retrieval rate is to be computed. As categories are having different sample sizes, we average over the retrieval rates that are measured for each category individually, thereby avoiding a bias towards classes with more images. Berg et al. [8] have calculated a reasonable baseline performance of 16% using texton histograms. Moreover their approach which is based on shape correspondence achieved a classification rate of 48%. Using a constellation model Fei-Fei et al. performed at about 16%. Finally, Holub et al. [17] extend the generative constellation model approaches with a discriminative method and a fusion of several interest point detectors to achieve 40.1%.

Baseline Performance Without Compositions: Object categorization is based on an intermediate compositional image representation in our approach. The following experiments estimate a baseline performance of the system without this hidden representational layer. Therefore we neglect all compositions and consider only the bag of features representation $\mathbf{g}^I$ of the whole image, introduced in Section 2.4.

The basic evaluation scenario is as follows: For each class up to 50 training images are randomly selected (the coupled classifiers are weighted to compensate for the unequal priors) and the remainder is taken as test set (minimally 10 images in a class and over 4000 in total). To estimate the retrieval rate and its error 5-fold cross-validation is performed, i.e. the same algorithm is applied to 5 different training and test set compositions. Figure 3(b) shows the resulting category confusion table for the case of a feature bag which consists of 100 prototypes. This simple model achieves a retrieval rate of $33.3 \pm 0.9\%$.

To evaluate its dependence on the size of the codebook from Section 2.1 the simple bag of features approach is now evaluated with different numbers of clusters. Figure 3(a) shows the retrieval rates under varying model complexity. In the case of 1000 prototypes this model yields a retrieval rate of $\mathbf{38.4 \pm 1.3\%}$. Compare this with the maximal performance of 29% that [17] obtain with their discriminative method on the basis of a single interest point detector (like our simple model presented in this section) and the 40.1% of the combination of all three detectors. As the localized histograms are fairly low-dimensional descriptors, comparably small codebooks do already yield considerable retrieval rates. This is advantageous for modeling compositions robustly which are obviously

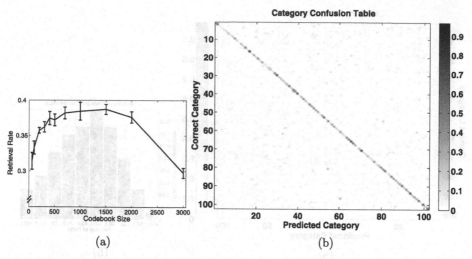

Fig. 3. (a) Retrieval rates for a bag of features approach with codebooks of different sizes. (b) Category confusion table for a bag of features approach with 100 prototypes. The retrieval rate is $33.3 \pm 0.9\%$.

consisting of fewer parts than a complete image and justifies our choice of a 100 prototype representation in the full compositional architecture.

Categorization Performance of the Compositional Model: Subsequently, the full compositional model is learned to categorize images. Evaluation under 5-fold cross-validation yields a retrieval rate of **$53.6 \pm 0.88\%$** which compares favorably with the 48% of Berg et al. [8]. Additionally, we note that the overall retrieval rate per image without averaging over categories is $67.3 \pm 2.1\%$. Figure 4(a) depicts the respective category confusion table. When comparing this plot with the one for the simple bag of features approach from above it is evident that the number of incorrectly classified images has significantly decreased. The categories with lowest performance are "octopus", "wildcat", and "ant", the best ones are "car", "dollar bill", and "accordion". Amongst the off-diagonal elements the confusions "water-lilly" vs. "lotus", "ketch" vs. "schooner", and "lobster" vs. "crayfish" are the most prominent ones. All of these confusions are between pairs that are either synonymous or at least semantically very close. To conclude, the observable gain in resolving ambiguities between classes emphasizes the advantage of an intermediate compositional image representation in contrast to a direct categorization.

Evaluating Compositions: The following evaluates the relevant compositions that have been learned. Firstly, Figure 4(b) plots the number of parts that are typically grouped to form a composition. On average there are approximately 57 parts coupled together. This is a significant increase compared to the tuple groupings formed in [7].

The next experiment intends to visualize the learned compositions. Since these are agglomerations of localized histograms that cannot be displayed

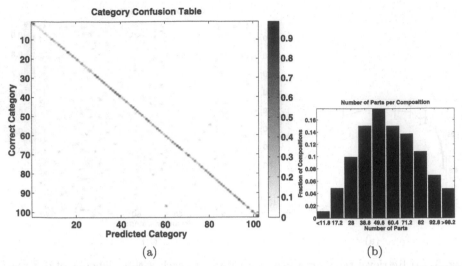

(a) (b)

Fig. 4. (a) Category confusion table of the compositional model. The retrieval rate is $53.6 \pm 0.88\%$. (b) Distribution of the number of parts assigned to each composition.

directly an indirect method has to be pursued. We therefore plot image regions from the test images that have been detected to contain a specific composition. A displayed region is then simply the rectangular hull of all parts that have been agglomerated to a composition. As space in this paper does not permit to present the full set, Figure 5 visualizes a subset of all learned compositions by showing 3 candidate regions for each. The zones are therefore scaled to equal sizes. Observe that compositions are reflecting quite different, abstract concepts: There are those that nicely correspond to salient structures in a single category Figure 5(a)-(c). In the latter case there are however also representatives from another category (motorbike) that show a visually similar pattern. Figure 5(d) and (e) exhibit more extended feature sharing. In (d) the triangular structures of airplane rudders and schooners are captured, while (e) combines sails of different boat categories and butterfly wings. The composition in (f) grasps roundish, metallic structures and (g) elongated, repetitive patterns of windsor chairs and menorahs. The next two compositions are an example of textures. The latter however also seems to model the presence of sharp edges, while (j) captures characteristic contours of pianos and staplers. An example for drawings is given in (k), while (l) seems to model the abstract concept of feet of chairs, pianos, and insects. In conclusion various kinds of low level properties are combined to represent fairly abstract concepts that help to discriminate between categories.

Localizing Object Constituents: Subsequently the relevance of individual compositions for the task of categorizing an image is to be evaluated. Therefore, the relevant object constituents are to be identified and localized. We measure how the categorization performance varies when a single composition is removed. Relevance is then proportional to the decrease in categorization probability of

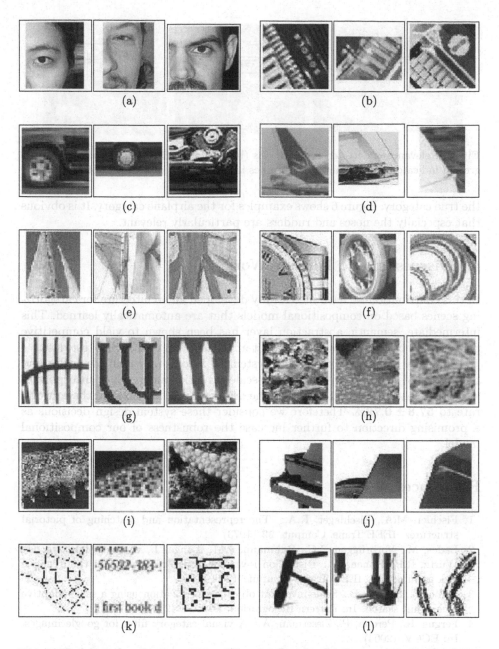

Fig. 5. Visualization of compositions: The pictures show the rectangular hulls of test image regions associated with different compositions. Different, abstract concepts captured by compositions: (a) Parts of faces, (b) accordions, and (c) cars, motorbikes. Feature sharing for complex structures of airplanes and schooners in (d), and of boat sails and butterfly wings in (e). (f) roundish structures. (g) elongated patterns of chairs and menorah. (h), (i) texture with and without a sharp edge, respectively. (j) contours. (k) drawings. (l) feet of chairs, pianos, and insects.

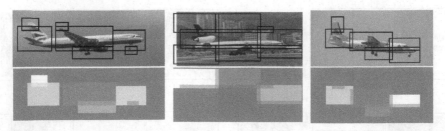

Fig. 6. Relevance of detected compositions (black boxes). Brighter patches than background indicate high relevance, darker ones indicate compositions are not useful.

the true category. Figure 6 shows examples for the airplane category. It is obvious that especially the noses and rudders are particularly relevant.

4   Discussion and Further Work

In this contribution we have successfully developed an architecture for categorizing scenes based on compositional models that are automatically learned. This intermediate, semantic abstraction layer has been shown to yield competitive performance compared to other current approaches on challenging test data.

Currently we are extending the system to incorporate multiple scales and hierarchies of compositions. The multi-scale extension alone, which incorporates additional features extracted on half the original scale, has boosted the retrieval rate to $57.8 \pm 0.79\%$. Therefore we consider these system design decisions as a promising direction to further increase the robustness of our compositional model.

References

1. Fischler, M.A., Elschlager, R.A.: The representation and matching of pictorial structures. IEEE Trans. Comput. **22** (1973)
2. Lades, M., Vorbrüggen, J.C., Buhmann, J.M., Lange, J., von der Malsburg, C., Würtz, R.P., Konen, W.: Distortion invariant object recognition in the dynamic link architecture. IEEE Trans. Comput. **42** (1993)
3. Leibe, B., Schiele, B.: Scale-invariant object categorization using a scale-adaptive mean-shift search. In: Pattern Recognition, DAGM. (2004)
4. Fergus, R., Perona, P., Zisserman, A.: A visual category filter for google images. In: ECCV. (2004)
5. Fei-Fei, L., Fergus, R., Perona, P.: Learning generative visual models from few training examples: An incremental bayesian approach tested on 101 object categories. In: CVPR Workshop GMBV. (2004)
6. Agarwal, S., Awan, A., Roth, D.: Learning to detect objects in images via a sparse, part-based representation. IEEE Trans. Pattern Anal. Machine Intell. **26** (2004)
7. Ommer, B., Buhmann, J.M.: Object categorization by compositional graphical models. In: EMMCVPR. (2005)

8. Berg, A.C., Berg, T.L., Malik, J.: Shape matching and object recognition using low distortion correspondence. In: CVPR. (2005)
9. Geman, S., Potter, D.F., Chi, Z.: *Composition Systems*. Technical report, Division of Applied Mathematics, Brown University, Providence, RI (1998)
10. Biederman, I.: Recognition-by-components: A theory of human image understanding. Psychological Review **94** (1987)
11. Ommer, B., Buhmann, J.M.: A compositionality architecture for perceptual feature grouping. In: EMMCVPR. (2003)
12. Lowe, D.G.: Perceptual Organization and Visual Recognition. Kluwer Academic Publishers, Norwell, MA (1985)
13. Lowe, D.G.: Distinctive image features from scale-invariant keypoints. Int. J. Computer Vision **60** (2004)
14. Veltkamp, R.C., Tanase, M.: Content-based image and video retrieval. In: A Survey of Content-Based Image Retrieval Systems. Kluwer (2002)
15. Dance, C., Willamowski, J., Fan, L., Bray, C., Csurka, G.: Visual categorization with bags of keypoints. In: ECCV Workshop on Stat. Learn. in Comp. Vis. (2004)
16. Weber, M., Welling, M., Perona, P.: Unsupervised learning of models for recognition. In: ECCV. (2000)
17. Holub, A.D., Welling, M., Perona, P.: Combining generative models and fisher kernels for object class recognition. In: ICCV. (2005)
18. Felzenszwalb, P.F., Huttenlocher, D.P.: Pictorial structures for object recognition. Int. J. Computer Vision **61** (2005)
19. Heisele, B., Serre, T., Pontil, M., Vetter, T., Poggio, T.: Categorization by learning and combining object parts. In: NIPS. (2001)
20. Borenstein, E., Sharon, E., Ullman, S.: Combining top-down and bottom-up segmentation. In: CVPR Workshop on Perceptual Organization in Comp. Vis. (2004)
21. Viola, P., Jones, M.: Rapid object detection using a boosted cascade of simple features. In: CVPR. (2001)
22. Mikolajczyk, K., Schmid, C.: Scale & affine invariant interest point detectors. Int. J. Computer Vision **60** (2004)
23. Winkler, G.: Image Analysis, Random Fields and Markov Chain Monte Carlo Methods—A Mathematical Introduction. 2nd edn. Springer (2003)
24. Torralba, A., Murphy, K.P., Freeman, W.T.: Sharing visual features for multiclass and multiview object detection. In: CVPR. (2004)
25. Roth, V., Tsuda, K.: Pairwise coupling for machine recognition of hand-printed japanese characters. In: CVPR. (2001)
26. Hastie, T., Tibshirani, R.: Classification by pairwise coupling. In: NIPS. (1998)

EMD-L_1: An Efficient and Robust Algorithm for Comparing Histogram-Based Descriptors

Haibin Ling[1] and Kazunori Okada[2]

[1] Computer Science Dept., Center for Automation Research, University of Maryland, College Park, Maryland 20770, USA
hbling@umiacs.umd.edu
[2] Imaging and Visualization Department, Siemens Corporate Research, Inc.
755 College Rd. E. Princeton, New Jersey, 08540, USA
kazunori.okada@siemens.com

Abstract. We propose a fast algorithm, EMD-L_1, for computing the Earth Mover's Distance (EMD) between a pair of histograms. Compared to the original formulation, EMD-L_1 has a largely simplified structure. The number of unknown variables in EMD-L_1 is $O(N)$ that is significantly less than $O(N^2)$ of the original EMD for a histogram with N bins. In addition, the number of constraints is reduced by half and the objective function is also simplified. We prove that the EMD-L_1 is formally equivalent to the original EMD with L_1 ground distance without approximation. Exploiting the L_1 metric structure, an efficient tree-based algorithm is designed to solve the EMD-L_1 computation. An empirical study demonstrates that the new algorithm has the time complexity of $O(N^2)$, which is much faster than previously reported algorithms with super-cubic complexities. The proposed algorithm thus allows the EMD to be applied for comparing histogram-based features, which is practically impossible with previous algorithms. We conducted experiments for shape recognition and interest point matching. EMD-L_1 is applied to compare shape contexts on the widely tested MPEG7 shape dataset and SIFT image descriptors on a set of images with large deformation, illumination change and heavy noise. The results show that our EMD-L_1-based solutions outperform previously reported state-of-the-art features and distance measures in solving the two tasks.

1 Introduction

Histogram-based descriptors are used widely in various computer vision tasks such as shape matching [1, 22, 23, 13], image retrieval [15, 8, 18, 16], texture analysis [19, 9]. For comparing these descriptors, *bin-to-bin* distance functions, such as L_p distance, χ^2 statistics, and KL divergence, are most commonly used. These approaches assume that the domain of the histograms are already aligned. However, in practice, such assumption can be violated due to various factors, such as shape deformation, lighting variation, heavy noise, etc. The *Earth Mover's Distance* (EMD) [20] is a *cross-bin* dissimilarity function that addresses the above alignment problem by solving the *transportation problem* as a special case of

A. Leonardis, H. Bischof, and A. Pinz (Eds.): ECCV 2006, Part III, LNCS 3953, pp. 330–343, 2006.

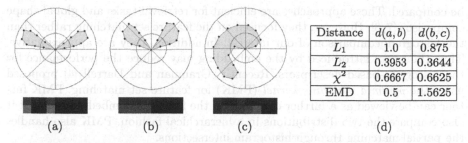

Distance	$d(a,b)$	$d(b,c)$
L_1	1.0	0.875
L_2	0.3953	0.3644
χ^2	0.6667	0.6625
EMD	0.5	1.5625

(a)   (b)   (c)   (d)

Fig. 1. An example where bin-to-bin distances meet problems. (a), (b) and (c) show three shapes with log-polar bins on them and corresponding shape context histograms. (d) lists the distances between them using different distance functions.

linear programming (LP). Beyond the color signature application proposed by Rubner et al. [20] originally, we claim that EMD is useful for more general class of histogram descriptors such as SIFT [15] and shape context [1].

Fig. 1 shows an example with shape context [1]. EMD correctly describes the perceptual similarity of (a) and (b), while the three bin-to-bin distance functions (L_1, L_2 and χ^2) falsely state that (b) is closer to (c) than to (a). Despite this favorable robustness property, EMD has seldom been applied to general histogram-based local descriptors to our knowledge. The main reason lies in its expensive computational cost, which is super-cubic[1] for a histogram with N bins.

Rubner et al. [20] proposed using the *transportation simplex* (TS) [6] to solve the EMD. They showed that TS has a super-cubic average time complexity. In [20], EMD is applied to compact signatures instead of raw distributions directly. This approach is efficient and effective especially for distributions with sparse structures, e.g., color histograms in the CIE-Lab space in [20]. However, the histogram-based descriptor is generally not sparse and can not be modelled compactly. This forces the EMD algorithm to be applied to the raw distribution directly. In real vision problems, the number of comparisons between these descriptors is very large, which forbids the use of TS algorithm. Cohen and Guibas [2] studied the problem of computing a transformation between distributions with minimum EMD. Levina and Bickel [11] proved that EMD is equivalent to the Mallows distance when applied to probability distributions. The L_1 formulation had been introduced by Wesolowsky [24] and then Cohen and Guibas [2]. In this paper we extended it to general histograms.

Indyk and Thaper [7] proposed a fast algorithm for image retrieval by embedding the EMD metric into a Euclidean space. Grauman and Darrell [3] extended the approach for contour matching. The embedding is performed using a hierarchical distribution analysis. A fast nearest neighbor retrieval is achieved through locality-sensitive hashing. EMD can be approximated by measuring the L_1 distance in the Euclidean space after embedding. The time complexity of the embedding is $O(Nd \log \Delta)$, where N is the size of feature sets, d is the dimension of the feature space and Δ is the diameter of the union of the two feature sets to

---

[1] By super-cubic, we mean a complexity between $O(N^3)$ and $O(N^4)$

be compared. These approaches are efficient for retrieval tasks and global shape comparison [7, 3]. However, they focused on the feature set matching rather than the histogram comparison of our interest. In addition, they are approximative. Thus the errors introduced by the embedding may reduce the performance for the histogram-based descriptors. Recently, Grauman and Darrell [4] proposed using the *pyramid matching kernel* (PMK) for feature set matching. PMK further can be viewed as a further extension of the fast EMD embedding in that it also compare the two distributions in a hierarchical fashion. PMK also handles the partial matching through histogram intersections.

The contribution of this paper is twofold. First, we propose a new fast algorithm, *EMD-L_1*, to compute EMD between histograms with L_1 ground distance. The formulation of EMD-L_1 is much simpler than the original EMD formulation. It has only $O(N)$ unknown variables, which is less than the $O(N^2)$ variables required in the original EMD. Furthermore, EMD-L_1 has only half the number of constraints and a more concise objective function. Unlike previous approximative algorithms, we formally prove that EMD-L_1 is equivalent to the original EMD with L_1 ground distance. An efficient tree-based algorithm is designed to solve EMD-L_1 and an empirical study shows that the time complexity of EMD-L_1 is $O(N^2)$, which significantly improves the previous super-cubic algorithm.

Second, the speedup gained by EMD-L_1 enables us to compute the exact EMD directly for histograms without reducing the discriminability. For the first time, EMD is applied to compare histogram-based local descriptors. We tested EMD-L_1 in two experiments. First, it is applied to the inner-distance shape context [13] for shape matching on the widely tested MPEG7 shape dataset, where EMD-L_1 achieves a better score than all previously reported results. Second, EMD-L_1 is applied to the SIFT [15] descriptors for feature matching on images with large distortion. Again, EMD-L_1 demonstrates excellent performance. In addition, it also shows that EMD-L_1 performs similar to the original EMD with L_2 ground distance, while the latter is much slower.

The rest of the paper is organized as follows. Sec. 2 reviews the EMD and derives its formulation for histograms. Sec. 3 first gives the formulation of EMD-L_1. Then, the equivalence between EMD-L_1 and EMD with L_1 ground distance is proved. Finally a fast algorithm for EMD-L_1 is proposed, followed by an empirical study of time complexity. Sec. 4 describes the experiments of applying the EMD-L_1 to shape recognition and interest point matching. Sec. 5 concludes.

2   The Earth Mover's Distance (EMD)

2.1   The EMD Between Signatures

The Earth Mover's Distance (EMD) is proposed by Rubner et al. [20] to measure the dissimilarity between *signatures*. Signatures are extracted from distributions via clustering. A signature of size N is defined as a set $S = \{s_j = (w_j, m_j)\}_{j=1}^N$. Where m_j is the position of the j-th element and w_j is its weight.

Given two signatures $P = \{(p_i, u_i)\}_{i=1}^m$ and $Q = \{(q_j, v_j)\}_{j=1}^n$ with size m, n respectively, the EMD between them is modeled as a *transportation problem*.

The elements in P are treated as "supplies" located at u_i's and element in Q as "demands" at v_j's. p_i and q_j indicate the amount of supply and demand respectively. The EMD is the minimum (normalized) work required for this task. It is defined as

$$EMD(P,Q) = \min_{F=\{f_{..}\}} \frac{\sum_{i,j} f_{ij} d_{ij}}{\sum_{i,j} f_{ij}}$$

such that $\sum_j f_{ij} \leq p_i$, $\sum_i f_{ij} \leq q_j$, $\sum_{i,j} f_{ij} = \min\{\sum_i p_i, \sum_j q_j\}$ and $f_{ij} \geq 0$. $F = \{f_{ij}\}$ is the set of *flows*. f_{ij} represents the amount transported from the i-th supply to the j-th demand. d_{ij} is a distance between the position u_i and v_j called the *ground distance*.

2.2   The EMD Between Histograms

Histograms can be viewed as a special type of signatures in that each bin corresponding to an element in a signature. Specifically, the histogram values are treated as the weights w_j in a signature S, and the grid locations (indices of bins) are treated as positions m_j in S.

In the following we will discuss two dimensional histograms which are widely used for shape and image descriptors. Higher dimensional cases can be derived similarly. Wlog, we use the following assumptions and notations.

- The histogram has m rows and n columns and $N = m \times n$ bins.
- The index set for bins is defined as $\mathcal{I} = \{(i,j) : 1 \leq i \leq m, 1 \leq j \leq n\}$. We use (i,j) to denote a bin or a node corresponding to it.
- The index set for flows is defined as $\mathcal{J} = \{(i,j,k,l) : (i,j) \in \mathcal{I}, (k,l) \in \mathcal{I}\}$.
- $P = \{p_{ij} : (i,j) \in \mathcal{I}\}$ and $Q = \{q_{ij} : (i,j) \in \mathcal{I}\}$ are the two histograms to be compared.
- Histograms are normalized to 1, i.e., $\sum_{i,j} p_{ij} = 1$, $\sum_{i,j} q_{ij} = 1$.

Now the EMD between two histograms P and Q becomes

$$EMD(P,Q) = \min_{F=\{f_{...;...}:(i,j,k,l)\in\mathcal{J}\}} \sum_{\mathcal{J}} f_{i,j;k,l} d_{i,j;k,l} \qquad (1)$$

$$\text{s.t.} \begin{cases} \sum_{(k,l)\in\mathcal{I}} f_{i,j;k,l} = p_{ij} & \forall(i,j) \in \mathcal{I} \\ \sum_{(i,j)\in\mathcal{I}} f_{i,j;k,l} = q_{kl} & \forall(k,l) \in \mathcal{I} \\ f_{i,j;k,l} \geq 0 & \forall(i,j,k,l) \in \mathcal{J} \end{cases} \qquad (2)$$

Where F is the flow from P to Q, i.e., $f_{i,j;k,l}$ is a flow from bin (i,j) to (k,l). Note that we use "flow" to indicate both the set of flows in a graph and a single flow between two nodes, when there is no confusion. A flow F satisfying (2) is called *feasible*. The ground distance $d_{i,j;k,l}$ is usually defined by L_p distance

$$d_{i,j;k,l} = \|(i,j)^\top - (k,l)^\top\|_p = (|i-k|^p + |j-l|^p)^{1/p} \qquad (3)$$

3   EMD-L_1

This section presents the EMD-L_1, a more efficient formulation of the EMD between histograms. We first show that, by using L_1 or Manhattan distance as the ground distance, the EMD-L_1 is drastically simplified compared to the original one. Then, we prove that EMD-L_1 is equivalent to the original EMD with L_1 ground distance. Finally an efficient algorithm and an empirical complexity study are presented.

3.1   EMD with L_1 Ground Distance

As shown later in Sec. 4.2 and Fig. 7(b), EMD's with L_1 and L_2 ground distances performs similarly for our purpose, while the former is much faster. Therefore, we are interested in L_1 ground distance. In the rest of the paper, L_1 ground distance is implicitly assumed. With L_1 ground distance, formula (3) becomes

$$d_{i,j;k,l} = |i - k| + |j - l|.$$

Note that the ground distance now takes only integer values. For convenience of discussion, the flow index set $\mathcal{J}$ is divided into three disjointed parts $\mathcal{J} = \mathcal{J}_0 \bigcup \mathcal{J}_1 \bigcup \mathcal{J}_2$, each of them corresponds to one of three flow types.

- $\mathcal{J}_0 = \{(i,j,i,j) : (i,j) \in \mathcal{I}\}$ is for flows between bins at same location. We call this kind of flow *s-flows* for the short of *self-flow*.
- $\mathcal{J}_1 = \{(i,j,k,l) : (i,j,k,l) \in \mathcal{J}, d_{i,j;k,l} = 1\}$ is for flows between neighbor bins. We call this kind of flow *n-flows*.
- $\mathcal{J}_2 = \{(i,j,k,l) : (i,j,k,l) \in \mathcal{J}, d_{i,j;k,l} > 1\}$ is for other flows which are called *f-flows* because of their *far* distances.

An important property of the L_1 ground distance is that each positive f-flow can be replaced with a sequence of n-flows. This is because L_1 distance forms a shortest path system along the integer lattice. For example, given an f-flow $f_{i,j;k,l}$, $i{\leq}k, j{\leq}l$, the L_1 ground distance has the following decomposition

$$d_{i,j;k,l} = d_{i,j;i,l} + d_{i,l;k,l} = \sum_{j \leq x < l} d_{i,x;i,x+1} + \sum_{i \leq y < k} d_{y,l;y+1,l} .$$

Accordingly, the shortest path from (i,j) to (k,l) can be decomposed into neighbor edges. It follows that, without changing the total weighted flow $\sum_{f \in F} fd$, $f_{i,j;k,l}$ can be set to zero by first increasing all n-flows along the path $[(i,j), (i,j+1), \ldots, (i,l), (i+1,l), \ldots, (k,l)]$ by $f_{i,j;k,l}$. This is illustrated in Fig. 2

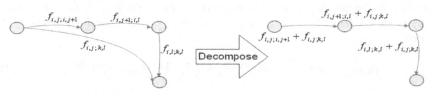

Fig. 2. Decompose an f-flow $f_{i,j;k,l}$, $k = i + 1, l = j + 2$. Only related flows are shown.

S-flows are also redundant due to their zero ground distances. With these intuitions, we propose a new formulation of EMD, *EMD-L_1*, as below

$$EMD_{L_1}(P,Q) = \min_{G=\{g\cdots;\cdots:(i,j,k,l)\in\mathcal{J}_1\}} \sum_{\mathcal{J}_1} g_{i,j;k,l} \qquad (4)$$

$$\text{s.t.} \begin{cases} \sum_{k,l:(i,j,k,l)\in\mathcal{J}_1} (g_{i,j;k,l} - g_{k,l;i,j}) = b_{ij} & \forall(i,j)\in\mathcal{I} \\ g_{i,j;k,l} \geq 0 & \forall(i,j,k,l)\in\mathcal{J}_1 \end{cases} \qquad (5)$$

Where $b_{ij} = p_{ij} - q_{ij}$ is the difference between the two histograms. We call a flow G satisfying (5) a *feasible* flow analogous to that in the original EMD.

EMD-L_1 has large simplifications over the original EMD (1), including

1. There are only about $O(N)$ variables in (4), one order of magnitude less than that in (1). This is critical for speedup since the number of variables is a dominant factor in the time complexity of all LP algorithms [6]. In addition, the space efficiency gained by this is very favorable for large histograms.
2. The number of equality constraints is reduced by half. This is another important factor for the efficiency of the LP algorithms.
3. All the ground distances involved in the EMD-L_1 are ones. This is practically useful, because it saves multiplications during computation and allows the use of integer operations to handle the coefficients.

Note that these simplifications can be extended to higher dimensional cases. For example, the unknown variables for 3D histograms is $6N$ thus still of $O(N)$ complexity. These simplifications are used to design a fast tree-based algorithm.

3.2 Equivalence Between EMD-L_1 and Original EMD

We now prove the equivalence between the EMD-L_1 and the original EMD with L_1 ground distance. The equivalence is in the sense of the weighted total flows. That is, a flow G for EMD-L_1 and a flow F in the original EMD is said to be equivalent if $\sum_{\mathcal{J}_1} g_{i,j;k,l} = \sum_{\mathcal{J}} d_{i,j;k,l} f_{i,j;k,l}$, i.e., they have same total weighted flow. The following proposition states the equivalence in which we are interested.

Proposition. Given two histograms P and Q as defined above

$$EMD(P,Q) = EMD_{L_1}(P,Q) . \qquad (6)$$

The discussion in the last subsection hints that, for any flow F for the original EMD, an equivalent flow G for EMD-L_1 can be created by eliminating f-flows and s-flows. This implies $EMD(P,Q) \geq EMD_{L_1}(P,Q)$. Now we need to verify the other direction. Given a flow G for EMD-L_1, find an equivalent F for the original EMD. The key issue is how to satisfy the constraints (2) in the original EMD. To do this, we use a "merge" procedure instead of the decomposition. The idea is to merge input and output flows at each bin such that either input or output flow survives as a result. This is demonstrated in Fig. 3. Notice that we only need an F to have a total weight not greater than that of G. This makes the merge procedure much simpler, since we can just merge any pair of input and output flows.

Proof. It suffices to prove
$$EMD(P,Q) \geq EMD_{L_1}(P,Q) \text{ and } EMD(P,Q) \leq EMD_{L_1}(P,Q).$$

Part I. Proof of $EMD(P,Q) \geq EMD_{L_1}(P,Q)$.

It suffices to prove that for any feasible flow $F = \{f_{i,j;k,l} : (i,j,k,l) \in \mathcal{J}\}$ for the original EMD, there exists an equivalent feasible flow $G = \{g_{i,j;k,l} : (i,j,k,l) \in \mathcal{J}_1\}$ for EMD-L_1, i.e.

$$\sum_{\mathcal{J}} f_{i,j;k,l} d_{i,j;k,l} = \sum_{\mathcal{J}_1} g_{i,j;k,l} \tag{7}$$

For any F satisfying (2), we create an auxiliary flow $F' = \{f'_{i,j;k,l:(i,j,k,l) \in \mathcal{J}}\}$. First, F' is initialized by F. F' has three properties which will be maintained during its evolution

$$\begin{cases} \sum_{\mathcal{J}} f'_{i,j;k,l} d_{i,j;k,l} = \sum_{\mathcal{J}} f_{i,j;k,l} d_{i,j;k,l} \\ \sum_{k,l} (f'_{i,j;k,l} - f'_{k,l;i,j}) = b_{ij} & \forall (i,j) \in \mathcal{I} \\ f'_{i,j;k,l} \geq 0 & \forall (i,j,k,l) \in \mathcal{J} \end{cases} \tag{8}$$

Then, we evolve F' to make all f-flows vanish. For every positive f-flow $f'_{i,j;k,l}$ in F', we decompose it into a sequence of n-flows as illustrated in Fig. 2. In detail, assume $i \leq k, j \leq l$ (other cases are similar), the three modifications to F' are conducted in the given order

$$\begin{cases} f'_{i,x;i,x+1} \leftarrow f'_{i,x;i,x+1} + f'_{i,j;k,l} & \forall x, j \leq x < l \\ f'_{y,l;y+1,l} \leftarrow f'_{y,l;y+1,l} + f'_{i,j;k,l} & \forall y, i \leq y < k \\ f'_{i,j;k,l} \leftarrow 0 \end{cases} \tag{9}$$

It is clear that (8) always holds because (9) does not change it. After all the f-flows vanish, we build G from F'

$$g_{i,j;k,l} = f'_{i,j;k,l} , \ \forall (i,j,k,l) \in \mathcal{J}_1 \tag{10}$$

From (8) it follows that G satisfies (5) and (7).

Part II. Proof of $EMD(P,Q) \leq EMD_{L_1}(P,Q)$.

It suffices to prove that, for any $G = \{g_{i,j;k,l} : (i,j,k,l) \in \mathcal{J}_1\}$ satisfying (5), there exists $F = \{f_{i,j;k,l} : (i,j,k,l) \in \mathcal{J}\}$ satisfying (2), such that

$$\sum_{\mathcal{J}} f_{i,j;k,l} d_{i,j;k,l} \leq \sum_{\mathcal{J}_1} g_{i,j;k,l} \tag{11}$$

For any G satisfying (5), we create an auxiliary flow $G' = \{g'_{i,j;k,l} : (i,j,k,l) \in \mathcal{J}\}$. G' is first initialized by G

$$g'_{i,j;k,l} = \begin{cases} g_{i,j;k,l} & \forall (i,j,k,l) \in \mathcal{J}_1 \\ 0 & \forall (i,j,k,l) \in \mathcal{J}_0 \bigcup \mathcal{J}_2 \end{cases}$$

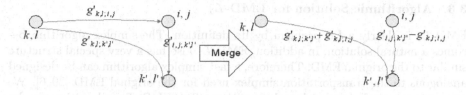

Fig. 3. Flow merging, where $b_{ij} > 0$, $g'_{i,j;k',l'} > g'_{k,l;i,j} > 0$

G' has three properties which will be maintained during its evolution

$$\begin{cases} \sum_{\mathcal{J}} g'_{i,j;k,l} d_{i,j;k,l} \leq \sum_{\mathcal{J}_1} g_{i,j;k,l} \\ \sum_{k,l \in \mathcal{I}} (g'_{i,j;k,l} - g'_{k,l;i,j}) = b_{ij} & \forall (i,j) \in \mathcal{I} \\ g'_{i,j;k,l} \geq 0 & \forall (i,j,k,l) \in \mathcal{J} \end{cases} \quad (12)$$

Note that in the first equation of (12) "$\leq$" is used instead of "$=$".

Now we will evolve G' targeting the equality constraints (2) in the original EMD. This is done by the following procedure.

> Procedure: Merge G'
>   FOR each grid node (i,j)
>   WHILE exists flow $g'_{k,l;i,j} > 0$ AND flow $g'_{i,j;k',l'} > 0$ DO

$$\begin{cases} \delta \leftarrow \min\{g'_{i,j;k',l'}, g'_{k,l;i,j}\} \\ g'_{k,l;k',l'} \leftarrow g'_{k,l;k',l'} + \delta \\ g'_{k,l;i,j} \leftarrow g'_{k,l;i,j} - \delta \\ g'_{i,j;k',l'} \leftarrow g'_{i,j;k',l'} - \delta \end{cases} \quad (13)$$

>   END WHILE
>   END FOR

Fig. 3 shows an example of merging. The four steps in (13) need to be applied in the order as given. Moreover, each run of (13) removes at least one non-zero flow, so the procedure is guaranteed to terminate.

Because of the triangle inequality $d_{k,l;k',l'} \leq d_{k,l;i,j} + d_{i,j;k',l'}$, (13) will only decrease the left hand side of the first inequality in (12) and hence will not change it. The second equation in (12) also holds because (13) changes the input and output flows of a node with the same amount (δ). The third condition in (12) is obvious.

An important observation due to (12) and the procedure is

$$\begin{cases} g'_{i,j;k,l} = 0 & \forall (i,j,k,l) \in \mathcal{J} \text{ if } b_{ij} \leq 0 \\ g'_{k,l;i,j} = 0 & \forall (i,j,k,l) \in \mathcal{J} \text{ if } b_{ij} \geq 0 \end{cases} \quad (14)$$

Now we build F from G':

$$f_{i,j;k,l} = \begin{cases} \min\{p_{ij}, q_{kl}\} & \forall (i,j,k,l) \in \mathcal{J}_0 \\ g'_{i,j;k,l} & \forall (i,j,k,l) \in \mathcal{J}_1 \bigcup \mathcal{J}_2 \end{cases} \quad (15)$$

From (14), (12) and (15), we have that F satisfies (2) and (11). ∎

3.3   Algorithmic Solution for EMD-L_1

EMD-L_1 is clearly a LP problem by its definition. The simplex algorithm becomes a natural solution. In addition, EMD-L_1 also has a very special structure similar to the original EMD. Therefore, a fast simplex algorithm can be designed analogous to the transportation simplex used for the original EMD [20, 6]. We propose an even faster tree-based algorithm, *Tree-EMD*. The algorithm can be derived from the fast simplex algorithm. It takes the benefit of the simplex while exploiting a tree structure for further speedup. In addition, Tree-EMD has a more intuitive interpretation. Finally, the tree structure also makes coding easy for different dimensions. Due to the space limitation, we only briefly describe the outlines of the algorithm and left the details to its longer version [14].

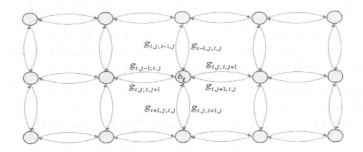

Fig. 4. The EMD-L_1 as a network flow problem for 3×5 histograms

   To gain intuition, EMD-L_1 is modeled as a graph $\mathcal{G} = < V, B, G >$ as illustrated in Fig. 4. $V = \{v_{ij} : (i,j) \in \mathcal{I}\}$ is the set of nodes in the graph. $B = \{b_{ij} : (i,j) \in \mathcal{I}\}$ is the weights associated to V, $\sum_{\mathcal{I}} b_{ij} = 0$. G is the set of flows between neighbor nodes. The task is to find the minimum flow such that all nodes have zero weights after applying the flow.

   Before describing Tree-EMD, we give some definitions derived from the classic simplex algorithm [6]. A flow G is called *feasible* if (5) holds. A feasible flow G is called a *basic feasible tree* (BFT) if G has only $mn-1$ elements that can be non-zero and they form a tree. Such elements are called *basic variable*(BV) flows.

   Notes: 1) The loops and trees in this paper are undirected, although flows do have directions. 2) A BFT is actually a *spanning tree* since there are mn nodes in the graph.

   The task becomes to find a feasible flow G with minimum total flow $\sum_{g \in G} g$. It can be shown that there exists an optimal BFT G [14]. Therefore, the search space of the optimum solution can be restricted within the set of BFT's.

   Tree-EMD is an iterative algorithm for searching the optimum BFT tree. First, an initial BFT tree G is built using the greedy algorithm. Then, G is iteratively replaced by a better BFT tree with smaller flow until the optimum is reached. In each iteration, an *entering* flow $g_{i_0,j_0;k_0,l_0}$ is found and added to G. Accordingly, a *leaving* BV flow $g_{i_1,j_1;k_1,l_1}$ is picked to avoid loops. G is then modified by adding $g_{i_0,j_0;k_0,l_0}$ and removing $g_{i_1,j_1;k_1,l_1}$ and adjusting flow values to keep it as a BFT. The iteration is guaranteed to terminate at a global minimum due to its underlying simplex algorithm.

The most important variables in Tree-EMD are u_{ij}'s for nodes v_{ij}'s and $c_{i,j;k,l}$ for flows $g_{i,j;k,l}$'s. They have following relations

$$c_{i,j;k,l} = 1 - u_{i,j} + u_{k,l} \qquad \forall (i,j,k,l) \in \mathcal{J}_1 \qquad (16)$$

$$c_{i,j;k,l} = 1 - u_{i,j} + u_{k,l} = 0 \quad \text{if } g_{i,j;k,l} \text{ is a BV flow} \qquad (17)$$

We now discuss several key issues in the algorithm.

1. *Optimality test*: A BFT G is optimum iff $c_{i,j;k,l} \geq 0$, $\forall (i,j,k,l) \in \mathcal{J}_1$.
2. *Finding $g_{i_0,j_0;k_0,l_0}$*: $(i_0, j_0, k_0, l_0) = \text{argmin}_{(i,j,k,l) \in \mathcal{J}_1} c_{i,j;k,l}$.
3. *Finding $g_{i_1,j_1;k_1,l_1}$*: First, find the loop formed by adding $g_{i_0,j_0;k_0,l_0}$ into G. Then $g_{i_1,j_1;k_1,l_1}$ is the flow in the loop with minimum flow value and reversed direction of $g_{i_0,j_0;k_0,l_0}$.
4. *Updating G*: First, adding $g_{i_0,j_0;k_0,l_0}$ in G. Then modify flow values along the loop mentioned above ($g_{i_1,j_1;k_1,l_1}$ becomes zero). After that, remove $g_{i_1,j_1;k_1,l_1}$ and adjust the links in G accordingly.

Table 1. Tree-EMD

Step 0 /*Define some key variables*/
   r: the root of the tree
   p^*: the root of the subtree to be updated
Step 1 /*Initialization*/
   Initialize BFT by a greedy initial solution
   $p^* \leftarrow r$
Step 2 /*Iteration*/
   WHILE(1)
      /*Recursively update **u** in the subtree rooted at p^*) */
      FOR any child q of p^*
         Update u_{ij} at node q according to (17)
         Recursively update q's children
      END FOR
      /*Optimality test*/
      Compute $c_{i,j;k,l}$'s
      IF (optimum is reached)   goto Step 3   END IF
      /*Find a new improved BF solution*/
      Find entering BV flow $g_{i_0,j_0;k_0,l_0}$
      Find loop by tracing from v_{i_0,j_0} and v_{k_0,l_0} to their common ancestor
      Find the leaving BV $g_{i_1,j_1;k_1,l_1}$
      Update flow values in G along the loop
      Maintain the tree, include removing $g_{i_1,j_1;k_1,l_1}$, adding $g_{i_0,j_0;k_0,l_0}$
         and updating links.
      Set p^* as the root of subtree where u_{ij}'s need to be updated.
   END WHILE
Step 3 Compute the total flow as the EMD distance.

---

5. *Updating u_{ij}'s*: Fix u_{ij} of the root to zero. Other u_{ij}'s can be computed starting from the root by using (17). In fact, only a small amount of u_{ij}'s in a subtree need to be updated in more iterations.
6. *Updating $c_{i,j;k,l}$'s*: When u_{ij}'s determined, use formula (16).

A brief description of Tree-EMD is given in Table 1.

3.4   Empirical Study for Time Complexity

To study the time complexity of the proposed algorithm, we conduct an empirical study similar to that in [20]. First, two sets of 2D random histograms for each size $n \times n$, $2 \leq n \leq 20$ are generated. For each n, 1000 random histograms are generated for each set. Then, the two sets are paired and the average time to compute EMD for each size n is recorded. We compare EMD-L_1 (with tree-EMD) and the original EMD (with TS²). In addition, EMD-L_1 is tested for 3D histograms with similar settings, except $2 \leq n \leq 8$. The results are shown in Fig. 5. From (a) it is clear that EMD-L_1 is much faster than the original one. (b) shows that EMD-L_1 has a complexity around $O(N^2)$, where N is the number of bins (n^2 for 2D and n^3 for 3D).

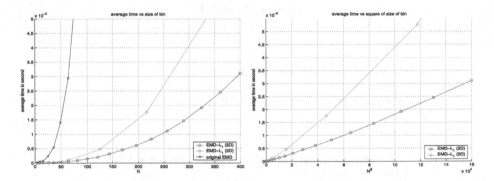

Fig. 5. Empirical time complexity study of EMD-L_1 (Tree-EMD). Left: In comparison to the original EMD (TS). Right: Average running time vs. square of histogram sizes.

4   Experiments

4.1   Shape Matching with Shape Context

EMD-L_1 is tested for shape matching by applying it to the inner-distance shape context (IDSC)[13]. IDSC is an extension of shape context (SC)[1] by using the shortest path distances. These studies used χ^2 distance for comparing the shape descriptors. In [13], IDSC is used for contour comparison with a dynamic programming (DP) scheme. We use the same framework, except for replacing the χ^2 distance with the EMD-L_1. In addition, the lower bound of EMD [20] is used for speeding up the dynamic programming.

---

² With Rubner's code, http://ai.stanford.edu/~rubner/emd/default.htm

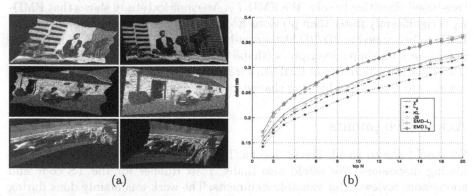

Fig. 6. Typical shape images from the MPEG7 CE-Shape-1, one image per class

Table 2. Retrieval rate (bullseye) of different methods for the MPEG7 CE-Shape-1

Alg.	CSS[17]	Vis. Parts[10]	SC[1]	Curve Edit[21]	Gen. Mod.[23]	IDSC[13]	EMD-L_1
Score	75.44%	76.45%	76.51%	78.17%	80.03%	85.40%	86.56%

The MPEG7 CE-Shape-1 [10] database is widely used for benchmarking different shape matching algorithms. The data set contains 1400 silhouette images from 70 classes. Each class has 20 different shapes (e.g. Fig. 6). The performance is measured by the Bullseye test. Every image in the database is matched with all other images and the top 40 most similar candidates are counted. At most 20 of the 40 candidates are correct hits. The Bullseye score is the ratio of the number of correct hits of all images to the highest possible number of hits (20x1400).

We use the same experimental setup as [13]. The bullseye score is listed in Tab. 2 with previously reported results. The excellent performance, outperforming the previous best scores, demonstrates the effectiveness of EMD-L_1.

4.2   Image Feature Matching

This subsection describes our experiment using the EMD-L_1 for interest point matching. The experiment was conducted on a set of ten image pairs containing synthetic deformation, noise and illumination change. Some testing images are shown in Fig. 7 (a).

Interest point. We use Harris corners [5] for the matching experiments. The reason for this choice is that, due to the large deformation, noise and lighting change, it is hard to apply other interest point detectors. Furthermore, we focus more on comparing descriptors than the interest points. For each image, we pick 300 points with the largest cornerness responses.

Fig. 7. (a) Some testing images with synthetic deformation, illumination change and noise. (b) ROCs for EMD-L_1 and other dissimilarity functions on SIFT.

Descriptors. We use the SIFT proposed by Lowe [15] as the descriptors. SIFT is a very popular histogram-based descriptor. In our case, since scale invariant detectors are not available, a fixed support region is used (with diameter 41, similar to the setting used in [16]. SIFT is a three dimensional weighted histogram, 4 for each spatial dimensions and 8 for gradient orientation.

Evaluation criterion. For each pair of images together with their interest points, we first automatically obtained the ground truth correspondence from the synthesis procedure. Then, every interest point in Image 1 is compared with all interest points in Image 2 by comparing the SIFT extracted on them. An interest point p_1 in Image 1 is treated as a correct match of another point p_2 in Image 2 if the displacement of p_1 is within a fixed distance of p_2. The detection rate among the top N matches is used to study the performance. The detection rate is defined as: $r = \dfrac{\#\text{ correct matches}}{\#\text{ possible matches}} = \dfrac{\#\text{ correct matches}}{\#\text{ points in Image 1}}$.

Experiment results. We tested the EMD-L_1 along with several bin-to-bin distance measures, including χ^2, KL-divergence (symmetric), Jensen-Shannon(JS) divergence [12], L_2, etc. The EMD with L_2 ground distance is also tested for comparison. A Receiver Operating Characteristic (ROC) based criterion is used to show the detection rates versus N, which is the number of most similar matches allowed. The ROC curves for the experiment are shown in Fig. 7 (b). The EMD-L_1 outperforms all other bin-to-bin metrics. In addition, EMD-L_1 and EMD with L_2 ground distance have very similar performance, though the former takes about 25 seconds per pair while the latter takes about 2100 seconds.

5   Conclusion

We propose a fast algorithm, EMD-L_1 for computing Earth Mover's Distance (EMD) between histograms with L_1 ground distance. The new algorithm reformulates the EMD into a drastically simplified version by using the special structure of L_1 metric on histograms. We proved that EMD-L_1 is equivalent to the EMD with L_1 ground distance for histograms. We then designed an efficient tree-based algorithm to solve the EMD-L_1. An empirical study shows that EMD-L_1 is significantly faster than previous EMD algorithms. The speedup allows the EMD to be applied to 2D/3D histogram-based features for the first time. Experiments on both shape descriptors (shape context [1]) and image features (SIFT [15]) show the superiority of EMD-L_1 for handling the matching tasks with large deformation, noise and lighting change, etc.

Acknowledgments

We would like to thank David Jacobs, Leo Grady, and Kevin Zhou for stimulating discussions. We would also thank Yossi Rubner for the TS code and anonymous reviewers for valuable comments. The work was mainly done during Haibin Ling's internship at Siemens Corporate Research. Haibin Ling also thank NSF grant (ITR-03258670325867) for supporting.

References

1. S. Belongie, J. Malik and J. Puzicha. "Shape Matching and Object Recognition Using Shape Context", *IEEE Trans. on PAMI*, 24(24):509-522, 2002.
2. S. Cohen, L. Guibas. "The Earth Mover's Distance under Transformation Sets", *ICCV*, II:1076-1083, 1999.
3. K. Grauman and T. Darrell, "Fast Contour Matching Using Approximate Earth Mover's Distance", *CVPR*, I:220-227, 2004
4. K. Grauman and T. Darrell. "The Pyramid Match Kernel: Discriminative Classification with Sets of Image Features". *ICCV*, II:1458-1465, 2005.
5. C. Harris and M. Stephens, "A combined corner and edge detector", *Alvey Vision Conference*, 147-151, 1988.
6. F. S. Hillier and G. J. Lieberman, *Introduction to Mathematical Programming*. McGraw-Hill, New York, NY, 1990.
7. P. Indyk and N. Thaper, "Fast Image Retrieval via Embeddings", *In 3rd Workshop on Statistical and computational Theories of Vision*, Nice, France, 2003
8. Y. Ke and R. Sukthankar. "PCA-SIFT: a more distinctive representation for local image descriptors", *CVPR*, II:506-513, 2004.
9. S. Lazebnik, C. Schmid, and J. Ponce, "A sparse texture representation using affine-invariant regions," *IEEE Trans. PAMI*, 27(8):1265-1278, 2005.
10. L. J. Latecki, R. Lakamper, and U. Eckhardt, "Shape Descriptors for Non-rigid Shapes with a Single Closed Contour", *CVPR*, I:424-429, 2000.
11. E. Levina and P. Bickel. "The Earth Mover's Distance is the Mallows Distance: Some Insights from Statistics", *ICCV*, 251-256, 2001.
12. J. Lin. "Divergence measures based on the Shannon entropy". *IEEE Trans. on Information Theory*, 37(1):145-151, 1991.
13. H. Ling and D. W. Jacobs, "Using the Inner-Distance for Classification of Articulated Shapes", *CVPR*, II:719-726, 2005.
14. H. Ling and K. Okada. "An Efficient Earth Mover's Distance Algorithm for Robust Histogram Comparison", in submission, 2006.
15. D. Lowe, "Distinctive Image Features from Scale-Invariant Keypoints," *IJCV*, 60(2), pp. 91-110, 2004.
16. K. Mikolajczyk and C. Schmid, "A Performance Evaluation of Local Descriptors," *IEEE Trans. on PAMI*, 27(10):1615-1630, 2005.
17. F. Mokhtarian, S. Abbasi and J. Kittler. "Efficient and Robust Retrieval by Shape Content through Curvature Scale Space," *Image Databases and Multi-Media Search*, 51-58, World Scientific, 1997.
18. E. N. Mortensen, H. Deng, and L. Shapiro, "A SIFT Descriptor with Global Context", *CVPR*, I:184-190, 2005.
19. S. Peleg, M. Werman, and H. Rom. "A Unified Approach to the Change of Resolution: Space and Gray-level", *IEEE Trans. on PAMI*, 11:739-742, 1989.
20. Y. Rubner, C. Tomasi, and L. J. Guibas. "The Earth Mover's Distance as a Metric for Image Retrieval", *IJCV*, 40(2):99-121, 2000.
21. T. B. Sebastian, P. N. Klein and B. B. Kimia. "On Aligning Curves", *IEEE Trans. on PAMI*, 25(1):116-125, 2003.
22. A. Thayananthan, B. Stenger, P. H. S. Torr and R. Cipolla, "Shape Context and Chamfer Matching in Cluttered Scenes", *CVPR*, I:127-133, 2003.
23. Z. Tu and A. L. Yuille. "Shape Matching and Recognition-Using Generative Models and Informative Features", *ECCV*, III:195-209, 2004.
24. G. Wesolowsky. "The Weber Problem: History and Perspectives", *Location Science*, 1(1):5-23, 1993.

2D and 3D Multimodal Hybrid Face Recognition

Ajmal Mian, Mohammed Bennamoun, and Robyn Owens

School of Computer Science and Software Engineering,
The University of Western Australia,
35 Stirling Highway, Crawley, WA 6009, Australia
{ajmal, bennamou, robyn}@csse.uwa.edu.au
http://web.csse.uwa.edu.au

Abstract. We present a 2D and 3D multimodal hybrid face recognition algorithm and demonstrate its performance on the FRGC v1.0 data. We use hybrid (feature-based and holistic) matching for the 3D faces and a holistic matching approach on the 2D faces. Feature-based matching is performed by offline segmenting each 3D face in the gallery into three regions, namely the eyes-forehead, the nose and the cheeks. The cheeks are discarded to avoid facial expressions and hair. During recognition, each feature in the gallery is automatically matched, using a modified ICP algorithm, with a complete probe face. The holistic 3D and 2D face matching is performed using PCA. Individual matching scores are fused after normalization and the results are compared to the BEE baseline performances in order to provide some answers to the first three conjectures of the FRGC. Our multimodal hybrid algorithm substantially outperformed others by achieving 100% verification rate at 0.0006 FAR.

1 Introduction

Machine recognition of human faces has fascinated many researchers because of its potential applications in scenarios where fingerprinting or iris scanning are impractical (e.g. surveillance) or undesirable due to problems of social acceptance [7]. Considerable work has been done in this area for over three decades [14] which has resulted in a number of face recognition algorithms. These algorithms are categorized from two different perspectives, namely the type of data and the type of approach they use. From the first perspective, face recognition algorithms are divided into (1) 2D face recognition (which use 2D greyscale or colour images), (2) 3D face recognition (which use 3D range images or pointclouds of faces) and (3) multimodal face recognition algorithms (which use both 2D and 3D facial data) e.g [8]. Bowyer et al. [4] give a detailed survey of 3D and multimodal face recognition algorithms and state that multimodal face recognition outperforms both 2D and 3D face recognition alone. A comprehensive survey of 2D face recognition algorithms is given by Zhao et al. [14]. They also categorize face recognition into (1) holistic, (2) feature-based (referred to as region-based in this paper) and (3) hybrid matching face recognition algorithms. Holistic algorithms match the faces as a whole whereas region-based algorithms match local regions of the faces e.g. eyes and nose. Hybrid algorithms perform recognition on the

A. Leonardis, H. Bischof, and A. Pinz (Eds.): ECCV 2006, Part III, LNCS 3953, pp. 344–355, 2006.

Table 1. First three experiments of FRGC. Gallery and probe correspond to the database face and the face to be tested respectively. "Controlled" means controlled illumination and normal expression.

	Gallery	Probe
Experiment 1	Single controlled 2D image	Single controlled 2D image
Experiment 2	Four controlled 2D images	Four controlled 2D images
Experiment 3	Single 3D image (shape & texture)	Single 3D image (shape & texture)

basis of both holistic and region-based matching. It is argued that the hybrid methods "could potentially offer the best of the two types of methods" [14].

One of the major limitations in comparing different face recognition algorithms is that most researchers perform their experiments on different datasets. In most cases these datasets are very sparse and insufficient to provide statistically significant inference. To overcome this problem the Face Recognition Grand Challenge (FRGC) [10] was designed, with an objective to pursue the development of face recognition algorithms by providing sufficient datasets, challenge problems and standard benchmarks so that the performance of different algorithms can be compared on similar benchmarks. The first three challenge problems (or experiments) of FRGC which are related to this paper are listed in Table 1. FRGC also states five conjectures [10], the first three of which regard 2D versus 3D face recognition. For completeness, the relevant conjectures are summarized below (> stands for "performance will be better than" and "texture" means the 2D luminance image acquired by a 3D sensor).

Conjecture I-A: Exp3 (shape only) > Exp3 (texture only). 3D face recognition will perform better than 2D face recognition at equal resolution.

Conjecture I-D: Exp3 (shape only) > Exp1. 3D face recognition will perform better than higher resolution 2D face recognition.

Conjecture I-E: Exp3 (shape + texture) > Exp1. Multimodal (2D and 3D) face recognition will perform better than higher resolution 2D face recognition.

Conjecture II: The opposite of I-D and I-E.

Conjecture III-A: Exp2 > Exp3 (shape + texture). 2D face recognition using four high resolution images will perform better than multimodal (2D and 3D) face recognition at lower resolution.

Conjecture III-B: Exp2 > Exp3 (shape only). 2D face recognition using four high resolution images will perform better than 3D face recognition at lower resolution.

In this paper, we present a multimodal hybrid face recognition approach and perform Experiment 3 (see Table 1) on the FRGC v1.0 dataset (frontal views of faces). Our algorithm is multimodal as it utilizes both the shape and texture data of a face. At the same time it is hybrid as it performs recognition on the basis of region-based and holistic matching. In order to provide some answers to the above listed conjectures, we compare our results to those of Experiment 1, 2 and 3 (see Table 1) when using the BEE (Biometric Experimentation Environment) baseline algorithms (PCA-based face recognition [12]). Comparison is performed using the FRGC criterion i.e. verification rate at 0.001 FAR (False Acceptance Rate). Our multimodal hybrid algorithm significantly outperforms the BEE baseline performance by achieving 100% verification rate at 0.0006 FAR which is well below the FRGC benchmark of 0.001 FAR. Our results clearly support Conjecture I-A, I-D and I-E and go against Conjectures II and III. In other words, 3D face recognition using our region-based matching algorithm performs better than PCA based 2D face recognition.

1.1   Overview of Multimodal Hybrid Face Recognition

Most sensors, including the Minolta scanner which was used to acquire the FRGC data, give a 3D pointcloud of the face along with its registered coloured texture map. We use the texture map for 2D holistic face recognition using the BEE baseline PCA algorithm. The 3D facial data consist of the x, y and z components of the pointcloud of the face. Taking the z component alone results in the range image of the face where each pixel value represents the depth of the corresponding facial point. The range image of the face is used separately for holistic 3D face recognition using the BEE baseline PCA algorithm. Additionally, the 3D pointcloud of the face is segmented into three disjoint regions, namely the eyes-forehead, the nose, and the cheeks, in order to perform a region-based matching [9]. For region-based matching, a modified version of the ICP algorithm [1] is used. An advantage of using this algorithm is that a partial region (e.g. nose) from the gallery can be matched directly with a complete probe face without segmenting the probe. Only the eyes-forehead (referred to as "forehead" hereafter) and the nose are used for region-based matching in order to avoid facial expressions and artifacts resulting from facial hair. These matching processes result in four similarity matrices which are normalized and subsequently fused. A min-max rule is used for normalization and a multiplication rule is used for fusion. The resulting similarity matrix is normalized once again and used to calculate the verification and identification rates of our algorithm. Fig. 1 shows the block diagram of our multimodal hybrid face recognition algorithm. The region-based 3D matching (left blocks of Fig. 1) algorithm was initially proposed in [9] however it is explained in Section 2 for completeness.

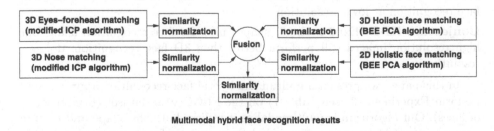

Fig. 1. Illustration of our multimodal hybrid face recognition algorithm

2   3D Region-Based Matching Algorithm

2.1   Offline Preprocessing

A face is first detected in its 2D image using Viola and Jones' algorithm [13] and both the 2D and its corresponding 3D images are cropped. The resolution of FRGC 3D faces is very high (480 × 640). Therefore, we downsampled the spatial data (by a factor of $\frac{1}{4}$) by eliminating alternate rows and columns. Each 3D face is preprocessed to remove spikes and noise. Spikes are removed by converting the 3D pointcloud of a face into a triangular mesh and removing triangles with long edges. This is followed by the elimination of disconnected points. The resulting mesh is smoothed using Taubin's algorithm [11] (50 iterations using the mesh toolbox of The Robotics Institute, CMU). Unlike the BEE baseline algorithms, which rely on prespecified landmarks on the gallery as well as the probe faces for their normalization, **our region-based matching approach is fully automatic** and requires no user intervention during the online recognition phase. However, during offline preprocessing, we manually identify six landmarks on each gallery face for its segmentation (Fig. 2). Note that this does not affect the automatism of our approach since this operation is only performed during the offline preprocessing phase. Moreover, this identification of landmarks can be replaced with an automatic feature detection algorithm [2] in order to automate the offline process as well.

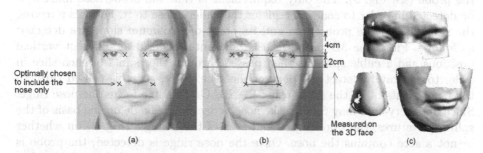

Fig. 2. Six points are manually identified on a gallery face (i.e. off-line) to segment its corresponding 3D face into three disjoint regions i.e. eyes-forehead, nose and cheeks (reproduced from [9]).

Fig. 3. (a) 2D coloured image of an eyes-forehead region. (b) Skin map after skin detection. (c) The corresponding 3D eyes-forehead region before skin detection and after skin detection (d). Note that small holes have been interpolated (reproduced from [9]).

The identified landmarks are used to segment the gallery face into three disjoint regions, namely the forehead, the nose, and the cheeks (Fig. 2). The forehead region may contain artifacts caused by the eyes and hair (see Fig. 3-a and c). The latter causes more problems since it covers more area. To remove these artifacts a skin detection algorithm [3] is used to detect the skin pixels in the 2D coloured image of the forehead region. Points in the 3D forehead region which do not correspond to the skin pixels are removed (see Fig. 3-d). The threshold for skin detection is tuned to minimize false positives so that the non-skin pixels are rejected with a high probability.

2.2   Online Nose Matching

During online recognition, the probe face is first detected using Viola and Jones' algorithm [13] and preprocessed as explained in Section 2.1. However, a prior segmentation of the probe is not required. This makes the online matching process fully automatic. Next, each gallery nose is registered to the probe for matching. Registration is performed in two steps. First, a gallery nose is coarsely registered to the probe nose by aligning their ridge lines and points of maximum slope. Next, the registration is refined with our modified version of the ICP algorithm [1] (explained in Section 2.3). Advantages of using this algorithm are that the gallery and probe need not cover exactly the same area of the face nor are they required to have the same resolution. A gallery nose, for example, can be registered to the nose of a complete probe face without having to segment the probe (see Fig. 5). The only requirement is that the probe nose must first be detected in order to coarsely register the gallery nose to it. For this purpose, the ridge line of the probe nose and its point of maximum slope are detected as follows. First, the 3D probe face is horizontally sliced at different vertical positions and a cubic spline is then passed through the points of each slice in order to accurately detect the peak of the slice. Next, a line is passed through the peak points of all the slices using RANSAC. This line forms the nose ridge. Since not every slice may contain the nose, a decision is made on the basis of the spline curvatures, the side lengths and area of the triangle (Fig. 4) on whether or not a slice contains the nose. Once the nose ridge is detected, the probe is vertically sliced along the nose ridge, a cubic spline is passed through the slice

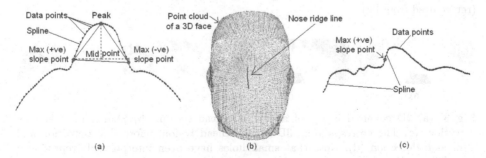

Fig. 4. Online nose detection in the 3D probe face (reproduced from [9])

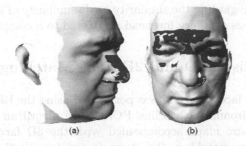

Fig. 5. A correct match between a 3D probe face (shaded white) and a gallery (shaded dark blue) (a) nose and (b) forehead. Note that some holes may have been interpolated.

data points and the point of maximum slope is detected on the spline. The ridge lines and points of maximum slope of the probe and gallery noses are aligned and the registration is then refined with our modified version of the ICP algorithm [1]. The average registration error e_N normalized with the resolution of the probe is taken as the matching score between the two (a lower value of e_N means a better match). Fig. 5-a shows a gallery nose registered to a complete probe face.

2.3   Online Forehead Matching

Forehead matching is performed by registering each gallery forehead to the probe without segmenting the probe. This process is also fully automatic. Since, the forehead and nose of each gallery face exist in the same coordinate basis, the rigid transformation resulting from the nose matching can be used as the coarse registration for the forehead matching. This registration is further refined with our modified version of the ICP algorithm. Our modified ICP algorithm establishes correspondences between the nearest points of the probe and a gallery region whose mutual distance is below a threshold t_c. Correspondences whose mutual distance is more than t_c are considered outliers and are therefore removed. A high initial value (four times the resolution of the probe) is chosen for t_c which is then reduced as the registration is refined. To speed up the correspondence search, a kd-tree data structure is used. After few iterations (when the registration error falls below a threshold), a region of interest (within the neighborhood of the gallery region) is cropped in the probe face to gain further computational efficiency. A conservative threshold is chosen for this purpose to avoid removing the overlapping region of the probe. The registration is refined iteratively until the correspondences between the probe and the gallery reaches a maximum saturation value. Next, t_c is further reduced and the above process is repeated. At the final stage, the stopping criterion of the algorithm is changed to the minimization of the registration error. Moreover at this stage, in the case of the forehead only, the correspondences are established between points which are close in the xy plane. In other words, correspondences are established along the approximate viewing direction. Points which are close in the xy plane but far in the z-dimension are still considered corresponding points as they provide useful information regarding the similarity or dissimilarity of the gallery and the probe. Fig. 5-b shows a gallery forehead registered to a complete probe face.

3   Online Holistic 3D and 2D Face Matching

Holistic 3D and 2D face matching was performed using the BEE (Biometric Experimentation Environment) baseline PCA-based algorithm [12]. For 2D face matching, the texture maps accompanied with the 3D face data were used, whereas for 3D face matching, the range image (see Section 1.1) of the 3D faces was used. The parameters of the PCA algorithm were separately tuned in the case of 2D and 3D face matching in order to maximize their individual performance (i.e. verification rate at 0.001 FAR). The BEE algorithm utilizes prespecified landmarks on the faces, which are provided along with the data in a metadata file, for their normalization. Note that we did not use these landmarks for the online region-based matching as it is fully automatic and does not require manually specified landmarks. The BEE algorithm normalizes the faces with respect to pose and illumination and scales them to 150×130 spatial pixels each. A mask is used to crop out unwanted pixels. The normalized faces are then projected onto the PCA space and matched using the Mahalanobis distance.

4   Fusion

Each matching process results in a similarity matrix $\mathbf{S}_i$ (where i denotes a modality) of size $P \times G = 668 \times 275$ (where P is the number of tested probes and G is the number of faces in the gallery). An element s_{rc} (at row r and column c) of a matrix $\mathbf{S}_i$ denotes the similarity score between probe number r and gallery face number c. Each $\mathbf{S}_i$ has a negative polarity in our case i.e. a smaller value of s_{rc} means high similarity. The similarity matrices resulting from the 3D nose matching, 3D forehead matching, 3D holistic face matching and 2D holistic face matching are normalized before fusion. Since none of the similarity matrices had outliers a simple min-max rule (Eqn. 1) was used for normalizing each one of them on a scale of 0 to 1.

$$\mathbf{S}'_i = \frac{\mathbf{S}_i - \min(\mathbf{S}_i)}{\max(\mathbf{S}_i - \min(\mathbf{S}_i)) - \min(\mathbf{S}_i - \min(\mathbf{S}_i))} \quad \text{where} \quad i = 1 \ldots n \quad (1)$$

$$\mathbf{S} = \prod_{i=1}^{n} \mathbf{S}'_i \quad (2)$$

$$\mathbf{S}' = \frac{\mathbf{S} - \min(\mathbf{S})}{\max(\mathbf{S} - \min(\mathbf{S})) - \min(\mathbf{S} - min(\mathbf{S}))} \quad (3)$$

In Eqn. 1 and Eqn. 3, $\max(\mathbf{S}_i)$ and $\min(\mathbf{S}_i)$ mean the overall minimum and maximum value (i.e. a scalar) of the entries of matrix $\mathbf{S}_i$ respectively. In Eqn. 2, n is the number of modalities used. The normalized similarity matrices $\mathbf{S}'_i$ are then fused using a multiplication rule (Eqn. 2) to get a combined similarity matrix **S** which is normalized using the min-max rule (Eqn. 3) once again. **S′** is used to calculate the combined performance of the used modalities. We also tested a weighted sum rule for fusing the similarity matrices with the weights adjusted according to the confidence in each modality. However, this technique gave slightly worse results compared to the multiplication rule.

5 Results

The FRGC v1.0 [10] data contain multiple high resolution 2D images of 275 subjects. For Experiment 1 and 2, 2D images of subjects are acquired with a high resolution camera (4 megapixel) under controlled illumination and expressions. For Experiment 3, multiple 3D snapshots (3D shape and texture) of 275 subjects are acquired under a controlled environment. For the sake of comparison, we fixed the gallery size to 275 subjects and the number of tested probes to 668 for each experiment. For each experiment, a brute force matching approach was used i.e. every probe was matched with every gallery face to get a 668 × 275 similarity matrix. Although brute force matching could have been avoided through the use of some indexing scheme, it was still performed to get dense non-match scores [10] in order to derive statistically more significant inferences.

5.1 Multimodal Hybrid Face Recognition Results

Fig. 6 shows the individual and combined results Receiver Operating Characteristic (ROC) curve and identification rate) of our multimodal hybrid face recognition on Experiment 3. The region based matching was performed using our modified ICP algorithm whereas the holistic face recognition was performed using the BEE baseline PCA algorithm. Our results show that the forehead shape matching has the best performance which indicates that this region contains the most discriminating information regarding a face. These results support the findings of Zhao et al. [14] which state that the upper part of the face is more

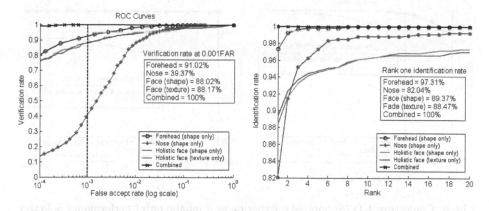

Fig. 6. Individual and combined results of the multimodal hybrid face recognition. The holistic face recognition is performed using the BEE baseline PCA algorithm.

important for recognition compared to the lower part. As expected, the performance of the nose shape matching is the lowest due to the sparsity of information in this region. However, a significant improvement in performance is achieved when the results of the nose are fused with those of the forehead (see Fig. 8). The overall performance of our multimodal hybrid face recognition algorithm is very high with a combined verification rate of 100% reached at 0.0006 FAR (well below the 0.001 FAR benchmark of FRGC).

One of the important findings of our results is that when the region-based (forehead and nose) shape matching results are fused with the holistic face matching (shape only) results, no significant improvement in performance is achieved. Therefore, we excluded the holistic 3D face matching while comparing our results to the BEE baseline performances on Experiment 1 and 2.

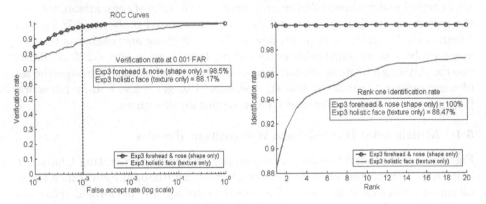

Fig. 7. Conjecture 1-A (Supported): Experiment 3 (shape only) performance is better than Experiment 3 (texture only) when region-based matching of shape is performed with our modified ICP algorithm and the BEE baseline PCA algorithm is used for holistic matching of texture.

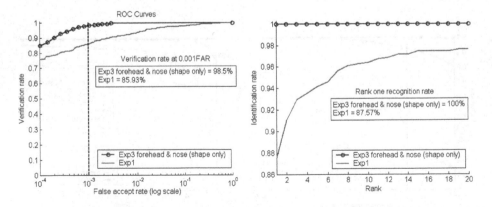

Fig. 8. Conjecture 1-D (Supported): Experiment 3 (shape only) performance is better than Experiment 1 when region-based shape matching is performed with our modified ICP algorithm and BEE baseline PCA algorithm is used for holistic 2D face matching.

5.2   Conjecture I and II

Fig. 7 and 8 show that Experiment 3 (shape only) using the region-based approach gives far better verification and identification performance compared to Experiment 3 (texture only) as well as Experiment 1 using the BEE baseline PCA algorithm. Moreover, Fig. 9 shows that Experiment 3 (shape and texture) using our multimodal hybrid matching approach gives better performance compared to Experiment 1 using the BEE baseline PCA algorithm. These results support Conjecture I-A, I-D and I-E respectively and oppose Conjecture II. Put another way, 3D face recognition (with or without texture) significantly outperforms PCA based 2D face recognition (at equal or higher resolution).

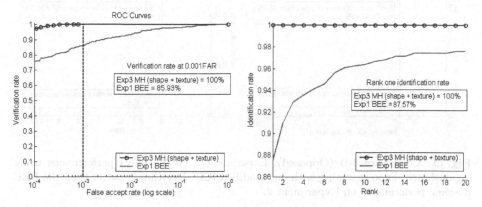

Fig. 9. Conjecture 1-E (Supported): Experiment 3 (shape and texture) performance using our multimodal hybrid (MH) face recognition algorithm is better compared to Experiment 1 using the BEE baseline PCA algorithm.

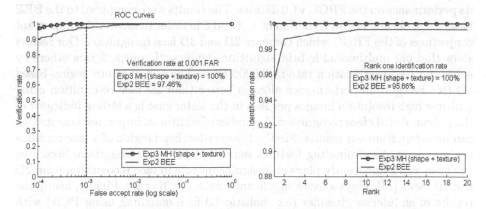

Fig. 10. Conjecture 3-A (Opposed). Experiment 3 (shape and texture) performance using our multimodal hybrid (MH) face recognition algorithm performance is better than the BEE baseline performance on Experiment 2.

5.3   Conjecture III

Fig. 10 and Fig. 11 show that regardless of whether texture information is used, our algorithm outperforms the BEE baseline performance on Experiment 2 where four high resolution images per gallery and probe are used. These results oppose Conjecture III-A and III-B. In other words, our results show that 3D face recognition (with or without texture) outperforms PCA based 2D face recognition even when multiple high resolution images per face are used in the latter case.

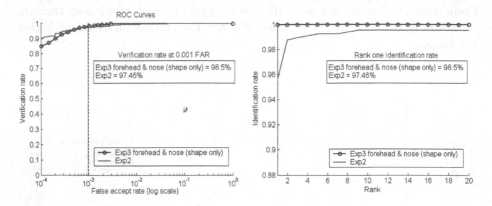

Fig. 11. Conjecture 3-B (Opposed). Experiment 3 (shape only) performance using region-based shape matching with our modified ICP algorithm is better than the BEE baseline performance on Experiment 2.

6   Analysis and Conclusion

We presented a multimodal hybrid face recognition algorithm and demonstrated its performance on the FRGC v1.0 dataset. The results were compared to the BEE baseline performances on Experiment 1, 2 and 3 in order to answer the important conjectures of the FRGC which compare 2D and 3D face recognition. Our results show that our multimodal hybrid algorithm significantly outperforms others by achieving 100% verification rate at 0.0006 FAR. The fact that our region-based 3D face recognition performance alone is better than 2D face recognition using multiple high resolution images per face in the latter case is a strong indicator of the potential of 3D face recognition. A number of additional important conclusions can be drawn from our results. Firstly, the eyes-forehead region of a face contains the maximum discriminating features important for face recognition. Secondly, the nose which apparently plays an insignificant role in face recognition from 2D frontal views [14], plays a more significant role in the 3D case. Finally, fusing the results of an inferior classifier (e.g. holistic 3D face matching using PCA) with that of a superior classifier (e.g. region-based 3D face matching using ICP) when operating on the same modality (i.e. 3D face in our example) does not improve performance as much as when the results of classifiers which operate on different modalities (e.g. 3D and 2D face) are fused. Recall that the region-based 3D face matching was performed at $\frac{1}{4}$ of the original resolution of the FRGC data. Using full resolution is likely to further improve the performance. Based on our findings we would like to add the following conjecture to the FRGC.

Conjecture MBO: Exploiting multimodal hybrid matching techniques has the potential to give the best face recognition performance.

Our conjecture gives rise to a number of questions. What combination of modalities (e.g. 2D face, 3D face and IR image of the face) should be used? For each modality, what is the best possible segmentation of the face to perform region-based matching? What is the best matching algorithm for each modality and region? Finally, what fusion technique will produce the best results? These questions give directions for focusing future research of the FRGC.

Acknowledgments

We would like to thank Ashley Chew for setting up the Biometrics Experimentation Environment, CMU for the Mesh Toolbox and F. Boussaid for the skin detection code. This research is sponsored by ARC grant DP0664228.

References

1. P. J. Besl and N. D. McKay, "Reconstruction of Real-world Objects via Simultaneous Registration and Robust Combination of Multiple Range Images," *IEEE TPAMI*, Vol. 14(2), pp. 239–256, 1992.
2. C. Boehnen and T. Russ, "A Fast Multi-Modal Approach to Facial Feature Detection", *IEEE WACV*, 2005.
3. F. Boussaid, D. Chai and A. Bouzerdoum, "A Current-mode VLSI Architecture for Skin Detection", *ISSPA*, Vol. 1, pp. 629 – 632, 2003.
4. K. W. Bowyer, K. Chang and P. Flynn, "A Survey Of Approaches to Three-Dimensional Face Recognition," *IEEE ICPR*, pp. 358–361, 2004.
5. K. I. Chang, K. W. Bowyer and P. J. Flynn, "Face Recognition Using 2D and 3D Facial Data," *MMUA*, pp. 25–32, 2003.
6. J. Huang, B. Heisele and V. Blanz, "Component-based Face Recognition with 3D Morphable Models", *AVBPA*, 2003.
7. A. K. Jain, A. Ross and S. Prabhakar, "An Introduction to Biometric Recognition," *IEEE TCSVT*, Vol. 14(1), pp. 4–20, 2004.
8. X. Lu, A. K. Jain and D. Colbry, "Matching 2.5D Face Scans to 3D Models," *IEEE TPAMI*, Vol. 28(1), pp. 31–43, 2006.
9. A. S. Mian, M. Bennamoun and R. A. Owens, "Region-based Matching for Robust 3D Face Recognition," *BMVC*, Vol. 1, pp. 199–208, 2005.
10. P. J. Phillips, P. J. Flynn, T. Scruggs, K. W. Bowyer, J. Chang, K. Hoffman, J. Marques, J. Min and W. Worek, "Overview of the Face Recognition Grand Challenge", *IEEE CVPR*, 2005.
11. G. Taubin, "Curve and Surface Smoothing without Shrinkage," *ICCV*, pp. 852–857, 1995.
12. M. Turk and A. Pentland, "Eigenfaces for Recognition", *JOCN*, Vol. 3, 1991.
13. P. Viola and M. J. Jones, "Robust Real-Time Face Detection", *IJCV*, Vol. 57(2), pp. 137–154, 2004.
14. W. Zhao, R. Chellappa, P.J. Phillips, and A. Rosenfeld, "Face Recognition: A Literature Survey", *ACM Computing Survey*, pp. 399–458, 2003.

Robust Attentive Behavior Detection by Non-linear Head Pose Embedding and Estimation

Nan Hu[1,*], Weimin Huang[2], and Surendra Ranganath[3]

[1] University of Kentucky, Electrical & Computer Engineering,
Lexington, KY 40506
nan.hu@uky.edu
[2] Institute for Infocomm Research (I²R), 21 Heng Mui Keng Terrace,
Singapore 119613
wmhuang@i2r.a-star.edu.sg
[3] National University of Singapore, Electrical & Computer Engineering,
4 Engineering Drive 3, Singapore 117576
elesr@nus.edu.sg

Abstract. We present a new scheme to robustly detect a type of human attentive behavior, which we call frequent change in focus of attention (FCFA), from video sequences. FCFA behavior can be easily perceived by people as temporal changes of human head pose (normally the pan angle). For recognition of this behavior by computer, we propose an algorithm to estimate the head pan angle in each frame of the sequence within a normal range of the head tilt angles. Developed from the ISOMAP, we learn a non-linear head pose embedding space in 2-D, which is suitable as a feature space for person-independent head pose estimation. These features are used in a mapping system to map the high dimensional head images into the 2-D feature space from which the head pan angle is calculated very simply. The non-linear person-independent mapping system is composed of two parts: 1) Radial Basis Function (RBF) interpolation, and 2) an adaptive local fitting technique. The results show that head orientation can be estimated robustly. Following the head pan angle estimation, an entropy-based classifier is used to characterize the attentive behaviors. The experimental results show that entropy of the head pan angle is a good measure, which is quite distinct for FCFA and focused attention behavior. Thus by setting an experimental threshold on the entropy value we can successfully and robustly detect FCFA behavior.

1 Introduction

Human attentive behavior is a means to express mental state [1], from which an observer can infer their beliefs and desires. Attentive behavior analysis by computer seeks to mimic an observer's perception.

We propose a novel attentive behavior analysis technique to classify two kinds of human attentive behaviors, i.e. a frequent change in focus of attention (FCFA)

---

* This work was done when the author was at I²R.

A. Leonardis, H. Bischof, and A. Pinz (Eds.): ECCV 2006, Part III, LNCS 3953, pp. 356–367, 2006.

and focused attention. We would expect that FCFA behavior requires a frequent change of head pose, while focused attention means that the head pose will be in limited orientations for the observation period. Hence, this motivates us to detect head pose in each frame of a video sequence, so that the change of head pose can be analyzed and subsequently classified.

Applications can be easily found in video surveillance and monitoring, or a remote learning environment [2], where system operators are interested in the attentive behavior of the learners. If learners are found to be distracted, it may be a helpful hint to change or modify the teaching materials.

One category of research related to our work is head pose estimation, such as [3,4]. Generally, head pose estimation methods can be categorized into two classes: 1) feature-based approaches, such as [5], and 2) view-based approaches, such as [6,7]. Feature-based techniques try to locate facial features in an image from which it is possible to calculate the actual head orientation. These features can be obvious facial characteristics like eyes, nose, mouth etc. View-based techniques, on the other hand, analyze the entire head image in order to decide a person's head orientation.

An ideal way to detect human's attentive behavior is to estimate the eye gaze, such as [8], where Stiefelhagen used a Hidden Markov Model (HMM) to estimate the gaze and further infer the focus of attention. However, in many cases, the eye area in the image is not large enough to detect gaze.

Another way is to model the head pose by dimensionality reduction methods such as PCA, Isometric Feature Mapping (ISOMAP) [9] and Locally Linear Embedding (LLE) [10], which have been used to solve vision problems. Pless [11] used ISOMAP to visualize the image space for toy images and to find the video trajectory for bird flying videos. Elgammal et al. [12] built a generative model from LLE to reconstruct incomplete human walking sequences as well as to generate laughing faces. Vlachos et al. [13] modified the ISOMAP algorithm itself for classification and visualization. Efros [14] enhanced the ISOMAP by solving the leakage problem.

Here we propose a novel scheme for the estimation of head pan orientation and behaviour detection. Our algorithm works with an uncalibrated, single camera, and can give accurate and robust estimate of the pan orientation even when the person's head is totally or partially turned back to the camera. As showing later, our method requires only very few images to be labeled in the training data in contrast to other methods which need intensive labeling of face or head. In addition, our method works very well on low resolution video sequences. This makes its use possible in monitoring systems where high resolution images are hard to acquire.

2 Methodology

The algorithm for head pan angle estimation consists of: i) unified embedding to find the 2-D feature space and ii) parameter learning to find a person-independent mapping. This is then used in an entropy-based classifier to detect

358 N. Hu, W. Huang, and S. Ranganath

FCFA behavior. We use a simple foreground segmentation and edge detection method to extract the head in each frame of the sequence. However, our method can also be used with different head tracking algorithms (see a review in [15]).

All the image sequences used were obtained from fixed video cameras. To successfully estimate the head pan angle regardless of the tilt angle, for every person in the training set, we obtained three video sequences where the heads faced horizontally, or somewhat downwards and upwards while panning. Obtained sequences were first Gaussian filtered and histogram equalized to reduce the effects of varying illumination and noise. Since the size of the head within a sequence or between different sequences could vary, we normalized them to a fixed size of $n_1 \times n_2$. Preprocessed sample sequences for one person are shown in Fig. 1.

    (i) Facing horizontally   (ii) Facing downwards   (iii) Facing upwards

Fig. 1. Normalized sample sequences used in our proposed method

2.1 Unified Embedding

Nonlinear Dimensionality Reduction. Since the image sequences primarily exhibit head pose changes, we believe that even though the images are in high dimensional space, they must lie on some manifold with dimensionality much lower than the original. Recently, several new non-linear dimensionality reduction techniques have been proposed, such as Isometric Feature Mapping (ISOMAP) [9] and Locally Linear Embedding (LLE) [10]. Both methods have been shown to successfully embed manifolds in high dimensional space onto a low dimensional space in several examples.

Fig. 2(a) shows the 2-D embedding of the sequence sampled in Fig. 1(ii) using the K-ISOMAP (K varies according to the density of the nearest neighbors in our experiments) algorithm. As can be noticed from Fig. 2(a), the embedding can discriminate between different pan angles and forms an ellipse-like manifold. The frames with head pan angles close to each other in the images are also close

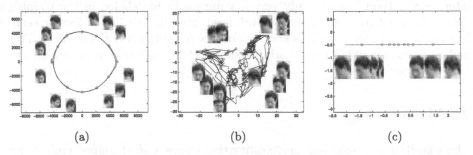

        (a)   (b)   (c)

Fig. 2. 2-D embedding of the sequence sampled in Fig. 1(ii) (a) by ISOMAP, (b) by PCA, (c) by LLE.

in the embedded space. One point to be emphasized is that we do not use the temporal relationships to achieve the embedding, since the goal is to obtain an embedding that preserves the geometry of the manifold.

Fig. 2(b) and (c) showed the corresponding results using the classic linear dimensionality reduction method of principal component analysis (PCA) and the non-linear dimensionality reduction method of LLE on the same sequence. We also choose 2-D embedding to make them comparable. As can be seen, ISOMAP keeps the intrinsic property of the head pose change in the manifold according to the pan orientation in an ellipse, while PCA and LLE don't. Hence we adopt the ISOMAP framework.

Embedding Multiple Manifolds. Although the ISOMAP can effectively represent a hidden manifold in high dimensional space into a low dimensional embedded space as shown in Fig. 2(a), it fails to embed multiple people's data together into one manifold. Since typically intra-person differences are much smaller than inter-person differences, the residual variance minimization technique used in ISOMAP tries to preserve large contributions from inter-person variations. This is shown in Fig. 3 where ISOMAP is used to embed two people's manifolds (care has been taken to ensure that all the inputs are spatially registered). Here, the embedding shows separate manifolds (note one manifold has degenerated into a point because the embedding is dominated by inter-person distances which are much larger than intra-person distances.) Besides, another fundamental problem is that different persons will have different-looking manifolds as can be seen in Fig. 5 (though they are essentially ellipse-like).

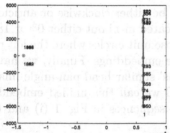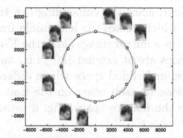

Fig. 3. Embedding obtained by ISOMAP on the combination of two person's sequences

Fig. 4. The results of the ellipse (solid line) fitted on the sequence (dotted points)

To embed multiple persons' data to find a useful, common 2-D feature space, each person's manifolds are first embedded individually using ISOMAP. An interesting point here is that, although the appearance of the manifolds for each person differs, they are all ellipse-like. We then find a best fitting ellipse [16] to represent each manifold before we further normalize it. Fig. 4 shows the results of the ellipse fitted on the manifold of the sequence sampled in Fig. 1(ii). The parameters of each ellipse are then used to scale the coordinate axes of each embedded space to obtain a unit circle.

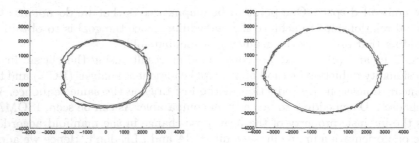

Fig. 5. Separate embedding of two manifolds for two people's head pan images

After normalizing the coordinates in every person's embedded manifolds into a unit circle, we find an interesting property that on every person's unit circle the angle between any two points is roughly the same as the difference between their corresponding pan angles in the original images. However, when using ISOMAP to embed each person's manifold individually, it cannot be ensured that different person's frontal faces are close in angle in each embedded space. Thus, further normalization is needed to make all persons' frontal face images to be located at the same angle in the manifold so that they are comparable and it is meaningful to build a unified embedded space. To do this, we first manually label the frames in each sequence with frontal views of the head. To reduce the labeling error, we label all the frames with a frontal or near frontal view, take the mean of the corresponding coordinates in the embedded space, and rotate it so that the frontal faces are located at the 90° angle. In this way, we align all the person's frontal view coordinates to the same angle.

Next, since the embedding can turn out to be either clockwise or anticlockwise, which makes the left profile frames be located at about either 0° or 180°, we form a mirror image along the Y-axis for those unit circles where the left profile faces are at around 180°, i.e., anticlockwise embeddings. Finally, we have a unified embedded space where different persons' similar head pan angle images are close to each other on the unit circle, and we call this unified embedding space the feature space. Fig. 6 shows the two sequences in Fig. 1 (i) and (iii)

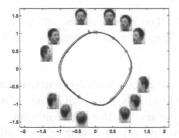
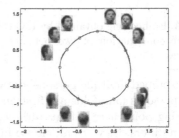

Fig. 6. Unified embedding space for sequences shown in Fig.1 (i) and (iii) whose low-dimensional embedded manifolds have been normalized (shown separately)

Table 1. A complete description of our unified embedding algorithm

Step	Description
1	*INDIVIDUAL EMBEDDING* Define $Y^P = \{\mathbf{y}_1^P, \cdots, \mathbf{y}_n^P\}$ the vector sequence of length n_P in the original measurement space for person P. ISOMAP is used to embed Y^P to a 2-D embedded space. $Z^P = \{\mathbf{z}_1^P, \cdots, \mathbf{z}_n^P\}$ are the corresponding coordinates in the 2-D embedded space for person P.
2	*ELLIPSE FITTING* For person P, we use an ellipse to fit Z^P, resulting in the ellipse with parameters: center $\mathbf{c}_e^P = (c_x^P, c_y^P)^T$, major and minor axes a^P and b^P respectively, and orientation Φ_e^P.
3	*MULTIPLE EMBEDDING* For person P, let $\mathbf{z}_i^P = (z_{i1}^P, z_{i2}^P)^T$, $i = 1, \cdots, n_P$. We rotate, scale and translate every $\mathbf{z}_i^P$ to obtain $\mathbf{z}_i^{*} = \begin{pmatrix} 1/a^P & 0 \\ 0 & 1/b^P \end{pmatrix} \left(\begin{pmatrix} cos\Phi_e^P & -sin\Phi_e^P \\ sin\Phi_e^P & cos\Phi_e^P \end{pmatrix} \mathbf{z}_i^P - \mathbf{c}_e^P \right)$. Identify the frontal face frames for Person P, and the corresponding $\{\mathbf{z}_i^{*P}\}$ of these frames. The mean of these points is calculated, and the embedded space is rotated so that this mean value lies at the 90 degrees angle. After that, we choose a frame l showing left profile and test whether $\mathbf{z}_l^{*}$ is close to 0 degrees. If not, we set $\mathbf{z}_i^{*} = \begin{pmatrix} -1 & 0 \\ 0 & 1 \end{pmatrix} \cdot \mathbf{z}_i^{*}$.

normalized into the unified embedding space. The details of obtaining the unified embedded space are given in Table 1.

2.2 Person-Independent Mapping

RBF Interpolation. After the unified embedding as described in Table 1, we learn a nonlinear interpolative mapping from the input images to the corresponding coordinates in the feature space by using Radial Basis Functions (RBF).

We combine all the persons' sequences together, $\Gamma = \{Y^{P_1}, \cdots, Y^{P.}\} = \{\mathbf{y}_1, \cdots, \mathbf{y}_{n_0}\}$, and their corresponding coordinates in the feature space, $\Lambda = \{Z^{*1}, \cdots, Z^{*.}\} = \{\mathbf{z}_1^*, \cdots, \mathbf{z}_{n_0}^*\}$, where $n_0 = n_{P_1} + \cdots + n_{P.}$ is the total number of input images. For every single point in the feature space, we take the interpolative mapping function to have the form

$$f(\mathbf{y}) = \omega_0 + \sum_{i=1}^{M} \omega_i \cdot \psi(\|\mathbf{y} - \mathbf{c}_i\|). \tag{1}$$

where $\psi(\cdot)$ is a Gaussian basis function, ω_i are real coefficients, $\mathbf{c}_i$ are centers of the basis functions on R^D (original input space), $\|\cdot\|$ is the norm on R^D.

We used k-means clustering [17] algorithm to find the centers and variances σ_i^2 of the basis functions.

To decide the number of basis function to use, we experimentally tested various values of M and calculated the mean squared error of the RBF output. We found $M = 14$ to be a good choice.

Let $\psi_i = \psi(\|\mathbf{y} - \mathbf{c}_i\|)$ and by introducing an extra basis function $\psi_0 = 1$, (1) can be written as

$$f(\mathbf{y}) = \sum_{i=0}^{M} \omega_i \psi_i. \tag{2}$$

With points in the feature space denoted as $\mathbf{z}_i^* = (z_{i1}^*, z_{i2}^*)$, after obtaining the centers $\mathbf{c}_i$, and widths σ_i^2 of the basis functions, to determine the weights ω_i, we solve a set of overdetermined linear equations

$$f_l(\mathbf{y}_i) = \sum_{j=0}^{M} \omega_{lj} \cdot \psi(\|\mathbf{y}_i - \mathbf{c}_j\|) = z_{il}^*, \quad i = 1, \cdots, n_0, \tag{3}$$

where $l = 1, 2$. ω_{lj}'s are obtained by using standard least squares.

Adaptive Local Fitting. In a generic human attentive behaviour sequence, the head poses will be geometrically continuous along the temporal axis when located or mapped onto the learned manifold. Based on this observation, an adaptive local fitting (ALF) technique is proposed, assuming temporal continuity and temporal local linearity assumption, to correct unreasonable mappings, as well as to smooth the outputs of RBF interpolation. Our ALF algorithm is composed of two parts: 1) adaptive outlier correction; 2) locally linear fitting.

In adaptive outlier correction, estimates which are far away from those of their S (an even number, e.g. $S = 2s_0$) temporally nearest neighbor (S-TNN) frames are defined as outliers. Let $\mathbf{z}_t$ be the output of the RBF interpolator for the t-th frame, and $D_S(t)$ be the distance between $\mathbf{z}_t$ and the mean of its TNNs $\{\mathbf{z}_{t-k}| - s_0 \le k \le s_0, k \ne 0\}$:

$$D_S(t) = \left\| \mathbf{z}_t - \frac{1}{S} \sum_{k=-s_0, k \ne 0}^{s_0} \mathbf{z}_{t-k} \right\|, \tag{4}$$

where $\|\cdot\|$ is the norm on the 2-D feature space.

For the t-th frame, we wait until the $(t+s_0)$-th image (to obtain all S-TNNs) for updating. We then calculate the relative difference $R_S(t)$ between $D_S(t)$ and $D_S(t-1)$ as:

$$R_S(t) = \left| \frac{D_S(t)}{D_S(t-1)} - 1 \right|. \tag{5}$$

To check for outliers, we set a threshold R_0. Different values of R_0 can make the system tolerant to different degrees of sudden change in the head pose. If $R_S(t) \ge R_0$, we deem point $\mathbf{z}_t$ to be an outlier, and set $\mathbf{z}_t = \text{median}(\mathbf{z}_{t-s_0}, \cdots, \mathbf{z}_{t-1}, \mathbf{z}_{t+1}, \cdots, \mathbf{z}_{t+s_0})$.

In locally linear fitting, we assume local linearity within a temporal window of length L. We employed the technique suggested in [18] for linear fitting to smooth the output of RBF interpolation.

After the above process, the head pan angle can be easily estimated as

$$\theta_t = \tan^{-1}\left(\frac{z_{t2}}{z_{t1}}\right). \qquad (6)$$

2.3   Entropy Classifier

Here we propose a simple method to detect FCFA behavior in a video sequence, given the head pan angle estimated for each frame as in (6). The head pan angle range of $0°$-$360°$ is divided into Q equally spaced angular regions. Given a video sequence of length N, a pan angle histogram with Q bins is calculated as

$$p_i = \frac{n_i}{N}, \quad i = 1, 2, \cdots, Q \qquad (7)$$

where n_i is the number of pose angles which fall into the i-th bin. The head pose entropy E of the sequence is then estimated as

$$E = -\sum_{i=1}^{Q} p_i \log p_i. \qquad (8)$$

For focused attention, we expect that the entropy will be low, and become high for FCFA behavior. Hence we can set a threshold on E to detect FCFA.

3   Experiments

In the first experiment, we tested the generalization ability of our person-independent mapping function to determine head pan angles. To test our algorithm's ability to detect FCFA behavior, we performed a second experiment using new video data exhibiting simulated FCFA and focused attention.

3.1   Data Description and Preprocessing

The data we used is composed of two parts: 1) Sequences used to investigate person independent mapping to estimate pose angle (these sequences were also used to train the system for FCFA detection); 2) Sequences exhibiting FCFA and focused attention behavior. All image sequence data were obtained from fixed video cameras. To simplify the problem, we set the camera to be approximately level with the heads. As described in Section 2, the size of the head images is normalized to $n_1 \times n_2 = 24 \times 16$ in preprocessing.

For parameter learning, we used 7 persons' sequences, a subset of which is shown in Fig. 1. The corresponding lengths of the 7x3=21 sequences are from 322 to 1462, totally 13832 frames in the sequences. One frontal face is labeled in each sequences for the manifold embedding.

For use in classification and detection of FCFA behavior, we obtained 14 more sequences, where six exhibited FCFA and eight exhibited focused attention. The corresponding lengths of the 14 sequences are from 311 to 3368.

3.2   Pose Estimation

To test our person-independent mapping method, we used leave-one-out cross-validation (LOOCV). Fig. 7 shows the results of the person-independent mapping to estimate the head pan angle in each frame for the three sequences corresponding to Fig. 1 where all 18 sequences of the other 6 persons' were used in parameter learning. The green lines correspond to the reference curve. This is obtained by calculating the projection of the test sequence into the unified 2-D embedded space. The head pan angles on the reference curve are very similar to what a human being perceives. This reference curve is for comparison with the pan angles estimated from the person-independent RBF interpolation system shown with red lines. It can be seen that the latter are very good approximations to the reference curve. The values above the small head images are the head pan angles of those images calculated from person-independent mapping.

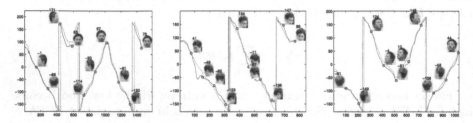

Fig. 7. LOOCV results of our person-independent mapping system to estimate head pan angle where the sequences sampled in Fig. 1 were used as the testing data. The pan angles can be corretly estimated within a normal range of the tilt angles. Green lines correspond to the reference curve, while red lines show the pan angles estimated by the person-independent mapping. The numbers above the images are the pan angles estimated by our system. (The 3 sequences were tested separately because there was no temporal continuity among these sequences).

We found that our proposed person-independent mapping system works well even if the face displays small facial expressions. This is the case for one of the people in our database, where he appears to be smiling.

3.3   Validation on FCFA and Focused Attention Data

After testing the framework for person-independent head pan angle mapping system, we tested its use for detecting FCFA behavior. We processed every sequence in the person-independent mapping system to estimate the pan angle in each frame and then calculated the pan angle entropy value E for that sequence as described in Section 2.3. To visualize the pose angles in sequences of FCFA and focused attention, we combined the estimated pose angle with temporal information to draw the trajectories as shown in Fig. 8 for one FCFA sequence and in Fig. 9 for one focused attention sequence. Here the roughly circular trajectory in Fig. 8 depicts the FCFA behavior of a person looking around, while for focused attention when a person is looking roughly in two directions, the trajectory in Fig. 9 depicts the situation quite well.

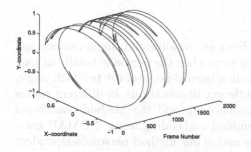 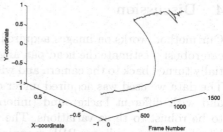

Fig. 8. One trajectory of FCFA behavior   **Fig. 9.** One trajectory of focused attention behavior

Table 2. The entropy value of head pose for the simulated sequences

Sequence	1	2	3	4	5	6	7	8
FCFA		3.07	3.00	3.31	3.24	3.18	2.72	
Focused Attention	1.17	1.91	1.66	1.43	1.73	1.19	2.37	1.47

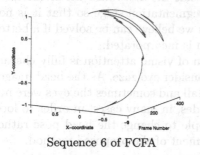 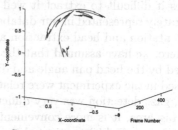

Sequence 6 of FCFA   Sequence 7 of focused attention

Fig. 10. Trajectories for Sequence 6 of FCFA (left) and Sequence 7 of focused attention (right)

Table 2 shows the corresponding value of E for the 14 sequences calculated using $Q = 36$ angular bins. It can be seen that the entropy values of FCFA are distinct from those of focused attention. By setting a threshold of $E_0 = 2.5$, we can detect FCFA behavior perfectly in the 14 sequences. However, for Sequence 6 of FCFA and Sequence 7 of focused attention (trajectories shown in Fig. 10), the entropy values are near the threshold E_0. As can be seen, for Sequence 6 of FCFA, the range of the person's head pan is over 180° but less than 360°, while for Sequence 7 of focused attention, the range is less than 180° but close to it. Thus, we suggest that they are assigned to a new class between FCFA behavior and focused attention behavior. To be noted that a small head change (nodding, slight shaking) will be still recognized as focused behaviour, which is due to the tolerance of the proposed method against the small tile and quantization of the orientation in the entropy calculation.

4 Discussion

Our method works on images acquired from an uncalibrated single camera and can robustly estimate the head pan angle even when the person is totally or partially turned back to the camera and within a normal range of the head tilt angle. The data we used was acquired under different illuminations, in different rooms and with different background (inhomogeneous), and the method was found to be robust to these variations. The unified embedding using ISOMAP combined with the nonlinear RBF mapping makes our method person-independent regardless of whether the person is in our database. In addition, our system is also robust to small facial expression changes, since the training data we used to learn the non-linear mapping includes those where the person is smiling.

If the input data is well represented by the training data, the estimation results will be quite accurate, such as the left and right figures in Fig. 7. However, since our person-independent mapping system is based on an interpolative RBF system, the results may degrade if the test images or sequences were not well represented in the original training space.

As can be seen in the middle figure in Fig. 7, the LOOCV results are not as good as the other two. The reason may be that the downward tilt of the faces makes it difficult to extract it well in the segmentation stage so that it is not accurately represented in our database. This we believe can be solved if a better segmentation and head extraction algorithm is incorporated.

Here, we have assumed that the direction of visual attention is fully characterized by the head pan angle and did not consider eye gaze. As the head images we used in the experiment were relatively small and sometimes the eyes were not clear, gaze detection was very difficult. Besides, in many cases, in order to look at a big area, it is more convenient for people to change the head pose rather than eye gaze, which motivated the development of the proposed method.

5 Conclusion

We have presented an attentive behavior detection system, where we used ISOMAP to embed each individual's high dimensional head image data into a low dimensional (2-D) space. By ellipse fitting, and normalizing by rescaling, rotating, and mirror imaging if needed, the individual embedded space is converted to a unified embedded space for multiple people. A RBF interpolation technique is used to find a person-independent mapping for new input head image data into the unified embedding space, i.e. our feature space. For head image sequences, we proposed an adaptive local fitting algorithm to remove outliers and to smooth the output of RBF interpolation, which enhanced the robustness of our system. The head pan angle estimate in each frame is then obtained by a simple coordinate-angle converter. To detect FCFA behavior from video sequences, the entropy of the head pan angle estimates over the entire sequence is used to classify the sequence as a FCFA or a focused attention behavior. The experimental results showed that our method robustly estimate the head pan angle even when the head is turned back to the camera and within a normal range of the head tilt angles. By setting a threshold on the entropy of head pan angle, we can successfully detect FCFA behavior.

Future work includes extending our method to a system that can also work with large facial expressions. Finding a 3-D embedding for both tilt and pan angle of an individual is also a possible future work.

References

1. Blumberg, B., et. al.: Creature smarts: the art and architecture of a virtual brain. proc. Game Developers Conf. (2000) 147–166
2. Webpage: (http://www.isinspect.org.uk/reports/2004/0374_04_r.htm)
3. Rae, R., Ritter, H.: Recognition of human head orientation based on artificial neural networks. IEEE Trans. Neural Networks 9 (1998) 257–265
4. Zhao, L., Pingali, G., Carlbom, I.: Real-time head orientation estimation using neural networks. proc. Int'l Conf. Image Processing 1 (2002) 297–300
5. Matsumoto, Y., Zelinsky, A.: An algorithm for real-time stereo vision implementation of head pose and gaze direction measurement. FG 2000 (2000) 499–505
6. Srinivasan, S., Boyer, K.L.: Head pose estimation using view based eigenspaces. ICPR 2002 4 (2002) 302–305
7. Everingham, M., Zisserman, A.: Identifying individuals in video by combining generative and discriminative head models. In: Proceedings of the International Conference on Computer Vision. (2005) 1103–1110
8. Stiefelhagen, R., Yang, J., Waibel, A.: Modeling focus of attention for meeting indexing. ACM Multimedia (1999) 3–10
9. Tenenbaum, J., de Silva, V., Langford, J.: A global geometric framework for nonlinear dimensionality reduction. Science 290 (2000) 2319–2323
10. Roweis, S., Saul, L.: Nonlinear dimensionality reduction by locally linear embedding. Science 290 (2000) 2323–2326
11. Pless, R.: Image spaces and video trajectories: Using isomap to explore video sequences. ICCV'03 2 (2003) 1433–1440
12. Elgammal, A., Lee, C.: Separating style and content on a nonlinear manifold. CVPR'04 (2004) 478–485
13. Vlachos, M., et al.: Non-linear dimensionality reduction techniques for classification and visualization. proc. 8th ACM SIGKDD Int'l Conf. on Knowledge Discovery and Data Mining (2002) 645–651
14. Efros, A., et al.: Seeing through water. In Neural Information Processing Systems (NIPS 17) (2004) 393–400
15. Yang, M., Kriegman, D., Ahuja, N.: Detecting faces in images: A survey. IEEE Trans. PAMI 24 (2002) 34–58
16. Fitzgibbon, Pilu, M., R.Fisher: Direct least-square fitting of ellipses. IEEE Trans. PAMI 21 (1999) 476–480
17. Duda, R., Hart, P., Stork, D.: Pattern Classification. 2 edn. John Wiley & Sons, Inc. (2000)
18. Hutcheson, M.: Trimmed Resistant Weighted Scatterplot Smooth. Master's Thesis, Cornell University (1995)

Human Pose Tracking
Using Multi-level Structured Models

Mun Wai Lee and Ram Nevatia

Institute for Robotics and Intelligent System,
University of Southern California,
Los Angeles, CA 90089, USA
{munlee, nevatia}@usc.edu

Abstract. Tracking body poses of multiple persons in monocular video
is a challenging problem due to the high dimensionality of the state space
and issues such as inter-occlusion of the persons' bodies. We proposed a
three-stage approach with a multi-level state representation that enables
a hierarchical estimation of 3D body poses. At the first stage, humans
are tracked as blobs. In the second stage, parts such as face, shoulders
and limbs are estimated and estimates are combined by grid-based belief propagation to infer 2D joint positions. The derived belief maps are
used as proposal functions in the third stage to infer the 3D pose using
data-driven Markov chain Monte Carlo. Experimental results on realistic
indoor video sequences show that the method is able to track multiple
persons during complex movement such as turning movement with inter-
occlusion.

1 Introduction

Human body pose tracking is important for many applications, including understanding human activity and other applications in video analysis. For example
in surveillance applications, people are often the main object of interest in the
monitored scenes. Analyzing the body poses of the people allows for inference of
the people's activities and their interactions. In the general case, analyzing body
poses involves estimating the positions of the main body components such as the
head, torso, and limbs, and the angles of joints such as shoulders and elbows.

Existing research work on human pose estimation is motivated by different
applications. In human motion capture and human computer interaction, one can
simplify the problem by using multiple cameras and controlling the environment
and the subject's appearance. In our work however, we focus on applications for
video understanding and surveillance that deal with uncontrolled scenes with
only a single camera; multiple persons may also be present. This is a difficult
problem for many reasons including variations in individual body shapes and
choice of clothing. Furthermore, the humans need to be segmented from the
background and self-occlusions need to be considered. The presence of multiple
persons in the scene makes the problem more complex as people may occlude
each other.

A. Leonardis, H. Bischof, and A. Pinz (Eds.): ECCV 2006, Part III, LNCS 3953, pp. 368–381, 2006.

Our aim is to recover body and limb positions and orientations, i.e. their poses, in 3D from monocular video sequences without any special markers on the body. We use a model-based approach to overcome the above difficulties. By modeling separately the human body and other aspects of the image generation process (including dynamics, image projection, and observation process model), fewer training images can be used to handle more varying environments. An analysis-by-synthesis approach is often used to evaluate hypotheses of the state that represents the pose parameters but efficient search for the state solution in a high dimension space is a key issue. For a sequence, we can use the dynamic model to reduce the search space; nonetheless, we must still estimate the initial state and re-initialize when tracking becomes unreliable. In this paper, we present a novel three-stage approach for 3D pose estimation and tracking of multiple people from a monocular sequence (See Fig. 1). To improve the search efficiency, a *hierarchical* approach is used since some parameters are easier to estimate than others. In addition, bottom-up detection of body components is used to reduce the search space. We focus on sequences on a meeting room environment. The camera is stationary and the resolution is such that a persons height is about 200 to 250 pixels.

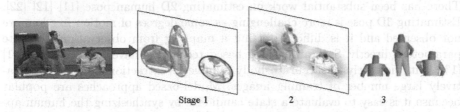

Stage 1   2   3

Fig. 1. Three stages approach. From left: (*i*) input, (*ii*) Stage 1: blobs tracking, (*iii*) Stage 2: 2D inference, (*iv*) Stage 3: 3D inference. The scene consists of three persons in a meeting room cnvironment. The poses are estimated in a hierarchical coarse-to-fine manner.

In the first stage, moving people are detected and tracked as *elliptical blobs*. A coarse *histogram-based appearance model* for each person is learned during tracking so that when one person occludes another, we can determine the depth ordering from the appearance. This stage provides a coarse estimation of the persons' positions, sizes and the occluding layers.

In the second stage, part detection modules are used to locate the faces, shoulders and limbs. Inferences from these local component detections are integrated in a *belief network*; a *belief propagation* technique is used to estimate the marginalized belief of each state. Restricting the second stage to 2D inference enables us to use *grid-based representations* for the belief functions that can handle complex distributions efficiently. This approach is different from the *nonparametric belief propagation* method (NBP) [6] [10] [14] [17] , as we do not use Monte Carlo sampling or a mixture-of-Gaussians approximation.

In the third stage, a method based on *data-driven Markov chain Monte Carlo* (DD-MCMC) [21] is used to estimate the full 3D body poses in each frame.

A state candidate is evaluated by generating synthesized humans (we assume an orthographic projection and known camera orientation) and comparing it to the input image. With this generative approach, we can consider nonlinear constraints such as inter-occlusion and non-self-penetration. To search the state space efficiently, the Markov chain transition uses proposal functions generated from the previous stage (estimates of 2D joint positions).

With these three stages, the body poses of each frame are estimated with multiple hypotheses. The body trajectories of the people can be estimated by combining results of multiple frames. A human dynamic model is used to apply temporal constraints of body kinematics. A *dynamic programming* technique is used to compute the optimal trajectories of the persons motion.

Part of the implementation of Stage 3 is based on our earlier work on pose estimation for a single person in mainly upright and frontal poses [8]. This work extends the method to dynamic pose estimation of multiple persons in sequences and includes more difficult scenarios such as turning movements as well as occlusions among people.

1.1 Related Work

There has been substantial work on estimating 2D human pose [11] [12] [22]. Estimating 3D pose is more challenging as some degrees of motion freedom are not observed and it is difficult to find a mapping from observations to state parameters directly. Several learning based techniques have been proposed [1] [13], but these rely on accurate body silhouette extraction and having relatively large number of training images. Model-based approaches are popular because it is easy to evaluate a state candidate by synthesizing the human appearance. In [3], *particle filtering* is used for 3D pose tracking with multiple cameras by approximating the state posterior distribution with a set of samples. It is however difficult to extend this to tracking monocular view because of significant ambiguities in depth. In [15], a *mixture density propagation* approach is used to overcome the depth ambiguities of articulated joints seen in monocular view. A *hybrid Monte Carlo* technique is used in [2] for tracking walking people. Nonetheless, the issue of pose initialization is not addressed in these techniques.

The *non-parametric belief propagation* (NBP) method [10] [17] has been used for pose estimation [6] [14] and hand tracking [18]. A *mean field Monte Carlo* algorithm is also proposed in [20] for tracking articulated body. These techniques use a graphical model, with each node representing a body joint. Inference is made by propagating beliefs along the network. Our method uses belief propagation only at the second stage to bootstrap the 3D inference at the third stage where a complete analysis, including self-occlusion, is performed. Recently, bottom-up, local parts detection has been used as a data-driven mechanism for the pose estimation [6] [9] [12] and this has now been recognized as an important component in a body pose estimation solution and is the main motivation for this work.

2   Human Ellipse Tracking

We describe in this section the first stage of our approach which involves the tracking of humans whose shape is approximated as ellipses in the video. The objective here is to determine the number of people in the scene, estimate coarsely their positions and sizes and infer the depth ordering when they overlap with each other in the image.

Given a sequence, the static background is learned using an *adaptive mixture model* approach [16] and the foreground moving blobs are extracted by background subtraction. Human ellipses are detected and tracked by matching them with the foreground. A human blob is represented by a simple ellipse that has five parameters: positions, width, height and rotation. The matching between the ellipses and foreground is described by a *cost function* based on region matching of the estimated ellipses with the foreground (see Fig. 2). A track is initiated automatically by the presence of an unmatched foreground blob of sufficiently large size. At each time frame, the states are updated by performing a block search to minimize the cost function. We assume that the ellipse size changes slowly and that the ellipses are allowed to overlap each other. A color histogram is used to represent the appearance of a human blob and is learned by adaptive updating. When the ellipses overlap, we determine the depth order by comparing the overlapped region with the learned color histograms.

This is a simple method to track the human blobs as the first coarse stage to estimate human pose and is adequate for uncrowded scenes.

Fig. 2. Human blobs tracking. *Left*: extracted foreground. *Right*: estimated ellipses representing human blobs with inference of depth order.

3   Inference of 2D Joint Positions

The second stage aims to make efficient inference of 2D image position of body joints, using results from various body component detections, as well as the dependency between the various joints. We use a graphical model to represent the human body. For a single frame, this graphical model is a tree where each node corresponds to the image position of a body joint and each edge represents the pair-wise dependency between the adjacent joints, as shown in Fig. 3. We let the state of the ith body joint be denoted by $r_i = (u_i, v_i)$. These states are approximates of the 3D pose.

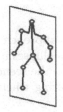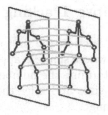

Fig. 3. *Left:* Graphical model in 2nd stage; *right:* extension to two frames showing temporal constraints. Note: observation nodes are not shown here.

3.1 Observation Function

For each node, there is a corresponding observation function, denoted by $\phi_i(r_i) = \phi_i(u_j, v_j)$. These functions are generated from various detection modules applied to the current frame. The observations include the outputs of human blob ellipse detector, face, torso, head-shoulder contour matching and skin blob extraction (Fig. 4); part detectors are described in more detail in [7][8]. Our proposed framework can be used with other detection modules proposed in the literature, for example in [11][12][14][16][22]. In general, these observations may contain localization noise, outliers, missed detections, and data association ambiguities in the presence of multiple persons. In [14], a mixture-of-Gaussians was used to approximate the observation function, but observations from multiple views were used to provide greater accuracy. For a monocular view, the observation function can be quite complex, and such an approximation scheme is inadequate. We therefore use a grid-based method to represent the observation function.

Fig. 4. Parts detection. (a) face-body tracker, (b) head-shoulder contour, (c) skin color blobs (for face and hand).

3.2 Potential Function

For each pair of adjacent nodes connected by an edge (i, j), there is a potential function denoted by $\psi_{i,j}(r_i, r_j)$ that encodes the joint distribution of neighbouring states. This potential function is shift invariant and can be simplified as a 2D function: $\psi_{i,j}(r_i, r_j) = \psi_{i,j}(u_i - u_j, v_i - v_j)$. We use an approximate grid representation for each potential function. In our current implementation, the grid is of the same size as the image.

The potential functions are however dependent on the image scale. We denote by s the scale representing the image height of a person when in a standing pose. The scale is estimated by the width of the detected human ellipse, denoted by $w_{ellipse}$, which is insensitive to occlusion of the lower body. Given the scale, the conditional potential function can be expressed as

$$\psi_{i,j}(r_i, r_j|s) = \hat{\psi}_{i,j}\left(\frac{u_i - u_j}{s}, \frac{v_i - v_j}{s}\right),$$

where $\hat{\psi}_{i,j}(\cdot)$ is a scale invariant function. Therefore, when learning the potential functions, the training data is normalized by scale.

The potential function, marginalized by scale, can be expressed as:

$$\psi_{i,j}(r_i, r_j) = \int \psi_{i,j}(r_i, r_j|s)p(s|w_{ellipse})ds,$$

where $w_{ellipse}$ is the width of the ellipse detected in the first stage and $p(s|w_{ellipse})$ is the posterior probability of scale given the width. In practice, the observed ellipse provides a fairly reliable estimate of the scale, so that the observation function can be approximated by $p(s|w_{ellipse}) = \delta(s - s')$, where $\delta(\cdot)$ is the delta function, $s' = \lambda w_{ellipse}$ is the estimated scale, and λ is a constant estimated from training data. The potential function can now be simplified as:

$$\psi_{i,j}(r_i, r_j) = \hat{\psi}_{i,j}\left(\frac{u_i - u_j}{s'}, \frac{v_i - v_j}{s'}\right).$$

3.3   Grid-Based Belief Propagation

Belief propagation is a statistical inference technique used to estimate the state belief in the graphical model as in [10][14][17][18]. At each iteration, each node passes messages to its neighbors. A message from ith node to the jth node is denoted by $m_{i,j}(r_j)$ and is expressed as:

$$m_{i,j}(r_j) = \int \psi_{i,j}(r_i, r_j)\phi_i(r_i) \prod_{k \in \Gamma_i \setminus j} m_{ki}(r_i)dr_i,$$

where r_i is an image position of the ith node and Γ_i is the set of neighbors of ith node. The belief of the ith node is given as:

$$b_i(r_i) \propto \phi_i(r_i) \prod_{k \in \Gamma_i} m_{ki}(r_i).$$

By using 2D grid representations for the observation functions, potential functions, messages and beliefs, the belief propagation computation is simplified. The message is expressed as:

$$m_{i,j}(u_j, v_j) = \sum_{u_i} \sum_{v_i} \psi_{i,j}(u_i - u_j, v_i - v_j)\phi_i(u_i, v_i) \prod_{k \in \Gamma_i \setminus j} m_{ki}(u_i, v_i).$$

This is a discrete convolution and can be rewritten as:

$$m_{i,j}(u_j, v_j) = \psi_{i,j}(u, v) \otimes \left[\phi_i(u, v) \prod_{k \in \Gamma \backslash j} m_{ki}(u, v) \right],$$

where the symbol $\otimes$ represents the convolution operation. The belief is now written as:

$$b_i(u_j, v_j) \propto \phi_i(u_j, v_j) \prod_{k \in \Gamma} m_{ki}(u_j, v_j).$$

We call these 2D belief functions as *belief maps* and they can be computed efficiently by using the *fast Fourier transform* for the discrete convolution. The maps are used as proposal functions in Stage 3 described later.

For a single frame, the graphical model is a tree. Each iteration involves a parallel updating of all the nodes. The number of iterations required for belief propagation is equal to the longest path between nodes, or the diameter of the graph. In our case, six iterations are sufficient.

The graphical model is extended to multiple frames, (see Fig. 3). Let r_i^t denotes the state of ith node at time t. The temporal potential function of this node between consecutive frames is denoted by $\psi_{T,i}(r_i^t, r_i^{t-1})$. This function is time invariant and can also be expressed as a grid representation:

$$\psi_{T,i}(r_i^t, r_i^{t-1}) = \psi_{T,i}(u_i^t - u_i^{t-1}, v_i^t - v_i^{t-1}).$$

The resulting graphical model now contains loops and the belief updating process becomes a *loopy belief propagation* which in general does not guarantee convergence. However, in practice, our network always converges during experiment. This is because the temporal potential function serves as a temporal smoother and this prevents oscillations. In our experiment, we observed

Fig. 5. Inference of 2D face positions. (a) Face detection from different cues with many false alarms, (b) initial face belief map before belief propagation, (c)-(e) face belief maps for each person after belief propagation. Dark regions indicate higher probability values.

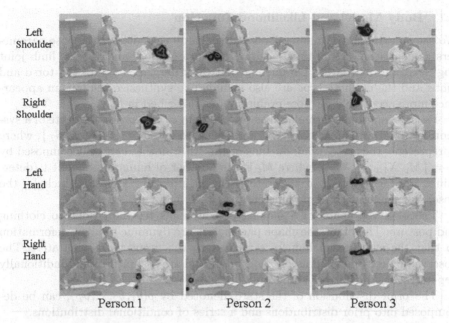

| | Person 1 | Person 2 | Person 3 |

Left Shoulder

Right Shoulder

Left Hand

Right Hand

Fig. 6. Further examples of belief maps, each row for each body joint and each column for each person

that ten iterations are sufficient for convergence. Fig. 5 and Fig. 6 shows examples of belief maps for each person in the scene. In these maps, some ambiguities still exist; but the beliefs are much better compared to initial observation function.

The computations of messages and beliefs are deterministic. In comparison, nonparametric belief propagation uses Monte Carlo sampling which is less suitable in a multiple persons scene where the observations are more ambigious and distributions are complex.

4   3D pose inference

3D pose estimation is performed at the third stage. Estimating these object-centered parameters is important for providing view-invariant pose recognition and infering spatial relations between objects in the scene, for example during a pointing gesture. We use a model-based approach and MCMC inference technique. The belief maps generated in Stage 2 are used to generate data-driven proposal in this third stage.

In this section, we describe the key components including the human model, the observation, and the formulation of the prior distribution and likelihood function. We have extended a previous work [8] by formulating a joint prior distribution and a joint likelihood function for all persons in the scene.

4.1   Body Model and Likelihood Function

We use an articulated limb model of human body that defines the pose parameters as consisting of the torso position and orientation, and various limb joint angles. Additional latent parameters that describe the shape of the torso and limbs and the clothing type are also included to synthesize the human appearance more accurately for pose evaluation, as described in [7].

Pose estimation is formulated as the problem of estimating the state of a system. State for a sequence with T frames is represented by $\{\theta_1, \theta_2, ..., \theta_T\}$, where θ_t represents the states of all humans at the tth frame. It can be decomposed by $\theta_t = \{M_t, X_{1,t}, ..., X_{M,t}\}$ where M_t is the number of human at time it t (determined in Stage 1), $X_{m,t}$ is the state of the mth person. This state includes the pose, shape and clothing parameters.

The observed shape of a moving person tends to change due to clothing and posture. Therefore, the shape parameters are dynamic to allow deformation so that the synthesized human is aligned to the input more accurately. The observed images, denoted as $\{I_1, I_2, ..., I_T\}$, and are assumed to be conditionally dependent on the current states only.

The prior distribution of the state, denoted by $p(\theta_1, \theta_2, ..., \theta_T)$, can be decomposed into prior distributions and a series of conditional distributions.

$$p(\theta_1, \theta_2, ..., \theta_T) = \frac{1}{z} \prod_{m=1}^{M_1} p(X_{m,1}) \prod_{t=1}^{T-1} \prod_{m=1}^{M.} p(X_{m,t+1}|X_{m,t})$$

where Z is a normalization constant (we simplified the above expression by assuming all tracks start from $t{=}1$). The prior distribution is learned from a training set of human poses in static image and sets of motion capture data. The conditional distribution is based on a zeroth-order dynamic model and is approximated by a normal distribution.

$$p(X_{m,t+1}|X_{m,t}) \approx \mathrm{N}(X_{m,t+1} - X_{m,t}, \Sigma), \tag{1}$$

where Σ is the covariance matrix of the dynamic model and is learned from motion capture data.

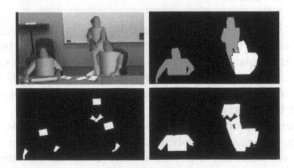

Fig. 7. Joint likelihood. *Top left:* predicted human poses; *top right:* predicted foreground regions; *bottom left:* predicted skin regions; *bottom right:* predicted non-skin regions.

A state candidate θ_t is evaluated by a likelihood function denoted by $p(I_t|\theta_t)$. We formulate the image likelihood function as consisting of four components, based on (i) region coherency, (ii) color dissimilarity with background, (iii) skin color and (iv) foreground matching, respectively.

$$p(I_t|\theta_t) = L_{region}(I_t, \theta_t) \times L_{color}(I_t, \theta_t) \times L_{skin}(I_t, \theta_t) \times L_{foreground}(I_t, \theta_t)$$

These likelihood components are described in detail in [7][8]; we have extended them to a joint likelihood measure for all humans in the scene that considers the inter-occlusion among them. Fig. 7 illustrates some of the synthesized variables that are generated when computing the likelihood measure.

4.2 Proposal Mechanisms

Different proposal mechanisms are used for the Markov chain transitions. We follow the procedure described in [8] and provide only a brief summary here for completeness. The MCMC approach uses a proposal function to generate state candidates. In theory, one can generate a candidate for the whole sequence of states $\{\theta_1, \theta_2, ..., \theta_T\}$ but such schemes have high computation complexity and difficult to implement. Instead, at each Markov transition, we update only the state of one person at one frame, $X_{m,t}$. From a current state, $X'_{m,t}$, a new state candidate, $X^*_{m,t}$, is generated by three types of evidence:

1. The estimation of previous state, $X_{m,t-1}$, can be propagated using a human dynamic model to generate candidates for the current state. We denote this proposal as $q(X^*_{m,t}|X_{m,t-1})$.

2. The candidates can be generated from the belief maps derived in the second stage. This is an adaptation of a bottom-up data-driven approach [21] that has now been used for a number of computer vision tasks [19][23]. In each belief map, the value at each pixel position represents the importance sampling probability of the corresponding joint's image position. The maps are used to generate pose candidates in a *component-based Metropolis-Hastings* approach. In [7], it is shown how this framework can be adapted for estimating 3D kinematics parameters by constructing reversible jumps using the belief maps and inverse kinematics computation; and it approximately satisfies the detailed balance requirement for MCMC. We denote this proposal function as $q(X^*_{m,t}|I_{m,t}, X'_{m,t})$, where $I_{m,t}$ represents the set of belief maps for the mth person derived in Stage 2.

3. Using backward-propagation, the next state estimates, can also be used to generate candidates for the current state. We denote this proposal as $q(X^*_{m,t}|X_{m,t+1})$.

The proposal distribution is denoted by $q(X^*_{m,t}|X_{m,t-1}, I_{m,t}, X_{m,t+1}, X'_{m,t})$, where $X'_{m,t}$ is the current Markov chain state. For simplicity, the distribution can be decomposed into its components:

$$q(X^*_{m,t}|X_{m,t-1}, I_{m,t}, X_{m,t+1}, X'_{m,t})$$
$$= \alpha_1 q(X^*_{m,t}|X_{m,t-1}) + \alpha_2 q(X^*_{m,t}|I_{m,t}, X'_{m,t}) + \alpha_3 q(X^*_{m,t}|X_{m,t+1}) + \alpha_4 q(X^*_{m,t}|X'_{m,t})$$

where $\alpha_1, \alpha_2, \alpha_3, \alpha_4$ are the mixing ratios for the different components. The last component, $q(X^*_{m,t}|X'_{m,t})$, represents a proposal distribution derived from the current Markov state. It is implemented to involve both the random-walk sampler [5] and the flip kinematic jump [15] that is designed to explore the depth space [7].

4.3   Dynamic Proposals

Dynamic proposal mechanism involves generating a state candidate for the current frame, $X^*_{m,t}$, either from the estimates in the previous frame, $X_{m,t-1}$, or in the next frame, $X_{m,t+1}$. For the following discussion, we focus on the former.

The state estimation in the previous frame is represented by a set of state samples $\{X^1_{m,t-1}, X^2_{m,t-1}, ...\}$ generated by the Markov chain search. These samples are clustered to form a compact set of representative samples

$$\{X^{(1)}_{m,t-1}, X^{(2)}_{m,t-1}, ..., X^{(N)}_{m,t-1}\},$$

where N is the number of mixture components. We use $N=50$ in our experiments. These components are weighted according to their cluster sizes. To generate a candidate for the current frame, a sample $X^{(*)}_{m,t-1}$ is selected from the set of mixture components in the previous frame based on their normalized weights $\{w^{(1)}_{m,t-1}, w^{(2)}_{m,t-1}, ..., w^{(N)}_{m,t-1}\}$. Using a zeroth-order dynamic model, the state candidate is generated by sampling a normal distribution centered at $X^{(*)}_{m,t-1}$, with Σ as the covariance matrix from Equation (1).

4.4   Extracting Pose Trajectory

The previous section describes state estimation for each frame. The set of generated Markov samples can be represented compactly using a mixture model as described earlier. Using dynamic programming, an estimated trajectory of the each person can be obtained by "traversing" along the sequence and selecting a set of poses from these mixture components as in [8].

5   Experimental Results

In this section, we describe the experimental setup and discuss the result. We used a realistic sequence depicting a meeting room scene[1] [4]. We annotated the video manually to aid in evaluation by locating the image positions of the body joints. The depths of these joints, relative to the hip, were also estimated. The annotation data are used for evaluation only and not for training.

A set of training data is used to learn the prior distribution of state parameters, potential functions, dynamic model and observation models. These include motion capture data and annotated video sequences; and they are from sources

---

[1] The video was provided to us by the National Institute for Standards and Technology of the U.S. Government.

different from the test sequences and are of different scenes. The position of the table in the meeting room is annotated manually and provided to the system, and this information is used to infer occlusion of the body by the table.

5.1 Pose Tracking Results

The results of pose estimation are shown in Fig. 8. The initialization of each human model is automatic. The shape of the human model was initialized as the mean of the shape prior distribution.

As the results show, the proposed method is able to initialize and track the human poses robustly. The system is able to recover after partial self-occlusion or inter-occlusion. Estimation of the salient components including the face, torso and hands are fairly accurate. These help to boost the estimation of the other joints that are either less salient (e.g. elbows) or are temporarily occluded.

Some instances of temporary failure are observed due to lack of reliable observation, especially for the lower arms. Nonetheless, the results demonstrate the robustness of our approach in recovering from these partial failures.

For evaluation, we compare the estimated joint position with the annotated data. In the tth frame, we compute the 2D Euclidean distance error (in pixels) for the jth joint, denoted by e_t^j . A weighted average error, denoted by E_t, is defined by:

$$E_t = \left[\sum_{j=1}^{K} w_j e_t^j \Big/ \sum_{j=1}^{K} w_j \right],$$

where K is the number of joints used for evaluation and $\{w_j | j = 1, ..., K\}$ are the weights. The weights are chosen to approximate the relative size of the corresponding body parts, and the values are: 1.0 for torso and neck; 0.6 for shoulders, elbows and knees; 0.4 for wrists and ankles; 0.3 for head; and 0.2 for hand-tips. We ignore those joints that are always occluded, namely the lower

Fig. 8. Multiple persons pose tracking in meeting room scene

body joints of the sitting persons. The error for the pose estimation is 22.51 pixels or about 15.5cm (one pixel is approximately 0.69cm).

The experiment was performed on a 2.8GHz Intel PC in Windows XP and C++ programming code. For each frame, 1000 Markov state samples were generated in the third stage. The total processing for each frame took on average 5 minutes. We believe the computation can be improved significantly with later code optimization and the use of graphics hardware which we are currently exploring.

5.2 Discussion

We have shown how a novel three-stage approach using multi-level models can estimate and track poses accurately in highly realistic scene. This method allows us to perform a hierarchical estimation to overcome difficulties associated with realistic scene of multiple persons. By limiting the 2nd stage to 2D inference and using a grid-based representation, our method can efficiently integrate bottom-up observations with belief propagation using deterministic computation. Overall, the computation cost is slightly higher compared with that in [14] where nonparametric belief propagation is used to infer 3D pose directly (both methods run at several minutes per frame), but our system handles monocular views and considers inter-occlusion and non self-penetration constraints which we believe are essential for general applications related to event recognition and stored-video analysis.

The test sequences are different from the training data we used; this shows some generality of this model-based approach. A strength of this method is the ability to perform automatic initialization and recover from partial track failures due to occlusion. This is achieved without prior learning of the person's specific appearance or movement; these constraints are important in video understanding applications.

Acknowledgment

This research was funded, in part, by the Advanced Research and Development Activity of the U.S. Government under contract # MDA-904-03-C-1786.

References

1. A. Agarwal, B. Triggs: "3D human pose from silhouettes by relevance vector regression," *CVPR* 2004.
2. K. Choo, D.J. Fleet: "People tracking with hybrid Monte Carlo," *ICCV* 2001.
3. J. Deutscher, A. Davison, I. Reid: "Automatic partitioning of high dimensional search spaces associated with articulated body motion capture," *CVPR* 2001.
4. J.S. Garofolo, C.D. Laprun, M. Michel, V.M. Stanford, E. Tabassi: "The NIST Meeting Room Pilot Corpus," *Proc. 4th International Conference on Language Resources and Evaluation* (LREC-2004), Lisbon, Portugal, May 26-28 2004.

5. W. Gilks, S. Richardson, D. Spiegelhalter: *Markov Chain Monte Carlo in Practice.* Chapman and Hall, 1996.
6. G. Hua, M. Yang, Y. Wu: "Learning to estimate human pose with data driven belief propagation," *CVPR* 2005.
7. M. Lee, I. Cohen: "Proposal Maps driven MCMC for Estimating Human Body Pose in Static Images," *CVPR* 2004.
8. M. Lee, R. Nevatia: "Dynamic Human Pose Estimation using Markov chain Monte Carlo Approach," *Motion* 2005.
9. G. Mori, X. Ren, A. Efros, J. Malik: "Recovering Human Body Configurations: Combining Segmentation and Recognition," *CVPR* 2004.
10. M. Isard: "PAMPAS: Real-valued graphical models for computer vision," *CVPR* 2003.
11. D. Ramanan, D. A. Forsyth: "Finding and tracking people from the bottom up," *CVPR* 2003.
12. T. J. Roberts, S. J. McKenna, I. W. Ricketts: "Human Pose Estimation Using Learnt Probabilistic Region Similarities and Partial Configurations," *ECCV* 2004.
13. G. Shakhnarovich, P. Viola, T. Darrell: "Face pose estimation with parameter sensitive hashing," *ICCV* 2003.
14. L. Sigal, S. Bhatia, S. Roth, M. J. Black, M. Isard: "Tracking Loose-limbed People," *CVPR* 2004.
15. C. Sminchisescu, B. Triggs: "Kinematic Jump Processes for Monocular Human Tracking," *CVPR* 2003.
16. C. Stauffer, W.Grimson: "Adaptive background mixture models for real-time tracking," *CVPR* 1999.
17. E.B. Sudderth, A.T. Ihler, W.T. Freeman, A.S. Willsky: "Nonparametric belief propagation," *CVPR* 2003.
18. E.B. Sudderth, M.I. Mandel, W.T. Freeman, A.S. Willsky: "Distributed occlusion reasoning for tracking with nonparametric belief propagation," *NIPS* 2004.
19. Z.W. Tu, S.C. Zhu: "Image Segmentation by Data-Driven Markov Chain Monte Carlo," *PAMI* 24(5), pp. 657-672, 2002.
20. Y. Wu, G. Hua, T. Yu: "Tracking articulated body by dynamic Markov network," *CVPR* 2003.
21. "S. Zhu, R. Zhang, Z. Tu: "Integrating bottom-up/top-down for object recognition by data driven Markov chain Monte Carlo," *CVPR* 2000.
22. J. Zhang, R. Collins, Y. Liu: "Representation and Matching of Articulated Shapes," *CVPR* 2004.
23. T. Zhao, R. Nevatia: "Tracking Multiple Humans in Crowded Environment," *CVPR* 2004.

Context-Aided Human Recognition – Clustering

Yang Song and Thomas Leung

Fujifilm Software (California), Inc.,
1740 Technology Drive, Suite 490, San Jose, CA 95110, USA
{ysong, tleung}@fujifilmsoft.com

Abstract. Context information other than faces, such as clothes, picture-taken-time and some logical constraints, can provide rich cues for recognizing people. This aim of this work is to automatically cluster pictures according to person's identity by exploiting as much context information as possible in addition to faces. Toward that end, a clothes recognition algorithm is first developed, which is effective for different types of clothes (smooth or highly textured). Clothes recognition results are integrated with face recognition to provide similarity measurements for clustering. Picture-taken-time is used when combining faces and clothes, and the cases of faces or clothes missing are handled in a principle way. A spectral clustering algorithm which can enforce hard constraints (positive and negative) is presented to incorporate logic-based cues (e.g. two persons in one picture must be different individuals) and user feedback. Experiments on real consumer photos show the effectiveness of the algorithm.

1 Introduction

Being able to identify people is important for automatic organizing and retrieving photo albums and for security applications, where face recognition has been playing a major role. But reliable face recognition is still a challenging problem after many research efforts [5], especially when imaging condition changes. On the other hand, information besides faces (called 'context' relative to face) can provide rich cues for recognizing people.

Generally speaking, there are three types of context information. The first type is appearance-based, such as a person's hair style or the clothes he is wearing; the second type is logic-based, for instance, different faces in one picture belong to different persons or some people are more likely to be pictured together (e.g. husband and wife); the third type is the meta-data for pictures such as the picture-taken-time. This context information is often used by human observers consciously or unconsciously. It is very tempting to investigate how to build algorithms which can utilize this context information effectively to improve human recognition accuracy.

The aim of this work is to automatically organize pictures according to person's identity by using faces and as much context information as possible. Assuming we have a face recognition engine, we want to improve upon it via contexts. We want to develop a clustering algorithm which can put persons in the pictures

A. Leonardis, H. Bischof, and A. Pinz (Eds.): ECCV 2006, Part III, LNCS 3953, pp. 382–395, 2006.

into groups (clusters). The ideal results will be that all the images of the same individual are in one cluster and images from different individuals are in different clusters. Towards this end, we need to answer the following three questions: 1) what context information to use? 2) what is the clustering algorithm? 3) how to put context information into the clustering algorithm?

Regarding to the first question, we use the appearance-based and logic-based context explicitly, and the picture taken time implicitly. For the appearance-based context, clothes provide an important cue for recognizing people in the same event (or on the same day) when clothes are not changed. They are complimentary to faces and remain very useful when face pose changes, poor face quality, and facial expression variations occur. Therefore, it is intuitively appealing to use clothes information. However, in practice, due to different types of clothes (solid colored or heavily textured) and changes in clothes imaging condition (occlusions, pose changes, lighting changes, etc), it is not a trivial matter to use clothes information effectively. We strive to develop an effective clothes recognition method in this paper. For the logic-based context, we want to enforce some hard constraints. A constraint is hard when it must be satisfied in order for a clustering result to be correct. For example, the fact that different faces in one picture belonging to different individuals is a hard constraint.

Many clustering algorithms have been developed, from traditional K-means to the recently popular spectral clustering ([10, 14, 8, 15]). One major advantage of spectral clustering methods over K-means ([8]) is that K-means easily fails when clusters do not correspond to convex regions (similar for mixture of models using EM, which often assumes that the density of each cluster is Gaussian). In human clustering, imaging conditions can change from different aspects, hence one cluster doesn't necessarily form a convex region. Therefore a spectral clustering algorithm is favored.

Now we are facing the question of how to put the context information into the clustering algorithm. The base of a spectral clustering algorithm is the similarity measure between nodes (for human recognition, each node represents a person image). It is a natural thought to combine clothes recognition results with face recognition results as the similarity measurements. But due to occlusion or pose changes, either face or clothes information may be missing or when different people wear the same clothes on the same day, the clothes information can become unreliable. We propose a principled way to handle these cases. The next issue is how to enforce the hard constraints? For K-means, hard constraints can be enforced as in [13]. Though spectral clustering methods have the aforementioned advantage over K-means, it is hard to enforce hard constraints. In [15], a solution of imposing positive constraints (two nodes must belong to the same cluster) is addressed, but there is no guarantee that the positive constraints will be respected and the problem of enforcing negative constraints (two nodes cannot belong to the same cluster) remains open. In this paper, by taking advantages of both K-means and spectral clustering methods, we devise a spectral clustering method which can enforce hard constraints.

In [18], clothes information is used for annotating faces. Our work differs from that in (1) a new clothes recognition algorithm is developed, and the results from face and clothes recognition are integrated in a principled way; (2) a constrained spectral clustering algorithm, which can enforce hard constraints, is proposed, so that other context cues (e.g. persons from one picture should be in different clusters) and user feedback can be imposed.

The rest of the paper is organized as follows. The clothes recognition method is presented in Section 2. Section 3 describes how to combine clothes recognition results with face recognition into one similarity measurement. Section 4 depicts the spectral clustering algorithm and how to put some logic-based context cues (i.e. enforcing hard constraints) into the clustering algorithm. Experimental results are presented in Section 5. Finally, Section 6 gives concluding remarks.

2   Clothes Recognition

Clothes recognition is to judge how similar two pieces of clothes image are and therefore to indicate how likely they are from the same individual. There are three major steps for clothes recognition: clothes detection and segmentation, clothes representation (or feature extraction), and similarity computation based on extracted features.

2.1   Clothes Detection and Segmentation

Clothes detection and segmentation is to obtain the clothes part from an image. For recognition purpose, precise contours of clothes are not necessary, but we need to get the representative part and get rid of clutters.

An initial estimation of the clothes location can be obtained by first running face detection [1] and taking some parts below the head. However, this is often unsatisfactory due to occlusion by another person or by the person's self limbs (skin) or presence of other objects in the environment. To improve upon the initial estimations, the following two steps are therefore performed. One is to segment clothes among different people via maximizing the difference of neighboring clothes pieces, which can be computed by the χ^2 distance of color histograms in CIElab space. Assuming that the 'true' clothes are not far away from the initial guess, candidate locations can be obtained by shifting and resizing the initial estimation. The candidates which can maximize the difference are chosen. Figure 1 shows an example.

The next step is to get rid of clutters not belonging to clothes. Clutters are handled in two ways. For predictable clutters like human skin, a common cause of occlusion, we build a skin detector using techniques similar to what described

---

[1] Here we obtain a quick initial guess of the clothes location from face detection. Face detection [9, 12, 2] can currently achieve better accuracy than face recognition so results derived from face detection can be complimentary to face recognition results. For example, profile faces can be detected (so are the corresponding clothes), but they present a challenge for state-of-the-art face recognition algorithms.

(a)   (b)

Fig. 1. (a) initial estimation from face detection (shown by the dashed yellow lines, small red circles show the eye positions); (b) refined segmentation by maximizing the difference between people (shown by the solid green lines)

in next section. More details on skin detection will be given in Section 2.4. For more random clutters not persistent across pictures, we diminish their influence in the feature extraction step (Section 2.2).

2.2 Clothes Representation (or Feature Extraction)

After extracting clothes from an image, the next issue is to represent it quantitatively: clothes representation (or feature extraction). In the literature, there are generally two types of features being extracted: local features and global features. Local features have recently received a lot of research attention (such as [6, 1, 7, 11]) and have been successfully used in some recognition systems. However, most local features are selected based on some kind of local extrema (e.g. with 'maximum entropy' or 'maximum change'), which cannot work if the clothes under consideration is a smooth colored region without textures or patterns (e.g. a single-colored T-shirt). Then how about global features like color histogram and/or orientation histogram? Color histogram suffers when lighting changes. Clothes are often folded and therefore create false edges and self-shadows, which create difficulties for orientation histograms. Thus some more effective features are desired. To take advantage of global representations (which can be more robust to pose changes), the features extracted will be histograms of 'something'. But unlike color histograms or orientation histograms, we want the 'something' to be representative patches for clothes under consideration and to exclude random clutters. In order to achieve that, we devise the following feature extraction method - the representive patches are learned automatically from a set of clothes.

The method uses code-word (representative patches) frequency as feature vectors. The code-words are learned as follows. Overlapped small image patches (e.g. 7x7 pixel patches with two neighboring patches 3 pixels apart) are taken from each normalized clothes piece (according to the size of faces - from face detection module). All the patches from all the clothes pieces in the image set are gathered. If a small patch is of 7x7 pixels, and the total number of small patches is N, we have N 147-dimensional (3 color channels for each pixel) vectors.

In order to get rid of noise and make the computation efficient, principle component analysis (PCA) is used to reduce the dimensionality of these vectors.

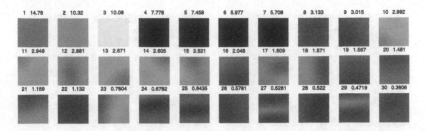

Fig. 2. Examples of code-words obtained. The occurrence frequency of these code-words in a clothes piece is used as the feature vector.

Each small patch is represented by projections under the first k (we use $k = 15$) principle components. Vector quantization (e.g. K-means clustering) is then run on these N k-dimensional vectors to obtain code-words. The Mahalanobis distance, given by $d(x_1, x_2) = \sqrt{(x_1 - x_2)^T \Sigma^{-1}(x_1 - x_2)}$ for any two vectors x_1 and x_2 (where Σ is the covariance matrix), is used for K-means clustering. The number of code-words (i.e. the number of clusters for K-means) can vary according to the complexity of the data. 30 code-words are used in our experiments. Figure 2 shows code-words obtained (i.e. centers of k-means clustering) for the image set including the image in Figure 1.

By vector quantization, each small patch is quantized into one of the code-words, and one clothes piece can be represented by the vector describing the frequency of these code-words. Suppose that the number of code-words is C, then this code-word frequency vector is C-dimensional, $V_{thiscloth} = [v_1, \cdots v_i, \cdots, v_C]$, with each component $v_i = \frac{n_i^{\cdots\cdots}}{n^{\cdots\cdots\cdots}}$, where $n_i^{thiscloth}$ is the number of occurrence of code-word i in the clothes piece and $n^{thiscloth}$ is the total number of small patches in the clothes piece.

The above feature extraction method has the following advantages for clothes recognition. 1) The clustering process selects consistent features as representative patches (code-words) and is more immune to background clutters which are not consistently present since small image patches from non-persistent background are less likely to form a cluster. 2) It uses color and texture information at the same time, and it can handle both smooth and highly textured regions. 3) Code-word frequency counts all the small patches and does not rely on any particular features. Hence it can handle pose changes to a certain degree. 4) Compared to color histograms, it is more robust to lighting changes. Image patches corresponding to the same clothes part can have different appearance due to lighting changes. For example, a green patch can have different brightness and saturation. Through PCA dimension reduction and using Mahalanobis distance, these patches are more likely to belong to the same cluster than to the same color bin for color histogram.

2.3 Similarity Computation

The similarity between two pieces of clothes is computed in a way similar to [11]. Each component of the code-word frequency vector is multiplied by $\log(\frac{1}{w_.})$, where w_i is the percentage of small patches quantized into code-word i among all the N patches. By putting these weights, higher priorities are given to those code-words (features) occurring less frequently. This is based on the idea that less frequent features can be more distinctive therefore more important.

The similarity score of two pieces of clothes is given by the normalized scalar product (cosine of angle) of their weighted code-word frequency vectors.

2.4 Skin Detection

As described in section 2.1, skin is a common type of clutter. However, general skin detection is not a trivial matter due to lighting changes. Fortunately for a set of images, skin from faces and from limbs usually looks similar. Therefore a skin detector can be learned from faces.

Learning Skin Code-words from Faces. The representive skin patches (code-words for skin detection) are learned from faces. First, small skin patches are obtained from faces (majorly cheek part). Each small skin patch is represented by the mean of each color channel. K-means clustering are then performed on these 3-dimensional vectors. The centers from k-means clustering form the code-words for skin detection.

Detect Skin in Clothes. In order to decide whether a small patch is skin or not, we first get its mean of three color channels, and then compute its Mahalanobis distance to each code-word. If the smallest distance is less than a pre-defined threshold and the patch satisfies certain smoothness criterion, the patch is taken as skin. The smoothness of a patch is measured by the variance of luminance. Only those non-skin patches will be used for further computation.

3 Integrating Clothes Context with Face Recognition

The clothes recognition scheme presented in the previous section tells how similar a pair of clothes pieces are. To achieve higher human recognition accuracy, clothes cues are to be integrated with face cues. These combination results provide similarity measurements for clustering (section 4).

For any pair of person images, let x_f be the score from face recognition (e.g. [5]), x_c be the score from clothes recognition. Let random variable Y indicate whether the pair is from the same person or not: $Y = 1$ means from the same person and $Y = 0$ means otherwise. We want to estimate the probability of the pair belonging to the same individual given certain face and clothes scores $P(Y = 1|x_f, x_c)$. In linear logistic regression,

$$P(Y = 1|x_f, x_c) = \frac{1}{1 + \exp(-w_f x_f - w_c x_c - w_0)} \quad (1)$$

where $\bar{w} = [w_f, w_c, w_0]$ are parameters to be learned. The best $\bar{w}$, which maximizes the log-likelihood of a set of training examples, can be obtained iteratively through Newton-Raphson's method.

In testing, for any pair of face recognition and clothes recognition scores, we plug them into equation (1), and get $P(Y = 1|x_f, x_c)$, i.e., the probability of being from the same person. Other cue combination algorithms, such as using Fisher linear discriminant analysis and mixture of experts ([4]), were also experimented. They gave close results for our application though the mixture of experts method is potentially more powerful. Linear logistic regression is adopted here because it is simple and works well. It also provides a good way for handling the cases of face or clothes information missing.

3.1   Recognition When Face or Clothes Are Missing

While one advantage of using clothes context is to help improve human recognition accuracy, another is that it makes human recognition possible when face recognition results are unavailable (e.g. faces are occluded or profile to back view of faces). Clothes information can also be missing due to occlusion or become unreliable for images taken on different days (events) or when different people in the same picture wearing the same clothes. Hence we need to handle the case of face or clothes information missing. The similarity measurements under all the situations (with face recognition only, clothes recognition only, and face and clothes combined) need to be compatible so that they can be compared directly and fairly.

Using the same notations as in the previous section, when face or clothes scores are missing, $P(Y = 1|x_c)$ or $P(Y = 1|x_f)$ needs to be computed. The compatibility requirement is satisfied if $P(Y = 1|x_f)$ and $P(Y = 1|x_c)$ are the marginal probabilities of $P(Y = 1|x_f, x_c)$. By Bayesian rule and equation (1),

$$P(Y = 1|x_c) = \int_{x} \frac{1}{1 + \exp(-w_f x_f - w_c x_c - w_0)} P(x_f|x_c)\, dx_f$$

If we assume that $x_f = C \cdot x_c + C_0$ for some constant C and C_0, i.e., $P(x_f|x_c) = \delta(x_f - C x_c - C_0)$, then

$$P(Y = 1|x_c) = \frac{1}{1 + \exp(-w_f \cdot C \cdot x_c - w_f \cdot C_0 - w_c x_c - w_0)}$$

$$= \frac{1}{1 + \exp(-w_c' x_c - w_0')} \tag{2}$$

Therefore, $P(Y = 1|x_c)$ is also in the form of a logistic function, so does $P(Y = 1|x_f)$. The parameters of these logistic functions such as w_c', and w_0' can be estimated in a similar fashion to those of equation (1).

Note that equation (2) is derived assuming that face scores are a linear function of clothes scores so that only clothes information determines the similarity between a pair of person images. This could be a reasonable assumption when face information missing. We tested the compatibility of computed $P(Y = 1|x_f, x_c)$, $P(Y = 1|x_f)$ and $P(Y = 1|x_c)$ in experiments.

3.2 Handling the Case of People Wearing the Same Clothes

People wearing the same (or similar) clothes poses difficulties for incorporating clothes information. Two persons in one picture usually are not the same individual. Thus if in one picture, two persons wear the same (or similar) clothes, we need to discard the clothes information. The clothes information also becomes possibly misleading when the pair-wise similarity between other clothes pieces and either of those two is high. The clothes information is therefore treated as missing for these cases, and similarities are computed as in section 3.1.

4 Human Clustering with Hard Constraints

The previous sections depict a clothes recognition algorithm as well as how to integrate clothes context with faces into one similarity measure. These pair-wise similarity measurements provide grounds for clustering. This section focuses on the clustering algorithm and how to put logic-based contexts (such as some hard constraints) into clustering.

4.1 Spectral Clustering

Spectral clustering methods cluster points by eigenvalues and eigenvectors of a matrix derived from the pair-wise similarities between points. Spectral clustering is often looked as a graph partitioning problem: each point is a node in the graph and similarity between points gives weight of the edge. In human clustering, each point is a person's image, and similarity measurements are from face and/or clothes recognition.

One effective spectral clustering method used in computer vision is normalized cuts [10], with generalization in [15]. The normalized cuts criterion is to maximize links (similarities) within each cluster and to minimize links between clusters. Suppose that we have a set of points $S = \{s_1, \ldots, s_N\}$, and we want to cluster them into K clusters. Let W be the $N \times N$ weight matrix with each term W_{ij} being the similarity between points s_i and s_j, and let D denote the diagonal matrix with the i-th diagonal element being the sum of W's i^{th} row (i.e. the degree for the ith node). The clustering results can be represented by a $N \times K$ partition matrix X, with $X_{ik} = 1$ if and only if point s_i belongs to the kth cluster and 0 otherwise. Let X_l denote the lth column vector of X, $1 \leq l \leq K$. X_l is the membership indicator vector for the lth cluster. Using this notations, the normalized cut criterion is to find the best partition matrix X^* which can maximize $\varepsilon(X) = \frac{1}{K} \sum_{l=1}^{K} \frac{X_l^\top W X_l}{X_l^\top D X_l}$.

Relaxing the binary partition matrix constraint on X and using Rayleigh-Ritz theorem, it can be shown that the optimal solution in the continuous domain are derived through the K largest eigenvectors of $D^{-1/2} W D^{-1/2}$. Let v_i be the ith largest eigenvector of $D^{-1/2} W D^{-1/2}$, and $V^K = [v_1, v_2, \ldots, v_K]$. Then the continuous optimum of $\varepsilon(X)$ can be achieved by X^*_{conti}, the row normalized version of V^K (each row of X^*_{conti} has unit length). In fact, the optimal solution is not unique - the optima are a set of matrices up to an orthonormal transformation: $\{X^*_{conti}O : O^T O = I_K\}$, where I_K is the $K \times K$ identity matrix.

In [15], a repulsion matrix is introduced to model the dissimilarities between points. The clustering goal becomes to maximize within-cluster similarities and between-cluster dissimilarities, but to minimize their compliments. Let A be the matrix quantifying similarities (affinity matrix), R be the matrix representing dissimilarities (repulsion matrix), and D_A and D_R be the diagonal matrices corresponding to the row sum of A and R respectively. Define $\hat{W} = A - R + D_R$ and $\hat{D} = D_A + D_R$, then the goal is to find the partition matrix X which can maximize $\frac{1}{K} \sum_{l=1}^{K} \frac{X_{\cdot}^{!} \hat{W} X_{\cdot}}{X_{\cdot}^{!} \hat{D} X_{\cdot}}$. The continuous optima can be found through the K largest eigenvectors of $\hat{D}^{-1/2} \hat{W} \hat{D}^{-1/2}$ in a similar fashion to the case of without a repulsion matrix.

Since a continuous solution can be found by solving eigensystems, the above methods are fast and can achieve global optimum in the continuous domain. However, for clustering, a continuous solution needs to be discretized. In [15], discretization is done iteratively to find the binary partition matrix $X^*_{discrete}$ which can minimize $\|X_{discrete} - X^*_{conti}O\|^2$, where $\|M\|$ is the Frobenius norm of matrix M: $\|M\| = \sqrt{tr(MM^T)}$, O is any orthonormal matrix, and $X^*_{conti}O$ is a continuous optimum.

4.2   Incorporating More Context Cues: Enforcing Hard Constraints

Some logic-based contexts can be expressed as hard constraints, e.g., one useful negative hard constraint is that different persons in one picture should be different individuals. It is desirable to be able to enforce these constraints in human clustering. However, incorporating priors (such as hard constraints) poses a challenge for spectral clustering algorithms. In [16, 15], a method to impose positive constraints (two points mush belong to the same cluster) was proposed, but the constraints may be violated in the discretization step. To the best of our knowledge, there is no previous work which can enforce negative hard constraints (two points cannot be in the same cluster) in spectral clustering methods. This section explores how to enforce hard constraints, negative as well as positive.

Using the same notations as in section 4.1, if s_i and s_j are in the same picture, we want to make sure s_i and s_j are in different clusters. To achieve that, the corresponding term in the affinity matrix A_{ij} is set to be zero. A repulsion matrix R is also used to enhance the constraints: R_{ij} is set to be 1 if s_i and s_j cannot be in the same cluster. However, this is not enough: there is no guarantee that the hard constraints are satisfied. We resort to the discretization step.

A constrained K-means algorithm is presented in [13] to integrate hard constraints into K-means clustering. We want to take advantage of that: we propose to use constrained K-means in the discretization step to enforce hard constraints. Our work was inspired by [8], where K-means was used in the discretization step. But in [8], a repulsion matrix was not used, the use of K-means with a repulsion matrix was not justified, regular K-means instead of constrained K-means was used, and therefore no constraints were imposed.

In the following, we will first justify the use of K-means (with or without a repulsion matrix), and therefore the use of constrained K-means. We take each row of X^*_{conti} as a point, and perform K-means clustering [2]. If the ith row of X^*_{conti} belongs to the kth cluster, then assign the original point s_i to the kth cluster. We argue that this K-means clustering can achieve as good results as the best partition matrix $X^*_{discrete}$ minimizing $\|X_{discrete} - X^*_{conti}O\|^2$.

Proposition 1. For any orthonormal matrix O, row vectors of $X^*_{conti}O$ and X^*_{conti} have the same K-means clustering results under the following condition: if c_l is the lth initial center for X^*_{conti}, then c_lO is the lth initial center for $X^*_{conti}O$.

Proposition 2. Suppose $X^*_{discrete}$ and O^* are the discrete partition matrix and rotation matrix minimizing $\|X_{discrete} - X^*_{conti}O\|^2$. If rows of $K \times K$ identity matrix I_K are taken as cluster centers, then one iteration of K-means clustering on row vectors of $X^*_{conti}O^*$ achieves the same clustering results as what represented by partition matrix $X^*_{discrete}$. Further, if $\|X^*_{discrete} - X^*_{conti}O^*\|^2$ is small, then the cluster centers will not go far away from rows of I_K, and therefore the K-means clustering on rows of $X^*_{conti}O^*$ will converge to the same clustering results as $X^*_{discrete}$.

From propositions 1 and 2, if $\|X^*_{discrete} - X^*_{conti}O^*\|^2$ is small, and rows of $(O^*)^{-1}$ are taken as initial cluster centers, then K-means clustering on X^*_{conti} achieves the same results as $X^*_{discrete}$. Small $\|X^*_{discrete} - X^*_{conti}O^*\|^2$ means that the points actually form good clusters, otherwise no clustering algorithm can work well. A good approximation of $(O^*)^{-1}$ can be found by finding orthogonal vectors among rows of X^*_{conti}.

K-means clustering on rows of X^*_{conti} with proper initializations (or through multiple initializations) can achieve as good results [3] as minimizing $\|X_{discrete} - X^*_{conti}O\|^2$. On the other hand, hard constraints can be enforced by constrained K-means. So to incorporate hard constraints, K-means is a better discretization method.

Using constrained K-means in discretization step is to take row vectors of X^*_{conti} as points and run constrained K-means on them. In each iteration of the constrained K-means algorithm [13], when a point is assigned to a cluster, two criteria are used: (1) distance to the center of the cluster; and (2) whether the hard constraint is satisfied. A point is assigned to the closest cluster not violating hard constraints. Therefore, the constrained K-means guarantees that the hard constraints are satisfied.

---

[2] One might wonder what the difference is between performing K-means clustering on the original points and here at the discretization step. K-means clustering can work here because previous steps in spectral clustering have possibly transformed non-convex clusters into convex clusters (See more examples in [8]).

[3] In [17], similar observation is presented through simulation, for the case of regular K-means and without a repulsion matrix.

5   Experiments

Experiments are performed on real consumer photos. Collections from three families are used (Table 1). Face detection ([2]) is first run on these photos, and persons' identities are manually labeled to provide ground truth for evaluation (only those individuals with 8 or more pictures are labeled). The data include a variety of scenes such as vacations in theme parks, a group of friends mountain climbing, having parties, fun activities at home, and children's sports event.

5.1   Proposed Clothes Features vs. Color Histogram

The proposed clothes features (sections 2.2 and 2.3) are compared with color histograms (using χ^2 distance in CIElab space). To make the comparison fair, the same clothes detection and segmentation method (section 2.1) is used. Figure 3(a) shows the results by receiver operating characteristics (ROC) curves on five days' images (from families 1 and 2), with around 100 pictures. Any pair of clothes pieces from the same person the same day are considered as a positive example, and any pair of clothes pieces from different people are considered as a negative example. These results show that the proposed method outperforms color histograms. More detailed studies reveal that the advantages of the new feature representation are more dominant when lighting condition changes.

5.2   Integrating Clothes and Hard Constraints with Face Recognition

Clothes recognition results are to be combined with face recognition to provide pair-wise similarity measurements for clustering. Raw face scores are obtained from a face recognition module ([3, 5]). Logistic regression is used to combine face and clothes recognition results (section 3). The parameters of those logistic functions are learned using data from another family with around 200 faces and clothes pieces.

Figure 4 shows an illustrative example using images from a children's party. Figure 4(b) is from face recognition only. Figure 4(c) gives results using additional contexts (clothes recognition and enforcing the constraint that different persons in one image must belong to different clusters). Five clusters are used,

Table 1. Summary of image data. Time span of each collection is shown in the second column. The third column gives the total number of days when the pictures were taken.

	time span	number of days	number of pictures with person	number of faces labeled	number of persons (clusters)	number of faces for each person
family 1	Apr-Aug 2002	13	182	342	8	126,68,45,35,26,16,15,11
family 2	May-Nov 2003	14	149	224	16	42,16,16,16,16,14,13,12,11, 11,11,11,10,10,9,9,8
family 3	May-Dec 2002	22	165	203	3	85,69,49

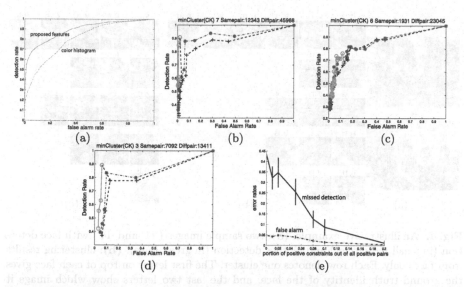

Fig. 3. **(a)**: ROC curves: the proposed clothes features (EER: 20.1%) vs. color histograms (EER:28.3%). **(b), (c), and (d)**: clustering results on family collections 1, 2, and 3 (Table 1), respectively. Blue dashed (with '+'): face recognition only; red dashdot (with '*'): clothes combined with faces, but without constraints; green solid curves (with 'o'): clothes and faces combined, and with constraints enforced. The most upper-right points of blue dashed (with '+') and red dashdot (with '*') curves correspond to the number of clusters being one, and from right to left with the increase of number of clusters. The minimum number of clusters for all the samples to satisfy hard negative constraints is displayed on the title 'minCluster(CK)'. The first point (from top right) of each green solid curve ('o') gives the results for that minimum number of clusters. The dashed curve in each graph connects results under that minimum number of clusters. 'Samepair' and 'Diffpair' on the title mean the total number of positive and negative pairs, respectively. **(e)**: results of adding positive constraints. The vertical bars on the curves give standard deviation (from 30 runs for each fixed proportion).

which is the minimum number of clusters in order to satisfy the hard constraint. Figure 4 illustrates the benefits of using contexts. For instance, in the top row of Figure 4(b), there are faces from persons 'M' and 'R', and two faces from one image are in the same cluster ('R I4' and 'M I4'). This is corrected by using contexts as shown in Figure 4(c).

For **images collected on multiple days**, the affinity matrix is constructed as follows. For any pair of person images, if they are from pictures taken on the same day, both face and clothes information are used; otherwise, only face information is used. Clothes information is treated as missing if clothes are occluded or different people wear similar clothes. To enforce the negative hard constraint that two persons in one picture must be different individuals, repulsion matrix and constraint K-means are applied.

We use Rand index ([13]) to characterize clustering performance. Suppose we have N pieces of person images, any clustering results can be viewed as a collection of $N * (N - 1)/2$ pairwise decisions. A false alarm happens when a

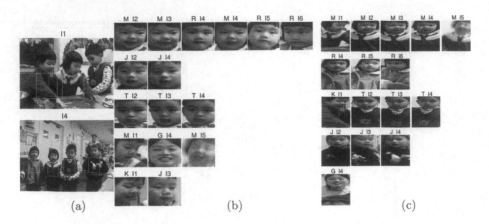

Fig. 4. An illustrative example. (**a**): two sample images ('I1' and 'I4') with face detection (in small red circles) and clothes detection (in green lines). (**b**): clustering results from faces only. Each row denotes one cluster. The first letter on top of each face gives the ground truth identity of the face, and the last two letters show which image it comes from. (**c**): results from faces plus contexts (clothes recognition and the hard constraint that two faces in one image belonging to different clusters).

pair actually from different individuals, but the algorithm claims they are the same individual. A true positive (detection) is when a pair actually from the same individual and the algorithm also claims so.

Clustering performance varies with the number of clusters. We experiment with different number of clusters: from one cluster to two times of the ground truth number of clusters (see Table 1). In applications, the desired number of clusters may be input by the user. Figure 3(b), (c), and (d) show the results on family collections 1, 2, and 3, respectively. From these curves, we can see that (1) clustering performance generally improves with the use of clothes; (2) the compatibility of logistic functions in section 3 is verified to a certain degree since similarities from face and clothes and similarities from face only are used in one affinity matrix, which outperforms the affinity matrix from face only; (3) hard constraints can help improve the results. Note that the performance improvements due to hard constraints are more dominant in Figure 3(b) and (d) than in (c). One possible reason is that the set of labeled faces from family 2 belong to 16 individuals. So for any random pair, the probability of belonging to different individuals is high, and hard negative constraints provide less information.

Positive constraints (meaning that a pair of person images must belong to the same individual) can also be applied. In practice, positive constraints are available through user feedback. Here we randomly choose a certain number of positive pairs to simulate the situation. Figure 3(e) shows experimental results on images from family 2. The ground truth number of clusters, 16, is used. Figure 3(e) indicates that positive constraints can improve clustering performance, especially for the detection rates.

6   Conclusions and Future Work

In this paper, we have developed a clothes recognition method which can work well for different types of clothes (smooth or highly textured), and under imaging condition changes. A principled way is provided to integrate clothes recognition results with face recognition results, and the cases when face or clothes information is missing are handled naturally. A constrained spectral clustering algorithm, which can utilize face, clothes and other context information (e.g. persons from one picture should be in different clusters), has been presented. Hard constraints are enforced in the spectral clustering algorithm so that logic-based context cues and user feedbacks can be used effectively. Picture-taken-time is used when face and clothes recognition results are combined. Experiments on real consumer photos show significant performance improvements. Future work includes exploring how to select the number of clusters automatically, although in human clustering applications, it can possibly be input by users.

References

1. R. Fergus, P. Perona, and A. Zisserman, "Object class recognition by unsupervised scale-invariant learning", In *CVPR*, 2003.
2. S. Ioffe, "Red eye detection with machine learning", In *Proc. ICIP*, 2003.
3. S. Ioffe, "Probabilistic linear discriminant analysis", In *Proc. ECCV*, 2006.
4. M.I. Jordan and R.A. Jacobs, "Hierarchical mixtures of experts and the em algorithm", *Neural Computation*, 6:181–214, 1994.
5. T. Leung, "Texton correlation for recognition", In *ECCV*, 2004.
6. D. Lowe, "Object recognition from local scale-invariant features", In *ICCV*, 1999.
7. K. Mikolajczyk and C. Schmid, "A performance evaluation of local descriptors", In *CVPR*, 2003.
8. A.Y. Ng, M.I. Jordan, and Y. Weiss, "On spectral clustering: Analysis and an algorithm", In *NIPS 14*, 2002.
9. H. Schneiderman and T. Kanade, "A statistical method for 3d object detection applied to faces and cars", In *Proc. CVPR*, 2000.
10. J. Shi and J. Malik, "Normalized cuts and image segmentation", In *Proc. CVPR*, pages 731–7, June 1997.
11. J. Sivic and A. Zisserman, "Video google: A text retrieval approach to object matching in videos", In *Proc. ICCV*, 2003.
12. P. Viola and M. Jones, "Rapid object detection using a boosted cascade of simple features", In *Proc. CVPR*, 2001.
13. K. Wagstaff, C. Cardie, S. Rogers, and S. Schroedl, "Contrained k-means clustering with background knowledge", In *Proc. ICML*, 2001.
14. Y. Weiss, "Segmentation using eigenvectors", In *Proc. ICCV*, 1999.
15. Stella X. Yu, *Computational Models of Perceptual Organization*, Ph.d. thesis, Carnegie Mellon University, 2003.
16. S.X. Yu and J. Shi, "Grouping with bias", In *NIPS*, 2001.
17. S.X. Yu and J. Shi, "Multiclass spectral clustering", In *Proc. ICCV*, 2003.
18. L. Zhang, L. Chen, M. Li, and H. Zhang, "Automated annotation of human faces in family albums", In *MM'03*, 2003.

Robust Expression-Invariant Face Recognition from Partially Missing Data

Alexander M. Bronstein, Michael M. Bronstein, and Ron Kimmel

Dept. of Computer Science, Technion – Israel Institute of Technology,
Haifa 32000, Israel
{alexbron, bronstein}@ieee.com, ron@cs.technion.ac.il

Abstract. Recent studies on three-dimensional face recognition proposed to model facial expressions as isometries of the facial surface. Based on this model, expression-invariant signatures of the face were constructed by means of approximate isometric embedding into flat spaces. Here, we apply a new method for measuring isometry-invariant similarity between faces by embedding one facial surface into another. We demonstrate that our approach has several significant advantages, one of which is the ability to handle partially missing data. Promising face recognition results are obtained in numerical experiments even when the facial surfaces are severely occluded.

1 Introduction

Face recognition deals with the problem of identifying a human subject using information describing his or her face. A description of a subject to be identified (*probe*), is compared to those stored in the database of subjects with known identity (usually referred to as *gallery*). The probe is accepted if identified with one of the gallery subject, or otherwise rejected, based on some distance function. Ideally, there should be no false acceptances or false rejections.

Recently, three-dimensional (3D) face recognition has become an emerging modality, trying to use 3D geometry of the face for accurate identification of the subject. While traditional two-dimensional (2D) face recognition methods suffer from sensitivity to factors such as illumination, head pose and the use of cosmetics, 3D methods appear to be more robust to these factors. Yet, the problem of *facial expressions* is a major issue in 3D face recognition, since the geometry of the face significantly changes as a result of facial expressions. One of the focuses of the recent Face Recognition Grand Challenge (FRGC) competition is robustness to facial expressions [1, 2].

In [3], we introduced an expression-invariant 3D face recognition method. Our main thesis is the *isometric model*, according to which facial expressions are modelled as isometries of the facial surface. The subject's identity is associated with the intrinsic geometry of the surface (i.e. its metric structure), which appears to be nearly expression-invariant [3]. Getting rid of the extrinsic geometry of the surface and using its intrinsic geometry only, an expression-invariant representation of the face is constructed. We used the approach presented by Elad

A. Leonardis, H. Bischof, and A. Pinz (Eds.): ECCV 2006, Part III, LNCS 3953, pp. 396–408, 2006.

and Kimmel [4]. Mapping the surface in an isometric way into $\mathbb{R}^3$, where the original geodesic distances are replaced with the Euclidean ones, one creates a representation of the intrinsic geometry, which can be simply handled as a rigid surface. Such a mapping is termed *isometric embedding*. Elad and Kimmel used a numerical procedure called *multidimensional scaling* (MDS) [5] to compute the embedding.

Face recognition based on the isometric embedding approach is simple and computationally-efficient (in [3], a real-time system that acquires and matches two surfaces in less than 5 *sec* was obtained). The disadvantage is the fact that in general, a surface cannot be isometrically embedded into $\mathbb{R}^m$, and therefore, such a mapping introduces an inevitable distortion of the distances (*embedding error* or *metric distortion*), which reduces the recognition accuracy. Attempts to reduce the embedding error were made in [6, 7, 8] by resorting to non-Euclidean embedding spaces. In [8], it was conjectured that smaller embedding error results in better face recognition accuracy. This conjecture was proved experimentally using two-dimensional spheres with different radii as the embedding space.

The main limitation of the different embedding spaces used beforehand was the demand that the geodesic distances are expressed *analytically*. This practically limits the possibilities to spheres and flat domains. It is obvious, however, that the embedding of one surface into another results in *zero* metric distortion if the surfaces are isometric. If the surfaces are not isometric, the embedding error could be a measure of how different their intrinsic geometry is.

Unfortunately, a facial surface has a complicated metric structure and the geodesic distances can not be expressed analytically. The price we have to pay in order to perform embedding into such spaces is that the geodesic distances must be computed numerically. However, the apparent advantages seem to justify it. In addition to higher accuracy, this kind of embedding allows to compare *partially missing* surfaces. This is especially important in practical 3D face recognition, where due to acquisition imperfections the facial surfaces can be occluded. The ability to handle partially missing data also frees us from the need to perform sophisticated cropping identical for all faces, which is required in [3].

This paper consists of five sections. In Section 2, we review the expression-invariant face recognition method based on the isometric model. In Section 3, we introduce the notion of partial embedding and outline a recent generalization of MDS as a way to compute it [9]. Section 4 outlines a hierarchical matching scheme for one-to-many face recognition with very large databases. Section 5 is devoted to experimental results. We show that our approach works accurately even in a setting where the facial surface is severely occluded. Section 6 concludes the paper.

2 Expression-Invariant Face Recognition

Our starting point is the isometric model of facial expressions, introduced in [3]. The facial surface is described as a smooth compact connected two-dimensional Riemannian manifold (surface), denoted by S. The *minimal geodesics* between

$s_1, s_2 \in \mathcal{S}$ are curves of minimum length on $\mathcal{S}$ connecting s_1 and s_2. The geodesics are denoted by $C_{\mathcal{S}}^*(s_1, s_2)$. The *geodesic distances* refer to the lengths of the minimum geodesics and are denoted by $d_{\mathcal{S}}(s_1, s_2) = \text{length}(C_{\mathcal{S}}^*(s_1, s_2))$. A transformation $\psi : \mathcal{S} \to \mathcal{Q}$ is called an *isometry* if $d_{\mathcal{S}}(s_1, s_2) = d_{\mathcal{Q}}(\psi(s_1), \psi(s_2))$ for all $s_1, s_2 \in \mathcal{S}$. In other words, an isometry preserves the intrinsic metric structure of the surface.

The isometric model, assuming facial expressions to be isometries of some "neutral facial expression", is based on the intuitive observation that the facial skin stretches only slightly. All expressions of a face are assumed to be *intrinsically* equivalent (i.e. have the same metric structure), and *extrinsically* different. Broadly speaking, the intrinsic geometry of the facial surface can be attributed to the subject's identity, while the extrinsic geometry is attributed to the facial expression. The isometric model tacitly assumes that the expressions preserve the *topology* of the surface. This assumption is valid for most regions of the face except the mouth. Opening the mouth changes the topology of the surface by virtually creating a "hole", which was treated in [10] by imposing topological constraints.

The goal of expression-invariant face recognition, under the assumption of the isometric model, is to perform an isometry-invariant matching of facial surfaces. In other words, we are looking for some distance function $d(\mathcal{S}, \mathcal{Q})$ to compare between two facial surfaces $\mathcal{S}$ and $\mathcal{Q}$, such that $d(\mathcal{S}, f(\mathcal{S})) = 0$ for all isometries f of $\mathcal{S}$. Since the geodesic distances are an obvious isometry-invariant, one could think of $d(\mathcal{S}, \mathcal{Q})$ comparing the geodesic distances on $\mathcal{S}$ and $\mathcal{Q}$. However, in practice only *sampled* versions of the surfaces are available, and therefore we have the intrinsic geometry of $\mathcal{S}$ and $\mathcal{Q}$ represented as *finite metric spaces* $(\{s_1, ..., s_N\}, \mathbf{\Delta}_{\mathcal{S}})$ and $(\{q_1, ..., q_M\}, \mathbf{\Delta}_{\mathcal{Q}})$, where the $N \times N$ matrix $\mathbf{\Delta}_{\mathcal{S}} = (d_{\mathcal{S}}(s_i, s_j))$ and the $M \times M$ matrix $\mathbf{\Delta}_{\mathcal{Q}} = (d_{\mathcal{Q}}(q_i, q_j))$ denote the pair-wise geodesic distances (which, in practice, must be computed numerically) between the samples of $\mathcal{S}$ and $\mathcal{Q}$. There is no guarantee that different instances of the same facial surface are sampled at the same points, nor that the number of samples is the same. Moreover, even if the samples are the same, they can be ordered arbitrarily. This ambiguity, which theoretically requires examining all the permutations between the points on the two surfaces, makes impractical the use of the geodesic distances *per se* for isometry-invariant surface matching. Yet, we point to a recent fundamental paper by Mémoli and Sapiro [11], which relates the permutation-based distance between surfaces represented as point clouds to the Gromov-Hausdorff distance and shows a probabilistic framework allowing to approximate it without computing all the permutations.

2.1   Isometric Embedding

An alternative proposed by Elad and Kimmel [4] and adopted in [3] for face recognition is to avoid dealing explicitly with the matrix of geodesic distances and represent $\mathcal{S}$ as a subset of $\mathbb{R}^m$, such that the original intrinsic geometry is approximately preserved. Such a procedure is called an *isometric embedding*. The image of $\mathcal{S}$ under the embedding is referred to as the *canonical form* of $\mathcal{S}$, and

$\mathbb{R}^m$ as the *embedding space*. As a result of isometric embedding, the canonical forms of all the isometries of $\mathcal{S}$ are identical, up to the isometry group in $\mathbb{R}^m$ (rotations, translations and reflections), which is easy to deal with. The distance $d(\mathcal{S}, \mathcal{Q})$ is computed by comparing the canonical forms of $\mathcal{S}$ and $\mathcal{Q}$ in a rigid way.

In the discrete setting, isometric embedding is a mapping between two finite metric spaces

$$\varphi : (\{s_1, ..., s_N\} \subset \mathcal{S}, \boldsymbol{\Delta}_{\mathcal{S}}) \to (\{x_1, ..., x_N\} \subset \mathbb{R}^m, \mathbf{D}), \tag{1}$$

such that $d_{\mathcal{S}}(s_i, s_j) = d_{\mathbb{R}^\cdot}(x_i, x_j)$ for all $i, j = 1, ..., N$. Here $d_{\mathbb{R}^\cdot}$ denotes the Euclidean metric, and $\mathbf{D} = (d_{\mathbb{R}^\cdot}(x_i, x_j))$ is the matrix of pair-wise geodesic distances between the points in the embedding space. In practice, this matrix is computed approximately using the *fast marching method* (FMM) [12].

2.2 Multidimensional Scaling

Unfortunately, it appears that a general surface like the human face usually cannot be isometrically embedded into $\mathbb{R}^m$ of any finite dimension [13], and therefore, such an embedding introduces a distortion of the geodesic distances, referred to as the *embedding error*. Yet, though an exact isometric embedding of $\mathcal{S}$ into $\mathbb{R}^m$ does not exist, it is possible to compute an approximately isometric embedding, which minimizes the embedding error. In [4], the *raw stress* [5] was used

$$\sigma_{\text{raw}}(\mathbf{X}; \boldsymbol{\Delta}_{\mathcal{S}}) = \sum_{i > j} \left(d_{\mathbb{R}^\cdot}(\mathbf{x}_i, \mathbf{x}_j) - d_{\mathcal{S}}(s_i, s_j) \right)^2 . \tag{2}$$

as the embedding error criterion. Here $\boldsymbol{\Delta}_{\mathcal{S}}$ denotes the geodesic distances matrix of the surface $\mathcal{S}$, and $\mathbf{X}$ is a $N \times m$ matrix of coordinates in $\mathbb{R}^m$. The solution

$$\mathbf{X}_{\mathcal{S}} = \underset{\mathbf{X}}{\operatorname{argmin}} \, \sigma_{\text{raw}}(\mathbf{X}; \boldsymbol{\Delta}_{\mathcal{S}}) \tag{3}$$

obtained by gradient descent minimization of the stress is the discrete canonical form of $\mathcal{S}$, and the whole process is called *multidimensional scaling* (MDS). The optimization problem (3) is non-convex and therefore convex optimization algorithms cannot guarantee global convergence. Yet, this problem can be usually resolved using good intialization or employing multiscale or multigrid optimization [14].

2.3 Canonical Form Matching

The similarity function between two surfaces $\mathcal{S}$ and $\mathcal{Q}$ in the canonical forms (CF) algorithm is computed as the Euclidean distance between the vector of P-th order high-dimensional moments of the corresponding canonical forms $\mathbf{X}_{\mathcal{S}}$ and $\mathbf{X}_{\mathcal{Q}}$ after alignment [15]

$$d_{\text{CF}}(\mathcal{S}, \mathcal{Q}) = \sum_{p_1 + ... p_\cdot \leq P} \left(\mu_{p_1, ..., p_\cdot}^{\mathbf{X}_{\mathcal{S}}} - \mu_{p_1, ..., p_\cdot}^{\mathbf{X}_{\mathcal{Q}} \mathbf{R} + \mathbf{b}} \right)^2 , \tag{4}$$

where

$$\mu^{\mathbf{X}}_{p_1,\ldots,p.} = \sum_{i=1}^{N} \prod_{j=1}^{m} x_{ij}^{p.}, \tag{5}$$

is the $(p_1, ..., p_m)$-th moment* of $\mathbf{X}$, and $\mathbf{X}_Q \mathbf{R} + \mathbf{b}$ is an m-dimensional Euclidean transformation (rotation, reflection and translation) aligning the canonical forms $\mathbf{X}_S$ and $\mathbf{X}_Q$. In [4], the alignment transformation is obtained by centering the canonical forms, diagonalizing their matrices of second-order moments, and reordering the axes such that the variance values in each axis are decreasing. Alternatively, the alignment can be performed using three fiducial points [3].

2.4 Remarks

The CF approach does not allow exact isometry-invariant surface matching, as the embedding is not exactly isometric and inevitably introduces an error. In other words, generally $d_{\mathrm{CF}}(f(\mathcal{S}), \mathcal{S}) > 0$ for a surface $\mathcal{S}$ and its isometry f. The algorithm is sensitive to the definition of the boundaries of the surfaces, and does not allow for matching of surfaces with different topologies, or more generally, partial matching.

The alignment ambiguity and the use of rigid matching algorithms for the canonical forms poses a restriction on the number of the surface samples. It must be sufficiently large ($N \sim 1000$) in order for the alignment and matching to work accurately. In [3], we found that 2500 samples were required for face recognition with a reasonable recognition rate. The number of points is a major issue in terms of computational complexity, as the cost of the stress and its gradient computation is $\mathcal{O}(N^2)$, while the computation of the geodesic distance matrix is at least $\mathcal{O}(N^2)$.

Another major issue in face recognition with large databases is precomputation of distances between faces. Using the method of moments, in the CF approach it is possible to precompute the moments signatures for all faces in the gallery. When a new probe face has to be matched, its moment signature is computed and efficiently matched to the gallery signatures.

3   Generalized Multidimensional Scaling

The main thesis of this paper is measuring the intrinsic similarity of two facial surfaces by embedding them into each other, based on [9]. Embedding two isometric surfaces into each other results in *zero* embedding error. In the general case when two surfaces are not isometric, the embedding error is a measure of their similarity. Conceptually, the difference between Euclidean and partial embedding is presented in Figure 1.

We assume to be given the model surface $\mathcal{S}$ from the gallery, sampled at N points, and the probe surface $\mathcal{Q}$ sampled at M points (typically, $M \ll N$). Possibly, $\mathcal{Q}$ is partially missing. We are looking for a mapping

$$\varphi : (\{q_1, ..., q_N\} \subset \mathcal{Q}, \mathbf{\Delta}_\mathcal{Q}) \to (\{s_1, ..., s_N\} \subset \mathcal{S}, \mathbf{\Delta}_\mathcal{S}),$$

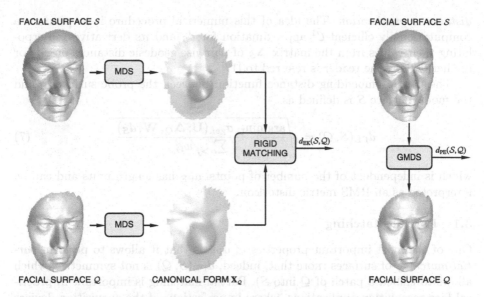

Fig. 1. Schematic representation of face recognition using expression-invariant canonical forms obtained using MDS (left), and the proposed method of embedding one facial surface into another using GMDS (right)

such that $d_Q(q_i, q_j)$ is as close as possible to $d_S(\varphi(q_i), \varphi(q_j))$ for all $i, j = 1, ..., N$. Note that d_S is assumed continuous here, as $s_i = \varphi(q_i)$ can be an arbitrary point. In practice, the values of d_S must be approximated numerically. We refer to such φ as *partial embedding* of Q into S.

In order to compute the partial embedding, we use a procedure similar to MDS, which we call the *generalized* MDS or GMDS [9]. Since our new embedding space S is a general 2D manifold, we have to represent the points on S in their parametric coordinates. Let us assume that Q is given in parametric from by the mapping $\mathbf{u} \in I \subset \mathbb{R}^2 \rightarrow S$, where I is the parametrization domain, which can be assumed to be $[0, 1] \times [0, 1]$. Similarly to the Euclidean case, the *generalized stress* is defined as [9]

$$\sigma_{\text{gen}}(\mathbf{U}; \Delta_Q, \mathbf{W}, d_S) = \sum_{i>j} w_{ij} \left(d_S(\mathbf{u}_i, \mathbf{u}_j) - d_Q(q_i, q_j) \right)^2. \qquad (6)$$

Here $\mathbf{u}_i$, $i = 1, ..., M$ denote the vectors of parametric coordinates of s_i, and $\mathbf{W} = (w_{ij})$ is a symmetric matrix of non-negative weights. In case of full matching, $w_{ij} = 1$ are used. When the probe is partially missing, the weights must be chosen differently [9].

Minimization of the stress is performed iteratively, like in the former case, using gradient-descent type methods or more sophisticated optimization algorithms [16]. Note that, in practice, d_S is available only between N samples of S. Hence, it must be approximated for all the rest of the points. This computation is critical for the GMDS. For that goal we developed the *three-point geodesic distance approximation.* The idea of this numerical procedure is to produce a computationally efficient $\mathcal{C}^1$-approximation for d_S and its derivatives, interpolating their values from the matrix $\boldsymbol{\Delta}_S$ of pairwise geodesic distances on S. For further details, the reader is referred to [17].

The partial embedding distance function between the probe surface Q and the model surface S is defined as

$$d_{\mathrm{PE}}(S, Q) = \sqrt{\frac{\mathrm{argmin}_{\mathbf{U}} \, \sigma_{\mathrm{gen}}(\mathbf{U}; \boldsymbol{\Delta}_Q, \mathbf{W}, d_S)}{\sum_{i>j} w_{ij}}}, \tag{7}$$

which is independent of the number of points. d_{PE} has length units and can be interpreted as an RMS metric distortion.

3.1 Partial Matching

One of the most important properties of d_{PE} is that it allows to perform *partial matching* of surfaces (note that, indeed, $d_{\mathrm{PE}}(S, Q)$ is not symmetric, which allows to embed a patch of Q into S). Partial matching is important in practical face recognition applications, where imperfections of the acquisition devices and occlusions of the face (e.g. when the subject is wearing glasses) result in a partially missing probe surfaces.

Let us assume that we wish to compare two facial surfaces: a model S and a probe Q, which is acquired with occlusions such that only a patch $Q' \subset Q$ is available. If Q' is sufficiently large, $d_{\mathrm{PE}}(S, Q') \approx d_{\mathrm{PE}}(S, Q)$; the difference can be bounded by the diameter of $Q \setminus Q'$ [9]. Yet, it is tacitly assumed that the geodesic distances on Q' are given by $d_{Q'}(q_1, q_2) = d_Q|_{Q'}(q_1, q_2)$ (this notation implies that $d_{Q'}(q_1, q_2) = d_Q(q_1, q_2)$ for all $q_1, q_2 \in Q'$). However, $d_{Q'}$ is computed numerically on Q' and can be inconsistent with $d_Q|_{Q'}$. The problem potentially arises for example with geodesics that touch the boundary $\partial Q'$; such geodesics can be different on Q and Q' (see Figure 2), and the corresponding distance is therefore inconsistent. To resolve this problem, we assign zero weight $w_{ij} = 0$ to every pair of points (q_i, q_j) such that $d_{Q'}(q_i, \partial Q') + d_{Q'}(q_j, \partial Q') < d_{Q'}(q_i, q_j)$ For more details, the reader is referred to [17].

3.2 Comparison to the Canonical Forms Approach

A major difference of the CF and the PE algorithms is that in the former, isometric embedding is used only as an intermediate stage to obtain an isometry-invariant representation of the surfaces, whereas in our approach isometric embedding is used directly to compute the similarity between surfaces. The consequences of this difference are several. First, the *codimension* of the canonical form in the embedding space is at least one. In PE, the codimension is always zero. Secondly, embedding into Euclidean space still leaves the degrees of freedom of an Euclidean isometry (rotation, translation and reflection). In embedding into a general surface, if it is rich enough, such ambiguity usually does not exist. Thirdly, this ambiguity requires alignment of the CF canonical forms, which is avoided in PE. Due to the fact that the metric distortion serves

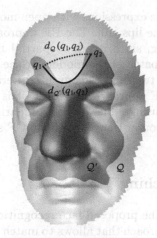

Fig. 2. Partial matching problem. Shown in blue dotted is a geodesic between the points $q_1, q_2 \in \mathcal{Q}$; the corresponding inconsistent geodesic on $\mathcal{Q}'$ is shown in black.

Table 1. Comparison of partial embedding and the canonical forms algorithm

	Canonical forms	Partial Embedding
Accuracy	up to minimum distortion caused by the embedding space	up to numerical errors
Distance function	moments or ICP	embedding error is used as distance
Alignment	required to resolve rotation, translation and reflection ambiguity	no alignment ambiguity
Partial matching	difficult	natural
Precomputation	possible using moment signatures	possible to some extent using hierarchial matching
Samples	∼ 1000	10 ∼ 100
Preprocessing	requires geometrically-consistent cropping of the facial surfaces using geodesic mask; particularly sensitive to lip cropping in case of open-mouth expressions	the probe can be an arbitrary patch of the facial surface
Numerical core	FMM, MDS	FMM, GMDS

as a dissimilarity measure in PE rather than a side effect (as in CF), a small number of surface samples suffices for accurate matching, and practically, as few as tens of points were enough in all of our face recognition experiments.

Another major issue is preprocessing. The performance of the CF approach depends heavily on the facial surface preprocessing, since it is important that the probe and the model surfaces contain the same region of the face. In [3], a *geodesic mask* was used to crop the facial surfaces. The problem is especially acute if one wishes to handle expressions with open mouth and uses a topological constraint by cutting off the lips [10]. The PE approach, on the other hand, is insensitive to preprocessing, since it allows partial matching. Practically, the probe can be an arbitrary patch of the model surface.

Since d_{PE} between any two faces is computed iteratively, it is impossible to precompute it as in the CF approach. However, it is still possible to speed-up the matching significantly using a hierarchial comparison. We address this issue in Section 4. The comparison of the PE and the CF approaches is summarized in Table 1.

4   Hierarchial Matching

An apparent limitation of the proposed face recognition method stems from the fact that, unlike the CF approach that allows to match canonical forms using moment signatures, the partial embedding distance cannot be precomputed. ¿From this point of view, our approach is similar to methods proposing the use of the iterative closest point algorithm (ICP). Taking, for example, about $1\,sec$ per comparison, matching a probe to a gallery of $100,000$ faces would take about 30 hours on a single CPU. Such computational complexity makes the one-to-many face recognition scenario infeasible. However, our method can still be used for one-to-many face recognition with very large databases by taking advantage of a hierarchical matching scheme, which is briefly outlined here.

Let the gallery database consist of K_0 faces, $\left\{\mathcal{S}_1^0,...,\mathcal{S}_{K_0}^0\right\}$. We aggregate groups of faces close in the sense of d_{PE}, replacing them with a single representative, as usually done in vector quantization [18]. The number of faces forming an aggregate can be either constant or adaptive, and depends on the specific aggregation algorithm used. As a result, a smaller set $\left\{\mathcal{S}_1^1,...,\mathcal{S}_{K_1}^1\right\}$ is obtained. Repeating the procedure iteratively, a tree-like structure is created, where at the top level there is a relatively small set $\left\{\mathcal{S}_1^L,...,\mathcal{S}_{K_L}^L\right\}$ of representative faces. Here L denotes the number of levels in the tree. Such hierarchial representation can be computed off-line once for a given database. Adding new faces to it can be made very efficient using techniques from heap and sorting trees, requiring $\mathcal{O}\left(\log K\right)$ comparisons.

Hierarchical comparison of a probe face to the entire database is performed in a top-down manner: first, the probe $\mathcal{Q}$ is compared to K_L top-level faces $\left\{\mathcal{S}_i^L\right\}$; $\mathcal{S}_i^L$ minimizing $d_{PE}\left(\mathcal{S}_i^L,\mathcal{Q}\right)$ is selected, and the probe is compared to its subtree. The process is repeated until the lowest level is reached. Such a scheme allows to perform face recognition with only $\mathcal{O}\left(\log K\right)$ matches and is suitable for one-to-many comparison scenarios with very large database of faces.

5   Results

The presented face recognition algorithm was tested on a set of 30 subjects from the Notre Dame 3D face database used in the FRGC competition [1, 2].

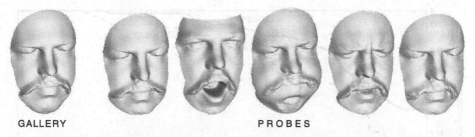

GALLERY   PROBES

Fig. 3. Gallery (leftmost) and four probe faces of a representative subject in the database

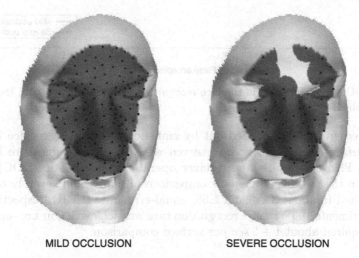

MILD OCCLUSION   SEVERE OCCLUSION

Fig. 4. Left: probe face with mild occlusions; right: the same probe face with severe occlusions. Surface samples are denoted by black dots.

The gallery consisted of one neutral expression per subject; five instances with moderate facial expressions were used as probes for each subject, yielding the total of 180 faces (see Figure 3). Gallery faces were cropped with a wide rectangular mask, which included most of the facial surface. These surfaces were subsequently sampled on a regular Cartesian grid consisting of approximately 2500 points. Pairwise geodesic distances between these points were measured using an efficient modification of parametric FMM [12, 12, 19] requiring about $1\,sec$ for computing a 2500×2500 distance matrix. Two sets of probes were created: in the first experiment, the probe faces were cropped using a narrow geodesic mask, which excluded hair and other unrelated details, covering most of the relevant parts of the face (Figure 4, left). In the second experiment, random parts of the surface were intentionally removed, resulting in severe occlusions of the facial surface (see example in Figure 4, right). In both experiments, the surfaces were sampled at 53 points using *furthest point sampling* strategy [20].

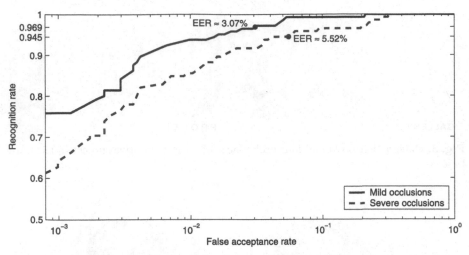

Fig. 5. ROC curves obtained in the face recognition experiment with mild (solid) and severe (dashed) occlusions

Face recognition was carried out by embedding the probe surface into the gallery surface using GMDS[1]; d_{PE} served as a dissimilarity measure between the faces. Figure 5 depicts the receiver operator characteristic (ROC) curves obtained in the two experiments. Comparison of mildly and severely occluded faces resulted in about 3.1% and 5.5% equal-error rate (EER), respectively. In both experiments 100% rank-1 recognition rate was achieved. Our non-optimized C code required about $1 \div 5\,sec$ per surface comparison.

6   Conclusions

Following the isometric model of facial expression introduced in [3], we proposed a novel expression-invariant face recognition algorithm. The main idea of our approach is to embed the probe facial surface into that of the model. Faces belonging to the same subject are nearly isometric and thus result in low embedding error, whereas different subjects are expected to have different intrinsic geometry, and thus produce higher embedding error. Unlike the previous approaches, our method does not introduce unnecessary metric distortions due to the embedding itself. Moreover, the probe and the model are not required to contain the same amount of information; matching a probe with partially missing data is natural to our approach. To the best of our knowledge, it is the first method to allow partial isometry-invariant matching of surfaces in general and of facial geometry in particular.

The numerical core of our face recognition method is the GMDS procedure, which has the same computational complexity as that of the standard MDS

---

[1] The GMDS MATLAB implementation will be available for download from http://tosca.cs.technion.ac.il as a part of the TOSCA (Toolbox for Surface Comparison and Analysis) Project.

procedure. Although our algorithm does not permit pre-computation of simple efficiently comparable signatures, we outlined a hierarchical matching strategy that enables the use of our approach for one-to-many face recognition in large databases.

Promising face recognition results were obtained on a small database of 30 subjects even when the facial surfaces were severely occluded. In sequel studies, we intend to demonstrate the performance of our approach on larger databases with extreme facial expression. Noting that GMDS is capable of finding intrinsic correspondence between two facial surfaces, our approach can be readily extended to handle texture as well, similarly to [21].

References

1. K. Chang, K. W. Bowyer, and P. J. Flynn. Face recognition using 2D and 3D facial data. In *ACM Workshop on Multimodal User Authentication*, pages 25–32, 2003.
2. P. J. Flynn, K. W. Bowyer, and P. J. Phillips. Assessment of time dependency in face recognition: an initial study. In *Audio- and Video-Based Biometric Person Authentication*, pages 44–51, 2003.
3. A. M. Bronstein, M. M. Bronstein, and R. Kimmel. Three-dimensional face recognition. *Intl. J. Computer Vision*, 64(1):5–30, August 2005.
4. A. Elad and R. Kimmel. On bending invariant signatures for surfaces. *IEEE Trans. PAMI*, 25(10):1285–1295, 2003.
5. I. Borg and P. Groenen. *Modern multidimensional scaling - theory and applications*. Springer-Verlag, Berlin Heidelberg New York, 1997.
6. J. Walter and H. Ritter. On interactive visualization of high-dimensional data using the hyperbolic plane. In *Proc. ACM SIGKDD Int. Conf. Knowledge Discovery and Data Mining*, pages 123–131, 2002.
7. A. M. Bronstein, M. M. Bronstein, and R. Kimmel. On isometric embedding of facial surfaces into $\mathbb{S}^3$. In *Proc. Int'l Conf. Scale Space and PDE Methods in Computer Vision*, number 3459 in Lecture Notes on Computer Science, pages 622–631. Springer, 2005.
8. A. M. Bronstein, M. M. Bronstein, and R. Kimmel. Expression-invariant face recognition via spherical embedding. In *Proc. ICIP*, 2005.
9. A. M. Bronstein, M. M. Bronstein, and R. Kimmel. Generalized multidimensional scaling: a framework for isometry-invariant partial surface matching. *Proc. Nat. Acad. Sci.*, 103(5):1168–1172, January 2006.
10. A. M. Bronstein, M. M. Bronstein, and R. Kimmel. Expression-invariant representations for human faces. Technical Report CIS-2005-01, Dept. of Computer Science, Technion, Israel, June 2005.
11. F. Mémoli and G. Sapiro. A theoretical and computational framework for isometry invariant recognition of point cloud data. *Foundations of Computational Mathematics*, 2005. to appear.
12. R. Kimmel and J. A. Sethian. Computing geodesic on manifolds. In *Proc. US National Academy of Science*, volume 95, pages 8431–8435, 1998.
13. N. Linial, E. London, and Y. Rabinovich. The geometry of graphs and some its algorithmic applications. *Combinatorica*, 15:333–344, 1995.
14. M. M. Bronstein, A. M. Bronstein, R. Kimmel, and I. Yavneh. A multigrid approach for multidimensional scaling. In *Proc. Copper Mountain Conf. Multigrid Methods*, 2005.

15. A. Tal, M. Elad, and S. Ar. Content based retrieval of VRML objects - an iterative and interactive approach. In *Proc. Eurographics Workshop on Multimedia*, 2001.
16. D. Bertsekas. *Nonlinear programming*. Atlanta Scientific, 2 edition, 1999.
17. A. M. Bronstein, M. M. Bronstein, and R. Kimmel. Effcient computation of the Gromov-Hausdorff distance for smooth surfaces. Technical Report CIS-2006-01, Dept. of Computer Science, Technion, Israel, January 2006.
18. A. Gersho and R. M. Gray. *Vector quantization and signal compression*. Kluwer Academic Publishers, Boston, 1992.
19. A. Spira and R. Kimmel. An efficient solution to the eikonal equation on parametric manifolds. *Interfaces and Free Boundaries*, 6(3):315–327, 2004.
20. Y. Eldar, M. Lindenbaum, M. Porat, and Y. Y. Zeevi. The farthest point strategy for progressive image sampling. *IEEE Trans. Image Processing*, 6(9):1305–1315, 1997.
21. G. Zigelman, R. Kimmel, and N. Kiryati. Texture mapping using surface flattening via multi-dimensional scaling. *IEEE Trans. Visualization and computer graphics*, 9(2):198–207, 2002.

An Integral Solution to Surface Evolution PDEs Via Geo-cuts

Yuri Boykov[1], Vladimir Kolmogorov[2], Daniel Cremers[3], and Andrew Delong[1]

[1] University of Western Ontario, Canada
{yuri, adelong3}@csd.uwo.ca
[2] University College London, UK
vnk@adastral.ucl.ac.uk
[3] University of Bonn, Germany
cremers@cs.ucla.edu

Abstract. We introduce a new approach to modelling gradient flows of contours and surfaces. While standard variational methods (e.g. level sets) compute local interface motion in a *differential* fashion by estimating local contour velocity via energy derivatives, we propose to solve surface evolution PDEs by explicitly estimating *integral* motion of the whole surface. We formulate an optimization problem directly based on an integral characterization of gradient flow as an infinitesimal move of the (whole) surface giving the largest energy decrease among all moves of equal size. We show that this problem can be efficiently solved using recent advances in algorithms for global hypersurface optimization [4, 2, 11]. In particular, we employ the *geo-cuts* method [4] that uses ideas from integral geometry to represent continuous surfaces as cuts on discrete graphs. The resulting interface evolution algorithm is validated on some 2D and 3D examples similar to typical demonstrations of level-set methods. Our method can compute gradient flows of hypersurfaces with respect to a fairly general class of continuous functionals and it is flexible with respect to distance metrics on the space of contours/surfaces. Preliminary tests for standard L_2 distance metric demonstrate numerical stability, topological changes and an absence of any oscillatory motion.

1 Introduction

As detailed in [4, 11, 12], discrete minimum cut/maximum flow algorithms on graphs can be effectively used for optimization of a fairly wide class of functionals defined on contours and surfaces in continuous metric spaces. So far, graph based methods were presented as a global optimization alternative to local variational optimization methods such as the level set method. Efficient algorithms for finding global optima have a number of advantages over local optimization methods. However, in some cases it is necessary to observe gradual changes of a contour/surface that they display under gradient flow (or gradient descent). For example, gradient flow models dynamics of many natural phenomena in physics. In computer vision, ability to track gradual changes in segmentation allowed variational methods to successfully incorporate shape priors [8, 14].

A. Leonardis, H. Bischof, and A. Pinz (Eds.): ECCV 2006, Part III, LNCS 3953, pp. 409–422, 2006.

In this paper we propose a new integral approach to computing gradient flow of interfaces with respect to a fairly general class of energy functionals. The proposed algorithm generates a timely sequence of cuts corresponding to gradient flow of a given contour. Note that the proposed method is not a new implementation of level set methods but rather an alternative numerical method for evolving interfaces. Our method does not use any level set function to represent contours/surfaces. Instead, it uses an implicit contour/surface representation via geo-cuts [4]. As the level set method, our approach handles topological changes of the evolving interface.

2   Variational Methods and PDEs in Computer Vision

Numerous computer vision problems can be addressed by variational methods. Based on certain assumptions regarding the image formation process, one formulates an appropriate cost functional which is subsequently minimized by implementing the Euler-Lagrange equations in a gradient flow partial differential equation (PDE). This technique has become standard in various fields of computer vision ranging from motion estimation [9, 3, 17, 13], over image enhancement [15, 16] to segmentation [10, 6]. While not all PDEs are derived from a variational approach, in this work we will focus on the class of PDEs which correspond to the gradient flow to an underlying variational principle.

Despite their enormous success in the local optimization of a large class of cost functionals, PDEs suffer from certain drawbacks. In particular, they are inherently differential approaches, they rely on the notion of an energy gradient which – in many cases — requires intense numerical computations. The numerical discretization of PDEs requires a careful choice of appropriate time step sizes. Extensive research went into determining conditions which guarantee stability of the respective implementations. In practice, meaningful time step sizes are often chosen based on various heuristics.

In contrast to this differential approach, we develop in this paper an integral approach to solving a certain class of gradient flow PDEs. To this end we revert to efficient combinatorial optimization methods acting on a discrete space. In a number or recent papers [4, 2, 11], it was shown that various optimization problems defined on surfaces in continuous spaces can be efficiently solved by discrete combinatorial optimization methods. In contrast to these works, the present paper is not focussed on determining the global optima of respective cost functions, but rather on actually modelling the local gradient descent evolution of the corresponding variational approaches. In this sense, we hope to further bridge the gap between continuous variational approaches and discrete combinatorial approaches to optimization.

3   From Differential to Integral Approach

Our main goal is an algorithm for computing gradient flows for hypersurfaces based on novel optimization techniques [4, 2, 11] which are fundamentally different from standard variational methodology. Gradient flow for contours and surfaces amounts to evolving an initial boundary under Euler-Lagrange equation of a given energy functional. Such propagation of surfaces corresponds to many natural phenomena and it can be derived from the laws of physics. Standard variational calculus justifies the corresponding PDE in the context of (local) energy optimization and provides numerical methods (including level-sets) for solving it directly via finite difference or finite element schemes. In contrast, our new approach solves the corresponding PDE indirectly.

Our approach to gradient flow was motivated by the numerical stability of global optimization methods in [4, 2, 11]. In this paper we show how to turn them into robust surface evolution methods that may overcome some of the numerical limitations of standard variational techniques. Note that variational methods rely on estimates of energy derivatives in order to compute each point's local *differential* motion (velocity). In contrast, our main idea is to compute *integral* motion of the surface as a whole. In particular, geo-cuts [4] allow to compute such motion by means of integral geometry without estimating derivatives.

When trying to model surface evolutions by global optimization approaches, we are faced with the following discrepancy between local and global optimization methods: while existing global optimization methods [4, 2, 11] are merely focussed on finding the boundary with the lowest energy, the gradient approaches make use of the energy *gradient*, i.e. they focus on the maximal energy reduction per change in the boundary. Therefore, any algorithm for computing gradient flow needs to have means to incorporate a measure of the boundary change.

3.1   Distances Between Contours

There are numerous metrics to measure change between boundaries. In fact, the question of which metric on the space of contours should be used has been largely ignored in the context of calculus of variation. Most so-called gradient descent evolutions implicitly assume an L_2 inner product. Several recent advances were made regarding the derivation of Euler-Lagrange equations with respect to more sophisticated contour metrics, focussed either on using the correct metric [19], or on designing novel gradient flows with certain desirable properties [7]. A very similar freedom in the choice of metric on the space of contours will also arise in our novel integral formulation of boundary evolution.

Note that motion of a contour C in a differential framework is described by a (normal) vector field $v = \frac{dC}{dt}$ where velocity vector v_s is given for every contour point s. Then, standard L_2 measure for boundary change is defined as $||\frac{dC}{dt}||^2 = \int_C |v_s|^2 ds = \langle \frac{dC}{dt}, \frac{dC}{dt} \rangle$ using Euclidean inner product $\langle, \rangle$. As mentioned above, employing other inner products on the space of contours will entail different kinds of gradient flows of a contour.

In order to avoid local differential computations, we will represent the motion of a contour C by integral measures of boundary change: a distance metric on the space of contours that for any two contours C and C_0 assigns a (nonnegative) distance value $dist(C, C_0)$. Such distance metric could be consistent with ideas for measuring boundary change in the differential framework if for $C \to C_0$

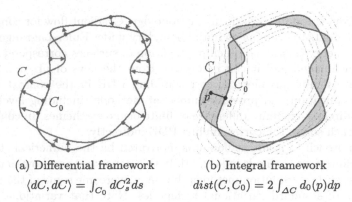

(a) Differential framework   (b) Integral framework

$$\langle dC, dC \rangle = \int_{C_0} dC_s^2 ds \qquad\qquad dist(C, C_0) = 2 \int_{\Delta C} d_0(p) dp$$

Fig. 1. L_2 distance between two near-by contours. In the integral framework $dist(C, C_0)$ is equal to a weighted area of the highlighted region. The weight of each point p is given by a distance $d_0(p)$ to the nearest point on C_0.

$$dist(C, C_0) = \langle dC, dC \rangle + o(||dC||^2) \qquad\qquad (1)$$

where $dC = C - C_0$ is a field of (normal) vectors defined on points in C_0 and connecting them with points on C as shown in Figure 1(a). In other words: The integral distance metric is consistent with the differential approach if the two metrics are identical up to higher order terms.

Example 1. (L_2 *metrics*) Figure 1 illustrates relationship between differential and integral approaches to measuring boundary change between two contours for the most standard case of L_2 inner product $\langle , \rangle$. The corresponding distance metric on the space of contours in $\mathcal{R}^2$ is

$$dist(C, C_0) = 2 \cdot \int_{\Delta C} d_0(p) dp$$

where p are points in $\mathcal{R}^2$, function $d_0(p)$ is a distance from p to the nearest point on C_0 (*distance map*), and ΔC is a region between two contours. Then, (1) holds because integrating the distance function $2d_0(p)$ along a (normal) direction connecting some point $s \in C_0$ and a point $q \in C$ gives $||q - s||^2 = dC_s^2$. ∎

Our general integral approach to front propagation is described in the next subsection. The method is well defined for any distance metric on the space of contours. However, if one wants to model the gradient flow corresponding to a differential formulation with a given inner product $\langle , \rangle$ then the consistent distance metric (1) should be used.

3.2 Integral Formulation of Gradient Flow

Our method for solving PDEs for contours or surfaces evolution is motivated as follows. Gradient flow (descent) of an interface C under any given energy functional $F(C)$ can be intuitively viewed as a temporal sequence of infinitesimal steps where each step gives the largest decrease of the contour energy among all steps of the same size. This almost banal interpretation of the gradient descent suggests that the contour C_{t+dt} corresponding to an infinitesimal step in the gradient descent from a contour C_t can be obtained by solving the following constrained optimization problem:

$$\min_{C\, :\, dist(C,C_t)=\epsilon} F(C)$$

for some (arbitrarily) small value $\epsilon > 0$ fixing the distance $dist(C, C_t)$ from the contour C_t. Equivalently, the method of Lagrangian multipliers shows that C_{t+dt} should also solve unconstrained optimization problem

$$\min_{C} \ F(C) + \lambda \cdot dist(C, C_t)$$

for some (arbitrarily) large value of parameter λ. These formulations for C_{t+dt} do not establish an explicit relationship between the temporal step size dt and the values of ϵ or λ. We just know that for each small dt there is some corresponding small $\epsilon = \epsilon(dt)$ or some corresponding large $\lambda = \lambda(dt)$.

In fact, it is not difficult to establish an exact relationship between λ and dt using a well known PDE for evolution of an interface C under a gradient flow (descent) with respect to a given energy functional $F(C)$. Our general approach to computing gradient flows will be based on optimization of energy (2).

Theorem 1. *Consider a family of contours C_t minimizing energy*

$$E_t(C) = F(C) + \frac{1}{2(t - t_0)} \cdot dist(C, C_0) \tag{2}$$

where metric $dist(C, C_0)$ is consistent with some inner product $\langle , \rangle$ according to equation (1). Then, as $t \to t_0$

$$C_t = C_0 + v \cdot (t - t_0) + o(\Delta t)$$

where vector field $v = -\frac{dF}{dC}$ is a gradient of F with respect to inner product $\langle , \rangle$. That is, as $t \to t_0$ the contour C_t solves the standard gradient flow PDE

$$\frac{\partial C}{\partial t} = -\frac{dF}{dC} \tag{3}$$

Proof. Since $E_t(C) = F(C) + \frac{1}{2(t-t_0)}\langle C - C_0, C - C_0 \rangle$ then any contour C optimizing E_t should satisfy

$$0 = \frac{dE_t}{dC} = \frac{dF}{dC} + \frac{1}{(t - t_0)} \cdot (C - C_0).$$

Thus, optimality of C_t for E_t implies $C_t - C_0 = -(t - t_0) \cdot \frac{dF}{dC}$ which is equivalent to the standard gradient flow equation (3) as $t \to t_0$. ∎

Standard variational (differential) methods for computing contour evolution under gradient flow, including level sets, explicitly estimate the derivative $\frac{dF}{dC}$ and use finite differences or finite elements to approximate the PDE (3). Theorem 1 suggests an alternative integral approach to computing gradient flows. Assuming that C_0 is a current state of the contour, we can obtain an optimal contour C_t minimizing (2) for some small time step $\Delta t = (t-t_0)$. The gradient flow problem is solved by a sequence of optimal steps $\{C_0 \rightarrow C_t\}$ where at each new iteration C_0 is reset to the optimal contour computed in the previous step.

Optimization of E_t may look like a difficult task. However, our integral approach is practical because a wide class of continuous functionals $F(C)$ and metrics $dist(C, C_0)$ in energy (2) can be efficiently optimized by recent global methods [4, 2, 11]. In particular, Section 4 describes details of a discrete approximation algorithm for gradient flows based on geo-cuts [4]. This algorithm is based on implicit representation of continuous contours as cuts on discrete graphs. Optimization of continuous contour/surface energy (2) via geo-cuts avoids explicit differentiation of E_t and relies on efficient combinatorial algorithms.

3.3   Discussion and Relation to Previous Approaches

Note that energy E_t in (2) can be globally minimized using geo-cuts [4] when the first term, hypersurface functional $F(C)$, includes anisotropic Riemannian length/area and any regional bias. It is important, however, that energy (2) contains another term $dist(C, C_0)$. This second term is critical for implementing gradient flow instead of global minimization of functional $F(C)$. Note that $dist(C, C_0)$ enforces shape stabilization and slows down the contour generating gradual motion instead of a jump into a global minima. As shown in Example 1 from Section 3.1, standard gradient flow with respect to L_2 inner product corresponds to shape constraint $dist(C, C_0)$ penalizing deviation of C from C_0 according to the area between the contours weighted by the distance from C_0. In fact, this is a simple regional bias that can be easily incorporated into geo-cuts. Additional details are given in Section 4.

Our approach can also compute gradient flow with respect to inner products different from L_2. One has to determine the distance metric $dist(C, C_0)$ consistent with the corresponding inner product as in equation (1).

Generally speaking, one can use our general framework for propagating hypersurfaces by optimizing energy (2) with an arbitrary distance metric $dist(C, C_0)$. In this case the method may not really correspond to any true gradient flow but it may still generate some gradual motion of an interface. That may be sufficient for many practical applications in computer vision that do not need exact gradient flow. The results in [19, 7] suggest that using specialized distance metrics could be beneficial in applications.

Interestingly, some existing discrete algorithms for active contours are special cases of our general approach for some specific distance metric $dist(C, C_0)$.

Example 2. (DP snakes) A well-known dynamic programming approach to 2D snakes [1] uses control points to represent discrete snake C. Then, a typical snake energy functional $F(C)$ is iteratively minimized by dynamic programming over positions of control points. In order to simulate gradient-descent-like motion, the algorithm in [1] allows each point to move only in a small box around their current position. Intuitively speaking, this idea does capture the spirit of gradient flow motion. However, as easily follows from our theories in Section 3.2, the motion generated in [1] corresponds to energy (2) with a $0 - 1$ boxy distance metric on a space of snakes $dist(C, C_0) = \prod_p \delta_{|dC. |>\epsilon}$ where ϵ is a given box size and $dC_p = C(p) - C_0(p)$ is a shift of snake's control point p. This distance metric is not consistent with any inner product (bilinear form). Therefore, the corresponding algorithm does not generate a true gradient flow[1]. At the same time, our theories suggest a simple correction to the problem; In order to get a true L_2 gradient flow, DP-snakes algorithm [1] could amend box-based move constraints with a quadratic motion penalty $dist(C, C_0) = \sum_p dC_p^2$ which can be easily handled by dynamic programming.

Example 3. (Fixed Band Graph-Cuts) An approach to segmentation in [18] is very similar to DP-snakes algorithm in [1]. Dynamic programming in DP-snakes is replaced by graph cuts but [18] still uses the idea of a fixed size "box". Since graph cuts do not use control points to represent contours and instead rely on implicit binary graph-partitioning representation, the boxes around control points are replaces by a small band around a current cut. Otherwise, the active contour algorithm presented in [18] can be described through energy (2) with the same $0 - 1$ boxy distance metric $dist(C, C_0) = \delta_{|dC|. >\epsilon}$ where $|dC|_h$ is the Hausdorff distance between C and C_0. It follows that the method in [18] does not correspond to gradient flow for any reasonable inner product. In fact, fixed-band approach in [18] is likely to generate a jerky non-smooth motion. In contrast, our theoretical framework allows a principled approach to contour evolution via graph cuts. Using proper distance $dist(C, C_0)$ consistent with some (continuous) inner product $\langle , \rangle$ allows to control geometric artifacts that may arise in front propagation using discrete optimization techniques.

4   Computing Gradient Flow Via Geo-Cuts

As discussed before, there are a number of algorithms that can (globally) minimize continuous functional (2) and practically implement our approach to solving gradient flow PDEs. This paper concentrates on a solution based on geo-cuts [4].

4.1   Review of Geo-cuts

Geo-cuts is a graph based approach to minimizing continuous functionals $E(C)$ based on representing contours as cuts on a discrete graph (Fig. 2). Nodes in this graph correspond to sampled points in space. A cut is a binary labeling of

---

[1] A standard DP snake [1] under Euclidean length functional $F(C)$ will not generate a true mean curvature motion. In particular, this snake may not converge to a circle before collapsing into a point.

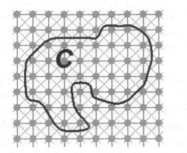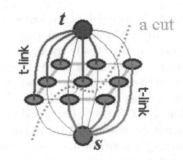

Fig. 2. Geo-cuts: Any continuous contour C corresponds to a cut on a graph. Edge weights define discrete *cut metric* assigning length to C based on the cost of the corresponding cut. With appropriately chosen weights, cut metric approximates any continuous anisotropic Riemannian metric.

these nodes. In the context of continuous contour representation, binary labels $\{1,0\}$ say if the point (node) is inside or outside of the contour. Note that this implicit representation of continuous contours does not say precisely where the boundary is between the two neighboring graph nodes (points in space) with different labels. In fact, the lack of sub-pixel accuracy does not cause problems for geo-cuts because they do not use estimates of local gradients/derivatives, e.g. curvature, and rely on methods of integral geometry instead.

There are also two special nodes, *terminals* s and t (source and sink). Graph edges are *n-links* and *t-links*, as in Fig. 2. Typically, n-links encode regularization term in the energy (length or area) while t-links encode regional bias.

The first step in the geo-cuts approach is to construct a graph whose cut metric approximates that of functional $E(C)$. Such construction exists for a fairly large class of continuous functionals E, as shown in [4, 12]. In general, $E(C)$ can be any submodular (graph-representable) functional over contours/surfaces. In particular, it can include the following terms:

- Geometric length/area under a fairly wide class of continuous metrics (including any anisotropic Riemannian metric);
- Flux with respect to any continuous vector field;
- Regional term integrating arbitrary potential function over the interior of C.

After constructing an appropriate graph, the cut with the smallest cost can be computed very efficiently via min cut/max flow algorithms.

We now apply this framework to the problem of computing gradient flow at time t given current contour C_0. In order to minimize functional $E_t(C)$ in eq. (2), we need to approximate terms $F(C)$ and $dist(C, C_0)$ with a discrete cut metric. According to the characterization above, the first term $F(C)$ can be any submodular functional over contours/surfaces. This covers a widely used special case when F is a geometric length/area in a Riemannian metric induced by the image. Let us consider the second term.

As discussed in section 3.1, we have some freedom in choosing function $dist(C, C_0)$. There are many distance measures corresponding to different inner products $\langle , \rangle$. For example, in order to incorporate standard L_2 inner product we can use the distance function described in example 1. It can be rewritten as

$$dist(C, C_0) = -2 \cdot \int_{int(C_0)} d_0(p)dp + 2 \cdot \int_{int(C)} d_0(p)dp \qquad (4)$$

where $int(C)$ is the interior of C and $d_0(p)$ is now the *signed* distance map; it is negative inside C_0 and positive outside. The first term above is a constant independent of C. The second term is a regional bias that can be incorporated into geo-cuts using t-links. Note that we can use non-Euclidean signed distance maps to implement metrics on the space of contours different from L_2.

4.2 Minimizing Energy E_t with Geo-cuts

Our approach to gradient flows amounts to finding small moves $C(t)$ from $C(0) = C_0$ for $(t - t_0) < \delta t$ and then resetting time and energy (2) for $C_0' = C(t)$. Section 4.3 describes this *move-reset* algorithm. In this section, however, we assume that C_0 is fixed and discuss properties of a timely sequence of cuts $\{C(t)|t \geq 0\}$ where each particular cut $C(t)$ is a global minima of $E_t(C)$ for a given t. For simplicity of notation we will assume that $t_0 = 0$.

It can be shown that the time axis can be split into a finite number of intervals $[t_i, t_{i+1}]$ such that there is cut C_i which is optimal for all $t \in [t_i, t_{i+1}]$. Our goal is therefore to find a sequence of critical time instances $t_1, t_2, t_3, \ldots, t_n$ when an optimal cut changes. We will also need to find the corresponding sequence of optimal cuts $C_1, C_2, C_3, \ldots, C_n$. Note that the initial contour C_0 will be an optimal cut for any $t \in [0, t_1]$. Also, "final cut" C_n is a global minimizer of functional $F(C)$. It may happen that C_0 is already a global minimum, in which case $n = 0$. Below we list a number of useful facts about this sequence of cuts.

Remark 1. It is possible to prove that

$$F(C_0) > F(C_1) > F(C_2) > \ldots > F(C_n)$$

Therefore, the energy will never increase during the algorithm. This will prevent any oscillatory behaviour present in some implementations of level sets.

Remark 2. Similar to the continuous case, the gradient flow (gradient descent) algorithm above is related to the following constrained optimization problem (where C is now a discrete cut and $F(\cdot)$ encodes cut metric):

$$\min_{C \, : \, dist(C_0, C) = \epsilon} F(C) \qquad (5)$$

More precisely, an optimal solution C_t for energy (2) at any given time $t > 0$ solves the constrained minimization problem above for

$$\epsilon_t = dist(C_0, C) \qquad (6)$$

Indeed, suppose that there is some other cut C such that $dist(C_0, C) = \epsilon_t$ and $F(C) < F(C_t)$. Then, $F(C) + \frac{1}{2t}dist(C_0, C) < F(C_t) + \frac{1}{2t}dist(C_0, C)$ and we have a contradiction to the fact that C_t is optimal for energy (2).

Equation (6) explicitly determines the "size" of each gradient descent step $\epsilon_i = dist(C_0, C_i)$ generated by our algorithm. It is easy to show that

$$0 < \epsilon_1 < \epsilon_2 < \ldots < \epsilon_n < \infty$$

Remark 3. An interesting observation is that C_1 (the first cut different from initial solution C_0) is a solution for

$$\min_{C \neq C_0} \frac{F(C) - F(C_0)}{dist(C_0, C)}$$

The proof is based on the fact that at time t_1 energy (2) has two distinct optimal cuts C_1 and C_0. Thus, $F(C_0) = F(C_1) + \frac{1}{2t_1}dist(C_0, C_1)$ and the proof follows from a standard "binary search" algorithm for ratio optimization. It also follows that the corresponding optimal value of the ratio is equal to $-\frac{1}{2t_1}$. Note that the optimal (minimal) ratio value has to be negative (non-positive). Indeed, unless C_0 is a global minimizer of $F(\cdot)$ we have at least one cut (e.g. C_1) where the value of the ratio is negative (since $F(C_1) < F(C_0)$). Note that optimization of the ratio above is meaningful in discrete formulation only. It can be shown that in the continuous case the ratio above converges to $-\infty$ as $C \to C_0$.

Remark 4. The first cut C_1 is the most accurate gradient descent step from C_0 as it corresponds to the smallest step size ϵ_1. Ideally, we want to compute the optimal solution of (5) for the smallest value of ϵ while ϵ_1 is the smallest step size where our graph cut algorithm can detect an optimal move. The size of that smallest step ϵ_1 is possibly due to approximation errors in our discrete graph-cut formulation and may depend on graph "resolution".

4.3   Summary of Gradient Flow Algorithm

It follows that the gradient flow is approximated the best when we reset to initial cut $C_0' = C_1$ and update the energy (2) after each small move C_1. In practice we may not need to be so conservative but that needs to be checked experimentally.

It is possible to show that

$$\epsilon_1 \approx (2t_1 \cdot ||\nabla F||)^2 = (2t_1 \cdot ||\frac{dF}{dC}(C_0)||)^2 \tag{7}$$

Indeed, using remark 3 and expression $\epsilon_1 = dist(C_0, C_1) \approx ||C_1 - C_0||^2$ we get

$$-\frac{1}{2t_1} = \frac{F(C_1) - F(C_0)}{\epsilon_1} \approx \frac{\langle \nabla F, C_1 - C_0 \rangle}{\epsilon_1} \approx -\frac{||\nabla F|| \cdot ||C_1 - C_0||}{\epsilon_1} \approx -\frac{||\nabla F||}{\sqrt{\epsilon_1}}$$

Equation (7) allows to determine a stopping criteria for our algorithm when we converged to a local minima where $\nabla F = 0$. In practice we may stop if the gradient of F is smaller than some predefined threshold, $||\nabla F|| < \delta$, which corresponds to the stopping condition

$$dist(C_0, C_1) < (2t_1 \cdot \delta)^2$$

5   Experimental Validation

Although the focus of our paper is mainly theoretical, we have generated preliminary results to show that gradient flow can indeed be approximated with an integral representation of length and hypersurfaces. The image sequences that follow were generated by combining the geo-cuts method for computing $F(C)$ and a signed distance map for computing $dist(C, C_0)$ as in (4). The distance map is computed in such a way that for pixels p at the boundary of cut C_0 there holds $d_0(p) = \pm 0.5$. (Pixel p is said to be at the boundary if it is 4-connected to some pixel q in the other segment). In our tests we compute the first cut C_1 and reset $t_0' = t_1, C_0' = C_1$. We use an implementation of maxflow graph-cuts [5] as a tool for optimizing the energy. Note that in the figures below we show only selected time frames of the gradient flow motion computed by out method.

In Figures 3, 6 and 7 we have intentionally used low-resolution grids to illustrate that even extremely coarse integral representations can yield accurate gradient flow motion, despite a lack of sub-pixel accuracy. Our test results on

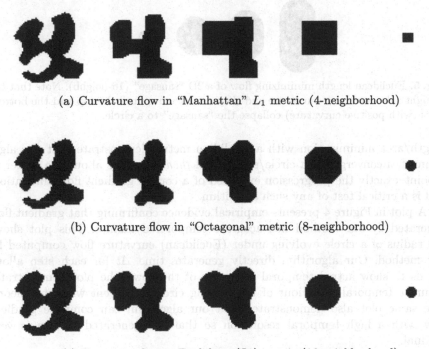

(a) Curvature flow in "Manhattan" L_1 metric (4-neighborhood)

(b) Curvature flow in "Octagonal" metric (8-neighborhood)

(c) Curvature flow in Euclidean (L_2) metric (16-neighborhood)

Fig. 3. Length minimizing (curvature) flow of a 2D contour under different homogeneous metrics. Pixalization reflects the actual resolution used in the experiments and demonstrates that our discrete geo-cuts representation of contours generates accurate gradient flow without explicitly tracking the contour with sub-pixel accuracy as in level-sets.

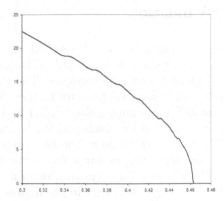

Fig. 4. Empirical plot of a radius of a circle under curvature flow. Theoretically, this function is $r(t) = \sqrt{const - 2t}$.

Fig. 5. Euclidean length minimizing flow of a 2D "sausage" (16-neighb). Note that the straight sides have zero curvature and they do not move until the top and the bottom sides (with positive curvature) collapse the "sausage" to a circle.

length/area minimization with a Euclidian metric demonstrate that our algorithm *first* converges to a circle/sphere and *then* converges about the center to a point–exactly the progression expected of a correct gradient flow simulation, and is a critical test of any such algorithm.

A plot in Figure 4 presents empirical evidence confirming that gradient flow generated by our method has accurate temporal dynamics. This plot shows the radius of a circle evolving under (Euclidean) curvature flow computed by our method. Our algorithm directly generates time Δt for each step allowing us to show actual temporal dynamics of the flow. The plot demonstrates accurate temporal behaviour of the moving circle consistent with the theory. The same plot also demonstrates that our algorithm can compute gradient flow with a high temporal resolution so that the generated motion is very gradual.

Figure 5 provides additional evidence of our method's accuracy. We compute (Euclidean) curvature flow of a "sausage" which gradually moves from the ends where the curvature is non-zero while the straight sides do not move until the sausage turns into a circle. This result would be impossible to obtain with a DP-snake [1] or fixed-band graph cuts [18]. For example, each step of the algorithm in [18] will uniformly erode the "sausage" from all sides. The "sausage" will

Fig. 6. Length minimizing flow of a 2D contour (blue) under image-based anisotropic Riemannian metric (16-neighborhood)

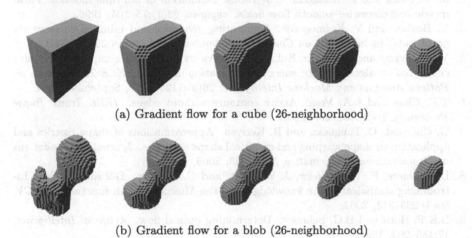

(a) Gradient flow for a cube (26-neighborhood)

(b) Gradient flow for a blob (26-neighborhood)

Fig. 7. Euclidean area minimizing flow of a surface in 3D. Voxalization reflects the actual resolution.

collapse into a line interval (not into a point) in jumpy moves of equal size (band width).

Our tests with image-based Riemannian metrics (e.g. see Figure 6) have confirmed that topological changes in contours occur in a similar manner to level-set methods, and that contours do not exhibit oscillatory motion but instead remain fixed at local minima.

As of this writing, we have yet to experiment with more justified ways of both controlling the time steps and the manner in which the distance map(s) are used. One potential source of inaccuracy lies in the fact that the distance map can be determined only with precision 0.5, since we use discrete representation of contours via geo-cuts. The influence of this effect is most significant near the boundary of contour C_0. This suggests that using the first cut C_1 is not necessarily the most accurate method. The problem, however, may be solved by using cuts C_k for bigger time step $t_k > t_1$. This idea can be combined with supersampling the grid graph. Despite this potential difficulty, the experiments indicate that even our preliminary implementation gives very encouraging results, which show that geo-cuts approach may provide a numerically stable method for solving gradient flow PDEs.

References

1. Amir A. Amini, Terry E. Weymouth, and Ramesh C. Jain. Using dynamic programming for solving variational problems in vision. *IEEE Transactions on Pattern Analysis and Machine Intelligence*, 12(9):855–867, September 1990.
2. Ben Appleton and Hugues Talbot. Globally minimal surfaces by continuous maximal flows. *IEEE transactions on Pattern Analysis and Pattern Recognition (PAMI)*, 28(1):106–118, January 2006.
3. M. J. Black and P. Anandan. The robust estimation of multiple motions: Parametric and piecewise–smooth flow fields. *cvgip-iu*, 63(1):75–104, 1996.
4. Y. Boykov and V. Kolmogorov. Computing geodesics and minimal surfaces via graph cuts. In *Int. Conf. on Computer Vision*, volume I, pages 26–33, 2003.
5. Yuri Boykov and Vladimir Kolmogorov. An experimental comparison of min-cut/max-flow algorithms for energy minimization in vision. *IEEE Transactions on Pattern Analysis and Machine Intelligence*, 26(9):1124–1137, September 2004.
6. T.F. Chan and L.A. Vese. Active contours without edges. *IEEE Trans. Image Processing*, 10(2):266–277, 2001.
7. G. Charpiat, O. Faugeras, and R. Keriven. Approximations of shape metrics and application to shape warping and empirical shape statistics. *Journal of Foundations of Computational Mathematics*, 5(1):1–58, 2005.
8. D. Cremers, F. Tischhäuser, J. Weickert, and C. Schnörr. Diffusion Snakes: Introducing statistical shape knowledge into the Mumford–Shah functional. *IJCV*, 50(3):295–313, 2002.
9. B.K.P. Horn and B.G. Schunck. Determining optical flow. *Artificial Intelligence*, 17:185–203, 1981.
10. M. Kass, A. Witkin, and D. Terzolpoulos. Snakes: Active contour models. *International Journal of Computer Vision*, 1(4):321–331, 1988.
11. D. Kirsanov and S.-J. Gortler. A discrete global minimization algorithm for continuous variational problems. *Harvard CS. Tech. Rep.*, TR-14-04, July 2004.
12. V. Kolmogorov and Y. Boykov. What metrics can be approximated by geo-cuts, or global optimization of length/area and flux. In *ICCV*, October 2005.
13. P. Kornprobst, R. Deriche, and G. Aubert. Image sequence analysis via partial differential equations. *Journal of Math. Imaging and Vision*, 11(1):5–26, 1999.
14. Nikos Paragios. Shape-based segmentation and tracking in cardiac image analysis. *IEEE Transactions on Medical Image Analysis*, pages 402–407, 2003.
15. P. Perona and J. Malik. Scale-space and edge-detection. *IEEE Trans. on Pattern Analysis and Machine Intelligence*, 12(7):629–639, 1990.
16. J. Weickert. *Anisotropic diffusion in image processing*. Teubner, Stuttgart, 1998.
17. J. Weickert and C. Schnörr. A theoretical framework for convex regularizers in PDE–based computation of image motion. *IJCV*, 45(3):245–264, 2001.
18. N. Xu, R. Bansal, and N. Ahuja. Object segmentation using graph cuts based active contours. In *CVPR*, volume II, pages 46–53, 2003.
19. Anthony Yezzi and Andrea Mennucci. Conformal metrics and true "gradient flows" for curves. In *IEEE Intl. Conf. on Comp. Vis.*, 2005.

Detecting Doctored JPEG Images Via DCT Coefficient Analysis

Junfeng He[1], Zhouchen Lin[2], Lifeng Wang[2], and Xiaoou Tang[2]

[1] Tsinghua University, Beijing, China
heroson98@tsinghua.edu.cn
[2] Microsoft Research Asia, Beijing, China
{zhoulin, lfwang, xitang}@microsoft.com

Abstract. The steady improvement in image/video editing techniques has enabled people to synthesize realistic images/videos conveniently. Some legal issues may occur when a doctored image cannot be distinguished from a real one by visual examination. Realizing that it might be impossible to develop a method that is universal for all kinds of images and JPEG is the most frequently used image format, we propose an approach that can detect doctored JPEG images and further locate the doctored parts, by examining the double quantization effect hidden among the DCT coefficients. Up to date, this approach is the only one that can locate the doctored part automatically. And it has several other advantages: the ability to detect images doctored by different kinds of synthesizing methods (such as alpha matting and inpainting, besides simple image cut/paste), the ability to work without fully decompressing the JPEG images, and the fast speed. Experiments show that our method is effective for JPEG images, especially when the compression quality is high.

1 Introduction

In recent years, numerous image/video editing techniques (e.g. [1]-[12]) have been developed so that realistic synthetic images/videos can be produced conveniently without leaving noticeable visual artifacts (e.g. Figures 1(a) and (d)). Although image/video editing technologies can greatly enrich the user experience and reduce the production cost, realistic synthetic images/videos may also cause problems. The B. Walski event [17] is an example of news report with degraded fidelity. Therefore, developing technologies to judge whether the content of an image/video has been altered is very important.

Watermark [13] has been successful in digital right management (DRM). However, doctored image/video detection is a problem that is different from DRM. Moreover, plenty of images/videos are not protected by watermark. Therefore, watermark-independent technologies for doctored image/video detection are necessary, as pointed out in [14, 19]. Farid *et al.* have done some pioneering work on this problem. They proposed testing some statistics of the images that may be changed after tempering [14] (but did not develop effective algorithms that use these statistics to detect doctored images), including the interpolation relationship among the nearby pixels if resampling happens when synthesis, the double quantization (DQ) effect of two JPEG compression

A. Leonardis, H. Bischof, and A. Pinz (Eds.): ECCV 2006, Part III, LNCS 3953, pp. 423–435, 2006.
© Springer-Verlag Berlin Heidelberg 2006

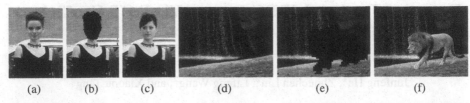

(a)   (b)   (c)   (d)   (e)   (f)

Fig. 1. Examples of image doctoring and our detection results. (a) and (d) are two doctored JPEG images, where (a) is synthesized by replacing the face and (b) is by masking the lion and inpainting with structure propagation [9]. (b) and (e) are our detection results, where the doctored parts are shown as the black regions. For comparison, the original images are given in (c) and (f).

steps with different qualities before and after the images are synthesized, the gamma consistency via blind gamma estimation using the bicoherence, the signal to noise ratio (SNR) consistency, and the Color Filter Array (CFA) interpolation relationship among the nearby pixels [15]. Ng [18] improved the bicoherence technique in [14] to detect spliced images. But temporarily they only presented their work on testing whether a given 128×128 patch, rather than a complete image, is a spliced one or not. Lin et al. [19] also proposed an algorithm that checks the normality and consistency of the camera response functions computed from different selections of patches along certain kinds of edges. These approaches may be effective in some aspects, but are by no means always reliable or provide a complete solution.

It is already recognized that doctored image detection, as a *passive* image authentication technique, can easily have counter measures [14] if the detection algorithm is known to the public. For example, resampling test [14] fails when the image is further resampled after synthesis. The SNR test [14] fails if the same noise is added across the whole synthesized image. The blind gamma estimation [14] and camera response function computation [19] do not work if the forger synthesizes in the irradiance domain by converting the graylevel into irradiance using the camera response functions [19] estimated in the component images, and then applying a consistent camera response function to convert the irradiance back into graylevel. And the CFA checking [15] fails if the synthesized image is downsampled into a Bayer pattern and then demosaicked again. That is why Popescu and Farid conclude at the end of [14] that developing image authentication techniques will increase the difficulties in creating convincing image forgeries, rather than solving the problem completely. In the battle between image forgery and forgery detection, the techniques of both sides are expected to improve alternately.

To proceed, we first give some definitions (Figure 2). A "doctored" image (Figure 2(a)) means part of the content of a real image is altered. Note that this concept does not include those wholly synthesized images, e.g. an image completely rendered by computer graphics or by texture synthesis. But if part of the content of a real image is replaced by those synthesized or copied data, then it is viewed as "doctored". In other words, that an image is doctored implies that it must contain two parts: the undoctored part and the doctored part. A DCT block (Figure 2(b)), or simply called a "block", is a group of pixels in an 8×8 window. It is the unit of DCT that is used in JPEG. A DCT grid is the horizontal lines and the vertical lines that partition an image into blocks when doing JPEG compression. A doctored block (Figure 2(c)) refers to

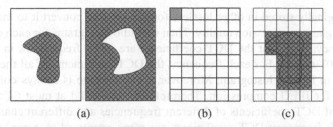

(a)   (b)   (c)

Fig. 2. Illustrations to clarify some terminologies used in the body text. (a) A doctored image must contain the undoctored part (blank area) and the doctored part (shaded area). Note that the undoctored part can either be the background (left figure) or the foreground (right figure). (b) A DCT block is a group of pixels in an 8×8 window on which DCT is operated when compression. A DCT block is also call a block for brevity. The gray block is one of the DCT blocks. The DCT grid is the grid that partition the image into DCT blocks. (c) A doctored block (shaded blocks) is a DCT block that is inside the doctored part or across the synthesis edge. An undoctored block (blank blocks) is a DCT block that is completely inside the undoctored part.

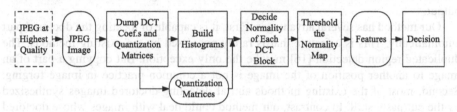

Fig. 3. The work flow of our algorithm

a block in the doctored part or along the synthesis edge and an undoctored block is a block in the undoctored part.

Realizing that it might be impossible to have a universal algorithm that is effective for all kinds of images, in this paper, we focus on detecting doctored JPEG images only, by checking the DQ effects (detailed in Section 2.2) of the double quantized DCT coefficients. Intuitively speaking, the DQ effect is the exhibition of periodic peaks and valleys in the histograms of the DCT coefficients. The reason we target JPEG images is because JPEG is the most widely used image format. Particularly in digital cameras, JPEG may be the most preferred image format due to its efficiency of compression. What is remarkable is that the doctored part can be automatically located using our algorithm. This capability is rarely possessed by the previous methods.

Although DQ effect is already suggested in [14, 20] and the underlying theory is also exposed in [14, 20], those papers actually only *suggested* that DQ effect can be utilized for image authentication: those having DQ effects are possibly doctored. This is not a strong testing as people may simply save the same image with different compression qualities. No workable algorithm was proposed in [14, 20] to tell whether an image is doctored or not. In contrast, our algorithm is more sophisticated. It actually detects the parts that *break* the DQ effect and deems this part as doctored.

Figure 3 shows the work flow of our algorithm. Given a JPEG image, we first dump its DCT coefficients and quantization matrices for YUV channels. If the image is originally stored in other lossless format, we first convert it to the JPEG format at the highest compression quality. Then we build histograms for each channel and each frequency. Note that the DCT coefficients are of 64 frequencies in total, varying from (0,0) to (7,7). For each frequency, the DCT coefficients of all the blocks can be gathered to build a histogram. Moreover, a color image is always converted into YUV space for JPEG compression. Therefore, we can build at most $64 \times 3 = 192$ histograms of DCT coefficients of different frequencies and different channels. However, as high frequency DCT coefficients are often quantized to zeros, we actually only build the histograms of low frequencies of each channel. For each block in the image, using a histogram we compute one probability of its being a doctored block, by checking the DQ effect of this histogram (more details will be presented in Section 3.2). With these histograms, we can fuse the probabilities to give the normality of that block. Then the normality map is thresholded to differentiate the possibly doctored part and possibly undoctored part. With such a segmentation, a four dimensional feature vector is computed for the image. Finally, a trained SVM is applied to decide whether the image is doctored. If it is doctored, then the segmented doctored part is also output.

Our method has several advantages. First, it is capable of locating the doctored part automatically. This is a feature that is rarely possessed by the existing methods. The duplicated region detection [16] may be the only exception. But copying a part of an image to another position of the image is not a common practice in image forging. Second, most of the existing methods aim at detecting doctored images synthesized by the cut/paste skill. In contrast, our method could deal with images whose doctored part is produced by different kinds of methods such as inpainting, alpha matting, texture synthesis and other editing skills besides image cut/paste. Third, our algorithm directly analyzes the DCT coefficients without fully decompressing the JPEG image. This saves the memory cost and the computation load. Finally, our method is much faster than the bi-coherence based approaches [14, 18], iterative methods [14], and the camera response function based algorithm [19].

However, it is not surprising that there are cases under which our method does not work:

1. The original image to contribute the undoctored part is not a JPEG image. In this case the DQ effect of the undoctored part cannot be detected.
2. Heavy compression after image forgery. Suppose the JPEG compression quality of the real image is Q_1, and after it is doctored, the new image is saved with compression quality of Q_2. Generally speaking, the smaller Q_2/Q_1 is, the more invisible the DQ effect of the undoctored part is, hence the more difficult our detection is.

The rest of this paper is organized as follows. We first give the background of our approach in Section 2, then introduce the core part of our algorithm in Section 3. Next we present the experimental results in Section 4. Finally, we conclude our paper with discussions and future work in Section 5.

2   Background

2.1   The Model of Image Forgery and JPEG Compression

We model the image forgery process in three steps:

1. Load a JPEG compressed image I_1.
2. Replace a region of I_1 by pasting or matting a region from another JPEG compressed image I_2, or inpainting or synthesizing new content inside the region.
3. Save the forged image in any lossless format or JPEG. When detection, we will re-save the image as JPEG with quantization steps being 1 if it is saved in a lossless format[1].

To explain the DQ effect that results from double JPEG compression, we shall give a brief introduction of JPEG compression. The encoding (compression) of JPEG image involves three basic steps [14]:

1. Discrete cosine transform (DCT): An image is first divided into DCT blocks. Each block is subtracted by 128 and transformed to the YUV color space. Finally DCT is applied to each channel of the block.
2. Quantization: the DCT coefficients are divided by a quantization step and rounded to the nearest integer.
3. Entropy coding: lossless entropy coding of quantized DCT coefficients (e.g. Huffman coding).

The quantization steps for different frequencies are stored in quantization matrices (luminance matrix for Y channel or chroma matrix for U and V channels). The quantization matrices can be retrieved from the JPEG image. Here, two points need to be mentioned:

1. The higher the compression quality is, the smaller the quantization step will be, and vice versa;
2. The quantization step may be different for different frequencies and different channels.

The decoding of a JPEG image involves the inverse of the pervious three steps taken in reverse order: entropy decoding, de-quantization, and inverse DCT (IDCT). Unlike the other two operations, the quantization step is not invertible as will be discussed in Section 2.2. The entropy encoding and decoding step will be ignored in the following discussion, since it has nothing to do with our method.

Consequently, when an image is doubly JPEG compressed, it will undergo the following steps and the DCT coefficients will change accordingly:

1. The first compression:
   (a) DCT (suppose after this step a coefficient value is u).
   (b) the first quantization with a quantization step q_1 (now the coefficient value becomes $Q_{q_1}(u) = [u/q_1]$, where $[x]$ means rounding x to the nearest integer).

---

[1] Note that most of the existing image formats other than JPEG and JPEG2000 are lossless.

2. The first decompression:
   (a) dequantization with q_1 (now the coefficient value becomes $Q_{q_1}^{-1}(Q_{q_1}(u)) = [u/q_1] q_1$.
   (b) inverse DCT (IDCT).
3. The second compression:
   (a) DCT.
   (b) the second quantization with a quantization step q_2 (now the coefficient value u becomes $Q_{q_1 q_2}(u) = [[u/q_1] q_1/q_2]$).

We will show in the following section that the histograms of double quantized DCT coefficients have some unique properties that can be utilized for forgery detection.

2.2 Double Quantization Effect

The DQ effect has been discussed in [14], but their discussion is based on quantization with the floor function. However, in JPEG compression the rounding function, instead of the floor function, is utilized in the quantization step. So we provide the analysis of DQ effect based on quantization with the rounding function here, which can more accurately explain the DQ effect caused by double JPEG compression.

Denote h_1 and h_2 the histograms of DCT coefficients of a frequency *before* the first quantization and *after* the second quantization, respectively. We will investigate how h_1 changes after double quantization. Suppose a DCT coefficient in the u_1-th bin of h_1 is relocated in a bin u_2 in h_2, then

$$Q_{q_1 q_2}(u_1) = \left[\left[\frac{u_1}{q_1} \right] \frac{q_1}{q_2} \right] = u_2.$$

Hence,

$$u_2 - \frac{1}{2} \le \left[\frac{u_1}{q_1} \right] \frac{q_1}{q_2} < u_2 + \frac{1}{2}.$$

Therefore,

$$\left\lceil \frac{q_2}{q_1} \left(u_2 - \frac{1}{2} \right) \right\rceil - \frac{1}{2} \le \frac{u_1}{q_1} < \left\lfloor \frac{q_2}{q_1} \left(u_2 + \frac{1}{2} \right) \right\rfloor + \frac{1}{2},$$

where $\lceil x \rceil$ and $\lfloor x \rfloor$ denote the ceiling and floor function, respectively.

If q_1 is even, then

$$q_1 \left(\left\lceil \frac{q_2}{q_1} \left(u_2 - \frac{1}{2} \right) \right\rceil - \frac{1}{2} \right) \le u_1 < q_1 \left(\left\lfloor \frac{q_2}{q_1} \left(u_2 + \frac{1}{2} \right) \right\rfloor + \frac{1}{2} \right).$$

If q_1 is odd, then

$$q_1 \left(\left\lceil \frac{q_2}{q_1} \left(u_2 - \frac{1}{2} \right) \right\rceil - \frac{1}{2} \right) + \frac{1}{2} \le u_1 \le q_1 \left(\left\lfloor \frac{q_2}{q_1} \left(u_2 + \frac{1}{2} \right) \right\rfloor + \frac{1}{2} \right) - \frac{1}{2}.$$

In either cases, the number $n(u_2)$ of the original histogram bins contributing to bin u_2 in the double quantized histogram h_2 depends on u_2 and can be expressed as:

$$n(u_2) = q_1 \left(\left\lfloor \frac{q_2}{q_1} \left(u_2 + \frac{1}{2} \right) \right\rfloor - \left\lceil \frac{q_2}{q_1} \left(u_2 - \frac{1}{2} \right) \right\rceil + 1 \right). \qquad (1)$$

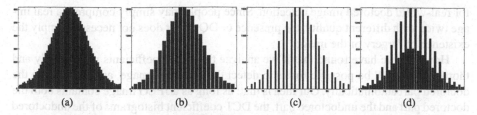

(a)   (b)   (c)   (d)

Fig. 4. The left two figures are histograms of single quantized signals with steps 2 (a) and 5 (b). The right two figures are histograms of double quantized signals with steps 5 followed by 2 (c), and 2 followed by 3 (d). Note the periodic artifacts in the histograms of double quantized signals.

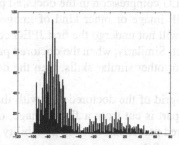

Fig. 5. A typical DCT coefficient histogram of a doctored JPEG image. This histogram can be viewed as the sum of two histograms. One has high peaks and deep valleys and the other has a random distribution. The first "virtual" histogram collects the contribution of undoctored blocks, while the second one collects the contribution of doctored blocks.

Note that $n(u_2)$ is a periodic function, with a period:

$$p = q_1/\gcd(q_1, q_2),$$

where $\gcd(q_1, q_2)$ is the greatest common divider of q_1 and q_2. This periodicity is the reason of the periodic pattern in histograms of double quantized signals (Figures 4(c) and (d) and Figure 5).

What is notable is that when $q_2 < q_1$ the histogram after double quantization can have periodically missing values (For example, when $q_1 = 5$, $q_2 = 2$, then $n(5k+1) = 0$. Please also refer to Figure 4(c).), while when $q_2 > q_1$ the histogram can exhibit some periodic pattern of peaks and valleys (Figures 4(d) and 5). In both cases, it could be viewed as showing peaks and valleys periodically. This is called the *double quantization (DQ) effect*.

3   Core of Our Algorithm

3.1   DQ Effect Analysis in Doctored JPEG Images

Although DQ effect has been suggested for doctored image detection in [14, 20], by detecting the DQ effect from the spectrum of the histogram and using the DQ effect as the indicator of doctored images, [14, 20] actually did not develop a workable algorithm for real-world doctored image detection. Since people may simply compress a real image twice with different quality, the presence of DQ effect does not necessary imply the existence of forgery of the image.

However, we have found that if we analyze the DCT coefficients more deeply and thoroughly, it will be possible for us to detect the doctored image, and even locate the doctored part automatically. Our idea is that: as long as a JPEG image contains both the doctored part and the undoctored part, the DCT coefficient histograms of the undoctored part will still have DQ effect, because this part of the doctored image is the same as that of the double compressed original JPEG image. But the histograms of doctored part will not have DQ effects. There are several reasons:

1. Absence of the first JPEG compression in the doctored part. Suppose the doctored part is cut from a BMP image or other kind of images rather than JPEG ones, then the doctored part will not undergo the first JPEG compression, and of course does not have DQ effect. Similarly, when the doctored part is synthesized by alpha matting or inpainting, or other similar skills, then the doctored part will not have DQ effect either.

2. Mismatch of the DCT grid of the doctored part with that of the undoctored part. Suppose the doctored part is cut from a JPEG image, or even the original JPEG image itself, the doctored part is still of little possibility to have DQ effect. Recall the description in Section 2.1, one assumption to assure the existence of DQ effect is that the DCT in the second compression should be just the inverse operation of IDCT in the first decompression. But if there is mismatch of the DCT grids, then the assumption is violated. For example, if the first block of a JPEG image, i.e. the block from pixel (0,0) to pixel (7,7), is pasted to another position of the same image, say to the position from pixel (18,18) to (25,25), then in the second compression step, the doctored part will be divided into four sub-blocks: block (18,18)-(23,23), block (24,18)-(25,23), block (18,24)-(23,25), and block (24,24)-(25,25). None of these sub-blocks can recover the DCT coefficients of the original block.

3. Composition of DCT blocks along the boundary of the doctored part. There is little possibility that the doctored part exactly consists of 8×8 blocks, so blocks along the boundary of the doctored part will consist of pixels in the doctored part and also pixels in the undoctored part. These blocks also do not follow the rules of DQ effect. Moreover, some post-processing, such as smoothing or alpha matting, along the boundary of the doctored part can also cause those blocks break the rules of DQ effect.

In summary, when the doctored part is synthesized or edited by different skills, such as image cut/past, matting, texture synthesis, inpaiting, and computer graphics rendering, there might always exist one or more reasons, especially the last two, that cause the absence of DQ effect in the doctored part. Therefore, the histogram of the whole doctored JPEG image could be regarded as the superposition of two histograms: one has periodical peaks and valleys, and the other has random bin values in the same period. They are contributed by the undoctored part and the doctored part, respectively. Figure 5 shows a typical histogram of a doctored JPEG image.

3.2 Bayesian Approach of Detecting Doctored Blocks

From the analysis in Section 3.1, we know that doctored blocks and undoctored blocks will have different possibility to contribute to the same bin in one period of a histogram h. Suppose a period starts from the s_0-bin and ends at the $(s_0 + p - 1)$-th bin, then the possibility of an undoctored block which contributes to that period appearing in the $(s_0 + i)$-bin can be estimated as:

$$P_u(s_0 + i) = h(s_0 + i)/\sum_{k=0}^{p-1} h(s_0 + k), \qquad (2)$$

because it tends to appear in the high peaks and the above formula indeed gives high values at high peaks. Here, $h(k)$ denotes the value of the k-th bin of the DCT coefficient histogram h. On the other hand, the possibility of a doctored block which contributes to that period appearing in the bin $(s_0 + i)$ can be estimated as:

$$P_d(s_0 + i) = 1/p, \qquad (3)$$

because its distribution in one period should be random. From the naive Bayesian approach, if a block contributes to the $(s_0 + i)$-th bin, then the posteriori probability of it being a doctored block or an undoctored block is:

$$P(\text{doctored}|s_0 + i) = P_d/(P_d + P_u), \text{ and} \qquad (4)$$

$$P(\text{undoctored}|s_0 + i) = P_u/(P_d + P_u), \qquad (5)$$

respectively.

In the discussion above, we need to know the period p in order to compute P_u or P_d. It can be estimated as follows. Suppose s_0 is the index of the bin that has the largest value. For each p between 1 and $s_{max}/20$, we compute the following quantity:

$$H(p) = \frac{1}{i_{max} - i_{min} + 1} \sum_{i=i...}^{i...} [h(i \cdot p + s_0)]^{\alpha},$$

where $i_{max} = \lfloor (s_{max} - s_0)/p \rfloor$, $i_{min} = \lceil (s_{min} - s_0)/p \rceil$, s_{max} and s_{min} are the maximum and minimum index of the bins in the histogram, respectively, and α is a parameter (can be simply chosen as 1). $H(p)$ evaluates how well the supposed period p gathers the high-valued bins. The period p is finally estimated as: $p = \arg\max_{p} H(p)$. If $p = 1$, then this histogram suggests that the JPEG image is single compressed. Therefore, it cannot tell whether a block is doctored or not and we should turn to the next histogram.

If $p > 1$, then each period of the histogram assigns a probability to every block that contributes to the bins in that period, using equation (4). And this is done for every histogram with estimated period $p > 1$. Consequently, we obtain a normality map of blocks of the image under examination, each pixel value of which being the accumulated posterior probabilities.

3.3 Feature Extraction

If the image is doctored, we expect that low normality blocks cluster. Any image segmentation algorithm can be applied to do this task. However, to save computation, we simply threshold the normality map by choosing a threshold:

$$T_{opt} = \arg\max_T \left(\sigma / (\sigma_0 + \sigma_1) \right), \tag{6}$$

where given a T the blocks are classified into to classes C_0 and C_1, σ_0 and σ_1 are the variances of the normalities in each class, respectively, and σ is the squared difference between the mean normalities of the classes. The formulation of (6) is similar to the Fisher discriminator in pattern recognition.

With the optimal threshold, we expect that those blocks in class C_0 (i.e. those having normalities below T_{opt}) are doctored blocks. However, this is still insufficient for confident decision because any normality map can be segmented in the above manner. However, based on the segmentation, we can extract four features: T_{opt}, σ, $\sigma_0 + \sigma_1$, and the connectivity K_0 of C_0. Again, there are many methods to define the connectivity K_0. Considering the computation load, we choose to compute the connectivity as follows. First the normality map is medium filtered. Then for each block i in C_0, find the number e_i of blocks in class C_1 in its 4-neighborhood. Then $K_0 = \sum_i \max(e_i - 2, 0)/N_0$, where N_0 is the number of blocks in C_0. As we can see, the more connected C_0 is, the smaller K_0 is. We use $\max(e_i - 2, 0)$ instead of e_i directly because we also allow narrowly shaped C_0: if e_i is used, round shaped C_0 will be preferred.

With the four-dimensional feature vector, i.e. T_{opt}, σ, $\sigma_0 + \sigma_1$, and K_0, we can safely decide whether the image is doctored by feeding the feature vector into a trained SVM. If the output is positive, then C_0 is decided as the doctored part of the image.

4   Experiments

The training and evaluation of a doctored image detection algorithm is actually quite embarrassing. If the images are donated by others or downloaded from the web, then we cannot be completely sure about whether they are doctored or original because usually we cannot tell them by visual inspection. Even the donator claims that s/he does not make any change to the image, as long as the image is not produced by him or her, it is still unsafe. To have a large database, may be the only way is to synthesize by ourselves, using the images that are also captured by ourselves. However, people may still challenge us with the diversity of the doctoring techniques and the doctored images. Therefore, temporarily maybe the best way is to present many detection results that we are sure about the ground truth.

We synthesized 20 images using the Lazy Snapping tool [11], the Poisson Matting tool [8], the image completion tool [9], and the image inpainting tool (it is a part of the image completion tool), and trained an SVM using these images. Then we apply our algorithm and the SVM to detect the images that are contributed by authors of some Siggraph papers. As we believe in their claims that they are the owner of the images, we take their labelling of doctored or undoctored as the ground truth.

Fig. 6. Some detection results of our algorithm. The images are all taken from Siggaph papers. The first two images are doctored by inpainting. The last two images are doctored by matting. The left columns are the doctored images. The third column are the original images. The normality maps and the masks of doctored parts are shown in the middle column. For comparison, the normality maps of original images are also shown on the right-most column. Visual examination may fail for these images.

434   J. He et al.

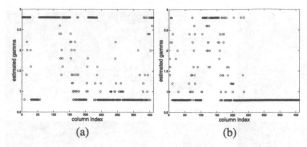

(a)   (b)

Fig. 7. The estimated column-wise gammas using the blind gamma estimation algorithm in [14]. (a) and (b) correspond to Figures 6(i) and (k), respectively. The horizontal axis is the column index and the vertical axis is the gamma value. The gamma is searched from 0.8 to 2.8 with a step size 0.2. By the methodology in [14], Figure 6(k) is more likely to be classified as doctored than Figure 6(i) is because the gamma distribution in (b) is more abnormal than that in (a).

Figure 6 shows some examples of successful detection. Given the doctored images shown in the first column, human inspection may fail. However, our algorithm can detect the doctored parts almost correctly. In comparison, the normalities of the original images do not show much variance.

Our algorithm is fast. Analyzing an image of a size 500×500 only requires about 4 seconds on our Pentium 1.9GHz PC, with unoptimized codes. For comparison, Figures 7 (a) and (b) show the estimated gammas for each column of Figures 6(i) and (k), respectively, using the blind gamma estimation algorithm proposed in [14]. Our algorithm only took 4.1 seconds to analyze Figure 6(i) or (k) and gave the correct results, while the blind gamma estimation algorithm [14] took 610 seconds but the detection was still erroneous.

5   Discussions and Future Work

With the improvement of image/video editing technologies, realistic images can be synthesized easily. Such eye-fooling images have caused some problems. Thus it is necessary to develop technologies that detect or help us detect those doctored images. Observing that JPEG is the most frequently used image format, especially in digital cameras, we have proposed an algorithm for doctored JPEG image detection by analyzing the DQ effects hidden among the histograms of the DCT coefficients. The four advantages possessed by our algorithm, namely automatic doctored part determination, resistent to different kinds of forgery techniques in the doctored part, ability to work without full decompression, and fast detection speed, make our algorithm very attractive.

However, more investigations are still needed to improve our approach. For example, a more accurate definition of (2) should be:

$$P_u(s_0 + i) = n(s_0 + i) / \sum_{k=0}^{p-1} n(s_0 + k).$$

But we need to know q_1 and q_2 in order to compute $n(k)$ according to (1). Actually q_2 can be dumped from the JPEG image. Unfortunately, q_1 is lost after the first decompression and hence has to be estimated. Although Lukas and Fridrich [20] have proposed an algorithm to estimate the first quantization matrix, the algorithm is too restrictive and may not be reliable. Hence we are exploring a simple yet practical method to estimate q_1. Moreover, since counter measures can be easily designed to break our detection (e.g. resizing the doctored JPEG image or compressing the doctored image heavily after synthesis), we still have to improve our algorithm by finding more robust low-level cues.

Acknowledgment. The authors would like to thank Dr. Yin Li, Dr. Jian Sun, and Dr. Lu Yuan for sharing us test images, Mr. Lincan Zou for collecting the training samples, and Dr. Yuwen He and Dr. Debing Liu for providing us the code to dump the DCT coefficients and the quantization matrices in the JPEG images.

References

1. A. Agarwala *et al.* Interactive Digital Photomontage. *ACM Siggraph 2004*, pp. 294-301.
2. W.A. Barrett and A.S. Cheney. Object-Based Image Editing. *ACM Siggraph 2002*, pp. 777-784.
3. Y.-Y. Chuang *et al.* A Bayesian Approach to Digital Matting. *CVPR 2001*, pp.II: 264-271.
4. V. Kwatra *et al.* Graphcut Textures: Image and Video Synthesis Using Graph Cuts. *ACM Siggraph 2003*, pp. 277-286.
5. C. Rother, A. Blake, and V. Kolmogorov. Grabcut - Interactive Foreground Extraction Using Iterated Graph Cuts. *ACM Siggraph 2004*, pp. 309-314.
6. Y.-Y. Chuang *et al.* Video Matting of Complex Scenes. *ACM Siggraph 2002*, pp. 243-248.
7. P. Pérez, M. Gangnet, and A. Blake. Poisson Image Editing. *ACM Siggraph 2003*, pp. 313-318.
8. J. Sun *et al.* Poisson Matting. *ACM Siggraph 2004*, pp. 315-321.
9. J. Sun, L. Yuan, J. Jia, H.-Y. Shum. Image Completion with Structure Propagation. *ACM Siggraph 2005*, pp. 861-868.
10. Y. Li, J. Sun, H.-Y. Shum. Video Object Cut and Paste. *ACM Siggraph 2005*, pp. 595-600.
11. Y. Li *et al.* Lazy Snapping. *ACM Siggraph 2004*, pp. 303-308.
12. J. Wang *et al.* Interactive Video Cutout. *ACM Siggraph 2005*, pp. 585-594.
13. S.-J. Lee and S.-H. Jung. A Survey of Watermarking Techniques Applied to Multimedia. *Proc. 2001 IEEE Int'l Symp. Industrial Electronics (ISIE2001)*, Vol. 1, pp. 272-277.
14. A.C. Popescu and H. Farid. Statistical Tools for Digital Forensics. *6th Int'l Workshop on Information Hiding*, Toronto, Canada, 2004.
15. A.C. Popescu and H. Farid. Exposing Digital Forgeries in Color Filter Array Interpolated Images. *IEEE Trans. Signal Processing*, Vol. 53, No. 10, pp. 3948-3959, 2005.
16. A.C. Popescu and H. Farid. Exposing Digital Forgeries by Detecting Duplicated Image Regions. Technical Report, TR2004-515, Dartmouth College, Computer Science.
17. D.L. Ward. Photostop. Available at: http://angelingo.usc.edu/issue01/politics/ward.html
18. T.-T. Ng, S.-F. Chang, and Q. Sun. Blind Detection of Photomontage Using Higher Order Statistics. *IEEE Int'l Symp. Circuits and Systems (ISCAS)*, Vancouver, Canada, May 2004, pp. 688-691.
19. Z. Lin, R. Wang, X. Tang, and H.-Y. Shum. Detecting Doctored Images Using Camera Response Normality and Consistency, *CVPR 2005*, pp.1087-1092.
20. J. Lukas and J. Fridrich. Estimation of Primary Quantization Matrix in Double Compressed JPEG Images, *Proc. Digital Forensic Research Workshop 2003*.

A Learning Based Approach for 3D Segmentation and Colon Detagging

Zhuowen Tu[1], Xiang (Sean) Zhou[2], Dorin Comaniciu[1], and Luca Bogoni[2]

[1] Integrated Data Systems Department, Siemens Corporate Research,
750 College Road East, Princeton, NJ, USA
[2] CAD Solutions, Siemens Medical Solutions,
51 Calley Stream Parkway, Malvern, PA, USA

Abstract. Foreground and background segmentation is a typical problem in computer vision and medical imaging. In this paper, we propose a new learning based approach for 3D segmentation, and we show its application on colon detagging. In many problems in vision, both the foreground and the background observe large intra-class variation and inter-class similarity. This makes the task of modeling and segregation of the foreground and the background very hard. The framework presented in this paper has the following key components: (1) We adopt *probabilistic boosting tree* [9] for learning discriminative models for the appearance of complex foreground and background. The discriminative model ratio is proved to be a pseudo-likelihood ratio modeling the appearances. (2) Integral volume and a set of 3D Haar filters are used to achieve efficient computation. (3) We devise a 3D topology representation, *grid-line*, to perform fast boundary evolution. The proposed algorithm has been tested on over 100 volumes of size $500 \times 512 \times 512$ at the speed of $2 \sim 3$ minutes per volume. The results obtained are encouraging.

1 Introduction

There have been many 3D segmentation methods proposed recently [4, 11, 14]. In these methods, Gaussian/mixture/non-parametric i.i.d. forms, or Markov random fields are often adopted to model the appearances/textures of patterns of interest. Often, they have problems in dealing with situations in which the foreground and the background are complex and confusing.

Virtual colonoscopy is a new technology being developed to find polyps in 3D CT data. However, patients currently are required to physically cleanse their colons before the examination, which is very inconvenient. By tagging the residual materials (stool) to make them bright in CT volumes, we can remove stool electronically [3, 15]. This process is also called *colon detagging*, which can be done if we can successfully perform colon segmentation since residual materials are always inside the colon. However, residual materials observe large variations in appearance depending upon where they are, what the patients eat, and how they are tagged. Fig. (1) shows a view of a typical 3D CT volume. There are two types of objects inside a colon, air and stool. Though most of them appear to be

A. Leonardis, H. Bischof, and A. Pinz (Eds.): ECCV 2006, Part III, LNCS 3953, pp. 436–448, 2006.

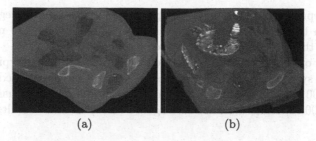

(a)   (b)

Fig. 1. Examples of clean and tagged CT volumes. (a) gives a view of a physically cleansed volume. The bright parts are bones in this volume. (b) is a view of an uncleansed volume. The bright parts on the upper part of the volume are tagged materials and the lower parts are bones same as in (a).

either very dark (air) or very bright (if successfully tagged), there are still a large portion of residual materials which have similar intensity values as tissues due to poor tagging. Also, some colon walls are bright due to the interference of the surrounding tagged stool. In addition, there are two types of tagging methods, liquid or solid, in which residual materials have very different textures. Fig. 9 shows some examples. For an input volume, we don't know what type of tagging it is and it can even a mixture of both. All these factors make the task of colon detagging very challenging.

In this paper, we propose a learning based algorithm for 3D segmentation and show its application on colon detagging. The algorithm learns the appearance models for the foreground and the background based on a large set annotated data by experts. The system therefore is highly adaptive and nearly has no parameter to tune. To account for the large intra-class variation, we adopt *probabilistic boosting-tree* [9] to learn the discriminative models. One common solution in 3D segmentation is to define/learn high-level shape models and use them as priors in defining a posterior distribution. High-level knowledge or more specifically, contextual information, plays a key role in telling whether some part belongs to colon or background. However, not only is high-level knowledge very hard to capture, but also it introduces additional computational burden in the inference phase. Instead, we put the support of contextual information implicitly in discriminative models, which are nicely turned into pseudo-likelihood appearance model ratio. This is done by learning/computing the discriminative models of each voxel based on its surrounding voxels. The use of PBT approach has several advantages over many existing discriminative methods [2,1]. First, it inherits the merit in the boosting methods which select and fuse a set of weak classifiers from a very large pool of candidates. Second, it outputs a unified discriminative probability through a hierarchical structure. Third, combined with integral volume and 3D Haar filters, it achieves rapid computation.

Here, we design a 3D representation, *grid-line*, for boundary evolution. In spirit, it is similar to the discrete surface model proposed by Malandain et al. [7].

Instead of representing the topology implicitly [12], we code the region topology explicitly on the grid node of each slice of a volume. Thus, the neighborhood structure of the boundaries can be traced explicitly.

Training of the discriminative models is performed on 10 typical volumes. The overall system is capable of robustly segmenting uncleansed colon for a volume of $500 \times 512 \times 512$ in $2 \sim 3$ minutes on a modern PC. It has been tested on around 100 volumes with fixed setting and we report some results in Sect. (6).

2   Problem Formulation

In this section, we give the problem formulation for 3D segmentation and show that the pseudo-likelihood ratio is essentially a discriminative model ratio, which can be learned and computed by a discriminative learning framework. We start our discussion with an ideal model and show that the pseudo-likelihood model is an approximation to it.

2.1   An Ideal Model

For an input volume, $\mathbf{V}$, the task of foreground and background segmentation in 3D is to infer what voxels belong to the foreground and what voxels belong to the background. The solution W can be denoted as

$$W = ((R_{-1}, \theta_{-1}), (R_{+1}, \theta_{+1})),$$

where $R_{-1}, R_{+1}, \theta_{-1}$, and θ_{+1} are the domains (voxel set) and model parameters for the background and the foreground respectively. We have $R_{-1} \bigcup R_{+1} = \Lambda$ where Λ defines the 3D lattice of the input $\mathbf{V}$, which is the set of all the voxels. $R_{-1} \cap R_{+1} = \emptyset$. The optimal solution W^* can be inferred by the Bayesian framework

$$W^* = \arg max_W \, p(W|\mathbf{V})$$
$$= \arg max_W \, p(\mathbf{V}|(R_{-1}, \theta_{-1}), (R_{+1}, \theta_{+1})) \cdot p((R_{-1}, \theta_{-1}), (R_{+1}, \theta_{+1})). \quad (1)$$

This requires the knowledge about the complex appearance models of the foreground and the background, their shapes, relations, and configurations. This "ideal" model is often out of reach in reality.

2.2   Pseudo-likelihood Models

A popular model for segmentation is the Mumford-Shah model [8]

$$\int_\omega (u - u_0)^2 dx dy + \mu \int_{\Omega/C} |\nabla u|^2 dx dy + \nu |C|.$$

The first term is the fidelity term encouraging the estimation u to be similar to the observation u_0, the second term penalizes big change in u, and the third term favors compact regions. Many similar models assume i.i.d. likelihood in modeling the texture. They are usually hard to resolve the confusion between the foreground and the background. The first column in Fig. (4) shows two slices along different planes in a volume. The second column in Fig. (4) displays the results by doing thresholding at an optimal value. We observe the "ring" effect due to the influence of tagged materials to the air. These interface voxels have similar intensity patterns as the background. Intuitively, the decision of where to place the colon boundary should be made jointly according to the overall shape and appearance of a colon. This information can be accounted in the "ideal" models discussed before. However, we don't know what ideal models are and it is very difficult to learn and compute them in reality. Therefore, we seek approximations to the "ideal" models.

Let a segmentation result now be $W = (R_{-1}, R_{+1})$, where R_{-1} and R_{+1} are the domains for the background and foreground respectively. Instead, we can put the contextual information into a model as

$$\hat{p}(W|\mathbf{V}) \propto \prod_{s \in R_{-1}} p(\mathbf{V}(s), y = -1|\mathbf{V}(N(s)/s)) \cdot \prod_{s \in R_{+1}} p(\mathbf{V}(s), y = +1|\mathbf{V}(N(s)/s))$$

$$\cdot \ p(R_{-1}, R_{+1}), \tag{2}$$

where $N(s)$ is the sub-volume centered at voxel s, $N(s)/s$ include all the voxels sub-volume except for s, and $y \in \{-1, +1\}$ is the label for each voxel, and $p(R_{-1}, R_{+1})$ defines the shape prior of the colon border. Our goal is to find the optimal W^* that maximizes the posterior $\hat{p}(W|\mathbf{V})$. Next, we show how to learn these models. Let

$$-\log \hat{p}(W|\mathbf{V}) = E_1 + E_2 + E_c$$

where E_c is a constant and does not depend on R_{-1} and R_{+1},

$$E_2 = -\log p(R_{-1}, R_{+1}),$$

and

$$E_1 = -\sum_{s \in R_{-1}} \log p(\mathbf{V}(s), y = -1|\mathbf{V}(N(s)/s)) - \sum_{s \in R_{+1}} \log p(\mathbf{V}(s), y = +1|\mathbf{V}(N(s)/s))$$

$$= -\sum_{s \in \Lambda} \log p(\mathbf{V}(s), y = -1|\mathbf{V}(N(s)/s)) - \sum_{s \in R_{+1}} \log \frac{p(y = +1|\mathbf{V}(N(s)))p(y = -1)}{p(y = -1|\mathbf{V}(N(s)))p(y = +1)}.$$

$$\tag{3}$$

This is done by taking a common part for $p(\mathbf{V}(s), y = -1|\mathbf{V}(N(s)/s)$ in R_{+1}. The first term in the above equation does not depend on R_{-1} and R_{+1}. Therefore, maximizing the probability $\hat{p}(W|\mathbf{V})$ is equivalent to minimizing the energy

$$E = -\sum_{s \in R_{+1}} \log \frac{p(l = +1|\mathbf{V}(N(s)))}{p(l = -1|\mathbf{V}(N(s)))} - |R_{+1}| \cdot \log \frac{p(y = -1)}{p(y = +1)} - \log p(R_{-1}, R_{+1}),$$

$$\tag{4}$$

where $|R_{+1}|$ is the size of volume of R_{+1}. Here, the models capturing the appearances of foreground and background are nicely turned into the discriminative probability model (classification) ratio. Note that $p(y = +1|\mathbf{V}(N(s)))$ is the posterior probability of a voxel s belonging to the foreground (colon) given the sub-volume centered at s. The optimal segmentation W^* is the one that minimizes the above energy E.

3   Learning Discriminative Models

Now the task is to learn and compute the discriminative model $p(y|\mathbf{V}(N(s)))$ for each voxel s given a sub-volume centered at s. As shown in Fig. (2), both the foreground and the background show complex patterns. Therefore, in order to make a firm decision, we need to combine various types of information together, e.g., intensities, gradients, and the surrounding voxels in the sub-volume.

AdaBoost algorithm [5] proposed by Freund and Schapire combines a number of weak classifiers into a strong classifier $H(x) = sign(f(x)) = sign(\sum_{t=1}^{T} \alpha_t h_t(x))$. Moreover, it is proved that AdaBoost and its variations are asymptotically approaching the posterior distribution [6].

$$p(y|x) \leftarrow q(y|x) = \frac{exp\{2yf(x)\}}{1 + exp\{2yf(x)\}}. \tag{5}$$

However, AdaBoost algorithm is still shown to be rigid and hard to deal with large intra-class variation. We adopt a new learning framework, probabilistic boosting tree [9], to learn complex discriminative models.

 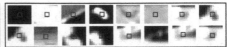

(a) Slice view of background sub-volume.   (b) Slice view of colon sub-volume.

Fig. 2. Slice view of 3D sub-volumes of background and colon. We consider the center voxel here. They observe large intra-class variability and inter-class similarity.

3.1   Probabilistic Boosting-Tree

The details of the discussion of PBT can be found in [9]. It has also been applied to learn affinity maps in perceptual grouping in [10]. We use it to learn appearance models here. The algorithm is intuitive. It recursively learns a tree. At each node, a strong classifier is learned using a standard boosting algorithm. The training samples are then divided into two new sets using the learned classifier, the left one and the right one, which are then used to train a left sub-tree and right sub-tree respectively. Under this model, positive and negative samples are naturally divided into sub-groups. Fig. (3b) illustrates an abstract version

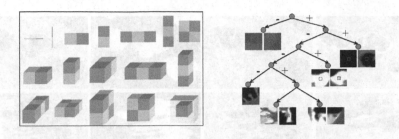

(a) 1D, 2D, and 3D Haar filters (b) Illustration of a PBT learned

Fig. 3. (a) shows various Haar filters in 1D, 2D, and 3D used. (b) illustrates an abstract version of a tree learned.

of a tree learned. Samples which are hard to classify are passed further down leading to the expansion of the tree. Since each tree node is a strong classifier, it can deal with samples of complex distributions. Compared with other existing hierarchical discriminative models, PBT learns a strong classifier at each tree node and outputs a unified posterior distribution.

During the testing stage, the overall discriminative model is computed as

$$p(y|x) = \sum_{l_1} \tilde{p}(y|l_1, x) q(l_1|x) = \sum_{l_1, l_2} \tilde{p}(y|l_2, l_1, x) q(l_2|l_1, x) q(l_1|x)$$

$$= \sum_{l_1,...,l.} \tilde{p}(y|l_n, ..., l_1, x), ..., q(l_2|l_1, x) q(l_1|x).$$

The procedure is consistent with the training stage. For each sample, it computes a probability at each node. Then the sample is sent to either the left, the right, or both sides of the tree based on this probability. At the top of the tree, information is accumulated from its descendants and an overall posterior distribution is reported. It is worth to mention that the Vapnik-Chervonenkis dimension theory shows that the test error is bounded by

$$TESTERR(\alpha) \leq TRAINERR(\alpha) + \sqrt{\frac{h(\log(2N/h + 1 - \log(\eta))}{N}},$$

where N is the number of training samples and h is the VC dimension of a classifier. In PBT, h is decided by the complexity of weak classifiers d, the number of classifiers on each tree node T, and the maximum depth of the tree L. By extending a derivation from [5]

$$h(PBT) \leq 2(d+1)(T+1) \log_2[e(T+1)](2^L - 1).$$

In this application, to keep the test error under check, we set the maximum depth of the tree to be 9 and train a classifier with half a million samples through bootstrapping.

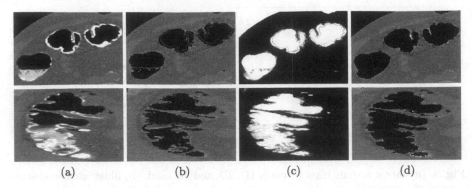

$$\text{(a)} \qquad\qquad \text{(b)} \qquad\qquad \text{(c)} \qquad\qquad \text{(d)}$$

Fig. 4. a) shows two slice views of part of a volume. b) illustrates the results by thresholding at an optimal value. We can clearly see some "ring" effects and a big part of colon in the second row is not removed. c) displays the saliency (probability) maps $p(y = +1|\mathbf{V}(N(s)))$. The higher the intensity values, the more likely it belongs to the foreground colon. d) illustrates the results by thresholding on $p(y = +1|\mathbf{V}(N(s)))$ at 0.5. The results are much better than direct thresholding in (b) though it is bit jagged. This is ameliorated by using the $p(y = |\mathbf{V}(N(s)))$ as a soft value with a local shape prior in the energy minimization formulation. Fig. (8) shows improved results by the overall algorithm.

3.2   Weak Classifiers and Features

Each training sample is of size $31 \times 31 \times 31$ and we want to learn a classification model $p(y|\mathbf{V}(N(s)))$ for the center voxel s. PBT selects and combines a set of weak classifiers into a strong classifier out of a large number of candidates. For a training sample, the features are the intensity and gradient values, curvatures at the center voxel and its surrounding voxels. Also, we design 1D, 2D, and 3D Haar filters at various locations with different aspect ratios, which are shown in Fig. (3). Therefore, local and context information are combined to give an overall decision on how likely a voxel is on the colon or not. There are around 25,000 candidate features each of which corresponds to a weak classifier.

For an input volume, we compute *integral volume* first, similar to the *integral image* used in [13]. At each location (x_1, y_1, z_1), an integral volume is computed $\int_{x_1} \int_{y_1} \int_{z_1} V(x, y, z) dx dy dz$. The computational cost of computing Haar filters is therefore largely reduced since every time we only need to sum up the values of corners of the Haar in the integral volume. Also, due to the tree structure as shown in Fig. (3).b, majority of the sub-volumes are only passed onto the top levels. Fig. (4) shows some results. We see the improvement on the place where context information is needed. Training of discriminative models is performed on 10 typical volumes (by liquid and solid tagging) with a couple of rounds of bootstrapping. We also implemented two other approaches, one node AdaBoost and a cascade of AdaBoost. The training errors for both the methods are significantly worse than that by PBT. For the cascade approach, the training error can not decrease too much after 4 levels due to the confusing patterns of the foreground and the background.

4   3D Representation for Boundary Evolution

Once we compute the discriminative model $p(y|\mathbf{V}(N(s)))$ for each voxel s, we then need to search the optimal segmentation that minimizes the energy E in eqn. (4). If we only do thresholding at 0.5 based on $p(y = +1|\mathbf{V}(N(s)))$, as shown in Fig. (4).d, the colon borders are not so smooth.

A popular implementation for boundary evolution in variational method is by level-set approaches [12]. Here, we design another 3D representation, *grid-line*, for fast boundary evolution, which is in spirit similar to [7]. Instead of representing the topology implicitly by different level sets, we code the topologies explicitly on the grid node of each slice of a volume. Thus, the neighborhood structure of the boundaries can be traced explicitly. Fig. (5) illustrates an example. For each voxel in the volume $\mathbf{V}$, we explicitly code its label by $+1$ if it is on the foreground (colon part), and -1 if is on the background. With the label map only, it does not easily facilitate the process of boundary evolution. We also code the segmentation topology at each slice along XY, XZ, and YZ planes. On each slice, boundary nodes have 4 corners with two types of labels. We code each possible situation for a boundary node on the grid. This is illustrated in Fig. (5c). Given any grid node on the boundary, we can obtain its most immediate nodes (clockwise or counter clockwise)) based on the configuration of the current node and its 4 connected neighboring nodes (special care needs to be taken on the nodes along the edge of the volume). Therefore, at each grid node on the boundary, we can explicitly compute its normal direction, curvature etc. Also, the explicit 3D representation allows us to have the property that the foreground is connected. This is often a desirable property in object specific 3D segmentation in which occlusion usually does not exist.

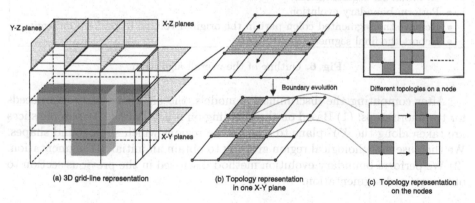

(a) 3D grid-line representation   (b) Topology representation in one X-Y plane   (c) Topology representation on the nodes

Fig. 5. A 3D topology representation for boundary evolution. In the volume shown in (a), we explicitly code the label of each voxel being either on the foreground, $+1$, or on the background, -1. In addition, we code the topology of each grid node of slices at the XY, XZ, and YZ planes. This is illustrated in (b). (c) lists various possible topologies of a grid node on the boundary. We also show an example of a boundary move in (b) and (c).

The term $p(R_{-1}, R_{+1})$ for shape prior is left undefined in eqn. (4). Indeed, part of the shape information is implicitly modeled in the discriminative model $p(y|\mathbf{V}(N(s)))$. Intuitively, the possibility of a voxel label is decided by its own intensity and the appearances of its surrounding voxels based on various features including gradients and curvatures. This implicitly reinforces certain degree of spatial coherence. In addition, we put an explicit shape prior term to encourage the boundaries to be smooth. Let A be the surface between R_{-1} and R_{+1}

$$- \log p(R_{-1}, R_{+1}) = \alpha \int_A ds$$

By Euler-Lagrange equation on E in eqn. , we obtain eqn. (4), we have

$$\frac{dE}{ds} = -(\log \frac{p(y = +1|\mathbf{V}(N(s)))}{p(y = -1|\mathbf{V}(N(s)))} + \log \frac{p(y = -1)}{p(y = +1)} + \alpha H)\mathbf{n}$$

where H and $\mathbf{n}$ are the mean curvature and normal direction at s respectively. The boundary evolution is performed using the above evolution equation based on the grid-line representation discussed above.

5   Outline of the Algorithm

The outline of the overall algorithm is illustrated below.

- Given an input volume, compute $p(y|\mathbf{V}(N(s)))$ for each voxel s.
- Perform thresholding on $p(y|\mathbf{V}(N(s)))$.
- Find seed regions in 2D slices and perform morphological region growing to obtain an initial 3D segmentation.
- Perform boundary evolution.
- Remove the segmented colon part in the original volume to perform detagging.
- Report the final segmentation results.

Fig. 6. Outline of the overall algorithm

After computing the discriminative models, the algorithm further proceeds for two more steps: (1) Based on thresholding on $p(y = |\mathbf{V}(N(s)))$, sample slices are taken along the XY plane to select some regions which show round shapes. We then use morphological region growing to obtain an initial 3D segmentation. (2) We perform boundary evolution method discussed in the previous section to obtain refined segmentation.

6   Experiments

We use 10 typical volumes for training. Fig. (8) shows the results by our method on a testing volume and those by Mumford-Shah model. We see some improvements on the place where context information is needed. The boundaries obtained are smoother than using just classification in the last row of Fig. (4).

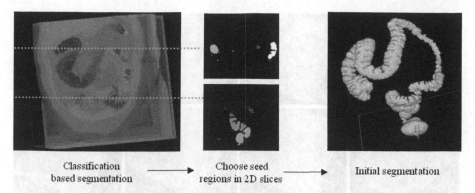

Classification based segmentation ⟶ Choose seed regions in 2D slices ⟶ Initial segmentation

Fig. 7. Initial segmentation. The image in the left column shows the volumes by thresholding at 0.5 for $p(y = +1|\mathbf{V}(N(s)))$. We then obtain a number of slice images on the thresholded volumes along the XY planes. The colon part in these slices appear to be more or less round. Some seed regions are the selected based on its size and shape. These are shown in the middle of the figure. An initial segmentation, shown in the right, is then obtained using morphological region growing.

Original Slices   Mumford-Shah   Proposed Method

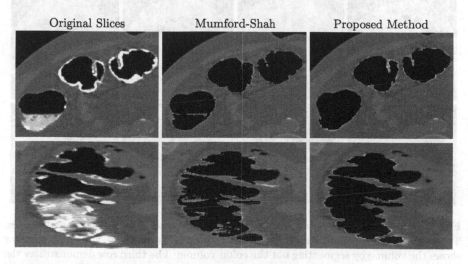

Fig. 8. The first column shows two original slices. The second column some results by Mumford-Shah model. The results by the proposed algorithm is shown in the third column.

We have tested the reported algorithm on 100 volumes with the same setting and the results are very promising. Four of which are shown in Fig. (9). The first 3 volumes are by solid tagging and the last one is by liquid tagging. Since it is very hard to obtain the ground truth for even a single 3D volume, we measure the error by comparing the results with manual annotation at some typical slices by experts. We use randomly selected 20 volumes with 15 slices in each volume. The measurement is taken by the difference of the overlaps $error = (miss(R_{+1}) + miss(R_{-1}))/|\mathbf{V}|$, where $miss(R_{+1})$ is the number of miss

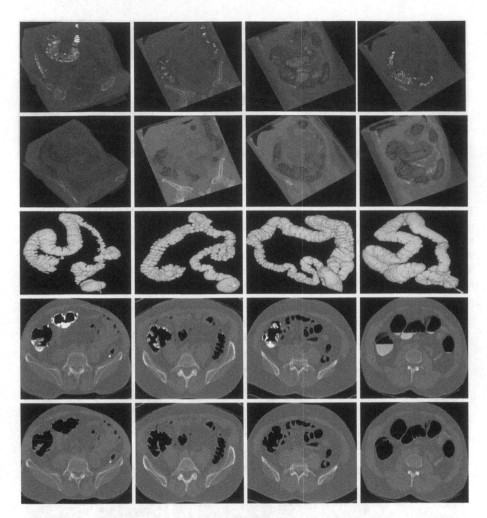

Fig. 9. Some results on colon segmentation. The first rows shows some input volumes. The first three uses solid tagging and the last one uses liquid tagging. The second row shows the volume by segmenting out the colon volume. The third row demonstrates the colon part only. The fourth row illustrates some 2D slice views of the original volume. The last row shows the corresponding views after detagging.

segmented voxels in the foreground and $miss(R_{-1})$ is the number of miss segmented voxels in the background. The error rate is lower than 0.1% by the algorithm. If we only consier those voxels that are within certain distance of the true boundary, the error rate is 5.2% while it is 20.3% for direct thresholding. Bones in these volumes appear to be very bright and their local sub-volumes look very like tagged materials. An example can be seen in Fig. (1). In our algorithm, the seed selection stage avoids picking up bones since they don't have round structures in 2D slices. Also, by enforcing the foreground regions to be connected in the boundary evolution, bones will not be touched in the boundary evolution stage. This is an important feature in our method. Existing methods [3, 15] only deal with liquid tagging, like the one in the fifth column in Fig. (9), which is relatively easy. Also, they usually do not distinguish between bones and colons, leading bones being mistakenly removed.

7 Discussion

In the paper, we have introduced a new learning based framework for 3D segmentation and shown its application on colon detagging. We use a probabilistic boosting tree (PBT) method to learn pseudo-likelihood models for the complex patterns. Integral volume and 1D, 2D, and 3D Haar wavelets are designed for fast computation. A 3D representation is used to efficiently evolve the boundary. This gives rise to a system capable of automatically segmenting colon volume of $512 \times 512 \times 400$ in $2 \sim 3$ minutes. There is no need to specify liquid or slid tagging, and the system is fully automatic. Also, the system learns the model based on a large database of annotation, which makes it very general and highly adaptive. It can be used in many problems in medical imaging and computer vision.

Our algorithm still has some problems to deal with situations where stool is very poorly tagged. The sub-volume used in computing the discriminative models is yet not big enough to capture big scope of context. Increasing it size will largely increase the complexity of the learner. It still remains to see how to combine high-level shape prior to further improve the results.

References

1. K. P. Bennett and J. A. Blue, "A Support Vector Machine Approach to Decision Trees", *Proc. of IJCNN*, 1998.
2. L. Breiman, J. H. Friedman, R. A. Olshen, and C. J. Stone, "Classification and Regression Trees", *Wadsworth International, Belmont, Ca*, 1984.
3. D. Chen, Z. Liang, M. Wax, L. Li, B. Li, and A. Kaufman, "A Novel Approach to Extract Colon Lumen from CT Images for Virtual Colonoscopy", *IEEE Tran. Medical Imaging*, vol. 19, no. 12, 2000.
4. R.H. Davies, C.J. Twining, T.F. Cootes, J.C. Waterton, C.J. Taylor, "3D Statistical Shape Models Using Direct Optimisation of Description Length", *ECCV*, 2002.
5. Y. Freund and R. Schapire, "A Decision-theoretic Generalization of On-line Learning And an Application to Boosting", *J. of Comp. and Sys. Sci.*, 55(1), 1997.
6. J. Friedman, T. Hastie and R. Tibshirani, "Additive logistic regression: a statistical view of boosting", Dept. of Statistics, Stanford Univ. Technical Report. 1998.
7. G. Malandain, G. Bertrand, N. Ayache, "Topological Segmentation of Discrete Surfaces", *Intl. J. of Computer Vision*, 10(2), 1993.
8. D. Mumford and J. Shah, "Optimal approximation by piecewise smooth functions and associated variational problems", *Comm. Pure Appl. Math.*, 42:577685, 1989.
9. Z. Tu, "Probabilistic Boosting-Tree: Learning Discriminative Models for Classification, Recognition, and Clustering", *Proc. of ICCV*, 2005.
10. Z. Tu, "An Integrated Framework for Image Segmentation and Perceptual Grouping", *Proc. of ICCV*, 2005.

11. S. Pizer et al., "Deformable M-Reps for 3D Medical Image Segmentation", *Intl. J. of Computer Vision*, 55(2), 2003.
12. J.A. Sethian, *Level Set Methods and Fast Marching Methods*, Cambridge University Press, 1999.
13. P. Viola and M. Jones, "Fast Multi-view Face Detection", *Proc. of CVPR*, 2001.
14. A. Yezzi and S. Soatto, "Stereoscopic segmentation", *Intl. J. of Computer Vision*, 53(1), 2003.
15. M. E. Zalis, J. Perumpillichira, and P. F. Hahn, "Digital Subtraction Bowel Cleansing for CT Colonography Using Morphological and Linear Filtration Methods", *IEEE Trans. Medical Imaging*, vol. 23, no. 11, 2004.

Fast, Quality, Segmentation of Large Volumes – Isoperimetric Distance Trees

Leo Grady

Siemens Corporate Research,
Department of Imaging and Visualization,
755 College Rd. East,
Princeton, NJ 08540
Leo.Grady@siemens.com

Abstract. For many medical segmentation tasks, the contrast along most of the boundary of the target object is high, allowing simple thresholding or region growing approaches to provide nearly sufficient solutions for the task. However, the regions recovered by these techniques frequently leak through bottlenecks in which the contrast is low or nonexistent. We propose a new approach based on a novel speed-up of the isoperimetric algorithm [1] that can solve the problem of leaks through a bottleneck. The speed enhancement converts the isoperimetric segmentation algorithm to a fast, linear-time computation by using a tree representation as the underlying graph instead of a standard lattice structure. In this paper, we show how to create an appropriate tree substrate for the segmentation problem and how to use this structure to perform a linear-time computation of the isoperimetric algorithm. This approach is shown to overcome common problems with watershed-based techniques and to provide fast, high-quality results on large datasets.

1 Introduction

Modern medical datasets are often so large that only the most simple, efficient segmentation algorithms may be employed to obtain results in a reasonable amount of time. Consequently, the present body of sophisticated, global segmentation algorithms are typically unsuitable in this context. In practice, thresholding, region growing [2] and watershed [3] algorithms appear to be the only approaches that are feasible under these circumstances.

Often, especially with CT data, simple intensity thresholding (or region growing) is almost sufficient to segment the entire object. However, the problem frequently occurs that the thresholded object is weakly connected to (i.e., touching) another object of equal intensity, leading to the common "leaking" problem associated with region growing. Therefore, an important problem for medical image segmentation is the fast segmentation of a mask into constituent parts via bottleneck detection within the mask. We will refer to this problem as the **mask segmentation** problem, where the mask is assumed to have been given by a simple thresholding or region growing process. Watershed algorithms, based either

A. Leonardis, H. Bischof, and A. Pinz (Eds.): ECCV 2006, Part III, LNCS 3953, pp. 449–462, 2006.

on intensity or the distance transform of the mask, are usually the algorithm of choice for breaking the mask into desired parts. Although this approach can be successful, watershed algorithms have a few common problems: 1) Small amounts of noise in the mask may lead to an overabundance of watershed regions (requiring a subsequent merging procedure), 2) Two objects may be included inside a single watershed region, 3) No measure of segmentation quality is included in the algorithm.

The recent isoperimetric algorithm for graph partitioning [1] has been successfully applied to image segmentation [4] and is specifically designed to use global information to cut a graph (mask) at bottlenecks, while remaining robust to noise, requiring only foreground seeds for initialization and offering a measure of partition quality. Although the isoperimetric algorithm is efficient enough for images or small volumes, ultimately requiring solution to a sparse linear system of equations, the size of medical volumes demands a faster approach. In this paper we show that the linear system associated with the isoperimetric algorithm may be solved in low-constant linear time if the underlying graph is a tree, propose an easily-computable tree from input data (which we call a **distance tree**), and show that our use of the isoperimetric algorithm with distance trees provides a fast, global, high-quality segmentation algorithm that correctly handles situations in which a watershed algorithm fails. For the remainder of this work, we shall refer to the approach of applying the isoperimetric graph partitioning algorithm to the mask-derived distance tree as the IDT (Isoperimetric Distance Tree) algorithm.

This paper is organized as follows: Section 2 gives context for the present algorithm by reviewing previous work. Section 3 recalls the isoperimetric algorithm for graph partitioning, shows how an underlying tree offers a linear-time solution, introduces the distance tree concept and summarizes the IDT algorithm. Section 4 compares the present algorithm to watersheds on several illustrative examples and provides results and runtimes for the IDT algorithm on real-world medical data. Section 5 draws conclusions and outlines future work.

2   Previous Work

The prior literature on segmentation is extremely large. Additionally, the special properties of trees have resulted in their use in many different contexts. Here, we attempt to review only those most relevant previous works in the context of segmentation on large datasets.

Level sets have attracted recent interest in the computer vision literature for general-purpose image segmentation [5]. However, in the context of segmenting large medical volumes, recent approaches still range from minutes to hours [6]. Furthermore, levels set techniques have not, to our knowledge, been applied to our present problem of mask segmentation.

For the task of mask segmentation, there is really only one option that is currently employed on a full resolution mask: the watershed algorithm [3]. Despite the speed of watershed approaches, there are several common problems, as outlined in the previous section. In Section 4 we show that the proposed IDT algorithm does not suffer from these problems, which maintaining the speed of a watershed approach.

Minimal/maximal spanning trees have seen extensive use in the computer vision literature since as early as Zahn [7] and Urquhart [8]. Despite the speed of these techniques, they are often insufficient for producing high-quality segmentations of a weakly-connected graph, as illustrated by the authors themselves. Although some papers have used gradient-based minimal spanning trees for segmentation [9] and others have used distance map-based maximal spanning trees for centerline extraction [10] the use of such a tree as the setting for computing a linear-time isoperimetric segmentation is novel. We note that the intense computations associated with finding solutions to Markov Random Fields have also led to approximations defined on trees (Bethe trees) instead of a full lattice [11]. Additionally, the use of quadtrees is ubiquitous in split-and-merge segmentation techniques [12] but, unlike the present approach, the algebraic or topological properties of the tree are typically not of any particular significance.

The recently-developed isoperimetric method of graph partitioning [1] has demonstrated that quality partitions of a graph may be determined quickly and that the partitions are stable with respect to small changes in the graph (mask). Additionally, the same method was also applied to image segmentation, showing quality results [4]. Other methods of graph partitioning have gained prominence in the computer vision literature, most notably the normalized cuts algorithm [13], max-flow/min-cut [14] and the random walker algorithm [15]. However, each of these algorithms is far too computationally expensive to be applied on the full medical image volume, even after thresholding a mask. Additionally, using a tree as the underlying graph is not suitable in any of these algorithms, since normalized cuts would still require an expensive eigenvector computation (albeit somewhat faster on a tree [16]), max-flow/min-cut will cut at the weakest edge in the tree (making it equivalent to Zahn's algorithm [7]) and random walker would simply return a cut such that voxels with a shorter distance to each seed (with respect to the tree) would be classified with the label of that seed.

3   Method

In this section, we review the isoperimetric algorithm of [1], show that the computations may be performed in linear time if the underlying graph is a tree, introduce the distance tree and summarize the entire IDT algorithm.

The isoperimetric algorithm is formulated on a graph where, in the image processing context, each node represents a voxel and edges connect neighboring voxels in a 6-connected lattice. Formally, a **graph** is a pair $G = (V, E)$ with vertices $v \in V$ and edges $e \in E \subseteq V \times V$. An edge, e, spanning two vertices, v_i and v_j, is denoted by e_{ij}. Let $n = |V|$ and $m = |E|$ where $|\cdot|$ denotes cardinality. A **weighted graph** has a value (here assumed to be nonnegative and real) assigned to each edge called a **weight**. The weight of edge e_{ij}, is denoted by $w(e_{ij})$ or w_{ij} and represents the strength of affinity between neighboring voxels.

3.1 Isoperimetric Graph Partitioning

The isoperimetric graph partitioning algorithm of [1] was motivated by the solution to the classical isoperimetric problem, namely: *Given an area of fixed size, what shape has the minimum perimeter?* In $\mathbb{R}^2$, the answer has been known since ancient times to be a circle. However, on an arbitrary manifold, particularly with an unusual metric, the solution is not always obvious. In particular, it is known that the solution to the isoperimetric problem often partitions the manifold at bottleneck points, as exhibited in Cheeger's classic paper on the subject [17].

Unfortunately, on a discrete manifold (represented as a graph), the solution to the isoperimetric problem is known to be NP-Hard [1]. However, one may give a sense of how close a particular partition is to the solution of the isoperimetric problem by defining the **isoperimetric ratio** as the ratio of the perimeter of a node set to the number of nodes in the set and looking for a partition that minimizes this ratio [1].

The isoperimetric algorithm for graph partitioning may be developed by writing the isoperimetric ratio as

$$h_G(x) = \min_x \frac{x^T L x}{x^T r}, \tag{1}$$

subject to $x^T r \leq \frac{n}{2}$, where r is the vector of all ones, x represents a vector indicating node membership in a set $S \subseteq V$, i.e.,

$$x_i = \begin{cases} 0 & \text{if } v_i \in S, \\ 1 & \text{if } v_i \in \overline{S}. \end{cases} \tag{2}$$

The $n \times n$ matrix L is the **Laplacian** matrix [18] of the graph, defined as

$$L_{v.v.} = \begin{cases} d_i & \text{if } i = j, \\ -w(e_{ij}) & \text{if } e_{ij} \in E, \\ 0 & \text{otherwise.} \end{cases} \tag{3}$$

where d_i denotes the weighted **degree** of vertex v_i

$$d_i = \sum_{e..} w(e_{ij}) \ \forall \, e_{ij} \in E. \tag{4}$$

The notation $L_{v.v.}$ is used to indicate that the matrix L is indexed by vertices v_i and v_j.

With these definitions, the numerator of the ratio in (1) represents the sum of the weights of the edges spanning S and $\overline{S}$, while the denominator gives the cardinality of S.

By relaxing the binary definition of x and minimizing the numerator of (1) with respect to x, given the cardinality constraint $|V| - x^T r = k$, one is left with a singular system of equations. The singularity may be overcome by arbitrarily assigning one node, v_g, (termed the **ground** in [1] by way of a circuit analogy) to S, resulting in the nonsingular system

$$L_0 x_0 = r_0, \tag{5}$$

where the subscript indicates that the row corresponding to v_g has been removed (or the row and column, in the case of L_0).

Given a real-valued solution to (5), one may convert this solution into a partition by finding the threshold that produces a partitioning with minimal isoperimetric ratio, which requires trying only n thresholds. When trying thresholds in order to measure the isoperimetric ratio of the resulting segmentation, we employ a denominator of $x^T r$ if $x^T r < \frac{n}{2}$ and $(n - x^T r)$ otherwise. It was proved in [1] that this strategy produces a connected object and shown that the ground node behaves as a specification of the *foreground*, while the background is determined from the thresholding of the solution to (5).

In the present context, we are only interested in the geometry of the graph (mask), and therefore, during the solution to (5) we treat all $w_{ij} = 1$.

3.2 Trees

Although the solution of the linear system in (5) is fast, since the matrix is sparse, symmetric and positive-definite (allowing for the use of such memory efficient methods as conjugate gradients), the enormity of data that comprises current medical volumes demands an even faster approach.

Since it is known that a matrix with a sparsity pattern representing a tree has a zero-fill Gaussian elimination ordering [19], we propose to replace the

Original	1st elimination	2nd elimination	3rd elimination	Final elimination

$$
\begin{bmatrix} 1 & -1 & 0 & 0 & 0 \\ -1 & 2 & 0 & 0 & -1 \\ 0 & 0 & 1 & 0 & -1 \\ 0 & 0 & 0 & 1 & -1 \\ 0 & -1 & -1 & -1 & 3 \end{bmatrix}
\begin{bmatrix} 1 & -1 & 0 & 0 & 0 \\ 0 & 1 & 0 & 0 & -1 \\ 0 & 0 & 1 & 0 & -1 \\ 0 & 0 & 0 & 1 & -1 \\ 0 & -1 & -1 & -1 & 3 \end{bmatrix}
\begin{bmatrix} 1 & -1 & 0 & 0 & 0 \\ 0 & 1 & 0 & 0 & -1 \\ 0 & 0 & 1 & 0 & -1 \\ 0 & 0 & 0 & 1 & -1 \\ 0 & 0 & -1 & -1 & 2 \end{bmatrix}
\begin{bmatrix} 1 & -1 & 0 & 0 & 0 \\ 0 & 1 & 0 & 0 & -1 \\ 0 & 0 & 1 & 0 & -1 \\ 0 & 0 & 0 & 1 & -1 \\ 0 & 0 & 0 & -1 & 1 \end{bmatrix}
\begin{bmatrix} 1 & -1 & 0 & 0 & 0 \\ 0 & 1 & 0 & 0 & -1 \\ 0 & 0 & 1 & 0 & -1 \\ 0 & 0 & 0 & 1 & -1 \\ 0 & 0 & 0 & 0 & 0 \end{bmatrix}
$$

Fig. 1. Gaussian elimination of the Laplacian matrix of a tree with ordering given by the numbers inside the nodes. Note that the resulting Gaussian elimination has the same sparsity structure as the original matrix when a no-fill ordering is used (e.g., as computed by Algorithm 1). This is why we need only compute the no-fill ordering, and not the full Gaussian elimination, in order to solve the linear system required by the isoperimetric algorithm. Note that the Laplacian matrix is singular — the last elimination produces a row of all zeros. Once the graph has been grounded, as in (5), this is no longer a concern e.g., if node 5 were grounded, the elimination would stop after the third elimination and $x_5 = 0$ would be used to recover the remaining values of the solution. Top row: Elimination of the tree — the figures depict the graph represented by the lower triangle of the matrix. Bottom row: Laplacian matrix of the tree after each elimination step.

Algorithm 1. Produce a no-fill ordering of a tree

1: void compute_ordering(degree, tree, ground, ordering)
2: $k \Leftarrow 0$
3: degree[root] $\Leftarrow 0$ {Fixed so that ground is not eliminated}
4: ordering[$N - 1$] $\Leftarrow$ ground
5: **for** each node in the graph **do**
6:     **while** degree[current_node] equals 1 **do**
7:         ordering[k] $\Leftarrow$ current_node
8:         degree[current_node] $\Leftarrow$ degree[current_node]-1
9:         current_node $\Leftarrow$ tree[current_node]
10:         degree[current_node] $\Leftarrow$ degree[current_node]-1
11:         $k \Leftarrow k + 1$
12:     **end while**
13:     $k \Leftarrow k + 1$
14: **end for**

---

standard lattice edge set with a *tree*. A zero-fill Gaussian elimination ordering means that the system of linear equations may be solved in two passes, with storage equal to n, since all entries in the matrix that were initially zero remain zero during the Gaussian elimination. Specifically, the ordering may be found in linear time by eliminating the nodes with (unweighted) degree of one (i.e., leaf nodes in the tree) and recursively eliminating nodes which subsequently have degree one until a root node is reached. In this case, a convenient root node is the ground. Algorithm 1 accomplishes the ordering in linear time, where the array **tree** contains, for each node, the index of one neighbor (with no edges overrepresented) and the array **degree** contains the degree of each node in the tree. This representation is possible since a tree has $n - 1$ edges (where the root would contain a '0').

Figure 1 illustrates a small tree with corresponding L and elimination. Once the elimination ordering is computed, the system in (5) may be solved by taking a forward pass over the nodes to modify the right hand side (i.e., the elimination of Figure 1) and then a backward pass to compute the solution. Algorithm 2 finds a solution to (5) in linear time, given a tree and an elimination ordering. Note that, as stated above, we assume that all $w_{ij} = 1$ and that the graph geometry (i.e., mask shape) encodes the pertinent information.

Consequently, when the graph is a tree, a low-constant linear time algorithm is available to compute a no-fill Gaussian elimination ordering, solution of (5) and subsequent thresholding to produce a partition. We note also that Branin has shown how to produce an explicit inverse for the Cholesky factors of a grounded Laplacian matrix [20]. Recall that the Cholesky factors are the results of Gaussian elimination for a symmetric, positive-definite matrix, i.e., from an LU matrix decomposition, $L = U = C$ for a symmetric, positive-definite matrix, where C is the Cholesky factor. However, the above procedure is simpler and more memory efficient than explicitly constructing the inverses of the Cholesky factors.

Algorithm 2. Given a tree, solve (5)

1: solve_system(ordering, diagonal, tree, r, output)
2: {Forward pass}
3: $k \Leftarrow 0$
4: **for** each non-ground node **do**
5:     r[tree[ordering[k]]] $\Leftarrow$ r[ordering[k]]/diagonal[ordering[k]]
6:     $k \Leftarrow k + 1$
7: **end for**
8:
9: output[ordering[N$-$1]] $\Leftarrow$ r[ordering[N$-$1]]/diagonal[ordering[$N-1$]]
10:
11: {Backward pass}
12: $k \Leftarrow$ N-2 {Last non-ground node}
13: **for** each non-ground node **do**
14:     output[ordering[k]] $\Leftarrow$ output[tree[ordering[k]]] +
        r[ordering[k]]/diagonal[ordering[k]]
15:     $k \Leftarrow k - 1$
16: **end for**

3.3   Distance Trees

In the above section, we have shown that by using a tree as the underlying graph structure (instead of the usual lattice), a very fast, linear-time solution to (5) may be obtained. We take the position that the desired cut will be a solution to the isoperimetric problem (i.e., the cut will minimize the isoperimetric ratio) and therefore we want to select a tree such that a threshold of the solution to (5) will produce the desired cut.

The most important property of a tree, such that the solution will examine the desired cut is: The path within the tree between the foreground point and the remaining voxels in the foreground object do not pass through any voxels in the background. i.e., the foreground is *connected* within the tree. If this condition is satisfied, and the background is also connected within the tree, then the foreground and background are connected with a single edge (since there may be no loops in a tree).

A tree satisfying the above desiderata may be constructed if the following conditions are satisfied: 1) The foreground object is connected, 2) Gradient ascent on the distance map from each node stabilizes at a node in the same set (i.e., foreground nodes stabilize on a foreground node and background nodes stabilize on a background node), 3) The distance value at all neighboring nodes that stabilize to different peaks is smallest along the true foreground/background boundary. The tree may be constructed by assigning to each edge in the lattice the weight

$$w_{ij} = D(v_i) + D(v_j), \qquad (6)$$

where $D(v_i)$ denotes the distance map [12] at node v_i, and then compute the *maximal spanning tree* [21]. The above desirable situation may also be restated in terms of the watershed algorithm [3]. If the foreground/background boundary occurs on the boundary of watershed basins and the height (in terms of D) of the basins separating the foreground/background boundary is larger than the basin boundaries internal to the foreground or background regions then the MST will span the foreground/background with a single edge. We note, however, that the above condition is simply sufficient to produce a tree with a connected foreground, although not necessary. Since a watershed algorithm also requires that the desired boundary lie on a watershed boundary, the isoperimetric algorithm is expected to work whenever a watershed algorithm would work, given a simply connected mask, but may additionally work in more difficult cases.

We term the maximal spanning tree of the image with weights given by (6) as the **distance tree**. We note that, as with a watershed algorithm, it would also be possible to employ different choices of function in (6). With respect to the watershed literature, the most common choices would be a distance map [12] of a masked part of the image, image gradient strength or image intensity. Furthermore, these different choices may be combined via multiplication of their respective weights. For purposes of the mask segmentation problem considered here, we restrict ourselves to distance maps.

3.4 Summary of IDT

The IDT algorithm proposed here may be summarized in the following steps:

1. Obtain a mask from the image data (e.g., via thresholding or region growing).
2. Compute a distance map on the mask.
3. Obtain a problem-specific ground (foreground) point.
4. Compute the maximal spanning tree (using Kruskal, Prim, etc.) on the lattice with edge weights given by (6).
5. Compute a no-fill ordering using Algorithm 1.
6. Solve the system in (5) using Algorithm 2.
7. Check n thresholds of the solution to (5) and choose the one such that the resulting segmentation minimizes the isoperimetric ratio of (1).

All of the above steps have a $\mathcal{O}(n)$ complexity, except for computation of the maximal spanning tree, which has a complexity of $\mathcal{O}(n \log(n))$ (for a lattice). However, as demonstrated in Section 4, the algorithm performs quickly in practice.

We note that several nodes may be used as the ground points, requiring their removal from the L matrix in (5) and fixing their values to zero in the solution procedure of Section 3.2. If desired, background seeds may also be incorporated by only considering thresholds below the x values of the background seeds. Since the x value of the ground will be zero, which will be the smallest x value of any node [1], the threshold will be guaranteed to separate the foreground from the background. Note also that the checking done by the algorithm for partition quality (i.e., the last step in the above summary) is done using the *original* graph (mask), not simply the tree.

4 Results

In this section, we first show several synthetic examples of mask segmentation problems where a region-growing or watershed algorithm would fail but the IDT algorithm succeeds. Finally, several examples are given with real data.

4.1 Synthetic Examples

In Section 1, several common problems with watershed algorithms were outlined. Specifically, a watershed approach fails if both objects fall in the same watershed region and produces an overabundance of watershed regions in noisy images (requiring an additional merging process).

In Figure 2 the problem of two touching circles is examined. Figure 2 illustrates the distance map and distance tree for two touching circles both with and without noise. Despite the small amount of noise added to the shape and the obviousness of the bottleneck, a watershed approach is left with many watershed regions, requiring an additional merging process to find the correct solution. However, the distance tree is relatively unchanged with noise and

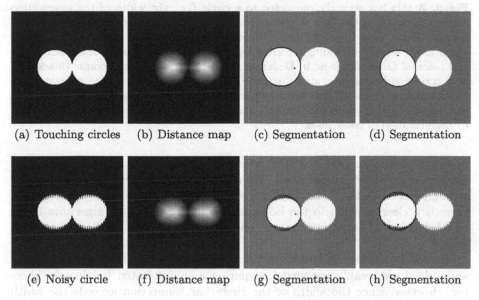

  (a) Touching circles   (b) Distance map   (c) Segmentation   (d) Segmentation

  (e) Noisy circle   (f) Distance map   (g) Segmentation   (h) Segmentation

Fig. 2. A simple case of two touching circles with noise. Although the distance map of the two circle image in (a) has one watershed basin corresponding to each circle, the small amount of noise associated with figure (e) results in many watershed basins within each circle. Consequently, an additional merging process would need to be employed by a watershed approach in order to obtain the desired segmentation. In contrast, no modification is necessary for the IDT approach. Figures (c,d,g,h) give segmentation results of the IDT algorithm. Each figure shows the user-supplied foreground point represented by a small black dot and the resulting foreground segment outlined in black. Note that no shape assumption was used — The IDT algorithm effectively segments the mask at bottlenecks.

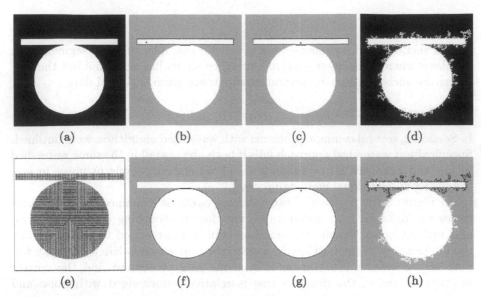

(a)   (b)   (c)   (d)

(e)   (f)   (g)   (h)

Fig. 3. A thin bar strongly connected to a circle (i.e., the width of the intersection exceeds the width of the bar). A watershed approach is incapable of separating the bar from the circle, since they both fall in the same watershed region. In contrast, the IDT algorithm is capable of finding a correct segmentation with a variety of ground points and noise. a) Original image, b) Distance tree, c–f) Various ground points (black dot) with corresponding segmentation (indicated by black line). Note that placement of the ground node near the desired boundary does not disrupt the segmentation. g) Noise was added to the mask to produce this multiply-connected example of the bar/circle. h) Segmentation of noisy mask.

Figure 2 illustrates that the IDT approach correctly segments the mask, regardless of noise or ground point. We note that this touching circles example strongly resembles the "dumbbell" manifold described by Cheeger [17] for which there is a clear solution to the isoperimetric problem, i.e., an algorithm based on minimizing the isoperimetric ratio should be expected to handle this problem well.

Figure 3 describes an entirely different scenario. Again, two objects (a circle and a bar) are weakly connected, requiring a sophisticated bottleneck detector. However, since the width of the circle/bar connection exceeds the width of the bar, both objects occupy the same watershed basin. Therefore, even a sophisticated basin-merging procedure (necessary for the situation of Figure 2) is incapable of assisting in the present situation, since both the circle and the bar occupy the same basin. However, as shown in Figure 3, such a situation is not a problem for the IDT algorithm. Specifically, choosing a ground (foreground point) in either the circle or the bar will produce the same circle/bar separation.

4.2   Real-World Volumes

The above results on synthetic examples suggest that the IDT algorithm should be expected to produce fast, quality results on large volumes. In this section, we explore the questions of quality and speed for large medical volumes. Segmentation examples were chosen to highlight the versatility of the IDT approach. All computation times reflect the amount of time required to perform all steps of the IDT algorithm given in Section 3.4. Since a Euclidean distance map was unnecessary for our algorithm, we employed a fast L1-metric distance map [22]. The maximal spanning tree was computed using a standard algorithm [21].

We first apply the IDT approach to a set of 2D examples with notoriously unreliable boundaries — ultrasound images. The mask was generated by thresholding out the dark regions and placing a ground point in the desired chamber. Note that no background seeds were placed. The results of the segmentation are displayed in Figure 4. Although the touching circles example of Figure 2

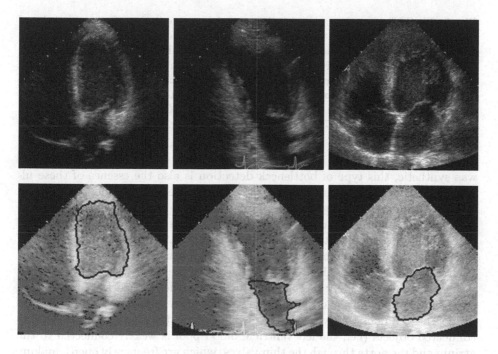

Fig. 4. Application of the IDT segmentation to 2D examples with notoriously unreliable boundaries — ultrasound images. The mask given to the IDT consisted of all pixels with an intensity below a given threshold. The ground (foreground) point was in the center of each object. Note the similarity of this problem to the touching circles example of Figure 2, since the heart chambers are weakly connected to each other through the open valve. All images were 240 × 320 with approximately 92% of the pixels inside the mask and required approximately 0.3s to process. Note that the top-row represents the images with their original (input) intensities, while the intensities in the bottom row were whitened to enhance the visibility of the contours.

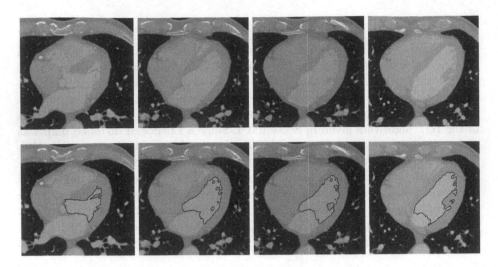

Fig. 5. The IDT algorithm applied to left ventricle segmentation of a mask produced by thresholding the volume to separate the blood pool from the background. A single ground point was placed inside the left ventricle and the IDT algorithm was run in 3D. No background seeds were given. Note that, with the open valve to the left atrium (and the aorta), this problem resembles the touching circles scenario of Figure 2. Top row: Slices from the original volume. Bottom row: Segmentation (outlined in black). The time required to perform the segmentation on this $256 \times 256 \times 181$ volume with 1,593,054 voxels inside the mask was 7.37s. Note that the papillary muscles were excluded from the blood pool mask.

was synthetic, this type of bottleneck detection is also the essence of these ultrasound segmentations since the heart chambers are weakly connected to each other through open valves and noisy boundaries.

The CT volume of Figure 5 is also suited to this segmentation approach. By thresholding the volume at the level of the blood pool, a mask was produced such that each chamber was weakly connected to each other by open or thin valves. Consequently, it was possible to apply the IDT to the mask with a ground point inside the desired chamber (in this case, the left ventricle). Figure 5 shows several slices of the segmentation of the left ventricle, using a ground (foreground) point inside the chamber. As with the ultrasound data, the mask contains weakly connected objects (i.e., the left ventricle blood pool is weakly connected to the atrium and the aorta through the thin valves, which are frequently open), making this task analogous to the touching circles example, for which the IDT was shown to behave robustly. Note that no background seeds were necessary to produce these segmentations.

Although it is possible to threshold bone in CT data, calcified blood vessels frequently also cross threshold and, more importantly, are pressed close against the bone. Consequently, the separation of bone from vessel inside the mask is a challenging task. However, as was shown in the bar/circle synthetic example of Figure 3, the IDT approach is capable of separating two tightly pressed

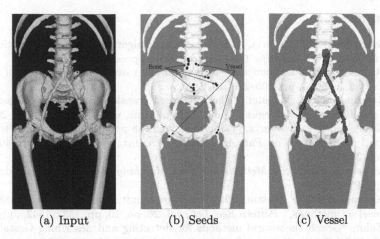

(a) Input   (b) Seeds   (c) Vessel

Fig. 6. The IDT algorithm applied to interactive vessel/bone separation. This problem is difficult because bone and vessel have similar intensities and strongly touch each other (i.e., have a weak boundary) in several places, as in the bar/circle separation problem of Figure 3. (a) Original 3D mask obtained by thresholding. (b) User-specified seeds (ground) of vessel (foreground) and bone (background). (c) Resulting vessel segmentation shaded in gray.

structures, even in noisy masks and when the point of contact is larger than the bar (vessel). Figure 6 shows the results of applying the IDT interactively to separate a blood vessel from bone. In this case, multiple grounds (i.e., vessel seeds) were placed and, additionally, background seeds (i.e., bone seeds) were also used to constrain the thresholding procedure.

5   Conclusion

The challenge of quickly segmenting regions of interest within large medical volumes frequently forces the use of less-sophisticated segmentation algorithms. Often, thresholding or region growing approaches are nearly sufficient for the required segmentation task, except that one is left with a weakly connected mask that a smart bottleneck detector is capable of parsing. Since watershed algorithms are used almost exclusively in this setting, and there are significant concerns with this approach, we have proposed a new algorithm based on operating the recent, sophisticated isoperimetric algorithm [1] on a tree derived from the mask geometry. This approach is shown to be fast, widely-applicable, high-quality, robust to noise and initialization, require specification of only a foreground seed and is not bound by the limitations of the watershed algorithm.

Further work includes investigation of other useful tree structures (e.g., based on functions other than a distance map), determining the suitability of graph structures with a level of connectivity between the lattice and the tree and domain-specific applications of this general approach to mask segmentation.

References

1. L. Grady and E. L. Schwartz, "The isoperimetric algorithm for graph partitioning," *SIAM Journal on Scientific Computing*, 2006, in press.
2. C. R. Brice and C. L. Fennema, "Scene analysis using regions," *Artificial Intelligence*, vol. 1, no. 3, pp. 205–226, 1970.
3. J. Roerdink and A. Meijster, "The watershed transform: definitions, algorithms, and parallellization strategies," *Fund. Informaticae*, vol. 41, pp. 187–228, 2000.
4. L. Grady and E. L. Schwartz, "Isoperimetric graph partitioning for image segmentation," *IEEE Trans. on Pat. Anal. and Mach. Int.*, vol. 28, no. 3, pp. 469–475, March 2006.
5. J. A. Sethian, *Level Set Methods and Fast Marching Methods*. Cambridge University Press, 1999.
6. K. Krissian and C.-F. Westin, "Fast sub-voxel re-initialization of the distance map for level set methods," *Pattern Rec. Let.*, vol. 26, no. 10, pp. 1532–1542, July 2005.
7. C. Zahn, "Graph theoretical methods for detecting and describing Gestalt clusters," *IEEE Transactions on Computation*, vol. 20, pp. 68–86, 1971.
8. R. Urquhart, "Graph theoretical clustering based on limited neighborhood sets," *Pattern Recognition*, vol. 15, no. 3, pp. 173–187, 1982.
9. P. F. Felzenszwalb and D. P. Huttenlocher, "Efficient graph-based image segmentation," *Int. J. of Computer Vision*, vol. 59, no. 2, pp. 167–181, Sept. 2004.
10. M. Wan, Z. Liang, Q. Ke, L. Hong, I. Bitter, and A. Kaufman, "Automatic centerline extraction for virtual colonoscopy," *IEEE Trans. on Medical Imaging*, vol. 21, no. 12, pp. 1450–1460, December 2002.
11. C.-H. Wu and P. C. Doerschuk, "Tree approximations to Markov random fields," *IEEE Trans. on Pat. Anal. and Mach. Int.*, vol. 17, no. 4, pp. 391–402, April 1995.
12. A. Jain, *Fundamentals of Digital Image Processing*. Prentice-Hall, Inc., 1989.
13. J. Shi and J. Malik, "Normalized cuts and image segmentation," *IEEE Trans. on Pat. Anal. and Mach. Int.*, vol. 22, no. 8, pp. 888–905, Aug. 2000.
14. Y. Boykov and M.-P. Jolly, "*Interactive graph cuts* for optimal boundary & region segmentation of objects in N-D images," in *Proc. of ICCV 2001*, 2001, pp. 105–112.
15. L. Grady and G. Funka-Lea, "Multi-label image segmentation for medical applications based on graph-theoretic electrical potentials," in *Computer Vision and Mathematical Methods in Medical and Biomedical Image Analysis, ECCV 2004*, no. LNCS3117. Prague, Czech Republic: Springer, May 2004, pp. 230–245.
16. P. E. John and G. Schild, "Calculating the characteristic polynomial and the eigenvectors of a tree," *MATCH*, vol. 34, pp. 217–237, Oct. 1996.
17. J. Cheeger, "A lower bound for the smallest eigenvalue of the Laplacian," in *Problems in Analysis*, R. Gunning, Ed. Princeton, NJ: Princeton University Press, 1970, pp. 195–199.
18. R. Merris, "Laplacian matrices of graphs: A survey," *Linear Algebra and its Applications*, vol. 197, 198, pp. 143–176, 1994.
19. K. Gremban, "Combinatorial preconditioners for sparse, symmetric diagonally dominant linear systems," Ph.D. dissertation, Carnegie Mellon University, Pittsburgh, PA, October 1996.
20. F. H. Branin, Jr., "The inverse of the incidence matrix of a tree and the formulation of the algebraic-first-order differential equations of an RLC network," *IEEE Transactions on Circuit Theory*, vol. 10, no. 4, pp. 543–544, 1963.
21. A. Gibbons, *Algorithmic Graph Theory*. Cambridge University Press, 1989.
22. A. Rosenfeld and J. L. Pfaltz, "Sequential operations in digital picture processing," *J. of the Assoc. for Computing Machinery*, vol. 13, no. 4, pp. 471–494, Oct. 1966.

Segmentation of High Angular Resolution Diffusion MRI Modeled as a Field of von Mises-Fisher Mixtures

Tim McGraw[1], Baba Vemuri[2], Robert Yezierski[3], and Thomas Mareci[4]

[1] West Virginia University,
Dept. of Computer Science and Electrical Engineering, Morgantown, WV
tmcgraw@csee.wvu.edu
[2] University of Florida,
Dept. of Computer and Information Sciences and Engineering, Gainesville, FL
vemuri@cise.ufl.edu
[3] University of Florida, Dept. of Neuroscience,
Dept. of Orthodontics, Gainesville, FL
ryezierski@dental.ufl.edu
[4] University of Florida, Dept. of Biochemistry,
Gainesville, FL
thmareci@ufl.edu

Abstract. High angular resolution diffusion imaging (HARDI) permits the computation of water molecule displacement probabilities over a sphere of possible displacement directions. This probability is often referred to as the orientation distribution function (ODF). In this paper we present a novel model for the diffusion ODF namely, a mixture of von Mises-Fisher (vMF) distributions. Our model is compact in that it requires very few variables to model complicated ODF geometries which occur specifically in the presence of heterogeneous nerve fiber orientation. We also present a Riemannian geometric framework for computing intrinsic distances, in closed-form, and performing interpolation between ODFs represented by vMF mixtures. As an example, we apply the intrinsic distance within a hidden Markov measure field segmentation scheme. We present results of this segmentation for HARDI images of rat spinal cords – which show distinct regions within both the white and gray matter. It should be noted that such a fine level of parcellation of the gray and white matter cannot be obtained either from contrast MRI scans or Diffusion Tensor MRI scans. We validate the segmentation algorithm by applying it to synthetic data sets where the ground truth is known.

1 Introduction

High angular resolution diffusion imaging (HARDI) has become a popular diffusion imaging mechanism lately in the research communities of MR imaging and analysis. Diffusion tensor models have been used in the past to explain the local geometry of the diffusivity function characterizing the tissue being imaged.

A. Leonardis, H. Bischof, and A. Pinz (Eds.): ECCV 2006, Part III, LNCS 3953, pp. 463–475, 2006.
© Springer-Verlag Berlin Heidelberg 2006

A diffuson tensor model primarily assumes a single dominant direction of diffusion and hence is well suited for modeling tissue that exhibits unidirectional diffusivity behavior. In general however, more general mathematical models are needed to represent the diffusivity function which may exhibit X-shaped local geometry corresponding to crossing fibers or bifurcating fibers. The DTI model is well known for its deficiency in coping with such complex local geometries and HARDI is one way to overcome this problem. Several research articles have been published that describe techniques for processing HARDI data sets. For example, Tuch [1, 2] developed the HARDI acquisition and processing and later Frank [3] used the spherical harmonics expansion of the HARDI data to characterize the local geometry of the diffusivity profiles. Neither one of these methods address the issue of segmenting the field of probability distributions. A level-set approach to segmenting HARDI data has been given by Jonasson et al. [4].

Several research groups have actively pursued the problem of segmenting DTI data sets. Some have used scalar-valued maps computed from DTI and applied standard level-set based scalar image segmentation methods to them [5] while, Feddern et al., [6] extended the geodesic active contour model to accomodate tensor field segmentation. A region-based active contour was used with a Frobenius norm based tensor distance in Wang et. al., [7] and Rousson et. al., [8] developed an extension of the classical surface evolution scheme by incorporating region based statistics computed from the tensor field. Recently, Wang et. al., [9, 10] introduced an affine invariant tensor dissimilarity and used it to reformulate the active contour implementation of the Mumford-Shah piecewise constant version [11] and the piecewise smooth version [12] of the segmentation model to suit tensor field segmentation. The piecewise constant DTI segmentation model was generalized by Lenglet et al. [13] to the case of regions with piecewise constant non-unit variances.

Since HARDI data have the ability to resolve fiber crossings, it would be natural to expect a better parcellation of the fiber connectivity pattern than that obtained using DTI. In this paper, we will present results on synthetic data sets that will demonstrate the truth of this hypothesis. We will also present segmentation results on real HARDI data acquired from a rat spinal cord. These results were visually validated, but quantitative validation of real data segmentation will be the focus of future work.

2   Modeling Diffusion

In DTI, data are modeled in terms of the diffusion tensor. The apparent diffusion coefficient is a quadratic form involving the tensor, and the diffusion displacement pdf is a Gaussian with covariance matrix equal to a constant multiple of the inverse of the tensor. For HARDI, we will model neither the diffusivity nor the displacement pdf, but will instead model the diffusion ODF.

In order to design efficient algorithms, we wish to find a continuous parametric model for the ODF with a small number of parameters, which is capable of describing diffusion in the presence of intravoxel orientational heterogeneity.

To put our proposed model in perspective we will first review some models for diffusion used in previous literature.

Gaussian mixture models (GMM) are one of the most commonly used models for multimodal distributions. The GMM is a convex combination of Gaussian density functions, $N(\mathbf{x}|\mu_i, \Sigma_i)$. Each Gaussian component is characterized by a 3×3 covariance matrix, Σ_i, which has 6 independent elements. For diffusion data, all components have a mean $\mu = 0$.

The GMM, $P(\mathbf{x}) = \sum_{i=1}^{m} w_i N(\mathbf{x}|\mu_i, \Sigma_i)$, where m is the number of components in the mixture, can describe the 3-dimensional diffusion displacement pdf. Each Gaussian component has its own 3×3 covariance matrix, Σ_i, which will have 6 independent elements. For diffusion data, all components will have $\mu_i = 0$.

However, we are primarily concerned with the directional characteristics of diffusion. This can be characterized by the marginal distribution, $P(\theta, \phi)$ obtained by integrating over the radial component of $P(\mathbf{x})$. Additionally, with the GMM, we must be careful to impose the positive-definiteness constraint on the covariance matrix of each component of the mixture. Previously Fletcher and Joshi [14] have described geodesic analysis on the space of diffusion tensors. The analysis includes an algorithm for computing the intrinsic mean of diffusion tensors. Later in this paper we will describe a similar analysis on the space of ODFs which will result in much simpler algorithms.

The spherical harmonic (SH) expansion is a useful representation for complex-valued functions on the sphere. We can represent the diffusion with the expansion $d(\theta, \phi) = \sum_{l=0}^{L} \sum_{m=-l}^{l} a_{l,m} Y_{l,m}(\theta, \phi)$, where $Y_{l,m}$ are the spherical harmonic basis functions. Note that the coefficients $a_{l,m}$ are complex-valued, so that the storage requirement is double that of an equivalent model with real variables, and the arithmetic operations are more costly as well. Frank [15] suggests an expansion truncated at order $L = 4$ (or higher) to describe multiple fiber diffusion. This requires at least 15 complex-valued coefficients per voxel. In general, the order L expansion can describe diffusion with $L/2$ fiber directions. Özarslan [16] has developed an extremely fast algorithm for computing a SH expansion for the ODF given a SH expansion of the diffusivity. Chen et al. [17] have previously presented a technique for estimating a regularized field of apparent diffusion coefficient (ADC) profiles as a SH expansion.

The diffusion tensor imaging model described previously represents diffusion using a rank-2 tensor. Diffusion has been described more generally by Özarslan et al. [18,19] by considering tensors of higher rank. A cartesian tensor of rank I will, in general, have 3^I components. Due to symmetry, the number of distinct components in a high rank diffusion tensor will be much smaller. By generalizing the concept of trace, it is possible to quantify the anisotropy of diffusion described by tensors of arbitrary rank [20].

Since tensors of odd rank imply negative diffusion coefficients, only even rank tensors are appropriate for describing diffusion. For diffusion tensors of rank 4,6, and 8, the number of distinct components are 15, 28, and 45 respectively. It is not clear how to extract fiber directions from higher rank tensors.

2.1   von Mises-Fisher Mixture Model

Many statistical approaches involve data over $\Re^n$. Since we are dealing with multivariate data over the sphere, S^2, we wish to express the data using distributions over this domain. Distributions over spherical domains are discussed in detail by Mardia and Jupp [21].

In this section we will present a directional model for the ODF in terms of von Mises-Fisher distributions. This model has fewer variables than the previously discussed models, allows the fiber directions to be extracted easily, involves constraints which are simpler to satisfy, and leads to a closed-form for several useful measures. The von Mises distribution over the circle can be generalized

Fig. 1. Example vMF distributions ($\kappa = 1$, 5, 15, 25) with same mean direction, μ

to spheres of arbitrary geometry by keeping the log of the distribution linear in the random variable $\mathbf{x}$ as in

$$M_p(\mathbf{x}|\mu,\kappa) = \left(\frac{\kappa}{2}\right)^{p/2-1} \frac{1}{2\pi\Gamma(p/2)I_{p/2-1}(\kappa)} \exp(\kappa\mu^T\mathbf{x}) \qquad (1)$$

where $|\mathbf{x}| = 1$ and $|\mu| = 1$, κ is the concentration parameter and I_k denotes the modified Bessel function of the first kind, order k. The concentration parameter, κ, quantifies how tightly the function is distributed around the mean direction μ. For $\kappa = 0$ the distribution is uniform over the sphere. The distributions are unimodal and rotationally symmetric around the direction μ.

For $p = 3$ the distribution is called the von Mises-Fisher (vMF) distribution, and can be written

$$M_3(\mathbf{x}|\mu,\kappa) = \frac{\kappa}{4\pi\sinh(\kappa)} \exp(\kappa\mu^T\mathbf{x}). \qquad (2)$$

A useful characteristic of the vMF distribution is that the product of two vMFs may also be written as an unnormalized vMF. Since

$$\exp(\kappa_i\mu_i^T\mathbf{x})\exp(\kappa_j\mu_j^T\mathbf{x}) = \exp((\kappa_i\mu_i + \kappa_j\mu_j)^T\mathbf{x}) \qquad (3)$$

we have

$$M_3(\mathbf{x}|\mu_i,\kappa_i)M_3(\mathbf{x}|\mu_j,\kappa_j) \propto M_3(\mathbf{x}|(\frac{\kappa_i\mu_i + \kappa_j\mu_j}{\rho(\kappa_i,\kappa_j,\mu_i,\mu_j)}),\rho(\kappa_i,\kappa_j,\mu_i,\mu_j)),$$

$$\rho(\kappa_i,\kappa_j,\mu_i,\mu_j) = \sqrt{\kappa_i^2 + \kappa_j^2 + 2\kappa_i\kappa_j(\mu_i \cdot \mu_j)}. \qquad (4)$$

Since the vMF distribution is unimodal, we require a combination of these distributions to represent a general ODF. In fact, since the ODF is antipodally symmetric, we will need a mixture to describe diffusion in even a single fiber region. Since the antipodal pair have $\mu_1 = -\mu_2$, we can specify a mixture with only 3 variables per component: the two spherical coordinate angles describing μ, and κ. The general ODF will have the form

$$ODF(\mathbf{x}) = \sum_{i=1}^{m} w_i M_3(\mathbf{x}|\mu_i, \kappa_i) \tag{5}$$

where m is the number of components in the mixture. Choosing a convex combination of vMF distributions, the weights have the property $\sum_{i=1}^{m} w_i = 1$ and $w_i \geq 0$. This ensures that the mixture still has nonnegative probabilities, and will integrate to 1. Since vMF distributions obey the property (3), the product of two von Mises-Fisher mixture models is also proportional to a vMF mixture model.

It can also be shown [22] that the Renyi entropy (order α) of the vMF mixture has closed form (for certain values of α). This is useful since the entropy of the mixture model can be used as measure of anisotropy. It can also be shown, using property (3), that there is a closed-form equation for the L_2 distance between two vMF mixtures.

2.2   Fitting the vMF Mixture

In this section we describe a nonlinear least-squares technique for computing the vMF mixture model. We will assume that we have been given a discrete set of samples of the ODF. We seek a mixture of vMFs which agrees with these samples in the least-squares sense while obeying the constraints imposed on the vMF parameters.

Using the spherical coordinates $\mathbf{x} = [\cos\theta\sin\phi, \sin\theta\sin\phi, \cos\phi]^T$ and $\mu = [\cos\alpha\sin\beta, \sin\alpha\sin\beta, \cos\beta]^T$, we may write the vMF in polar form:

$$M_3(\theta, \phi|\alpha, \beta, \kappa) = \frac{\kappa}{4\pi\sinh(\kappa)} \exp(\kappa[\cos\phi\cos\beta + \sin\phi\sin\beta\cos(\theta - \alpha)]) \tag{6}$$

The energy function we will seek to minimize is

$$\min_{w,\kappa,\mu} \sum_{i=1}^{N} [p(x_i) - \sum_{j=1}^{m/2} \frac{w_j}{2} (M(x_i|\kappa_j, \mu_j) + M(x_i|\kappa_j, -\mu_j))]^2$$

$$-\gamma_1 \sum_{j=1}^{m/2} \log(w_j) + \gamma_2 (1 - \sum_{j=1}^{m/2} w_j)^2 - \gamma_3 \sum_{j=1}^{m/2} \log(\kappa_j) \tag{7}$$

where the first term is the least-squares error. Note that we are fitting the data, $p(\mathbf{x})$, to a mixture of $m/2$ antipodal vMF pairs. The second term, with weight γ_1, is a barrier function which constrains the weights, w_j, to be greater than zero. The third term, with weight γ_2, constrains the sum of the weights to be 1. The fourth term, with weight γ_3, is a barrier function which constrains the concentration parameters, κ_j, to be greater than zero. Equation (7) is solved using Levenberg-Marquardt.

It is likely that most voxels will fit a mixture of 4 vMF pairs (4 fiber orientations per voxel) quite well. In this case the mixture of 8 vMF distributions requires only 15 real-valued parameters to completely describe due to pairwise antipodal symmetry. Once we have fit the vMF mixture to the ODF, we can directly extract the fiber directions, $\{\mu\}$.

3   The Space of vMF Distributions

The von Mises-Fisher distribution is parameterized by two variables: the concentration parameter $\kappa \in \Re^+$ and $\mu \in S^2$. For each point in $\Re^+ \times S^2$ there is a corresponding vMF distribution. The curved geometry of this space of vMF distributions will influence how we formulate distances, geodesics, interpolation functions and means. A general treatment of the geometry of the spaces formed by parametric distributions is given by Amari [23, 24].

3.1   Riemannian Geometry

The space of vMF distributions forms a differentiable manifold, a space which locally behaves like Euclidean space. A Riemannian manifold is a smooth manifold supplied with a Riemannian metric. This metric takes the form of an inner product, $\langle v, w \rangle_p$ defined on the tangent space, T_pM, for each point, p, on the manifold, M. The Riemannian metric allows us to measure the length of a curve, $\gamma(t)$ between two points, p, q on M.

$$L(\gamma) = \int_p^q (\langle \gamma'(t), \gamma'(t) \rangle_{\gamma(t)})^{\frac{1}{2}} dt \tag{8}$$

We will see how the notions of metric, distance, geodesics, interpolation and mean are all related. The mean can be defined in terms of the distance, d, as the point, μ, which satisfies

$$\min_{\mu \in M} \sum_{i=1}^{N} d^2(\mu, x_i). \tag{9}$$

Interpolation can be defined in terms of a weighted mean, so we can interpolate between the distributions p, q by minimizing

$$\min_{\mu \in M} td(\mu, p) + (1 - t)d(\mu, q). \tag{10}$$

3.2   Riemannian Exp and Log Maps

Let M be some manifold, and T_pM be the tangent space at $p \in M$. Consider all geodesics going through the point, p, on M. Given a tangent vector, $v \in T_pM$, it is known that there is a unique geodesic, γ, such that $\gamma(0) = p$, and $\gamma'(0) = v$.

If the manifold is geodesically complete, as it is in our case, the Riemannian exponential map, $\text{Exp}_p : T_pM \to M$, can be defined as $\text{Exp}_p(v) = \gamma(1)$.

The Riemannian log map is the inverse of the exponential map, $\text{Log}_p : M \to T_pM$. This map only exists in the region near p where the Exp map is invertible. If the log map, Log_p exists at q, we can write the Riemannian distance between p and q as $d(p,q) = \| \text{Log}_p(q) \|_p$.

3.3 Overview of the Geodesic Analysis

In this section we will give a brief overview of the geodesic analysis of the space of vMF mixtures. The complete analysis is given by McGraw [22]. Similar analysis has been presented by Fletcher and Joshi [14] for the space of diffusion tensors, and by Fletcher et al. [25] for the space of shapes represented by medial atoms. An outline of our analysis is given below:

1. Show that $\Re^+$ and S^2 are symmetric spaces.
2. Show that $M = \Re^+ \times S^2$ is a symmetric space.
3. Find a transitive Lie group action on M.
4. Formulate arbitrary geodesics on M by applying the Lie group action to a known geodesic.
5. Formulate the Exp and Log maps for M.

A symmetric space [26] is a connected Riemannian manifold such that at each point on the manifold there exists a distance preserving mapping which reverses geodesics through that point. Such a mapping can be computed for the spaces $\Re^+$ and S^2. It can also be shown that the direct product of symmetric spaces is also a symmetric space.

Now we can consider a vMF distribution to be a point in a symmetric space. If M_1 and M_2 are two metric spaces and $x_1, y_1 \in M_1$ and $x_2, y_2 \in M_2$, then the metric for $M_1 \times M_2$ is $d((x_1, x_2), (y_1, y_2))^2 = d(x_1, y_1)^2 + d(x_2, y_2)^2$. This result allows us to formulate distances between vMF distributions in terms of distances on the spaces $\Re^+$ and S^2.

The action of group G on M is called transitive if for any two $x, y \subset M$ there exists a $g \in G$ such that $g \cdot x = y$. If the group action is transitive then M can be shown to be a homogeneous space, and the action of G does not change distances on M : $d(g \cdot p, g \cdot q) = d(p, q)$. Geodesics on a homogeneous space can then be computed by applying the group action to other geodesics.

3.4 Exp and Log Maps for vMF Distributions

We have used the fact that the direct product of symmetric spaces is also a symmetric space to deduce that the space of vMF distributions is symmetric. Now we will use this fact to compute the Exp map for vMFs. For spaces which are expressed as direct products, we can write the exponential map as the direct product of the exponential maps for the constituent spaces. For a single vMF, let $p = (\kappa, \mu)$ represent the distribution $M_3(\mathbf{x}|\kappa, \mu)$, and $v = (a, u) \in T_pM$ be the tangent vector. Then

$$\mathrm{Exp}_p(v) = \left(\kappa \exp(a), Q \begin{bmatrix} u_x \frac{\sin \|u\|}{\|u\|} \\ u_y \frac{\sin \|u\|}{\|u\|} \\ \cos \|u\| \end{bmatrix} \right)^T \tag{11}$$

where Q is the orthogonal matrix which transforms μ to $[0,0,1]^T$. The distance between vMFs can be written using the Log maps as

$$d((\kappa_i, \mu_i), (\kappa_j, \mu_j)) = \sqrt{\log(\frac{\kappa_j}{\kappa_i})^2 + (\cos^{-1}(\mu_i \cdot \mu_j))^2}. \tag{12}$$

An example of interpolation between two vMF distributions computed using the Exp and Log maps is shown in Figure 2.

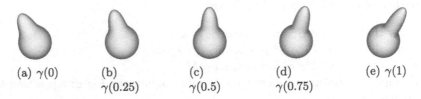

(a) $\gamma(0)$ (b)   (c)   (d)   (e) $\gamma(1)$
                  $\gamma(0.25)$ $\gamma(0.5)$ $\gamma(0.75)$

Fig. 2. Points along the geodesic between two vMF distributions

4   The Space of vMF Mixtures

Now, let us investigate the space of mixtures of vMF distributions. The mixture model of m components is given in Equation (5). At first, it may seem that we can simply extend the results of the previous section, and consider these mixtures to come from the space $(\Re^+ \times \Re^+ \times S^2)^m$. However, considering the set of weights as an point in $(\Re^+)^m$ ignores the convexity constraint on the weights. The space $(\Re^+)^m$ includes linear combinations of vMFs whose weights do not sum to 1.

Instead, we consider the square roots of the weights, $\{\sqrt{w_1}...\sqrt{w_m}\}$. The convexity constraint now becomes $\sum_{i=1}^m \sqrt{w_i}^2 = 1$ with $w_i >= 0$. So, we can consider the space of the square roots of the weights to be a hypersphere, S^{m-1}. Then, the space of mixtures with m components is $S^{m-1} \times (\Re^+ \times S^2)^m$.

4.1   Exp and Log Maps for the Space of vMF Mixtures

For the vMF mixture, the exponential map is the direct product of the exponential maps for each vMF, and the exponential map for S^{m-1}. Since we are quite unlikely to have more than 4 fiber orientations present within a single voxel, we will consider further the case of mixtures having 8 antipodal pairs, or 4 independent weights. In this case, the space of the square roots of $\{w\}$ is the unit hypersphere S^3. Fortunately, the space S^3 is well studied, since this is equivalent to the space of unit quaternions. In fact, S^3 forms a Lie group with respect to the quaternion multiplication operator.

The exponential map for S^3 is

$$\text{Exp}_p(v) = \left(\frac{\sin(\frac{1}{2}\|v\|)}{\|v\|} v, \cos(\frac{1}{2}\|v\|) \right)^T \tag{13}$$

and the log map is given by

$$\text{Log}_p(q) = \frac{2\cos^{-1}(q_w)}{|q_{vec}|} q_{vec} \tag{14}$$

where q_{vec} and q_w are the vector and scalar parts respectively of the quaternion q. We may now simply extend the results of the previous section to formulate the distance between mixtures. An example of interpolation between mixtures is shown in Figure 3.

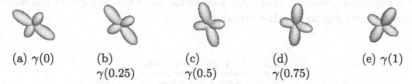

(a) $\gamma(0)$ (b)   (c)   (d)   (e) $\gamma(1)$
$\gamma(0.25)$ $\gamma(0.5)$ $\gamma(0.75)$

Fig. 3. Points along the geodesic between two vMF mixtures

Previously, the intrinsic mean problem has been solved with a gradient descent algorithm [27, 25, 28]. The gradient of the energy function in Equation (9) can be written in terms of the Log map. The algorithm, as given by Fletcher and Joshi [25] is

Given: $x_1, ..., x_N \in M$
Find: $\mu \in M$, the intrinsic mean
$\mu_0 = x_1$
repeat
$\Delta\mu = \frac{\tau}{N} \sum_{i=1}^{N} \text{Log}_{\mu.}(x_i)$
$\mu_{t+1} = \text{Exp}_{\mu.}(\Delta\mu)$
until $\|\Delta\mu\| < \epsilon$

5   Application to Segmentation

The mean and distance formulations discussed in the previous section can be quite useful in the context of model-based segmentation. In this section we will present results obtained using the hidden Markov measure field (HMMF) model, though the model we have developed may be used with many other segmentation schemes. This method, presented by Marroquin et al. [29], is a variation on the Markov random field segmentation model, but has fewer variables and can solved without slow stochastic methods. We use the gradient projection Newtonian descent algorithm for finding the resulting optimization problem.

5.1   Results

The proposed vMF fitting technique was applied to a synthetic dataset. This data simulated anisotropic Gaussian diffusion in a medium with a single dominant orientation. The orientation varies spatially according to a sinusoidal function. The result of the fitting is shown in Figure 4. The angular difference between the known dominant orientation and the mean direction, μ, of the dominant vMF component was computed at each voxel. The average angular error was 0.026 degrees. The results of the HMMF segmentation using the geodesic distance applied to synthetic HARDI data are presented below. The first two datasets are piecewise constant vMF fields with two regions. The results are presented in Figure 5a and b. Figure 5a shows the segmentation obtained from a field where the two regions differ in direction. In Figure 5b, the regions differ only in the concentration parameter, κ. There are no classification errors. In Figure 5c the results for segmentation of vMF mixtures is shown. The data consists of several piecewise constant areas and a crossing. Here the algorithm has correctly segmented each region and the crossing.

Fig. 4. vMF model fit to synthetic data

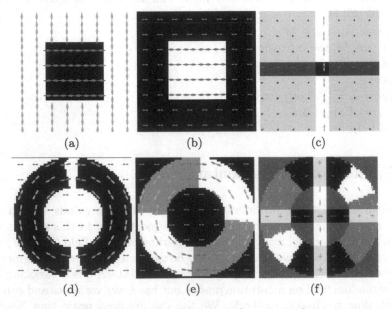

(a)   (b)   (c)

(d)   (e)   (f)

Fig. 5. HMMF segmentation of synthetic data

Next the algorithm was tested on curved regions. A synthetic dataset consisting of a circular region with vMFs oriented tangentially was created. A two region segmentation was computed in Figure 5d, and a three phase segmentation was computed in Figure 5e. Note that the two phase segmentation has identified nearly the entire circular region, even though the segmentation model is piecewise constant. Three regions was sufficient to segment the entire circular region.

The algorithm was then tested on a dataset with curved geometry and crossings. The results are shown in Figure 5f. In this case, the algorithm was able to discriminate between adjacent regions with multiple directions.

Finally the algorithm was applied to the lumbar region of a rat spinal cord. The data were acquired at the McKnight Brain Institute on a 14.1 Tesla Bruker Avance Imaging system with a diffusion weighted spin echo pulse sequence. Imaging parameters were : effective TR = 2000 ms, Δ = 17.5 ms, δ = 1.5 ms. Diffusion-weighted images were acquired with 46 different gradient directions with b = 1500 and a single image was acquired with $b \approx 0$. The image field of view was 60 x 60 x 300 μm^3, and the acquisition matrix was 72 x 72 x 40.

The RMS difference between the vMF model and a 6th order spherical harmonic expansion of the ODF are shown in Table (1). The spherical harmonic expansion was computed using the diffusion orientation transformation described by Özarslan et al. [16]. The RMS differences were computed for real and synthetic data in regions with one and two fibers per voxel. The single-fiber synthetic data show the best fitting results. The single and double-fiber fitting errors for the real data are comparable.

Table 1. RMS fitting error between vMF model and 6th order SH expansion

	Single Fiber	Double Fiber
Synthetic Data	0.0003	0.0013
Real Data	0.0018	0.0022

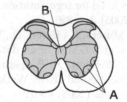

Fig. 6. Segmentation of spinal cord dataset (left) and anatomy from atlas (right)

The results of the segmentation are shown in the left side of Figure 6. The anatomical atlas shown in the right side of Figure 6 shows the the gray matter and white matter in an axial slice of the lumbar region of the spinal cord in gray and white respectively. Several of the distinct regions of the gray matter we would like to be able to segment are depicted in this image. Due to the low resolution of the data, we are unable to segment some of the finer structures.

We are, however, able to distinguish the lateral motor neurons (labeled A in the atlas) and the dorsal gray commissure (labeled B in the atlas) from the remainder of the gray matter.

6 Conclusion

We have introduced a novel model for orientational diffusion with mixtures of von Mises-Fisher distributions. This model leads to closed-form expressions for distances and anisotropy measures. A geodesic framework for working with this model was also presented. The results were applied within the hidden Markov measure field segmentation framework, and the results were presented for synthetic and real data. The technique was able to distinguish between regions of gray matter in the rat spinal cord which correspond to known anatomy.

Acknowledgements

This research was supported in part by the grant NIH-NS42075 and by Siemens Corporate Research (Princeton, NJ). We wish to thank Sara Berens and Evren Özarslan for the spinal cord data.

References

1. Tuch, D.S., Weisskoff, R.M., Belliveau, J.W., Wedeen, V.J.: High angular resolution diffusion imaging of the human brain. In: Proc. of the 7th Annual Meeting of ISMRM, Philadelphia, PA (1999) 321
2. Tuch, D.S., Reese, T.G., Wiegell, M.R., Wedeen, V.J.: Diffusion MRI of complex neural architecture. Neuron 40 (2003) 885–895
3. Frank, L.R.: Characterization of anisotropy in high angular resolution diffusion-weighted MRI. Magn. Reson. Med. 47 (2002) 1083–1099
4. Jonasson, L., Hagmann, P., Bresson, X., Thiran, J.P., Wedeen, V.J.: Representing diffusion mri in 5d for segmentation of white matter tracts with a level set method. In: IPMI. (2005) 311–320
5. Zhukov, L., Museth, K., Breen, D., Whitaker, R., Barr, A.: Level set modeling and segmentation of DT-MRI brain data. J. Electronic Imaging 12 (2003)
6. Feddern, C., Weickert, J., Burgeth, B.: Level-set methods for tensor-valued images. In: Proc. Second IEEE Workshop on Geometric and Level Set Methods in Computer Vision. (2003) 65–72
7. Wang, Z., Vemuri, B.C.: Tensor field segmentation using region based active contour model. In: ECCV (4). (2004) 304–315
8. Rousson, M., Lenglet, C., Deriche, R.: Level set and region based surface propagation for diffusion tensor mri segmentation. In: ECCV Workshops CVAMIA and MMBIA. (2004) 123–134
9. Wang, Z., Vemuri, B.C.: An affine invariant tensor dissimilarity measure and its applications to tensor-valued image segmentation. In: CVPR (1). (2004) 228–233
10. Wang, Z., Vemuri, B.C.: DTI segmentation using an information theoretic tensor dissimilarity measure. IEEE Trans. Med. Imaging 24 (2005) 1267–1277

11. Chan, T.F., Vese, L.A.: A level set algorithm for minimizing the mumford-shah functional in image processing. In: VLSM '01: Proceedings of the IEEE Workshop on Variational and Level Set Methods (VLSM'01), Washington, DC, USA, IEEE Computer Society Press, New York (2001) 161–170
12. Tsai, A., Yezzi, A., Willsky, A.: Curve evolution implementation of the Mumford-Shah functional for image segmentation, denoising, interpolation, and magnification. Volume 10. (2001) 1169–1186
13. Lenglet, C., Rousson, M., Deriche, R., Faugeras, O.D., Lehericy, S., Ugurbil, K.: A Riemannian approach to diffusion tensor images segmentation. In: IPMI. (2005) 591–602
14. Fletcher, P.T., Joshi, S.C.: Principal geodesic analysis on symmetric spaces: Statistics of diffusion tensors. In: ECCV Workshops CVAMIA and MMBIA. (2004) 87–98
15. Frank, L.R.: Anisotropy in high angular resolution diffusion-weighted MRI. Magn. Reson. Med. **45** (2001) 935–939
16. Özarslan, E., Shepherd, T., Vemuri, B.C., Blackband, S., Mareci, T.: Resolution of complex tissue microarchitecture using the diffusion orientation transform. Technical report, (University of Florida)
17. Chen, Y., Guo, W., Zeng, Q., Yan, X., Huang, F., Zhang, H., He, G., Vemuri, B.C., Liu, Y.: Estimation, smoothing, and characterization of apparent diffusion coefficient profiles from high angular resolution DWI. In: CVPR (1). (2004) 588–593
18. Özarslan, E., Mareci, T.H.: Generalized diffusion tensor imaging and analytical relationships between diffusion tensor imaging and high angular resolution diffusion imaging. Magn. Reson. Med. **50** (2003) 955–965
19. Özarslan, E., Vemuri, B.C., Mareci, T.: Fiber orientation mapping using generalized diffusion tensor imaging. In: IEEE Symp. on Biomedical Imaging (ISBI), Washington DC (2004) 1036–1038
20. Özarslan, E., Vemuri, B.C., Mareci, T.H.: Generalized scalar measures for diffusion MRI using trace, variance and entropy. Magn. Reson. Med. **53** (2005) 866–876
21. Mardia, K.V., Jupp, P.: Directional Statistics. 2nd edn. John Wiley and Sons Ltd., New York (2000)
22. McGraw, T.: Denoising, Segmentation and Visualization of Diffusion Weighted MRI. PhD dissertation, University of Florida, Gainesville, FL (2005)
23. Amari, S.: Information geometry on hierarchy of probability distributions. IEEE Trans. Information Theory **47** (2001) 1701–1711
24. Amari, S., Nagaoka, H.: Methods of information geometry. AMS, Providence, RI (2000)
25. Fletcher, P.T., Lu, C., Pizer, S.M., Joshi, S.: Principal geodesic analysis for the study of nonlinear statistics of shape. IEEE Transactions on Medical Imaging **23** (2004) 995–1005
26. Klingenberg, W.: Riemannian Geometry. de Gruyter, Berlin (1982)
27. Pennec, X., Fillard, P., Ayache, N.: A Riemannian framework for tensor computing. International Journal of Computer Vision **65** (2005) to appear
28. Karcher, H.: Riemannian center of mass and mollifier smoothing. Comm. Pure Appl. Math. **30** (1977) 509–541
29. Marroquin, J.L., Santana, E.A., Botello, S.: Hidden Markov measure field models for image segmentation. IEEE Trans. Pattern Anal. Mach. Intell. **25** (2003) 1380–1387

Globally Optimal Active Contours, Sequential Monte Carlo and On-Line Learning for Vessel Segmentation

Charles Florin[1], Nikos Paragios[2], and Jim Williams[1]

[1] Imaging & Visualization Department,
Siemens Corporate Research, Princeton, NJ, USA
755 College Road East, Princeton, NJ 08540, USA
[2] MAS - Ecole Centrale de Paris, Grande Voie des Vignes,
F-92 295 Chatenay-Malabry Cedex, France

Abstract. In this paper we propose a Particle Filter-based propagation approach for the segmentation of vascular structures in 3D volumes. Because of pathologies and inhomogeneities, many deterministic methods fail to segment certain types of vessel. Statistical methods represent the solution using a probability density function (pdf). This pdf does not only indicate the best possible solution, but also valuable information about the solution's variance. Particle Filters are used to learn the variations of direction and appearance of the vessel as the segmentation goes. These variations are used in turn in the particle filters framework to control the perturbations introduced in the Sampling Importance Resampling step (SIR). For the segmentation itself, successive planes of the vessel are modeled as states of a Particle Filter. Such states consist of the orientation, position and appearance (in statistical terms) of the vessel. The shape of the vessel and subsequently the particles pdf are recovered using globally active contours, implemented using circular shortest paths by branch and bound [1] that guarantees the global optimal solution. Promising results on the segmentation of coronary arteries demonstrate the potential of the proposed approach.

1 Introduction

Segmentation of vascular structures is a problem that arises in numerous situations in medical imaging, in particular for cardiac applications. Coronary arteries are thin vessels responsible for feeding the heart muscle in blood, and their segmentation provides a valuable tool for clinicians to diagnose diseases such as calcifications, and stenosis. Because of the low contrast conditions, and the coronaries vicinity to the blood pool, segmentation is a difficult task.

Since Computer Tomography (CT) and Magnetic Resonance (MR) imaging of the heart are now widely available, the number of patients imaged has significantly increased these past few years. Clinicians are now interested in periodically getting new images from the same patients to measure the development and severity of vascular diseases and their effects on the heart function. Such information is used to optimize the time of surgical operation and the effectiveness of treatments.

Vessel segmentation techniques consist of model-free and model-based methods. Skeleton-based techniques are the most primitive among the model-free [29] and aim

A. Leonardis, H. Bischof, and A. Pinz (Eds.): ECCV 2006, Part III, LNCS 3953, pp. 476–489, 2006.

at detecting the vessel skeletons, from which the whole vessel tree is reconstructed. Vessel enhancement using a multiscale-structural term derived from the image intensity Hessian matrix [27, 12] and differential geometry-driven methods [19] refer to a different class of model-free approaches that characterize tubular structures using the ratios between the Hessian matrix eigenvalues. Voxels that best fit the characterization are rendered brighter than the others, and the resulting image enhance tubular structures.

In [3], an anisotropic filtering technique, called *Vesselness Enhancement Diffusion*, is introduced that can be used to filter noisy images preserving vessels boundaries. The diffusivity function relies on the *vesselness* function introduced in [12] to filter along the vessel principal direction and not across. In the resulting image, the background is smoothed, whereas the vessel remains unchanged. The flux maximization criterion, a step forwards, was introduced in [31] and was exploited for vessel segmentation in [6] in low contrast conditions using vessel measures introduced in [12].

Region growing methods [33] progressively segment the vessels from a seed point, based on intensity similarity between adjacent pixels. These methods work fine for homogeneous regions, but not for pathological vessels, and may leak into other structures of similar intensity. Morphological operators [11] can be applied to correct a segmentation, smooth its edges or eventually fill holes in the structure of interest, but fail to account for prior knowledge. Tracking approaches [17, 30] are based on the application of local operators to track the vessel. Given a starting condition, such methods recover the vessel centerline through processing information on the vessel cross section [16]. Various forms of edge-driven techniques, similarity/matching terms between the vessel profile in successive planes, as well as their combination, were considered to perform tracking.

On the other hand, model-based techniques use prior knowledge and features to match a model with the input image and extract the vessels. The knowledge may concern the whole structure, or consist in modeling locally the vessel. Vessels template matching techniques (*Deformable Template Matcher*) [25] have been investigated. The structure model consists of a series of connected nodes that is deformed to best match the input image. Generalized Cylindrical models are modified in Extruded Generalized Cylinders in [23] to recover vessels in angiograms. For curvy vessels, the local basis used for classical generalized cylinders may be twisted, and a non-orthogonality issue may occur. This problem is solved keeping the vessel cross section orthogonal to the centerline, and the two normal vectors always on the same side of the tangent vector spine, as the algorithm moves along the vessel.

Nevertheless, since vessels vary enormously from one patient to another, deformable models are preferred to template models. Deformable models can either be parametric or geometric. Parametric deformable models [26] can be viewed as elastic surfaces (often called *snakes*), and cannot handle topological changes. Geometric deformable models [4, 28], on the contrary, can change their topology during the process and therefore are well suited to vessel segmentation. Like snakes, deformable models aim at minimizing the energy computed along the model. Level sets [24] are a way to apply deformable model to non-linear problems, such as vessel segmentation [21]. One can refer to the fast marching algorithm and its variant for vessel segmentation using the minimal path principle [2, 5] to determine the path of minimal length between two points, backtracking from one point toward the other crossing the isosurfaces perpendicularly. To discourage leaking, a local shape term that constrains the diameter of the vessel was proposed in [22]. One should also mention the method introduced in [20], where the optimization of a co-dimension two active contour was presented to segment brain vessels.

One can claim that existing approaches suffer from certain limitations. Local operators, region growing techniques, morphological filters as well as geometric contours might be very sensitive to local minima and fail to take into account prior knowledge on the form of the vessel. Parallel to that, cylindrical models, parametric active contours and template matching techniques may not be well suited to account for the non-linearity of the vessel structure, and require particular handling of branchings and bifurcations. Tracking methods can often fail in the presence of missing and corrupted data, or sudden changes. Level sets are very computational time-consuming and the Fast Marching algorithm loses all the local implicit function properties.

To improve segmentation results, a new method must account for non-linearities coming from branchings, pathologies, and acquisition artifacts, such as motion blur or CT beam hardening. This excludes any type of parametric models, or linear models, which would require special handling for bifurcations and non-linearities. Furthermore, the low contrast condition that features the coronaries drove the authors toward a method that would handle multiple hypotheses, and keep only the few most probable. The segmentation result would not be a deterministic result, but rather the most probable state of a vessel among several suppositions. Last, but not least, medical imaging is a field with vast prior knowledge; therefore, the new method must account for prior knowledge - if available -.

In this paper, we propose a particle-based approach to vessel segmentation where we re-formulate the problem of recovering successive planes of the vessel in a probabilistic fashion with numerous possible states. To this end, given an initial state for the vessel position, several hypotheses are generated uniformly in the feature space, and evaluated according to the observed data. From these hypothesis, a probability density function (pdf) can be defined, and used as a prior for a more efficient distribution of the hypothesis. Such an approach:

- combines edge-driven and region-based tracking metrics,
- recovers at each plane the optimal segmentation solution, that is the global minimum of the designed cost function,
- accounts for the structural and appearance non-linearity of the vessel,
- addresses pathological cases, and can incorporate prior local knowledge on the vessel structure.

The final paradigm consists of a fast multiple hypothesis propagation technique where the vessel structure as well as its appearance are successfully recovered. Such a framework allows to naturally address the non-linearity of the geometry and the appearance of coronaries and is compared in a favorable fashion with the existing approaches. The remainder of this paper is organized as follows. In section 2, we motivate vessel segmentation, introduce the feature space, and describe the measure used to quantify the quality of a given hypothesis. Random sampling and Particle Filters for tracking are introduced in section 3 while section 4 presents the overall system actually used to track vessels. Experimental results and discussion are part of the last section.

2   Vessel Segmentation

Cardio-vascular diseases are the leading cause of deaths in the USA (39%) and therefore there is a constant demand for improvement of diagnostic tools to detect and measure anomalies in the coronary tree. Such tools aid early diagnosis of the problem and therefore prevention that can significantly decrease the mortality rate due to cardiac diseases. One can consider the problem of vessel segmentation as a tracking problem of tubular structures in 3D volumes. Thus, given a starting position, the objective is to consider a feature vector that, upon its successful propagation, provides a complete segmentation of the coronaries. The statistical interpretation of such an objective refers to the introduction of a probability density function (pdf) that uses previous states to predict possible new positions of the vessel and image features to evaluate the new position. To this end, we define

- a state/feature vector, that defines the local geometry of a coronary artery
- an iterative process to update the density function, to predict the next state
- a distance between prediction and actual observation, to measure the quality of a given feature vector with respect to the image data.

2.1   The State/Feature Vector

One can define the state of the vessel at a given time as follows:

$$\underbrace{\mathbf{x} = (x_1, x_2, x_3)}_{position}, \underbrace{\Theta = (\theta_1, \theta_2, \theta_3)}_{orientation}, \underbrace{\mathbf{p}_{vessel}}_{appearance}$$

where the vessel state vector consists of the 3D location of the vessel $\mathbf{x}$, the tangent vector Θ, and the parameters required for the pdf estimation of the appearance of the vessel $\mathbf{p}_{vessel}$, as a mixture of two gaussians:

$$\mathbf{p}_{vessel} = ((P_B, \mu_B, \sigma_B), (P_C, \mu_C, \sigma_C)) \tag{1}$$

It is reasonable to assume irregularity in the appearance of the vessel because of the presence of calcifications, stents, stenosis and diseased vessel lumen [FIG. (1)]. Therefore simple parametric statistical models on the appearance space will fail to account for the statistical properties of the vessel and more complex distributions are to be considered. We consider a Gaussian mixture model that consists of two components to represent the evolving distribution of the vessel, the contrast enhanced blood (P_B, μ_B, σ_B) and the high density components, such as calcifications or stent, (P_C, μ_C, σ_C) subject to the constraint $[P_C + P_B = 1]$ leading to the following state vector:

$$\omega = (\mathbf{x}, \Theta, (P_B, \mu_B, \sigma_B), (P_C, \mu_C, \sigma_C)) \tag{2}$$

Such a state vector is to be recored for subsequent planes leading to complete reconstruction of the vessel tree. However, neither the planes position and orientation, nor the actual position of the vessel within this plane is known. In order to recover the most prominent plane position, a constrained multiple hypotheses framework will be used

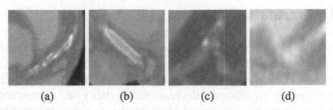

(a)   (b)   (c)   (d)

Fig. 1. (a) calcification, (b) stent (high intensity prosthesis), (c) branching with obtuse angles, (d) stenosis (sudden reduction of vessel cross section diameter)

according to a particle filter implementation. Such a framework will be explained at a later section.

Let us assume for the moment that the plane position is known as well as its orientation. Vessel segmentation consists of recovering the area of image within this plane that corresponds to the vessel. Snakes [18] as well as their geometric alternatives have been popular techniques to address such a demand. Despite numerous improvements, such methods often converge to local minimum. Such a limitation was addressed in [1] - known as circular shortest path algorithm by branch and bound - once appropriate initial conditions have been given to the process, that in our case could be satisfied.

2.2 Circular Shortest Paths and 2D Vessel Segmentation

The *Circular Shortest Paths by Branch and Bound* (CSP) [1] is a binary search-tree technique to recover the globally optimal active contour, given a point inside the contour and a potential map. First of all, let us note that the problem of finding the globally optimal active contour is equivalent to computing the minimal *weight* path (given a Riemannian metric) that connects a point at angle $\theta = 0$ to its equivalent at $\theta = 2\pi$ across the log-polar transform of the original image, see [FIG. (2)]. Given a Riemannian metric g (usually equal to the image gradient), the *weight* W of a path $\mathbf{P}$ is defined as:

$$W(\mathbf{P}) = \int_{\mathbf{P}} g\left(\mathbf{P}(s)\right) ds. \tag{3}$$

Given a start point p_0 at $\theta = 0$, the end point $p_{2\pi}$ at $\theta = 2\pi$ of the minimal *noncircular* path is defined as

$$p = argmin_{\mathbf{P}(2\pi)=p} W(\mathbf{P}). \tag{4}$$

This end point $p_{2\pi}$ is very quickly found using the well-known Dijkstra [7] algorithm, with the Riemannian metric g ([EQ. (3)]) playing the role of potential map. To demonstrate the use of a binary search-tree, a property needs to be stated at that point, whose proof is straightforward (see [1]):

> for two subsets $S_1 \subseteq S_2$, the minimal path $\mathbf{P}_2$ of S_2 has a lower weight than the minimal path $\mathbf{P}_1$ of S_1, otherwise stated as $W(\mathbf{P}_2) \leq W(\mathbf{P}_1)$.

A corollary is:

> for any point set S, the weight of the minimal path $\mathbf{P}$ (circular or not) is a lower bound of the minimal *circular* path weight. Therefore, if $\{S_1, S_2\}$ is a partition of S, and $W(\mathbf{P}_1) \leq W(\mathbf{P}_2)$, the minimal *circular* path of S has its starting point p_0 (and obviously ending point $p_{2\pi}$ as well) in the subset S_1.

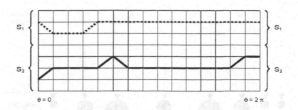

Fig. 2. Discreet grid of a log-polar image, with a circular path (dashed, subset S_1) and a noncircular path (plain, subset S_2)

Consequently, a binary search-tree is used in the CSP algorithm. First, any set of initial points $S = \{p_0\}$ is divided into two subsets $S_1 = \{p_0\}_1$ and $S_2 = \{p_0\}_2$; second, the minimal *noncircular* paths P_1 and P_2 are computed using [EQ. (4)] for the two subsets. This procedure is then repeated with the subset of minimal path until the subsets are reduced to a single point. At the bottom of the binary search-tree, the subsets are reduced to singletons, and their minimal path are naturally *circular*. The Globally Optimal Circular Shortest Path is obtained that way. The low cost complexity (for width u and height v, $O(u^{1.6}v)$ average time, or less than a milisecond for 15x15 pixels cross section profile, see [FIG. (4)]) makes this method very attractive for repetitive testings, such as the particle filters presented in [SEC. (3)]. It also reduces the dimensionality of the feature space, compared to model-based methods (elliptic models, tubular models,...) .

The CSP algorithm is an efficient technique to image segmentation for closest structures under the assumption that a point is given in the structure interior. Since segmentation in our case is approached as a multiple hypotheses testing, one can assume that each hypotheses generation could provide a start point to the CSP that is a necessity for the construction of the log-polar image. The multiple hypotheses generation could be done in a number of fashions. Sequential Monte Carlo is the prominent technique that associates evolving densities to the different hypotheses, and maintains a number of them. Particle filters is the most prominent technique to implemented such a strategy.

3 Particle Filters

3.1 Particle Filters: Generalities

Particle Filters [8, 15] are a sequential Monte-Carlo technique that is used to estimate the Bayesian posterior probability density function (pdf) with a set of samples [13, 32]. In terms of a mathematical formulation, such a method approximates the posterior pdf by M random measures $\{x_t^m, m = 1..M\}$ associated to M weights $\{w_t^m, m = 1..M\}$, such that

$$p(x_t|z_{1:t}) \approx \sum_{m=1}^{M} w_t^m \delta(x_t - x_t^m). \tag{5}$$

where each weight w_t^m reflects the importance of the sample x_t^m in the pdf, given the observations sequence $z_{1:t}$, as shown in [FIG. (3)]. Using Bayes rule, one can sequentially estimate $p(x_t|z_{1:t})$ from $p(x_{t-1}|z_{1:t-1})$, knowing $p(x_t|x_{t-1})$ and measuring $p(z_t|x_t)$:

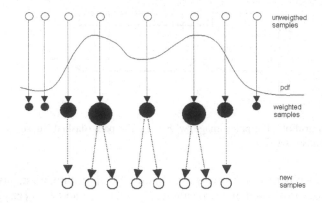

Fig. 3. The resampling process: a random selection chooses the samples with the highest weights where a local perturbation is applied

$$p(x_t|z_{1:t}) \propto p(z_t|x_t)p(x_t|z_{1:t-1})$$

$$\propto p(z_t|x_t) \int p(x_t|x_{t-1})p(x_{t-1}|z_{1:t-1})dx_{t-1}$$

$p(z_t|x_t)$ is discussed in [SEC. (4.1)], while a novel method to locally estimate $p(x_t|x_{t-1})$ is presented in [SEC. (3.3)]. The samples x_t^m are drawn using the principle of *Importance Density* [14], of pdf $q(x_t|x_{1:t}^m, z_t)$, and it is shown that their weights w_t^m are updated according to

$$w_t^m \propto w_{t-1}^m \frac{p(z_t|x_t^m)p(x_t^m|x_{t-1}^m)}{q(x_t^m|x_{t-1}^m, z_t)}. \tag{6}$$

Once a set of samples has been drawn, $p(x_t^m|x_{t-1}^m, z_t)$ can be computed out of the observation z_t for each sample, and the estimation of the posteriori pdf can be sequentially updated. Such a process will remove most of the particles and only the ones that express the data will present significant weights. Consequently the model will lose its ability to track significant changes on the pdf; therefore a resampling procedure has to be executed on a regular basis. Such a process will preserve as many samples as possible with respectful weights. One can find in the literature several resampling techniques. We chose the most prominent one, Sampling Importance Resampling, for its simplicity to implement, and because it allows more hypothesis with low probability to survive, compared to more selective techniques such as Stratified Resampling [10].

3.2 Sampling Importance Resampling

The Sampling Importance Resampling (SIR) algorithm [13] consists of choosing the prior density $p(x_t|x_{t-1})$ as importance density $q(x_t|x_{1:t}^m, z_t)$. This leads to the following condition, from [EQ. (6)]

$$w_t^m \propto w_{t-1}^m p(z_t|x_t^m). \tag{7}$$

The samples are updated by setting $x_t^m \propto p(x_t|x_{t-1}^m)$, and perturbed according to a random noise vector ϵ, so that $x_t^m \propto p(x_t|x_{t-1}^m)$. The SIR algorithm is the most widely used resampling method because of its simplicity from the implementation point of view. Nevertheless, the SIR uses mostly the prior knowledge $p(x_t|x_{t-1})$, and does not take into account the most recent observations z_t. Such a strategy could lead to an overestimation of outliers. On the other hand, because SIR resampling is performed at each step, fewer samples are required, and thus the computational cost may be reduced with respect to other resampling algorithms. Finally, in practice, the estimation of ϵ's law is difficult, and prior knowledge is usually required. A novel method is proposed in the following section [SEC. (3.3)] to circumvent this issue, by locally estimating $p(x_t|x_{t-1}^m)$.

3.3 Reinforced SIR: The State Transition Noise Pdf

After a particle x_{t-1}^m has been selected by the SIR algorithm, a random noise vector ϵ is added (see previous section [SEC. (3.2)]). A straightforward solution consists in using prior knowledge to estimate the law of ϵ once for all. This method presents two difficulties: first, prior knowledge may be limited and/or hard to obtain, second, vessels are linear structures only very locally, therefore the law of ϵ may greatly vary from one patient to another. In the technique presented in this paper, the distribution of ϵ is updated at every time step. At a given time step, each particle x_{t-1}^m selected by the SIR generates N offsprings by adding a random noise vector, uniformly distributed, and moving it forward (in the direction of the vessel, given by the particle hypothesis). Once their probability is estimated, these N offsprings particles provide a pdf $(p(x_t|x_{t-1}^m))$ which is then used for the distribution of the random vector ϵ.

The final paradigm for resampling follows the procedure:

1. first, particles are selected randomly according to their probability, as in any SIR procedure
2. second, the selected particles generates N new offsprings uniformly distributed
3. these offsprings probabilities are estimated, and a pdf is then drawn for each SIR selected particle
4. finally, this pdf is used to generate a random noise vector ϵ that perturbs the SIR selected particles

In other words, once the SIR selected a particle x_{t-1}^m to be resampled, $p(x_t|x_{t-1}^m, z_t)$ is estimated in a way similar to [EQ. (5)]:

$$p(x_t|x_{t-1}^m, z_t) \approx \sum_{i=1}^{N} w_t^i \delta(x_t - x_t^i),$$
(8)

where the x_t^i are generated from $x_{t-1}^m + \epsilon_i$, with the ϵ_i uniformly distributed. The weights w_t^i are estimated from the observation z_t.

This method presents two main advantages. First, as the noise vector ϵ is random, the advantages of SIR over exhaustive search are preserved. Second, the distribution of ϵ is updated at every time step, and for every particle, avoiding the disadvantages of having a noise distribution that would be determined once for all from prior knowledge. Vessels can be straight and suddenly become tortuous, or can have a very homogeneous shape/appearance before encountering a very inhomogeneous region. This *Reinforced SIR* captures the conditions change and adapts the noise vector distribution.

4   Particle Filters and Vessel Tracking

We now consider the application of such non linear model to vessel segmentation and tracking. Without loss of generality one can assume that the root of a coronary is known, either provided by the user or through some automatic procedure. Simple segmentation of that area can provide an initial guess on the statistical properties of the vessel

$$\mathbf{p}_{vessel} = \left(\left(P_B, \mu_B, \sigma_B \right), \left(P_C, \mu_C, \sigma_C \right) \right) \tag{9}$$

using an expectation/maximization process. Then, one can consider the problem of vessel segmentation equivalent to the recovery of successive cross-sections, along with the position of the vessel at any given cross-section. Such an approach is equivalent to finding a deterministic number of sequential states $\omega_\tau = (\mathbf{x}_\tau, \Theta_\tau, \mathbf{p}_{vessel})$, which belong to the feature space (see [SEC. (2.1)]) where we use the notion of Particle Filters.

The multiple hypotheses nature of the method requires a metric definition to validate their correctness. Given, the current state and the perturbation law we produce a number of new states following this law. Such states refer to a new plane, as well as a center point for the elliptic structure and therefore the CSP algorithm can be used to provide the most prominent area for the vessel given these initial conditions. We use this area and two metrics that aim to account for the shape and appearance of the vessel toward validation of the considered hypotheses.

4.1   Prediction and Observation: Distance

To this end, we are using mostly the image terms, and in particular the intensities that do correspond to the vessel in the current cross-section. The observed distribution of this set is approximated using a Gaussian mixture model according to the expectancy-maximization principle. Each hypothesis is composed by the features given in [EQ. (2)], therefore, the probability measure is essentially the likelihood of the observation z, given the appearance A model. The following measures (abusively called probabilities) are normalized so that their sum over all particles is equal to one.

– Probability measure for shape
Once the vessel's edge is detected using *Circular Shortest Path* [SEC. (2.2)], a measure of contrast, called the *ribbon measure*, R is computed:

$$\begin{cases} R = -\infty \ , & \mu_{int} \leq \mu_{ext} \\ R = \frac{\mu_{\cdots} - \mu_{\cdots}}{\mu_{\cdots} + \mu_{\cdots}}, & otherwise \end{cases}$$

while the correctness of the prediction is given by:

$$p(z|S) = e^{-\frac{|\cdot|}{\cdot 0}}$$

where μ_{int} is the mean intensity value for the voxels in the vessel, and μ_{ext} is the intensities mean value for the voxels in a band outside the vessel, such that the band and the vessel's lumen have the same area.

Fig. 4. Three vessels cross sections detected using the ribbon measure

Since the coronary arteries are brighter than the background, the best match maximizes R (see [FIG. (4)]).

– Probability measure for appearance

For the vessel lumen pixels distribution $\mathbf{p}_{vessel}$ [EQ. (1)], the probability is measured as the distance between the hypothesized distribution and the distribution actually observed.

The distance we use is the symmetrized Kullback-Leibler distance D between the model $p(x) = \mathbf{p}_{vessel}$ and the observation $q(x)$, obtained from the CSP segmentation:

$$D = \int p(x) log(\frac{p(x)}{q(x)}) + q(x) log(\frac{q(x)}{p(x)}) dx,$$

$$p(z|A) = e^{-\frac{|\cdot|}{\circ}}.$$

The combination of edge-driven and region-based metrics measures the fitness of the observation to the prior knowledge included in the state vector.

4.2 Branching Detection

When a branching occurs, the particles split up in the two daughter branches, and then track them separately (see [FIG. (5)]). As branchings are never perfectly balanced, one of the branches attracts most of the particles after few resampling steps. To avoid the collapse of one of the modes, two techniques are available: either to increase the number of particles in the weakest branch, or to treat the two branches separately. The second approach is preferred in this paper. To this end, a simple K-means clustering on the joint space (position+orientation) of the particles is considered. When the two clusters are well separated, the number of particles is doubled and equally dispatched in the two branches. The segmentation goes on, according to [EQ. (6)], with a bi-modal distribution.

The K-means algorithm [9] partitions N points, x_n, into K disjoint clusters, of centers μ_j, minimizing the sum-of-squares

$$J = \sum_{j=0}^{K} \sum_{n=0}^{N} |x_n - \mu_j|^2.$$

The K-mean procedure alternates two steps: first each point is associated to the nearest center μ_j, then each center is moved in the barycenter of the cluster.

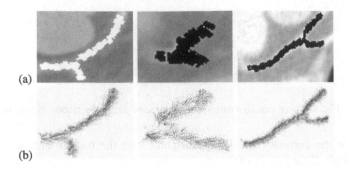

(a)

(b)

Fig. 5. (a) branching points between LCX and LAD for three patients with the particles' mean state overlaid, (b) the particles , clustered using K-means, follow up the two branches

Table 1. Results table showing the percentage of branches correctly segmented, over a dataset of 34 patients, using Particle Filters (PF) and Front Propagation (FP)

vessel name	RCA	Acute Marginal	LAD	First Septal	LCX	Obtuse Marginal
% of branches, using PF	100%	85.3%	100%	94%	100%	94%
% of branches, using FP	64%	18%	53%	32%	39%	22%

4.3   Implementation and Validation

Regarding the initial configuration, the use of approximatively $1,000$ particles gave sufficient results for our experiments. We perform a systematic resampling according to the Sampling Importance Resampling every time the effective sampling size $N_{eff} = \sum_i 1/w_i^2$ (where w_i is the weight of the ith particle) falls below half the number of particles. As mentioned in Section 3.1, the preference for SIR, compared to Stratified Resampling [10], is motivated by the robustness of the segmentation. The *reinforced SIR* strategy exposed in [SEC. (3.3)] gives better results, for a constant number of particles.

Validation is a difficult part for any coronary segmentation method. The algorithm has been evaluated on 34 patients, and has successfully recovered all the main arteries (RCA, LAD, LCX) for each patient as shown in the following table, while a small portion of visual results are also presented in [FIG. (6)].

The percentage in the above table corresponds to the number of branches segmented by Particle Filters and identified by a human expert. For comparison purposes, the same test is performed using Front Propagation based on the image Hessian matrix [27]. These results were achieved with a one-click initialization; a method based on a PCA on the intensity volume gives the approximative initial direction. All patients presented some kind of artery pathologies in one, at least, of their coronary vessels. This means the Particle Filter successfully segmented both healthy and unhealthy coronaries. The method seems to outperform regarding the detection of the main branchings, while in some cases smaller branchings at the lowest parts of the vessel tree, have been missed. Nevertheless, one can argue that their clinical use is of lower importance. However, current studies focus on the issue of branchings for narrow vessels in very low contrast conditions. The comparative study demonstrate the Particle Filters capability to outperform deterministic hessian based methods in cases with corrupt data (pathologies).

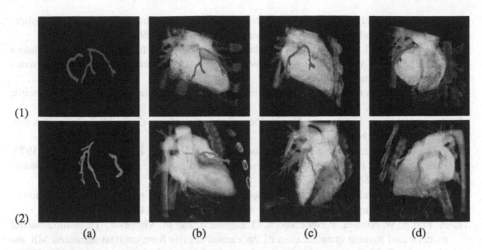

Fig. 6. Segmentation of the Left anterior descending coronary artery and Right coronary artery in CTA (in red) for four patients (1) & (2); (a) coronary tree, (b,c,d) Different $3D$ views superimposed to the cardiac volume are presented.

5 Discussion

In this paper, we have shown that Particle Filters can be used for vascular segmentation. In the context of vascular segmentation, Particle Filters sequentially estimate the pdf of segmentations in a particular feature space. The case of coronary arteries was considered to validate such an approach where the ability to handle discontinuities on the structural (branching) as well as appearance space (calcifications, pathological cases, etc.) was demonstrated. The main advantage of such methods is the non-linearity assumption on the evolution of samples. Experiments were conducted on several healthy and diseased patients CTA data sets, segmenting the *Left Main Coronary Artery* and the *Right Coronary Artery* [FIG. (6)].

Introducing further prior knowledge in the segmentation process is the most prominent future direction. One can see such a contribution in two parallel paths. First, building better models that account for the appearance of the vessel seems to be a necessity toward capturing the coronaries at the lowest parts of the vessel tree. The current model is based on the global statistics of the appearance of the vessel and one can claim is a meaningful measure for vessel cross sections with a certain area.

References

1. B. Appleton and C. Sun. Circular shortest paths by branch and bound. 36(11):2513–2520, November 2003.
2. B. Avants and J. Williams. An adaptive minimal path generation technique for vessel tracking in cta/ce-mra volume images. In *MICCAI*, pages 707–716, 2000.
3. C. Cañero and P. Radeva. Vesselness enhancement diffusion. *Pattern Recognition Letters*, 24(16):3141 – 3151, 2003.
4. V. Caselles, F. Catté, B. Coll, and F. Dibos. A geometric model for active contours in image processing. *Numerische Mathematik*, 66(1):1–31, 1993.

5. T. Deschamps and L. D. Cohen. Fast extraction of minimal paths in 3D images and applications to virtual endoscopy. *Medical Image Analysis*, 5(4):281–299, December 2001.
6. M. Descoteaux, L. Collins, and K. Siddiqi. Geometric Flows for Segmenting Vasculature in MRI: Theory and Validation. In *Medical Imaging Computing and Computer-Assisted Intervention*, pages 500–507, 2004.
7. E. W. Dijkstra. A note on two problems in connexion with graphs. *Numerische Mathematik*, 1:269–271, 1959.
8. A. Doucet, J. de Freitas, and N. Gordon. *Sequential Monte Carlo Methods in Practice*. Springer-Verlag, New York, 2001.
9. R Duda and P. Hart. *Pattern Classification and Scene Analysis*. John Wiley and Sons, 1973.
10. P. Fearnhead and P. Clifford. Online inference for well-log data. *Journal of the Royal Statistical Society*, 65:887–899, 2003.
11. M. Figueiredo and J. Leitao. A nonsmoothing approach to the estimation of of vessel controus in angiograms. *IEEE Transactions on Medical Imaging*, 14:162–172, 1995.
12. A. Frangi, W. Niessen, P. Nederkoorn, O. Elgersma, and M. Viergever. Three-dimensional model-based stenosis quantification of the carotid arteries from contrast-enhanced MR angiography. In *Mathematical Methods in Biomedical Image Analysis*, pages 110–118, 2000.
13. N. Gordon. Novel Approach to Nonlinear/Non-Gaussian Bayesian State Estimation. *IEE Proceedings*, 140:107–113, 1993.
14. N. Gordon. On Sequential Monte Carlo Sampling Methods for Bayesian Filtering. *Statistics and Computing*, 10:197–208, 2000.
15. N. Gordon. A Tutorial on Particle Filters for On-line Non-linear/Non-Gaussian Bayesian Tracking. *IEEE Transactions on Signal Processing*, 50:174–188, 2002.
16. M. Hart and L. Holley. A method of Automated Coronary Artery Trackin in Unsubtracted Angiograms. *IEEE Computers in Cardiology*, pages 93–96, 1993.
17. M. Isard and A. Blake. Contour Tracking by Stochastic Propagation of Conditional Density. In *European Conference on Computer Vision*, volume I, pages 343–356, 1996.
18. M. Kass, A. Witkin, and D. Terzopoulos. Snakes: Active Contour Models. In *IEEE International Conference in Computer Vision*, pages 261–268, 1987.
19. K. Krissian, G. Malandain, N. Ayache, R. Vaillant, and Y. Trousset. Model based detection of tubular structures in 3d images. *Computer Vision and Image Understanding*, 80:130–171, 2000.
20. L. Lorigo, O. Faugeras, E. Grimson, R. Keriven, R. Kikinis, A. Nabavi, and C. Westin. Codimension-Two Geodesic Active Controus for the Segmentation of Tubular Structures. In *IEEE Conference on Computer Vision and Pattern Recognition*, pages I:444–451, 2000.
21. R. Malladi and J. Sethian. A Real-Time Algorithm for Medical Shape Recovery. In *International Conference on Computer Vision*, pages 304–310, 1998.
22. D. Nain, A. Yezzi, and G. Turk. Vessel Segmentation Using a Shape Driven Flow. In *Medical Imaging Copmuting and Computer-Assisted Intervention*, 2004.
23. T. O´ Donnell, T. Boult, X. Fang, and A. Gupta. The Extruded Generalized Cylider: A Deformable Model for Object Recovery. In *IEEE Conference on Computer Vision and Pattern Recognition*, pages 174–181, 1994.
24. S. Osher and N. Paragios. *Geometric Level Set Methods in Imaging, Vision and Graphics*. Springer Verlag, 2003.
25. R. Petrocelli, K. Manbeck, and J. Elion. Three Dimentional Structue Recognition in Digital Angiograms using Gauss-Markov Models. *IEEE Computers in Radiology*, pages 101–104, 1993.
26. D. Rueckert, P. Burger, S. Forbat, R. Mohiadin, and G. Yang. Automatic Tracking of the Aorta in Cardiovascular MR images using Deformable Models. *IEEE Transactions on Medical Imaging*, 16:581–590, 1997.

27. Y. Sato, S. Nakajima, H. Atsumi, T. Koller, G. Gerig, S. Yoshida, and R. Kikinis. 3D Multi-scale line filter for segmentation and visualization of curvilinear structures in medical images. In *Conference on Computer Vision, Virtual Reality and Robotics in Medicine and Medial Robotics and Computer-Assisted Surgery*, pages 213–222, 1997.
28. J. Sethian. A Review of the Theory, Algorithms, and Applications of Level Set Methods for Propagating Interfaces. *Cambridge University Press*, pages 487–499, 1995.
29. E. Sorantin, C. Halmai, B. Erbohelyi, K. Palagyi, K. Nyul, K. Olle, B. Geiger, F. Lindbichler, G. Friedrich, and K. Kiesler. Spiral-CT-based assesment of Tracheal Stenoses using 3D Skeletonization. *IEEE Transactions on Medical Imaging*, 21:263–273, 2002.
30. K. Toyama and A. Blake. Probabilistic Tracking in a Metric Space. In *IEEE International Conference in Computer Vision*, pages 50–59, 2001.
31. A. Vasilevskiy and K. Siddiqi. Flux Maximizing Geometric Flows. In *IEEE International Conference in Computer Vision*, pages I: 149–154, 2001.
32. W. West. Modelling with mixtures. In J. Bernardo, J. Berger, A. Dawid, and A. Smith, editors, *Bayesian Statistics*. Clarendon Press, 1993.
33. P. Yim, P. Choyke, and R. Summers. Grayscale Skeletonization of Small Vessels in Magnetic Resonance Angiography. *IEEE Transactions on Medical Imaging*, 19:568–576, 2000.

Optimal Multi-frame Correspondence with Assignment Tensors

R. Oliveira, R. Ferreira, and J.P. Costeira

Instituto de Sistemas e Robótica - Instituto Superior Técnico
{rco, ricardo, jpc}@isr.ist.utl.pt
http://www.isr.ist.utl.pt

Abstract. Establishing correspondence between features of a set of images has been a long-standing issue amongst the computer vision community. We propose a method that solves the multi-frame correspondence problem by imposing a rank constraint on the observed scene, i.e. rigidity is assumed. Since our algorithm is based solely on a geometrical (global) criterion, it does not suffer from issues usually associated to local methods, such as the aperture problem.

We model feature matching by introducing the *assignment tensor*, which allows *simultaneous* feature alignment for *all* images, thus providing a coherent solution to the calibrated multi-frame correspondence problem in a single step of linear complexity. Also, an iterative method is presented that is able to cope with the non-calibrated case. Moreover, our method is able to seamlessly reject a large number of outliers in every image, thus also handling occlusion in an integrated manner.

1 Introduction

The establishment of correspondence between image features extracted from different viewpoints of the same scene is an essential step to the the 3D reconstruction process. In fact, most reconstruction algorithms rely on previously established correspondences to determine 3D structure. Clear examples of this are classical factorization algorithms such as [15] and more recent methods as [6], [14] and [7]. A notable exception is presented in [3], where correspondences are not explicitly extracted - maximum likelihood structure and motion are calculated using an EM framework.

The difficulty of the correspondence problem is associated to its combinatorial nature. Furthermore, matching in multiple frames presents an additional difficulty to the traditional correspondence problem: coherence between every pairwise correspondence has to be guaranteed. Several models have been proposed in order to obtain a matching solution with an acceptable computational cost. In [12] and [8], the n-frame correspondence problem is formulated as a maximum-flow problem and is solved through graph cut algorithms. Different approaches involving graphs have been presented in [13] and in [5].

A natural way to associate a cost function to the correspondence problem is to exploit a constant characteristic of an important class of 3D scenes: rigidity. The

A. Leonardis, H. Bischof, and A. Pinz (Eds.): ECCV 2006, Part III, LNCS 3953, pp. 490–501, 2006.
© Springer-Verlag Berlin Heidelberg 2006

use of rigidity presents the advantage of leading to intrinsically *global* algorithms; moreover, it naturally overcomes the aperture problem, since features are not characterized by their specific local properties. This geometric constraint can be translated into a rank constraint on the matrix containing the coordinates of the extracted features (the measurement matrix). Actually, it can be shown that when features in different viewpoints are correctly aligned (and only then) this matrix is highly rank-deficient - [9], [11]. Rank-deficiency for multi-frame correspondence has also been exploited in [10].

A first approach to correspondence exploiting rigidity has been made in [9], where the authors use a cost function based on the determinant of the measurement matrix to match features in a pair of images. This approach, although theoretically sound, has two main shortcomings: it is unable to handle the multi-image case and the cost function is intrinsically non-linear, presenting a high computational burden. In [11] the authors presented a new algorithm based on an alternative cost function, which would detect rank-deficiency based on the sum of the non-dominant singular values of the measurement matrix. This cost function allows the rigidity constraint to be applied to a multi-frame system. However, to obtain an acceptable computational complexity rank is imposed iteratively by matching each image individually with the remaining frames. Since rank is a global constraint this is not a desirable formulation. Moreover, occlusion cannot be modeled even within the iterative framework.

In this text, we propose a solution that generalizes the concept of assignment matrix used in our previous work to establish correspondences between the features in each of the frames. We introduce the assignment tensor that defines all correspondences in a single structure. With this formulation, linear complexity is retained even when dealing with more than two images, while occlusion is easily modeled.

2   Problem Formulation

We present in this paper a formulation that is capable of dealing with the multi-frame correspondence problem in the factorization context. Our objective is to align the observations in each image in a matrix W so that corresponding features share the same column. Optimal alignment is achieved by exploiting the intrinsic rank-deficiency associated to a correctly matched W.

Since our method relies solely on global geometric constraints of the scene, we place no constraints on the feature points selected - in particular, they do not have to contain significant texture in their vicinity. To emphasize this issue, our matching candidates are extracted from generic contour points, i.e. in areas prone to the aperture problem, and not from corners.

The method described herein assumes an orthographic camera, although it is easily extendable to any generic affine camera. In fact, the only factor limiting the camera model is the validity of the rank-defficiency condition on W.

2.1 The Assignment Tensor

Feature correspondence in a system containing n_f viewpoints is uniquely defined by a 2D point in each of the viewpoints such that all 2D points in the set are the projections of the same 3D feature. Bearing this in mind, it is straightforward to represent each correspondence in an n_f-dimensional structure - the *assignment tensor*. For the sake of simplicity, and without loss of generality, we will present these properties for the 3 image case. Extension to an arbitrary number of images is straightforward.

Suppose the three frames have p_1, p_2 and p_3 features, respectively. Each dimension of the assignment tensor contains a number of entries equal to the number of matching candidates (i.e. 2D features) in the associated frame: $i = 1, ..., p_1$, $j = 1, ..., p_2$, $k = 1, ..., p_3$. $T_{ijk} = 1$ iff the ith, j^{th} and k^{th} features in the first, second and third frames respectively are projections of the same 3D point, i.e., if they represent a correct match. Otherwise, $T_{ijk} = 0$.

We represent the three-frame case as an example in Fig. 1 below.

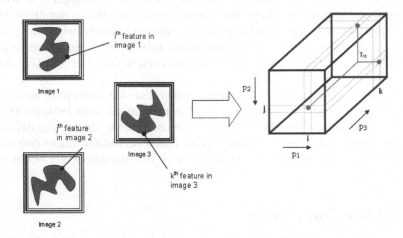

Fig. 1. The assignment tensor for the three-frame case. If feature i in the first image, j in the second and k in third are a valid correspondence, then $T_{ijk} = 1$.

Although the tensor establishes correspondence for all frames, the match between any subset of images can also be easily determined by summing over the dimensions not associated to the aforementioned images. In the 3-frame case, the relation P_{mn} between features in frame m and n can be easily obtained, as shown below (note that in this special case P_{mn} actually reduces to an assignment matrix). As will become evident in the next sections, the fact that any pairwise correspondence (represented by an *assignment matrix*) can be extracted from the assignment tensor is of key importance to our algorithm, as is the fact that the expression for each assignment matrix is linear in the elements of T. For the three image case, all pairwise correspondences are represented by the assignment matrices in Fig. 1:

$$P_{12} = \sum_{k=1}^{p_3} T_{ijk}, \quad P_{13} = \sum_{j=1}^{p_2} T_{ijk}, \quad P_{23} = \sum_{i=1}^{p_1} T_{ijk}. \tag{1}$$

To achieve a correct result, the assignment tensor must respect constraints that are intrinsic to the correspondence problem, such as unicity - a certain feature can be matched to *at most* one feature in another image. When matching a pair of images, this constraint is formulated by demanding that the sum of the rows/columns of the assignment matrix be less or equal to one. A similar set of constraints applies to the assignment tensor. In this case, it is required that *the sum over any dimension is less or equal to one*. This forces each feature to correspond to at most another feature in each of the remaining frames. For the three image case, the restrictions apply in the following manner:

$$\forall j,k \sum_{i=1}^{p_1} T_{ijk} \leq 1, \quad \forall i,k \sum_{j=1}^{p_2} T_{ijk} \leq 1, \quad \forall i,j \sum_{k=1}^{p_3} T_{ijk} \leq 1, \quad T_{ijk} \in \{0,1\}. \tag{2}$$

To avoid the trivial (and undesirable!) result of a null assignment tensor, a minimum number p_t of ones (i.e. matches) is forced on the tensor. This is done through the following restriction:

$$\sum_{i=1}^{p_1} \sum_{j=1}^{p_2} \sum_{k=1}^{p_3} T_{ijk} = p_t \tag{3}$$

The expressions for the three-frame case will be directly applied in the section dedicated to experiments.

2.2 Feature Point Representation

Observations on each frame are represented as a set of image coordinates containing the orthogonal projection of 3D feature points in the scene. Assuming p_f feature points, we represent the u and v image coordinates of a frame f in the u^f and v^f vectors. We assume that each set of p_f feature points is corrupted by a certain number of outliers which will have to be rejected. The data corresponding to frame f is thus represented by $2 \times p_f$ matrix w_f containing the u^f and v^f vectors.

Measurements corresponding to several frames can be vertically stacked in order to create a measurement matrix W_f that incorporates the projection of the feature points up to scene f. However, outliers in each frame have to be rejected beforehand; moreover, the remaining points have to be aligned so that corresponding features share the same column in W_f. Matrix P_f simultaneously aligns the feature points and rejects the outliers in the corresponding measurement matrix w_f. W_f can consequently be written as

$$
W_f = \begin{bmatrix} w_1 \, P_1 \\ w_2 \, P_2 \\ \vdots \; \vdots \\ w_f \, P_f \end{bmatrix} = \begin{bmatrix} \begin{bmatrix} u_1^1 \cdots u_{p_1}^1 \\ v_1^1 \cdots v_{p_1}^1 \end{bmatrix} P_{1\,[p_1 \times p_1]} \\ \begin{bmatrix} u_1^2 \cdots u_{p_2}^2 \\ v_1^2 \cdots v_{p_2}^2 \end{bmatrix} P_{2\,[p_2 \times p_1]} \\ \vdots \qquad \vdots \\ \begin{bmatrix} u_1^f \cdots u_{p.}^f \\ v_1^f \cdots v_{p.}^f \end{bmatrix} P_{f\,[p. \times p_1]} \end{bmatrix} \tag{4}
$$

We assume that only the best p_0 matches are to determined, where $p_0 \leq p_k, \forall k$. In (4), each P_k, for $k \geq 2$, represents a rank-p_0 assignment matrix which determines the correspondences between the first and the kth frame. It has been seen in the previous section that these assignment matrices can easily be written as a linear expression of the terms of T as defined in (1). Under these assumptions, each assignment matrix is defined by the conditions in (5).

$$
\begin{array}{ll}
P_{k..} = \{0,1\}, \forall i = 1...p_k, \forall j = 1...p_0 & \sum_i P_{k..} \leq 1, \forall j = 1...p_1 \\
\sum_j P_{k..} \leq 1, \forall i = 1...p_k & \sum_{i,j} P_{k..} = p_0
\end{array} \tag{5}
$$

Note that P_1 has a slightly different structure: it is a rank-p_0 matrix where ones are only allowed in the diagonal. Consequently, unlike the other P_k, it does not *permute* columns, it only forces certain columns of w_1 (corresponding to features that become occluded and thus do not have a match) to zero. As a result, W_f will have a set of null columns. This does not have any influence in subsequent calculations - in particular, this does not alter rank.

2.3   The Rank Constraint

It has been shown in [15] that a measurement matrix similar to the one presented in (2) is highly rank deficient. More specifically, when including translation W_f is at most rank-4. To this end it is however assumed that image coordinates corresponding to the same 3D feature point occupy the same column. In the presence of incorrect alignment, the resulting W_f is (generally) of higher rank. Note that in the presence of a limited amount of noise the rank-4 constraint for a correctly matched W_f may still be assumed as valid, as shown in [9].

Our problem is thus equivalent to *finding the correct assignment tensor T*. The tensor yields a set of assignment matrices P_k - each of these matrices aligns the corresponding w_k, so that a rank-4 W_f is generated.

2.4   The Cost Function

The multi-frame correspondence problem can be stated as the search for the assignment tensor that yields the optimal (pairwise) assignment matrices P_k as described in (1). The assignment matrices are optimal in a sense that these result in a rank-4 W_f (recall that W_f is a function of the assignment matrices). We consider the SVD decomposition of $W_f = Q\Sigma V^T$ and define Z as

$$Z = W_f W_f^T = \begin{bmatrix} w_1 P_1 P_1^T w_1^T & w_1 P_1 P_2^T w_2^T & \cdots & w_1 P_1 P_f^T w_f^T \\ w_2 P_2 P_1^T w_1^T & w_2 P_2 P_2^T w_2^T & \cdots & w_2 P_2 P_f^T w_f^T \\ \vdots & \vdots & & \vdots \\ w_f P_f P_1^T w_1^T & w_f P_f P_2^T w_2^T & \cdots & w_f P_f P_f^T w_f^T \end{bmatrix} \tag{6}$$

Recall that the aim of our algorithm is to find the matching solution that creates the best rank-4 W_f in the least-squares sense. This can be achieved by minimizing the sum of all eigenvalues λ_i of Z, with the exception of the four largest ones. This is a heuristic similar to the one used in [4], where rank minimization is achieved through minimization of the dual of the spectral norm. The eigenvalues of Z can be obtained, by definition, as the result of the following expression, where q_i represents the ith column of Q, i. e. the ith eigenvector of Z:

$$\lambda_i = q_i^T Z(P_1, P_2, ..., P_f) q_i, P_1 \in \mathcal{D}, P_2 \in \mathcal{P}^2, ..., P_f \in \mathcal{P}^f \tag{7}$$

where $\mathcal{P}^f$ represents the set of rank-p_0 assignment matrices of dimension $[p_f \times p_1]$ and $\mathcal{D}$ represents the set of rank-p_0 diagonal matrices of dimension $[p_1 \times p_1]$. The eigenvectors of Z are assumed known because these are the columns of Q, that under the factorization context is related to motion. In a calibrated system, Q is thus not a variable. For a rank-deficient Z, each of the non-dominant eigenvectors is a base vector for the null space of the column space of W_f defining in fact camera movement.

Our matching problem must thus be formalized as the search for the optimal set of assignment matrices $P_1^*, ..., P_f^*$ (e.g. optimal assignment tensor) such that:

$$P_1*, ..., P_f^* = \arg \min_{P_1, ..., P.} \left(\sum_{i>4} \lambda_i(P_1, ..., P_f) \right) = \arg \min_{P_1 ..., P.} \left(\sum_{i>4} q_i^T Z(P_1, ..., P_f) q_i \right) \tag{8}$$

3   Minimizing the Cost Function Using Linear Programming

In general, solving the multi-frame correspondence problem through the minimization of (8) is a very tough problem. In particular, when considering only isolated assignment matrices, as was done in [11], the cost function in (8) is clearly quadratic, since there are certain terms (the crossed terms $w_i P_i P_k^T w_k^T, i \neq k$) which cannot be expressed as a linear function of the elements of the associated assignment matrices. Note that this is *not* an intrinsic property of the problem, but rather a consequence of an inadequate formulation: in fact, when working with single assignment matrices there are restrictions which are not considered. This is not the case with the assignment tensor, which takes into account all the inter-frame restrictions. In the present formulation, the crossed terms actually do have a linear form in the terms of the tensor - in other words, we can solve the correspondence problem as a linear problem. Moreover, we show that this problem can be easily solved through relaxation. In this section, the tensor formulation of the correspondence problem will be used to generate a linear formulation in the elements of T for the cost function presented in the previous section.

3.1 Unicity Constraints Revisited

The unicity constraints governing the structure of the assignment tensor, as they have been presented in (2), are awkward to use in the following calculations. We will consequently derive an equivalent formulation for these constraints.

We recall that the unicity condition requires that the sum over any dimension of the assignment tensor be *at most* one. Although these restrictions are trivially extendable to an arbitrary number of frames we will once more focus on the three-frame case, which allows a simple insight on the technique. This formulation would amount to:

$$\forall j, k, m, n, \sum_{i=1} T_{ijk}.T_{imn} = \left(\sum_{i=1} T_{ijk}.T_{imn} \right).\delta_{jm}\delta_{kn},$$

$$\forall i, k, l, n, \sum_{j=1} T_{ijk}.T_{ljn} = \left(\sum_{j=1} T_{ijk}.T_{ljn} \right).\delta_{il}\delta_{kn}, \qquad (9)$$

$$\forall i, j, l, m, \sum_{k=1} T_{ijk}.T_{lmk} = \left(\sum_{k=1} T_{ijk}.T_{lmk} \right).\delta_{il}\delta_{jm},$$

In practice, this formulation is equivalent to saying that any two vectors in the same dimensions are orthogonal. This in turn will prevent two non-zero elements of the tensor of sharing the same dimension, thus enforcing the unicity conditions.

3.2 Solving for the Assignment Tensor

In this section we show that the cost function can be written as a linear program, thus effectively solving multi-frame correspondence with a low computational cost. Recall that the cost function has the following structure (the index i represents the order of the eigenvectors of Z):

$$\sum_{i>4} q_i^T W_f W_f^T q_i \qquad (10)$$

Our objective is to extract the optimal assignment tensor T, which is uniquely determined by the optimal set of assignment matrices $P_2, ..., P_f$. Given a tensor T, the *vec* operator stacks its dimensions successively (from the first to the last) in order to form a vector: $x = vec(T)$.

Note the relation between T and the structure of the assignment matrices $(P_2, ..., P_f)$: the elements of these matrices are a linear function of the elements of T, as explained in section 2.1. Furthermore, products of matrices (such as $P_2 P_3^T$) actually represent pairwise correspondences (in this case between the second and third frame - P_{23}) and are thus also a linear cost function of x - the simplification becomes evident when using the constraints in the form presented in (9). Given each of the q_i, we can thus rearrange (10) as a linear function of x. Optimal correspondence will consequently be given by (11), where $\mathcal{T}$ represents the set of all assignment tensors of dimension $p_1 \times p_2 \times p_3$ and rank p_0; in the generic case, the number of dimensions contained in the dimension set is determined by the number of frames in the system.

$$x* = \arg \min_x c.x, \quad s.t. \ x = vec(T), T \in \mathcal{T} \tag{11}$$

The coefficient vector c can be calculated directly from the original formulation of the cost function by developing the expression in (10) in order to the elements of the assignment tensor. The calculation of c for the three image case is presented in the Appendix.

The formulation presented in (11) still remains an *integer* minimization problem and as such has no efficient solution. However, in the continuous domain there are algorithms that allow the solution to this problem to be obtained in a simple and swift manner. Fortunately, it can easily be shown that the assignment tensor possesses equivalent properties that allow an exact relaxation to take place - all that is needed is to demonstrate that the matrix containing the restrictions on the vector x is totally unimodular, as shown in [2].

The resulting problem is thus equivalent to the original, but for this class of problems (linear programming problems) there exist several efficient algorithms that can provide an adequate solution such as the simplex algorithm.

This method of solving the integer optimization problem has originally been proposed in [9].

4   Extensions to the Algorithm

4.1   The Non-calibrated Case

Up to this point, Q has been considered as known. However, an iterative solution has been devised which allows the solution of non-calibrated systems with small baselines provided a reasonably good initialization is available. Under this assumption, an initial estimate of the q_i is used to solve an approximate matching problem, which in turn returns an improved value for the q_i. This process is repeated until convergence is achieved; a similar method has already been published by the authors in [11].

Note that in the non-calibrated case two sets of unknowns are present: the elements of T and the columns of Q. Our iterative optimization scheme is analogous to a cyclic coordinate descent algorithm, in the sense that it optimizes a set of unknowns while keeping the remaining unknowns constant.

4.2   The Support Tensor

As can be inferred from the previous sections, the size of the linear program to be solved in order to obtain a matching solution can be potentially rather large. If some *a priori* knowledge is available, improbable matches can be excluded, thus reducing the dimensionality of the problem. To this end, a support tensor is used, which is a binary structure in which *allowable* matches are marked. All null variables are consequently eliminated from the x vector, thus rendering a smaller x^c vector.

5   Experiments

We describe in this section a set of experiments in order to validate the algorithm that has been presented. An experiment with real data provides a proof-of-concept solution, while demonstrating the ability of the algorithm to function under less than optimal conditions (i.e., with noise and deviations to the theoretical model). A non-calibrated example is also presented that illustrates how absence of information regarding motion may be circumvented.

5.1   The LEGO Grid

In this experiment three images of a LEGO grid are used. The grid defines two perpendicular planes in the 3D space. In this experiment, only contour points in the images are considered. In the first image, 99 points from the contour are selected as features. Note that the features are selected in areas where the contour is a straight line , so as to demonstrate the robustness of the method to the aperture problem. In the remaining images, the matching candidates are simply the contours of the images. In order to illustrate the handling of occlusion, parts of the contour have been removed in the second and third frames in order to create a situation under which some features in the first image do not have a valid match. No ground-truth is available, but correspondences can be verified by visual inspection.

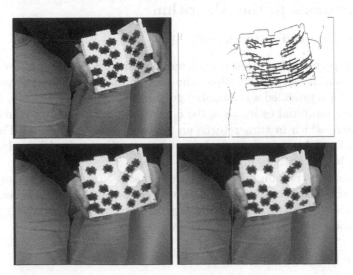

Fig. 2. Results for the LEGO Grid data set. Counter-clockwise from upper left: First image with features selected in red; second and third images with matching candidates in green and correspondences in red; feature trajectories in the third image.

Note that only a minimal error is noticeable by visual inspection, despite the fact that the camera was modeled as orthographic and that only approximate values were available for the q_i. Features which did not have valid matching candidates were successfully rejected. In this experiment a support tensor based on epipolar geometry was applied, so that candidates for each feature only exist in the vicinity of its epipolar lines. In total, ca. 3600 matching candidates were available for the 99 features in each of the frames. Using support, only 11000 matches were possible - consequently, *only a subset of the total number of matching candidates is an actual candidate for each feature*. It should be underlined that the use of the support tensor does not alter the result of the experiment; however, it does speed it up considerably - this problem, including support computation, can be solved in less than 15 min. on MATLAB. The actual matching algorithm, implemented in C, takes but a few seconds.

5.2 The Hotel Sequence

In this experiment information about camera motion is inexistent in the sequence, except in the first three frames. In the first two images 43 points (37 features and 6 points without matching candidates) have been singled out. Every image is matched against the first two using approximate values for motion information, i.e. the q_i. These are extrapolated based on the movement of frames already matched. These estimates are then iterated upon as referred in section 4.1. Note

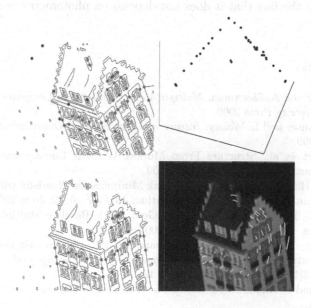

Fig. 3. Results for the Hotel data set. Counter-clockwise from upper left: First image with features in red and occluded points in blue; last image with correspondences in red; last image with trajectories; point cloud resulting from reconstruction, viewed from above.

that this is a simplified version of the presented algorithm, used only to illustrate the possibility of applying this work to uncalibrated images sequences; as such, matches are done pairwise to accelerate the procedure. Support based on maximum disparity between images is used.

No significant error is noticeable in this experiment, as the 37 features are correctly tracked and the 6 occluded points are rejected in every frame. Reconstruction based on the matches is precise. Each of the frames presents a total of ca. 11000 matching candidates, which after application of support reduces to only 1100 points.

6   Conclusions

We have presented in this text a novel approach to multi-view matching that allows correspondence to be obtained with linear complexity. This is achieved through a generalization of the concept of assignment matrix to the multidimensional assignment tensor. This tensor shares most of the properties of the assignment matrix, while adding constraints that allow a coherent solution between frames to be enforced. A cost function based on rigidity, as understood under the factorization context, has been used in conjunction with the assignment tensor to successfully determine correspondence between images. This cost function not only yields a global solution but also overcomes the aperture problem, owing to the fact that it does not depend on photometry as most present methods.

References

1. R. Hartley and A. Zisserman. *Multiple View Geometry in Computer Vision*. Cambridge Univerity Press 2000.
2. G. Nemhauser and L. Wolsey. *Integer and Cobinatorial Optimization*, John Wiley & Sons 1999.
3. F. Dellaert et al., Structure From Motion Without Correspondence. *In Proc. CVPR*, South Carolina, USA, June 2000
4. M. Fazel, H. Hindi and S. Boyd. A Rank Minimization Heuristic with Application to Minimum Order System Approximation. In *Proc. ACC*, June 2001.
5. V. Ferrari, T. Tuytelaars and L. van Gool. Wide-Baseline Multiple-View Correspondences. In *Proc. ICCV*, October 2003.
6. A. Heyden, R. Berthilsson and G. Sparr. An iterative factorization method for projective structure and motion from image sequences. *Image and Vision Computing*(17), 13(1), pp. 981-991, November 1999.
7. M. Irani and P. Anandan. Factorization with Uncertainty. In —textitProc. ECCV, June 2000.
8. V. Kolmogorov and R. Zabih. Multi-camera Scene Reconstruction via Graph Cuts. In *Proc. ECCV*, May 2002.
9. J. Maciel and J. Costeira. A Global Solution to Sparse Correspondence Problems. *IEEE Transactions on Pattern Analysis and Machine Intelligence*, Vol. 25(2), February 2003.

10. D. Martinec and T. Pajdla. 3D Reconstruction by Fitting Low-Rank Matrices with Data. In *Proc. CVPR*, June 2005.
11. R. Oliveira, J. Costeira and J. Xavier. Optimal Point Correspondence through the Use of Rank Constraints. *In Proc. CVPR*, San Diego, USA, June 2005.
12. S. Roy and I. Cox. A Maximum-Flow Formulation of the N-Camera Stereo Correspondence Problem. In *Proc. ICCV*, January 1998.
13. K. Shafique and M. Shah. A Non-Iterative Greedy Algorithm for Multi-frame Point Correspondence. In *Proc. ICCV*, October 2003.
14. P. Sturm and B. Triggs. A factorization based algorithm for multi-image projective structure and motion. In *Proc. ECCV*, pp. 709-720, April 1996.
15. C. Tomasi and T. Kanade. Shape from motion from image sreams under orthography: a factorization method. *IJCV*,9(2):137-154, November 1992.

Appendix

In this section an explicit expression for the coefficient vector of the linear program in (11) is presented, for the three-frame case. Each c_i is divided into a set of terms as in (12) corresponding, respectively, to the terms depending only on P_2, and P_3, and to the terms in $P_2 P_3{}^T$, $P_1 P_1^T$, $P_2 P_2{}^T$ and $P_3 P_3{}^T$.

$$c_i = 2c_{P_2} + 2c_{P_3} + 2c_{P_2 P_3} + c_P 1P1 + c_{P_2 P_2} + c_{P_3 P_3},$$

$$c_{P_2} = 1_{[1 \times p_3]} \otimes \left(q_{i_{1:2}}{}^T w_1 \otimes q_{i_{3:4}}{}^T w_2 \right)$$

$$c_{P_3} = \left(q_{i_{5:6}}{}^T w_3 \otimes q_{i_{1:2}}{}^T w_1 \right) \otimes 1_{[1 \times p_2]}$$

$$c_{P_1 P_1} = 1_{[1 \times p_3]} \otimes \left(\left((q_{i_{1:2}}^T w_1) \bullet (q_{i_{1:2}}^T w_1) \right) \otimes 1_{[1 \times p_2]} \right)$$

$$c_{P_2 P_3} = vec_r \left((q_{i_{5:6}}{}^T w_3) \otimes (q_{i_{3:4}}{}^T w_2) \right)$$

$$c_{P_2 P_2} = vec \left(1_{[p. \times p_3]} \otimes \left(diag \left((I_{[p_2 \times p_2]} \otimes q_{i_{3:4}}{}^T w_2) E_2 E_2{}^T \left(I_{[p_2 \times p_2]} \otimes w_2{}^T q_{i_{3:4}} \right) \right) \right)^T \right)$$

$$c_{P_3 P_3} = vec \left(\left(diag \left((I_{[p_3 \times p_3]} \otimes q_{i_{5:6}}{}^T w_3) E_3 E_3{}^T \left(I_{[p_3 \times p_3]} \otimes w_3{}^T q_{i_{5:6}} \right) \right) \right)^T \otimes 1_{[p. \times p_2]} \right)$$

$$E_i = \left[e_1 e_1^T \cdots e_{p.} e_{p.}^T \right]^T \tag{12}$$

The vec_r operator acts in a similar way to vec, except that it stacks the rows of a matrix instead of its columns. e_i represents the ith versor in the p_i-dimensional space. The complete c is constructed by the sum of all c_i.

Kernel-Predictability: A New Information Measure and Its Application to Image Registration

Héctor Fernando Gómez-García, José L. Marroquín, and Johan Van Horebeek

Center for Research in Mathematics (CIMAT),
Apartado Postal 402,
Guanajuato, Gto. 36000, México
{hector, jlm, horebeek}@cimat.mx

Abstract. A new information measure for probability distributions is presented; based on it, a similarity measure between images is derived, which is used for constructing a robust image registration algorithm based on random sampling, similar to classical approaches like mutual information. It is shown that the registration method obtained with the new similarity measure shows a significantly better performance for small sampling sets; this makes it specially suited for the estimation of non-parametric deformation fields, where the estimation of the local transformation is done on small windows. This is confirmed by extensive comparisons using synthetic deformations of real images.

1 Introduction

Image registration is a fundamental task in many fields like medical image processing, analysis of satellital images, and robot vision, among others (see [1][2][3] and references contained there in). Moreover, the methods used to register images, can be adapted to solve other important problems like motion segmentation, stereoscopic registration and the tracking of objects in motion.

When registering two images, I_1 and I_2 , one tries to find the transformation T that applied to I_1 aligns it spatially to I_2. Many registration methods suppose that the intensity of every point is conserved between frames, that is, the equality $I_1[T(x)] = I_2(x)$ is assumed for all the points x; this is known as the *Optical Flow Constraint*, and there is a huge number of registration methods based on this assumption, [4][5][6][7]. However, situations are found very easily where this constraint is violated, for example when the illumination sources change between frames, when the surfaces of the illuminated objects are not lambertian or when registering medical images acquired by different modalities. In these cases, image registration by the maximization of *Mutual Information* (*MI*) has been widely used because it does not assume a functional relationship between the intensities of the images; instead, it is based on the fact that if aligned, the maximal dependency (information) between the images intensities is found.

A. Leonardis, H. Bischof, and A. Pinz (Eds.): ECCV 2006, Part III, LNCS 3953, pp. 502–513, 2006.
© Springer-Verlag Berlin Heidelberg 2006

Given two images, I_1 and I_2, their mutual information is defined as:

$$MI(I_1, I_2) = H(I_1) + H(I_2) - H(I_1, I_2) \qquad (1)$$

where $H(\cdot)$ is the entropy function defined over the probabilities of the images intensities. For a discrete random variable, the entropy function is written as:

$$H(I) = -\sum_{i=1}^{N} p_i \log p_i \qquad (2)$$

with $p_i = p(I = b_i)$, where b_i is the i-th valid intensity value, and for continuous random variables the entropy is written as:

$$H(I) = -\int_{-\infty}^{\infty} p(b) \ln[p(b)] db \,.$$

The first applications of MI to the image registration problem, were published simultaneously by Viola et al. [8] and Collignon et al. [9], both in the middle of the last decade. Since then, a great number of publications have appeared extending the initial work to problems like nonparametric multimodal image registration [10][11], registration of stereoscopic pairs [12][13] or feature tracking in images [14].

In general, methods based on the maximization of MI, start with an initial transformation T^0, leading to a MI value MI^0, and using a proper optimization method, a sequence of transformations is generated in such a way that the associated MI is increased until convergence. During the optimization process, the increment in MI can be calculated with the expression:

$$\Delta(MI) = \Delta H[I_1(T)] + \Delta H(I_2) - \Delta H[I_1(T), I_2] \,.$$

If the discrete version of the entropy is considered, this is a function of the entries of the probability vector; using a Taylor series expansion, a linear approximation for the increment in entropy is given by:

$$\Delta(H) = -\sum_{i=1}^{N} [1 + \log p_i] \Delta p_i$$

and because the coefficient $[1 + \log p_i]$ is big for small probability values, this increment is highly determined by small features in the images to be registered (which are generally associated with small probability values). This can trap the registration algorithm in local optima, generated when aligning small features, particularly if the small probabilities are not accurately computed. This makes it difficult to apply MI in cases where only a limited sampling is available, for example when measuring entropy at a local level in images, which is important in interesting problems like nonparametric image registration, and in the segmentation of motion between frames, where local measures must be done in order to learn the local motion models and to have enough spatial definition at the motion interfaces.

Another problem related to the application of MI, occurs when working with images with a large background compared to the region of interest, as frequently happens in medical image problems. Under this circumstance the sum of the marginal entropies can become larger than the joint entropy, leading to an increase of MI, instead of decreasing it in misregistration. Studholme et al. [15] proposed the use of a normalized version of the MI to overcome this disadvantage. This measure is known as *Normalized Mutual Information* (NMI):

$$NMI(I_1, I_2) = \frac{H(I_1) + H(I_2)}{H(I_1, I_2)} . \tag{3}$$

In this work, we propose the use of a new information measure for probability distributions, which we call *Kernel-Predictability* (KP). KP, evaluated in the marginal and joint distributions of two images, is integrated in a similarity measure between images, normalized as (3), and applied to the registration problem. Unlike entropy, the increment of this measure when updated by an optimization method, is mostly determined by the larger entries of the probability vector, which is reflected in a higher robustness in problems where only limited sampling is available. Our proposal is discussed in the next section and in section 3 its performance in image registration problems is compared to that obtained under maximization of MI and NMI. The experimental results show that an important reduction in registration errors is obtained by the use of our method compared to MI and NMI.

2   Kernel-Predictability

In order to introduce our information measure for a given distribution F, consider the following guessing game: someone generates a value x_1 from F and we guess x_1 by generating (independently) a value x_2 from F. We denote by $K(x_1, x_2)$ the obtained reward. More generally, considering various games, we can define the average reward $E(K(X_1, X_2))$. We suppose that the reward function favors guesses close to the true value, i.e., $K(\cdot, \cdot)$ is a decreasing function of the distance between x_1 and x_2. Under this assumption it is clear that the less uncertainty is contained in F, the higher will be the average reward.

The above motivates the following measure for a given distribution F:

$$KP(F) = E[K(X_1, X_2)] = \int_{R^{\cdot}} \int_{R^{\cdot}} K(x_1, x_2) dF(x_1) dF(x_2) . \tag{4}$$

The last integral is a *regular statistical functional* of degree two (two is the number of arguments in K) [16][17], and the real function K is called the *kernel*. This functional measures the predictability of the random variables distributed according to F, weighted by K, and we denominate it *Kernel − Predictability*.

For the discrete case, this becomes:

$$KP(\mathbf{p}) = \sum_{i=1}^{M} \sum_{j=1}^{M} K_{ij} p_i p_j = \mathbf{p}^T \mathbf{K} \mathbf{p} \tag{5}$$

where M is the number of the different values taken by the random variable X and $\mathbf{K}$ is the matrix which stores in the entry K_{ij}, the reward given for guessing the value x_i when the generated value was x_j. This reward must be maximal, say K_M, when $i = j$, and if it does not depend on i (if we don't have preference to guess any particular value of X), $K_{ii} = K_M$, $\forall i$ and $K_M > K_{ij}$ if $i \neq j$. In general, K_{ij} must be selected as a decreasing function of the distance between the values x_i and x_j.

Observe that if only a unit reward is given for an exact guess, i.e. $\mathbf{K}$ is the identity matrix, KP reduces to the l^2 norm of the probability vector, and $KP(\mathbf{p}) = 1 - G(\mathbf{p})$, where $G(\cdot)$ is the well known *Gini* index of Machine Learning [18]. Opposite to the Gini index and other information measures like the discrete entropy which are invariant under a permutation of the values of the measurement scale, KP can incorporate the quantitative nature of the measurement scale by means of a proper reward function that expresses how close the guess is to the true value.

$KP(\cdot)$ is maximal for random variables which take a fixed value with probability one, by the next inequality:

$$KP(\mathbf{p}) = \sum_i \sum_j K_{ij} p_i p_j \leq K_M \sum_i \sum_j p_i p_j = K_M$$

note that K_M is the value of KP for variables with $p_i = 1$ for any particular value i and $p_j = 0$ for all $j \neq i$.

Taking again $\mathbf{K} = \mathbf{I}$, the minimal KP is obtained for uniformly distributed variables, as can easily be proved. It should be noted that KP is a predictability measure, so it behaves in an inverse way compared to the entropy, which is an uncertainty measure.

Returning to the case $\mathbf{K} = \mathbf{I}$, we can measure the increment in kernel-predictability, which may be associated to the optimization process:

$$\Delta(KP) = 2 \sum_{i=1}^{M} p_i \Delta p_i .$$

From this equation one can see that the increment in KP is mainly determined by the larger entries of the probability vector, and for that reason, by the more important features in the images to be registered. This is an important difference with respect to entropy.

2.1 Estimation of the Kernel-Predictability

In practice, it is not always possible to know exactly the distribution function required to evaluate (4) and (5), so an estimation of KP must be done based on a sampling set composed by n independent and identically distributed random variables, $\mathbf{X} = \{X_1, X_2, \ldots, X_n\}$,with $X_i \sim F$, $\forall i$. Two estimators to approximate (4) are:

$$\widehat{KP} = \frac{1}{\binom{n}{2}} \sum_{i=1}^{n-1} \sum_{j=i+1}^{n} K(X_i, X_j) \tag{6}$$

$$\widehat{KP'} = \frac{1}{\left(\frac{n}{2}\right)^2} \sum_{i=1}^{n/2} \sum_{j=n/2+1}^{n} K(X_i, X_j) . \tag{7}$$

In the first estimator, all possible pairs of variables in $\mathbf{X}$ appear in the sum; in the second, the set $\mathbf{X}$ is divided in two subsets and the kernel is evaluated at each couple formed by taking one variable from the first set and other variable from the second one. Both estimators are unbiased, and if the kernel K is symmetric then $\widehat{KP}$ has the minimal variance among all the unbiased estimators, as shown in [16][17]. $\widehat{KP'}$ has more variance than $\widehat{KP}$ but is cheaper to evaluate. Both variances tend to the same value when the sampling set is increased in size; for these reasons, we use the estimator $\widehat{KP'}$ in the present work.

2.2   Image Registration with Kernel-Predictability

Using KP, one can define a similarity measure between images $I_1(T)$ and I_2, in the following way:

$$SKP(I_1(T), I_2) = \frac{KP[F(I_1(T), I_2)]}{KP[F(I_1(T))] + KP[F(I_2)]} . \tag{8}$$

This similarity measure makes a comparison between the predictability of the joint distribution and that of the marginal distributions for the images $I_1(T)$ and I_2. The registration is done by searching for the transformation T^* with maximal SKP, $T^* = \arg max_T[SKP(I_1(T), I_2)]$, due to the fact that the joint distribution of the aligned images gets an ordered and more predictable structure than the one obtained with misregistered images. As done with NMI, our similarity measure is normalized to make it more robust in problems with different content of background and information of interest.

In [19], a measure called Kernel Density Correlation (KDC) is proposed for image registration; that measure shares some similarity with the approximation (7) to the functional (4); however important differences should be noted: firstly, for the approximation of KP (defined in the functional 4), more estimators can be used besides (7), e.g. equation (6), so KP is more general than KDC; moreover in [19] KDC is used for image registration taking the cartesian product of the points in the two images, penalizing the differences in intensities for points that are near in the overlapping coordinates, which implies that this method cannot be applied for multimodal image registration problems; in our case we are using the KP measure to search for peaked joint distributions of intensities in the corresponding regions, which is quite different, and indeed permits its use for multimodal registration.

The similarity defined in (8) can be estimated using the alternatives given above to approximate the KP. In particular, we sample uniformly the coordinates of the images, generating the set $\mathbf{X} = \{X_1, X_2, \ldots, X_n\}$; then, evaluate the intensities of the image I_2 over this set, and the intensities of the image I_1 over the set $T(\mathbf{X})$. Using the estimator (7), the approximation to (8) can be written in the following way:

$$\widehat{SKP}(I_1(T), I_2) = \frac{\sum_{i=1}^{\cdot \cdot 2} \sum_{j=\cdot \cdot 2+1} K_2(I_J^i - I_J^j)}{\sum_{i=1}^{\cdot \cdot 2} \sum_{j=\cdot \cdot 2+1} K_1(I_T^i - I_T^j) + \sum_{i=1}^{\cdot \cdot 2} \sum_{j=\cdot \cdot 2+1} K_1(I_2^i - I_2^j)}$$

$$= \frac{\widehat{KP_J'}}{\widehat{KP_J'} + \widehat{KP_2'}}$$

(9)

where $I_J^i = (I_1[T(X_i)], I_2(X_i))$, $I_2^i = I_2(X_i)$, $I_T^i = I_1[T(X_i)]$, K_2 is the kernel used to measure the predictability of the joint distribution of $I_1(T)$ and I_2 and K_1 for the marginal distributions of $I_1(T)$ and I_2. For example, if gaussian kernels are used, then:

$$K_2(I_J^i - I_J^j) = \exp\left\{ -\frac{\|I_J^i - I_J^j\|^2}{2\sigma_2^2} \right\}$$

(10)

$$K_1(I^i - I^j) = \exp\left\{ -\frac{(I^i - I^j)^2}{2\sigma_1^2} \right\}.$$

(11)

The maximization can be done using gradient ascent, starting with an initial transformation T^0 and actualizing it with the relation:

$$T^{t+1} = T^t + \lambda \frac{d}{dT^i} \widehat{SKP}(I_1(T^t), I_2)$$

with:

$$\frac{d}{dT} \widehat{SKP}(I_1(T), I_2) = \frac{1}{\widehat{KP_T'} + \widehat{KP_2'}} \frac{d}{dT} \widehat{KP_J'} - \frac{\widehat{KP_J'}}{(\widehat{KP_T'} + \widehat{KP_2'})^2} \frac{d}{dT} \widehat{KP_T'}$$

and in particular, when using the kernels (10) and (11), the last derivatives are:

$$\frac{d}{dT} \widehat{KP_J'} = -\frac{1}{\sigma_2^2} \sum_{i=1}^{n/2} \sum_{j=n/2+1}^{n} \exp\left\{ -\frac{\|I_T^i - I_T^j\|^2}{2\sigma_2^2} \right\} (I_T^i - I_T^j) \frac{d}{dT}(I_T^i - I_T^j)$$

$$\frac{d}{dT} \widehat{KP_T'} = -\frac{1}{\sigma_1^2} \sum_{i=1}^{n/2} \sum_{j=n/2+1}^{n} \exp\left\{ -\frac{\|I_T^i - I_T^j\|^2}{2\sigma_1^2} \right\} (I_T^i - I_T^j) \frac{d}{dT}(I_T^i - I_T^j).$$

3 Results

This section shows the results obtained by solving the image registration problem, with the application of the similarity measure defined in (9). These results are compared with those obtained by the maximization of MI and NMI. For both versions of mutual information, the entropy was estimated using Parzen windows to approximate the probability densities, following [8]. These approximations are:

$$H(I_2) \qquad = -\frac{2}{n} \sum_{i=1}^{n/2} \ln \left\{ \frac{2}{n} \sum_{j=n/2+1}^{n} K_1(I_2^i - I_2^j) \right\}$$

$$H[I_1(T)] \qquad = -\frac{2}{n} \sum_{i=1}^{n/2} \ln \left\{ \frac{2}{n} \sum_{j=n/2+1}^{n} K_1(I_T^i - I_T^j) \right\}$$

$$H[I_1(T), I_2] = -\frac{2}{n} \sum_{i=1}^{n/2} \ln \left\{ \frac{2}{n} \sum_{j=n/2+1}^{n} K_2(I_J^i - I_J^j) \right\}.$$

The use of Parzen windows is more suitable, when working with limited sampling, than other approaches used to estimate the entropy (e.g. normalized histograms); an additional advantage is that, the approximate similarity measures become differentiable, facilitating the optimization process. Gaussian kernels, (10) and (11), were used to approximate the entropies in MI and NMI (using integration constants to normalize the densities as is required by the Parzen windows) and the corresponding kernel-predictability measure. To make the 3 methods comparable, all the corresponding variances were set to equal values. As is done with the estimation of the KP values, two different, equally sized sampling sets of coordinates are used to estimate the entropy, again following the proposal in [8]. It should be noted that when using Parzen windows the continuous version of the entropy is used; this version can be negative depending on the domain of the variables, and the NMI can be maximal for a negative sum of the marginal entropies and a small negative joint entropy, to avoid this problem the images were scaled to [0,100]. All the methods were optimized using gradient ascent.

3.1   Global Multimodal Image Registration

In the first set of experiments, the 3 methods were tested, using 2 two-dimensional MR images, obtained by the simulator at the Montreal Neurological Institute [20], shown in figure 1. The first image corresponds to a modality T1, with 9% of noise level, and 40% of spatial inhomogeneities in intensity; the second corresponds to a modality T2. A set of 50 random rigid transformations was created, and applied to the T2 MR image. The T1 MR image was used as I_1, so the transformation was always started with the identity. The values for the rotation angles θ were chosen uniformly distributed, $\theta \sim U\{-30°, 30°\}$, and the translation vectors t, taking $t \sim U\{-25, 25\}$ (in pixels). Each sampling set was created taking at random coordinates uniformly distributed in the overlapping region of the images; when this kind of sampling is done, then the part of I_2 which is in the overlap depends on the actual transformation T, and in order to use gradient ascent, the derivative of I_2 with respect to the transformation must be calculated; but I_2 does not depend directly on T, so the gradient of the 3 similarity measures with respect to T was approximated using central finite differences. Though a rigid transformation was applied to the images, the

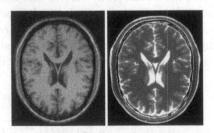

Fig. 1. Images (217 × 181 pixels) used for the global transformations experiments

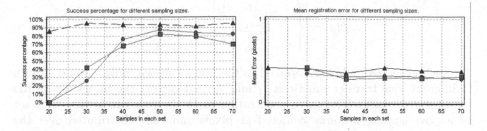

Fig. 2. Success percentage (left) and mean registration error (right) for MI (squares), NMI (circles) and SKP(triangles)

registrations were done searching for the best affine transformation in order to avoid the nonlinearity of the rigid transformations with respect to the rotation angle. In the experiments, the size of the sampling sets was progressively varied, and for each sampling size, the set of 50 registration problems was run.

Figure 2, shows the percentage of successful registrations and the mean registration error obtained for the 3 algorithms. The registration error was measured adding the length of the difference between the applied and the estimated vectors for all the pixels, and then taking the mean value; if the mean value was smaller than 1 pixel, then the registration was considered as successful, and only the successful registrations were considered in the computation of the mean error in the set of 50 transformations. As one can see, one obtains comparable errors using KP, but a significantly higher success rate, specially for small sampling sets, which means that one can obtain performances similar to MI and NMI at a significantly smaller computational cost.

3.2   Local Multimodal Image Registration

The above results suggest that KP should exhibit significantly better performance than MI and NMI when the size of the sampling set is limited by the problem itself; this is the case when the methods are applied for the estimation of nonparametric (local) deformation fields.

To test the performance of the three methods under local multimodal image registration in two-dimensional images, 10 different transformation fields were generated, synthesized by means of two rectangular grids of 5×5 nodes (one grid for each component of the translation vectors) and centering over each node a cubic B-spline function. The nodal values were assigned randomly with values uniformly distributed over a certain interval, in such a way that for each pixel (x, y) a translation vector $[u(x, y), v(x, y)]$ was defined in the following way:

$$
\begin{aligned}
u(x,y) &= \sum_i \sum_j U_{ij}\beta[k_1(x - x_i)]\beta[k_2(y - y_j)] \\
v(x,y) &= \sum_i \sum_j V_{ij}\beta[k_1(x - x_i)]\beta[k_2(y - y_j)]
\end{aligned}
\tag{12}
$$

with $U_{ij}, V_{ij} \sim U\{-7, 7\}$, for all centering nodes (x_i, y_j), k_d is the proportion of nodes versus the image dimension in the direction d; and:

$$\beta(z) = \begin{cases} \frac{2}{3} - |z|^2 + \frac{|z|^3}{2}, & |z| < 1. \\ \frac{(2-|z|)^3}{6}, & 1 \le |z| < 2 \\ 0, & |z| \ge 2. \end{cases}$$

Each generated field, was applied to the images shown in figs. 3 and 4, with 2 different tone transfer functions f_1 and f_2 that distort the intensities of the transformed images. The three registration methods were run locally on a set of nonoverlapping windows centered at pixels uniformly distributed over the images, in order to find the best translation vector that explains the true field $[u(x,y), v(x,y)]$ for each point (x,y); the center points were separated 10 pixels of each other in every direction (the images are 128×128 pixels of size). All the measures were estimated locally, i.e. using only the pixels placed within each window of size $w \times w$. The 2 sampling sets were built by assigning alternatively pixels in the window to each sampling set (each of the sampling sets had $\frac{w^2}{2}$ pixels). The window size was progressively reduced and the registrations repeated for each field. The performance of the three methods was measured using the mean angular error, as proposed by [21]; for that we extend the estimated, $d_e = (u_e, v_e)$, and true vectors $d_t = (u_t, v_t)$ to $d'_e = (u_e, v_e, 1)$ $d'_t = (u_t, v_t, 1)$ now representing the displacement in space and time for every pixel; the angular error is calculated by: $err = \arccos(\frac{d'_e \cdot d'_t}{\|d'_e\| \|d'_t\|})$. Figures 3 and 4, summarize the results obtained by the three methods.

Our registration method can be applied effectively in nonparametric registration problems, as is confirmed in the table 1 which summarizes the results of the application of the 3 measures for the computation of a dense transformation field.

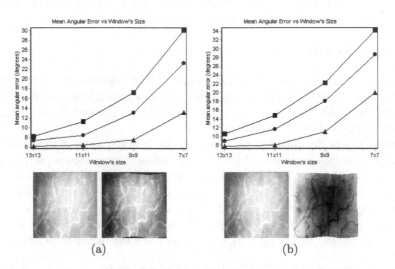

(a)   (b)

Fig. 3. Mean angular error for MI (squares), NMI (circles) and SKP(triangles). The subfigure (a) summarizes the results obtained using the tone transfer function $f_1(i) = 100(\frac{i}{100})^{1.35}$, and the subfigure (b) $f_2(i) = 100[1 - (\frac{i}{100})^{1.35}]$, $i \in [0, 100]$. The second row shows the original and the transformed images in each case.

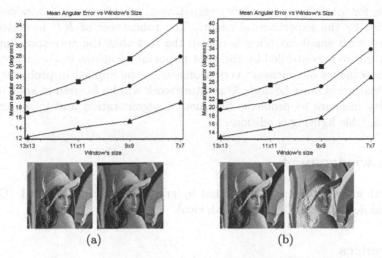

Fig. 4. Mean angular error for MI (squares), NMI (circles) and SKP(triangles). The subfigure (a) summarizes the results obtained using the tone transfer function $f_1(i) = 100(\frac{i}{100})^{1.35}$, and the subfigure (b) $f_2(i) = 100[1 - (\frac{i}{100})^{1.35}]$, $i \in [0, 100]$. The second row shows the original and the transformed images in each case.

Table 1. Mean angular error for nonparametric registration

Image	SKP	NMI	MI
Figs. 3(a)	13.31 $^\circ$	17.96 $^\circ$	20.52 $^\circ$
Figs. 3(b)	14.89 $^\circ$	19.06 $^\circ$	20.97 $^\circ$
Figs. 4(a)	28.40 $^\circ$	33.09 $^\circ$	36.14
Figs. 4(b)	29.19 $^\circ$	34.29 $^\circ$	36.27 $^\circ$

For each of the 3 similarities, the registration was done maximizing the sum of the similarity evaluated in small squared windows centered on each pixel and adding an elastic regularization term. The width of the windows was set to 5 pixels. As was done in the last experiment, 10 synthetic random fields were generated using cubic B-spline functions, but now taking grids with 15×15 nodes for each dimension; each field was applied to the images shown in figs. 3 and 4, with 2 different tone transfer functions, f_1 and f_2. The 3 methods were run for each field and the mean angular error was evaluated.

As can be seen, an important reduction in the registration errors is obtained using our proposal, making it very promising to be applied in local registration problems.

4 Conclusions and Future Work

The similarity measure based in kernel-predictability presented in this paper allows for registrations with errors equivalent to those obtained with MI and NMI but using significantly less sampling. For this reason, our proposal is more effective for local (nonparametric) registration, based on small windows as is confirmed by the experimental results. The robustness of KP in registration problems with small sampling is due to the fact that the corresponding similarity measure is controlled by the most important features in the images. This robustness makes our measure very promising to be applied in problems where local registration must be done. Our future work will be focused in applying this similarity measure to problems like motion segmentation and image tracking under variable lighting conditions.

Acknowledgement

The authors were partially supported by grant 46270 of CONACyT (Consejo Nacional de Ciencia y Tecnología, México).

References

1. Gottesfeld, L.: A survey of image registration techniques. ACM Computing Surveys, 24(4) (1992) 325–376.
2. Maintz, A., Viergever, M. A.: A survey of medical image registration. Medical Image Analysis, 2(1) (1998) 1-36.
3. Josien, P. W., Pluim, J. B., Maintz, A., Viergever, A.: Mutual information based registration of medical images: a survey. IEEE Transactions on Medical Imaging, 22(8) (2003) 986–1004.
4. Horn B.K.P., Schunck B.G.: Determining optical flow. Artificial Intelligence, 17 (1981) 185–203.
5. Szeliski, R., Coughlan, J.: Spline-based image registration. International Journal of Computer Vision, 22(3) (1997) 199–218.
6. Thirion, J-P.: Image matching as a diffusion process: an analogy with Maxwell's demons. Medical Image Analysis, 2(3) (1998) 243–260.
7. Aubert, G., Deriche, R., Kornprobst, P.: Computing optical flow via variational techniques. SIAM Journal on Applied Mathematics, 60(1) (2000) 156–182.
8. Viola, P., Wells III, W.: Alignment by Maximization of Mutual Information. ICCV, (1995) 16–23.
9. Collignon, A., Maes, F., Delaere, D., Vandermeulen, D., Suetens, P., Marchal, G.: Automated multi-modality image registration based on information theory. Information Processing in Medical Imaging. Y. Bizais, C. Barillot, and R. Di Paola, Eds. Dordrecht, The Netherlands. Kluwer, (1995) 263–274.
10. Hermosillo, G., Chefd'hotel, C., Faugeras, O.: Variational methods for multimodal image matching. International Journal of Computer Vision 50(3) (2002) 329–343.
11. DAgostino, E., Maes, F., Vandermeulen, D., Suetens, P.: A viscous fluid model for multimodal image registration using mutual information. MICCAI, (2002) 541–548.
12. Geoffrey, E.: Mutual information as a stereo correspondence measure. Technical Report MS-CIS-00-20, University of Pennsylvania, 2000.
13. Kim, J., Kolmogorov, V., Zabih, R.: Visual correspondence using energy minimization and mutual information. ICCV, (2003) 1033–1040.
14. Dowson, N., Bowden, R.: Metric Mixtures for Mutual Information Tracking. ICPR (2) (2004) 752–756.

15. Studholme, C., Hill, D. L. G., Hawkes, D. J.: An overlap invariant entropy measure of 3D medical image alignment. Pattern Recognit, 32(1) (1999) 71–86.
16. Lee, A. J.: U-Statistics, Theory and Practice. Marcel Dekker Inc. New York, (1990).
17. Lehman, E.L.: Elements of Large Sample Theory. Springer Verlag, New York, (1999).
18. Hastie, T., Tibshirani, R., Friedman, J.: The Elements of Statistical Learning. Springer Verlag, New York, (2003).
19. Maneesh Singh, Himanshu Arora, Narendra Ahuja.: Robust registration and tracking using kernel density correlation. CVPRW, 11(11) (2004) 174.
20. http://www.bic.mni.mcgill.ca/brainweb/
21. Barron, J. L., Fleet, D. J., Bauchemin, S. S.: Performance of Optical Flow Technics. IJCV, 12(1) (1994) 43–77.

Algebraic Methods for Direct and Feature Based Registration of Diffusion Tensor Images

Alvina Goh and René Vidal

Center for Imaging Science, Department of BME, Johns Hopkins University,
308B Clark Hall, 3400 N. Charles St., Baltimore, MD 21218, USA
agoh@jhu.edu, rvidal@cis.jhu.edu

Abstract. We present an algebraic solution to both direct and feature-based registration of diffusion tensor images under various local deformation models. In the direct case, we show how to linearly recover a local deformation from the partial derivatives of the tensor using the so-called Diffusion Tensor Constancy Constraint, a generalization of the brightness constancy constraint to diffusion tensor data. In the feature-based case, we show that the tensor reorientation map can be found in closed form by exploiting the spectral properties of the rotation group. Given this map, solving for an affine deformation becomes a linear problem. We test our approach on synthetic, brain and heart diffusion tensor images.

1 Introduction

Diffusion Tensor Imaging (DTI) is a relatively new 3-D imaging technique that measures the diffusion of water molecules in human and animal tissues. As the directional dependence of water diffusion rates is closely related to the structural anisotropy of the medium, DTI can be potentially used to infer the organization and orientation of tissue components. This has generated much enthusiasm and high expectations, because DTI is presently the only available approach to non-invasively study the three-dimensional architecture of white matter tracts, and quantify physical and geometrical properties of neuronal fibers in vivo.

Unfortunately, current image processing and computer vision algorithms are unable to take full advantage of what DTI offers. The main reason is that, unlike conventional images, DTI not only measures the intensity at each voxel, but also the orientation. Orientation at each voxel is represented mathematically with a symmetric positive semi-definite (SPSD) tensor field $D : \mathbb{R}^3 \rightarrow \mathrm{SPSD}(3) \subset \mathbb{R}^{3 \times 3}$ that measures the diffusion in a direction $v \in \mathbb{R}^3$ as $v^T D v$. Since the image data live on a 6-dimensional space with nontrivial geometry, problems such as filtering, smoothing, edge detection, matching, segmentation, registration, etc., need to be reconsidered in light of the new mathematical structure of the data.

Up until now, most of the research on DTI has focused on fiber tracking and segmentation. *Fiber tracking* refers to the problem of extracting 3-D curves on the image that follow the main orientation of the tensor field at each voxel. By assuming that the largest principal axis of the diffusion tensor (DT) aligns with the predominant fiber orientation, one can obtain a 3-D vector field representing

A. Leonardis, H. Bischof, and A. Pinz (Eds.): ECCV 2006, Part III, LNCS 3953, pp. 514–525, 2006.

the fiber orientation at each voxel. Fiber tracking is then equivalent to finding integral curves of this vector field. Existing fiber tracking methods include streamline techniques [1], tensor deflection [2], PDE-based curve evolution [3, 4], and dynamic programming [5]. *Segmentation* refers to the problem of grouping the fibers into tracts. For example, in images of the spinal cord, bundles of fibers have different functions, and one would like to cluster all fibers having the same or similar functions. Existing segmentation methods either assume that fiber tracts have already been extracted and segment these curves according to a certain cost function, or else segment the tensor data directly using various metrics on SPSD(3) [6, 7], such as the Euclidean distance between two fibers, or the ratio of the length of corresponding portions of the fibers to the overall length of the pairs [8]. In [9], fibers are reduced to a feature vector extracted from the statistical moments of the fibers, and segmentation is done by applying normalized cuts [10] to these feature vectors. [11] first reduces tensor data to a scalar anisotropic measure, and then applies a level set segmentation method.

Although registration of conventional 2-D and 3-D scalar images is a relatively well understood problem, registration of DT images is a problem that has received much less attention. The main difference between registration of scalar images and registration of tensor images is that in addition to estimating a local deformation model, e.g., translational, rigid or affine, one must also reorient each tensor so that it remains consistent with the surrounding anatomical structure in the image. In [12], several tensor reorientation approaches are proposed. The most commonly used method is the Finite Strain scheme [7, 13, 14], which, given an affine transformation A, reorients the tensor using the rotational component of A. Existing methods for registration of DT images are based on minimizing a cost function [15], such as sum-of-squared differences [13, 14], correlation [13], Euclidean distance [7] or diffusion profile [7], under an affine deformation model combined with the finite strain reorientation method. However, such methods are usually computationally intensive, and require good initialization.

The objective of this paper is to develop simple linear registration algorithms that can be used for initializing computationally intensive methods. The main contribution is to show that for the standard Euclidean metric in SPSD(3), the DTI registration problem can be solved in closed form, both directly from diffusion tensor data as well as from feature-point correspondences. Our direct approach is based on the so-called Diffusion Tensor Constancy Constraint (DTCC), a generalization of the well-known brightness constancy constraint (BCC) to DT data. We show that for various local deformation models, such as translational, rigid, and affine, together with the finite strain reorientation scheme, the DTCC leads to a *linear* relationship between the parameters of the deformation, the DT data and its first order partial derivatives. Our feature-based approach assumes that we are given a set of point correspondences in two images. We show that the tensor reorientation map can be computed directly from the singular value decompositions (SVD) of two corresponding tensors. Once this map has been computed, solving for a rigid or affine deformation becomes a linear problem. We test our approach on synthetic, brain and heart DT images.

2   Direct Registration of Diffusion Tensor Images

In this section, we present an algebraic method for registering two diffusion tensor images $D_1 \in \mathrm{SPSD}(3)$ and $D_2 \in \mathrm{SPSD}(3)$ under various local deformation models. We also extend our method to a multi-resolution framework using a coarse-to-fine refinement strategy.

We assume that the coordinates of the voxels in the two images, $x_1, x_2 \in \mathbb{R}^3$, are locally related by an affine deformation model

$$x_2 = Ax_1 + t, \tag{1}$$

where $A \in \mathbb{R}^{3 \times 3}$ and $t \in \mathbb{R}^3$. This local deformation model not only transforms the voxel coordinates, but also reorients the tensor data. We model the tensor reorientation with the Finite Strain (FS) method [7, 13, 14], which uses the Polar Decomposition Theorem [16] to express the affine matrix A as the product of a rotation matrix $R \in SO(3)$ and a strain matrix $S \in \mathrm{SPSD}(3)$, i.e. $A = RS$. The tensor is then reoriented using the rotational component of A as

$$D_2 = RD_1R^\top. \tag{2}$$

By combining the local deformation model with the tensor reorientation model, we obtain the following Diffusion Tensor Constancy Constraint (DTCC)

$$D_2(Ax + t) = RD_1(x)R^\top. \tag{3}$$

In order to locally register D_1 and D_2 in the presence of noise, at each voxel y we seek the parameters (A, t) that minimize the Frobenius norm of the error between the two tensors

$$J = \sum_{x \in \Omega(y)} \mathrm{trace}\big(D_2(Ax + t) - RD_1(x)R^\top\big)^2, \tag{4}$$

where $\Omega(y) \subset \mathbb{R}^{3 \times 3}$ is a neighborhood of voxel y at which the affine model is valid. While there are many possible metrics in $\mathrm{SPSD}(3)$ [6, 7], we have chosen the Frobenius norm, because it enables us to solve the registration problem in closed form for various 3-D deformation models, such as translational, rigid and affine, as we will show in the next subsections.

2.1   3-D Translational Model

In this subsection, we assume that the deformation is translational, i.e. $A = R = S = I$. Under this deformation model, the DTCC (3) reduces to

$$D_2(x + t) = D_1(x). \tag{5}$$

After expanding the left hand side in Taylor series, we obtain

$$D_2(x + t) \approx D_2(x) + D_x d_1 + D_y d_2 + D_z d_3, \tag{6}$$

where $\boldsymbol{x} = (x, y, z)^\top$, $\boldsymbol{t} = (d_1, d_2, d_3)^\top$, and (D_x, D_y, D_z) are the partial derivatives of the diffusion tensor at $\boldsymbol{x}$. Substituting (6) in (5) yields the following differential DTCC

$$D_x d_1 + D_y d_2 + D_z d_3 + D_t = \boldsymbol{0}_{3 \times 3}. \tag{7}$$

Notice that (7) is a natural generalization of the well-known brightness constancy constraint (BCC) $I_x u + I_y v + I_t = 0$ from scalar 2-D images $I(x, y, t)$ to DT images $D(x, y, z, t)$. However, an important difference is that while the BCC provides one equation in two unknowns, the DTCC provides 6 equations in 3 unknowns, because D_x, D_y, D_z are 3×3 symmetric matrices.

Thanks to the DTCC, we may rewrite our cost function (4) as:

$$J = \sum_\Omega \text{trace}\big(D_x d_1 + D_y d_2 + D_z d_3 + D_t\big)^2. \tag{8}$$

After differentiating J with respect to d_1, we obtain

$$\frac{\partial J}{\partial d_1} = 2 \sum_\Omega \text{trace}\big(D_x (D_x d_1 + D_y d_2 + D_z d_3 + D_t)\big),$$

and similarly for d_2 and d_3. By setting these derivatives to zero, we can linearly solve for the displacement $\boldsymbol{u} = (d_1, d_2, d_3)^\top$ from

$$G\boldsymbol{u} = -\boldsymbol{b}, \tag{9}$$

where

$$G = \sum_\Omega \begin{bmatrix} \text{trace}(D_x D_x) & \text{trace}(D_x D_y) & \text{trace}(D_x D_z) \\ \text{trace}(D_y D_x) & \text{trace}(D_y D_y) & \text{trace}(D_y D_z) \\ \text{trace}(D_z D_x) & \text{trace}(D_z D_y) & \text{trace}(D_z D_z) \end{bmatrix} \quad \text{and} \quad \boldsymbol{b} = \sum_\Omega \begin{bmatrix} \text{trace}(D_t D_x) \\ \text{trace}(D_t D_y) \\ \text{trace}(D_t D_z) \end{bmatrix}.$$

The similarity with the case of 2-D scalar images, where $\boldsymbol{u}$ is computed from a linear system of the form (9) with $G = \sum_\Omega \begin{bmatrix} I_x^2 & I_x I_y \\ I_x I_y & I_y^2 \end{bmatrix}$ and $\boldsymbol{b} = \sum_\Omega \begin{bmatrix} I_x I_t \\ I_y I_t \end{bmatrix}$, is immediate. However, in the scalar case $\text{rank}(G) = 1$ when Ω consists of a single pixel, while in the tensor-valued case $G \in \mathbb{R}^{3 \times 3}$ is full rank for a generic tensor field D, even if Ω consists of a single voxel. Hence, with generic data one can solve for $\boldsymbol{t}$ at each voxel independently. Obviously, in the presence of noise estimating $\boldsymbol{t}$ from a single voxel is not robust, thus in practice one assumes that $\boldsymbol{t}$ is constant on a neighborhood Ω of size much larger than one.

2.2 3-D Rigid Model

Assume now that the deformation model is a rigid-body transformation, i.e. $A = R \in SO(3)$ and $S = I$, and let $\boldsymbol{x} = (x, y, z)^\top$ and $\boldsymbol{t} = (d_1, d_2, d_3)^\top$. In this case, we use the well-known first order approximation [17] of the rotational component of the deformation $R = I + [\boldsymbol{w}]_\times$, where $[\boldsymbol{w}]_\times \in so(3)$ is the skew-symmetric matrix generating the cross product by $\boldsymbol{w} = (w_1, w_2, w_3)^\top$. After

A. Goh and R. Vidal

replacing this first order approximation into the expressions for the diffusion tensors D_1 and D_2, we obtain

$$D_2(Rx+t) \approx D_2(x + [w]_\times x + t)$$
$$\approx D_2(x) + D_x(e_1^\top [w]_\times x + d_1) + D_y(e_2^\top [w]_\times x + d_2) + D_z(e_3^\top [w]_\times x + d_3)$$
$$= D_2(x) + D_x(zw_2 - yw_3 + d_1) + D_y(xw_3 - zw_1 + d_2) + D_z(yw_1 - xw_2 + d_3)$$
$$RD_1(x)R^\top \approx (I + [w]_\times)D_1(x)(I + [w]_\times^\top) \approx D_1(x) + [w]_\times D_1(x) + D_1(x)[w]_\times^\top,$$

where $e_1 = (1,0,0)^\top$, $e_2 = (0,1,0)^\top$ and $e_3 = (0,0,1)^\top$. Therefore, the cost function (4) can be rewritten as

$$J = \sum_\Omega \text{trace}(U_1w_1 + U_2w_2 + U_3w_3 + U_4d_1 + U_5d_2 + U_6d_3 + D_t)^2, \qquad (10)$$

where

$$U_1 = -M_1 + yD_z - zD_y, \quad U_2 = -M_2 + zD_x - xD_z, \quad U_3 = -M_3 + xD_y - yD_x,$$
$$U_4 = D_x, \qquad\qquad\qquad U_5 = D_y, \qquad\qquad\qquad U_6 = D_z,$$
$$D_t = D_2(x) - D_1(x), \quad M_j = ([e_j]_\times D_1 + D_1[e_j]_\times^\top), \quad j = 1, \ldots, 3.$$

After taking derivatives of J with respect to $u = (w_1, w_2, w_3, d_1, d_2, d_3)^\top$ and setting them to zero, we obtain the following system of linear equations on u

$$Gu = -b, \qquad (11)$$

where $G_{ij} = \sum_\Omega \text{trace}(U_iU_j)$ for $i,j = 1, \ldots, 6$ and $b_i = \sum_\Omega \text{trace}(U_iD_t)$ for $i = 1, \ldots, 6$.

Notice that, with generic data, each voxel gives 6 linearly independent equations in 6 unknowns in u. This implies that $\text{rank}(G) = 6$, even if G is computed from a single voxel. Therefore, the minimum number of voxels needed to solve the registration problem is one, as in the translational case.

2.3 3-D Affine Model

Consider now the DTCC for the full affine deformation model

$$D_2(Ax + t) = RD_1(x)R^\top, \qquad (12)$$

where $A = RS$ with $R \in SO(3)$ and $S \in \text{SPSD}(3)$. If we approximate R and S up to first order as $R \approx I + [w]_\times$ and $S \approx I + \hat{s}$, where $\hat{s}$ is a symmetric matrix, we obtain the following first order approximation for $A \approx I + [w]_\times + \hat{s}$. This gives

$$D_2(Ax + t) \approx D_2(x) + D_x(e_1^\top [w]_\times x + e_1^\top \hat{s} x + d_1)$$
$$+ D_y(e_2^\top [w]_\times x + e_2^\top \hat{s} x + d_2) + D_z(e_3^\top [w]_\times x + e_3^\top \hat{s} x + d_3).$$

Note that the only differences between this expression and the corresponding one for the rigid model are the terms involving $\hat{s}$, which can be expressed as

$$s_{11}xD_x + s_{12}(yD_x + xD_y) + s_{13}(xD_z + zD_x) + s_{22}yD_y + s_{23}(zD_y + yD_z) + s_{33}zD_z.$$

Therefore, we may rewrite the cost function (4) as

$$J = \sum_{\Omega} \text{trace}(U_1 w_1 + U_2 w_2 + U_3 w_3 + U_4 d_1 + U_5 d_2 + U_6 d_3 + D_t +$$

$$U_7 s_{11} + U_8 s_{12} + U_9 s_{13} + U_{10} s_{22} + U_{11} s_{23} + U_{12} s_{33})^2, \qquad (13)$$

where $U_1, \ldots, U_6$ are defined as in the rigid case and

$$U_7 = xD_x, \qquad U_8 = yD_x + xD_y, \qquad U_9 = xD_z + zD_x,$$
$$U_{10} = yD_y, \qquad U_{11} = zD_y + yD_z, \qquad U_{12} = zD_z.$$

After differentiating the cost function J with respect to the unknown model parameters $u = (w_1, w_2, w_3, d_1, d_2, d_3, s_{11}, s_{12}, s_{13}, s_{22}, s_{23}, s_{33})^\top$ and setting the result to zero, we obtain the following linear system on u

$$Gu = -b, \qquad (14)$$

with $G_{ij} = \sum_{\Omega} \text{trace}(U_i U_j)$ for $i, j = 1, \ldots, 12$ and $b_i = \sum_{\Omega} \text{trace}(U_i D_t)$ for $i = 1, \ldots, 12$.

Notice that, with generic data, each voxel provides 6 linearly independent equations in 12 unknowns in u. This implies that $\text{rank}(G) = 6$ when G is computed from a single voxel. Therefore, the minimum number of voxels needed to solve the registration problem is two.

2.4   Multiscale Iterative Refinement

The algebraic registration method presented in the previous subsections assumes implicitly that the spatial-temporal discretization of the DT image is adequate for representing the deformation of the DT volume. When this is not the case, an approach that combines motion estimates across multiple scales is needed. The existing literature on estimation of optical flow from 2-D images provides various multiscale methods for motion estimation [18]. In our implementation, we adapt such methods to the case of DT data.

Our multiscale algorithm proceeds as follows:

1. Downsample D_1 and D_2 by a factor of 2^n and compute transformation u_n between the downsampled images by solving the linear system $G_n u_n = -b_n$.
2. Warp current D_1 to $D_1(x) \leftarrow R_n D_1(R_n S_n x + 2^n t_n) R_n^\top$, where (R_n, S_n, t_n) are the deformation parameters corresponding to u_n.
3. If $n \geq 1$, set $n \leftarrow n - 1$ and go to 1.
4. Set $u = \sum_{i=0}^{n}(w_1, w_2, w_3, 2^i d_1, 2^i d_2, 2^i d_3, s_{11}, s_{12}, s_{13}, s_{22}, s_{23}, s_{33})_i^\top$, where $u_i = (w_1, w_2, w_3, d_1, d_2, d_3, s_{11}, s_{12}, s_{13}, s_{22}, s_{23}, s_{33})_i^\top$.

Notice that in transforming the motion parameters from one scale to another only the translational part of the affine deformation is affected. This is because when scaling the voxel coordinates by a factor λ we obtain $\lambda x_2 = A\lambda x_1 + \lambda t$, thus t is scaled, but A is not.

3   Feature-Based Registration of Diffusion Tensor Images

Consider now the registration of diffusion tensor images from a set of point correspondences in two images $x_1 \leftrightarrow x_2$. If we are given 4 or more point correspondences, then recovering a global deformation model (A, t) from the equation $x_2 = Ax_1 + t$ is simply a linear problem. However, this linear solution does not make use of any tensor information, because the constraints due to tensor reorientation are not incorporated. Since a point correspondence $x_1 \leftrightarrow x_2$ naturally induces a tensor correspondence $D_1 \leftrightarrow D_2$, we propose a feature-based registration method that exploits both point and tensor correspondences. In fact, we show that in spite of the need for a tensor reorientation model, the registration problem can still be solved linearly.

3.1   Rigid Registration from Point and Tensor Correspondences

Under a rigid transformation $(R, t) \in SE(3)$, where $R \in SO(3)$ is the rotation and $t \in \mathbb{R}^3$ is the translation, the two images are related by the equations

$$x_2 = Rx_1 + t \qquad \text{and} \qquad D_2 = RD_1R^\top. \tag{15}$$

From the first equation in (15), note that if R were known, we could immediately solve for t as $x_2 - Rx_1$. Thus, solving the registration problem for a single voxel boils down to estimating the rotation matrix from the second equation in (15).

To this end, consider the SVD of the diffusion tensors $D_1 = U_1\Sigma_1U_1^\top$ and $D_2 = U_2\Sigma_2U_2^\top$. In the absence of noise, the equation $D_2 = RD_1R^\top$ implies that D_1 and D_2 share the same singular values, i.e. $\Sigma_1 = \Sigma_2$. In addition, we have

$$U_2\Sigma_2U_2^\top = RU_1\Sigma_1U_1^\top R^\top \implies \Sigma_2 = U_2^\top RU_1\Sigma_1U_1^\top R^\top U_2.$$

Therefore, if the three singular values of D_1 are different, we can immediately solve for the rotation as $R = U_2U_1^\top$ or $R = -U_2U_1^\top$, depending on whether $\det(U_2U_1^\top) = 1$ or not.

In the presence of noise, the matrices Σ_1 and Σ_2 will not necessarily coincide, thus we seek a rotation R that minimizes the error in (4), which in the case of a single correspondence is given by $\text{trace}(D_2 - RD_1R^\top)^2$. Minimizing this error is equivalent to solving the following optimization problem

$$\max_R \text{trace}(D_2RD_1R^\top) = \max_R \text{trace}(U_2\Sigma_2U_2^\top RU_1\Sigma_1U_1^\top R^\top). \tag{16}$$

We now prove that the solution to this optimization problem is $R = U_2U_1^\top$ or $R = -U_2U_1^\top$ as well. The proof will follow from the following theorem [19].

Theorem 1. Let $A, B \in \mathbb{R}^{n \times n}$. If both AB and BA are positive semidefinite, then there exists a permutation τ of the integers $1, 2, \ldots, n$, such that

$$trace(AB) = \sum_{i=1}^{n} \sigma_i(A)\sigma_{\tau(i)}(B) \leq \sum_{i=1}^{n} \sigma_i(A)\sigma_i(B),$$

where $\{\sigma_i(C)\}_{i=1}^n$ are the singular values of C arranged in non-decreasing order.

By applying Theorem 1 to equation (16) with $A = D_2$ and $B = RD_1R^\top$, we obtain

$$\text{trace}(D_2 RD_1 R^\top) = \sum_{i=1}^n \sigma_i(D_1)\sigma_{\tau(i)}(D_2) = \sum_{i=1}^n \sigma_i(\Sigma_1)\sigma_{\tau(i)}(\Sigma_2) \leq \text{trace}(\Sigma_1\Sigma_2).$$

If we now substitute $R = \pm U_2 U_1^\top$ on the left hand side we get

$$\begin{aligned}
\text{trace}(D_2 RD_1 R^\top) &= \text{trace}(U_2\Sigma_2 U_2^\top U_2 U_1^\top U_1\Sigma_1 U_1^\top U_1 U_2^\top) \\
&= \text{trace}(U_2\Sigma_2\Sigma_1 U_2^\top) = \text{trace}(\Sigma_2\Sigma_1).
\end{aligned}$$

Hence the rotation matrix $R = U_2 U_1^\top$ or $R = -U_2 U_1^\top$ achieves the maximum, as claimed. Notice that in order for the maximum to be unique, it is necessary that both D_1 and D_2 have different singular values, so that U_1 and U_2, hence R, are uniquely defined.

In the case of N correspondences, we seek to find the optimal rotation that minimizes $\sum_{i=1}^N \text{trace}(D_{2i} - RD_{1i}R^\top)^2$. We are not aware of an exact solution to this problem. We compute an approximate solution by averaging the rotations $R_i = U_{2i}U_{1i}^\top$ computed from the individual correspondences. We use the method in [20] for computing the average rotation.

3.2 Affine Registration from Point and Tensor Correspondences

We now extend the registration method from a rigid to an affine deformation

$$\boldsymbol{x}_2 = A\boldsymbol{x}_1 + \boldsymbol{t} \qquad \text{and} \qquad D_2 = RD_1R^\top.$$

First, we proceed as in the rigid case in order to obtain the rotation matrix R from the DTs. Since A can be expressed uniquely as $A = RS$, where $R \in SO(3)$ and $S \in \text{SPSD}(3)$, there are 6 independent parameters in S and 3 in $\boldsymbol{t}$. Since each point correspondence $(\boldsymbol{x}_1, \boldsymbol{x}_2)$ provides 3 equations, we will need 3 correspondences in order to solve for S and $\boldsymbol{t}$. More specifically, let $(\boldsymbol{x}_{11}, \boldsymbol{x}_{21})$, $(\boldsymbol{x}_{12}, \boldsymbol{x}_{22})$ and $(\boldsymbol{x}_{13}, \boldsymbol{x}_{23})$ be such correspondences. We can solve for S and $\boldsymbol{t}$ linearly from

$$\boldsymbol{x}_{21} = RS\boldsymbol{x}_{11} + \boldsymbol{t}, \qquad \boldsymbol{x}_{22} = RS\boldsymbol{x}_{12} + \boldsymbol{t}, \qquad \text{and} \qquad \boldsymbol{x}_{23} = RS\boldsymbol{x}_{13} + \boldsymbol{t}.$$

4 Experimental Results

We evaluate the performance of the proposed registration algorithm on a real DT image of the human brain [21]. The image size is $148 \times 190 \times 160$ voxels and the voxel size is $1\text{mm} \times 1\text{mm} \times 1\text{mm}$. The implementation is done in a hierarchy where we start downsampling at scale of 2^2. At this scale, a window Ω of size $5 \times 5 \times 5$ is used for the local computation of the deformation. For the subsequent scale of 2^1, the window size is $11 \times 11 \times 11$, followed by $21 \times 21 \times 21$ at the original resolution. Fig. 1 shows the estimated transformation at each

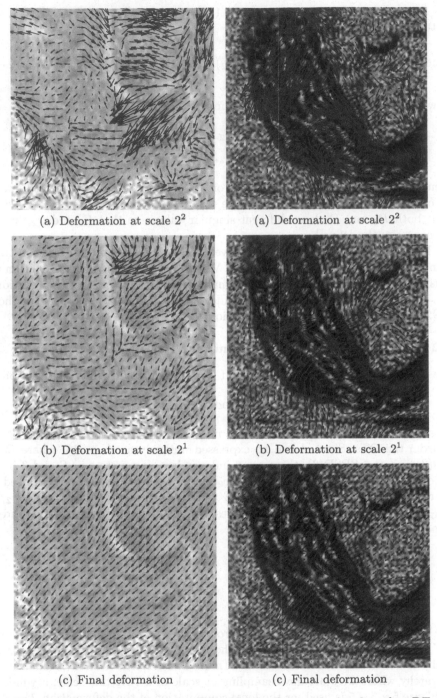

(a) Deformation at scale 2^2 (a) Deformation at scale 2^2

(b) Deformation at scale 2^1 (b) Deformation at scale 2^1

(c) Final deformation   (c) Final deformation

Fig. 1. Zoomed-in results for a DT brain image

Fig. 2. Zoomed-in results of a DT heart image

scale for a translational deformation of $t = (0, 8, 8)$ voxels. It can be seen that the DTCC-based method correctly estimates the direction of the deformation for most of the image, though it usually underestimates the magnitude. The method performs significantly poorer in regions where there is a sharp variation of the tensor field along a 1-D curve or a 2-D surface, e.g., in boundary regions, or regions where the tensor data has low variability. This is because the G matrix, from which the deformation field is estimated, is rank deficient in these regions. This is simply a generalization of the well-known *aperture problem* in standard 2-D images, which refers to the impossibility of estimating optical flow in regions with low texture using a local method.

Similar experiments are done on a DT image of a human heart obtained from [22]. Fig. 2 shows the estimated deformation field for a translational deformation of $t = (0, 5, 5)$. Notice that the performance of the algorithm on the heart dataset is worse than in the brain dataset. This is expected as the proportion of

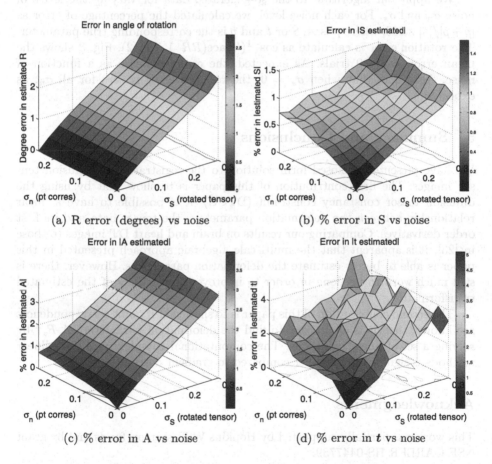

(a) R error (degrees) vs noise

(b) % error in S vs noise

(c) % error in A vs noise

(d) % error in t vs noise

Fig. 3. Error in estimated R, S, A and t vs σ_n and σ_s

the volume of the heart data that contains high variability and is away from the boundaries is significantly smaller.

Finally, we evaluate the proposed feature-based affine registration algorithm on synthetic data for varying levels of noise on the image data. We generate a $20 \times 20 \times 20$ volume containing the tensor $R_{\text{rand}} \text{diag}\{[10; 5; 2] + t_{\text{rand}}\} R_{\text{rand}}^\top$, where R_{rand} is a rotation matrix with an arbitrary rotation at each voxel and $t_{\text{rand}} \in \mathbb{R}^3$ is a translation vector whose entries are distributed uniformly in $[0, 1]$. Given an affine transformation (A, t) with $A = RS$, we construct the second volume by applying the transformation $x_2 = A x_1 + t + n$ to the voxel coordinates, where $n \sim N(0, \sigma_n^2 I)$, and the transformation $D_2 = R U_1 (\Sigma_1 + S_n) U_1^\top R^\top$ to the tensor data, where $D_1 = U_1 \Sigma_1 U_1^\top$ is the SVD of D_1 and $S_n = \sigma_s R_{\text{small}} \Sigma_1 R_{\text{small}}^\top$. σ_s is the amount of noise, and R_{small} is a rotation matrix generated via the exponential map by $R_{\text{small}} = \exp(\sigma_s |w_1| v)$, where $v \in \mathbb{R}^3$ is a unit random vector and $[w_1]_\times = \log U_1$.

We apply our algorithm to the so-generated data for varying the levels of noise σ_n and σ_s. For each noise level, we calculated the percentage of error as $|p - \hat{p}| / |\hat{p}| \times 100$, where p is A, S or t and $\hat{p}$ is the corresponding true parameter. The rotation error is calculate as $\cos^{-1}((\text{trace}(R\hat{R}^\top) - 1)/2)$. Fig. 3 shows the mean errors over 30 trials. As expected, the errors increase as a function of noise. Also, note that when $\sigma_s = 0$, the rotation error is zero for all σ_n, as expected.

5   Summary and Conclusions

We have presented a closed form solution to the registration of diffusion tensor images. The first contribution of this paper is to show that by using the diffusion tensor constancy constraint (DTCC), it is possible to have a linear relationship between the deformation parameters, the tensor data and its first order derivatives. Comparing our results on brain and heart DT images to those in [23], it is apparent that the multiscale algebraic approach presented in this paper is able to better estimate the deformation parameters. However, there is still much work to be done in order to improve the accuracy of the estimated transformation.

The second contribution of this paper is to show that if point correspondences are known, then it is again easy to find the deformation parameters A, R, t by solving a set of linear equations. The computational complexity of both linear methods is significantly smaller compared to gradient descent methods.

Acknowledgments

This work was partially supported by Hopkins WSE startup funds and by grant NSF CAREER IIS-0447739.

References

1. Mori, S., van Zijl, P.: Fiber tracking: principles and strategies - a technical review. NMR in Biomedicine **15** (2002) 468–480
2. Lazar, M., et al. : White matter tractography using diffusion tensor deflection. In: Human Brain Mapping 18:306-321. (2003)
3. Vemuri, B., et al. : Fiber tract mapping from diffusion tensor MRI. In: IEEE workshop on Variational and Level Set Methods in Computer Vision. (2001)
4. Lori, N.F., et al. : Diffusion tensor fiber tracking of human brain connectivity: aquisition methods, reliability analysis and biological results. NMR in Biomedicine **15** (2002) 494–515
5. Lal, R.: Probabilistic cortical and myocardinal fiber tracking in diffusion tensor imaging. Master's thesis, The Johns Hopkins University (2001)
6. Wang, Z., Vemuri, B.: An affine invariant tensor dissimilarity measure and its applications to tensor-valued image segmentation. IEEE Conference on Computer Vision and Pattern Recognition (2004)
7. Zhang, H., Yushkevich, P., Gee, J.: Registration of diffusion tensor images. IEEE Conference on Computer Vision and Pattern Recognition (2004)
8. Ding, Z., et al. : Classification and quantification of neuronal fiber pathways using diffusion tensor MRI. Magnetic Resonance in Medicine **49** (2003) 716–721
9. Brun, A., Knutsson, H., Park, H.J., Shenton, M.E., Westin, C.F.: Clustering fiber tracts using normalized cuts. In: MICCAI. (2004) 368–375
10. Shi, J., Malik, J.: Normalized cuts and image segmentation. IEEE Trans. on Pattern Analysis and Machine Intelligence **22** (2000)
11. Zhukov, L., Museth, K., Breen, D., Whitaker, R., Barr, A.: Level set segmentation and modeling of DT-MRI human brain data. Journal of Electronic Imaging (2003)
12. Alexander, D., et al. : Spatial transformation of diffusion tensor magnetic resonance images. IEEE Transactions on Medical Imaging **20** (2001) 1131–1139
13. Ruiz-Alzola, J., et al. : Nonrigid registration of 3D tensor medical data. Medical Image Analysis **6** (2002) 143–161
14. Guimond, A., et al. : Deformable registration of DT-MRI data based on transformation invariant tensor characteristics. In: IEEE International Symposium on Biomedical Imaging. (2002)
15. Park, H.J., et al. : Spatial normalization of diffusion tensor MRI using multiple channels. Neuroimage **20** (2003) 1995–2009
16. Gallier, J.: Geometric Methods and Applications for Computer Science and Engineering. Springer-Verlag New York (2001)
17. Murray, R.M., Li, Z., Sastry, S.S.: A Mathematical Introduction to Robotic Manipulation. CRC Press Inc. (1994)
18. Battiti, R., Amaldi, E., Koch, C.: Computing optical flow across multiple scales: An adaptive coarse-to-fine strategy. International Journal of Computer Vision **6** (1991) 133–145
19. Horn, R., Johnson, C.: Matrix Analysis. Cambridge University Press (1985)
20. Fletcher, P.T., et al. : Principal geodesic analysis for the study of nonlinear statistics of shape. IEEE Transactions on Medical Imaging **23** (2004) 995–1005
21. Kindlmann, G., Alexander, A.: Brain dataset, University of Utah, and University of Wisconsin-Madison. (http://www.sci.utah.edu/~gk/DTI-data/)
22. Helm, P.A., Winslow, R.L., McVeigh, E.: Cardiovascular DTMRI data sets. (http://www.ccbm.jhu.edu)
23. Goh, A., Vidal, R.: An algebraic solution to rigid registration of diffusion tensor images. In: IEEE International Symposium on Biomedical Imaging. (2006)

Rethinking the Prior Model for Stereo

Hiroshi Ishikawa[1] and Davi Geiger[2]

[1] Department of Information and Biological Sciences,
Nagoya City University,
Nagoya 467-8501, Japan
hi@nsc.nagoya-cu.ac.jp
[2] Courant Institute of Mathematical Sciences,
New York University,
New York, NY 10012, USA
geiger@cs.nyu.edu

Abstract. Sometimes called the smoothing assumption, the prior model of a stereo matching algorithm is the algorithm's expectation on the surfaces in the world. Any stereo algorithm makes assumptions about the probability to see each surface that can be represented in its representation system. Although the past decade has seen much continued progress in stereo matching algorithms, the prior models used in them have not changed much in three decades: most algorithms still use a smoothing prior that minimizes some function of the difference of depths between neighboring sites, sometimes allowing for discontinuities.

However, one system seems to use a very different prior model from all other systems: *the human vision system.* In this paper, we first report the observations we made in examining human disparity interpolation using stereo pairs with sparse identifiable features. Then we mathematically analyze the implication of using current prior models and explain why the human system seems to use a model that is not only different but in a sense diametrically opposite from all current models. Finally, we propose two candidate models that reflect the behavior of human vision. Although the two models look very different, we show that they are closely related.

1 Introduction

The main task in low-level vision is to filter out as much as possible irrelevant information that clutter the input image. There, disambiguation is one of the central problems, since resolving ambiguity eliminates great amount of later processing. Ambiguity arises because input images to a vision system usually do not contain enough information to determine the scene. Thus the vision system must have a prior knowledge on the kinds of scenes that it is likely to encounter in order to choose among possible interpretation of given data. In the case of stereo matching, where the correspondences between locations in the two or more images are determined and the depths are recovered from their disparity, ambiguity arising from such factors as noise, periodicity, and large regions of constant intensity makes it impossible in general to identify all locations in the two images with certainty. Thus, any stereo algorithm must have a way to resolve ambiguities and interpolate missing data. In the Bayesian formalism of stereo vision,

A. Leonardis, H. Bischof, and A. Pinz (Eds.): ECCV 2006, Part III, LNCS 3953, pp. 526–537, 2006.

this is given by the prior model. The prior model of a stereo matching algorithm is the algorithm's expectation on the surfaces in the world, where it makes assumptions about the probability to see each surface that can be represented in its representation system.

The prior model is an ingredient of stereo matching reasonably separate from other aspects of the process: whether a stereo system uses Dynamic Programming or Graph Cut or Belief Propagation, it explicitly or implicitly assumes a prior; and it is also usually independent of image formation model, which affects the selection of features in the images to match and the cost function to compare them. Also, in some algorithms, it is less obvious than in others to discern the prior models they utilize, especially when the smoothing assumption is implicit as in most local, window-based algorithms. In some cases, it is intricately entwined with the image formation model, as in the case where a discontinuity in disparity is encouraged at locations where there are intensity edges. As far as we could determine, however, the prior models that are used in stereo matching algorithms have not changed much in three decades. Computational models (Marr and Poggio[15, 16]; Grimson[8]; Poggio and Poggio[19]; Pollard, Mayhew, and Frisby[18]; Gillam and Borsting[7]; Ayache[1]; Belhumeur and Mumford[3]; Jones and Malik[10]; Faugeras[5]; Geiger, Ladendorf, and Yuille[6]; Belhumeur[2]) have generally used as the criterion some form of smoothness in terms of dense information such as the depth and its derivatives, sometimes allowing for discontinuities; among them, the most common by far is the minimization of the square difference of disparities between neighboring pixels, which encourage front-parallel surfaces.

Perhaps that most of the citations above are at least ten years old is indicative of the neglect the problem of prior model selection has suffered. The latest crop of algorithms, using Graph Cut (Roy and Cox[21, 20]; Ishikawa and Geiger[9]; Boykov et al.[4]; Kolmogorov and Zabih[12],) did not improve on the prior models, concentrating on the optimization. The excellent recent survey of stereo algorithms by Scharstein and Szeliski[22] does not classify the algorithms in their taxonomy by prior models–rightly, because there are not much difference in this respect among them.

Of course, by itself it might mean that the selection was exactly correct the very first time. However, it appears that there is a glaring exception to the widespread use of smoothing / front-parallel criterion as the prior model: *the human vision system*. In this paper, we first report the observations we made in examining human disparity interpolation using stereo pairs with sparse identifiable features. Then we mathematically analyze the implication of using current prior models and explain why the human system seems to use a model that is not only different but in a sense diametrically opposite from all current models. Finally, we propose two candidate models that reflect the behavior of human vision. Although the two models look very different, we show that they are closely related.

2   Experiment and Analysis

We used a stereogram, shown in Fig.1a, of textureless surface patches with explicit luminance contours to investigate the prior model the human vision uses. In these displays, there are very few features that can be depended upon when matching the points. The only distinguishing feature is the intensity edges on the circumference of the shape,

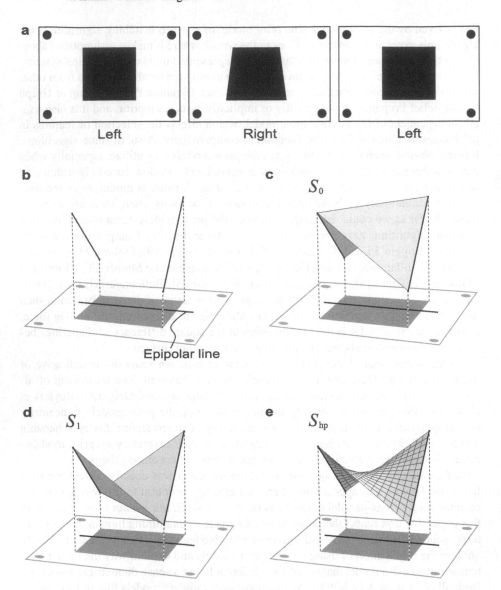

Fig. 1. The stereogram and possible surfaces. (**a**) A stereo pair. When the right images are cross-fused (or the left two images are fused divergently,) a three-dimensional surface is perceived. (**b**) The thick lines represent the disparity values unambiguously obtainable from local feature. (**c**), (**d**) The human brain tend to perceive either of these two. However, no current algorithm has this behavior. (**e**) Algorithms that seek to minimize gradient give a "soap bubble" surface like the one shown here. Models in which the prior on epipolar lines are independent line-by-line also give this solution.

where the discontinuous change in luminance occurs. There are no other cues that are ordinarily present, such as surface shade and partial occlusions (Gillam and Borsting[7]; Nakayama and Shimojo[17]; Malik[13]). Matching the edges gives the depth information illustrated in Fig. 1b. Everywhere else, each location in one image can perfectly match to a variety of locations in the other. This corresponds to the fact that any perfectly black surface spanning the two segments in Fig. 1b looks exactly the same.

Nevertheless, the perception human observers report is much less ambiguous. We examined shape judgments by human observers from the interpolated stereoscopic disparity. The details of the experiment can be found in the appendix. Most observers who viewed the stereogram reported the percept of one of the two surfaces shown in Fig. 1c and d, which we call S_0 and S_1. This result is in stark contrast to the smooth surface S_{hp}, shown in Fig. 1e, that is predicted by most extant computational models of stereo, as we explain in the following subsections.

2.1 One-Dimensional Models

First of all, any 1D interpolating model would predict the ruled surface S_{hp}. The three-dimensional geometry of image formation dictates the possible pairs of points in the image that can match each other (Fig. 2a). A point in a 3D scene and the two focal points determine a plane in the space. The projecting rays from the point through the focal points onto the retinae must lie on this plane. Thus, when the correspondence is not known, it can at least be said that a feature on one image can match only those locations on the other image that lie on the plane determined by the point and the two foci. Such possible matching points form a line called the epipolar line. Imagine a plane rotating around the line connecting the two foci: it sweeps the retinae, defining a set of corresponding epipolar lines. Geometrically, only points on the corresponding epipolar lines can match to each other. Thus, in theory, the stereopsis can be a 1D process that

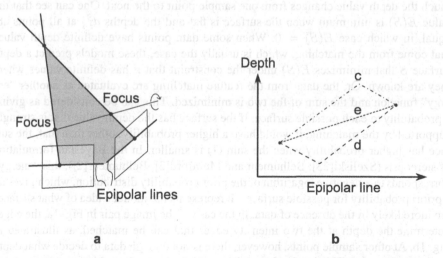

Fig. 2. (a) The geometry of stereopsis. Only points on the corresponding epipolar lines can match to each other. (b) The cross sections for solutions in Fig. 1c,d, and e on an epipolar line.

matches the locations on the two images line by line. One may be lead to postulate that the interpolation is also done one-dimensionally. However, the experiment shows that is not what is done in human perception. If the interpolation is done one-dimensionally on each epipolar line as Fig. 2b shows, the perceived surfaces S_0 and S_1 have forms that cannot be readily explained (c and d in Fig. 2b). Since the sole depth data given on each epipolar line are at the two endpoints, the only reasonable 1D interpolation is to connect the two points by a straight line, as indicated as e in Fig. 2b. As a whole, the lines give the smooth surface S_{hp}. Thus, theories that only use one-dimensional information do not predict the surfaces usually seen by human observers.

2.2   Gradient Minimization Models

In some computational models of stereopsis, epipolar lines are not independent. It would be useful to have an interaction between the matching on different epipolar lines even just for the sake of robustness in the presence of noise. Most current theories model the matching by a depth surface that gives a dense map of the depth at each point in the view. Mathematically, a depth surface S is typically represented by specifying the value of the depth $d_{i,j}^S$ at each of dense sample points, which usually are laid out as an equally-spaced grid $X = (i, j)$. In such models, distinguishing feature such as intensity edges can give a strong evidence of matches, determining the depth value $d_{i,j}^S$ at some of the sample points. Ever since Marr and Poggio[15, 16] and Pollard, Mayhew, and Frisby[18], most computational models of stereopsis used a weak smoothing scheme that in effect predicts a surface S that minimizes the total change in depth:

$$E(S) = \sum_X \{(d_{i+1,j}^S - d_{i,j}^S)^2 + (d_{i,j+1}^S - d_{i,j}^S)^2\}, \tag{1}$$

which approximates the total depth gradient $\int |\nabla d^S|^2$. Here, the sum evaluates how much the depth value changes from one sample point to the next. One can see that the value $E(S)$ is minimum when the surface is flat and the depths $d_{i,j}^S$ at all points are equal, in which case $E(S) = 0$. When some data points have definite depth values that come from the matching, which is usually the case, these models predict a depth surface S that minimizes $E(S)$ under the constraint that it has definite values where they are known. Or, the data from the feature matching are evaluated as another "energy" function and the sum of the two is minimized. This can be considered as giving a probability to each possible surface. If the surface has the depth value that is strongly supported by the matching, it would have a higher probability; other than that, the surface has higher probability when the sum (1) is smaller. In the Bayesian formulation of stereopsis (Szeliski[23]; Belhumeur and Mumford[3]; Belhumeur[2]), this "energy" corresponds to a negative logarithm of the prior probability distribution, which gives an a priori probability for possible surfaces. It represents the model's idea of what surfaces are more likely in the absence of data. In the case of the image pair in Fig. 1a, the edges determine the depth at the two intensity edges that can be matched, as illustrated in Fig. 1b. At other sample points, however, there is not enough data to decide what depth to give to the point. This is why the model must have some disambiguating process.

How would such models react to the stereo pair in Fig. 1a? The answer is that all current theories predict a surface similar to S_{hp}, rather than the most perceived surfaces

S_0 and S_1. This is because the gradient modulus $|\nabla d^S|$, at all points, is larger for S_0 and S_1 than for S_{hp}. This can be easily seen by simple calculation as follows.

Let $2l$ be the side of the square and $2h$ the height (the difference of the maximum and the minimum depth) of the surface. We set up a coordinate system where the four corners of the square have the coordinates $(x, y) = (\pm l, \pm l)$. Of the definite depths determined by matching the intensity edges, we assume that the two corners (l, l) and $(-l, -l)$ have the depth h and the other two have the depth $-h$. Thus, the boundary condition is the two line segments, shown in Fig. 1b, determined by the equations $x = l, d = \frac{h}{l}y, -l \le y \le l$ and $x = -l, d = -\frac{h}{l}y, -l \le y \le l$. Then, the depth and the depth gradient for the surfaces S_0 and S_1 are as follows:

$$
S_0 : \quad
\begin{aligned}
d^{S_0}(x, y) &= \begin{cases} \frac{h}{l}(x - y) + h & (x \le y) \\ \frac{h}{l}(-x + y) + h & (x \ge y) \end{cases} \\[2mm]
\nabla d^{S_0}(x, y) &= \begin{cases} (\frac{h}{l}, -\frac{h}{l}) & (x < y), \\ (-\frac{h}{l}, \frac{h}{l}) & (x > y) \end{cases}
\end{aligned}
$$

$$
S_1 : \quad
\begin{aligned}
d^{S_1}(x, y) &= \begin{cases} \frac{h}{l}(x + y) - h & (x \ge -y) \\ \frac{h}{l}(-x - y) - h & (x \le -y) \end{cases} \\[2mm]
\nabla d^{S_1}(x, y) &= \begin{cases} (\frac{h}{l}, \frac{h}{l}) & (x > -y), \\ (-\frac{h}{l}, -\frac{h}{l}) & (x < -y) \end{cases}
\end{aligned}
$$

Thus, we obtain $\sqrt{2}\frac{h}{l}$ as the gradient modulus for S_0 and S_1 everywhere on the square, except on the diagonal where it is not defined. On the other hand, the depth and its gradient for S_{hp} at point (x, y) are defined by

$$
S_{\text{hp}} : \quad
\begin{aligned}
d^{S_{\text{hp}}}(x, y) &= \frac{h}{l^2}xy \\[2mm]
\nabla d^{S_{\text{hp}}}(x, y) &= (\frac{h}{l^2}y, \frac{h}{l^2}x)
\end{aligned}
$$

Thus the gradient modulus for S_{hp} at point (x, y) is $\frac{h}{l^2}\sqrt{x^2 + y^2}$, which is smaller than $\sqrt{2}\frac{h}{l}$ wherever $x^2 + y^2$ is smaller than $2l^2$, which is the case inside the square. In fact, this observation rules out not only the energy (1) but also any energy that is the sum of an increasing function of the gradient modulus, which is to say most models.

2.3 Convex Models

To rule out the rest of the current prior models (and more), we can consider a functional of the form

$$
E(S) = \sum_X f(\delta d^S), \tag{2}
$$

where δd^S represents the derivative of some order of the depth function. For instance, the first-order case is the gradient such as in (1). The derivative δd^S, which in general is

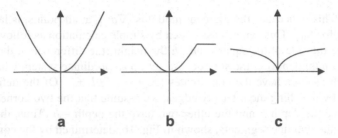

Fig. 3. Convex and non-convex functions of the magnitude. **(a)** A convex function. **(b)** A convex function with a cut-off value. **(c)** A concave function.

a vector, can be of any order, or a combination of several derivatives of different orders. Then, for a real number u between 0 and 1, we define a surface S_u that interpolates the two surfaces:

$$d^{S.} = (1 - u)d^{S_0} + ud^{S_1} \qquad (0 \le u \le 1).$$

We assume that f is a convex function of the derivative. In general, a function $f(x)$ that has the property

$$f((1 - u)x_0 + ux_1) \le (1 - u)f(x_0) + uf(x_1), \quad (0 \le u \le 1)$$

is said to be convex (see Fig. 3a.) If f is convex, then

$$E(S_u) \le (1 - u)E(S_0) + uE(S_1) \le \max\{E(S_0), E(S_1)\}$$

implies that any linear interpolation of the two surfaces has the value of $E(S)$ that is at least as small as the larger of the values for the two surfaces. Moreover, if the energy is symmetric with respect to the sign inversion of depth, it would give $E(S_0) = E(S_1)$; and if the energy is strictly convex, the extremes S_0 and S_1 would be maxima among all the interpolated surfaces, not minima. All convex theories of which we are aware satisfy the latter two conditions. We conclude that the perceived surfaces are not predicted by any theory that uses the minimization of the energy function of the form (2) with convex f for disambiguation. Most current theories, including thin plate and harmonic, employ a convex energy functional as their prior, when seen in this representation. The minimization problem of the continuous version of (1) (called the Dirichlet integral) has the hyperbolic paraboloid S_{hp} as the solution.

2.4   Non-convex Models

Note that d^S's total sum is determined by the boundary condition. In order to minimize a sum $f(x) + f(y)$ of a convex function $f(x)$ while keeping $x + y$ constant, the value should be distributed as much as possible. Thus convex energy functions such as (1) tend to round the corners and smooth the surface. What, then, about functions that are not convex? More recent theories of stereopsis use sophisticated priors that model discontinuity in depth and slope. One such model (Belhumeur[2]) minimizes the second derivative of depth, except for certain locus where it gives up and allows discontinuities in slope, or a crease, making it non-convex. In effect, it uses a function $f(x)$ such as

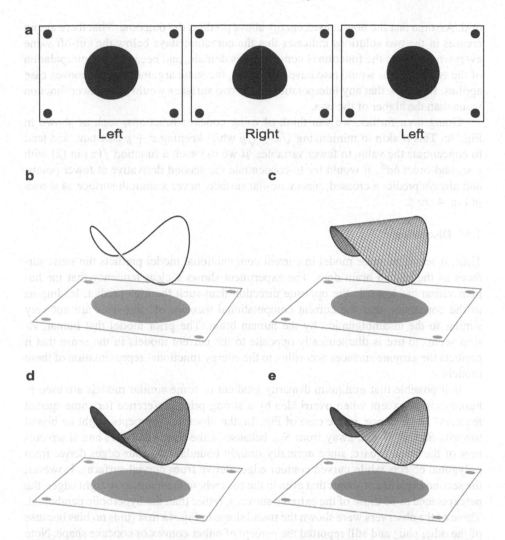

Fig. 4. Another stereogram further rules out possible theories. (a) Another stereo pair. (b) The unambiguous wire frame. (c), (d), and (e) are all possible surfaces that agree with the boundary condition. The human brain perceives either (c) or (d). Even algorithms that use non-convex functionals to allow discontinuities in depth and slope cannot have the solution (c) and (d) without having (e) as a better solution.

shown in Fig. 3b, which is still convex in low-modulus region but with a cut-off value beyond which the function value stays constant. This model actually can predict S_0 and S_1, with right parameter values, since both surfaces have zero second derivatives except at the crease, where the curvature can be as high as needed without any impact on the functional more than the cut-off value.

However, this model fails to predict the outcome on another stereogram, shown in Fig. 4a. Most observers reported a percept of one of the surfaces in either Fig. 4c or d. Assume that the non-convex energy above predicts the outcome. That there are no creases in the two solutions indicates that the curvature stays below the cut-off value everywhere. Since the function is convex in this domain, and because any interpolation of the two solutions would also have no creases, the same argument as the convex case applies. It follows that any interpolation of the two surfaces would have lower function value than the higher of the two.

Going even further, we can think of using concave functions, such as shown in Fig. 3c. This is akin to minimizing $\sqrt{x} + \sqrt{y}$ while keeping $x + y$ constant, and tend to concentrate the value to fewer variables. If we use such a function $f(x)$ in (2) with a second-order δd^S, it would try to concentrate the second derivative at fewer points, and always predict a creased, piecewise-flat surface, never a smooth surface as shown in Fig. 4c or d.

2.5 Discussion

Thus, it seems no prior model in current computational model predicts the same surfaces as the human brain does. The experiment shows a clear tendency that the human vision has towards the opposite direction than such theories predict, leading us to the conclusion that the current computational theories of stereopsis are not very similar to the disambiguation by the human brain. The prior model that human vision seems to use is diametrically opposite to the current models in the sense that it predicts the *extreme* surfaces according to the energy functional representation of these models.

Is it possible that minimum disparity gradient or some similar models are used in human vision except when overridden by a strong prior preference for some special features? For instance, in the case of Fig. 1a, the observers' percepts might be biased towards S_0 and S_1 and away from S_{hp} because of the linear contours and sharp corners of the black square, since normally straight boundary contour edges derive from polygonal objects while curved contour edges derive from curved surfaces. However, the second experiment shows that even in the case where there are no straight edges, the percepts tend to be those of the extreme surfaces, rather than the hyperbolic paraboloid. Three of the observers were shown the round shape in Fig. 4a first (thus no bias because of the other pair) and still reported the percept of either convex or concave shape. Note that the same computational models are excluded by the second experiment alone, by the same argument as above. Thus, even if there is a bias towards linear surfaces for linear contours and sharp corners, it is not enough to explain the observation, nor does it change our conclusion.

Also, it has been demonstrated (Mamassian and Landy[14]) that human perception prefers elliptic (egg shaped) to hyperbolic (saddle shaped). Since the prediction of current theories is hyperbolic, the observed departure from it may be because of this bias. However, note that all the surfaces that are preferred are parabolic, i.e., neither elliptic nor hyperbolic. This is remarkable since the parabolic case constitutes a set of measure zero in the space of all possible local shapes. Because of this, it is hard to argue that any tendency or bias toward elliptic brought the percept exactly to that rare position.

3 Alternatives

The consideration of parabolic nature of the surfaces that are perceived by the human vision leads to a model that reflects this respect of human vision. Namely, the Gaussian curvature of the four preferred surfaces in the two experiments is zero everywhere it is defined. Zero Gaussian curvature is a characteristic of parabolic points. Surfaces with zero Gaussian curvature are developable, meaning they can be made by rolling and bending a piece of paper. In other words, one possibility is that the human vision system tries to fit a paper on the boundary wire frame (the sparse frame that represent definite depth data shown in Fig. 1b and Fig. 4b in the case of the experiments).

Thus, minimizing the total sum of the absolute value or square of Gaussian curvature, for example, may predict the surfaces similar to those that are perceived by humans. Such a functional would be neither convex nor concave. It is also nonlinear, which means that the solutions depend on the starting location; that makes the analysis of such a problem nontrivial, which is why we said it *may* predict the surfaces.

From a very different point of view, it is also noteworthy that in both of the examples the two surfaces most perceived by the human brain are the front and back of the convex hull of the boundary wire frame. A set in a space is called convex when any line segment that connects two of its points is also contained in it. The convex hull of a set of points is the minimal convex set containing all the points. In the case of Fig. 1b, the convex hull is the tetrahedron defined by the four endpoints of the line segments with definite depth data. This leads us to another model: a model that predicts surfaces that are a face of the convex hull of the depth points that are determined by matching.

Now, although these two models are very different, it turns out that they are closely related. That is, the Gaussian curvature of the surface of the convex hull of a set (such as the boundary wire frame) at a point that does not belong to the original set is zero, wherever it is defined. We are not aware of any mention of this fact in the literature; so we present it here as a theorem:

Theorem. *Let A be a set in the three-dimensional Euclidean space, B its convex hull, and p a point in $\partial B \setminus A$, where ∂B denotes the boundary of B. Assume that a neighborhood of p in ∂B is a smooth surface. Then the Gaussian curvature of ∂B at p is zero.*

Proof. Since p is in the convex hull of A, there are finite number of points $q_1, \ldots, q_n$ in A and positive numbers $a_1, \ldots, a_n$ such that $p = \sum_{i=1}^{n} a_i q_i$ and $\sum_{i=1}^{n} a_i = 1$, where q_i's are all distinct and $n \geq 2$, since p is not in A. Also, since p is on the boundary ∂B of a convex set B, all points of B are in the same half space H whose boundary ∂H is the tangent plane of ∂B at p. Since p is on the plane ∂H and all q_i's are in H, it follows that all q_i's are on ∂H because a_i's are all positive. (To see this, imagine a coordinate system in which p is at the origin and ∂H is the x-y plane; consider the z coordinates of q_i's, which we can assume are all on or above the x-y plane; if any of them had a positive z coordinate, so would p.) Consider the convex hull C of $\{q_1, \ldots, q_n\}$. Then C is in B, since B is convex. It is also in ∂H, since all q_i's are. Thus, it follows $C \subset \partial B$ since $C \subset B \cap \partial H$. Since $n \geq 2$ implies that C is not a point, the plane ∂H is tangent to the surface ∂B around p along at least a line segment. Thus the Gaussian curvature of ∂B at p is zero.   □

This guarantees that, in a situation as in the experiments where there are points with definite depths and those with no information at all, we can take the convex hull of the points with depth information and take one of its faces to obtain a surface with minimum Gaussian curvature.

The minimization of Gaussian curvature seems a more familiar course for machine vision, while the convex-hull model gives some intuitive reason to think why these models might work better: the convex hull has the "simplest" 3D shape that is compatible with the data, much in the way the Kanizsa triangle (Kanizsa[11]) is the simplest 2D shape that explains incomplete contour information; and in the real world, most surfaces are in fact faces of some body; so it makes sense to try to interpolate the surfaces as such.

4   Conclusion

In this paper, we have reported the observations we made in examining human disparity interpolation using stereo pairs with sparse identifiable features. A mathematical analysis revealed that the prior models used in current algorithms don't have the same behavior as the human vision system; rather, they work in a diametrically opposite way. In discussing the implications of the findings, we have also proposed two quite different candidate models that reflect the behavior of human vision, and discussed the relations between them.

Acknowledgement. Hiroshi Ishikawa thanks the Suzuki Foundation and the Research Foundation for the Electrotechnology of Chubu for their support. Davi Geiger thanks NSF for the support through the ITR grant number 0114391.

References

1. N. Ayache. *Artificial Vision for Mobile Robots*. MIT Press. Cambridge, MA. 1991.
2. P. N. Belhumeur. "A Bayesian approach to binocular stereopsis". *Int. J. Comput. Vision* 19, pp. 237–262, 1996.
3. P. N. Belhumeur and D. Mumford."A Bayesian treatment of the stereo correspondence problem using half-occluded regions". In: *Proc. CVPR '92*, pp.506–512, 1992.
4. Y. Boykov, O. Veksler, R. Zabih. "Fast approximate energy minimization via graph cuts." *IEEE T. PAMI* 23, pp. 1222-1239, 2001.
5. O. Faugeras. *Three-Dimensional Computer Vision*. MIT Press. Cambridge, MA. 1993.
6. D. Geiger, B. Ladendorf, and A. Yuille. "Occlusions and binocular stereo". *Int. J. Comput. Vision* 14, pp. 211–226, 1995.
7. B. Gillam and E. Borsting. "The role of monocular regions in stereoscopic displays". *Perception* 17, pp. 603–608, 1988.
8. W. E. Grimson. *From Images to Surfaces*. MIT Press. Cambridge, MA. 1981.
9. H. Ishikawa and D. Geiger. "Occlusions, discontinuities, and epipolar lines in stereo." In *Fifth European Conference on Computer Vision*, Freiburg, Germany. 232–248, 1998.
10. J. Jones and J. Malik. *Image Vision Comput.* 10, pp. 699–708, 1992.
11. G. Kanizsa. *Organization in Vision*. Praeger. New York. 1979.
12. V. Kolmogorov and R. Zabih. "Computing Visual Correspondence with Occlusions via Graph Cuts." In *ICCV2001*, Vancouver, Canada. pp. 508–515.
13. J. Malik. "On Binocularly viewed occlusion Junctions". In: *Fourth European Conference on Computer Vision, vol.1*, pp. 167–174, 1996.

14. P. Mamassian and M. S. Landy. "Observer biases in the 3D interpretation of line drawings." *Vision Research* 38, pp. 2817-2832, 1998.
15. D. Marr and T. Poggio. "Cooperative computation of stereo disparity". *Science* 194, pp. 283–287, 1976.
16. D. Marr and T. Poggio. "A computational theory of human stereo vision". *Proc. R. Soc. Lond. B* 204, pp. 301–328, 1979.
17. K. Nakayama and S. Shimojo. "Da Vinci stereopsis: depth and subjective occluding contours from unpaired image points". *Vision Research* 30, pp. 1811–1825, 1990.
18. S. B. Pollard, J. E. W. Mayhew, and J. P. Frisby. "PMF: A stereo correspondence algorithm using a disparity gradient". *Perception*, 14, pp. 449–470, 1985.
19. G. Poggio and T. Poggio. "The Analysis of Stereopsis". *Annu. Rev. Neurosci.* 7, pp. 379–412, 1984.
20. S. Roy. Stereo without epipolar lines : A maximum-flow formulation. *Int. J. Comput. Vision* 34, pp. 147–162, 1999.
21. S. Roy and I. Cox. A maximum-flow formulation of the N-camera stereo correspondence problem. In *International Conference on Computer Vision*, Bombai, India. pp. 492–499, 1998.
22. D. Scharstein and R. Szeliski. "A Taxonomy and Evaluation of Dense Two-Frame Stereo Correspondence Algorithms". *Int. J. Computer Vision* 47, pp. 7–42, 2002.
23. R. Szeliski. "A Bayesian modelling of uncertainty in low-level vision". Kluwer Academic Press. Boston, MA. 1989.

Appendix. Methods

Seven observers naïve to the purpose of the experiment viewed the stereoscopic images in Fig. 1a and Fig. 4a. The images were presented on a 17-inch CRT monitor at a viewing distance of 1.5m through liquid crystal shutter goggles, which switch between opaque and transparent at 100Hz, synchronized to the monitor so that alternate frames can be presented to the left and right eyes, allowing stereoscopic displays. Images contained the black shape shown in the figures, the height of which was 10cm on the monitor surface. Four of the observers first viewed the image in Fig. 1a, and then Fig. 4a; the rest viewed the images in the reverse order. In each viewing, the observer was asked to describe what was perceived after 15 seconds; and then was asked to choose from the three pictures in Fig. 1c-e (when Fig. 1a is shown) or Fig. 4c-e. There was no discrepancy between what they described and what they chose. A few stereo pairs of color pictures were shown to each viewer prior to the experiment in order to ascertain that the observer is capable of binocular stereo perception. Only one of the observers reported the percept of a saddle-type shape (Fig. 1e). Other six viewers reported the percept of either convex (Fig. 1c) or concave (Fig. 1d) shape. One reported the percept of both of the convex and concave shapes.

Viewer	#1	#2	#3	#4	#5	#6	#7
Fig. 1a	convex	saddle	concave	concave	convex	convex	both
Fig. 4a	concave	saddle	concave	concave	convex	convex	convex
Which first?	Fig. 1a	Fig. 1a	Fig. 1a	Fig. 1a	Fig. 4a	Fig. 4a	Fig. 4a

Aligning Sequences and Actions by Maximizing Space-Time Correlations

Yaron Ukrainitz and Michal Irani

Department of Computer Science and Applied Mathematics,
The Weizmann Institute of Science,
Rehovot, Israel

Abstract. We introduced an algorithm for sequence alignment, based on maximizing local space-time correlations. Our algorithm aligns sequences of the same action performed at different times and places by different people, possibly at different speeds, and wearing different clothes. Moreover, the algorithm offers a unified approach to the problem of sequence alignment for a wide range of scenarios (e.g., sequence pairs taken with stationary or jointly moving cameras, with the same or different photometric properties, with or without moving objects). Our algorithm is applied directly to the dense space-time intensity information of the two sequences (or to filtered versions of them). This is done without prior segmentation of foreground moving objects, and without prior detection of corresponding features across the sequences. Examples of challenging sequences with complex actions are shown, including ballet dancing, actions in the presence of other complex scene dynamics (clutter), as well as multi-sensor sequence pairs.

1 Introduction

Given two video sequences of a dynamic scene, the problem of sequence alignment is defined as finding the spatial and temporal coordinate transformation that brings one sequence into alignment with the other, both in space and in time. In this work we focus on the alignment of sequences with similar dynamics, but with significantly different appearance properties. In particular, we address two applications in a single unified framework:

1. *Action Alignment*: The same action is performed at different times and places by different people, possibly at different speeds, and wearing different clothes (optionally with different sensors). We would like to recover the space-time transformation which best aligns the actions (the foreground moving object), regardless of their backgrounds or other dynamic scene clutter.
2. *Multi-sensor Alignment*: The same dynamic scene is recorded *simultaneously* by multiple cameras (of same or of different sensing modalities). In this case (of simultaneous recording) we would like to bring into alignment the entire scene (both the foreground moving objects and the background scene).

While sequences obtained by different sensors have significantly different spatial appearances, their temporal properties (scene or camera motion, trajectories of moving objects, etc.) are usually invariant to the sensing modalities, and are therefore shared by

A. Leonardis, H. Bischof, and A. Pinz (Eds.): ECCV 2006, Part III, LNCS 3953, pp. 538–550, 2006.

the two sequences. The same observation is true also for sequences of the same action performed by different people at different times and places. Such temporal changes are not captured in any individual frame. They are, however, contained in the space-time volumes generated by the two sequences. Sequence-to-sequence alignment is therefore a more powerful approach to handle those difficult scenarios than image-to-image alignment.

Several approaches to sequence alignment were suggested. Most of these methods assume that the video sequences are recorded simultaneously. Moreover, they are restricted to a particular scenario (e.g., moving objects [5], moving cameras [3], similar appearance properties [4]). Moreover, none of these methods is applicable to alignment of actions performed at different times and places.

Methods for aligning actions were also suggested (e.g., [10, 6, 2]). However, these require manual selection of corresponding feature points across the sequences. Some of them provide only temporal synchronization. In [11] an approach was proposed for detecting behavioral correlations in video under spatial and temporal *shifts*. Its output is a coarse space-time correlation volume. This approach does not account for spatial nor temporal scaling (nor more complex geometric deformations), nor was it used for aligning video clips (since video alignment requires sub-pixel and sub-frame accuracy).

In this paper we propose a unified approach to sequence alignment which is suited both for sequences recorded simultaneously (for a variety of scenarios), as well as for action sequences. Our approach is inspired by the multi-sensor image-alignment method presented in [8]. We extend it into space-time, and take it beyond multi-sensor alignment, to alignment of actions. Alignment in space and time is obtained by maximizing the local space-time correlations between the two sequences. Our method is applied directly to the dense space-time intensity information of the two sequences (or to filtered versions of them), without prior segmentation of foreground moving objects, and without prior detection of corresponding features across the sequences. Our approach offers two main advantages over existing approaches to sequence alignment:

1. It is capable of aligning sequences of the same *action* performed at different times and places by different people wearing different clothes, regardless of their photometric properties and other static or dynamic scene clutter.
2. It provides a unified approach to multi-sensor sequence alignment for a wide range of scenarios, including: (i) sequences taken with either stationary or jointly moving cameras, (ii) sequences with the same or different photometric properties, and (iii) sequences with or without moving objects. Our approach does assume, however, that the cameras are rigid with respect to each other (although they may move jointly).

The remainder of this work is organized as follows: Sec. 2 formulates the problem, Sec. 3 presents the space-time similarity measure between the two sequences. Sec. 4 presents the space-time alignment algorithm. Sec. 5 provides experimental results on real sequences. Sec. 6 discusses the robustness of the algorithm to noise and to other dynamic scene clutter.

2   Problem Formulation

Given two sequences, f and g, we seek the spatio-temporal parametric transformation p that maximizes a global similarity measure M between the two sequences after bringing them into alignment according to p. f and g may be either the original video sequences, or some filtered version of them, depending on the underlying application (see Sec. 5).

For each space-time point (x, y, t) in the sequence f, we denote its spatio-temporal displacement vector by $u = (u_1, u_2, u_3)$. u is a function of both the space-time point coordinates and the unknown parameter vector p, i.e., $u = u(x, y, t; p)$.

We assume that the *relative* internal and external parameters between the cameras are fixed (but unknown). The cameras may be either stationary or moving (jointly). In our current implementation we have chosen a 2D affine transformation to model the *spatial transformation* between corresponding frames across the two sequences (such a model is applicable when the scene is planar, or distant, or when the two cameras are relatively close to each other). A 1D affine transformation was chosen to model the *temporal transformation* between the two sequences (supporting sequences with different frame rates as well as a time offset between the sequences). The space-time transformation p therefore comprises of 8 parameters, where the first 6 parameters $(p_1, \ldots, p_6)$ capture the spatial 2D affine transformation and the remaining 2 parameters (p_7, p_8) capture the temporal 1D affine transformation. The spatio-temporal displacement vector $u(x, y, t; p)$ is therefore:

$$u(x, y, t; p) = \begin{bmatrix} u_1(x, y, t; p) \\ u_2(x, y, t; p) \\ u_3(x, y, t; p) \end{bmatrix} = \begin{bmatrix} p_1 x + p_2 y + p_3 \\ p_4 x + p_5 y + p_6 \\ p_7 t + p_8 \end{bmatrix}$$

This can be written more compactly as:

$$u(x, y, t; p) = X(x, y, t) \cdot p \tag{1}$$

where $p = (p_1, \ldots, p_8)$, and:

$$X(x, y, t) = \begin{bmatrix} x & y & 1 & 0 & 0 & 0 & 0 & 0 \\ 0 & 0 & 0 & x & y & 1 & 0 & 0 \\ 0 & 0 & 0 & 0 & 0 & 0 & t & 1 \end{bmatrix}.$$

3   The Similarity Measure

Sequences of actions recorded at different times and places, as well as sequences obtained by different sensing modalities (e.g., an IR and a visible light camera) have significantly different photometric properties. As such, their intensities are related by highly non-linear transformations.

In [8] the following observations were made for a multi-sensor *image* pair: (i) the intensities of images taken with sensors of different modalities are usually related by a highly non-linear global transformation which depends not only on the image intensity, but also on its image location. Such intensity transformations are not handled well by

Mutual Information (which assumes spatial invariance). Nevertheless, (ii) for very small corresponding image patches across the two images, their intensities are *locally* related by some *linear* intensity transformation. Since normalized-correlation is invariant to linear intensity transformations, it can be used as a *local* similarity measure applied to small image patches.

Our approach is based on extending this approach to space-time, and takes it beyond multi-sensor alignment, to alignment of actions. Local normalized correlations are computed within small *space-time patches* (in our implementation they were of size $7 \times 7 \times 7$). A *global* similarity measure is then computed as the sum of all those local measures in the entire sequence. The resulting global similarity measure is thus invariant to spatially and temporally varying non-linear intensity transformations.

Given two corresponding space-time patches/windows, w_f and w_g, one from each sequence, their local Normalized Correlation (NC) can be estimated as follows [7]: $NC(w_f, w_g) = \frac{\text{cov}(w., w.)}{\sqrt{\text{var}(w.)}\sqrt{\text{var}(w.)}}$, where *cov* and *var* stand for the covariance and variance of intensities. Squaring the NC measure further accounts for contrast reversal, which is common in multi-sensor sequence pairs. Our patch-wise local similarity measure is therefore:

$$C(w_f, w_g) = \frac{\text{cov}^2(w_f, w_g)}{\text{var}(w_f)\text{var}(w_g) + \alpha} \qquad (2)$$

where the constant α is added to account for noise (in our experiments we used $\alpha = 10$, but the algorithm is not particularly sensitive to the choice of α).

The *global* similarity measure M between two sequences (f and g) is computed as the sum of all the *local* measures C applied to small space-time patches around each pixel in the sequence:

$$M(f, g) = \sum_x \sum_y \sum_t C\left(w_f(x, y, t), w_g(x, y, t)\right) \qquad (3)$$

This results in a global measure which is invariant to highly non-linear intensity transformations (which may vary spatially and temporally over the sequences).

Our goal is to recover the global geometric space-time transformation which maximizes the global measure M between the two sequences. To do so, we reformulate the local measure C and the global measure M in terms of the unknown parametric transformation p. For each space-time point (x, y, t) in the sequence f and its spatio-temporal displacement vector $u = (u_1, u_2, u_3)$, the local normalized correlation measure of Eq. (2) can be written as a function of u:

$$C^{(x,y,t)}(u) = C\left(w_f(x, y, t), w_g(x + u_1, y + u_2, t + u_3)\right)$$

where $w_f(x, y, t)$ is the $7 \times 7 \times 7$ space-time window around pixel (x, y, t) in f, and $w_g(x + u_1, y + u_2, t + u_3)$ is the $7 \times 7 \times 7$ space-time window around pixel $(x + u_1, y + u_2, t + u_3)$ in g. We can therefore formulate the alignment problem as follows: Find p (the set of global spatio-temporal parameters) that maximizes the global similarity measure $M(p)$:

$$M(p) = \sum_{(x,y,t) \in f} C^{(x,y,t)}\left(u(x, y, t; p)\right) \qquad (4)$$

4   The Alignment Algorithm

4.1   The Maximization Process

We use Newton's method [9] for the optimization task. Local quadratic approximations of $M(p)$ are used in order to iteratively converge to the correct value of the space-time transformation p. Let p_0 be the current estimate of the transformation parameters p. We can write the quadratic approximation of $M(p)$ around p_0 as:

$$M(p) = M(p_0) + (\nabla_p M(p_0))^T \delta_p + \frac{1}{2}\delta_p^T H_M(p_0)\delta_p$$

where $\nabla_p M$ and H_M are the gradient and hessian of M, respectively (both computed around p_0), and $\delta_p = p - p_0$ is the unknown refinement step. By differentiating this approximation with respect to δ_p and equating to zero, we obtain the following expression for δ_p:

$$\delta_p = -\left(H_M(p_0)\right)^{-1} \cdot \nabla_p M(p_0) \tag{5}$$

From Eqs. (1) and (4) and the chain rule of differentiation, we can evaluate $\nabla_p M$ and H_M:

$$\nabla_p M(p) = \sum_{(x,y,t)\in f} \nabla_p C^{(x,y,t)}(u)$$

$$= \sum_{(x,y,t)\in f} \left(X^T \cdot \nabla_u C^{(x,y,t)}(u)\right) \tag{6}$$

$$H_M(p) = \sum_{(x,y,t)\in f} \left(X^T \cdot H_{C^{(\cdots)}}(u) \cdot X\right) \tag{7}$$

where $\nabla_u C^{(x,y,t)}$ and $H_{C^{(\cdots)}}$ are the gradient and hessian of $C^{(x,y,t)}(u)$, respectively, computed around $u_0 = u(x, y, t; p_0)$. Substituting Eq. (6) and Eq. (7) into Eq. (5), we get the following expression for the refinement step δ_p, in terms of the normalized correlation function $C^{(x,y,t)}(u)$:

$$\delta_p = -\left(\sum_{(x,y,t)\in f} X^T H_{C^{(\cdots)}}(u_0)X\right)^{-1} \cdot \sum_{(x,y,t)\in f} X^T \nabla_u C^{(x,y,t)}(u_0) \tag{8}$$

In order to calculate the refinement step of Eq. (8) we need to differentiate the normalized correlation function $C^{(x,y,t)}$ of each space-time point (x, y, t) around its currently estimated displacement vector $u_0 = u(x, y, t; p_0)$. This is done as follows: For each space-time point (x, y, t), a local normalized correlation function (volume) $C^{(x,y,t)}(u)$ is evaluated for a set of spatio-temporal displacements around u_0. Then, the first and second derivatives of $C^{(x,y,t)}$ with respect to $u = (u_1, u_2, u_3)$ are extracted in order to obtain $\nabla_u C^{(x,y,t)}$ and $H_{C^{(\cdots)}}$:

$$\nabla_u C^{(x,y,t)} = \left[\frac{\partial C^{(x,y,t)}}{\partial x} \quad \frac{\partial C^{(x,y,t)}}{\partial y} \quad \frac{\partial C^{(x,y,t)}}{\partial t}\right]^T$$

$$
H_{C^{(\cdot,\cdot\cdot)}} = \begin{bmatrix} \dfrac{\partial^2 C^{(\cdot,\cdot\cdot)}}{\partial x^2} & \dfrac{\partial^2 C^{(\cdot,\cdot\cdot)}}{\partial x \partial y} & \dfrac{\partial^2 C^{(\cdot,\cdot\cdot)}}{\partial x \partial t} \\[2ex] \dfrac{\partial^2 C^{(\cdot,\cdot\cdot)}}{\partial y \partial x} & \dfrac{\partial^2 C^{(\cdot,\cdot\cdot)}}{\partial y^2} & \dfrac{\partial^2 C^{(\cdot,\cdot\cdot)}}{\partial y \partial t} \\[2ex] \dfrac{\partial^2 C^{(\cdot,\cdot\cdot)}}{\partial t \partial x} & \dfrac{\partial^2 C^{(\cdot,\cdot\cdot)}}{\partial t \partial y} & \dfrac{\partial^2 C^{(\cdot,\cdot\cdot)}}{\partial t^2} \end{bmatrix} \tag{9}
$$

In practice, we evaluate $C^{(x,y,t)}(u)$ for displacements of $u_0 \pm 2$ in x, y, t (i.e., the correlation function is a volume of size $5 \times 5 \times 5$). To account for large misalignments, the above maximization scheme is performed within a coarse-to-fine data structure. The resulting algorithm is therefore as follows:

The Algorithm:
1. Construct a space-time Gaussian pyramid for each sequence (Sec. 4.3).
2. Find an initial guess p_0 for the space-time transformation parameters in the coarsest (smallest) pyramid level (Sec. 4.4).
3. Apply several maximization iterations in the current pyramid level until convergence. In each iteration do:
(a) Use the current parameter estimate p_0 from the last iteration to compute the refinement step δ_p (Eq. (8)).
(b) Update the current parameter estimate $p_0 = p_0 + \delta_p$.
(c) Test for convergence: If the change in the values of $M(p)$ for two successive iterations is small enough, go to step 4. Otherwise, go back to step 3.(a).
4. Proceed to the next pyramid level and go back to step 3.

4.2 Confidence-Weighted Regression

To further stabilize the maximization process, we consider only space-time points (x, y, t) in which the quadratic approximation of the normalized correlation function is *concave*. Other space-time points are ignored (are outliers), since they incorporate false information into the regression. Moreover, the contribution of each space-time point is weighted by its reliability, which is measured by the degree of concavity of the normalized correlation function at this point.

A twice-differentiable function is concave at a point if and only if the hessian of the function at the point is negative semidefinite [12], i.e., if all its kth order leading principal minors are non-positive for an odd k and non-negative for an even k. Therefore, the hessian matrix $H_{C^{(\cdot,\cdot\cdot)}(u_0)}$ of Eq. (9) is checked for negative semidefiniteness by:

$$
|H_{C(u_0)}| \le 0 \,, \quad \begin{vmatrix} \dfrac{\partial^2 C(u_0)}{\partial x^2} & \dfrac{\partial^2 C(u_0)}{\partial x \partial y} \\[2ex] \dfrac{\partial^2 C(u_0)}{\partial y \partial x} & \dfrac{\partial^2 C(u_0)}{\partial y^2} \end{vmatrix} \ge 0 \,, \quad \dfrac{\partial^2 C(u_0)}{\partial x^2} \le 0
$$

where $C(u_0) = C^{(x,y,t)}(u_0)$, and $|\cdot|$ denotes the determinant of a matrix. Only space-time points (x, y, t) in which the corresponding hessian $H_{C^{(\cdot,\cdot\cdot)}(u_0)}$ is negative semi-definite are considered as inliers in the maximization process. Let S denote this set of inlier space-time points. Each space-time point in S is further weighted by the determinant of its corresponding hessian, which indicates the degree of concavity at that point. This outlier rejection and weighting scheme is incorporated into the algorithm by extending Eq. (8):

$$\delta_p = -\left(\sum_{(x,y,t)\in S} w(\boldsymbol{u}_0) X^T H_{C(\boldsymbol{u}_0)} X \right)^{-1} \cdot \sum_{(x,y,t)\in S} w(\boldsymbol{u}_0) X^T \nabla_{\boldsymbol{u}} C(\boldsymbol{u}_0)$$

where $w(\boldsymbol{u}_0) = w^{(x,y,t)}(\boldsymbol{u}_0) = -\left| H_{C(\boldsymbol{u}_0)} \right|$.

4.3 The Space-Time Gaussian Pyramid

To handle large spatio-temporal misalignments between the two sequences, the optimization is done coarse-to-fine (in space and in time). Caspi and Irani [4] presented a space-time Gaussian pyramid for video sequences. Each pyramid level was constructed by applying a Gaussian low-pass filter to the previous level, followed by sub-sampling by a factor of 2. The filtering and sub-sampling phases were performed both in space and in time (i.e., in x, y and t). Our coarse-to-fine estimation is performed within such a data structure, with a small modification to handle sequences whose temporal and spatial dimensions are significantly different (otherwise, the coarsest pyramid level will be too coarse in one dimension, while not coarse enough in the other dimensions). Filtering and sub-sampling is first applied along the largest dimension(s), until it is of similar size to the other dimensions, and then proceeding as in [4]. To guarantee numerical stability, the coarsest (smallest) pyramid level is at least $30 \times 30 \times 30$.

4.4 The Initial Parametric Transformation p_0

An initial guess p_0 for the space-time parametric transformation is computed at the coarsest pyramid level. We seek for initial non-zero values only for the translational parameters of p in x, y and t (i.e., p_3, p_6 and p_8), leaving all the other parameters to be zero. This is done by evaluating the similarity measure M of Eq. (4) for each possible spatio-temporal integer shift within a search radius (in our implementation we used a radius of 25% of the sequence in each dimension). The translation parameters that provide the highest similarity value M are used in the initial guess p_0 for the transformation parameters. Initializing only p_3, p_6 and p_8 is usually sufficient for the initial guess. The remaining parameters in p tend to be smaller, and initializing them with zero-values usually suffice for convergence. All the parameters in p are updated during the optimization process. Note that although an "exhaustive" search is performed at the coarsest pyramid level, this process is *not* time consuming since the smallest spatio-temporal pyramid level is typically of size $30 \times 30 \times 30$.

5 Applications and Results

Recall that we focus on two applications of sequence alignment: (1) Alignment of action sequences, taken at different times and places, and (2) Alignment of sequences recorded simultaneously by different cameras, where the most difficult case is when these are sensors of different modalities. We use the same alignment algorithm for these two applications. However, we apply the algorithm to different sequence *representations*, which are obtained by pre-filtering the original input sequences with different linear filters. These prior filters emphasize the part of the data which we want to bring into alignment. The chosen filters for each application along with experimental results are presented next.

5.1 Multi-sensor Alignment

The common information across a multi-sensor pair of sequences (e.g., infra-red and visible-light) is the *details* in the scene (spatial or temporal). These are captured mostly by high-frequency information (both in time and in space). The multi-sensor pair differ in their photometric properties which are captured by low frequencies. Thus, to enhance the common detail information and suppress the non-common photometric properties, differentiation operators are applied to the sequences. Since directional information is important, the input sequences f and g are differentiated separately with respect to x, y and t, resulting in three sequences of directional derivatives (f_x, f_y, f_t and g_x, g_y, g_t). An absolute value is further taken to account for contrast reversal. Thus, the global similarity measure of Eq. (3) becomes:

$$M(f,g) = M\big(f_x^{abs}, g_x^{abs}\big) + M\big(f_y^{abs}, g_y^{abs}\big) + M\big(f_t^{abs}, g_t^{abs}\big)$$

Due to lack of space we omitted the figures of the multi-sensor alignment results from the paper. However, these results (i.e., multi-sensor sequences before and after space-time alignment) can be found on our web site: http://www.wisdom.weizmann.ac. il/~vision/SpaceTimeCorrelations.html. We display there different examples of multi-sensor pairs obtained under different scenarios – in one case the cameras are moving, while in another case the cameras are still and there are moving objects in the scene. All these sequence pairs were brought into space-time alignment using the above algorithm. Previous methods for sequence alignment were usually restricted to one type of scenario (either moving cameras [3] or moving objects [5]).

5.2 Action Alignment

Given two sequences that contain a similar action, performed by different people at different times and places, we would like to align only the action (i.e., the foreground moving objects), ignoring the different backgrounds and the photometric properties of the sequences. For example, given two sequences of walking people, we want to align only the walking people themselves, regardless of their backgrounds, the scale and orientation of the walking people, the walking speed, the illumination, and the clothing colors. The common information in two such sequences is captured mostly by the temporal variations (derivatives), and not by the spatial ones. Therefore, for the purpose of Action Alignment, Eq. (3) becomes:

$$M(f,g) = M\left(f_t^{abs}, g_t^{abs}\right) \tag{10}$$

The two sequences in Fig. 1.a and 1.b contain a person walking at different times and in different places (the cameras are stationary). There are four significant differences between the two input sequences: (1) their backgrounds are different (trees in one sequence, and a wall in the other), (2) the spatial scale of the walking person is

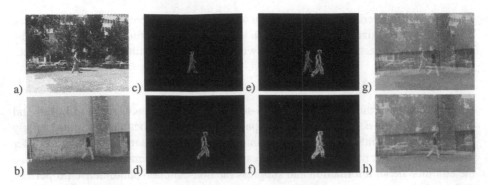

Fig. 1. Action alignment. (a) and (b) show frames 74 of the two input sequences, f and g. (c) and (d) show the absolute value of their temporal derivatives (f_t^{abs} in magenta and g_t^{abs} in green). (e) Initial misalignment (superposition of (c) and (d)). (f) Superposition of corresponding frames after alignment both in space and in time. The white color is a result of superposition of the green and magenta. (g) and (h) show superposition of the input sequences before and after alignment (one in green and one in magenta). For color figure and full video sequence see http://www.wisdom.weizmann.ac.il/~vision/SpaceTimeCorrelations.html.

significantly different (by approximately 36%), (3) the walking speed is different (be approximately 13%), and (4) the clothing colors are different. Figs. 1.c and 1.d show the absolute values of the temporal derivatives (f_t^{abs} and g_t^{abs}) of the input sequences. Fig. 1.e displays the initial misalignment between the two sequences through an overlay of 1.c and 1.d before alignment. Fig. 1.f shows the same display after alignment of the actions both in space and in time. The white color in Fig. 1.f is obtained from super-position of the green and magenta, which indicates good alignment (please see color figures and color sequences on our web site). Figs 1.g and 1.h display super-position of the two input video sequences before and after alignment, respectively (where one sequence is displayed in green and the other sequence is displayed in magenta).

The two sequences in Fig. 2.a and 2.b contain two different dancers that perform a similar ballet dance. Figs 2.c display super-position of the two input video sequences before alignment (where the first sequence is displayed in green and the second sequence is displayed in magenta). Initially, the two dancers are misaligned both in space and in time. 2.d shows a similar super-position after alignment. The two dancers are now aligned both in space and in time (although their movements are not identical).

Applications. This capability of aligning actions can be used for various applications, including: (i) Action/Event recognition: Given a sequence of an action and a database of sequences with different actions, find the action in the database that achieves best alignment with the query action, i.e., that yields the highest value for the measure M of Eq. (4). (ii) Identification of people by the way they behave: Given a sequence of a person performing some action, and a database of different people performing the same action, find the database sequence that provides the best alignment (maximal score M) with the query sequence. This will allow to identify the person in the query sequence. Carlsson [2] proposed an algorithm for recognizing people by the way they walk. However, his algorithm required manual marking of specific body locations in each

Fig. 2. Action alignment. (a) and (b) show several frames of the two input sequences, f and g (with same frame numbers). (c) shows superposition of (a) and (b) before alignment (f in green and g in magenta). (d) shows superposition of corresponding frames after alignment both in space and in time. This compensates for the *global parametric* geometric deformations (spatial scale, speed, orientation, position, etc.) The residual *non-parametric local* deformations highlight the differences in performance of the two dancers. For color figure and full video sequence see http://www.wisdom.weizmann.ac.il/~vision/SpaceTimeCorrelations.html.

frame of the two sequences, whereas our approach is automatic. (iii) Comparing performance and style of people in various sport activities.

Action Alignment vs. Background Alignment. The choice of the sequence representation is important. For example, consider the two input sequences in Fig. 3.a and 3.b. There are two different people walking against the same background (recorded at different times). Fig. 3.c shows the initial misalignment between the two input sequences. Note that both the walking people and their backgrounds are not aligned. Fig. 3.d shows the results of applying the alignment algorithm to the derivatives of the input sequences with respect to t alone (using the global similarity measure in Eq. (10)). As expected, only the actions are aligned, and the backgrounds are not aligned. Figure 3.e shows the results of applying the alignment algorithm to the derivatives of the same input sequences, but this time differentiated with respect to x and y. This is done by replacing Eq. (3) with:

$$M(f,g) = M\left(f_x^{abs}, g_x^{abs}\right) + M\left(f_y^{abs}, g_y^{abs}\right) \tag{11}$$

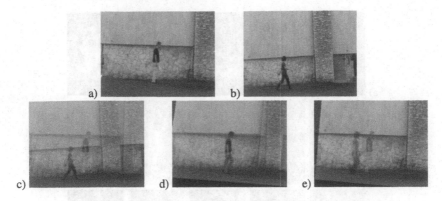

Fig. 3. Action alignment vs. background alignment. (a) and (b) show frame 45 of the two input sequences. (c) Initial misalignment (superposition of (a) and (b)). (d) Superposition after space-time alignment using temporal derivatives only (Eq. (10)). (e) Superposition after space-time alignment using spatial derivatives only (Eq. (11)). For color figure and full video sequence see http://www.wisdom.weizmann.ac.il/~vision/SpaceTimeCorrelations.html.

Since only the spatial variations of the sequences are used in the alignment process, the backgrounds are brought into alignment, while the walking people are not.

6   Robustness and Locking Property

One of the benefits of a coarse-to-fine estimation process is the "locking property", which provides robustness to noise, as well as the ability to lock onto a dominant space-time transformation. Burt *et al.* [1] discussed this effect in the context of *image alignment* in the presence of multiple motions. According to [1], since pyramids provide a separation of the spectrum into different frequency bands, motion components with different frequency characteristics tend to be separated. This separation causes the motion estimator to "lock" onto a single (dominant) motion component, even when other motions are present. A similar phenomena occurs in our sequence alignment algorithm, which tends to lock onto a *dominant space-time coordinate transformation* between the two sequences. Figs. 4 and 5 demonstrate the locking property.

Fig. 4 displays the robustness of our algorithm to noise. Gaussian noise with zero mean and a standard deviation of 40 gray-level units (out of 255) was added to the two input sequences of Fig. 1.a and 1.b. The resulting sequences are shown in Figs. 4.a and 4.b. Figs. 4.c and 4.d display the absolute values of the temporal derivatives of the input sequences. The presence of a significant noise is clearly seen in these figures. An overlay of 4.c and 4.d before alignment is shown in Fig. 4.e. Fig. 4.f displays an overlay of corresponding frames after alignment in space and in time. Good alignment is obtained despite the significant noise.

Fig. 5 displays the locking property in the case of multiple transparent layers. Again, we took the two input sequences of Fig. 1.a and 1.b, but this time mixed them with two different sequences that contain significant non-rigid motions (a waving flag and a waterfall). The first input sequence (Fig. 5.a) contains a walking person (with trees in the

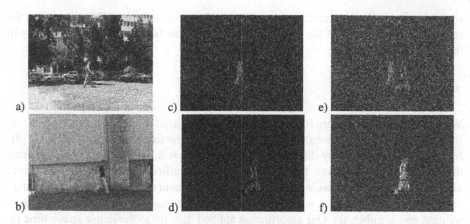

Fig. 4. Robustness to noise. (a) and (b) show frame 74 of the two noisy input sequences (see text for more details). (c) and (d) show the absolute value of the temporal derivatives of (a) and (b), respectively. (e) Initial misalignment (superposition of (c) and (d)). (f) Superposition after alignment in space and in time. For color figure and full video sequence see http://www.wisdom.weizmann.ac.il/~vision/SpaceTimeCorrelations.html.

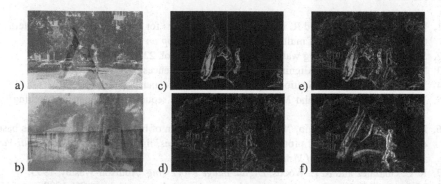

Fig. 5. The locking property. (a) Frame 61 of the first sequence: a mixture of the sequence of Fig. 1.a with a flag sequence. (b) Frame 61 of the second sequence: a mixture of the sequence of Fig. 1.b with a waterfall sequence. (c) and (d) show the absolute value of the temporal derivatives of (a) and (b), respectively. (e) Initial misalignment (superposition of (c) and (d)). (f) Superposition after alignment in space and in time. The algorithm locks onto the common walking action, despite the presence of other scene dynamics. For color figure and full video sequence see http://www.wisdom.weizmann.ac.il/~vision/SpaceTimeCorrelations.html.

background) mixed with a waving flag, and the second input sequence (Fig. 5.b) contains a walking person (with a wall in the background) mixed with a waterfall. Figs. 5.c and 5.d display the absolute values of the temporal derivatives of the input sequences. The presence of the multiple layers is clearly seen in these figures. An overlay of 5.c and 5.d before alignment is shown in Fig. 5.e. Fig. 5.f displays an overlay of corresponding frames after alignment in space and in time. The white color in Fig. 5.f indicates that the algorithm automatically locked on the common walking action, despite the other scene dynamics. The regression was applied to the entire sequence. This illustrates the strong locking property of the algorithm. The results can be seen much more clearly in the video on our web site.

7 Summary

We introduced an algorithm for sequence alignment, based on maximizing local space-time correlations. Our algorithm aligns sequences of the same action performed at different times and places by different people, possibly at different speeds, and wearing different clothes. Moreover, the algorithm offers a unified approach to the sequence alignment problem for a wide range of scenarios (sequence pairs taken with stationary or jointly moving cameras, with the same or different photometric properties, with or without moving objects). Our algorithm is applied directly to the dense space-time intensity information of the two sequences (or to filtered versions of them). This is done without prior segmentation of foreground moving objects, and without prior detection of corresponding features across the sequences.

References

1. P. Burt, R. Hingorani, and R. Kolczynski, "Mechanisms for isolating component patterns in the sequential analysis of multiple motion," in *Workshop on Visual Motion*, 1991.
2. S. Carlsson, "Recognizing walking people," in *IJRR*, vol. 22, pp. 359–370, 2003.
3. Y. Caspi and M. Irani, "Aligning non-overlapping sequences," *IJCV*, vol. 48, 2002.
4. Y. Caspi and M. Irani, "Spatio-temporal alignment of sequences," *T-PAMI*, 2002.
5. Y. Caspi, D. Simakov, and M. Irani, "Feature-based sequence-to-sequence matching," in *VMODS*, 2002.
6. M. A. Giese and T. Poggio, "Synthesis and recognition of biological motion patterns based on linear superposition of prototypical motion sequences," in *IEEE Workshop on Multi-View Modeling and Analysis of Visual Scenes*, 1999.
7. R. C. Gonzalez and R. E. Woods, *Digital Image Processing*. Addison-Wesley, 1993.
8. M. Irani and P. Anandan, "Robust multi-sensor image alignment," in *ICCV*, 1998.
9. W. Press, B. Flannery, S. Teukolsky, and W. Vetterling, *Numerical Recipes in C*. Cambridge Univ. Press, 1988.
10. C. Rao, A. Gritai, M. Shah, and T. Syeda-Mahmood, "View-invariant alignment and matching of video sequences," in *ICCV*, pp. 939–945, 2004.
11. E. Shechtman and M. Irani, "Space-time behavior based correlation," in *CVPR*, 2005.
12. G. Thomas and R. Finney, *Calculus and Analytic Geometry (9th Edition)*. Addison-Wesley, 1996.

Simultaneous Nonrigid Registration of Multiple Point Sets and Atlas Construction*

Fei Wang[1], Baba C. Vemuri[1], Anand Rangarajan[1],
Ilona M. Schmalfuss[2], and Stephan J. Eisenschenk[3]

[1] Department of Computer & Information Sciences & Engr.,
University of Florida, Gainesville
[2] Departments of Radiology, University of Florida, Gainesville
[3] Department of Neurology, University of Florida, Gainesville

Abstract. Estimating a meaningful average or mean shape from a set of shapes represented by unlabeled point-sets is a challenging problem since, usually this involves solving for point correspondence under a non-rigid motion setting. In this paper, we propose a novel and robust algorithm that is capable of simultaneously computing the mean shape from multiple unlabeled point-sets (represented by finite mixtures) and registering them nonrigidly to this emerging mean shape. This algorithm avoids the correspondence problem by minimizing the Jensen-Shannon (JS) divergence between the point sets represented as finite mixtures. We derive the analytic gradient of the cost function namely, the JS-divergence, in order to efficiently achieve the optimal solution. The cost function is fully symmetric with no bias toward any of the given shapes to be registered and whose mean is being sought. Our algorithm can be especially useful for creating atlases of various shapes present in images as well as for simultaneously (rigidly or non-rigidly) registering 3D range data sets without having to establish any correspondence. We present experimental results on non-rigidly registering 2D as well as 3D real data (point sets).

1 Introduction

In recent years, there has been considerable interest in the application of statistical shape analysis to problems in medical image analysis, computer graphics and computer vision. Regardless of whether shapes are parameterized by points, lines, curves etc., the fundamental problem of estimating mean and covariance of shapes remains. We are particularly interested in the unlabeled point-set parameterization since statistical shape analysis of point-sets is very mature [1]. Means, covariances and probability distributions on shape manifolds can now be defined and estimated.

The primary technical challenge in using point-set representations of shapes is the correspondence problem. Typically correspondences can be estimated once the point-sets are properly aligned with appropriate spatial transformations. If

---

* This research was in part funded by the NIH grants, RO1 NS046812 & NS42075 and NSF grant NSF 0307712.

A. Leonardis, H. Bischof, and A. Pinz (Eds.): ECCV 2006, Part III, LNCS 3953, pp. 551–563, 2006.

the objects at hand are deformable, the adequate transformation would obviously be a non-rigid spatial mapping. Solving for nonrigid deformations between point-sets with unknown correspondence is a hard problem. In fact, many current methods only attempt to solve for affine transformation for the alignment. Furthermore, we also encounter the issue of the bias problem in atlas creation. Since we have more than two sample point-sets to be aligned for creating an atlas, a question that arises is: How do we align all the point-sets in a symmetric manner so that there is no bias toward any particular point-set?

To overcome these aforementioned problems, we present a novel approach to simultaneously register multiple point-sets and construct the atlas. The idea is to model each point set by a kernel probability distribution, then quantify the distance between these probability distributions using an information-theoretic measure. The distance is optimized over a space of coordinate transformations yielding the desired registrations. It is obvious that once all the point sets are deformed into the same shape, the distance measure between these distributions should be minimized since all the distribution are identical to each other. We impose regularization on each deformation field to prevent over-deforming of each point-sets (e.g. all the point-sets may deform into a single data point). Jensen-Shannon divergence, first introduced in [2], serves as a model divergence measure between multiple probability distributions. It has some very desirable properties, researchers have used it as a dissimilarity measure for image registration and retrieval applications [3, 4].

The rest of this paper is organized as follows. The remainder of section 1 gives a brief review of the literature, focusing on difference between these methods and ours. Section 2 contains a description of our formulation using JS-divergence for our simultaneous nonrigid registration and atlas construction model. Experimental results on 2D as well as 3D point-sets are presented in Section 3.

1.1 Previous Work

Extensive studies on the atlas construction for deformable shapes can be found in literature covering both theoretical and practical issues relating to computer vision and pattern recognition. According to the shape representation, they can be classified into two distinct categories. One is the methods dealing with shapes represented by feature point-sets, and everything else is in the other category including those shapes represented as curves and surfaces of the shape boundary, and these curves and surfaces may be either intrinsicly or extrinsicly parameterized (e.g. using point locations and spline coefficients).

The work presented in [5] is a representative method using an intrinsic curve parameterization to analyze deformable shapes. Shapes are represented as elements of infinite-dimensional spaces and their pairwise difference are quantified using the lengths of geodesics connecting them on these spaces, the intrinsic mean (Karcher mean) can be computed as a point on the manifold (of shapes) which minimize the sum of square geodesic distance between this unknown point to each individual shape, which lies on the manifold. However the curves are limited by closed curves, and it has not been extended to the 3D surface shapes.

For methods using intrinsic curve or surface representations [5, 6], further statistical analysis on these representations is much more difficult than analysis on the point representation, but the reward maybe higher due to the use of intrinsic higher order representation.

Among these methods using point-sets parameterization, the idea of using nonrigid spatial mapping functions, specifically thin-plate splines [7, 8, 9], to analyze deformable shape has been widely adopted. Bookstein's work in [7], successfully initiated the research efforts on the usage of thin-plate splines to model the deformation of shapes. This method is landmark-based, it avoids the correspondence problem since the placement of corresponding points is driven by the visual perception of experts, however it suffers from the the typical problem besetting landmark methods, e.g. inconsistency. Several significant articles on robust and non-rigid point set matching have been published by Rangaranjan and collaborators [8] using thin-plate splines. The main strength of their work is the ability to jointly determine the correspondences and non-rigid transformation between each point sets to the emerging mean shape using deterministic annealing and soft-assign. However, in their work, the stability of the registration result is not guaranteed in the case of data with outliers, and hence a good stopping criterion is required. Unlike their approach, we do not need to first solve a correspondence problem in order to subsequently solve a non-rigid registration problem.

The active shape model proposed in [10] utilized points to represent deformable shapes. Their work pioneered the efforts in building point distribution models to understand deformable shapes [10]. Objects are represented as carefully-defined landmark points and variation of shapes are modeled using a principal component analysis. These landmark points are acquired through a more or less manual landmarking process where an expert goes through all the samples to mark corresponding points on each sample. It is a rather tedious process and accuracy is limited. In recent work [11], the authors attempt to overcome this limitation by attempting to automatically solve for the correspondences in a nonrigid setting. The resulting algorithm is very similar to the earlier work in [6] and is restricted to curves.

There are several papers in the point-sets alignment literature which bear close relation to our research reported here. For instance, Tsin and Kanade [12] proposed a kernel correlation based point set registration approach where the cost function is proportional to the correlation of two kernel density estimates. It is similar to our work since we too model each of the point sets by a kernel density function and then quantify the (dis)similarity between them using an information-theoretic measure, followed by an optimization of a (dis)similarity function over a space of coordinate transformations yielding the desired transformation. The difference lies in the fact that JS-divergence used in our work is a lot more general than the information-theoretic measure used in [12], and can be easily extended to multiple point-sets. More recently, in [13], Glaunes et al. convert the point matching problem into an image matching problem by treating points as delta functions. Then they "lift" these delta functions and diffeomorphically match them. The main problem for this technique is that they need a 3D spatial integral which must be numerically computed, while we do not need this due to the empirical computation of the JS-divergence. We will show it in the experimental results that our method, when applied to match point-sets, achieves very good performance in terms of both robustness and accuracy.

2   Methodology

In this section, we present the details of the proposed simultaneous atlas construction and non-rigid registration method. The basic idea is to model each point set by a probability distribution, then quantify the distance between these probability distributions using an information-theoretic measure. The distance measure is optimized over a space of coordinate transformations yielding the desired transformations. We will begin by presenting the finite mixtures used to model the probability distributions of the given point-sets.

2.1   Finite Mixture Models

Considering the point set as a collection of Dirac Delta functions, it is natural to think of a finite mixture model as representation of a point set. As the most frequently used mixture model, a Gaussian mixture [14] is defined as a convex combination of Gaussian component densities.

We use the following notation: The data point-sets are denoted by $\{X^p, p \in \{1, ..., N\}\}$. Each point-set X^p consists of points $\{x_i^p \in \mathcal{R}_D, i \in \{1, ..., n_p\}\}$. To model each point-set as a Gaussian mixture, we define a set of cluster centers, one for each point-set, to serve as the Gaussian mixture centers. Since the feature point-sets are usually highly structured, we can expect them to cluster well. Furthermore we can greatly improve the algorithm efficiency by using limited number of clusters. Note that we can choose the cluster centers to be the point-set itself if the size of point-sets are quite small. The cluster center point-sets are denoted by $\{V^p, p \in \{1, ..., N\}\}$. Each point-set V^p consists of points $\{v_i^p \in \mathcal{R}_D, i \in \{1, ..., K^p\}\}$. Note that there are K^p points in each V^p, and the number of clusters for each point-set may be different (in our implementation, the number of clusters were usually chosen to be proportional to the size of the point-sets). The cluster centers are estimated by using a clustering process over the original sample points x_i^p, and we only need to do this once before the process of joint atlas estimation and point-sets registration. The atlas points-set is denoted by Z. We begin by specifying the density function of each point set.

$$p(X^p|V^p, \alpha^p) = \prod_{i=1}^{n.} \sum_{a=1}^{K^.} \alpha_a^p p(x_i^p|v_a^p) \tag{1}$$

In Equation (1), the occupancy probability which is different for each data point-set is denoted by α^p. $p(X^p|V^p, \alpha^p)$ is a mixture model containing the component densities $p(x_i^p|v_a^p)$, where

$$p(x_i^p | v_a^p) = \frac{1}{(2\pi)^{\frac{1}{2}} \Sigma_a^{\frac{1}{2}}} \exp\left(-\frac{1}{2}(x_i^p - v_a^p)^T \Sigma_a^{-1}(x_i^p - v_a^p)\right) \tag{2}$$

Later, we set the occupancy probability to be uniform and make the covariance matrices Σ_a to be proportional to the identity matrix in order to simplify atlas estimation procedure.

Having specified the Gaussian mixtures of each point-set, we would like to compute a meaningful average/mean (shape) point-set Z, given all the sample sets and their associated distributions. Intuitively, if these point-sets are aligned correctly under appropriate nonrigid deformations, the resulting mixtures should be statistically similar to each other. Consequently, this raises the key question: how to measure the similarity/closeness between these distributions represented by Gaussian mixtures? We will answer this in the following paragraphs.

2.2 Jensen-Shannon Divergence for Learning the Atlas

Jensen-Shannon (JS) divergence, first introduced in [2], serves as a measure of cohesion between multiple probability distributions. It has been used by some researchers as a dissimilarity measure for image registration and retrieval applications [3, 4] with very good results. It has some very desirable properties, to name a few, 1) The square root of JS-divergence (in the case when its parameter is fixed to $\frac{1}{2}$) is a metric [15]; 2) JS-divergence relates to other information-theoretic functionals, such as the relative entropy or the Kullback divergence, and hence it shares their mathematical properties as well as their intuitive appeal; 3) The compared distributions using the JS-divergence can be weighted, which allows one to take into account the different sizes of the point set samples from which the probability distributions are computed; 4) The JS-divergence measure also allows us to have different numbers of cluster centers in each point-set. There is NO requirement that the cluster centers be in correspondence as is required by Chui et al [16]. Given n probability distributions $\mathbf{P_i}$, $i \in \{1, ..., n\}$, the JS-divergence of $\mathbf{P_i}$ is defined by

$$JS_\pi(\mathbf{P_1}, \mathbf{P_2}, ..., \mathbf{P_n}) = H(\sum \pi_i \mathbf{P_i}) - \sum \pi_i H(\mathbf{P_i}) \tag{3}$$

where $\pi = \{\pi_1, \pi_2, ..., \pi_n | \pi_i > 0, \sum \pi_i = 1\}$ are the weights of the probability distributions $\mathbf{P_i}$ and $H(P_i)$ is the Shannon entropy. The two terms on the right hand side of Equation (3) are the entropy of $\mathbf{P} := \sum \pi_i \mathbf{P_i}$ (the π- convex combination of the $\mathbf{P_i}$s) and the same convex combination of the respective entropies.

Assume that each point set X^p is related to Z via a function f^p, μ^p is the set of the transformation parameters associated with each function f^p. To compute the mean shape from these point-sets and register them to the emerging mean shape, we need to recover these transformation parameters to construct the mean shape. This problem can modeled as an optimization problem with the objective function being the JS-divergence between the distributions of the deformed point-sets, represented as $\mathbf{P}_i = p(f^i(X^i))$, the atlas construction problem can now be formulated as,

$$\min_{\mu^{\cdot}} JS_{\beta}(\mathbf{P}_1, \mathbf{P}_2, ..., \mathbf{P}_N) + \lambda \sum_{i=1}^{N} ||Lf^i||^2$$

$$= \min_{\mu^{\cdot}} H(\sum \beta_i \mathbf{P}_i) - \sum \beta_i H(\mathbf{P}_i) + \lambda \sum_{i=1}^{N} ||Lf^i||^2 \qquad (4)$$

In (4), the weight parameter λ is a positive constant the operator L determines the kind of regularization imposed. For example, L could correspond to a thin-plate spline, a Gaussian radial basis function, etc. Each choice of L is in turn related to a kernel and a metric of the deformation from and to Z.

Following the approach in [8], we choose the thin-plate spline (TPS) to represent the non-rigid deformation. Given n control points $\mathbf{x}_1, \ldots, \mathbf{x}_n$ in $\mathbb{R}^d$, a general nonrigid mapping $f : \mathbb{R}^d \rightarrow \mathbb{R}^d$ represented by thin-plate spline can be written analytically as: $f(x) = \mathbf{W}\mathbf{U}(\mathbf{x}) + \mathbf{A}\mathbf{x} + \mathbf{t}$ Here $\mathbf{A}\mathbf{x} + \mathbf{t}$ is the linear part of f. The nonlinear part is determined by a $d \times n$ matrix, $\mathbf{W}$. And $\mathbf{U}(\mathbf{x})$ is an $n \times 1$ vector consisting of n basis functions $U_i(\mathbf{x}) = U(\mathbf{x}, \mathbf{x}_i) = U(||\mathbf{x} - \mathbf{x}_i||)$ where $U(r)$ is the kernel function of thin-plate spline. For example, if the dimension is 2 ($d = 2$) and the regularization functional is defined on the second derivatives of f, we have $U(r) = 1/(8\pi)r^2 ln(r)$.

Therefore, the cost function for non-rigid registration can be formulated as an energy functional in a regularization framework, where the regularization term in equation 4 is governed by the bending energy of the thin-plate spline warping and can be explicitly given by $trace(\mathbf{W}\mathbf{K}\mathbf{W}^T)$ where $\mathbf{K} = (K_{ij})$, $K_{ij} = U(p_i, p_j)$ describes the internal structure of the control point sets. In our experiments, the clusters is used as control points. Other schemes to choose control points may also be considered. Note the linear part can be obtained by an initial affine registration, then an optimization can be performed to find the parameter $\mathbf{W}$.

Having introduced the cost function and the transformation model, now the task is to design an efficient way to estimate empirical JS-divergence from the Gaussian mixtures and derive the analytic gradient of the estimated divergence in order to achieve the optimal solution efficiently.

2.3 Estimating the Empirical JS

For simplicity, we choose $\beta_i = \frac{1}{N}, \forall i = \{1, 2, ..., N\}$. Let $Q_p^{x:} := \sum_{a=1}^{K} \alpha_a^p p(f^j(x_i^j)$ $|f^p(v_a^p))$ be a mixture model containing component densities $p(f^j(x_i^j)|f^p(v_a^p))$,

$$p(f^j(x_i^j)|f^p(v_a^p)) = \frac{1}{(2\pi)^{\frac{\cdot}{2}} \Sigma_a^{\frac{1}{2}}} \exp\left(-\frac{1}{2}(f^j(x_i^j) - f^p(v_a^p))^T \Sigma_a^{-1}(f^j(x_i^j) - f^p(v_a^p))\right) \quad (5)$$

Where $\{\Sigma_a, a \in \{1, ..., K\}\}$ is the set of cluster covariance matrices. For the sake of simplicity and ease of implementation, we assume that the occupancy probabilities are uniform ($\alpha_a^p = \frac{1}{K}$) and the covariance matrices Σ_a are isotropic, diagonal, and identical [$(\Sigma_a = \sigma 2 I_D)$]. Having specified the density function of the data, we can then rewrite Equation (4) as follows,

$$JS_{\beta}(\mathbf{P}_1, \mathbf{P}_2, ..., \mathbf{P}_N) = \frac{1}{N}\Big\{[H(\sum \frac{1}{N}\mathbf{P}_i) - \sum H(\mathbf{P}_1)]$$
$$+ [H(\sum \frac{1}{N}\mathbf{P}_i) - \sum H(\mathbf{P}_2)] + \cdots + [H(\sum \frac{1}{N}\mathbf{P}_i) - \sum H(\mathbf{P}_N)]\Big\} \qquad (6)$$

For each term in the equation, we can estimate the entropy using the weak law of large numbers, which is given by,

$$H(\sum \frac{1}{N}\mathbf{P}_\cdot) - H(\mathbf{P}_\cdot)) = -\frac{1}{n_\cdot}\sum_{\cdot=1} \log \frac{Q_1^{\cdot\cdot} + Q_2^{\cdot\cdot} + ... + Q_\cdot^{\cdot\cdot}}{N} + \frac{1}{n_\cdot}\sum_{\cdot=1}\log Q_\cdot^{\cdot\cdot}$$

(7)

$$= \frac{1}{n_\cdot}\sum_{\cdot=1}\log\frac{NQ_\cdot^{\cdot\cdot}}{Q_1^{\cdot\cdot} + Q_2^{\cdot\cdot} + ... + Q_\cdot^{\cdot\cdot}}$$

Combining these terms we have,

$$JS(\mathbf{P}_1, \mathbf{P}_2, ..., \mathbf{P}_\cdot \ ) = \Big\{\frac{1}{n_1}\sum_{\cdot=1}^{\cdot 1}\log\frac{NQ_1^{\cdot\cdot 1}}{Q_1^{\cdot\cdot 1} + Q_2^{\cdot\cdot 1} + ... + Q_\cdot^{\cdot\cdot 1}}$$

(8)

$$+ \frac{1}{n_2}\sum_{\cdot=1}^{\cdot 2}\log\frac{NQ_2^{\cdot\cdot 2}}{Q_1^{\cdot\cdot 2} + Q_2^{\cdot\cdot 2} + ... + Q_\cdot^{\cdot\cdot 2}} + \cdots + \frac{1}{n_\cdot}\sum_{\cdot=1}\log\frac{NQ_\cdot^{\cdot\cdot}}{Q_1^{\cdot\cdot} + Q_2^{\cdot\cdot} + ... + Q_\cdot^{\cdot\cdot}}\Big\}$$

2.4   Optimizing the Cost Function

Computation of the gradient of the energy function is necessary in the minimization process when employing a gradient-based scheme. If this can be done in analytical form, it leads to an efficient optimization method. We now present the analytic form of the gradient of the JS-divergence (our cost function):

$$\nabla JS = [\frac{\partial JS}{\partial\mu^1}, \frac{\partial JS}{\partial\mu^2}, ..., \frac{\partial JS}{\partial\mu^\cdot}]$$

(9)

Each component of the gradient maybe found by differentiating Eqn (8) with respect to the transformation parameters. In order to compute this gradient, let's first calculate the derivative of $Q_p^{x_\cdot}$ with respect to μ^l,

$$\frac{\partial Q_\cdot^{\cdot\cdot}}{\partial\mu^\cdot} = \begin{cases} \frac{1}{(2\cdot)^{\frac{\cdot}{2}}\cdot 3\cdot}\sum_{\cdot=1} -\exp\big(-\frac{1}{2\cdot^2}|\mathbf{F}_{\cdot\cdot}|^2\big)(\mathbf{F}_{\cdot\cdot}\cdot\frac{\cdots(\cdot\cdot)}{\mu^\cdot}) & \text{if } l = j \neq p \\ \frac{1}{(2\cdot)^{\frac{\cdot}{2}}\cdot 3\cdot}\sum_{\cdot=1}\exp\big(-\frac{1}{2\cdot^2}|\mathbf{F}_{\cdot\cdot}|^2\big)(\mathbf{F}_{\cdot\cdot}\cdot\frac{\cdots(\cdot\cdot)}{\mu^\cdot}) & \text{if } l = p \neq j \\ \frac{1}{(2\cdot)^{\frac{\cdot}{2}}\cdot 3\cdot}\sum_{\cdot=1}\exp\big(-\frac{1}{2\cdot^2}|\mathbf{F}_{\cdot\cdot}|^2\big)(\mathbf{F}_{\cdot\cdot}\cdot[\frac{\cdots(\cdot\cdot)}{\mu^\cdot} - \frac{\cdots(\cdot\cdot)}{\mu^\cdot}] & \text{if } l = p = j \end{cases}$$

(10)

where $\mathbf{F}_{jp} := f^j(x_i^j) - f^p(v_a^p)$. Based on this, it is straight forward to derive the gradient of the JS-divergence with respect to the transformation parameters μ^l, which is given by

$$\frac{\partial JS}{\partial\mu^\cdot} = \Big\{\frac{1}{n_1 N}\sum_{\cdot=1}^{\cdot 1}\Big(\log\frac{Q_1^{\cdot\cdot 1} + Q_2^{\cdot\cdot 1} + ... + Q_\cdot^{\cdot\cdot 1}}{N}\Big)\frac{\partial Q_\cdot^{\cdot\cdot 1}}{\partial\mu^\cdot}$$

(11)

$$+ \frac{1}{n_2 N}\sum_{\cdot=1}^{\cdot 2}\Big(\log\frac{Q_1^{\cdot\cdot 2} + Q_2^{\cdot\cdot 2} + ... + Q_\cdot^{\cdot\cdot 2}}{N}\Big)\frac{\partial Q_\cdot^{\cdot\cdot 2}}{\partial\mu^\cdot} + ...$$

$$+ \frac{1}{n_\cdot N}\sum_{\cdot=1}\Big(\log\frac{Q_1^{\cdot\cdot} + Q_2^{\cdot\cdot} + ... + Q_\cdot^{\cdot\cdot}}{N}\Big)\Big[\frac{\partial Q_1^{\cdot\cdot}}{\partial\mu^\cdot} + ... + \frac{\partial Q_\cdot^{\cdot\cdot}}{\partial\mu^\cdot}\Big] - \frac{1}{n_\cdot}\sum_{\cdot=1}\Big(\log Q_\cdot^{\cdot\cdot}\Big)\frac{\partial Q_\cdot^{\cdot\cdot}}{\partial\mu^\cdot}$$

$$+ ...... + \frac{1}{n_\cdot N}\sum_{\cdot=1}\Big(\log\frac{Q_1^{\cdot\cdot} + Q_2^{\cdot\cdot} + ... + Q_\cdot^{\cdot\cdot}}{N}\Big)\frac{\partial Q_\cdot^{\cdot\cdot}}{\partial\mu^\cdot}\Big\}$$

Since the analytic gradients with respect to these transformation parameters has be explicitly derived in equation (12), we can use them in gradient-based numerical optimization techniques like the Quasi-Newton method and the nonlinear Conjugate-Gradient method to yield a fast solution.

Note that our algorithm can be applied to registration problems other than the atlas construction, e.g. we can apply it to align any two point-sets in 2D or 3D, in this case, there is a model point-set and a scene point-set (N=2). The only modification to the above procedure is to keep the scene point-set fixed and we try to recover the motion from the model point-set to the scene point-set such that the JS-divergence between these two distributions is minimized. We will present experimental results on point-set alignment between two given point-sets as well as atlas construction from multiple point-sets in the next section.

3   Experiment Results

We now present experimental results on the application of our algorithm to both synthetic and real data sets. First, to demonstrate the robustness and accuracy of our algorithm, we show the alignment results by applying the JS-divergence to the point-set matching problem. Then, we will present the atlas construction results in the second part of this section.

3.1   Alignment Results

First, to test the validity of our approach, we perform a set of exact rigid registration experiments on both synthetic and real data sets without noise and outliers. Some examples are shown in Figure 1. The top row shows the registration result for a 2D real range data set of a road (which was also used in Tsin and Kanade's experiments [12]). The figure depicts the real data and the registered (using rigid motion). Top left frame contains two unregistered point sets superposed on each other. Top right frame contains the same point sets after registration using our algorithm. A 3D helix example is presented in the second row (with the same arrangement as the top row). We also tested our method against the KC method [12] and the ICP methods, as expected, our method and

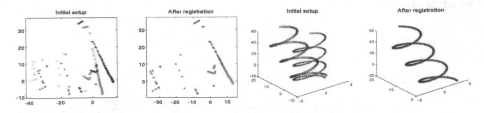

Fig. 1. Results of rigid registration in noiseless case. 'o' and '+' indicate the model and scene points respectively.

KC method exhibit a much wider convergence basin/range than the ICP and both achieve very high accuracy in the noiseless case.

Next, to see how our method behaves in the presence of noise and outliers, we designed the following procedure to generate a corrupted template point set from a model set. For a model set with n points, we control the degree of corruption by (1) discarding a subset of size $(1 - \rho)n$ from the model point set, (2) applying a rigid transformation $(\mathbf{R}, \mathbf{t})$ to the template, (3) perturbing the points of the template with noise (of strength ϵ), and (4) adding $(\tau - \rho)n$ spurious, uniformly distributed points to the template. Thus, after corruption, a template point set will have a total of τn points, of which only ρn correspond to points in the model set. Since ICP is known to be prone to outliers, we only compare our method with the more robust KC method in terms of the sensitivity of noise and outliers. The comparison is done via a set of 2D experiments. *At each of several noise levels and outlier strengths, we generate five models and six corrupted templates from each model for a total of 30 pairs at each noise and outlier strength setting.* For each pair, we use our algorithm and the KC method to estimate the known rigid

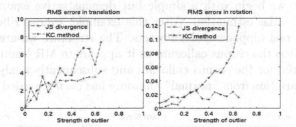

Fig. 2. Robustness to outliers in the presence of large noise. Errors in estimated rigid transform vs. proportion of outliers $((\tau - \rho)/(\rho))$ for both our method and KC method.

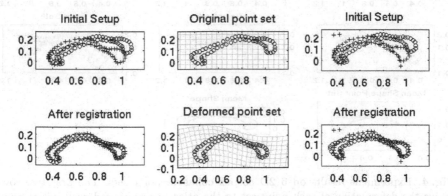

Fig. 3. Nonrigid registration of the corpus callosum data. Left column: two manually segmented corpus callosum slices before and after registration; Middle column: warping of the 2D grid using the recovered motion; Top right: same slices with one corrupted by noise and outliers, before and after registration.

transformation which was partially responsible for the corruption. Results show when the noise level is low, both KC and the presented method have strong resistance to outliers. However, we observe that when the noise level is high, our method exhibits stronger resistance to outliers than the KC method, as shown in Figure 2. We also applied our algorithm to nonrigidly register medical datasets (2D point-sets). Figure 3 depicts some results of our registration method applied to a set of 2D corpus callosum slices with feature points manually extracted by human experts. Registration result is shown in the left column with the warping of 2D grid under the recovered motion which is shown in the middle column. Our non-rigid alignment performs well in the presence of noise and outliers (Figure 3 right column). For the purpose of comparison, we also tested the TPS-RPM program provided in [8] on this data set, and found that TPS-RPM can correctly register the pair without outliers (Figure 3 top left) but failed to match the corrupted pair (Figure 3 top right).

3.2 Atlas Construction Results

In this section, we begin with a simple but demonstrative example of our algorithm for 2D atlas estimation. After this example, we describe a 3D implementations on real hippocampal data sets. The structure we are interested in this experiment is the corpus callosum as it appears in MR brain images. Constructing an atlas for the corpus callosum and subsequently analyzing the individual shape variation from "normal" anatomy has been regarded as potentially

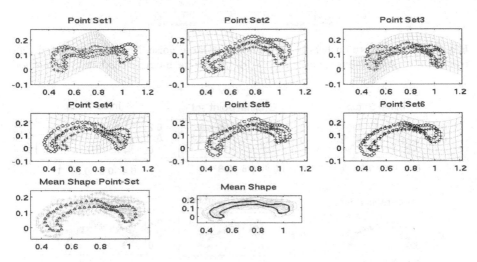

Fig. 4. Experiment results on 6 2D corpus collasum point sets. The first two rows shows the deformation of each point-set to the atlas, superimposed with initial point set (show in 'o') and deformed point-set (shown in '+'). Left image in the third row: The estimated atlas is shown superimposed over all the point-sets. Right: An atlas contour is traced and shown superimposed over all the original contours.

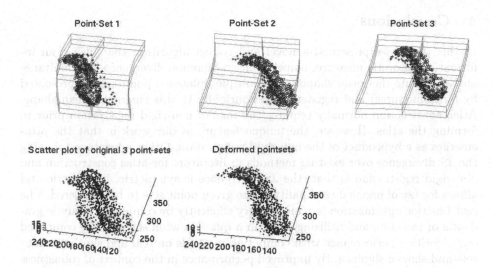

Fig. 5. Atlas construction from three 3D hipcampal point sets. The first row shows the deformation of each point-set to the atlas (represented as cluster centers), superimposed with initial point set (show in 'o') and deformed point-set (shown in '+'). Left image in the second row: Scatter plot of the original three hippocampal point-sets. Right: Scatter plot of all the warped point-sets.

valuable for the study of brain diseases such as agenesis of the corpus callosum(ACC), and fetal alcohol syndrome(FAS).

We manually extracted points on the outer contour of the corpus callosum from six normal subjects, (as shown Figure 4, indicated by "o"). The recovered deformation between each point-set and the mean shape are superimposed on the first two rows in Figure 4. The resulting atlas (mean point-set) is shown in third row of Figure 4, and is superimposed over all the point-sets. As we described earlier, all these results are computed simultaneously and automatically. This example clearly demonstrate that our joint matching and atlas construction algorithm can simultaneously align multiple shapes (modeled by sample point-sets) and compute a meaningful atlas/mean shape.

Next, we present results on 3D hippocampal point-sets. Three 3D point-sets were extracted from epilepsy patients with left anterior temporal lobe foci identified with EEG. An interactive segmentation tool was used to segment the hippocampus in the 3D anatomical brain MRI of the 3 subjects. The point-sets differ in shape, with the number of points $450, 421, 376$ in each point-set respectively. In the first row of Figure 5, the recovered nonrigid deformation between each hippocampal point-set to the atlas is shown along with a superimposition on all of the original data sets. In second row of the Figure 5, we also show the scatter plot of original point-sets along with all the point-sets after the non-rigid warping. An examination of the two scatter plots clearly shows the efficacy of our recovered non-rigid warping. Note that validation of what an atlas shape ought to be in the real data case is not feasible.

4   Conclusions

In this paper, we presented a novel and robust algorithm that utilize an information theoretic measure, namely Jensen-Shannon divergence, to simultaneously compute the mean shape from multiple unlabeled point-sets (represented by finite mixtures) and register them nonrigidly to this emerging mean shape. Atlas construction normally requires the task of non-rigid registration prior to forming the atlas. However, the unique feature of our work is that the atlas emerges as a byproduct of the non-rigid registration. Other advantages of using the JS-divergence over existing methods in literature for atlas construction and non-rigid registration is that, the JS-divergence is symmetric, is a metric and allows for use of unequal cardinality of the given point sets to be registered. The cost function optimization is achieved very efficiently by computing analytic gradients of the same and utilizing them in a quasi-Newton scheme. We compared our algorithm performance with competing methods on real and synthetic data sets and showed significantly improved performance in the context of robustness to noise and outliers in the data. Experiments were depicted with both 2D and 3D point sets from medical and non-medical domains. Our future work will focus on generalizing the non-rigid deformations to diffeomorphic mappings.

References

1. Small, C.: The Statistical theory of shape. Springer, New York (1996)
2. Lin, J.: Divergence measures based on the shannon entropy. IEEE Trans. Infor. Theory **37** (1991) 145–151
3. Hero, A., B. Ma, O.M., Gorman, J.: Applications of entropic spanning graphs. IEEE Trans. Signal Processing **19** (2002) 85–95
4. He, Y., Ben-Hamza, A., Krim, H.: A generalized divergence measure for robust image registration. IEEE Trans. Signal Processing **51** (2003) 1211–1220
5. Klassen, E., Srivastava, A., Mio, W., Joshi, S.H.: Analysis of planar shapes using geodesic paths on shape spaces. IEEE Trans. Pattern Anal. Mach. Intell. **26** (2003) 372–383
6. Tagare, H.: Shape-based nonrigid correspondence with application to heart motion analysis. IEEE Trans. Med. Imaging **18** (1999) 570–579
7. Bookstein, F.L.: Principal warps: Thin-plate splines and the decomposition of deformations. IEEE Trans. Pattern Anal. Mach. Intell. **11** (1989) 567–585
8. Chui, H., Rangarajan, A., Zhang, J., Leonard, C.M.: Unsupervised learning of an atlas from unlabeled point-sets. IEEE Trans. Pattern Anal. Mach. Intell. **26** (2004) 160–172
9. Belongie, S., Malik, J., Puzicha, J.: Shape matching and object recognition using shape contexts. IEEE Trans. Pattern Anal. Mach. Intell. **24** (2002) 509–522
10. Cootes, T.F., Taylor, C.J., Cooper, D.H., Graham, J.: Active shape models: their training and application. Comput. Vis. Image Underst. **61** (1995) 38–59
11. Hill, A., Taylor, C.J., Brett, A.D.: A framework for automatic landmark identification using a new method of nonrigid correspondence. IEEE Trans. Pattern Anal. Mach. Intell. **22** (2000) 241–251
12. Tsin, Y., Kanade, T.: A correlation-based approach to robust point set registration. In: ECCV2004(3). (2004) 558–569

13. Glaunes, J., Trouvé, A., Younes, L.: Diffeomorphic matching of distributions: A new approach for unlabelled point-sets and sub-manifolds matching. In: CVPR2004 (2). (2004) 712–718
14. McLachlan, G., Basford, K.: Mixture Model:Inference and Applications to Clustering. Marcel Dekker, New York (1988)
15. Endres, D.M., Schindelin, J.E.: A new metric for probability distributions. IEEE Trans. Inf. Theory **49** (2003) 1858–60
16. Chui, H., Rangarajan, A.: A new point matching algorithm for non-rigid registration. Computer Vision and Image Understanding (CVIU) **89** (2003) 114–141

Enforcing Temporal Consistency in Real-Time Stereo Estimation

Minglun Gong

Department of Math and Computer Science,
Laurentian University, Sudbury, ON, Canada

Abstract. Real-time stereo matching has many important applications in areas such as robotic navigation and immersive teleconferencing. When processing stereo sequences most existing real-time stereo algorithms calculate disparity maps for different frames independently without considering temporal consistency between adjacent frames. While it is known that temporal consistency information can help to produce better results, there is no efficient way to enforce temporal consistency in real-time applications.

In this paper the temporal correspondences between disparity maps of adjacent frames are modeled using a new concept called disparity flow. A disparity flow map for a given view depicts the 3D motion in the scene that is observed from this view. An algorithm is developed to compute both disparity maps and disparity flow maps in an integrated process. The disparity flow map generated for the current frame is used to predict the disparity map for the next frame and hence, the temporal consistency between the two frames is enforced. All computations are performed in the image space of the given view, leading to an efficient implementation. In addition, most calculations are executed on programmable graphics hardware which further accelerates the processing speed. The current implementation can achieve 89 million disparity estimations per second on an ATI Radeon X800 graphic card. Experimental results on two stereo sequences demonstrate the effectiveness of the algorithm.

1 Introduction

Stereo vision studies how to estimate disparity maps based on spatial correspondences among the input images captured at different views [2, 11]. It has been one of the most actively researched topics in computer vision with a variety of algorithms proposed in the past few years. Some of these have obtained excellent results by casting stereo vision as a global optimization problem and solving it using techniques such as graph cuts [7] and belief propagation [12].

Many applications, including robot navigation and immersive teleconferencing, require disparity maps to be generated in real-time. While global optimization techniques help to produce accurate disparity maps, they generally require long computation time. Most real-time stereo applications today either optimize each pixel locally using a simple winner-take-all (WTA) approach [4, 6, 8, 15-17] or optimize different scanlines separately using dynamic programming [3, 5].

When handling a stereo sequence, the above real-time algorithms process different frames in the sequence independently, without considering the temporal consistency

A. Leonardis, H. Bischof, and A. Pinz (Eds.): ECCV 2006, Part III, LNCS 3953, pp. 564–577, 2006.

between adjacent frames. Previous research has shown that that utilizing temporal consistency information helps to produce better results [1, 13, 18]. However, there is no efficient way to enforce temporal consistency in real-time stereo matching.

In this paper, the temporal consistency between disparity maps of adjacent frames is modeled using a new concept called disparity flow. Disparity flow is defined in the disparity space of a given view and can be considered as view-dependent scene flow [14]. Just as a disparity map is a 2D array of scalars describing the observation of the 3D geometry in the scene from a given view, a disparity flow map is a 2D array of 3D vectors depicting the observation of the 3D motion in the scene from a given view. Since both disparity maps and disparity flow maps are defined in the disparity space, using disparity flow maps to enforce temporal consistency is very efficient.

An algorithm is presented in this paper to compute both disparity maps and disparity flow maps in an integrated process. The disparity flow map obtained for the current frame is used to predict the disparity map for the next frame and hence the temporal consistency between the two frames is enforced. The disparity maps found also provide the spatial correspondence information which is used to cross-validate the disparity flow maps estimated for different views.

All computations involved in the algorithm can be performed in the image space of a given view. This allows for efficient implementation using programmable graphics hardware which further accelerates the processing speed. When handling binocular stereo sequences, the current implementation can produce disparity maps for both views at 17.8 frames per second (fps) on an ATI Radeon X800 graphic card, i.e., about 89 million disparity estimations per second (Mde/s).

1.1 Related Works

Several techniques have been proposed to obtain more accurate disparity maps from stereo sequences by utilizing consistency in the temporal domain [1, 13, 18]. Some of them assume either that the scenes are static/quasi-static or that the motion is negligible compared to the sampling frequency [1, 18]. These approaches can produce accurate disparity maps for static scenes based on stereo sequences captured under varying lighting conditions, but they have difficulty handling dynamic scenes or scenes with constant lighting.

How to enforce temporal consistency for dynamic scenes has been investigated in [9, 13]. In Tao et al.'s approach [13], the input images are segmented into homogeneous color regions and each segment is modeled using a 3D planar surface patch. The projections of a given planar patch on two adjacent frames are related by a temporal homography. The temporal homography, together with the spatial homography, is then used to estimate the parameters of the planar patch. Since their approach is segmentation-based both the accuracy of the results and the processing speed are limited by the image segmentation algorithm used.

Leung et al.'s approach [9] does not require image segmentation. The temporal consistency is enforced by minimizing the difference between the disparity maps of adjacent frames. However, since disparity changes are always penalized, this approach may have difficulties in handling scenes that contain large motions. This approach is also designed for offline processing only — it takes pre-captured stereo sequences as input and calculates the disparity maps for all frames at the same time.

Different from the above approaches, the proposed algorithm models temporal consistency in disparity space using the concept of disparity flow. This makes it possible to enforce temporal consistency in real-time online stereo calculation.

This paper is also related to existing graphics hardware based stereo matching techniques. Modern programmable graphics hardware allows developers to write their own computational kernels that can be executed in parallel on the Graphics Processing Units (GPUs). Several approaches have been proposed to accelerate the stereo matching computation using the processing power of GPUs [5, 15-17]. They typically use the graphics hardware's texture capability to compute the matching costs and then select optimal disparity values for different pixels. In [17], a very high processing speed of 289Mde/s has been achieved on an ATI 9800 card.

The proposed algorithm differs from existing GPU-based stereo approaches in that it estimates both disparity maps and disparity flow maps for the input stereo sequence. The disparity flow maps obtained depict the 3D motion of the scene and are used to enforce temporal consistency between disparity maps of adjacent frames. As yet, there seem to be no published reports on implementing a 3D motion estimation algorithm on the GPU.

2 Definition of Disparity Flow

A disparity flow map is a 2D array of 3D vectors defined on a particular view. Assume that at frame t and under a given view k, a pixel (u,v) has a disparity value d (the disparity can be defined either based on a stereo pair or more generally based on the inverse distance between the corresponding 3D point and the image plane of view k [10]). The triple $<u,v,d>$ is called the disparity space coordinate of the corresponding 3D point at frame t and under view k. Due to the motion of this 3D point, the disparity space coordinate of this point may change to $<u+\Delta u,v+\Delta v,d+\Delta d>$ at frame $t+1$. The difference between the two coordinates, $<\Delta u,\Delta v,\Delta d>$, is defined as the disparity flow of pixel (u,v) at frame t.

The relationships among disparity, disparity flow, and optical flow is illustrated in Fig. 1 using a binocular stereo scenario. Assume that, at time t, a physical point at

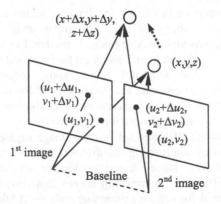

Fig. 1. Disparity flow under a binocular stereo scenario

location (x,y,z) in the scene is observed at pixel (u_1,v_1) in the first image and at pixel (u_2,v_2) in the second image. This point has a 3D motion $(\Delta x,\Delta y,\Delta z)$, which causes optical flows of $(\Delta u_1,\Delta v_1)$ and $(\Delta u_2,\Delta v_2)$ being observed in the two images. Now assume that, when observed from the first view, the disparity of the physical point is d_1 at time t and $d_1+\Delta d_1$ at time $t+1$. When observed from the second view, the disparity of the same point is d_2 and $d_2+\Delta d_2$ for time t and time $t+1$. According to the definition above, the disparity flow of pixel (u_1,v_1) is $<\Delta u_1,\Delta v_1,\Delta d_1>$, and that of pixel (u_2,v_2) is $<\Delta u_2,\Delta v_2,\Delta d_2>$. As a result, the first two coordinates in the disparity flow of a given pixel is simply the optical flow observed at that pixel, while the third coordinate is equal to the change in the corresponding 3D point's disparity value.

2.1 Constraints Between Disparity and Disparity Flow

While the disparity flow map provides temporal correspondences between disparity maps of adjacent frames, the disparity map also provides spatial correspondences between the disparity flow maps of different views. Two additional constraints can be derived based on these relations, which help to produce better disparity and disparity flow maps. In this section, these two constraints are formulated under a rectified left-and-right stereo scenario. It is noteworthy that similar constraints exist for arbitrary stereo pairs, though not in as concise a form.

First, a disparity flow map obtained at a given view can be used to enforce a temporal consistency constraint between the disparity maps of adjacent frames at the same view. Assume that the disparity and the disparity flow found for a given pixel (u,v) at view k are d and $<\Delta u,\Delta v,\Delta d>$, respectively. According to the definition of the disparity flow, this suggests that the corresponding 3D point moves from coordinates $<u,v,d>$ in the disparity space of view k to coordinates $<u+\Delta u,v+\Delta v,d+\Delta d>$. Therefore, the disparity of pixel $(u+\Delta u,v+\Delta v)$ in the next frame should be $d+\Delta d$, i.e., the following temporal consistency constraint holds:

$$\left. \begin{array}{l} D_t(u,v)=d \\ F_t(u,v)=\langle \Delta u,\Delta v,\Delta d \rangle \end{array} \right\} \Rightarrow D_{t+1}(u+\Delta u,v+\Delta v)=d+\Delta d \qquad (1)$$

where $D_t(u,v)$ and $F_t(u,v)$ are the disparity and disparity flow of pixel (u,v) at frame t.

Secondly, a disparity map obtained for a given frame also provides a spatial consistency constraint on disparity flow maps generated at different views for the same frame. As shown in Fig. 1, assume that pixel (u_2,v_2) in the right view is the corresponding pixel of (u_1,v_1) in the left view and that the disparity flows of these two pixels are $<\Delta u_1,\Delta v_1,\Delta d_1>$ and $<\Delta u_2,\Delta v_2,\Delta d_2>$, respectively. Then:

- the epipolar constraint gives:

$$\left. \begin{array}{l} v_1=v_2 \\ v_1+\Delta v_1=v_2+\Delta v_2 \end{array} \right\} \Rightarrow \Delta v_1=\Delta v_2$$

- since the two image planes are coplanar, the distances from the 3D point to both image planes are the same, i.e.:

$$d_1=d_2=d$$
$$\Delta d_1=\Delta d_2=\Delta d$$

- finally, based on the definition of the disparity, the following can be derived:

$$\left.\begin{array}{c} d = u_1 - u_2 \\ d + \Delta d = \left(u_1 + \Delta u_1\right) - \left(u_2 + \Delta u_2\right) \end{array}\right\} \Rightarrow \Delta u_1 = \Delta u_2 + \Delta d$$

Hence, the following spatial consistency constraint can be derived, which specifies the relations between the disparity flow maps for the left and the right views:

$$\left.\begin{array}{c} D^{right}\left(u,v\right) = d \\ \mathbf{F}^{right}\left(u,v\right) = \left\langle \Delta u, \Delta v, \Delta d \right\rangle \end{array}\right\} \Leftrightarrow \left\{\begin{array}{c} D^{left}\left(u+d,v\right) = d \\ \mathbf{F}^{left}\left(u+d,v\right) = \left\langle \Delta u + \Delta d, \Delta v, \Delta d \right\rangle \end{array}\right. \tag{2}$$

where $D^{left/right}(u,v)$ and $\mathbf{F}^{left/right}(u,v)$ are the disparity and disparity flow of pixel (u,v) in the left/right views, respectively.

3 The Proposed Real-Time Stereo Algorithm

In order to derive a simple and efficient algorithm for real-time applications, it is assumed that the input stereo sequences are pre-rectified. In addition, scenes are assumed to be Lambertian so that the constant brightness assumption holds. For simplicity, here the algorithm is discussed under a binocular (left-and-right) stereo setting. As shown in the experiments, when trinocular (left-center-top) stereo sequences are available the algorithm can also make use of the additional view to better solve the visibility problem.

The outline of the presented algorithm is shown in Fig. 2 In the following sections, different stages shown in the figure are discussed in detail.

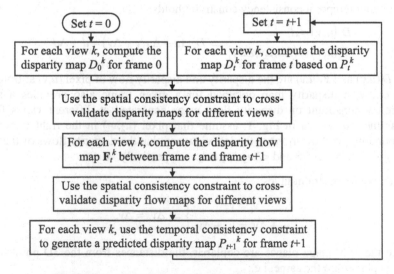

Fig. 2. The outline of the proposed real-time stereo algorithm

3.1 Compute a Disparity Map for the First Frame of Each View

For a given binocular stereo sequence, the algorithm starts by computing the disparity maps for the first frames of both views. Since there is no temporal consistency information available yet, the process used at this step is similar to existing GPU-based stereo algorithms [15-17]. Without losing generality, only the process for the right view in the left-and-right stereo pair is described in detail. This process involves three steps: matching costs calculation, cost aggregation, and disparity optimization.

The first step calculates the costs of assigning different disparity hypotheses to different pixels at the first frame (frame 0) of the right view. The obtained costs form a 3D matrix C_0^{right}, which is often referred as the disparity space. Based on the constant brightness assumption, the cost for each disparity assignment is calculated using the color differences between the corresponding pixels in the two views, i.e.:

$$\mathbf{C}_0^{right}[u,v,d] = \frac{\min\left(\left|I_0^{right}(u,v) - I_0^{left}(u+d,v)\right|, c_{\max}\right)}{c_{\max}}$$

where $I_t^k(u,v)$ is the color of pixel (u,v) at frame t of view k. $c_{\max}$ is a predefined value for maximum matching cost. For color images the average absolute difference among the three color channels is used. The final costs are normalized to the interval [0,1].

In order to achieve real-time performance the above cost calculation is conducted on the GPU. The input stereo images are treated as textures and a pixel shader is used to calculate the cost for different pixels under different disparity hypotheses. To fully utilize the vector processing capacity of the GPU, the pixel shader calculates the matching costs for four different disparity hypotheses in one rendering pass and packs the costs into the four color channels of the rendering target. For efficiency, the results obtained for the four different disparity hypotheses groups are tiled together and kept as a single 2D texture (see Fig. 3 as an example).

In the second step, the matching costs calculated based on a single pixel are propagated to its neighbors. Similar to existing stereo approaches, the shiftable square window is used [11]. The entire aggregation step is implemented on the GPU with four rendering passes involved. The first two rendering passes replace a current cost with the average cost of its local neighbors along horizontal and then vertical directions, which give the effect of mean filtering over a local square window. The next two passes replace a cost with the minimum cost of its local neighbors along horizontal and then vertical directions, which give the effect of a shift filter. In the experiments shown in this paper, 9×9 mean filter and 5×5 shift filter are used.

The third step searches for an optimal disparity map D_0^{right} based on the cost matrix C_0^{right}. To achieve real-time performance the simplest local WTA optimization is used to find the disparity value that gives the smallest matching cost at each pixel in the image. This process requires $D/4$ rendering passes, where D is the total number of disparity hypotheses. The first rendering pass takes the first tile in the 2D texture shown in Fig. 3 as input, computes for different pixels the smallest costs among those for the first four disparity hypotheses, and stores the costs and the corresponding disparity values in the green and red channels of the rendering target respectively. The remaining rendering passes step through other tiles in the texture

Fig. 3. The texture used for representing the 3D disparity space. The matching costs under 40 different disparity hypotheses are encoded using 10 tiles.

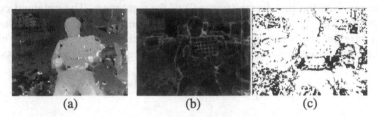

(a)   (b)   (c)

Fig. 4. The texture that encodes the result of disparity computation. The red channel (a) keeps the best disparity hypotheses, the green channel (b) stores the corresponding matching costs, and the blue channel (c) indicates whether the disparity values pass the validation. Image intensity in (a) is adjusted for better visibility.

and update the minimum costs and the best disparity values at different pixels. At the end of the process, the red channel of the output texture holds the disparity maps generated (shown in Fig. 4).

3.2 Cross-Validate Disparity Maps for Different Views

The WTA optimization is efficient but may produce noisy disparity maps. In order to distinguish correct disparity values from potentially incorrect ones, a cross-validation process is implemented to verify the disparity maps generated for the current frame t. According to the spatial consistency constraint (Eq. 2), the disparity value at pixel (u,v) in the right view is considered potentially incorrect if it fails the test below:

$$\left| D_t^{right}(u,v) - D_t^{left}\left(u + D_t^{right}(u,v), v\right) \right| \le 1$$

Please note that the above test condition does not require the corresponding disparity values in the two views to be exactly the same. This is reasonable as the true value normally lies in between two quantized disparity values. Similarly, the disparity map for the left view is validated using the following criteria:

$$\left| D_t^{left}(u,v) - D_t^{right}\left(u - D_t^{left}(u,v), v\right) \right| \le 1$$

The validation process is implemented on the GPU using one rendering pass for each view. When processing view k, the pixel shader takes both disparity maps as input, tests the disparity value of each pixel in view k, and sets the blue channel of each pixel to either '1' or '0' according to whether the corresponding disparity value passes the validation (see Fig. 4 as an example).

3.3 Compute a Disparity Flow Map for Each View

In the next stage, a disparity flow map between frame t and frame $t+1$ is computed for each of the two views. Again, only the process for the right view is described in detail. The one for the left view is similar.

Under the binocular stereo setting, if a pixel (u,v) in the right view has a disparity value of d and a disparity flow of $<\Delta u,\Delta v,\Delta d>$, in the next frame the corresponding 3D point should move to a location that projects to pixel $(u+\Delta u,v+\Delta v)$ in the right view and to pixel $(u+\Delta u+d+\Delta d,v+\Delta v)$ in the left view. Based on the constant brightness assumption, the correct disparity flow for pixel (u,v) should minimize the color difference between $I_t^{right}(u,v)$ and $I_{t+1}^{right}(u+\Delta u,v+\Delta v)$, as well as between $I_t^{right}(u,v)$ and $I_{t+1}^{left}(u+\Delta u+d+\Delta d,v+\Delta v)$. Similar to the disparity map computation process, the costs for assigning different disparity flow hypotheses to different pixels in the frame t of the right view are kept in a 5D matrix $\mathbf{B}_t^{right}$. This 5D matrix is referred as the disparity flow space in this paper and is calculated using:

$$\mathbf{B}_t^{right}[u,v,\Delta u,\Delta v,\Delta d] = \frac{\min\left(\begin{array}{l}\left|I_t^{right}(u,v) - I_{t+1}^{right}(u+\Delta u,v+\Delta v)\right| + \\ \left|I_t^{right}(u,v) - I_{t+1}^{left}(u+\Delta u+D_t^{right}(u,v)+\Delta d,v+\Delta v)\right|\end{array},2c_{max}\right)}{2c_{max}}$$

The above equation is calculated on the GPU using a process similar to the one for computing costs in the disparity space. For efficiency, the costs in the 5D disparity flow space are also packed into a 2D color texture. The color texture contains multiple tiles with each tile keeping the matching costs for all pixels under four different disparity flow hypotheses. Under this packing scheme, costs in a given tile can be calculated using a single rendering pass: the pixel shader takes I_t^{right}, D_t^{right}, I_{t+1}^{right}, and I_{t+1}^{left} as input textures, calculates the matching costs for the current pixel under the four disparity flow hypotheses, and stores the costs into different channels of the rendering target.

The next step is cost aggregation, in which the matching costs are convoluted on the GPU with a 9×9 mean filter, followed by a 5×5 shift filter. The aggregated matching costs are then used for searching optimal disparity flows using a GPU-based local WTA procedure. Similar to the one described in section 0, this procedure takes multiple rendering passes, with each rendering pass handling four disparity flow hypotheses. The output of the procedure is a 2D texture with the minimum matching

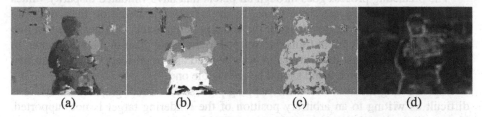

(a)   (b)   (c)   (d)

Fig. 5. The texture that encodes the result of disparity flow computation. The red (a), green (b), and blue (c) channels keep the Δu, Δv, and Δd components of the best disparity flow hypotheses. The alpha channel (d) stores the corresponding matching costs. Image intensities in (a), (b), and (c) are adjusted for better visibility.

cost for each pixel stored in its alpha channel and the three components of the corresponding disparity flow vector encoded in its red, green, and blue channels (see Fig. 5 as an example).

3.4 Cross-Validate Disparity Flow Maps for Different Views

Similar to the case of disparity map computation, the disparity flow maps generated using local WTA approach can be noisy. An additional validation process is used to distinguish correct disparity flows from potentially incorrect ones so that only the former ones are used to enforce the temporal consistency constraint.

Based on the spatial consistency constraint (Eq. 2), the disparity flow found for pixel (u,v) in the right view is considered potentially incorrect if it fails the test below:

$$\mathbf{F}_t^{right}(u,v) = \mathbf{F}_t^{left}\left(u + D_t^{right}(u,v),v\right) - \left\langle \mathbf{F}_t^{right}(u,v)\big|_d,0,0\right\rangle$$

where $\mathbf{F}|_d$ is the Δd component of the disparity flow vector.

Similarly, the disparity flow for the left view is validated using the following criteria:

$$\mathbf{F}_t^{left}(u,v) = \mathbf{F}_t^{right}\left(u - D_t^{left}(u,v),v\right) + \left\langle \mathbf{F}_t^{left}(u,v)\big|_d,0,0\right\rangle$$

The validation process is implemented on the GPU and takes one rendering pass for each view to be validated. The pixel shader takes both disparity flow maps as input textures and tests disparity flows for different pixels of the current view. The output is a copy of the original disparity flow map with information about whether a given disparity value passes the validation stored in the alpha channel of the corresponding pixel.

3.5 Predict a Disparity Map for the Next Frame of Each View

With both disparity maps and disparity flow maps calculated for frame t, it is now possible to predict the disparity maps for frame $t+1$ based on the temporal consistency constraint. For a given view k, the predicted disparity map P_{t+1}^k is calculated from D_t^k and $\mathbf{F}_t^k$ based on Eq. 1. To prevent error propagation, a pixel is used if and only if both the disparity value and the disparity flow found for this pixel are validated, i.e., they pass the corresponding cross-validation processes.

The predicting process goes through all pixels that have validated disparity values and disparity flows, warps these pixels to the next frame based on their disparity flows, and sets the disparity values for the corresponding pixels. It is possible that two or more pixels in the current frame are warped to the same pixel in the next frame. In such a case, the highest disparity value will be used as it represents the 3D point that is the closest to the camera and should be the visible one.

Implementing the above forward mapping process on current graphics hardware is difficult as writing to an arbitrary position of the rendering target is not supported. Hence, this process is implemented using a CPU-based procedure. Since the inputs of the procedure are the disparity map and disparity flow map and the output is a single predicted disparity map, there is very little overhead for transferring data between the system memory and the video memory.

|(a)|(b)|(c)|

Fig. 6. Disparity prediction process: (a) validated disparity map for frame t; (b) validated disparity flow map (Δu channel only) for frame t; (c) predicted disparity map for frame $t+1$. Green color indicates pixels that do not pass the validation.

3.6 Compute Disparity Maps Based on Previous Predictions

When predicted disparity maps are generated by previous calculations, the process used for computing the disparity maps differs slightly from the one described in section 0. When computing D_t^k for each give view k, the new process uses the predicted disparity map P_t^k as a guide so that validated matches found for the previous frame can help to solve ambiguities.

As shown in Fig. 6(c), even though the P_t^k is generated using only validated disparity values and disparity flows found for the previous frame, it may still contain mismatches. Therefore, if all disparity values predicted by P_t^k were selected into D_t^k directly, these mismatches would be propagated over different frames. To prevent error propagation, in the proposed algorithm the predicted disparity values are used to adjust matching costs only. The final disparity value calculated for a given view may differ from the original prediction.

The new disparity map computation process involves four steps: matching cost calculation, cost adjustment, cost aggregation, and disparity optimization. In the first step, a 3D matching cost matrix $\mathbf{C}_t^k$ is initialized based on the tth frames captured at different views. The same GPU-based procedure as the one described in section 0 is used here. The output of the procedure is a 2D texture, shown in Fig. 7(a), encoding the costs calculated.

The second step takes both $\mathbf{C}_t^k$ and P_t^k as input textures and updates the matching cost matrix using the following equation:

$$\mathbf{C}_t^k[u,v,d] = \begin{cases} \mathbf{C}_t^k[u,v,d] \times 3 & \text{If } P_t^k(u,v) \text{ is validated} \wedge P_t^k(u,v) \neq d \\ \mathbf{C}_t^k[u,v,d] & \text{Otherwise} \end{cases}$$

As suggested by the equation, if a disparity value $P_t^k(u,v)$ is predicted for pixel (u,v), the matching costs for all other disparity hypotheses d, $d \neq P_t^k(u,v)$, are tripled. This encourages disparity value $P_t^k(u,v)$ to be selected into the final disparity map D_t^k so that D_t^k is temporally consistent with D_{t-1}^k.

The cost adjustment step is implemented on the GPU using one rendering pass. The output of the shader is a 2D texture that encodes the adjusted matching costs. As shown in Fig. 7(c), the texture that encodes the adjusted matching costs has higher contrast than the one encoding the unadjusted costs. This suggests that there should be fewer ambiguous matches when using the adjusted costs to compute disparity map.

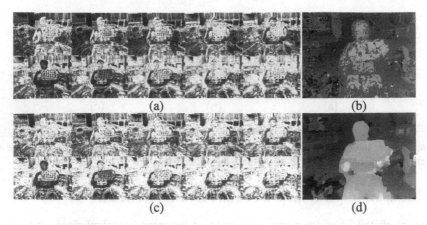

Fig. 7. Stereo matching based on previous prediction: (a) matching costs calculated using input images; (b) previous disparity map prediction P_t^k (the same image as Fig. 6(c)); (c) adjusted matching cost based on P_t^k; (d) the final disparity map D_t^k, in which many incorrect predictions shown in P_t^k are corrected

In the next two steps, the adjusted matching costs are aggregated before they are used for computing the disparity map. The same GPU-based procedures as the ones described in section 0 are used in these two steps. As shown in Fig. 7(d), since the disparity optimization step is based on the aggregated matching costs, isolated noise in the predicted disparity maps is corrected.

4   Experimental Results

The algorithm presented in this paper is tested using a variety of stereo sequences. Due to the space limits, only the results for two sequences are shown here. The first one is a color sequence captured using PointGrey's Bumblebee stereo camera; while the second one is a grayscale sequence captured using PointGrey's Digiclops camera. Both sequences are captured at 512×384 resolution, but are cropped and downsampled to 288×216 to focus on the moving persons as well as to remove the black border and oversampling caused by the rectification process. As shown in Fig. 8(a), both sequences are challenging due to the existence of textureless surfaces (whiteboard in both scenes), non-Lambertian reflection (highlighted background wall in the first scene and floor in the second scene), and areas with periodic textures (checkerboard pattern in the second scene).

The algorithm is configured to use the same set of parameters for both sequences. The disparity computation process considers 40 different disparity hypotheses. The search range for the disparity flow computation is set to [-4,4] for both horizontal and vertical directions, but is set to [-1,1] for the disparity direction since the motion along the disparity direction is much smaller. As a result, the total number of disparity flow hypotheses is 243.

As shown in Fig. 8(b), for both sequences the disparity maps generated using only the 15th frames captured at different views are quite noisy. Many mismatches are

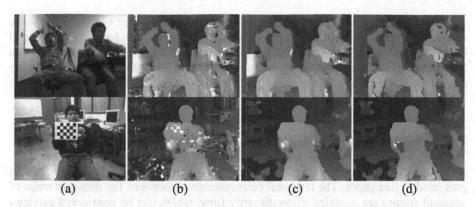

Fig. 8. Results comparison on the 15th frames of both sequences: (a) source images; (b) disparity maps generated without enforcing temporal consistency constraint; (c) disparity maps generated with temporal consistency constraint enforced; (d) cross-validated disparity maps using spatial consistency constraint

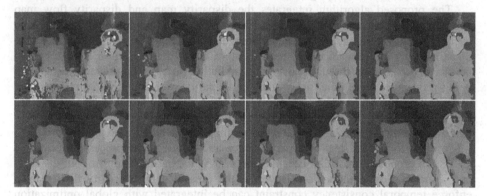

Fig. 9. Semi-dense disparity maps generated for the first eight frames in the binocular sequence. As more frames became available, there are fewer mismatches caused by ambiguities and fewer pixels with unvalidated disparities as well.

caused by ambiguities such as in the area of the checkerboard pattern in the second scene. Enforcing temporal consistency constraint helps to remove these mismatches. The disparity flows obtained, shown in Fig. 8(c), are much smoother and appear mostly accurate. Most of the remaining errors are caused by occlusions, which are filtered out in the semi-dense disparity maps obtained after the cross-validation process (shown in Fig. 8(d)). It is noteworthy that there are considerably fewer mismatches caused by occlusions in the results generated for the trinocular sequence as the algorithm can utilize the additional view to solve occlusions.

A screen captured animation is submitted with the paper. The animation compares the disparity sequences generated using both the single frame approach and the proposed approach. The latter shows noticeable improvements in temporal consistency. At the beginning of the animation one can also observe how mismatches are gradually removed from the estimation results as more frames become available (see Fig. 9 as an example).

In terms of the processing speed, testing shows that, for the binocular sequence above, the current implementation can generate disparity maps for both the left and the right views at 17.8 fps on a 3GHz P4 computer equipped with an ATI Radeon X800 card. This means that the algorithm can perform 89M disparity evaluations per second. It is worth noting that the disparity flow maps for the two views are also generated at the same time.

5 Conclusions

A real-time stereo matching algorithm that enforces temporal consistency constraint is presented in this paper. The temporal correspondences between the disparity maps of adjacent frames are modeled using disparity flow, which can be considered as view-dependent scene flow. The concept of disparity flow provides simple and efficient ways to enforce temporal consistency between disparity maps generated for the adjacent frames at the same view, as well as to cross-validate the spatial consistency between disparity flow maps generated for the same frame at different views.

The proposed algorithm integrates the disparity map and disparity flow map computations in an integrated process. As a result, both computations benefit from each other. In particular, when generating disparity map for the next frame, the disparity flow map obtained for the current frame is used to enforce the temporal consistency constraint through a disparity predicting process. To prevent mismatches being propagated over time, only validated disparity values and disparity flows are used in the disparity predicting process. Furthermore, the predicted disparity values are used to guide the disparity computation through the cost adjustment process instead of being used directly in the disparity map for the next frame.

In order to achieve real-time performance and to utilize the processing power of GPUs the proposed algorithm uses the simplest WTA optimization in both disparity and disparity flow computation. However, the idea of using disparity flow map to enforce temporal consistency constraint can be integrated with global optimization techniques as well. The resulting algorithm will be able to produce temporally consistent disparity maps for stereo sequences though not at real time speed.

Acknowledgements

The author would like to thank Mr. Cheng Lei and Mr. Liang Wang for capturing the stereo sequences used in this paper. This research is supported by NSERC and Laurentian University.

References

1. Davis, J., Nehab, D., Ramamoothi, R., and Rusinkiewicz, S.: Spacetime stereo: a unifying framework for depth from triangulation. *IEEE Transactions on Pattern Analysis and Machine Intelligence.* **27** (2005)
2. Dhond, U. R. and Aggarwal, J. K.: Structure from stereo - A review. *IEEE Transactions on Systems, Man and Cybernetics.* **19** (1989) 1489-1510.

3. Forstmann, S., Ohya, J., Kanou, Y., Schmitt, A., and Thuering, S.: Real-time stereo by using dynamic programming. *Proc. CVPR Workshop on Real-time 3D Sensors and Their Use*. Washington, DC, USA. (2004) 29-36.
4. Gong, M. and Yang, R.: Image-gradient-guided real-time stereo on graphics hardware. *Proc. International Conference on 3-D Digital Imaging and Modeling*. Ottawa, ON, Canada. (2005) 548-555.
5. Gong, M. and Yang, Y.-H.: Near real-time reliable stereo matching using programmable graphics hardware. *Proc. IEEE Conference on Computer Vision and Pattern Recognition*. San Diego, CA, USA. (2005) 924-931.
6. Hirschmuller, H., Innocent, P. R., and Garibaldi, J.: Real-time correlation-based stereo vision with reduced border errors. *International Journal of Computer Vision*. **47** (2002)
7. Hong, L. and Chen, G.: Segment-based stereo matching using graph cuts. *Proc. IEEE Conference on Computer Vision and Pattern Recognition*. Washington, DC, USA. (2004) 74-81.
8. Kanade, T., Yoshida, A., Oda, K., Kano, H., and Tanaka, M.: A stereo engine for video-rate dense depth mapping and its new applications. *Proc. IEEE Conference on Computer Vision and Pattern Recognition*. (1996) 196-202.
9. Leung, C., Appleton, B., Lovell, B. C., and Sun, C.: An energy minimisation approach to stereo-temporal dense reconstruction. *Proc. International Conference on Pattern Recognition*. Cambridge, UK. (2004) 72-75.
10. Okutomi, M. and Kanade, T.: A multiple-baseline stereo. *IEEE Transactions on Pattern Analysis and Machine Intelligence*. **15** (1993) 353-363.
11. Scharstein, D. and Szeliski, R.: A taxonomy and evaluation of dense two-frame stereo correspondence algorithms. *International Journal of Computer Vision*. **47** (2002) 7-42.
12. Sun, J., Li, Y., Kang, S. B., and Shum, H.-Y.: Symmetric stereo matching for occlusion handling. *Proc. IEEE Conference on Computer Vision and Pattern Recognition*. San Diego, CA, USA. (2005) 399-406.
13. Tao, H., Sawhney, H. S., and Kumar, R.: Dynamic depth recovery from multiple synchronized video streams. *Proc. IEEE Conference on Computer Vision and Pattern Recognition*. Kauai, Hawaii, USA. (2001)
14. Vedula, S., Baker, S., Rander, P., Collins, R., and Kanade, T.: Three-dimensional scene flow. *Proc. International Conference on Computer Vision*. (1999)
15. Woetzel, J. and Koch, R.: Real-time multi-stereo depth estimation on GPU with approximative discontinuity handling. *Proc. European Conference on Visual Media Production*. London, United Kingdom. (2004)
16. Yang, R. and Pollefeys, M.: Multi-resolution real-time stereo on commodity graphics hardware. *Proc. IEEE Conference on Computer Vision and Pattern Recognition*. Madison, WI, USA. (2003) 211-220.
17. Yang, R., Pollefeys, M., and Li, S.: Improved real-time stereo on commodity graphics hardware. *Proc. CVPR Workshop on Real-time 3D Sensors and Their Use*. Washington, DC, USA. (2004)
18. Zhang, L., Curless, B., and Seitz, S. M.: Spacetime stereo: shape recovery for dynamic scenes. *Proc. IEEE Conference on Computer Vision and Pattern Recognition*. Madison, WI, USA. (2003) 367-374.

The Alignment Between 3-D Data and Articulated Shapes with Bending Surfaces

Guillaume Dewaele, Frédéric Devernay, Radu Horaud, and Florence Forbes

INRIA Rhône-Alpes, 655, avenue de l'Europe,
38330 Montbonnot Saint-Martin, France

Abstract. In this paper we address the problem of aligning 3-D data with articulated shapes. This problem resides at the core of many motion tracking methods with applications in human motion capture, action recognition, medical-image analysis, etc. We describe an articulated and bending surface representation well suited for this task as well as a method which aligns (or registers) such a surface to 3-D data. Articulated objects, e.g., humans and animals, are covered with clothes and skin which may be seen as textured surfaces. These surfaces are both articulated and deformable and one realistic way to model them is to assume that they bend in the neighborhood of the shape's joints. We will introduce a surface-bending model as a function of the articulated-motion parameters. This combined articulated-motion and surface-bending model better predicts the observed phenomena in the data and therefore is well suited for surface registration. Given a set of sparse 3-D data (gathered with a stereo camera pair) and a textured, articulated, and bending surface, we describe a register-and-fit method that proceeds as follows. First, the data-to-surface registration problem is formalized as a classifier and is carried out using an EM algorithm. Second, the data-to-surface fitting problem is carried out by minimizing the distance from the registered data points to the surface over the joint variables. In order to illustrate the method we applied it to the problem of hand tracking. A hand model with 27 degrees of freedom is successfully registered and fitted to a sequence of 3-D data points gathered with a stereo camera pair.

1 Introduction

In this paper we address the problem of aligning 3-D data to articulated shapes. This problem resides at the core of a variety of methods, including object localization, tracking, e.g., human-body motion capture, model-to-data registration, etc. The problem is difficult for a number of reasons. First of all, there is a lack of a general framework for representing large varieties of objects, such as humans and their body parts, animals, etc. Second it is difficult to predict the appearance of such objects such that the tasks of identifying them in images and of locating them become tractable. Third, since they have a large number of degrees of freedom, the problem of estimating their pose is confronted with a difficult optimization problem that can be trapped in local minima.

A. Leonardis, H. Bischof, and A. Pinz (Eds.): ECCV 2006, Part III, LNCS 3953, pp. 578–591, 2006.
© Springer-Verlag Berlin Heidelberg 2006

A first class of methods addresses the problem of articulated object tracking [1]. A human motion tracker, for example, uses a previously estimated pose as a prior to predict the current pose and to update the model's parameters [2], [3], [4], [5], [6]. Objects may have large motion amplitudes between two video frames and their aspect may drastically change as one body part is occluded by another one or when it turns away from the camera's field of view [7], [8]. Image data are often ambiguous and it is not easy to separate the tracked object from the background or from other moving objects.

A second class of methods addresses the problem of aligning (or registering) a point data set to a rigid or a deformable object. The data may lie at some distance from the object and the shape of the object may change over time. There are two classes of techniques available for solving this problem. The first class describes the object as a point data set and estimates the motion parameters using point-to-point assignments [9]. This type of methods works well provided that point-assignments (that may well be viewed as *hidden variables*) are properly established. The second class of techniques describes the object as a parameterized surface (or a curve) and fits the latter to the data [10], [2], [3]. This type of methods works well provided that the data are not too far from the object, that the data are evenly distributed around the object and that they are not corrupted by large-amplitude noise or outliers. Indeed, the distance from a datum to a surface (whether algebraic or Euclidean) is a non-linear function of the model's parameters and the associated non-linear optimization problem does not have a trivial solution.

In this paper we address both object tracking and object registration. One one side we consider a 3-D point data set, e.g., data gathered with a stereo camera pair. On the other side we consider articulated objects with their associated surface and we assume that this surface is textured. The surface itself is parameterized by the joint parameters associated with an underlying kinematic chain. The texture points are loosely attached to the kinematic chain such that when the surface bends, the texture points slightly *slide* along the surface. The amount of sliding is controlled by a set of *bending parameters* such that the texture sliding is proportional to the amount of surface bending.

We introduce an align and fit method that proceeds as follows. *Alignment*: The data points are associated with texture points. This point-to-point assignment is modelled as a classification problem. The texture points are viewed as classes and each data point is assigned to one of these classes. Data classification is carried out by an EM algorithm that performs three tasks: it classifies the points, it rejects outliers, and it estimates the joint parameters. *Fit*: The surface is fitted to the registered data points by minimizing a distance function over the joint parameters. An example is shown on Figure 1.

The methodology described in this paper has several contributions. We introduce an object representation framework that is well suited for describing articulated shapes with bending surfaces. We cast the data-to-model association problem into a classification problem. We show that it is more judicious, both from theoretical and practical points of view, to allow for one-to-many data-to-model

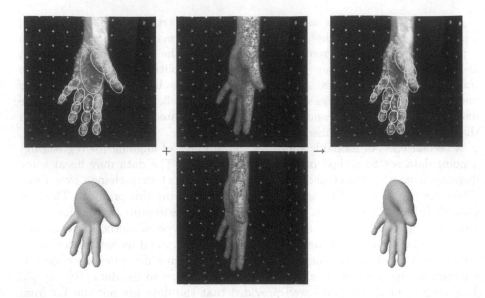

Fig. 1. This figure illustrates the alignment method described in this paper. *Left:* The articulated model (texture and surface) shown in its previously estimated pose, *Middle:* a set of 3-D data points obtained by stereo, and *Right:* the result of aligning the data (middle) with the model (left).

assignments, rather than pair-wise assignments, as is usually the case with most existing methods. We combine the advantages of point registration and of parameterized surface fitting. We emphasize that the *point-to-surface alignment* problem has primarily been addressed in the case of rigid and deformable objects, and has barely been considered in the case of articulated objects.

The idea of approximatively matching sets of points stems from [11]. [12]. These same authors propose a point matching algorithm able to deal with outliers [13]. However, they constrain the points to be assigned pair-wise which leads to some difficulties, as explained in section 4. The idea of using the EM algorithm [14] for solving the point matching problem was used by others [15], [16], [17]. However, previous work did not attempt to with articulated shapes. Moreover, the prolem of outlier rejection is not handled by their EM algorithms.

The remainder of this paper is organized as follows. Section 2 describes the articulated and bending surface model. Section 3 is a detailed account of the point-to-surface alignment method. In section 4, we compare our method with other similar methods and section 5 describes experiments performed with a 3-D hand tracker.

2   Articulated Shapes with Bending Surfaces

The object model that will be used throughout the paper has three main components:

- It has one or several kinematic chains linked to a common part, i.e., a base part. The kinematic joints are the model's parameters;
- A volumetric representation that describes the shape of each part of the kinematic chain as well as a surface embedding the whole object, and
- a texture that is described by a set of points loosely attached to the underlying surface, i.e., the texture is allowed to slide in the neighbourhood of the kinematic joints where the surface bends.

The kinematic model. A kinematic chain consists in P elementary parts which are referred by $Q_1...Q_P$ in this paper. These parts are linked by rotational joints. The motion of this chain can be described by a set of K parameters, one for each degree of freedom, $\Theta = \{\theta_1, ..., \theta_K\}$. The first six parameters will correspond to the 3-D position and orientation of the chain's base-part, and the remaining parameters correspond to the joints angles. The position and orientation of each part Q_p is therefore determined by by Θ. The kinematically-constrained motion of such a multi-chain articulated structure is conveniently described by the rigid motions, $T_p(\Theta)$, of its parts.

A hand, for example, can be described with 5 such kinematic chains, and a total of 16 parts and 27 degrees of freedom. The base-part (the palm) has six degrees of freedom which correspond to the free motion of the hand. There are five degrees of freedom for the thumb and four degrees of freedom for the other fingers. The thumb has two joints with two rotational degrees of freedom and one joint with one degree of freedom, while the other fingers have one joint with two degrees of freedom and two joints with one degree of freedom.

The 3-D shape model. We will associate a rigid shape to each elementary part Q_p of the kinematic chain. In principle, it is possible to use a large variety of shapes, such as truncated cylinders or cones, quadrics, superquadrics, and so forth. One needs to have in mind that it is important to efficiently compute the distance $d(\mathbf{X}, Q_p)$ from a point $\mathbf{X}$ to such a part.

In order to obtain a single and continuous surface describing the whole object, we will fuse these parts into a single one using isosurfaces. Isosurfaces are a very useful tool to create complex shapes, such as human-body parts, and have already been used in computer vision [10, 2]. To build this isosurface we will first associate a field function ϕ_p to each part Q_p of the model:

$$\phi_p(\mathbf{X}) = e^{-\frac{\cdot (\mathbf{X} \cdot Q \cdot)}{\cdot}} \tag{1}$$

The surface associated to the part Q_p can be described by the implicit equation $\phi_p(\mathbf{X}) = 1$. The fusion of the parts Q_p is obtained simply by summing up the field functions in one single field function $\phi(\mathbf{X}) = \sum_p \phi_p(\mathbf{X})$, and by considering the surface S defined by $\phi(\mathbf{X}) = 1$. The coefficient ν allows some amount of control of the fusion. In practice the summation will not be carried out over all the elements Q_p. Indeed, a blind summation over all the elementary parts will have the tendency to fuse them whenever they are close to each other, even if they are not adjacent within the kinematic chain. For example, one doesn't want two touching fingers to be glued together. To prevent this effect, whenever we determine the field at a surface point $\mathbf{X}$, e.g., $\phi(\mathbf{X})$, we look for the part $\mathcal{Q}_p$ that corresponds to the most important contribution $\phi_p(\mathbf{X})$, and we only consider the contribution of this part and the adjacent parts in the kinematic chain.

The distance between a point $\mathbf{X}$ and a part $\mathcal{Q}_p$ is evaluated through the formula $d(\mathbf{X}, \mathcal{Q}_p) = -\nu \, log(\phi_p(\mathbf{X}))$ Similarly, the distance from a point $\mathbf{X}$ to the isosurface $\mathcal{S}$ will be evaluated through the formula:

$$d(\mathbf{X}, \Theta) = -\nu \, log(\phi(\mathbf{X})) \qquad (2)$$

This distance depends on the position of the point $\mathbf{X}$ and on the parameters $\Theta = \{\theta_k\}_{1 \leq k \leq K}$. For points close to the surface one may take the first order Taylor expansion of the above expression, so that the quantity $-\nu(\phi_p(\mathbf{X}) - 1)$ is a good approximation of $d(\mathbf{X}, \Theta)$.

The hand model uses ellipsoids as basic volumes to describe each part. Ellipsoids are relatively simple objects and correspond quite precisely to the shape of the fingers' phalanxes. To estimate the distance from a point to an ellipsoid, one may use the algebraic distance, i.e., the quadratic form $\mathbf{X}^\top \mathcal{Q}_p \mathbf{X}$. Estimation of the Euclidean distance from a point to an ellipsoid requires to solve for a six degree polynomial. In practice we will use a pseudo-Euclidean distance which is more efficiently computed than the Euclidean distance, [7]. Finally, by fusing these ellipsoids together, we are able to build a realistic model of the hand.

Modelling bending surfaces. The description detailed so far yields a surface model that is parameterized by the kinematic-joint parameters. Nevertheless, this model contains no information about how to control the non-rigid behaviour of the texture lying onto the object's surface, when the joint parameters vary. Consider again the case of the hand. In between two phalanxes the skin will stretch on one side of the finger and will be compressed on the opposite side. In other terms, the skin will slide along the underlying bones whenever the finger is bent. This is a non-rigid motion and therefore this phenomenon will not be properly modelled if surface points are rigidly attached to a part $\mathcal{Q}_p$. We will use an approach similar to skinning techniques in graphics.

The motion of a point $\mathbf{X}$, that lies nearby the surface of the object, is modelled as a linear combination of the rigid motions T_p and T_r of two adjacent parts $\mathcal{Q}_p$ and $\mathcal{Q}_r$; We will use the field function $\phi_p(\mathbf{X_i})$ for weighting the contributions of these two motions:

$$\mathcal{T}(\mathbf{X}, \Theta) = \frac{(\phi_p(\mathbf{X}, \Theta))^a T_p(\Theta)\mathbf{X} + (\phi_r(\mathbf{X}, \Theta))^a T_r(\Theta)\mathbf{X}}{(\phi_p(\mathbf{X}, \Theta))^a + (\phi_r(\mathbf{X}, \Theta))^a} \qquad (3)$$

The parameter a allows to adjust the sliding when the distances to both $\mathcal{Q}_p$ and $\mathcal{Q}_r$ are of comparable value. A small value for a yields a nicely interpolated motion while the points remain attached to either $\mathcal{Q}_p$ or to $\mathcal{Q}_r$ for a large a. A few examples of how the sliding is controlled in this way are shown on figure 2. For the hand, we use $a = 2$.

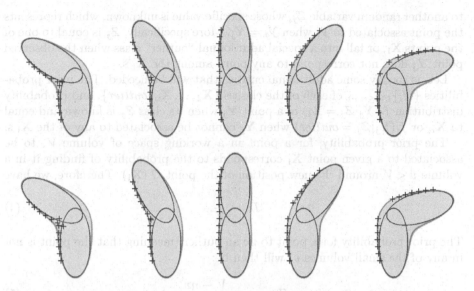

Fig. 2. The sliding of the texture onto a bending surface is controlled by the parameter a. For $a = 2$ (top) the texture nicely compresses and streches when the surface bends. For $a = 10$ (bottom) the texture is rigidly attached to the nearest rigid part.

3   3-D Point-to-Surface Alignment

The input data of our method consist in 3-D points extracted at time t and we denote these points by $\{\mathbf{Y_j}\}_{1 \leq j \leq m}$. The input model consists in an articulated surface. We want to estimate the articulated motion of this surface from its pose at time $t - dt$ to the its pose at time t. Moreover, the surface has a texture associated with it and the latter is desribed as a set of 3-D points that we denote by $\{\mathbf{X_i}\}_{1 \leq i \leq n}$. These points correspond to data points that were correctly fitted to the surface at $t - dt$, i.e., the distance from eachone of these points to the surface falls below a threshold ε. The latter depends on the accuracy with which one wants to estimate the motion parameters, the accuracy of the data, and the accuracy of the model. For the hand-tracking experiments we use $\varepsilon = 5mm$.

3.1   3-D Point Matching Via Classification

Given a set of *model* points $\{\mathbf{X_i}\}_{1 \leq i \leq n}$ and a set of *data* points $\{\mathbf{Y_j}\}_{1 \leq j \leq m}$, the goal is to estimate the transformation $\mathcal{T}$. Therefore, one needs to find correspondences between the priors and the candidates. This is known in statistics as a *missing data problem* that can be formulated as a classification problem. Each point $\mathbf{Y_j}$ should be either associated to one (or several) of the points $\mathbf{X_i}$, or be rejected as an outlier. Therefore, the $\mathbf{X_i}$'s can be seen as classes into which the $\mathbf{Y_j}$'s have to be classified or thrown out.

To recast the problem in a statistical framework, the $\{\mathbf{Y_j}\}_{1 \leq j \leq m}$ are the observed values of a set of random variables $\{\mathcal{Y}_j\}_{1 \leq j \leq m}$. Each $\mathcal{Y}_j$ is associated to another random variable $\mathcal{Z}_j$, whose specific value is unknown, which represents the point associated to $\mathcal{Y}_j$ when $\mathcal{Y}_j = \mathbf{Y_j}$. More specifically, $\mathcal{Z}_j$ is equal to one of the points $\mathbf{X_i}$, or fall into a special additionnal "outlier" class when the observed point $\mathbf{Y_j}$ does not correspond to any point among the $\mathbf{X_i}$'s.

Let us specify some additionnal entities that will be needed. The prior probabilities $\{\Pi_i\}_{1 \le i \le n+1}$ of each of the classes $\{\mathbf{X_1}, ..., \mathbf{X_n}, outlier\}$, and probability distribution $f_j(\mathbf{Y_j}|\mathcal{Z}_j = \mathbf{X_i})$ of a point $\mathbf{Y_j}$ when its class $\mathcal{Z}_j$ is known and equal to $\mathbf{X_i}$, or $f_j(\mathbf{Y_j}|\mathcal{Z}_j = outlier)$ when $\mathbf{Y_j}$ cannot be associated to any of the $\mathbf{X_i}$'s.

The prior probability, for a point in a working space of volume V, to be associated to a given point $\mathbf{X_i}$ corresponds to the probability of finding it in a volume $v < V$ around the new position of the point, $\mathcal{T}(\mathbf{X_i})$. Therefore, we have

$$\Pi_i = \frac{v}{V}. \tag{4}$$

The prior probability for a point to be an outlier (meaning that the point is not in any of the small volumes v) will then be:

$$\Pi_{outlier} = \frac{V - nv}{V}. \tag{5}$$

The probability distribution for $\mathcal{Y}_j$ can also be written quite easily. If this point $\mathcal{Y}_j$ corresponds to a point $\mathbf{X_i}$, its position $\mathbf{Y_j}$ should be close to the new position of this point (after the motion), $\mathcal{T}(\mathbf{X_i})$. We will choose a Gaussian distribution $\mathcal{N}$, centered in $\mathcal{T}(\mathbf{X_i})$ with variance σ^2:

$$f_j(\mathbf{Y_j}|\mathcal{Z}_j = \mathbf{X_i}) = \mathcal{N}(\mathbf{Y_j}; \mathcal{T}(\mathbf{X_i}), \sigma^2) \tag{6}$$

If the point $\mathcal{Y}_j$ is an outlier, this probability distribution should be uniform over the working space. So, if V is the volume of the working space,

$$\forall\, \mathbf{Y_j} \in V, \; f_j(\mathbf{Y_j}|\mathcal{Z}_j = outlier) = \frac{1}{V} \tag{7}$$

Using Bayes' formula, we can then write the distribution of the random variable $\mathcal{Y}_j$, which is :

$$f_j(\mathbf{Y_j}) = \sum_{i=1}^{n} \Pi_i\, f_j(\mathbf{Y_j}|\mathcal{Z_j} = \mathbf{X_i}) + \Pi_{outlier}\, f_j(\mathbf{Y_j}|\mathcal{Z_j} = outlier) \tag{8}$$

or, by specifying the different terms,

$$f_j(\mathbf{Y_j}) = \sum_{i=1}^{n} \frac{v}{V}\, \mathcal{N}(\mathbf{Y_j}; \mathcal{T}(\mathbf{X_i}), \sigma^2) + \frac{V - nv}{V^2} \tag{9}$$

For the volume v, we will use a sphere of radius σ, so that we have $v = 4\pi\sigma^3/3$. We can choose a working space large enough so that the quantity nv is negligeable when compared to V. We will use this remark later for simplification.

3.2   A Robust EM Algorithm

To simplify the notations, we will denote by Ψ the set of unknown parameters, i.e., the joint variables Θ defining the transformation T and the variance σ. We seek the parameters Ψ which maximize the likelihood $\mathcal{P}(\mathbf{Y}|\Psi)$, where the $\mathbf{Y_j}$'s are the measured positions of the points $\{\mathcal{Y}_j\}_{1 \leq j \leq m}$.

Due to the unknowns $\mathcal{Z}_j$, this is a *missing data problem* and the EM algorithm will be used. In addition of providing estimates of Ψ, the algorithm will provide values for the unknown $\mathcal{Z}_j$'s. We will use the following notation:

$$\alpha_{i,j} = \mathcal{P}(\mathcal{Z}_j = \mathbf{X_i}|\mathbf{Y}, \Psi) \tag{10}$$

Therefore, $\alpha_{i,j}$ denotes the probability that the class $\mathcal{Z}_j$ of the observed point $\mathbf{Y_j}$ corresponds to the prior point $\mathbf{X_i}$.

Starting with an initial guess Ψ^0, the EM algorithm proceeds iteratively and the iteration q consists in searching for the parameters Ψ that maximize the following term:

$$Q(\Psi|\Psi^q) = E \left[log(\mathcal{P}(\mathbf{Y}, \mathcal{Z}|\Psi)) \mid \mathbf{Y}, \Psi^q \right] \tag{11}$$

where Ψ^q is the prior estimation of Ψ available at the current iteration q. The expectation is taken over all the values of $\mathcal{Z}$, thus taking into account all possible values of the $\mathcal{Z}_j$'s. This process will be iterated until convergence. We will first develop $Q(\Psi|\Psi^q)$ for the distributions (6) and (7) that we defined in the previous section. First, one can write that:

$$\mathcal{P}(\mathbf{Y}, \mathcal{Z}|\Psi) = \prod_{j=1}^{m} \left(\prod_{i=1}^{n} (\Pi_i f_j(\mathbf{Y_j}|\mathcal{Z}_j = \mathbf{X_i}, T, \sigma))^{\delta_{\{\mathcal{Z}_j = \mathbf{X_i}\}}} \right. $$
$$\left. \times \ (\Pi_{outlier} f_j(\mathbf{Y_j}|\mathcal{Z}_j = outlier))^{\delta_{\{\mathcal{Z}_j = \cdots \cdots\}}} \right) \tag{12}$$

where $\delta_{\{\mathcal{Z}_j = \mathbf{X_i}\}}$ (resp. $\delta_{\{\mathcal{Z}_j = outlier\}}$) equals 1 when the class $\mathcal{Z}_j$ of the point $\mathcal{Y}_j$ is $\mathbf{X_i}$ (resp. is an outlier), and 0 otherwise. Note that in the second product, all terms but one are equal to 1. Therefore, we have:

$$log\left(\mathcal{P}(\mathbf{Y}, \mathcal{Z}|\Psi)\right) = \sum_{j=1}^{m} \left(\sum_{i=1}^{n} \left(log \ \Pi_i + log \ f_j(\mathbf{Y_j}|\mathcal{Z}_j = \mathbf{X_i}, T, \sigma)\right) \delta_{\{\mathcal{Z}_j = \mathbf{X_i}\}} \right.$$
$$\left. + \ (log \ \Pi_{outlier} + log \ f_j(\mathbf{Y_j}|\mathcal{Z}_j = outlier, T, \sigma)) \delta_{\{\mathcal{Z}_j = outlier\}} \right). \tag{13}$$

By reporting the expression (13) in (11), we obtain :

$$Q(\Psi|\Psi^q) = \sum_{j=1}^{n} \left(\sum_{i=1}^{m} \left(log \ \Pi_i + log \ f_j(\mathbf{Y_j}|\mathcal{Z}_j = \mathbf{X_i}, T, \sigma)\right) \mathcal{P}(\mathcal{Z}_j = \mathbf{X_i}|\mathbf{Y}, \Psi^q) \right.$$
$$\left. + \ (log \ \Pi_{outlier} + log \ f_j(\mathbf{Y_j}|\mathcal{Z}_j = outlier, T, \sigma)) \mathcal{P}(\mathcal{Z}_j = outlier|\mathbf{Y}, \Psi^q) \right). \tag{14}$$

This expression involves the probabilities $\alpha_{i,j}^q = \mathcal{P}(\mathcal{Z}_\mathbf{j} = \mathbf{X}_\mathbf{i}|\mathbf{Y}, \Psi^q)$ which, using the Bayes formula, can be written as:

$$\alpha_{i,j}^q = \frac{\Pi_i f_j(\mathbf{Y_j}|\mathcal{Z}_\mathbf{j} = \mathbf{X}_\mathbf{i}, \mathcal{T}^q, \sigma_q)}{\sum_{k=1}^n \Pi_k f_j(\mathbf{Y_j}|\mathcal{Z}_\mathbf{j} = \mathbf{X}_\mathbf{k}, \mathcal{T}^q, \sigma_q) + \Pi_{outlier} f_j(\mathbf{Y_j}|\mathcal{Z}_\mathbf{j} = outlier)} \quad (15)$$

where

$$f_j(\mathbf{Y_j}|\mathcal{Z}_\mathbf{j} = \mathbf{X}_\mathbf{i}, \mathcal{T}^q, \sigma_q^2) = \frac{1}{(2\pi\sigma_q^2)^{\frac{3}{2}}} e^{-\frac{\|\mathbf{Y_j}-\mathcal{T}^\cdot(\mathbf{X_i})\|^2}{2\cdot ?}}. \quad (16)$$

The expression of $\alpha_{i,j}^q$, i.e., the probability that a point $\mathbf{Y_j}$ is matched with the point $\mathbf{X_i}$, can be further developed using expressions (4), (5) and (7):

$$\alpha_{i,j}^q = \frac{e^{-\frac{\|\mathbf{Y_j}-\mathcal{T}^\cdot(\mathbf{X_i})\|^2}{2\cdot ?}}}{\sum_{k=1}^m e^{-\frac{\|\mathbf{Y_j}-\mathcal{T}^\cdot(\mathbf{X_k})\|^2}{2\cdot ?}} + c} \quad (17)$$

where

$$c = 3\sqrt{\frac{\pi}{2}}\left(1 - \frac{nv^q}{V}\right) \simeq 3\sqrt{\frac{\pi}{2}} \text{ since we assumed } nv^q \ll V. \quad (18)$$

This expression for the $\alpha_{i,j}^q$ is at the core of the robust method (outlier rejection):

- If the transformation $\mathcal{T}^q$ does not take any point $\mathbf{X_i}$, i.e., the action $\mathcal{T}^q(\mathbf{X_i})$, in a small volume of radius σ_q around $\mathbf{Y_j}$ then all the terms in the denominator's sum will be small compared to c. Therefore, all the coefficients $\alpha_{i,j}^q$ corresponding to the point $\mathbf{Y_j}$ will lean towards zero. We will see in the following section that it will mean that the point $\mathbf{Y_j}$ will not be taken into account for the estimation of the transformation $\mathcal{T}$.
- On the contrary, a point $\mathbf{X_i}$ taken by $\mathcal{T}^q$ within the neighborhood of $\mathbf{Y_j}$ will yield a value for $\alpha_{i,j}^q$ that is close to 1 (if only one point $\mathbf{X_i}$ is present in this neighborhood), and the association between $\mathbf{X_i}$ and $\mathbf{Y_j}$ will be used to determine $\mathcal{T}$.

3.3 Estimating the Transformation $\mathcal{T}^q$

It is now possible to derive a simpler expression of equation (14). Neither the coefficients Π_i, nor the second row of eq. (14) depend on the transformation $\mathcal{T}$. By substituting f_i in (14) by its expression (16), we obtain a new expression for $Q(\Psi|\Psi^q)$:

$$Q(\Psi|\Psi^q) = -\frac{1}{2\sigma_q^2}\sum_{i=1}^n\sum_{j=1}^m \alpha_{i,j}^q \|\mathbf{Y_j} - \mathcal{T}(\mathbf{X_i}, \mathbf{\Theta})\|^2 + C^{st} \quad (19)$$

where the constant term does not depend on the transformation $\mathcal{T}$. To maximize Q, the EM algorithm iterates a two-step procedure:

– *Expectation:* The probabilities $\alpha_{i,j}^q$ are evaluated using equation (17).
– *Maximization:* We seek the parameters Θ that maximize the criterion Q, given the $\alpha_{i,j}^q$'s previously evaluated. As it will be explained below, σ_q will not be evaluated through the maximization process. Its value will be evaluated through an annealing schedule.

These two steps are carried out until changes between T^q and T fall under a given threshold.

After developing the sum over j in equation (19) and after a few algebraic manipulation, one obtains that the maximization of (19) is equivalent to the minimization of:

$$E(\Theta) = \sum_{i=1}^{n} \lambda_i^q \|T(\mathbf{X_i}, \Theta) - \mathbf{G_i^q}\|^2 \qquad (20)$$

with:

$$\lambda_i^q = \sum_{j=1}^{m} \alpha_{i,j}^q \text{ and } \mathbf{G_i^q} = \frac{1}{\lambda_i^q} \sum_{j=1}^{m} \alpha_{i,j}^q \mathbf{Y_j} .$$

It is less complex and more efficient to minimize equation (20) rather than to maximize eq. x(19). Indeed, the summation is restricted to the priors $\mathbf{X_i}$. Moreover, it is straightforward to evaluate the Jacobian matrix associated with the transformation T given by equation (3). As the value of $E(\Theta)$ decreases, the model points $\mathbf{X_i}$ which do not have a data-point assignment will rapidly disappear from the summation since their associated coefficient λ_i rapidly converges to 0 as the value of σ_q decreases. On the contrary, for those priors $\mathbf{X_i}$ which do have *one or several* data-point assignments, their center of gravity, $\mathbf{G_i}$, will get closer to the data point $\mathbf{Y_j}$ which is the closest to $T(\mathbf{X_i})$.

Conventionally, EM algorithms also include the evaluation of σ_q during the maximisation step. In fact, it has been observed by us and by other authors that this does not lead to good alignment results. Very often, the values of σ^q evaluated by the maximization step, decrease too quickly, and the algorithm tends to get trapped in a local minimum. To prevent this, we will simply specify an annealing schedule for σ_q, in the spirit of simulated annealing techniques. The initial value, σ_0, will be set at the threshold previously defined, σ_m, which corresponds to the largest allowed motion of a point. At each step of the algorithm, σ_q will decrease geometrically, according to $\sigma_{q+1} = \kappa\sigma_q$ with $\kappa < 1$. The value σ should not fall below the variance σ_r of the noise associatd with the 3-D locations of the points (a few millimeters in our case), and the decrease of σ_q is stopped when it reaches this threshold σ_r. The decrease rate κ is chosen so that it takes about five steps to go from σ_m downto σ_r.

3.4 Surface Fitting

Now that outliers were rejected and that the articulated object moved such that the inliers are in the neighbourhood of the object's surface, it is worthile to perform surface fitting. This introduces small corrections and it is useful to prevent drift over time. We will simply refine the position of the model (through the parameters Θ) so that the 3-D points lie on the surface or as close as possible to this surface. The minimization criterium can be written as, [2], [7]:

$$E_s(\Theta) = \sum_{j=1}^{m} \beta_j d(\mathbf{Y_j}, \Theta)^2 \qquad (21)$$

where d is given by equation (2), and

$$\beta_j = e^{-\frac{\cdot(\mathbf{Y}_j)^2}{\cdot^2}} \qquad (22)$$

4   Comparison with Other Methods

The main and fundamental difference between our method and other methods such as [11], [12], [13], [15], and [16] resides both in the expression of the probabilities $\alpha_{i,j}$ provided by equation (17) and in the fact that these probabilites are subject to the constraint $\sum_j \alpha_{i,j} = 1$ i.e., *a summation over the data points*. This constraint imposes that to each model point $\mathbf{X_i}$ corresponds a unique data point $\mathbf{Y_j}$ but a data point may correspond to several model points.

The SoftAssign method described in [11] treats the data- and the model-points symmetrically, and hence it needs the additional constraint $\sum_i \alpha_{i,j} = 1$ i.e., *a summation over the model points*. From a statistical point of view, it means that one needs to consider two non-independent classifiers. A formal derivation for the $\alpha_{i,j}$'s is more delicate. In [11] [12] it is suggested to normalize the $\alpha_{i,j}$'s, alternating over i and over j, until convergence, the latter being insured by the Sinkhorn theorem. However this is computationally expensive. In addition, since the data and the model are treated symmetrically, it is crucial to reject outliers both from the data and from the model. This is done by adding one row and one column to the matrix $\alpha_{i,j}$. For example, a data point $\mathbf{Y_j}$ which is an outlier will have a "1" entry in the extra row and a model point $\mathbf{X_i}$ which is an outlier will have a "1" entry in the extra column. The normalization along the rows and along the columns should not affect, however, these extra row and column. Indeed, there should be several outliers and therefore there should be several 1's in each one of these extra row and column. We implemented this method and noticed that when the normalization is not applied to these extra row and column, the final solution depends a lot upon the initial entries of these row and column. If the initial probabilities to have outliers are too high, all the points will be classified as outliers. If these initial probabilities are too low, there will be no outliers.

5   Experimental Results

The method described in this paper was applied to the problem of tracking a hand model with 3-D data. We used a calibrated stereo camera pair together with a stereo algorithm. This algorithm provides a dense disparity map. Texture

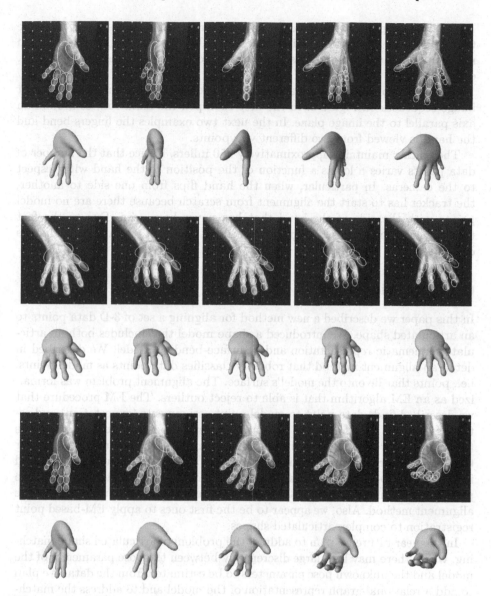

Fig. 3. Three different stereo video sequences of a hand. When the hand turns, the tracker has difficulties because the texture of the hidden side of the hand has not yet been included in the model. When the fingers bend, the hand may be tracked from both its sides.

points are extracted from both the left and right images using the Harris interest point detector. Since a dense disparity map is available, the texture points are easily matched and their 3-D positions estimated.

We gathered several stereoscopic video sequences at 20 frames per second. Each sequence has approximatively 100 frames. There are in between 500 and

1000 3-D data points associated with each stereo pair in the sequence. Notice that while some background points may be easily thrown out, there still remain many unrelevant points, such as those on the forearm (which is not modelled), e.g., Figure 1.

The results of applying the alignment method are shown on three different image sequences on Figure 3. In the first example, the hand rotates around an axis parallel to the image plane. In the next two examples the fingers bend and the hand is viewed from two different viewpoints.

The tracker maintains approximatively 250 inliers. Notice that the number of data points varies a lot as a function of the position of the hand with respect to the cameras. In particular, when the hand flips from one side to another, the tracker has to start the alignment from scratch because there are no model points with the side of the hand that has never been seen. Due to the fact that the hand-model has 27 degrees of freedom, it cannot capture all the hand's deformations.

6   Conclusion

In this paper we described a new method for aligning a set of 3-D data points to an articulated shape. We introduced a shape model that includes both an articulated kinematic representation and a surface-bending model. We described in detail an alignment method that robustly classifies data points as model points, i.e., points that lie onto the model's surface. The alignment problem was formalized as an EM algorithm that is able to reject outliers. The EM procedure that we described finds data-point-to-model-point assignments (expectation) and estimates the best transformation that maps the model points onto the data points (maximization). Our EM algorithm differs from previous attempts to solve for the point-registration problem: it has a built-in outlier rejection mechanism and it allows, one-to-many data classssifications (or data assignments). Relaxing the pair-wise assignment constraint results in a more efficient and more reliable alignment method. Also, we appear to be the first ones to apply EM-based point registration to complex articulated shapes.

In the near future we plan to address the problem of articulated shape matching, where there may be a large discrepancy between the pose parameters of the model and the unknown pose parameters to be estimated from the data. We plan to add a relational-graph representation of the model and to address the matching problem as the problem of both matching the model-graph to the data-graph and of finding the kinematic pose.

References

1. Gavrila, D.M.: The visual analysis of human movement: A survey. Computer Vision and Image Understanding **73** (1999) 82–98
2. Plaenkers, R., Fua, P.: Articulated soft objects for multi-view shape and motion capture. IEEE Transactions on Pattern Analysis and Machine Intelligence **25** (2003)

3. Herda, L., Urtasun, R., Fua, P.: Hierarchical implicit surface joint limits for human body tracking. Computer Vision and Image Understanding **99** (2005) 189–209
4. Deutscher, J., Blake, A., Reid, I.: Articulated body motion capture by annealed particle filtering. In: Computer Vision and Pattern Recognition. (2000) 2126–2133
5. Sminchisescu, C., Triggs, B.: Estimating articulated human motion with covariance scaled sampling. International Journal of Robotics Research **22** (2003) 371–379
6. Delamarre, Q., Faugeras, O.: 3d articulated models and multi-view tracking with physical forces. Computer Vision and Image Understanding **81** (2001) 328–357
7. Dewaele, G., Devernay, F., Horaud, R.: Hand motion from 3d point trajectories and a smooth surface model. In Pajdla, T., Matas, J., eds.: 8th European Conference on Computer Vision. Volume I of LNCS 3021., Springer (2004) 495–507
8. Athitsos, V., Sclaroff, S.: Estimating 3D hand pose from a cluttered image. In: CVPR '03: Proceedings of Conference in Computer Vision and Pattern Recognition. (2003)
9. Zhang, Z.: Iterative point matching for registration of free-form curves and surfaces. International Journal on Computer Vision **13** (1994) 119–152
10. Ferrie, F.P., Lagarde, J., Whaite, P.: Darboux Frames, Snakes, and Super-Quadrics: Geometry from the Bottom Up. IEEE Transactions on Pattern Analysis and Machine Intelligence **15** (1993) 771–784
11. Gold, S., Rangarajan, A.: A Graduated Assignment Algorithm for Graph Matching. IEEE Transactions on Pattern Analysis and Machine Intelligence **18** (1996) 377–388
12. Rangarajan, A., Chui, H., Bookstein, F.L.: The softassign procrustes matching algorithm. In: Information Processing in Medical Imaging (IPMI). (1997) 29–42
13. Chui, H., Rangarajan, A.: A new point matching algorithm for non-rigid registration. Computer Vision and Image Understanding **89** (2003) 114–141
14. Dempster, A.P., Laird, N.M., Rubin, D.B.: Maximum likelihood estimation from incomplete data via the EM algorithm (with discussion). Journal of the Royal Statistical Society, Series B **39** (1977) 1–38
15. Cross, A.D.J., Hancock, E.R.: Graph Matching With a Dual-Step EM Algorithm. IEEE Transactions on Pattern Analysis and Machine Intelligence **20** (1998) 1236–1253
16. Luo, B., Hancock, E.: A unified framework for alignment and correspondence. CVIU **92** (2003) 26–55
17. Granger, S., Pennec, X.: Multi-scale em-icp: A fast and robust approach for surface registration. In: ECCV02. (2002) IV: 418 ff.

Feature Harvesting for Tracking-by-Detection

Mustafa Özuysal, Vincent Lepetit, François Fleuret, and Pascal Fua

Computer Vision Laboratory,
École Polytechnique Fédérale de Lausanne (EPFL), 1015 Lausanne, Switzerland
{mustafa.oezuysal, vincent.lepetit, francois.fleuret, pascal.fua}@epfl.ch
http://cvlab.epfl.ch

Abstract. We propose a fast approach to 3–D object detection and pose estimation that owes its robustness to a training phase during which the target object slowly moves with respect to the camera. No additional information is provided to the system, save a very rough initialization in the first frame of the training sequence. It can be used to detect the target object in each video frame independently.

Our approach relies on a Randomized Tree-based approach to wide-baseline feature matching. Unlike previous classification-based approaches to 3–D pose estimation, we do not require an *a priori* 3–D model. Instead, our algorithm learns both geometry and appearance. In the process, it collects, or *harvests*, a list of features that can be reliably recognized even when large motions and aspect changes cause complex variations of feature appearances. This is made possible by the great flexibility of Randomized Trees, which lets us add and remove feature points to our list as needed with a minimum amount of extra computation.

1 Introduction

In many 3–D object-detection and pose estimation problems ranging from Augmented Reality to Visual Servoing, run-time performance is of critical importance. However, there usually is time to train the system before actually using it. It has recently been shown [1] that, given a 3–D model, statistical learning techniques [2] can be used during this training phase to achieve robust real-time performance by learning the appearance of features on the target object. As a result, at run-time, it becomes possible to perform wide-baseline matching quickly and robustly, which is then used to detect the object and compute its 3–D pose. Here we show that this approach extends naturally to the case where no *a priori* 3–D model is available, thus removing one of the major limitations of the original method and yielding the behavior depicted by Fig. 1.

The key ingredient of our approach is what we refer to as *feature harvesting*: Assuming that we can first observe the target object moving slowly, we define an ellipsoid that roughly projects at the object's location in the first frame. We extract feature points inside this projection and use the image patches surrounding them to train a first classifier, which is then used to match these initial features in the following frames. As more and more new frames become available, we

A. Leonardis, H. Bischof, and A. Pinz (Eds.): ECCV 2006, Part III, LNCS 3953, pp. 592–605, 2006.

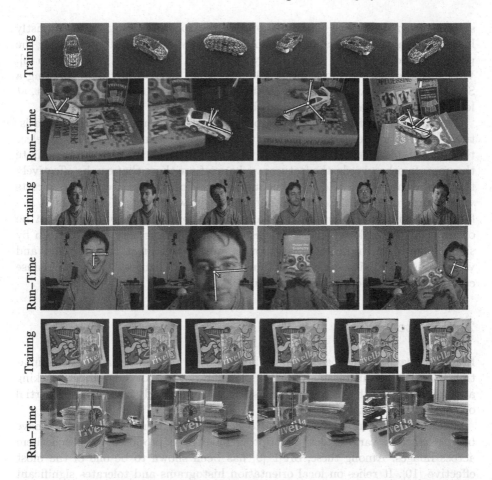

Fig. 1. Our approach to 3–D object detection applied to a toy car, a face, and a glass. In each one of the three cases, we show two rows of pictures. The first represents the training sequence, while the second depicts detection results in individual frames that are not part of the training sequence. We overlay the ellipsoid we use as our initial model on the images of the first row. The only required manual intervention is to position it in the very first image. To visualize the results, we attach a 3–D referential to the center of gravity of the ellipsoid and use the estimated 3–D pose to project it into the images. Note that, once trained, our system can handle large aspect, scale, and lighting changes. It can deal with the transparent glass as well as with the hand substantially occluding the car. And when a complete occlusion occurs, such as when the book completely hides the face, it simply returns no answer and recovers when the target object becomes visible again.

discard features that cannot be reliably found and add new ones to account for aspect changes. We use new views of the features we retain to refine the classifier and, each time we add or remove a feature, we update it accordingly. Once all the training frames have been processed, we run a bundle-adjustment algorithm on the tracked feature points to also refine the model's geometry. In short, starting from the simple ellipsoid shown in the top row of Fig. 1, we robustly learn both geometry and appearance. An alternative approach to initializing the process would have been to use a fully automated on-line SLAM algorithm [3]. We chose the ellipsoid both for simplicity's sake—successfully implementing a SLAM method is far from trivial—and because it has proved to be sufficient, at least for objects that can be enclosed by one.

The originality of our approach is to use exactly the same tracking and statistical classification techniques, first, to train the system and automatically select the most stable features and, second, to detect them at run-time and compute the pose. In other words, the features we harvest are those that can be effectively tracked by the specific wide-baseline matching algorithm we use. This contrasts with standard classification-based approaches in which classifiers are built beforehand, using a training set manually labeled and that may or may not be optimal for the task at hand. As a result, our system is very easy to train by simply showing it the object slowly moving and, once trained, both very fast and very robust to a wide range of motions and aspect changes, which may cause complex variations of feature appearances.

2   Related Work

In recent years, feature-based approaches to object recognition and pose estimation have become increasingly popular for the purpose of 3-D object tracking and detection [4, 5, 6, 7], mostly because they are relatively insensitive to partial occlusions and cluttered backgrounds.

These features are often designed to be affine invariant [8]. Once they have been extracted, various local descriptors have been proposed to match them across images. Among these, SIFT [9] has been shown to be one of the most effective [10]. It relies on local orientation histograms and tolerates significant local deformations. In [8], it is applied to rectified affine invariant regions to achieve perspective invariance. In [11], a similar result is obtained by training the system using multiple views of a target object, storing all the SIFT features from these views, and matching against all of them. However, computing such descriptors can be costly. Furthermore, matching is usually performed by nearest-neighbor search, which tends to be computationally expensive, even when using an efficient data structure [12].

Another weakness of these descriptors is that they are predefined and do not adapt to the specific images under consideration. [5] addresses this issue by building the set of the image neighborhoods of features tracked over a sequence. Kernel PCA is then performed on this set to compute a descriptor for each feature. This approach, however, remains computationally expensive.

By contrast, [1] proposes a classification-based approach that is both generic and faster. Since the set of possible patches around an image feature under changing perspective and lighting conditions can be seen as a class, it is possible to train a classifier—made of Randomized Trees (RT) [2]—to recognize feature points by feeding it samples of their possible appearances. In the case of

3–D objects, these samples are synthesized using a textured model of the target object. This is effective because it allows the system to learn potentially complex appearance changes. However, it requires building the 3–D model. This can be cumbersome if the object is either complex or made of a non-Lambertian material that makes the creation of an accurate texture-map non-trivial. If one is willing to invest the effort, it can of course be done but it is time consuming. The approach we introduce here completely does away with this requirement.

3   Randomized Trees for Feature Recognition

The approach we use as a starting point [1] relies on matching image features extracted from training images and those extracted from images acquired at run-time under potentially large perspective and scale variations. It formulates wide-baseline matching as a classification problem by treating the set of all possible appearances of each individual *object feature*, typically a 3–D point on the object surface, as a class. During training, given at least one image of the target object, *image features*, are extracted and associated to object features. These features are taken to be extrema of Laplacian extracted from the first few octaves of the images. This simple multi-scale extraction and the classifier work in tandem to recognize the features under large variation of both scale and appearance. Image patches surrounding the image features are then warped to generate numerous synthetic views of their possible appearance under perspective distortion, which are then used to train a set of Randomized Trees (RTs) [2]. These RTs are used at run-time to recognize the object features under perspective and scale variations by deciding to which class, if any, their appearance belongs.

The training procedure outlined above assumes that a fixed number of image features have been extracted *beforehand* and that their number does not change. This is not true in our case because image features can be added or discarded *during* training. Therefore, in the remainder of this section, we first recall the original formulation [1] and then extend it to allow the addition and removal of object features on the fly. RTs appear to be a very good trade-off between the efficiency of the recognition, and these possibilities of manipulations.

3.1   Wide Baseline Matching Using Randomized Trees

Let us consider a set of 3–D object features $\{\mathbf{M}_i\}$ that lie on the target object and let us assume that we have collected a number of image patches $f_{i,j}$ centered on the projections of $\mathbf{M}_i$ into image j, for all available i and j. The $\{f_{i,j}\}$ constitute the training set we use to train the classifier $\hat{\mathscr{R}}$ to predict to which $\mathbf{M}_i$, if any, a given image patch f corresponds, in other words, to approximate as well as possible the actual mapping $\mathscr{R}(f) = i$. At run-time, $\hat{\mathscr{R}}$ can then be used to recognize the object features by considering the image patch f around a detected image feature. Given the 3–D position of the $\mathbf{M}_i$, this is what is required to compute 3–D pose.

In principle any kind of classifier could have been used. RTs, however, are particularly well adapted because they naturally handle multi-class problems, while being both robust and fast. Multiple trees are grown so that each one yields a different partition of the space of image patches. The tree leaves contain an estimate of the posterior distribution over the classes, which is learned from training data. A patch f is classified by dropping it down each tree and performing an elementary test at each node, which sends it to one side or the other, and considering the sum of the probabilities stored in the leaves it reaches. We write

$$\hat{\mathscr{R}}(f) = \underset{i}{\text{argmax}} \sum_{T \in \mathcal{T}} \hat{P}_{L(T,f)}(\mathscr{R}(f) = i) \ , \tag{1}$$

where i is a label, the $\hat{P}_{L(T,f)}(\mathscr{R}(f) = i)$ are the posterior probabilities stored in the leaf $L(T, f)$ of tree T reached by f, and $\mathcal{T}$ is the set of Randomized Trees. Such probabilities are evaluated during training as the ratio of the number n_i^L of patches of class i in the training set that reach L and the total number n_i of patches of class i that is used in the training. This yields

$$\hat{P}_L(\mathscr{R}(f) = i) \simeq \frac{n_i^L/n_i}{S_L} \ , \tag{2}$$

where $S_L = \sum_j \frac{n_j^L}{n_j}$ is a normalization term that enforces $\sum_i \hat{P}_L(\mathscr{R}(f) = i) = 1$. We normalize by the number of patches because the real prior on the class is expected to be uniform, while this is not true in our training population. Although any kind of test could be performed at the nodes, simple binary tests based on the difference of intensities of two pixels have proved sufficient. Given two pixels $\mathbf{m_1}$ and $\mathbf{m_2}$ in f and their gray levels $I(f, \mathbf{m_1})$ and $I(f, \mathbf{m_2})$ after some Gaussian smoothing, these tests are of the form

$$\begin{aligned} &\text{If } I(f, \mathbf{m_1}) \leq I(f, \mathbf{m_2}) \text{ go to left child,} \\ &\text{otherwise} \qquad\qquad\qquad \text{go to right child.} \end{aligned} \tag{3}$$

This test is very simple and requires only pixel intensity comparisons. In practice, classifying a patch involves only a few hundreds of intensity comparisons and additions per patch, and is therefore very fast.

3.2   Randomized Trees and On-Line Training

The approach described above assumes that the complete training set is available from the beginning, which is not true in our case as object features may be added or removed while the classifier is being trained. Here we show how to overcome this limitation by modifying the tree-building algorithm in two significant ways.

First, in [1], the node tests are chosen so as to minimize leaf entropy, which is estimated according to the training set. Without the complete training set, this cannot be meaningfully done. Instead, we build the tree by randomly selecting the tests, that is to say the $\mathbf{m_1}$ and $\mathbf{m_2}$ locations of Eq. 3. The training data is only used to evaluate the $\hat{P}_L$ posterior probabilities in the leaves of these randomly generated trees. Surprisingly, this much simplified procedure, which is going to allow us to iteratively estimate the $\hat{P}_L$ values, results in virtually no loss of classification performance [13]. Interestingly, a similar result has also been reported in the context of 2–D object recognition [14].

Second, we introduce a mechanism for updating the tree when new views of an existing object feature are introduced or when an object feature is either added or removed, which the RT approach lets us do very elegantly as follows.

- **Incorporating New Views of Object Features.** Recall that, during the initial training phase, patches are dropped down the tree and the number of patches reaching leaf L is plugged into Eq. 2 to derive $\hat{P}_L$ for each class at leaf L. Given a new view, we want to use it to refine these probability estimates. To this end, we invert the previous step and compute the number of patches reaching leaf L as

$$ n_i^L = \hat{P}_L(\mathscr{R}(f) = i) \times n_i \times S_L. $$

  This only requires storing the normalization terms S_L at each leaf L and keeping the n_i counters for each class. We then use newly detected patches to increment n_i^L and n_i. When all the new patches have been processed, we again use Eq. 2 to obtain the refined values of $\hat{P}_L$. Note that we do not store the image patches themselves, which could cost a lot of memory for long training sequences.
- **Adding and Removing Object Features.** The flexible procedure outlined above can also be used to add, remove or replace the classes corresponding to specific object features during training. Removing class i and the corresponding object feature merely requires setting

$$ n_i^L = n_i = 0. $$

We can then replace the ith feature by a new one by simply changing the $\mathbf{M}_i$ 3–D coordinates introduced at the beginning of Section 3.1 to be those of the new object feature and using patches centered around the new projections of $\mathbf{M}_i$ to estimate $\hat{P}_L$.

These update mechanisms are the basic tools we use to recursively estimate the RTs while harvesting features, as discussed in the next section.

4   From Harvesting to Detection

In this section, we show that standard frame-to-frame tracking and independent 3–D detection in each individual frame can be formalized similarly and, therefore, combined seamlessly as opportunity dictates. This combination is what we refer to as tracking-by-detection. The originality of our approach is to use exactly the same image feature recognition technique at all stages of the process, first, to train the system and automatically select the most stable features and, second, to detect them at run-time.

We first give an overview of our method. We then explain how the tracking is performed *without* updating the classifier, and conclude with the complete "feature harvesting" framework.

4.1   Overview

As shown in the top row of Fig. 1, to initialize the training process, we position the ellipsoid that we use as an initial 3–D model so that it projects on the target object in the first frame. We then extract a number of image features from this first image and back-project them to the ellipsoid, thus creating an initial set of the $\{M_i\}$ object features of Section 3.1. By affine warping lightly the image patches surrounding the image features, we create the $f_{i,j}$ image patches that let us instantiate a first set of randomized trees.

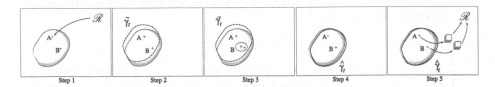

Fig. 2. The five steps of feature harvesting introduced at the beginning of Section 4.1

During training, new features detected on the object are integrated into the classifier. Because the number of such features can become prohibitively large when dealing with long training sequences, it is desirable to keep the ones that are successfully detected and recognized by the classifier most often, and remove the other ones. More precisely, given the set of trees trained using the first frame or more generally all frames up to frame $t-1$, we handle frame t using the five-step feature-harvesting procedure described below and illustrated by Fig. 2:

1. We extract image features from frame t and use the classifier to match them, which, in general, will only be successful for a subset of these features.
2. We derive a first estimate $\tilde{\gamma}_t$ of the camera pose from these correspondences using a robust estimator that lets us reject erroneous correspondences.
3. We use $\tilde{\gamma}_t$ to project unmatched image features from frame $t-1$ into frame t and match them by looking for the image features closest to their projections.
4. Using these additional correspondences, we derive a refined estimate $\hat{\gamma}_t$.
5. We use small affine warping of the patches around image features matched in frame t to update the classifier as discussed in Section 3.2. Features that have not been recognized often are removed to be replaced by new ones.

At run-time, we use the exact same procedure, with one single change: We stop updating the classifier, which simply amounts to skipping the fifth step.

4.2   3–D Tracking by Detection

Let us first assume that the classifier $\mathscr{R}$ has already been trained. Both tracking and detection can then be formalized as the estimation of the camera pose Γ_t from image features extracted from all previous images that we denote $I_{s\leq t}$. In other words, we seek to estimate the conditional density $p(\Gamma_t \mid I_{s\leq t})$.

A camera motion model —appearing as the term $p(\Gamma_t \mid \Gamma_{t-1})$ in the following derivations— should be chosen. It often assumes either constant velocity or constant acceleration. This is fine to regularize the recovered motion but can also lead to complete failure. This tends to occur after an abrupt motion or if Γ_{t-1} is incorrectly estimated, for example due to a complete occlusion. Γ_t can then have any value no matter what the estimate of Γ_{t-1} is. In such a case, we should consider the density of Γ_t as uniform and write $p(\Gamma_t \mid \Gamma_{t-1}) \propto \lambda$, which amounts to treating each frame completely independently. In our implementation, we use a mixture of these two approaches and take the distribution to be

$$p(\Gamma_t \mid \Gamma_{t-1}) \propto m(\Gamma_{t-1}, \Gamma_t) = \exp\left(-(\Gamma_t - \Gamma_{tq-1})^\top \Sigma^{-1} (\Gamma_t - \Gamma_{t-1})\right) + \lambda. \quad (4)$$

This lets us both enforce temporal consistency constraints and to recover from tracking failures by relying on single-frame detection results. In our implementation, the respective values of Σ and λ were chosen manually.

Unfortunately, introducing the term λ process precludes the use of standard particle filtering techniques. Our camera pose space has six dimensions, and the required number of particles, which grows exponentially with the number of dimensions, would be too large to make particle filters tractable. Therefore we have to restrict ourself to the estimation of the mode $\widehat{\gamma}_t$ of this density:

$$\widehat{\gamma}_t = \underset{\gamma}{\mathrm{argmax}}\ P(\Gamma_t = \gamma \mid I_{s \leq t}),$$

in which the expression of $P(\Gamma_t = \gamma \mid I_{s \leq t})$ can be found using the standard Bayesian tracking relation:

$$P(\Gamma_t = \gamma \mid I_{s \leq t}) \propto P(I_t \mid \Gamma_t = \gamma) P(\Gamma_t = \gamma \mid \Gamma_{t-1} = \widehat{\gamma_{t-1}}) P(\Gamma_{t-1} = \widehat{\gamma_{t-1}} \mid I_{s < t}). \quad (5)$$

As described in the overview, we apply a RANSAC based approach on the set $\widetilde{n}_t$ of correspondences obtained using the classifier to derive a first estimate $\widetilde{\gamma}_t$ for the camera pose. A new set $\widehat{n}_t$ is then made of the inliers of $\widetilde{n}_t$, and completed by projecting the unmatched object features with $\widetilde{\gamma}_t$ and matched each of them with the closest image feature. A numerical optimization is then performed to find $\widehat{\gamma}_t$ by minimizing the log-likelihood of $m(\widehat{\gamma_{t-1}}, \gamma) P(I_t \mid \Gamma_t = \gamma)$:

$$\widehat{\gamma}_t = \underset{\gamma}{\mathrm{argmin}} \sum_{n \in \widehat{n}} \|\mathbf{P}(\gamma)\mathbf{M}(n) - \mathbf{m}(n)\|^2 + \rho\left((\gamma - \widehat{\gamma_{t-1}})^\top \Sigma^{-1} (\gamma - \widehat{\gamma_{t-1}})\right) \quad (6)$$

where $\mathbf{P}(\gamma)$ is the projection matrix for the camera pose γ, ρ is the Tukey robust estimator that approximates the logarithm of (4), and $\mathbf{M}(n)$ and $\mathbf{m}(n)$ are respectively the object feature and the image feature for correspondence n.

The advantage of the classifier is that there is no need for the previous pose. However, this procedure can result in some jittering on the estimated pose over a sequence. To enforce temporal consistency and reduce the effect, when $\widehat{\gamma_{t-1}}$ is valid, we also consider transient object features which projections can be matched across I_{t-1} and I_t using standard cross-correlation. Their 3–D positions can be estimated from the rough model and $\widehat{\gamma_{t-1}}$ by back-projection. According to our experience, over two consecutive frames, this position is accurate enough to improve the recovered displacement. These additional correspondences are integrated in Eq. (6) for pose estimation exactly in the same way as the correspondences established with the classifier. Note that these correspondences are not required by our method, but they are useful to reduce the jittering effect.

4.3   Feature Harvesting

During training we use the same process but now the classifier is not initially available and we want to create it incrementally by "feature harvesting." This implies keeping or discarding object features such as those shown in Fig. 3. Let us first denote by r_t^* the best classifier obtained with the images $I_{s \le t}$ and the feature correspondences computed using the poses $\gamma_{s \le t}$:

$$r_t^* = \underset{r}{\mathrm{argmax}}\, P(\mathscr{R} = r \,|\, \Gamma_{s \le t} = \gamma_{s \le t},\, I_{s \le t}).$$

Here we show that r_t^* can be used to compute $\widehat{\gamma_{t+1}}$ under reasonable assumptions. We have:

$$P(\Gamma_{s \le t} = \gamma_{s \le t}, I_{s \le t})$$
$$= \sum_r P(\Gamma_{s \le t} = \gamma_{s \le t}, I_{s \le t}, \mathscr{R} = r) = \sum_r P(\Gamma_t = \gamma_t, I_t, \Gamma_{s < t} = \gamma_{s < t}, I_{s < t}, \mathscr{R} = r)$$
$$= \sum_r P(\Gamma_t = \gamma_t, I_t \,|\, \Gamma_{s < t} = \gamma_{s < t}, I_{s < t}, \mathscr{R} = r) P(\mathscr{R} = r \,|\, \Gamma_{s < t} = \gamma_{s < t}, I_{s < t}) \times$$
$$P(\Gamma_{s < t} = \gamma_{s < t}, I_{s < t})$$

All the classifiers have a negligible probability $P(\mathscr{R} = r \,|\, P_{s < t} = \gamma_{s < t}, I_{s < t})$ except for those concentrated around $r = r_{t-1}^*$. Otherwise, that would mean that other classifiers than r_{t-1}^* constructed with $\gamma_{s < t}, I_{s < t}$ would be as good as r_{t-1}^*,

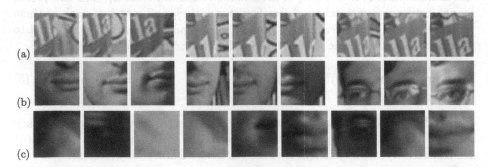

(a)

(b)

(c)

Fig. 3. The harvest. (a) Three sample patches for three distinct features on the glass. Note that the foreground is relatively constant while the background changes drastically. (b) Three sample patches for three distinct face features, obtained under changing light and orientation. (c) Patches corresponding to object features found to be unreliable and discarded during training.

which is not realistic since r_{t-1}^* has been built from these poses and images. Let us continue the derivation:

$$\simeq P(\Gamma_t = \gamma_t, I_t \mid \Gamma_{s<t} = \gamma_{s<t}, I_{s<t}, \mathcal{R} = r_{t-1}^*)P(\Gamma_{s<t} = \gamma_{s<t}, I_{s<t})$$
$$= P(I_t \mid \Gamma_t = \gamma_t, \Gamma_{s<t} = \gamma_{s<t}, I_{s<t}, \mathcal{R} = r_{t-1}^*) \times$$
$$P(\Gamma_t = \gamma_t \mid \Gamma_{s<t} = \gamma_{s<t}, I_{s<t}, \mathcal{R} = r_{t-1}^*)P(\Gamma_{s<t} = \gamma_{s<t}, I_{s<t})$$
$$\simeq P(I_t \mid \Gamma_t = \gamma_t, \mathcal{R} = r_{t-1}^*)P(\Gamma_t = \gamma_t \mid \Gamma_{s<t} = \gamma_{s<t})P(\Gamma_{s<t} = \gamma_{s<t}, I_{s<t})$$

because the incoming image does not depend on the poses except on the current one, and the current pose does not depend on the previous images neither on the classifier, which is reasonable. By applying the Bayes' theorem on the terms $P(\Gamma_{s\leq t} = \gamma_{s\leq t}, I_{s\leq t})$ and $P(\Gamma_{s<t} = \gamma_{s<t}, I_{s<t})$, we get:

$$P(\Gamma_{s\leq t} = \gamma_{s\leq t} \mid I_{s\leq t}) \simeq$$
$$\frac{P(I..)}{P(I.\leq\cdot)}P(I_t \mid P_t = \gamma_t, \mathcal{R} = r_{t-1}^*)P(\Gamma_t = \gamma_t \mid \Gamma_{t-1}{}_{s<t} = \gamma_{s<t})P(\Gamma_{s<t} = \gamma_{s<t} \mid I_{s<t})$$

And under standard probabilistic tracking hypotheses, we finally obtain:

$$P(\Gamma_t = \gamma_t \mid I_{s\leq t}) \propto$$
$$P(I_t \mid P_t = \gamma_t, \mathcal{R} = r_{t-1}^*)P(\Gamma_t = \gamma_t \mid \Gamma_{t-1} = \gamma_t)P(\Gamma_{t-1} = \gamma_{t-1} \mid I_{s<t})$$

which is the same expression as Eq. 5 used for tracking, except that the classifier r_{t-1}^* appears in the observation model. That means that the same method as in Section 4.2 can be used to estimate $\widehat{\gamma}_t$. Once this pose is found, r_{t-1}^* is updated using correspondences between object features and image features to give r_t^* as explained in Section 3.2.

To validate this training procedure, we performed the experiment depicted by Fig. 4, which clearly shows that the recovered camera trajectory does not drift.

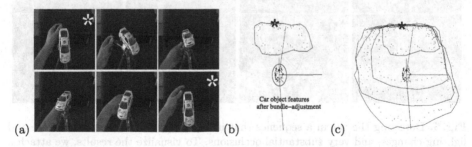

Fig. 4. (a) Sample frames from a training sequence where the toy car is fixed to a tripod and rotated four times. The frames marked with a star show the reference position which is reached in all four loops. (b) Recovered relative camera motion with respect to the toy car after the first loop. The trajectory is shown in the referential of the ellipsoid. The dots represent the trajectory before bundle-adjustment, the plain curve after. (c) Camera motion for all four loops. As can be seen, there is no drift. Note that all four loops go through the star.

5   Results

In this section we demonstrate the effectiveness and generality of our approach using three very different objects, a toy car, a face, and a partially-textured transparent glass. In all three cases, we follow the same procedure: We show the system the training sequence depicted by the top rows of Fig. 1, which is used to harvest features as discussed in Section 4.3. When all the training frames have been processed, we freeze the set of RTs we have built and proceed with the tracking-by-detection approach of Section 4.2. Our non-optimized implementation runs at 5Hz during tracking, and 1Hz during training. About 20% of the time is devoted to extracting and recognizing the features, and the remaining 80% by the pose estimation procedure. This could be considerably sped-up by using more efficient strategies [15].

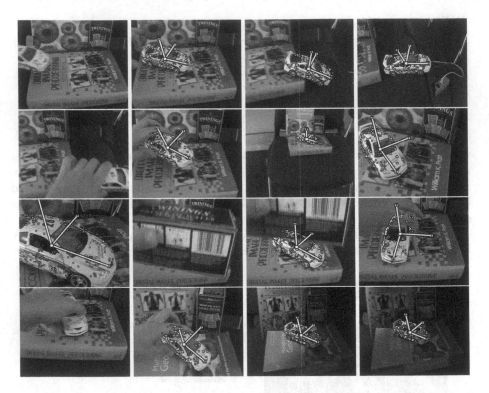

Fig. 5. Detecting the car in a sequence that involves abrupt motions, large scale and lighting changes, and very substantial occlusions. To visualize the results, we attach a 3–D referential to the center of gravity of the initial ellipsoid and use the estimated 3–D pose to project it into the images. We also overlay the projections of the harvested object feature points. The toy car is successfully detected in all frames except those where it is almost entirely occluded. And, because the object is re-detected in every frame, the system easily recovers after such a failure.

Fig. 6. Face results. Note that by contrast with previous face detection approaches, the face pose can be retrieved under (a) large rotations, (b) scale and lighting changes, and (c) different facial expressions. (d) After the occlusion by the book, the algorithm automatically recovers.

Fig. 7. Detecting a transparent object with partial texture. The squares in the first three images outline the patches around the features detected at three different scales in a test frame. The straight line segments connect the feature with the corresponding one in a frame of the training sequence. Since during training the system learned which parts of the patches are meaningful as shown in Fig. 3, the image features can be recognized even if the patch overlaps the background or the transparent parts. As shown in the fourth frame, the glass is successfully detected.

Figs 5, 6, and 7 show a number of frames extracted from test sequences of several hundreds frames—the toy sequence is made of about 1500 frames—in which our target objects translate and rotate. Because the object is re-detected in every frame, the algorithm is robust to abrupt motion and complete occlusion.

For example, after the third frame of Fig. 5, the car falls on the ground and has to be picked up. As soon as it becomes visible again, the system reacquires it. The same happens in the example of Fig. 6 after the subject hides his face behind the book. These examples highlight some of the strengths of our algorithm:

- **Robustness to cluttered background.** Once trained, the classifier is feature-specific enough so that it does not get confused by cluttered background as shown in Fig. 5.
- **Insensitivity to scale changes.** Thanks to the multi-scale approach to feature detection described at the beginning of Section 3, the algorithm can handle a very broad range of scales, including scales that were not part of the training sequence. As shown in several of the examples of Figs 5 and 6, the system keeps on successfully detecting even though the target object moves both much closer and much further.
- **Robustness to complex illumination effects.** In the case of the face, we deliberately changed the lighting when acquiring the training sequence of Fig. 1 to build lighting invariance into the classifier. As can be seen in the bottom rows of Fig. 6, this was successful and gives the system robustness to very marked lighting changes. While it was not necessary for the toy car because it has a simple shape, it experimentally appeared that a training sequence with such variations greatly improve the results.
- **Handling transparencies.** Finally, we can also handle the partially-textured transparent glass of Fig. 6 by using a suitable training sequence with a complex background. It lets the classifier learn that the parts of the patches surrounding feature points that overlap the transparent parts or the background are not relevant for classification purposes. Our algorithm can automatically reject feature points on transparent parts. At run-time features can thus be successfully recognized even if the background has changed.

6   Conclusion

Feature-based approaches to 3-D object detection that take advantage of *a priori* knowledge of the object's shape have consistently shown to be among the most effective. Their drawback is that building an accurate model that includes both 3-D and texture information, while usually possible, tends to be cumbersome. The approach proposed here exhibits the same reliability but completely does away with *a priori* 3-D model building. Instead, during an automated training phase, the system learns both geometry and appearance of object feature points that have been harvested because they can be reliably recognized.

In a more global context, learning based on the consistency between two unknown stochastic variables, in our case between the appearance and the pose and between two poses close in time, is known to tremendously reduce the required amount of expert knowledge. This paradigm has proved its power in speech processing with the Baum-Welch algorithm [16], and as our results demonstrate, is also suitable for object recognition and tracking.

We believe this to be an important step towards developing applications that can handle a hundreds or thousands of objects. Indeed, this will only be possible if only minimal amounts of manual intervention are required, which may preclude the building of 3–D models for all target objects.

References

1. Lepetit, V., Lagger, P., Fua, P.: Randomized Trees for Real-Time Keypoint Recognition. In: Conference on Computer Vision and Pattern Recognition, San Diego, CA (2005)
2. Amit, Y., Geman, D.: Shape Quantization and Recognition with Randomized Trees. Neural Computation **9** (1997) 1545–1588
3. Davison, A.: Real-Time Simultaneous Localisation and Mapping with a Single Camera. In: International Conference on Computer Vision. (2003) 1403–1410
4. S. Se and D. G. Lowe and J. Little: Mobile robot localization and mapping with uncertainty using scale-invariant visual landmarks. International Journal of Robotics Research **22** (2002) 735–758
5. Meltzer, J., Yang, M.H., Gupta, R., Soatto, S.: Multiple View Feature Descriptors from Image Sequences via Kernel Principal Component Analysis. In: European Conference on Computer Vision. (2004) 215–227
6. Skrypnyk, I., Lowe, D.G.: Scene modelling, recognition and tracking with invariant image features. In: International Symposium on Mixed and Augmented Reality, Arlington, VA (2004) 110–119
7. Lepetit, V., Fua, P.: Monocular model-based 3d tracking of rigid objects: A survey. Foundations and Trends in Computer Graphics and Vision **1** (2005) 1–89
8. Mikolajczyk, K., Tuytelaars, T., Schmid, C., Zisserman, A., Matas, J., Schaffalitzky, F., Kadir, T., Gool, L.V.: A comparison of affine region detectors. Accepted to International Journal of Computer Vision (2005)
9. Lowe, D.: Distinctive Image Features from Scale-Invariant Keypoints. International Journal of Computer Vision **20** (2004) 91–110
10. Mikolajczyk, K., Schmid, C.: A Performance Evaluation of Local Descriptors. In: Conference on Computer Vision and Pattern Recognition. (2003) 257–263
11. Pritchard, D., Heidrich, W.: Cloth motion capture. In: Eurographics. Volume 22. (2003) 263–271
12. Beis, J., Lowe, D.: Shape Indexing using Approximate Nearest-Neighbour Search in High-Dimensional Spaces. In: Conference on Computer Vision and Pattern Recognition, Puerto Rico (1997) 1000–1006
13. Lepetit, V., Fua, P.: Keypoint recognition using randomized trees. IEEE Transactions on Pattern Analysis and Machine Intelligence (2006) Accepted for publication.
14. Marée, R., Geurts, P., Piater, J., Wehenkel, L.: Random subwindows for robust image classification. In: Conference on Computer Vision and Pattern Recognition. (2005)
15. Chum, O., Matas, J.: Matching with PROSAC - Progressive Sample Consensus. In: Conference on Computer Vision and Pattern Recognition, San Diego, CA (2005) 220–226
16. Rabiner, L., Juang, B.H.: Fundamentals of Speech Recognition. Prentice Hall, Englewood Cliffs, NJ, USA (1993)

Effective Appearance Model and Similarity Measure for Particle Filtering and Visual Tracking

Hanzi Wang, David Suter, and Konrad Schindler

Institute for Vision Systems Engineering,
Department of Electrical and Computer Systems Engineering,
Monash University, Clayton Vic. 3800, Australia
{hanzi.wang, d.suter, konrad.schindler}@eng.monash.edu.au

Abstract. In this paper, we adaptively model the appearance of objects based on Mixture of Gaussians in a joint spatial-color space (the approach is called SMOG). We propose a new SMOG-based similarity measure. SMOG captures richer information than the general color histogram because it incorporates spatial layout in addition to color. This appearance model and the similarity measure are used in a framework of Bayesian probability for tracking natural objects. In the second part of the paper, we propose an Integral Gaussian Mixture (IGM) technique, as a fast way to extract the parameters of SMOG for target candidate. With IGM, the parameters of SMOG can be computed efficiently by using only simple arithmetic operations (addition, subtraction, division) and thus the computation is reduced to linear complexity. Experiments show that our method can successfully track objects despite changes in foreground appearance, clutter, occlusion, etc.; and that it outperforms several color-histogram based methods.

1 Introduction

Visual tracking in unconstrained environments is one of the most challenging tasks in computer vision because it has to overcome many difficulties arising from sensor noise, clutter, occlusions and changes in lighting, background and foreground appearance etc. Yet tracking objects is an important task with many practical applications such as smart rooms, human-computer interaction, video surveillance, and gesture recognition. Generally speaking, methods for visual tracking can be roughly classified into two major groups: deterministic methods and stochastic methods.

In deterministic methods (for example, the Mean Shift (MS) tracker [1]), the target object is located by maximizing the similarity between a template image and the current image. The localization is implemented by iterative search. These methods are computationally efficient, but they are sensitive to background distraction, clutter, occlusion, etc. Once they lose the target object, they can not recover from the failure on their own. This problem can be mitigated by stochastic methods, which maintain multiple hypotheses in the state space and in this way, achieve more robustness. For example, the Particle Filter (PF) [2, 3, 4] has been widely applied in visual tracking in recent years.

A particle filter tracks multiple hypotheses simultaneously and weights them according to a similarity measure (i.e., the observation likelihood function). This paper

A. Leonardis, H. Bischof, and A. Pinz (Eds.): ECCV 2006, Part III, LNCS 3953, pp. 606–618, 2006.

is essentially concerned with devising and calculating this likelihood function/similarity measure. Visual similarity can be measured using many features such as intensity, color, gradient, contour, texture, or spatial layout. A popular feature is color [1, 2, 4, 5, 6], due to its simplicity and robustness (against scaling, rotation, partial occlusion, and non-rigid deformation). Usually, the appearance of a region is represented by its color histogram, and the distance between the normalized color histograms of two regions is measured by the Bhattacharyya distance [2, 4].

Despite its popularity, the color histogram also has several disadvantages:

1) The spatial layout information of a tracked object is completely ignored (see figure 1(a)). As a result, a tracker based on color histograms is easily confused when two objects with similar colors but different spatial distributions get close to each other. An ad-hoc solution is to manually split the tracked region into several sub-regions (e.g., [4, 7]).

2) Since the appearance of the target object is reduced to a global histogram, the similarity measure (e.g., the Bhattacharyya coefficient) is not discriminative enough (see Fig. 1) [8].

3) For a classical color histogram based particle filter, the construction of the histograms is a bottleneck. The computation is quadratic in the number of samples.

In order to overcome the disadvantages of color histograms, we describe a Spatial-color Mixture of Gaussians (called SMOG) appearance model and propose a SMOG-based similarity measure in Sect. 2. The main advantage of SMOG over color histograms and general Gaussian Mixtures is in that both the color information and the spatial layout information are utilized in the objective function of SMOG. Therefore, the SMOG-based similarity measure is more discriminative.

When SMOG and the SMOG-based similarity measure are used in particle filters, one major bottleneck is the extraction of the parameters (weight, mean, and covariance) of SMOG for each particle. In Sect. 3, we propose an Integral Gaussian Mixture (IGM) technique as a fast way to extract these parameters and which also requires less memory storage than the integral histogram [9].

In Sect. 4, experiments showing the advantages of our method over other popular methods are provided. We summarize the paper in Sect. 5.

2   SMOG for Particle Filters

2.1   A Brief Review of the Particle Filter

Denoting by X_t and Y_t the hidden state and the observation respectively at time t. The goal is to estimate the posterior probability density function (pdf) $p(X_t)$ of the target object state given all available observations up to time t: $Y_{1:t} = \{Y_i, i=1, ...,t\}$. Employing the first-order Markovian assumption $p(X_t|X_{1:t-1}) = p(X_t|X_{t-1})$, the posterior distribution of the state variable can be formulated as follows:

$$p(X_t|Y_{1:t}) \propto L(Y_t \mid X_t) \int p(X_t|X_{t-1}) p(X_{t-1}|Y_{1:t-1}) dX_{t-1} \qquad (1)$$

Given the dynamic model $p(X_t|X_{t-1})$ and the observation likelihood model $L(Y_t | X_t)$, the posterior pdf distribution in Eq (1) can be recursively calculated.

The particle filter approximates the posteriori distribution $p(X_t| Y_{1:t})$ based on a finite set of random particles and associated weights $\{X_t^{(j)}, W_t^{(j)}\}_{j=1}^M$. If we draw particles from an importance density, i.e., $X_t^{(j)} \sim q(X_t^{(j)} | X_{t-1}^{(j)}, Y_{1:t})$, the weights of new particles become:

$$W_t^{(j)} \propto \frac{L(Y_t | X_t^{(j)}) p(X_t^{(j)} | X_{t-1}^{(j)})}{q(X_t^{(j)} | X_{t-1}^{(j)}, Y_{1:t})} \tag{2}$$

Then, the state estimate of the object at each frame can be obtained by either the mean state or a maximum a posteriori (MAP) estimate [10].

The observation likelihood function $L(Y_t | X_t)$ plays an important role in the particle filter. It determines the weights of particles and thereby could significantly influence the performance [11]. The likelihood function mainly affects the particle filter by the following ways:

1) It affects the way particles are re-sampled. Re-sampling is necessary to decrease the number of low weighted particles and to increase the ones with more potential particles. Particles are re-sampled according to their weights.
2) It affects the state estimate $\hat{X}_t$ of the target object.

Two popular likelihood function categories are: contour-based models (e.g., [12]) and color-based models (e.g. [1, 2, 4, 6]). Although the contour-based model can accurately describe the shape of a target, it performs poorly in clutter and the time complexity is high. In the color-based model, a color histogram (due to its robustness to noise, rotation, and partial occlusion, etc.) is frequently employed with the Bhattacharyya coefficient as a similarity measure. However, color histogram has some limitations, as we show next.

2.2 Limitations of Color-Histogram Based Similarity Measure

We illustrate the main disadvantage of the color histogram based similarity measure: it lacks information about the spatial layout of the target object, and is thus not discriminative enough.

Denote by $\phi_{O_t} = \{\phi_{O_t}^{(u)}\}_{u=1,...,m}$ and $\phi_{O_v} = \{\phi_{O_v}^{(u)}\}_{u=1,...,m}$ respectively the m-bin normalized color histograms of target model o_t and the target candidate o_v, the Bhattacharyya coefficient (i.e., the similarity measure) between the reference region and candidate region is:

$$\rho(\phi_{O_t}, \phi_{O_v}) = \sum_{u=1}^m \sqrt{\phi_{O_t}^{(u)} \phi_{O_v}^{(u)}} \tag{3}$$

In Fig. 1, we track a face comprising pixels within a red rectangle region in a video sequence from http://vision.stanford.edu/~birch/headtracker/seq/. Target candidates

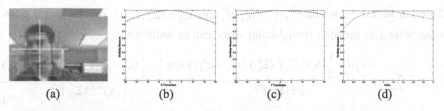

| (a) | (b) | (c) | (d) |

Fig. 1. Color-histogram based similarity measure. The score of the similarity measure over (b) x-translation; (c) y-translation; and (d) scaling. (see text below and compare with Fig. 2).

are generated by translating the rectangle from -20 to 20 horizontally or vertically, and by scaling the rectangle by a factor of 0.2 (the smaller green rectangle inside the target model) to 2 (the larger green rectangle inside the target model) in steps of 0.2. We use 8x8x8 color histogram bins. From Fig. 1, we can see that the similarity measure by Eq. (3) obtains very similar scores for different target candidates, and does not discriminate well between different candidate regions.

2.3 SMOG: A Joint Spatial-Color Appearance Model

Both the appearance model and the similarity measure are very important to the performance of particle filters. The color histogram, as described above, is one popular appearance model. Other popular models for foreground and/or background appearance include: the Gaussian [13], the kernel density [14, 15] and the MOG (Mixture of Gaussians) based appearance model [10, 16, 17, 18, 19, 20]. For example, [13] represented humans by blobs and modeled each blob by a Gaussian model.

The kernel density based model is robust to noise and does not require the calculation of parameters (such as weights, mean and covariance of the Gaussian model) but it is computationally expensive and requires a large storage space. It is also not trivial to update the appearance changes. The disadvantage of the general MOG-based model is that it treats each pixel independently without using any spatial information. Moreover, it requires setting the number of Gaussians and a learning rate. Despite these limits, it is popular because (1) it can model the multimodal distribution of the appearance; (2) it is computationally efficient; (3) it is easy to adapt to the changes of the appearance; and (4) it does not require a large storage space.

We model the appearance of an object with a joint spatial-color mixture of Gaussians. We refer to this approach as SMOG. We denote by $S_i=(x_i, y_i)$ and $C_i=\{C_i^j\}_{j=1,...,d}$ respectively the spatial feature (i.e., the 2D coordinates) and the color feature with d color channels (in RGB color space, $C_i=\{R_i,G_i,B_i\}$ and $d=3$) at pixel x_i. Thus, we can write the features of x_i as the Cartesian product of its position and color: $x_i = (S_i, C_i)$. We assume that the spatial feature (S) and the color feature (C) are independent to each other. For the mean and the covariance of the lth mode of the

Gaussian Mixtures, we have $\mu_{t,l} = (\mu_{t,l}^S, \mu_{t,l}^C)$ and $\Sigma_{t,l} = (\Sigma_{t,l}^S, \Sigma_{t,l}^C)$. The estimated density at the point x_i in the joint spatial-color space can be written as:

$$p_o(x_i) = \sum_{l=1}^{k} \omega_{t,l} \frac{\exp\left\{-\frac{1}{2}(S_i - \mu_{t,l}^S)^T (\Sigma_{t,l}^S)^{-1}(S_i - \mu_{t,l}^S)\right\}}{2\pi |\Sigma_{t,l}^S|^{1/2}} \frac{\exp\left\{-\frac{1}{2}(C_i - \mu_{t,l}^C)^T (\Sigma_{t,l}^C)^{-1}(C_i - \mu_{t,l}^C)\right\}}{(2\pi)^{d/2} |\Sigma_{t,l}^C|^{1/2}}$$

$$(4)$$

2.4 SMOG-Based Similarity Measure

We model the appearance of a target object O_t by SMOG with k modes. We initialize the parameters of SMOG for a target object $\{\omega_{t=1,l}^{O_t}, \mu_{t=1,l}^{S,O_t}, \mu_{t=1,l}^{C,O_t}, \Sigma_{t=1,l}^{S,O_t}, \Sigma_{t=1,l}^{C,O_t}\}_{l=1,\dots,k}$ by a K-means algorithm followed by a standard EM algorithm. Once we obtain the parameters of the target object, we either update these parameters in an "exponential forgetting" way or keep the parameters (if we detect that it is occluded by other objects) in the following frames ($t=2,3\dots$). At time t, we sample M particles (i.e., target candidates O_v) and evaluate the likelihood function in Eq. (1) for each particle. The parameters of each target candidate $\{\omega_{t,l}^{O_v}, \mu_{t,l}^{S,O_v}, \mu_{t,l}^{C,O_v}, \Sigma_{t,l}^{S,O_v}, \Sigma_{t,l}^{C,O_v}\}_{l=1,\dots,k}$ are calculated by:

1. Calculate the Mahalanobis distances between pixels $\{x_i\}$ in the target candidate $O_v = \{x_i\}_{i=1,\dots N}$ to each mode of SMOG of the target object O_t in color space:

$$D_i^2(C_i, \mu_{t,l}^{C,O_t}, \Sigma_{t,l}^{C,O_t}) = (C_i - \mu_{t,l}^{C,O_t})^T (\Sigma_{t,l}^{C,O_t})^{-1}(C_i - \mu_{t,l}^{C,O_t})$$

$$(5)$$

2. Label the pixels satisfying ANY($|D_l|_{l=1,\dots,k} \leq 2.5$) with the number of the mode to which the Mahalanobis distance is the least. For other pixels, label them with zero.

$$LB(x_i) = \arg\min_l |D_l|$$

$$(6)$$

3. Calculate the parameters $\{\omega_{t,l}^{O_v}, \mu_{t,l}^{S,O_v}, \mu_{t,l}^{C,O_v}, \Sigma_{t,l}^{S,O_v}, \Sigma_{t,l}^{C,O_v}\}_{l=1,\dots,k}$ of the target candidate by:

$$\omega_{t,l}^{O_v} = \left(\sum_{i=1}^{N} \delta(LB(x_i) - l)\right) \bigg/ \left(\sum_{l=1}^{k}\sum_{i=1}^{N} \delta(LB(x_i) - l)\right)$$

$$\mu_{t,l}^{O_v} = (\mu_{t,l}^{S,O_v}, \mu_{t,l}^{C,O_v}) = \left(\sum_{i=1}^{N} x_i \delta(LB(x_i) - l)\right) \bigg/ \left(\sum_{i=1}^{N} \delta(LB(x_i) - l)\right)$$

$$(7)$$

$$\Sigma_{t,l}^{O_v} = (\Sigma_{t,l}^{S,O_v}, \Sigma_{t,l}^{C,O_v}) = \left(\sum_{i=1}^{N} \left(x_i - \mu_{t,l}^{O_v}\right)^T \left(x_i - \mu_{t,l}^{O_v}\right)\delta(LB(x_i) - l)\right) \bigg/ \left(\sum_{i=1}^{N} \delta(LB(x_i) - l)\right)$$

where δ is the Kronecker delta function. The covariance matrix is taken to be a diagonal matrix for simplicity. One should normalize the coordinate space first so that the coordinates of pixels in the target candidate (and target object) are within the range [0, 1].

Let $\Lambda_{t,l}^S$ and $\Lambda_{t,l}^C$ be respectively the spatial and the color similarity measure between the lth mode of the target candidate O_v and the lth mode of the target object O_t. The SMOG-based similarity measure (as compared to the color-histogram based similarity measure in Eq. (3)) between two regions (O_v and O_t) in the joint spatial-color space is defined as:

$$\Lambda(O_t, O_v) = \sum_{l=1}^{k} \Lambda_{t,l}^S \Lambda_{t,l}^C \qquad (8)$$

where $\Lambda_{t,l}^S = \exp\left\{-\frac{1}{2}(\mu_{t,l}^{S,O_v} - \mu_{t,l}^{S,O_t})^T (\hat{\Sigma}_{t,l}^S)^{-1}(\mu_{t,l}^{S,O_v} - \mu_{t,l}^{S,O_t})\right\}$ with $(\hat{\Sigma}_{t,l}^S)^{-1} = (\Sigma_{t,l}^{S,O_v})^{-1} + (\Sigma_{t,l}^{S,O_t})^{-1}$

and $\Lambda_{t,l}^C = \min(\omega_{t,l}^{O_v}, \omega_{t,l}^{O_t})$.

The likelihood function in our method is given by:

$$L(Y_t \mid X_t) \propto \exp\left\{-\frac{1}{2\sigma_b^2}(1 - \Lambda(O_t, O_v))\right\} \qquad (9)$$

where σ_b is the observation variance.

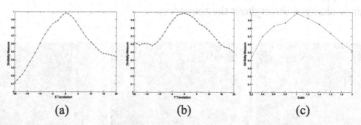

(a)   (b)   (c)

Fig. 2. The score by the SMOG-based similarity measure over (a) x-translation; (b) y-translation; and (c) scale

We repeat the experiment in Fig. 1 using SMOG. As shown in Fig. 2, the SMOG-based similarity measure (Eq. (8)) is more discriminative than the color-histogram based similarity measure in Eq. (3).

Recently, Birchfield et al. [21] proposed a method (Spatiograms), which captures the spatial information of the general histogram bins, and applied it to the Mean Shift (MS) tracker. The spatial mean and covariance *of each bin* is computed. In contrast, we consider the spatial layout and color distribution *of each mode* of SMOG. The number of the Gaussians (normally, k is set within the range from 3 to 7 in our case) is much less than the number of the histogram bins. SMOG is also more efficient in estimating density distribution of the data and in computation, and requires less storage space to build up an integral Gaussian mixtures image (as described in Sect. 3) than the integral histogram method [9].

2.5 Updating the Parameters of SMOG

We dynamically model the object appearance by updating the parameters of SMOG through a learning rate α. The assumption made here is that in the temporally neighboring frames (e.g., frame t and frame t-1), the appearance (including both spatial and color distributions) of an object does not change dramatically.

Similar to [10] and [17], we assume that the past appearance is exponentially forgotten and new information is gradually added to the appearance model.

To handle occlusion where image outliers exist, we use a heuristic way: we update the appearance only if the score of the similarity measure is larger than a threshold T_u. When occlusion is declared (i.e., the score is less than T_u), we stop updating the appearance model.

2.6 Choosing the Color Space

We employ the normalized color space in our method. The normalized chromaticity coordinates of (r, g, b) can be written as: $r=R/(R+G+B)$; $g=G/(R+G+B)$; $b=R/(R+G+B)$. The intensity information is also exploited. Thus we use (r, g, I) as the color feature in our method.

In Fig. 3, we show an experiment illustrating the advantage of (r, g, I) over (R, G, B) color space in dealing with illumination changes. (r, g, I) color space shows more robustness to the illumination change. In contrast, the method employing (R, G, B) achieved less accurate results and lost the target at the end.

Fig. 4 shows the adaptation of the proposed method to the appearance changes by updating the appearance model in subsection 2.5. Our method succeeds in adaptation to appearance changes throughout the sequence.

| $t=21$ | $t=34$ | $t=52$ |

Fig. 3. Tracking results employing RGB as color feature (in the first row) and *rgI* as color feature (in the second row)

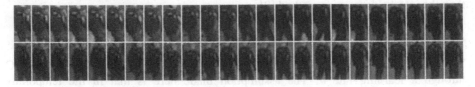

Fig. 4. The appearance of the tracked target changes with time increasing

3   Integral Gaussian Mixture for Higher Computational Efficiency

To efficiently calculate the similarity measure $\Lambda(O_t, O_v)$ (in Eq. (8)), we need to calculate $\left\{\omega_l^{O_v}, \mu_l^{s,O_v}, \Sigma_l^{s,O_v}\right\}_{l=1,\dots,k}$ for each target candidate. One possible way, which is usually used in the color-histogram based particle filters (such as [2, 4]), is to randomly sample a particle, and generate a target candidate, and then calculate the parameters corresponding to the candidate region. This is computationally inefficient because particles may have many overlapped regions and the same operator for each possible region can be repeated many times.

To overcome this inefficiency, integral methods exploiting rectangle features were introduced by Viola et al. [22] and more recently, were developed by Porikli [9]. In [22], a grey-level image is converted to integral image format (i.e., the value of each pixel is the sum of values of all pixels to the left and above of the current pixel). In [9], integral histogram is constructed by a recursive propagation of an aggregated histogram in a Cartesian data space.

We propose an Integral Gaussian Mixture (IGM) technique as a fast and efficient way to extract the parameters of SMOG for each particle. To calculate the parameters of the lth mode of a target candidate, we need to calculate $(n_l, \mu_{x,l}, \mu_{y,l}, \sigma_{x,l}^2, \sigma_{y,l}^2)$, i.e., the number of pixels whose label is l, the spatial mean and variance values in x and y coordinates.

We can write these quantities in the following form:

$$n_l = \sum_{i=1}^{N} \delta(LB(x_i) - l)$$

$$\mu_{x,l} = \left(\sum_{i=1}^{N} x_i \delta(LB(x_i) - l)\right)\Big/n_l \; ; \; \mu_{y,l} = \left(\sum_{i=1}^{N} y_i \delta(LB(x_i) - l)\right)\Big/n_l \quad (10)$$

$$\sigma_{y,l}^2 = \left(\sum_{i=1}^{N} x_i^2 \delta(LB(x_i) - l)\right)\Big/n_l - \mu_{x,l}^2 \; ; \; \sigma_{y,l}^2 = \left(\sum_{i=1}^{N} y_i^2 \delta(LB(x_i) - l)\right)\Big/n_l - \mu_{y,l}^2$$

and we have

$$\omega_l = n_l \Big/ \sum_{l=1}^{k} n_l \; ; \; \mu_l^S = (\mu_{x,l}, \mu_{y,l}); \Sigma_l^S = \begin{pmatrix} \sigma_{x,l}^2 & 0 \\ 0 & \sigma_{y,l}^2 \end{pmatrix} \quad (11)$$

The procedure of the IGM can be described as follows:

1. Predict the region $\tilde{R}$, that includes all particles (i.e., target candidates), in the 2D image.
2. Label each pixel $x_{\tilde{i}}$ in $\tilde{R}$ by step 1 and 2 in subsection 2.4.
3. Generate a GM image whose $\tilde{i}$th pixel is given by $x_{\tilde{i}} = \{x_{\tilde{i},l}\}_{l=1,...,k}$, where
   $x_{\tilde{i},l} = \delta(LB(x_{\tilde{i}}) - l)(1, x_{\tilde{i}}, x_{\tilde{i}}^2, y_{\tilde{i}}, y_{\tilde{i}}^2)$.
4. Build an IGM image, where each pixel is the sum of values of all pixels of the GM image to the left and above of the current pixel.
5. Calculate the parameters of each target candidate by four table lookup operations, which are similar to [22].

We find that once the IGM is built, the calculation of the likelihood function is very fast. Fig. 5 gives a rough estimation of the computational time (in MATLAB code) to evaluate the likelihood function for particles. From Fig. 5, we can see that the calculation of the color histogram based similarity measure in Condensation is

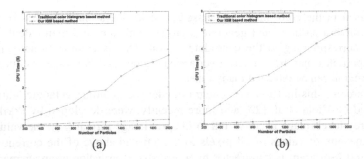

(a)   (b)

Fig. 5. The computational time v.s. the number of particles for the color histogram based method and the proposed method. Candidate region size in (b) is twice as that in (a).

computationally expensive and will be affected by both the number of particles and the size of target candidate regions. When we double the region size (Fig. 5 (b)) of the candidate region (Fig. 5 (a)), the computational time of the color histogram based Condensation increased by about 60%. In contrast, both the number of particles and the size of the target candidate regions have much less influence on the computational complexity of the proposed method: the processing time is about 10 to 20 times less than the color histogram based Condensation.

4 Experiments

We test the effectiveness of our method using a number of video sequences with different environments and conditions[1]. We compare with two popular color histogram based

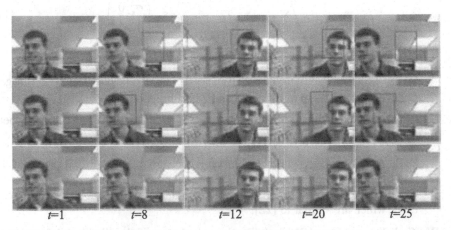

t=1   t=8   t=12   t=20   t=25

Fig. 6. Tracking results of the *face* sequence with the MS tracker (first row), Condensation (second row) and our method (third row)

---

[1] Some demo video sequences of our method can be obtained from http://users.monash. edu.au/~hanzi

methods: the Mean Shift tracker and Condensation. Note: we employ the (r, g, I) color space for all three methods. For the Mean Shift tracker and the Condensation tracker, we use 16x16x16 color histogram bins. For both Condensation and our method, we employ a random walk dynamic model (number of particles M=200).

In Fig. 6, the human face is moving to the left and right very quickly. The illumination on the face also changes. The background scene includes clutter and material of similar color to the face. As we can see in Fig. 6, the Mean Shift tracker fails to track the face very soon; the results of Condensation are not accurate and Condensation even fails to track the face in some frames because the color histogram based similarity measure is not discriminative enough (section 2.2). In comparison, our method, which considers both color and spatial information of the target object, never loses the target and achieves the most accurate results.

Fig. 7 and Fig. 8 show situations where two humans with very similar colors get close to each other and one occludes the other. In Fig. 7, when the man's face gets close to and occludes the girl's face, the results of both the MS tracker and Condensation are greatly influenced. In Fig. 8 (a), because the color histogram based similarity ignores the spatial information, both the MS tracker and Condensation break down when two players with similar colors, but different spatial distributions, get close to each other. In contrast, our method works well in both cases. Fig. 8 (b) shows that our method can still effectively track the human body even if it is almost completely occluded by another player.

Next, we test the adaptation of our method to appearance changes. In Fig. 9, a particularly challenging (with high clutter) video sequence is used. The head of a player is tracked even though it moves fast and the appearance of the head changes frequently (including occlusion, blurring, and changes in the spatial and color distributions of the appearance). Fig. 9 shows that our method has successfully tracked the target and adapted to the changes of the target appearance.

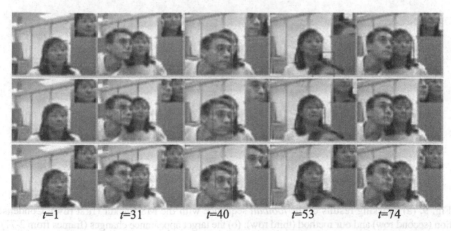

$t=1$ $t=31$ $t=40$ $t=53$ $t=74$

Fig. 7. Tracking results of the *girl* sequence with the MS tracker (first row), Condensation (second row) and our method (third row). The tracked face is shown in the upper-right window.

616   H. Wang, D. Suter, and K. Schindler

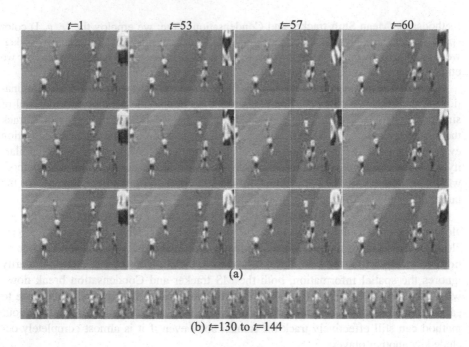

(a)

(b) *t*=130 to *t*=144

Fig. 8. Tracking results of the *soccer* sequence with three methods (a): the MS tracker (first row), Condensation (second row) and our method (third row). The tracked body is also shown in the upper-right window; (b) tracking results with occlusions by our method.

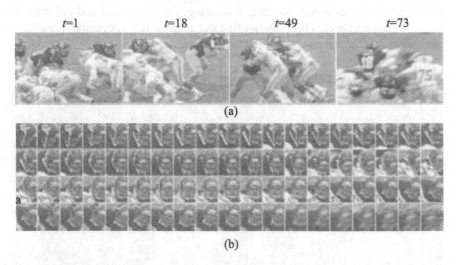

(a)

(b)

Fig. 9. (a) Tracking results of the *football* sequence with the MS tracker (first row), Condensation (second row) and our method (third row); (b) the target appearance changes (frames from 2-77)

5 Conclusion

We have described an effective appearance model (SMOG) in a joint spatial-color space and a new similarity measure based on SMOG. The SMOG appearance model and the SMOG-based similarity measure consider both the spatial distribution and the color distribution of objects: they utilize richer information than the general color histogram based appearance model and similarity measure.

We also propose an Integral Gaussian Mixture (IGM) technique, which greatly improves the computational efficiency of our method. Thus the number of particles and the size of target candidate region can be greatly increased, without significant change in the processing time of the proposed method.

We have successfully applied the SMOG appearance model and the SMOG-based similarity measure to the task of visual tracking in the framework of particle filters. Our tracking method can effectively handle clutter, illumination changes, appearance changes, occlusions, etc. Comparisons show that our method outperforms popular methods such as the general color histogram based MS tracker and Condensation.

Acknowledgements

We thank Dr. Chunhua Shen for his valuable comments, and the ARC for support (grant DP0452416).

References

1. Comaniciu, D., V. Ramesh, and P. Meer, *Kernel-based Object Tracking*. IEEE Trans. Pattern Analysis and Machine Intelligence, 2003. **25**(5): p. 564 - 577.
2. Nummiaroa, K., E. Koller-Meierb, and L.V. Gool, *An Adaptive Color-Based Particle Filter*. Image and Vision Computing, 2003. **21**: p. 99-110.
3. Isard, M. and A. Blake, *Condensation-Conditional Density Propagation for Visual Tracking*. International Journal of Computer Vision, 1998. **29**(1): p. 5-28.
4. Perez, P., et al. *Color-Based Probabilistic Tracking*. European Conference on Computer Vision. 2002. p. 661-675.
5. Shen, C., A.v.d. Hengel, and A. Dick. *Probabilistic Multiple Cue Integration for Particle Filter Based Tracking*. International Conference on Digital Image Computing - Techniques and Applications. 2003. p. 309-408.
6. McKenna, S.J., et al., *Tracking Groups of People*. Computer Vision and Image Understanding, 2000. **80**: p. 42-56.
7. Pérez, P., J. Vermaak, and A. Blake, *Data Fusion for Visual Tracking with Particles*. Proceedings of the IEEE, 2004. **92**(3): p. 495-513.
8. Yang, C., R. Duraiswami, and L. Davis. *Fast Multiple Object Tracking via a Hierarchical Particle Filter*. International Conference on Computer Vision. 2005. p. 212-219.
9. Porikli, F. *Integral Histogram: A Fast Way to Extract Histograms in Cartesian Spaces*. Computer Vision and Pattern Recognition. 2005. p. 829-836.
10. Zhou, S., R. Chellappa, and B. Moghaddam, *Visual Tracking and Recognition Using Appearance-Adaptive Models in Particle Filters*. IEEE Transactions on Image Processing, 2004. **11**: p. 1434-1456.

11. Lichtenauer, J., M. Reinders, and E. Hendriks. *Influence of the Observation Likelihood Function on Particle Filtering Performance in Tracking Applications.* IEEE International Conference on Automatic Face and Gesture Recognition. 2004. p. 767-772.
12. Isard, M. and A. Blake. *ICONDENSATION: Unifying Low-level and High-level Tracking in a Stochastic Framework.* European Conference on Computer Vision. 1998. p. 893-908.
13. Wren, C.R., et al., *Pfinder: real-time tracking of the human body.* IEEE Trans. Pattern Analysis and Machine Intelligence, 1997. **19**(7): p. 780-785.
14. Elgammal, A., et al., *Background and Foreground Modeling using Non-parametric Kernel Density Estimation for Visual Surveillance.* Proceedings of the IEEE, 2002. **90**(7): p. 1151-1163.
15. Yang, C., R. Duraiswami, and L.S. Davis. *Efficient Mean-Shift Tracking via a New Similarity Measure.* Computer Vision and Pattern Recognition. 2005. p. 176-183.
16. McKenna, S.J., Y. Raja, and S. Gong, *Tracking Colour Objects Using Adaptive Mixture Models.* Image and Vision Computing, 1999. **17**: p. 225-231.
17. Stauffer, C. and W.E.L. Grimson. *Adaptive Background Mixture Models for Real-time Tracking.* Computer Vision and Pattern Recognition. 1999. p. 246-252.
18. Han, B. and L. Davis. *On-Line Density-Based Appearance Modeling for Object Tracking.* International Conference on Computer Vision. 2005. p. 1492-1499.
19. Wu, Y. and T.S. Huang, *Robust Visual Tracking by Integrating Multiple Cues Based on Co-Inference Learning.* International Journal of Computer Vision, 2004. **58**(1): p. 55-71.
20. Khan, S. and M. Shah. *Tracking People in Presence of Occlusion.* Asian Conference on Computer Vision. 2000. p. 263-266.
21. Birchfield, S. and S. Rangarajan. *Spatiograms versus Histograms for Region-Based Tracking.* Computer Vision and Pattern Recognition. 2005. p. 1152-1157.
22. Viola, P. and M. Jones, *Robust Real-Time Face Detection.* International Journal of Computer Vision, 2004. **52**(2): p. 137-154.

Tracking and Labelling of Interacting Multiple Targets

Josephine Sullivan and Stefan Carlsson

Royal Institute of Technology, Stockholm, Sweden
{sullivan, stefanc}@nada.kth.se

Abstract. Successful multi-target tracking requires solving two problems - *localize* the targets and *label* their identity. An isolated target's identity can be unambiguously preserved from one frame to the next. However, for long sequences of many moving targets, like a football game, grouping scenarios will occur in which identity labellings cannot be maintained reliably by using continuity of motion or appearance. This paper describes how to match targets' identities despite these interactions.

Trajectories of when a target is isolated are found. These trajectories end when targets interact and their labellings cannot be maintained. The interactions (merges and splits) of these trajectories form a graph structure. Appropriate feature vectors summarizing particular qualities of each trajectory are extracted. A clustering procedure based on these feature vectors allows the identities of temporally separated trajectories to be matched. Results are shown from a football match captured by a wide screen system giving a full stationary view of the pitch.

1 Introduction

This paper addresses the problem of the surveillance and tracking of multiple persons over a wide area. Typical scenarios involve following pedestrians in traffic or other crowded environments such as airports and shopping malls. There is also the more specialized problem of tracking players in team sports, such as football or ice-hockey, which we specifically explore. The first challenge is defining a multiple camera set-up that ensures all the target objects are visible, at a required resolution, at all times. Such a camera set-up is shown in figure 2.

Over the last years, many algorithms and results have been presented [1, 2] with regard to the problem of multiple object tracking. Prevalent are algorithms based on kalman filtering [3, 4] and advanced techniques of particle filtering [5, 6, 7, 8]. These works demonstrate that the tracking of individual players is no problem as long as they are isolated. Situations of congestion and confusion due to multiple players occluding each other are generally resolved by exploiting continuity of motion, appearance and relative depth. However, these properties cannot be used to reliably solve all congested situations, see fig. 1. It is clear even extremely sophisticated trackers will eventually lose the identity of a track due to the complex scenarios that arise during a soccer game lasting 90 minutes. A

A. Leonardis, H. Bischof, and A. Pinz (Eds.): ECCV 2006, Part III, LNCS 3953, pp. 619–632, 2006.

Fig. 1. All the players from one team have congregated into a small area to celebrate a goal. In this situation the players' identities cannot be maintained by using continuity of motion, appearance or relative depth, irrespective of the camera viewpoint.

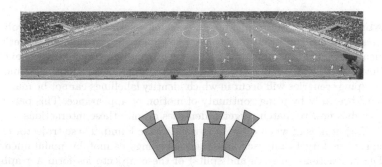

Fig. 2. Four cameras are on one side of the field. Each one looks at a portion of the pitch and the images obtained are stitched together using the inter camera homographies.

system for the automatic tracking of players over a whole game must, therefore, address the problem of automatic track label initialization and re-initialization.

With these observations in mind, consider the strategy put forward in this paper. Periods and trajectories when players are isolated are identified, which we term *player tracks*. The merge and splits between the *player tracks* are recorded to form a giant graph summarizing the game. A feature vector for each track, encoding a player's relative spatial position wrt his team-mates, is defined. The identity of the *player tracks* are then linked through analysis of the recorded merge and splits and clustering of the feature vectors associated with each track.

Paper Overview. The paper is organized as follows. Section 2 is devoted to explaining the imaging set-up and image processing performed to get an initial estimate of the player/target positions. The machinery used to temporally analyze these results is then introduced in addition to describing how a graph summarizing the interaction of the targets is obtained. Section 4 is concerned with resolving some of the split and merge situations that occur using the properties of continuity of motion, appearance and relative depth ordering. Finally a clustering procedure is described that allows the identity of temporally separated player trajectories to be linked. The paper ends with a discussion on the merits of the ideas put forward here and future avenues of research. Throughout results are displayed from analyzing 10 minutes of an international football match.

2   Video Capture and Processing

One of the innovations of this paper is the use of wide-screen video in our tracking/labelling algorithm. This video allows a wide field of view to be monitored at each time instant at a high resolution. This makes it possible to track simultaneously a large group of targets spread over a large area. This wide screen video is obtained by mounting several cameras (in our case 4) on a tripod with each camera directed towards a portion of the area of interest. As the optical centres of the cameras are aligned a homography relates the images between each camera. This imaging set-up allows us a full, stationary view of the area-of-interest, an ideal environment to perform background subtraction given a background image model. The next subsection describes how to find this background model.

2.1   Background Modelling

A probabilistic model for the image gradient of each pixel in the background is obtained. Note that the image gradient is learnt as opposed to the rgb values, as often a football team's uniform contains white, the colour of the pitch markings. Also using the image gradient increases robustness to changes in illumination.

Let $\mathbf{g}_x^t$ denote the image gradient at pixel x in frame t. Each background pixel's image gradient, $\mathbf{g}_x^b$, is modelled by a bivariate normal distribution with mean μ_x and diagonal covariance matrix Σ_x. The parameters of this distribution are learnt in the manner of Stauffer and Grimson [9]. Except we consider it as a batch process and learn the background for a time interval. The initial learning algorithm produces, for each pixel x, a mixture of Gaussians distribution to describe the values of $\mathbf{g}_x$ over a set of training images.

$$\mathbf{g}_x \sim \sum_{i=1}^{3} \beta_x^i \, \mathbf{N}_2(\mu_x^i, \Sigma_x^i) \tag{1}$$

with each $0 \le \beta_x^i \le 1$ and the β_x^i's summing to one. It is assumed that at a given location, x, the background is most commonly visible. To ensure this assumption

Fig. 3. The set of ellipses, $\mathcal{E}_t$, the highlighted regions, found by background subtraction

is true, as players frequently stand still for relatively lengthy periods of time, for a given time window of length T only every nth frame is used as input. Then set

$$(\mu_x, \Sigma_x) = (\mu_x^i, \Sigma_x^i) \text{ s.t. } \beta_x^i \geq \beta_x^j \text{ for } j = 1, 2, 3. \tag{2}$$

For a frame in the time window a pixel, x, is considered a foreground pixel if:

$$(g_x^t - \mu_x)^T \Sigma_x^{-1} (g_x^t - \mu_x) \geq \chi_{3,\alpha}^2, \quad 0 < \alpha < 1 \tag{3}$$

Let $\mathcal{F}_t$ ($\mathcal{B}_t$) be the set of foreground(background) pixels found at time t. Once $\mathcal{F}_t$ has been calculated, connected components are identified. A set $\mathcal{E}_t = \{E_t^i\}_{i=1}^{n}$ of ellipses is used to represent these components, see figure 3. We assume that each ellipse corresponds to at least one whole player. The raw connected components are processed by deleting small connected components or joining them to neighbouring larger ones to ensure this assumption is for the most part upheld.

3   Constructing the Target Interaction Graph

This section is devoted to the temporal analysis of the $\mathcal{E}_t$'s - spotting the merging and splitting of ellipses from one frame to the next. Detection of these splits and merges allows for the identification of ellipses corresponding to individual and multiple targets and then to the trajectories of individual players.

3.1   Finding Player Tracks

The first aim is to put the ellipse in $\mathcal{E}_t$ and $\mathcal{E}_{t+1}$ in correspondence. This requires the definition of a relation, $\sim$, between ellipses in $\mathcal{E}_t$ and $\mathcal{E}_{t+1}$. Let ellipses E_1 and E_2 be an exact match if their size and orientation are sufficiently similar and the displacement between their centres is sufficiently small. If $\exists E_{t+1}^j \in \mathcal{E}_{t+1}$ s.t. E_t^i and E_{t+1}^j are an exact match then $E_t^i \sim E_{t+1}^j$. If no such exact match exists for E_t^i in $\mathcal{E}_{t+1}$ then $E_t^i \sim E_{t+1}^j$ if

$$\text{Area}(E_t^i \cap E_{t+1}^j) > 0 \quad \& \quad E_{t+1}^j \text{ has no exact match in } \mathcal{E}_t. \tag{4}$$

Define a mapping F_t, matching each ellipse in $\mathcal{E}_t$ to its related ellipses in $\mathcal{E}_{t+1}$

$$F_t : \mathcal{I}_t \to \{a : a \subset \mathcal{I}_{t+1}\} \quad \text{s.t.} \quad j \in F_t(i) \Rightarrow E_t^i \sim E_{t+1}^j \tag{5}$$

where $\mathcal{I}_t = \{1, \cdots, n_t\}$ is the set of indices of the ellipses in $\mathcal{E}_t$ (see figure 4). A mapping B_t is then defined relating each ellipse in $\mathcal{E}_t$ to a subset of $\mathcal{E}_{t+1}$,

$$B_t : \mathcal{I}_{t+1} \to \{a : a \subset \mathcal{I}_t\} \quad \text{s.t.} \quad k \in B_t(i) \Rightarrow i \in F_t(k). \tag{6}$$

With F_t and B_t it is easy to define events that can happen or have happened at each ellipse at each frame given the cardinality of $F_t(i)$ and $B_t(i)$:

Signal	Event	Signal	Event
$|F_t(i)| > 1$	split	$|B_t(j)| > 1$	merge
$|F_t(i)| = 0$	disappear	$|B_t(j)| = 0$	appear
$|F_t(i)| = |B_t(F_t(i))| = 1$	stable		

(a) F_t (b) B_t

Fig. 4. The correspondences between the ellipses in one frame and those in the next

A maximal sequence of *stable* events sandwiched between non-*stable* events is termed a *track*. Formally, it is a temporal sequence, starting at t of n ellipses with indices **k**

$$\mathcal{T}(t, n, \mathbf{k}) = \{E_t^{k_0}, E_{t+1}^{k_1}, \cdots, E_{t+n-1}^{k_{n-1}}\} \tag{7}$$

that unambiguously match to one another s.t. for $i = 0, \cdots, n - 2$

$$|F_{t+i}(k_i)| = 1, \quad F_{t+i}(k_i) = k_{i+1}, \quad |B_{t+i}(k_{i+1})| = 1 \tag{8}$$

and a non-*stable* event occurs to go from $\mathcal{E}_{t-1}$ to $E_t^{k_0}$ and from $E_{t+n-1}^{k_{n-1}}$ to $\mathcal{E}_{t+n}$. During a track there is no change in the identity or number of the subjects represented by the ellipses concerned. It is clear, therefore, that if either of the following sequence of events occurs

$$track \rightarrow split \quad \text{or} \quad merge \rightarrow track \tag{9}$$

the involved *track* corresponds to multiple players. However, when the involved track appears in the sequence

$$\{split, \, appear\} \rightarrow track \rightarrow \{merge, \, disappear\} \tag{10}$$

it may correspond to exactly one player. If the track has long enough duration and the size of the ellipses during the track is on average not too big then the track is considered to be a *player track*. Each ellipse in a player track corresponds to exactly one player and the identity of this player remains fixed over the track.

The application of this analysis results in a partition of all ellipses, found from the background subtraction process, into *player tracks* or *multiple player tracks* and the interactions of these tracks through merges and splits.

Modelling Player Appearance. Frequently in multi-target applications the appearance of some or all of the targets will be distinctive. In a football game there are two teams and officials with distinct uniforms. With a pdf for the rgb values for each category it is possible to distinguish between them. These distributions, $p_{A,B,C}$, are learnt from a few labelled training examples. The likelihood that ellipse E_t^j is team A is defined, naively, as:

$$p(E_t^j|A) = \prod_{x \in E_t^j} p_A(\mathbf{I}_t^x) \tag{11}$$

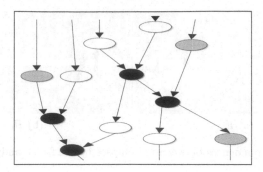

Fig. 5. The player interaction graph. White/gray nodes correspond to team A/B player tracks and black nodes to multiple player tracks. Edges indicate when tracks interact. Shown is a small section of the $\sim$ 5000 node graph describing the 10 minutes analyzed.

where $\mathbf{I}_t^x$ represents the rgb values of pixel x at time t. The ellipse is classified as the category with the maximal likelihood. Each ellipse in a player track, $\mathcal{T}(t, n, \mathbf{k})$, is classified accordingly. The label, λ, of the track is set to the category that occurs most frequently amongst its ellipses. All these ellipses are then set to the track label. As player tracks are quite long there is sufficient temporal evidence to compensate for less than perfect appearance models. Given the labelling of the tracks and their interactions through merging and splitting, the game can be summarized by a graph structure, see figure 5.

4   Linking Player Tracks

By examining the player interaction graph it is possible to isolate situations where n individual player tracks merge (potentially staggered over time) and then split into n individual player tracks (potentially staggered over time). These merge-split situations are resolved by finding the correct correspondence between the input and output tracks. This can often be done by exploiting the continuity of motion, appearance and/or relative depth ordering of the players involved.

4.1   Matching Input and Output Tracks

The set of input and output tracks with labels to be put in correspondence are:

$$\textbf{Input: } \{\mathcal{T}(t_{s_.}, n_{s_.}, \mathbf{k}^{s_.}), \lambda_{s_.}\}_{i=1}^n \quad \textbf{Output: } \{\mathcal{T}(t_{f_.}, n_{f_.}, \mathbf{k}^{f_.}), \lambda_{f_.}\}_{i=1}^n \quad (12)$$

For brevity we refer to $\mathcal{T}(t_{s_.}, n_{s_.}, \mathbf{k}^{s_.})$ as $\mathcal{T}_{s_.}$. We wish to find the assignment, M, of the inputs to the outputs. It is a bijective mapping $M : \{1, \cdots, n\} \to \{1, \cdots, n\}$ s.t. $M(i) = j$ implies that track $\mathcal{T}_{s_.}$ and $\mathcal{T}_{f_.}$ are the same player. Not all assignments are physically possible, thus M is a valid assignment iff all the input tracks and their matched output tracks have the same label and all the input tracks finish before their matched output tracks begin. Finding the correct assignment from the valid ones involves scoring each valid assignment and choosing the most plausible one. Our score is computed as follows.

For each valid assignment, M, we estimate the intermediate trajectories, $\mathcal{T}_{s.\rightarrow f.~(\cdot)}$'s between the matched player tracks $\mathcal{T}_{s.}$ and $\mathcal{T}_{f.~(\cdot)}$. There are numerous reasonable ways in which each $\mathcal{T}_{s.\rightarrow f.~(\cdot)}$ can be estimated. We return to this issue later in the section. For now we continue with the discussion of finding the correct valid assignment, assuming we have estimates for the $\mathcal{T}_{s.\rightarrow f.~(\cdot)}$'s. We define a score based on these estimated trajectories.

$$\mathrm{Sc}_M = \sum_{i=1}^{n}(\mathrm{Dist}(\mathcal{T}_{s.\rightarrow f.~(\cdot)}) + \alpha \mathrm{Pen}(\mathcal{T}_{s.\rightarrow f.~(\cdot)})) \tag{13}$$

where $\alpha > 0$ and has a large value. The first term $\mathrm{Dist}(\mathcal{T}_{s.\rightarrow f.~(\cdot)})$ is a measure of the distance traveled by the player during the hypothesized trajectory, measured using the estimated feet positions on the ground plane transformed via a homography to a rectified version of the pitch. The second term indicates whether the estimated trajectories are consistent with the image data:

$$\mathrm{Pen}(\mathcal{T}_i) = \begin{cases} 1 & \text{if } \mathcal{T}_i \text{ not consistent with relevant } \mathcal{F}_t\text{'s} \\ 0 & \text{otherwise.} \end{cases} \tag{14}$$

Due to space constraints we summarize in words our consistency measure. Its definition is based on deciding whether a sufficient number of a trajectory's ellipses intersect with a sufficient number of the foreground pixels. Once these scores have been calculated the valid assignment which does not incur the penalty α and whose intermediary trajectories cover the least distance is chosen.

4.2   Estimating Intermediary Tracks

We now focus on the task of estimating the intermediary trajectories $\{\mathcal{T}_{s.\rightarrow f.~(\cdot)}\}$. We exploit the properties of maintaining continuity of motion and relative depth ordering. At the first stage, we investigate if any of the intermediary tracks can

---

Data: A set of input and output player tracks as in eqn (12).

Algorithm:

1. Enumerate all the valid assignments $\{M_k\}_{k=1}^{K'}$.
2. For each M_k estimate the intermediary trajectories $\{\mathcal{T}_{s.\rightarrow f.~(\cdot)}\}$ based solely on linear interpolation. Score each assignment, eqn. (13), to obtain $\{\mathrm{Sc}_M.\}$.
3. $k' = \arg\min_k \mathrm{Sc}_M.$, if $\mathrm{Sc}_{M.,} < \alpha$ set $M = M_{k'}$ and go to step 6.
4. If $\mathrm{Sc}_{M.,} \geq \alpha$ repeat the process of finding the intermediary trajectories, but based on piecewise linear interpolation. Update the set of scores accordingly.
5. $k' = \arg\min_k \mathrm{Sc}_M.$, if $\mathrm{Sc}_{M.,} < \alpha$ set $M = M_{k'}$.
6. If M has been defined, for $i = 1, \cdots, n$ set

$$\mathcal{T}_{s.} = \mathcal{T}_{s.} \cup \mathcal{T}_{s.\rightarrow f.~(\cdot)} \cup \mathcal{T}_{f.~(\cdot)}. \tag{15}$$

Update the interaction graph as the matched tracks have been concatenated.

Fig. 6. Algorithm for resolving merge-split scenarios in the player interaction graph

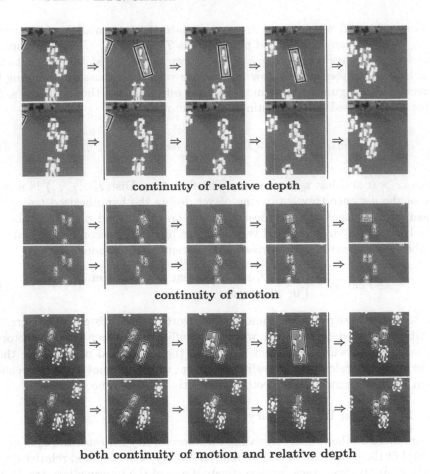

continuity of relative depth

continuity of motion

both continuity of motion and relative depth

Fig. 7. Examples of resolved merge and split situations. In each example the first row shows the split and merge scenario and the bottom row the found intermediary tracks.

be adequately described by a constant velocity motion model. To do this we linearly interpolate between the parameters of the last ellipse of $\mathcal{T}_{s.}$ and the first ellipse of $\mathcal{T}_{f.~(\cdot)}$. If there is sufficient image data evidence to support this trajectory, that is $\mathrm{Pen}(\mathcal{T}_{s.\to f.~(\cdot)}) = 0$, it is considered as feasible. Let $\mathcal{Z}_M$ be the set of the indices of the input tracks whose trajectory to its matched output track cannot be modeled by a constant velocity trajectory.

The intermediate tracks for the elements of $\mathcal{Z}_M$ have to be estimated. It is at this stage we impose maintaining relative depth ordering amongst players from the same team. Every mth frame in the interval $[t_S, t_F]$, the temporal extent of the intermediate trajectories, is considered for analysis, with $t_k = t_S + km$. For each t_k let the subset $\mathcal{Z}_M^k \subset \mathcal{Z}_M$ be the set of tracks that exists at this time instant. Let E_j^F be the final ellipse in each trajectory $\mathcal{T}_{s.}, j \in \mathcal{Z}_M$. Then define the region $\mathcal{R}_k(\{\mathbf{t}_j\})$ as the union of the ellipses $E_j^F, j \in \mathcal{Z}_M^k$ each displaced by $\mathbf{t}_j$. The aim at each t_k is to find the $\mathbf{t}_j$'s to maximize the intersection of $\mathcal{R}_k(\{\mathbf{t}_j\})$

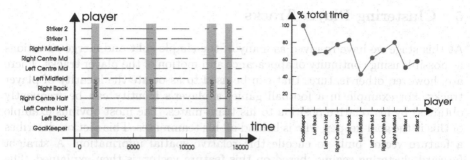

Fig. 8. The left graph shows the temporal extent of the player tracks ($\geq$ 250 frames) for team A players during the 10 minutes of the game examined. Events causing congestion are marked by the gray strips. The right graph shows for each player the percentage of time it has been assigned to a player track. For the remaining frames the players are assigned to multiple player tracks or short player tracks.

with the foreground pixels and minimize its intersection with the background pixels or mathematically to maximize wrt the t_j's:

$$\alpha_1 \, \text{Area}(\mathcal{R}_k(\{t_j\}) \cap \mathcal{F}_{t.}\,) - (1 - \alpha_1)\,\text{Area}(\mathcal{R}_k(\{t_j\}) \cap \mathcal{B}_{t.}\,) \qquad (16)$$

with $\alpha_1 > 0$, subject to the constraint that the depth ordering amongst players from the same team in $\mathcal{Z}_M$ is maintained from t_S throughout the t_k's. Given the translations at each t_k the full trajectories $\{\mathcal{T}_{s. \to f. \,(\cdot)}\}_{j \in \mathcal{Z}}$ are computed by interpolating between the displaced ellipses found at the fixed times.

We approximate this global optimization in a greedy manner. We first find the translation for the player closest to the camera by ensuring the displaced ellipse explains the relevant foreground pixels closest to the camera. Then similarly the translation for the player furthest away is found and then the inner players. It should be noted that we only analyze cases with $n \leq 5$, this generally implies that there are no more than 3 players from a single team are present. Figure 6 gives a more detailed overview of the interaction between our trajectory estimation and scoring. Throughout the sequence examined roughly 200 merge-split situations, of varying complexity, are resolved. Figure 7 shows a few results obtained. Solving these trajectories in this non-causal exhaustive manner proves to be very reliable.

Once all the possible simple merge and split situations have been solved, it is interesting to see how frequently a player is assigned to a *player track*. Figure 8 gives an overview of this information for our football game clip. The tracks are fairly evenly distributed throughout and are mainly only significantly interrupted by the major congestion scenarios of corner kicks and goals. One player "Left Midfield" is significantly less frequently in a player track. He is on the side of the field furtherest from the camera. Thus we see the effect of our lack of resolution on that side. It must be noted, though, that during the periods when a player is not assigned to a player track, he is assigned to a multiple player track. Given the interaction graph and player track identities, it is possible to ascertain the identities of the players in a multiple player track. The next sections are devoted to recreating the graph in figure 8(a) automatically.

5 Clustering Player Tracks

At this stage we have resolved as many of the simple split and merge situations as possible using continuity of appearance and motion of the player tracks. There are, however, other features that can be used to associate the identity of player tracks. For example in a football game, a player's identity can be frequently obtained by his relative position to his team-mates. The most obvious example of this is the goal-keeper, who is behind all his teammates. This section describes a feature vector built to encode this relative spatial information. A straight forward clustering regime, based on this feature vector, is then explained. The clustering aims to find clusters containing player tracks of the same identity. This allows for the identity of temporally separated player tracks to be linked and thus defines re-initialization points for each player throughout the game.

5.1 Player Track Feature Vector

The specific feature vector calculated to describe a player track is, of course, biased by the application domain. What follows is a football dependent feature vector. Though the same methodology could be applied to other applications.

Let $^A\mathcal{X}_t = \{^A\mathbf{x}_t^i\}_{i=1}^{11}$ be the x, y-coordinates of the team A players at frame t. For each $\mathbf{x}_t^i$ (dropping the A superscript for brevity) we construct a 4-dimensional vector $\mathbf{v}_t^i = (r_t^i, l_t^i, f_t^i, b_t^i)$ recording the number of players to the right, left, in front and behind player i, subject to a margin $\epsilon > 0$. As there are eleven players on each team $r_t^i + l_t^i \leq 10$ and $f_t^i + b_t^i \leq 10$. Thus there are 66^2 distinct possible v_t^i. To reduce this number the range from 0 to 10 is quantized into 6 bins $\{0,1\}, \{2,3\}, \cdots, \{9,10\}$. This quantization results in 21^2 distinct v_t^i. Each v_t^i is assigned an index, $id(v_t^i)$ between 0 and 440.

From the subset of ellipses of $\mathcal{E}_{t.+j}$ labelled as team A we can estimate $^A\mathcal{X}_{t.+j}$. These computations take place once the players' feet positions from each ellipse have been estimated and transformed to a rectified version of the pitch. Consider the player track, $\mathcal{T}_i = \mathcal{T}(t_i, n_i, \mathbf{k}^i)$. The relative spatial arrangement of this player during the track is encoded by the v-vector for each of its ellipses:

$$\mathcal{V}_{\mathcal{T}_i} = (id(v_{t.}^{k_0^i}), id(v_{t.+1}^{k_1^i}), \cdots, id(v_{t.+n.-1}^{k_{.n.-1}^i})) \tag{17}$$

Histogram $\mathcal{V}_{\mathcal{T}_i}$ to define a feature vector $\mathbf{f}_{\mathcal{T}_i} \in [0,1]^{441}$ with jth entry

$$\mathbf{f}_{\mathcal{T}_i}(j) = \frac{1}{n_i} \sum_{s=1}^{n.} \delta_{j, id(v_{.}^{.})} \tag{18}$$

The distance between two tracks is then defined as $D(\mathcal{T}_i, \mathcal{T}_l) = \|\mathbf{f}_{\mathcal{T}_i} - \mathbf{f}_{\mathcal{T}_l}\|^2$.

5.2 Clustering Procedure

Let $\mathcal{U} = \{\mathcal{T}_i\}_{i=1}^K$ be the set of team A trajectories with length > 10 seconds. This limit is chosen to ensure each trajectory has a reliably estimated feature vector. The goal is to partition $\mathcal{U}$ into L, 11 for football, clusters $\mathcal{C} = \{C_l\}$ s.t. each cluster corresponds exactly to one player. This partition is subject to the condition that one person can only be in one place at one time. Thus temporally overlapping trajectories cannot be assigned to the same cluster. An indicator function $\gamma(\mathcal{T}_i, \mathcal{T}_j)$ is set to 1 if $\mathcal{T}_i$ and $\mathcal{T}_j$ temporally overlap and 0 otherwise.

Cluster Initialization. We have no explicit model for each player. Therefore we rely upon un-supervised clustering. This necessitates proceeding carefully, especially initially. We want to ensure finding representative members for each cluster from which we can grow. For football, the longer a trajectory the more likely it is to incorporate the state of a player from several team formations. The clustering thus occurs in two stages - initialize the clusters and then expand them. The first stage initializes the clusters by examining only temporally very long trajectories which are fortuitously nicely separated in our chosen feature space. Explicit details of the algorithm are given in figure 9, essentially the algorithm finds compact clusters starting from tracks of decreasing temporal length. The results of applying this algorithm to the football data are displayed in figure 10. Thirteen clusters are found and each cluster contains only tracks of one identity.

Cluster Growing. The second stage of the clustering process involves expanding the initial clusters to include the other trajectories of non-trivial length and merging clusters when possible and necessary to reach the expected number of 11. To adequately describe the secondary clustering procedure some notation and concepts are now introduced. A temporally dependent subset, $a \subset \mathcal{U}$, is a subset in which every pair of member tracks temporally overlap. Then define $\mathcal{S}(\mathcal{U})$ as the set containing all such subsets of $\mathcal{U}$. An assignment, P_a, from a set

---

Data: A set of player trajectories $\{\mathcal{T}_{i_j}\}_{j=1}^{K_0} \subset \mathcal{U}$ with temporal lengths $n_{i_j} \geq 1000$.

Constraints: All members of a cluster are within a distance $\epsilon > 0$ of each other. No two members of a cluster can temporally overlap.

Algorithm: Let the set of clusters $\mathcal{C} = \emptyset$ and the set of unexplained trajectories $\mathcal{U}' = \{\mathcal{T}_{i_j}\}_{j=1}^{K_0}$. Initialize the counter variables $k = 0, l = 0$.

while $k \leq K_0$

1. Choose $\mathcal{T}_{i_0}$ the longest track in $\mathcal{U}'$.
2. Set $C_l = \{\mathcal{T}_{i_0}\}$.
   while $|C_l|$ is increasing
   – Find the longest track in $\mathcal{T}_{i_j} \in \mathcal{U}'$ such that

   $$\gamma(\mathcal{T}_{i_j}, \mathcal{T}_k) = 0 \ \& \ D(\mathcal{T}_{i_j}, \mathcal{T}_k) < \epsilon \ \ \forall \mathcal{T}_k \in C_l.$$

   – If such a $\mathcal{T}_{i_j}$ exists, set $C_l = C_l \cup \mathcal{T}_{i_j}$.
   end
3. Set $\mathcal{C} = \mathcal{C} \cup C_l$, $\mathcal{U}' = \mathcal{U}' \backslash C_l$, $l = l + 1$ and $k = k + |C_l|$.
end

Fig. 9. The initial clustering algorithm

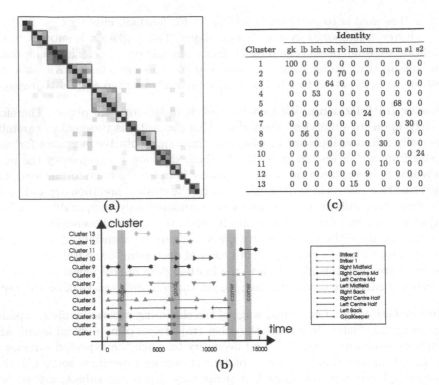

Cluster	\multicolumn{11}{c}{Identity}
	gk	lb	lch	rch	rb	lm	lcm	rcm	rm	s1	s2
1	100	0	0	0	0	0	0	0	0	0	0
2	0	0	0	0	0	70	0	0	0	0	0
3	0	0	0	64	0	0	0	0	0	0	0
4	0	0	53	0	0	0	0	0	0	0	0
5	0	0	0	0	0	0	0	68	0	0	0
6	0	0	0	0	0	0	24	0	0	0	0
7	0	0	0	0	0	0	0	0	0	30	0
8	0	56	0	0	0	0	0	0	0	0	0
9	0	0	0	0	0	0	0	0	30	0	0
10	0	0	0	0	0	0	0	0	0	0	24
11	0	0	0	0	0	0	0	10	0	0	0
12	0	0	0	0	0	0	9	0	0	0	0
13	0	0	0	0	0	15	0	0	0	0	0

Fig. 10. (a) The distance between every pair of player tracks >40 sec is shown. Ordering is according to the clusters found by the initial clustering. Darker values indicate smaller distances. **(b)** This graph displays the temporal extent and true identity of the player tracks in each cluster. The legend shows the color and symbol representing each identity. **(c)** This confusion table summarizes the homogeneity of the identities for a cluster's temporal extent. Each entry is the sum of the temporal lengths of the player tracks in a cluster of one identity, shown as a percentage of the total sequence time.

$a \in \mathcal{S}(\mathcal{U})$ is a one-to-one mapping $P_a : \{1, \cdots, |a|\} \rightarrow \{1, \cdots, L\}$ s.t. the ith track of a is assigned to cluster $P_a(i)$. P_a is valid if for each $\mathcal{T}_{a.} \in a$

$$\exists \mathcal{T}_l \in C_{P.\,(i)} \text{ s.t. } D(\mathcal{T}_l, \mathcal{T}_{a.}) < \epsilon_1 \quad \& \quad \mathcal{T}_l \in C_{P.\,(i)} \Rightarrow \gamma(\mathcal{T}_{a.}, \mathcal{T}_l) = 0 \qquad (19)$$

where $\epsilon_1 > 0$. The cost of such an assignment is

$$Sc(P_a) = \sum_{i=1}^{|a|} \min_{\mathcal{T}_. \in C_{.\,.}\,(\cdot)} D(\mathcal{T}_l, \mathcal{T}_{a.}). \qquad (20)$$

In essence the algorithm finds the valid assignments for temporally dependent subsets and chooses the assignment with least cost. Finding the best fit with respect to a temporal dependent subset offers greater robustness to using a greedy algorithm on individual tracks and is still computational feasible.

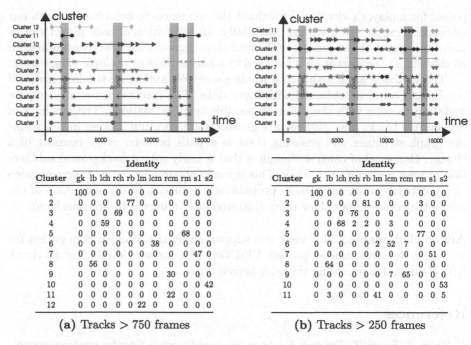

(a) Tracks > 750 frames

Cluster	gk	lb	lch	rch	rb	lm	lcm	rcm	rm	s1	s2
1	100	0	0	0	0	0	0	0	0	0	0
2	0	0	0	0	77	0	0	0	0	0	0
3	0	0	0	69	0	0	0	0	0	0	0
4	0	0	59	0	0	0	0	0	0	0	0
5	0	0	0	0	0	0	0	0	68	0	0
6	0	0	0	0	0	0	38	0	0	0	0
7	0	0	0	0	0	0	0	0	0	47	0
8	0	56	0	0	0	0	0	0	0	0	0
9	0	0	0	0	0	0	0	30	0	0	0
10	0	0	0	0	0	0	0	0	0	0	42
11	0	0	0	0	0	0	0	22	0	0	0
12	0	0	0	0	0	22	0	0	0	0	0

(b) Tracks > 250 frames

Cluster	gk	lb	lch	rch	rb	lm	lcm	rcm	rm	s1	s2
1	100	0	0	0	0	0	0	0	0	0	0
2	0	0	0	0	81	0	0	0	3	0	0
3	0	0	0	76	0	0	0	0	0	0	0
4	0	0	68	2	2	0	3	0	0	0	0
5	0	0	0	0	0	0	0	0	77	0	0
6	0	0	0	0	0	2	52	7	0	0	0
7	0	0	0	0	0	0	0	0	0	51	0
8	0	64	0	0	0	0	0	0	0	0	0
9	0	0	0	0	0	7	65	0	0	0	0
10	0	0	0	0	0	0	0	0	0	0	53
11	0	3	0	0	0	41	0	0	0	0	5

Fig. 11. Cluster growing results. The graphs and tables have the same format as figure 10. Column **(a)** shows the results when tracks of length > 750 are added to the initial clusters. In this case, homogeneity of identity in the clusters is maintained. However, when tracks of shorter length are added errors begin to occur, see column **(b)**. The columns of the right confusion table sum to the percentages displayed in figure 8 (b).

Results of applying the clustering algorithm are shown in figure 11. The left column shows the results of including the tracks with temporal lengths between 750 and 1000 frames and the right column the additional tracks over 250 frames. Results are good. Errors in the clustering begin to appear with the addition of the shorter length tracks. Most of the errors occur at the major events when the team switches between different formations. This would indicate that our feature vector should be extended to take the overall team formation into account.

6   Conclusions and Discussion

This paper presents an approach to multi-target tracking and labelling that is viable on long sequences with many targets, assuming there are no real-time constraints. At each stage the reliable information is extracted and built upon. Initially we find the trajectories when players are isolated, extend and concatenate these trajectories when possible by resolving merge-split situations. From these trajectories a large graph summarizing the player interactions throughout the game is built. The identities of the found, but temporally spread, trajectories are linked using a two-stage clustering scheme. This sets re-initialization points for a player's identity throughout the sequence. In combination with our interaction graph this gives us, potentially, an estimation of each player's position throughout the sequence, with a varying degree of accuracy depending on whether at a time instant he is assigned to a *player track* or *multiple player track*.

The methods are scalable to a whole game. We anticipate similar results, if not better, could be obtained with more data. The feature vector may require updating to cope with the different possible team formations. The labelling of the shorter tracks may also require greater sophistication, taking into account the graph structure and ensuring there is a path between every member of a cluster. One word of caution though is that a fairly robust background subtraction process underpins this work. This is made possible by our wide screen video and sports environment. A more probabilistic approach to the extraction of the initial trajectories may allow more cluttered environments to be considered.

Acknowledgments. This work was supported by the Swedish Foundation for Strategic Research funded project VISCOS. The authors would like to thank Eric Hayman for providing the wide-screen video.

References

1. Khan, Z., Balch, T., Dellaert, F.: An mcmc-based particle filter for tracking multiple interacting targets. In: European Conference on Computer Vision. (2004)
2. Gelgon, M., Bouthemy, P., Le Cadre, J.: Recovery of the trajectories of multiple moving objects in an image sequence with a pmht approach. J. Image & Vision Computing **23** (2005) 19–31
3. Xu, M., Orwell, J., Jones, G.: Tracking football players with multiple cameras. In: IEEE International Conference on Image Processing. (2004)
4. Iwase, S., Saito, H.: Parallel tracking of all soccer players by integrating detected positions in multiple view images. In: ICPR. (2004) 751–754
5. Vermaak, J., Doucet, A., Perez, P.: Maintaining multi-modality through mixture tracking. In: International Conference on Computer Vision. (2003)
6. Okuma, K., Taleghani, A., De Freitas, N., Little, J.J., Lowe, D.G.: A boosted particle filter: Multitarget detection and tracking. In: ECCV. (2004)
7. Needham, C., Boyle, R.: Tracking multiple sports players through occlusion, congestion and scale. In: BMVC. (2001)
8. Figueroa, P., Leite, N., Barros, R., Cohen, I., Medioni, G.: Tracking soccer players using the graph representation. In: ICPR. (2004) 787–790
9. Stauffer, C., Grimson, W.: Adaptive background mixture models for real-time tracking. In: Conference on Computer Vision and Pattern Recognition. (1999)

Level-Set Curve Particles*

Tingting Jiang and Carlo Tomasi

Department of Computer Science, Duke University, Durham NC 27708, USA
{ruxu, tomasi}@cs.duke.edu

Abstract. In many applications it is necessary to track a moving and
deforming boundary on the plane from infrequent, sparse measurements.
For instance, each of a set of mobile observers may be able to tell the
position of a point on the boundary. Often boundary components split,
merge, appear, and disappear over time. Data are typically sparse and
noisy and the underlying dynamics is uncertain. To address these issues,
we use a particle filter to represent a distribution in the large space of all
plane curves and propose a full-fledged combination of level sets and particle filters. Our main contribution is in controlling the potentially high
expense of multiplying the cost of a level set representation of boundaries
by the number of particles needed. Experiments on tracking the boundary of a colon in tomographic imagery from sparse edge measurements
show the promise of the approach.

1 Introduction

Many applications require tracking boundaries that move and deform over time,
whether these are the contours of an oil spill in the ocean, a plume of smoke,
a hurricane, a wildfire, the dividing cells under a microscope, a running crowd
of people, or the contours of an anatomical structure tracked across slices of
a volumetric medical image. With imagery, measurements of the boundary of
interest are typically dense and abundant. Even so, the presence of clutter often
requires estimating the boundaries stochastically, by letting a probability distribution entertain multiple hypotheses about the boundary's position and shape.
In other applications, observations are much more sparse and perhaps less frequent: a small number of mobile observers may know their own location through
GPS, and perhaps measure their distance from the boundary of interest through
imaging, range finding, or other sensors.

These problems have a common abstraction: a temporally discrete, possibly
spatially sparse distribution of noisy point measurements is used to infer the
shape and position of a boundary that moves and deforms on the plane under
the influence of only partially understood causes.

Conceptually, the solution ingredients are known: a dynamic system models
the underlying evolution phenomenon; stochastic estimation addresses sparsity

---

* This research was sponsored through a subcontract from Intelligent Automation,
Inc. under U.S. Army STTR Phase II Grant W911NF-04-C-0114, and through NSF
grant IIS-0534897.

A. Leonardis, H. Bischof, and A. Pinz (Eds.): ECCV 2006, Part III, LNCS 3953, pp. 633–644, 2006.

and uncertainty of the measurements; and level sets elegantly represent boundaries whose components merge, split, appear, and disappear. All these ingredients have been used with success. Their full combination, however, has not, because of its potentially high computational complexity: the high cost of level sets is charged to each of a large number of particles needed to represent a probability distribution in the space of plane curves. The number of particles required depends on how large the space of all possible plane curves is. With some assumptions and prior knowledge about the plane curves such as smoothness and initialization, the probability distribution of the plane curves can be represented by a particle filter of applicable size. However, the complexity of combining level sets and particle filter is still high.

In this paper we show a way to keep this complexity in check. This leads to a tracking method of great generality and flexibility, based on the core concept of *level-set curve particles*. This method capitalizes on the observation that many of the curves that populate the boundary distribution being tracked are very similar to each other. In our method, a number of *base curves* account for macroscopic differences between boundaries. Each base curve is then deformed by P *base perturbations* which provide an implicit representation of the 2^P deformations obtained by applying any subset of the P base perturbations to the base curve. Through this device, an exponential number of curves can be propagated and their likelihoods can be computed at linear cost in the framework of a particle filter. Resampling has still an exponential cost. However, the per-curve cost of resampling is trivial, while the per-curve cost of propagation is proportional to the size of the data structure needed to represent an entire level set, and the unit cost of likelihood estimation is proportional to the number of measurements. Saving on propagation has a huge effect on running time, and saving on likelihood computation has a significant effect when measurements are plentiful.

In the next Section, we review related work. Section 3 defines level-set curve particles and shows the tracking algorithm. Section 4 presents the experimental results and Section 5 concludes with a summary and plans for future work.

2   Related Work

Active contours [1, 2] are based on ideas developed initially for Brownian motion [3, 4], and later incorporated into *particle filters* (see [5] for a recent overview). These approaches capture the uncertain position of a boundary at time t by a probability distribution represented by a random sample of boundaries (*particles*). Each boundary is represented explicitly, e.g. with splines [6] and *propagated* forward in time through an assumed, uncertain motion model. Measurements update the particles through *resampling*, which weighs each particle by its posterior probability given the measurements. This is computed from the *likelihood* (conditional probability density of a measurement given a boundary) through Bayes' theorem. New particles are drawn from the posterior, and are ready for a new step of propagation. This cycle is analogous to the estimation loop of a Kalman filter [7], but maintains a multi-modal distribution rather than a Gaussian one.

Level sets [8, 9, 10] describe a boundary as the zero crossing of a function $\phi(\boldsymbol{x}, t)$ of space and time. While many functions ϕ share the same zero-crossing $\mathcal{B}$, computational considerations (see [11]) suggest using the signed distance function of $\mathcal{B}$, which is then maintained in a narrow *band* [12] around the boundary $\mathcal{B}$. The motion model is then a PDE for ϕ. The main strength of level sets is that they account effortlessly for changes of boundary topology, as exemplified in applications to image segmentation [13], object detection [14], tracking [15], shape modeling [16] and medical image segmentation [17], among others.

Recently, several papers [14, 18, 19, 20, 21, 22] have combined active contours and level sets. These papers create suitable artificial "forces" that draw an initial boundary towards a boundary of interest. These approaches essentially seek a new boundary in each frame, view a boundary as a deterministic object, and do not incorporate prior knowledge of boundary motion. This holds also for work based on "shape averages" [23, 22] where the deformation of a boundary is decomposed into an average motion plus a set of local deformations. More specifically, in [22] the propagation of the local deformations is still deterministic for each particle, with no way to add "noise" to model the uncertainty of the underlying dynamics.

In contrast, we combine active contours and level sets into a full-fledged particle filter for boundaries. Our *level-set curve particles* marry the power of stochastic estimation methods from active contours with the flexibility of nonparametric level sets.

3   Approach

3.1   Problem Statement

A dynamic boundary $\mathcal{B}$ is a variable number of moving and deforming closed curves on the plane. These curves may merge, split, appear, and disappear over time. The boundaries $\mathcal{B}^{(1)}$ and $\mathcal{B}^{(2)}$ at initial times 1 and 2 are assumed to be known. M mobile and controllable observers make noisy measurements of the position of a point on the boundary $\mathcal{B}$. The boundary tracking problem is to use the observations $\{Q_m^{(t)}\}_{m=1}^M$ made by the observers at times $t = 3, 4, \ldots$ to estimate the posterior probability distribution of the boundary $\mathcal{B}^{(t)}$ at these points in time. The Maximum A Posteriori (MAP) boundary estimate may optionally be computed when requested.

3.2   Level-Set Curve Particles

We use a set of $P + 1$ particles $\chi_t = \{\phi_p^{(t)}, w_p^{(t)}\}_{p=0}^P$ to represent the probability distribution of the boundary $\mathcal{B}^{(t)}$. Each particle is a signed distance function $\phi_p^{(t)} : \mathbb{R}^2 \to \mathbb{R}$ whose zero level set denotes an estimate of the boundary $\mathcal{B}^{(t)}$. A weight $w_p^{(t)}$ determined by the measurements is associated to each particle. Since all the particles are estimates of the same boundary, it can be expected that the signed distance function values are similar for most points on the plane.

For efficiency, we represent particles as a multiple perturbation of a "mother" particle $\phi_0^{(t)}$. The perturbations $\{\phi_p^{(t)}\}_{p=1}^P$ are "child" particles. For each $p > 0$, define a function $\Delta\phi_p^{(t)}$ such that $\phi_p^{(t)}$ and $\phi_0^{(t)} + \Delta\phi_p^{(t)}$ share the same zero level crossing and $\Delta\phi_p^{(t)}$ is nonzero only inside a small window $W_p^{(t)}$.

This construction yields $P + 1$ "explicit" particles. However, 2^P of particles can be obtained by combining the mother particle with subsets of the deformations $\Delta\phi_p^{(t)}$ for its children. For example, a particle $\phi_{1,2}^{(t)} = \phi_0^{(t)} + \Delta\phi_1^{(t)} + \Delta\phi_2^{(t)}$ can be obtained that concurrently deforms the mother particle in the union of the two windows $W_1^{(t)}$ and $W_2^{(t)}$. More generally, given the set of child indices $X = \{1, \ldots, P\}$, for every set Z in the power set of X we can define a new perturbation $\phi_Z^{(t)} = \phi_0^{(t)} + \sum_{j \in Z} \Delta\phi_j^{(t)}$ of the mother particle $\phi_0^{(t)}$.

The probability distribution of the boundary $\mathcal{B}^{(t)}$ is encoded by the set of parameters $\chi_t = \{\phi_0^{(t)}, \{W_p^{(t)}, \Delta\phi_p^{(t)}\}_{p=1}^P, \{w_p^{(t)}\}_{p=0}^P\}$ which now represents a much bigger sample. Of course, the challenge is to propagate, update, and resample the 2^P "implicit" particles by working only with the $P + 1$ "explicit" ones. The next Sections show how to do this.

3.3   Tracking Algorithm

The outline of the proposed tracking method is Algorithm 1. Let $Q_m^{(t)}$ denote the estimate of a point on boundary $\mathcal{B}^{(t)}$ returned by observer number m for $m = 1, \ldots, M$. Let χ_t be the level-set curve particle set at time step t. Since $\mathcal{B}^{(1)}$ and $\mathcal{B}^{(2)}$ are known, the corresponding signed-distance functions $\phi^{(1)}$ and $\phi^{(2)}$ can be computed. Tracking then starts from $t = 3$. The main parts of this algorithm are discussed next.

Algorithm 1. Tracking algorithm

INPUT: χ_{t-1} $(t > 2)$

OUTPUT: χ_t.

(1) Propagate χ_{t-1} to $\bar{\chi}_t$;

(2) Observers take measurements $\{Q_m^{(t)}\}_{m=1}^M$;

(3) Update $\bar{\chi}_t$;

(4) Resample and generate χ_t.

Initialization. Algorithm 1 must be initialized with an initial particle set χ_2 that is, with a set of functions $\{\phi_p^{(2)}\}_{p=0}^P$ each of which is a random perturbation of a given initial boundary estimate $\mathcal{B}^{(2)}$. All functions are given the same weight. To define perturbations, we need a notion of "closeness" between boundaries. Given $\epsilon > 0$ and a boundary $\mathcal{B}$, the neighborhood of $\mathcal{B}$ within distance ϵ is defined as $N_\epsilon(\mathcal{B}) = \{\mathcal{B}' : D(\mathcal{B}, \mathcal{B}') < \epsilon\}$ where $D(\mathcal{B}, \mathcal{B}')$ is the symmetric set difference between the areas enclosed by $\mathcal{B}$ and $\mathcal{B}'$ normalized by the area of $\mathcal{B}$.

We perturb $\mathcal{B}^{(2)}$ by adding a function δ to $\phi^{(2)}$. Then the zero crossing of $\phi' = \phi^{(2)} + \delta$ is the perturbed boundary $\mathcal{B}'$. To make $\mathcal{B}'$ continuous and within $N_\epsilon(\mathcal{B}^{(2)})$ for a given small $\epsilon > 0$, the function δ should be continuous and its

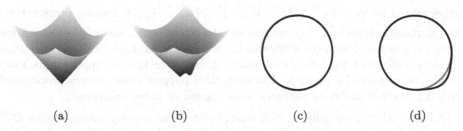

(a)   (b)   (c)   (d)

Fig. 1. (a) The signed distance function ϕ of a boundary $\mathcal{B}$. (b) The perturbed function ϕ'. (c) The initial boundary $\mathcal{B}$. (d) The perturbed boundary $\mathcal{B}'$ (dark).

values should be small. We choose $\delta(\boldsymbol{x}) = \alpha G_2(\boldsymbol{x}, \boldsymbol{y}, \boldsymbol{\Sigma})$, the product of a scalar α and a 2D Gaussian function $G_2(\boldsymbol{x}, \boldsymbol{y}, \boldsymbol{\Sigma})$ with mean $\boldsymbol{y}$ and diagonal covariance matrix $\boldsymbol{\Sigma}$. The vector $\boldsymbol{y}$ determines the center of the perturbation, $\boldsymbol{\Sigma}$ controls its extent, and α determines the amount of perturbation. All of these parameters are generated randomly. $\boldsymbol{y}$ is usually chosen close to $\mathcal{B}^{(2)}$, and α and $\boldsymbol{\Sigma}$ are chosen to satisfy $\mathcal{B}' \in N_\epsilon(\mathcal{B}^{(2)})$. A sample perturbation is shown in Fig. 1.

With this method we generate P boundaries $\mathcal{B}'_p (p = 1, \ldots, P)$ that perturb $\mathcal{B}^{(2)}$. From these, we compute P signed-distance functions $\phi'_p = \gamma(\phi^{(2)} + \delta_p)$ where $\gamma(\phi)$ denotes the signed distance function of the zero level set of ϕ. To construct the initial particle set χ_2, we define the mother particle $\phi_0^{(2)} = \phi^{(2)}$. The difference between each ϕ'_p and $\phi_0^{(2)}$ is $\Delta\phi_p^{(2)} = \phi'_p - \phi_0^{(2)}$. Each window $W_p^{(2)}$ is defined as the smallest rectangle which includes all the points $\boldsymbol{x}$ such that $|\Delta\phi_p^{(2)}(\boldsymbol{x})|$ is not trivial and $|\phi'_p(\boldsymbol{x})|$ is below a small positive threshold dependent on both the width of the narrow band and the dynamics of the boundary[1]. The perturbations $\Delta\phi_p^{(2)}(\boldsymbol{x})$ are then truncated to zero for $\boldsymbol{x}$ outside $W_p^{(2)}$. All particles are given the same initial weight $w_p^{(2)} = 1/(P+1)$. Given the initial particle set χ_2, we maintain the particle set χ_t over time through Algorithm 1.

Propagation. Suppose that the velocity of each point on the plane at time t is given as $\boldsymbol{v}(\boldsymbol{x})$. We wish to move all the points on the surface $\phi^{(t-1)}$ to $\bar{\phi}^{(t)}$ as $\phi^{(t-1)}(\boldsymbol{x}) = \bar{\phi}^{(t)}(\boldsymbol{x} + \boldsymbol{v}(\boldsymbol{x}))$. Assume that mother particle $\phi_0^{(t-1)}$ is propagated to $\bar{\phi}_0^{(t)}$, $\phi_0^{(t-1)}(\boldsymbol{x}) = \bar{\phi}_0^{(t)}(\boldsymbol{x} + \boldsymbol{v}(\boldsymbol{x}))$. Similarly, the difference between mother and child particles is propagated to $\Delta\bar{\phi}_p^{(t)}$. According to the above equation, $\bar{\phi}_Z^{(t)}(\boldsymbol{x} + \boldsymbol{v}(\boldsymbol{x})) = \phi_Z^{(t-1)}(\boldsymbol{x}) = \phi_0^{(t-1)}(\boldsymbol{x}) + \Sigma_{j \in Z}\Delta\phi_j^{(t-1)}(\boldsymbol{x}) = \bar{\phi}_0^{(t)}(\boldsymbol{x} + \boldsymbol{v}(\boldsymbol{x})) + \Sigma_{j \in Z}\Delta\bar{\phi}_j^{(t)}(\boldsymbol{x} + \boldsymbol{v}(\boldsymbol{x}))$. Therefore, we can define $\bar{\phi}_Z^{(t)} = \bar{\phi}_0^{(t)} + \Sigma_{j \in Z}\Delta\bar{\phi}_j^{(t)}$ if $\boldsymbol{x} \to \boldsymbol{x} + \boldsymbol{v}(\boldsymbol{x})$ is a one-to-one mapping, which implies that all "implicit" particles can be propagated by only explicitly propagating the mother particle and the differences between mother and child particles.

The windows $W_p^{(t-1)}$ are propagated by modifying them to $\overline{W}_p^{(t)}$ so as to properly enclose nonzero values of $\Delta\bar{\phi}_p^{(t)}$. The propagated particle set is now

---

[1] $W_p^{(2)}$ should be large enough to include all possible boundary points at the next time step. Derivation details for this threshold are omitted for lack of space.

represented by $\bar{\chi}_t = \{\bar{\phi}_0^{(t)}, \{\Delta\bar{\phi}_p^{(t)}, \overline{W}_p^{(t)}\}_{p=1}^P, \{w_p^{(t-1)}\}_{p=0}^P\}$. During propagation, the particle weights $w_p^{(t-1)}$ do not change. In our experiments, $v(\boldsymbol{x})$ at each time step t is generated from the difference between the maximum-likelihood particles of the previous two time steps $t-1$ and $t-2$. However, in some applications, $v(\boldsymbol{x})$ might be measured separately. For numerical purposes, we enforce propagated mother particle and child particles to be signed distance functions.

Update. After propagation, each observer returns a noisy measurement $Q_m^{(t)}$ of a point on the boundary. One simple likelihood function of a particle ϕ is $\Lambda_t(\phi) = \prod_{m=1}^M G(\phi(Q_m^{(t)}))$ where G is a Gaussian function whose standard deviation ζ depends on the noise statistics of the measurements, assumed to be mutually independent. And $\phi(Q_m^{(t)})$ denotes the function value of ϕ at point $Q_m^{(t)}$. If $|\phi(Q_m^{(t)})|$ is large, $Q_m^{(t)}$ is far away from the zero level set of ϕ and therefore the likelihood that the zero crossing of ϕ passes through point $Q_m^{(t)}$ is small. On the other hand, if $\phi(Q_m^{(t)}) = 0$, $Q_m^{(t)}$ lies exactly on the zero crossing of ϕ. Given $\Lambda_t(\phi)$, we can update the weight of each particle as $\bar{w}_p^{(t)} = w_p^{(t-1)} \cdot \Lambda_t(\bar{\phi}_p^{(t)})$. Since each child particle p only differs from the mother particle inside window $\overline{W}_p^{(t)}$, the ratio $H_p^{(t)} = \frac{\Lambda.(\bar{\phi}_p^{(\cdot)})}{\Lambda.(\bar{\phi}_0^{(\cdot)})}$ depends only on the difference between function values of $\bar{\phi}_0^{(t)}$ and $\bar{\phi}_p^{(t)}$ at the measurement points $Q_m^{(t)}$ inside window $\overline{W}_p^{(t)}$. So we can first calculate the likelihood $\Lambda_t(\bar{\phi}_0^{(t)})$ for the mother particle and then check for each child particle p whether there are any $Q_m^{(t)}$ inside $\overline{W}_p^{(t)}$. If not, the likelihoods of the mother and the child are same. Otherwise, calculate $H_p^{(t)}$ and get $\Lambda_t(\bar{\phi}_p^{(t)})$ by the above ratio equation. After update, the particle set $\bar{\chi}_t$ becomes $\{\bar{\phi}_0^{(t)}, \{\Delta\bar{\phi}_p^{(t)}, \overline{W}_p^{(t)}\}_{p=1}^P, \{\bar{w}_p^{(t)}\}_{p=0}^P\}$.

Resampling. In a standard particle filter, resampling is drawing (with replacement) from the set of particles with probabilities proportional to their weights. In our method, $P+1$ "explicit" particles represent 2^P "implicit" particles. From $\bar{\chi}_t$, only the weights of the "explicit" particles $\{\bar{w}_p^{(t)}\}_{p=0}^P$ are known. So we need to evaluate the weights of the "implicit" particles before resampling. First define $K_p^{(t)} = \frac{w_\cdot^{(\cdot)}}{w_0^{(\cdot)}}$ and similarly $\bar{K}_p^{(t)} = \frac{\bar{w}_\cdot^{(\cdot)}}{\bar{w}_0^{(\cdot)}}$ for each $p > 0$. We consider two cases:

Disjoint Windows. Assume $W_i^{(t)} \cap W_j^{(t)} = \emptyset$ for $i \neq j$, $i, j = 1, \ldots, P$ and for all t. For this case, we can draw the following conclusion:

Lemma 1. *Given* $Z \subseteq X = \{1, \ldots, P\}$, *let* $w(\phi_Z^{(t-1)}) = w_0^{(t-1)} \cdot \prod_{j \in Z} K_j^{(t-1)}$ *be the weight of the "implicit" particle* $\phi_Z^{(t)}$. *After propagation, if the corresponding windows* $\{\overline{W}_j^{(t)}\}_{j \in Z}$ *are disjoint, the weight of* $\bar{\phi}_Z^{(t)}$ *is* $w(\bar{\phi}_Z^{(t)}) = \bar{w}_0^{(t)} \cdot \prod_{j \in Z} \bar{K}_j^{(t)}$.

The proof is omitted here due to space limits. However, the result stands to reason because measurements in each window contribute independently to $w(\phi_Z^{(t)})$.

From Lemma 1, we see that if the condition $w(\phi_Z^{(t-1)}) = w_0^{(t-1)} \cdot \prod_{j \in Z} K_j^{(t-1)}$ is satisfied before propagation at time step t, the evaluation of $w(\bar{\phi}_Z^{(t)})$ is just the product of the weight of mother particle and $\bar{K}_j^{(t)}$ of each child particle in Z. This condition is iteratively satisfied if the windows are always disjoint. In this case, resampling can be done as follows. Let particle i correspond to an "implicit" particle ϕ_Z, where $Z_i \subseteq X, (1 \leq i \leq 2^P)$. Let $w_i = \bar{w}_0^{(t)} \cdot \prod_{j \in Z} \bar{K}_j^{(t)}$ be the weight for particle i and $\pi_i = \frac{w_\cdot}{\Sigma_{\cdot=1}^{2^\cdot} w_\cdot}$ be the normalized weight for particle i. We can draw with replacement from the 2^P particles with probabilities proportional to π_i. Suppose the newly generated weight for each particle is μ_i which might be different from π_i due to the limited number of samples. Since we only maintain the weights for $P + 1$ "explicit" particles instead of 2^P "implicit" particles , it is desirable to represent μ_i by a new set of K_p, i.e., each μ_i could be approximated as $\frac{\Pi_{\cdot \in \cdot} \cdot K_\cdot}{\Sigma_{\cdot=1}^{2^\cdot} \Pi_{\cdot \in \cdot} \cdot K_\cdot}$. Thus, the goal of resampling "implicit" particles is achieved by changing the weight of "explicit" particles. This leads to minimizing[2] the function $F(K_1, K_2, \ldots, K_P) = \sum_{i=1}^{2^\cdot} (\mu_i - \frac{\Pi_{\cdot \in \cdot} \cdot K_\cdot}{\Sigma_{\cdot=1}^{2^\cdot} \Pi_{\cdot \in \cdot} \cdot K_\cdot})^2$ by which we can find a new set of K_p to replace $\bar{K}_p^{(t)}$. Then the weight of each child particle is updated as $w_p^{(t)} = \bar{w}_0^{(t)} \cdot K_p$ while the weight of the mother particle does not change. After resampling, a new particle set $\chi_t = \{\phi_0^{(t)}, \{\Delta\phi_p^{(t)}, W_p^{(t)}\}_{p=1}^P, \{w_p^{(t)}\}_{p=0}^P\}$ is generated.

Remark. Two special cases need to be handled. If $K_p = 0$, the weight of particle p is very small and discarded. If K_p is very large, this perturbation will be generated with high probability, so it should be incorporated into the mother particle. In both cases, we need generate new particles to replace the ones that are eliminated. During resampling, we can also optionally find the particle with the maximum weight and return its zero level set as the MAP estimate of $\mathcal{B}^{(t)}$.

Intersecting Windows. Since windows move, even windows that are initially disjoint may eventually intersect. Now consider the case in which any two windows can intersect. Formally, $\exists j \neq k$, s. t. $W_j^{(t)} \cap W_k^{(t)} \neq \emptyset, j, k = 1, \ldots, P$. In this case, we need additional information to maintain the weights of the "implicit" particles. Specifically, at each time step t, given χ_t, define $\{S_{jk}^{(t)}\}$ as a set of $\binom{P}{2}$ real numbers s.t. $\forall Z \subseteq X, w(\phi_Z^{(t)}) = w_0^{(t)} \prod_{p \in Z} K_p^{(t)} \prod_{j,k \in Z, j \neq k} S_{jk}^{(t)}$. Then we have the following conclusion similar to Lemma 1:

Lemma 2. *Given $Z \subseteq X = \{1, \ldots, P\}$, suppose the combined particle $\phi_Z^{(t)}$ has weight $w(\phi_Z^{(t-1)}) = w_0^{(t-1)} \cdot \prod_{p \in Z} K_p^{(t-1)} \prod_{j,k \in Z, j \neq k} S_{jk}^{(t-1)}$ before propagation. After propagation, the weight of $\bar{\phi}_Z^{(t)}$ is $w(\bar{\phi}_Z^{(t)}) = \bar{w}_0^{(t)} \cdot \prod_{p \in Z} \bar{K}_p^{(t)} \prod_{j,k \in Z, j \neq k} \bar{S}_{jk}^{(t)}$ where $\bar{S}_{jk}^{(t)} = S_{jk}^{(t-1)} \cdot I_{jk}^{(t)}$ and $I_{jk}^{(t)} = exp(\sum_{Q^{(\cdot)} \in \overline{W}^{(\cdot)} \cap \overline{W}^{(\cdot)}} \frac{-2\Delta\bar{\phi}^{(\cdot)}(Q^{(\cdot)})\Delta\bar{\phi}^{(\cdot)}(Q^{(\cdot)})}{\zeta^2})$.*

This lemma tells us that if intersections between windows are allowed, in addition to maintaining χ_t, it is also necessary to maintain an intersection factor set $\{S_{jk}^{(t)}\}$

---

[2] Minimizing $F(K_1, K_2, \ldots, K_P)$ is an approximation. If we can draw unlimited samples, μ_i will be equal to π_i and therefore $\bar{K}_p^{(t)} = K_p$. When the number of samples is limited, $\{\bar{K}_p^{(t)}\}$ is a good starting point to find $\{K_p\}$, so convergence to a correct minimum is likely. We do not yet have a proof for this conjecture.

for every pair of child particles over time. $S_{jk}^{(t)}$ is updated as $\bar{S}_{jk}^{(t)} = S_{jk}^{(t-1)} \cdot I_{jk}^{(t)}$. With $\bar{S}_{jk}^{(t)}$, we could approximately optimize $\{\bar{K}_p^{(t)}\}$ by minimizing function $F'(K_1, K_2, \ldots, K_P)$ which is defined similarly to F except that the products of intersection factors are added as constants in F'. The cost of maintaining intersection factors $\{S_{jk}^{(t)}\}$ is $O(MP^2)$.

New Component. If some measurement $Q_m^{(t)}$ is far away from the zero level sets of the current (implicit) particles, it is possible that a new component of the dynamic boundary has appeared. To account for cases like this, we randomly generate a small boundary component near $Q_m^{(t)}$ and add it to the mother particle, so that all child particles inherit this component automatically. Results of adding new components are shown in Section 4.

Efficiency. We now analyze the computation cost of the proposed method. Assume that all level set functions are defined on a grid of size N. The computation cost of the signed-distance function γ is $O(N)$. For initialization, we generate P child particles based on the given mother particle. For each child particle, we randomly generate a 2D Gaussian perturbation, at a cost $O(N)$. Propagation advances $P+1$ particles by the motion field, at a cost $O(PN)$. For each "explicit" particle, evaluating the weight according to M measurements will takes $O(PM)$ at worst. Resampling evaluates the weights for all 2^P "implicit" particles and then resamples 2^P numbers to generate the new μ_i, so the cost of this stage is $O(2^P)$. Note however that this computation occurs on numbers instead of functions. So the constant factor that multiplies 2^P is small. For the case of intersecting windows, the cost of maintaining intersection factors $\{S_{jk}^{(t)}\}$ is $O(MP^2)$. Optimization of function F or F' is fast practically because $\{\bar{K}_p^{(t)}\}$ is very close to $\{K_p\}$. The generation of new components takes at most $O(MN)$ time. From this analysis, the total complexity for our tracking algorithm is $O(2^P + PN + PM + MN + MP^2)$. If we had used a standard particle filter with 2^P "explicit" particles the cost for propagation and update would be $O(2^P(N+M))$ which is much higher than that for the proposed approach.

4   Experiments

Experimentation with our proposed framework runs apparently into two conflicting requirements: On one hand, we want to demonstrate the performance of our tracker when the set of available measurements is sparse, because sparseness is one of the main challenges of this problem. On the other hand, we need reference ground truth against which we can measure performance, and this requires dense information about the true location of the boundary. In order to meet both requirements, we have tracked the boundaries in a data set where we have dense information, but where we simulate sparseness by withholding that information from our algorithm. Specifically, we have obtained a sequence of 355 slices from a Computerized Axial Tomography (CAT) scan of a human colon. The boundaries in this data are very complex (see Fig. 3(d)): the colon tube is convoluted, and its frequent turns make boundaries appear and disappear as we progress from one slice to the next. In our experiments, we detected each boundary with a standard edge detector. In Fig. 3(a)-(c), these "true" boundaries are drawn in red. These are our ground truth, to which the tracker has no direct access. Instead, the tracker obtains limited information through a set of observers, the green marks in the figure, and generates the "cyan" tracking results. Only 10 child particles are used in this experiment.

Fig. 2 illustrates the variety that 1 mother and 5 child particles can make. There are 32 combinations created some of which are very different from both mother and child particles. Fig. 3(a) shows tracking details during frames 7-10. The yellow window indicates the position where a new component is about to appear. The four small figures shows what happens inside the yellow window during frames 7-10. In particular, in frame 8 a cyan curve is generated close to the red (true) component because some measurement point reports that it is possible that a new boundary component has appeared there. Fig. 3(b) shows a connected component inside the yellow window splitting during frames 52-55. The tracking algorithm captures the topological change. Conversely, Fig. 3(c) shows two com-

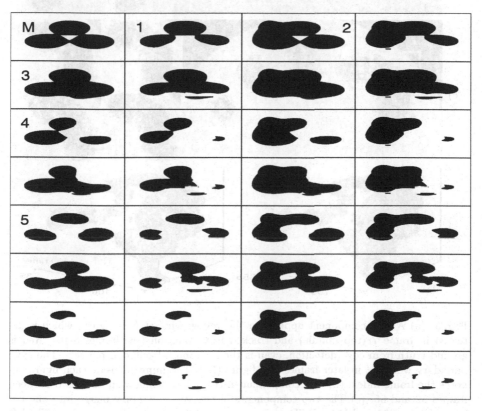

Fig. 2. A set of 32 "implicit" particles generated by one mother particle (top left) and 5 "child" particles (marked)

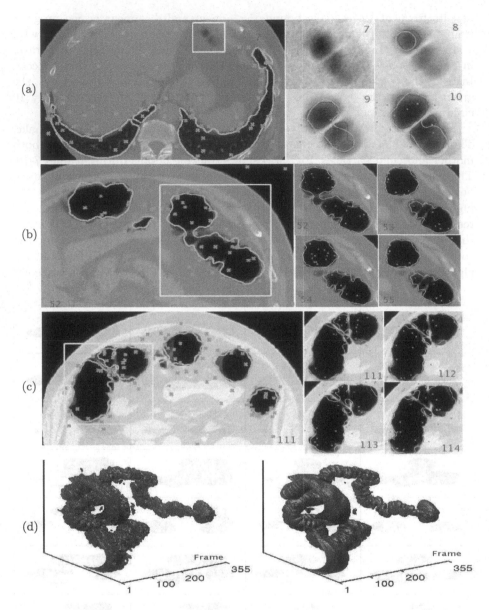

Fig. 3. (a) A new component appears in the yellow window (left figure) which is detected in frame 7 (top middle) and tracked from then on (see frames 8-10). Red is ground truth from edge detection, cyan is the maximum-likelihood particle. The cyan boundary will split in later frames (see figure (b)). The number inside each figure denotes the frame index. (b) The component in the yellow window splits in two between frames 52 and 55. (c) The two components in the yellow window merge into one between frames 111 and 114. (d) 3D reconstruction of the entire colon boundary. The left figure is based on the tracking result and the right is the ground truth.

ponents merging together during frames 111-114. The tracker, again, complies. Finally, Fig. 3(d) displays the 3D reconstruction from all the tracking results for 355 slices in the frame sequence and compares it to the ground truth obtained from edge detection. We use 100 measurement points in each slice, so the total number of measurements for the sequence is $100 \times 353 = 35,300$. The entire boundary has 363,069 points at pixel resolution, so the ratio between reconstructed points and measurements is about 10. The total tracking time for the sequence is 7121s, that is, about two hours for the sequence, or 20 seconds per frame. We are still far from real time performance. However, the code runs in Matlab and has several nested loops, so a substantial speedup is likely just by code optimization in C. Parallel implementation is of course trivially possible in obvious ways for particle filters. Now that preliminary experiments have shown the conceptual validity of our approach, we plan to turn some of our efforts to increasing efficiency through appropriate data structures and approximation algorithms as well.

5 Conclusions and Future Work

To our knowledge this is the first full-fledged formulation of particle filters for level sets. In our method, resampling has a cost proportional to the number of particles, but very small constant factors. The propagation cost is proportional to the *logarithm* of the number of particles, because P explicit particles represent 2^P particles implicitly. This is crucial, because the propagation cost per (explicit) particle is high for level sets. Preliminary experiments on tomographic imagery have shown the practicality of the approach by reconstructing a surface of $363,000$ points from only $35,300$ image measurements.

Immediate targets for future work are the improvement on the cost of maintaining the intersection factors for intersections windows and the use of multiple mother particles to represent macroscopic differences between particles. A multi-resolution hierarchy of overlapping particles is our ultimate goal in this respect. Now we are working on a finite-element perturbation strategy to make the tracking process more efficient. Incidentally, the approximation error for Finite Element Method is inherently better understood than that of mixture of Gaussian functions. Other plans for future work focus on the further reduction of constant factors and on the design of strategies for dispatching travelling observers as the boundaries move. Our experiments suggest in particular concentrating more observers close to high-curvature points on the boundary. This will make it possible, for instance, to send robots to autonomously track the moving boundary of an oil spill, wildfire, or cloud of pollutant. We intend to investigate the application of our methods to other domains as well.

References

1. Isard, M., Blake, A.: Condensation-conditional density propagation for visual tracking. IJCV **29** (1998) 5–28
2. Blake, A., Isard, M.: Active Contours. Springer, New York, NY (1999)

3. Einstein, A.: Zur Theorie der Brownschen Bewegung. Ann. d. Phys. **19** (1906) 180
4. Risken, H.: The Fokker-Planck Equation: Methods of Solution and Applications. Springer, New York, NY (1996)
5. Doucet, A., de Freitas, N., N. Gordon, editors: Sequential Monte Carlo in Practice. Springer, New York, NY (2001)
6. De Boor, C.: A Practical Introduction to Splines. Springer, New York, NY (2001)
7. Kalman, R.E.: A new approach to linear filtering and prediction problems. Trans. of the ASME J. on Basic Eng. **82** (1960) 34–45
8. Osher, S., Sethian, J.A.: Fronts propagating with curvature dependent speed: Algorithms based on Hamilton-Jacobi formulations. J. of Comp. Phys. **79** (1988) 12–49
9. Caselles, V., Morel, J.M., Sapiro, G., A. Tannenbaum, editors: Special issue on partial differential equations and geometrydriven diffusion in image processing and analysis. IEEE Trans. on Image Proc. **7** (1998) 269–473
10. Nielsen, M., Johansen, P., Olsen, O.F., J. Weickert, editors. In: Scale Space Theories in Computer Vision. Volume 1682. Springer, Berlin (1999)
11. Osher, S.J., Fedkiw, R.P.: Level Set Methods and Dynamic Implicit Surfaces. Springer, New York, NY (2002)
12. Adalsteinsson, D., Sethian, J.A.: A fast level set method for propagating interfaces. J. of Comp. Phys. **118** (1995) 269 – 277
13. Cremers, D., Soatto, S.: A pseudo-distance for shape priors in level set segmentation. 2nd IEEE Workshop on Variational, Geometric and Level Set Methods in Computer Vision (2003) 169–176
14. Paragios, N., Deriche, R.: Geodesic active contours and level sets for the detection and tracking of moving objects. IEEE Trans. PAMI **22** (2000) 266–280
15. Zhang, T., Freedman, D.: Tracking objects using density matching and shape priors. ICCV **2** (2003) 1050–1062
16. Malladi, R., Sethian, J.A., Vemuri, B.C.: Shape modeling with front propagation: A level set approach. IEEE Trans. on PAMI **17** (1995) 158–175
17. Tsai, A., Yezzi, A., Wells, W. Jr., Tempany, C., Tucker, D., Fan, A., Grimson, W.E., Willsky, A.: A shape-based approach to the segmentation of medical imagery using level sets. IEEE Trans. on Med. Im. **22(2)** (2003) 137–154
18. Caselles, V., Kimmel, R., Sapiro, G.: Geodesic active contours. IJCV **22** (1997) 61–79
19. Kichenassamy, S., Kumar, A., Olver, P., Tannenbaum, A., Yezzi, A.: Gradient flows and geometric active contour models. In: ICCV. (1995) 810–815
20. Bertalmio, M., Sapiro, G., Randall, G.: Morphing active contours. IEEE Trans. on PAMI **22** (2000) 733–737
21. Mansouri, A.: Region tracking via level set PDEs without motion computation. IEEE Trans. on PAMI **24** (2002) 947–961
22. Rathi, Y., Vaswani, N., Tannenbaum, A., Yezzi, A.: Particle filtering for geometric active contours with application to tracking moving and deforming objects. CVPR **2** (2005) 2–9
23. Yezzi, A.J., Soatto, S.: DEFORMOTION: Deforming motion, shape average and the joint registration and approximation of structures in images. IJCV **53(2)** (2003) 153–167

Author Index

Lecture Notes in Computer Science

For information about Vols. 1–3849

please contact your bookseller or Springer

Vol. 3899: S. Frintrop, VOCUS: A Visual Attention System for Object Detection and Goal-Directed Search. XIV, 216 pages. 2006. (Sublibrary LNAI).

Vol. 3898: K. Tuyls, P.J. 't Hoen, K. Verbeeck, S. Sen (Eds.), Learning and Adaption in Multi-Agent Systems. X, 217 pages. 2006. (Sublibrary LNAI).

Vol. 3897: B. Preneel, S. Tavares (Eds.), Selected Areas in Cryptography. XI, 371 pages. 2006.

Vol. 3896: Y. Ioannidis, M.H. Scholl, J.W. Schmidt, F. Matthes, M. Hatzopoulos, K. Boehm, A. Kemper, T. Grust, C. Boehm (Eds.), Advances in Database Technology - EDBT 2006. XIV, 1208 pages. 2006.

Vol. 3895: O. Goldreich, A.L. Rosenberg, A.L. Selman (Eds.), Theoretical Computer Science. XII, 399 pages. 2006.

Vol. 3894: W. Grass, B. Sick, K. Waldschmidt (Eds.), Architecture of Computing Systems - ARCS 2006. XII, 496 pages. 2006.

Vol. 3893: L. Atzori, D.D. Giusto, R. Leonardi, F. Pereira (Eds.), Visual Content Processing and Representation. IX, 224 pages. 2006.

Vol. 3891: J.S. Sichman, L. Antunes (Eds.), Multi-Agent-Based Simulation VI. X, 191 pages. 2006. (Sublibrary LNAI).

Vol. 3890: S.G. Thompson, R. Ghanea-Hercock (Eds.), Defence Applications of Multi-Agent Systems. XII, 141 pages. 2006. (Sublibrary LNAI).

Vol. 3889: J. Rosca, D. Erdogmus, J.C. Príncipe, S. Haykin (Eds.), Independent Component Analysis and Blind Signal Separation. XXI, 980 pages. 2006.

Vol. 3888: D. Draheim, G. Weber (Eds.), Trends in Enterprise Application Architecture. IX, 145 pages. 2006.

Vol. 3887: J.R. Correa, A. Hevia, M. Kiwi (Eds.), LATIN 2006: Theoretical Informatics. XVI, 814 pages. 2006.

Vol. 3886: E.G. Bremer, J. Hakenberg, E.-H.(S.) Han, D. Berrar, W. Dubitzky (Eds.), Knowledge Discovery in Life Science Literature. XIV, 147 pages. 2006. (Sublibrary LNBI).

Vol. 3885: V. Torra, Y. Narukawa, A. Valls, J. Domingo-Ferrer (Eds.), Modeling Decisions for Artificial Intelligence. XII, 374 pages. 2006. (Sublibrary LNAI).

Vol. 3884: B. Durand, W. Thomas (Eds.), STACS 2006. XIV, 714 pages. 2006.

Vol. 3882: M.L. Lee, K.-L. Tan, V. Wuwongse (Eds.), Database Systems for Advanced Applications. XIX, 923 pages. 2006.

Vol. 3881: S. Gibet, N. Courty, J.-F. Kamp (Eds.), Gesture in Human-Computer Interaction and Simulation. XIII, 344 pages. 2006. (Sublibrary LNAI).

Vol. 3880: A. Rashid, M. Aksit (Eds.), Transactions on Aspect-Oriented Software Development I. IX, 335 pages. 2006.

Vol. 3879: T. Erlebach, G. Persinao (Eds.), Approximation and Online Algorithms. X, 349 pages. 2006.

Vol. 3878: A. Gelbukh (Ed.), Computational Linguistics and Intelligent Text Processing. XVII, 589 pages. 2006.

Vol. 3877: M. Detyniecki, J.M. Jose, A. Nürnberger, C. J. '. van Rijsbergen (Eds.), Adaptive Multimedia Retrieval: User, Context, and Feedback. XI, 279 pages. 2006.

Vol. 3876: S. Halevi, T. Rabin (Eds.), Theory of Cryptography. XI, 617 pages. 2006.

Vol. 3875: S. Ur, E. Bin, Y. Wolfsthal (Eds.), Hardware and Software, Verification and Testing. X, 265 pages. 2006.

Vol. 3874: R. Missaoui, J. Schmidt (Eds.), Formal Concept Analysis. X, 309 pages. 2006. (Sublibrary LNAI).

Vol. 3873: L. Maicher, J. Park (Eds.), Charting the Topic Maps Research and Applications Landscape. VIII, 281 pages. 2006. (Sublibrary LNAI).

Vol. 3872: H. Bunke, A. L. Spitz (Eds.), Document Analysis Systems VII. XIII, 630 pages. 2006.

Vol. 3871: E.-G. Talbi, P. Liardet, P. Collet, E. Lutton, M. Schoenauer (Eds.), Artificial Evolution. XI, 310 pages. 2006.

Vol. 3870: S. Spaccapietra, P. Atzeni, W.W. Chu, T. Catarci, K.P. Sycara (Eds.), Journal on Data Semantics V. XIII, 237 pages. 2006.

Vol. 3869: S. Renals, S. Bengio (Eds.), Machine Learning for Multimodal Interaction. XIII, 490 pages. 2006.

Vol. 3868: K. Römer, H. Karl, F. Mattern (Eds.), Wireless Sensor Networks. XI, 342 pages. 2006.

Vol. 3866: T. Dimitrakos, F. Martinelli, P.Y.A. Ryan, S. Schneider (Eds.), Formal Aspects in Security and Trust. X, 259 pages. 2006.

Vol. 3865: W. Shen, K.-M. Chao, Z. Lin, J.-P.A. Barthès, A. James (Eds.), Computer Supported Cooperative Work in Design II. XII, 659 pages. 2006.

Vol. 3863: M. Kohlhase (Ed.), Mathematical Knowledge Management. XI, 405 pages. 2006. (Sublibrary LNAI).

Vol. 3862: R.H. Bordini, M. Dastani, J. Dix, A.E.F. Seghrouchni (Eds.), Programming Multi-Agent Systems. XIV, 267 pages. 2006. (Sublibrary LNAI).

Vol. 3861: J. Dix, S.J. Hegner (Eds.), Foundations of Information and Knowledge Systems. X, 331 pages. 2006.

Vol. 3860: D. Pointcheval (Ed.), Topics in Cryptology – CT-RSA 2006. XI, 365 pages. 2006.

Vol. 3858: A. Valdes, D. Zamboni (Eds.), Recent Advances in Intrusion Detection. X, 351 pages. 2006.

Vol. 3857: M.P.C. Fossorier, H. Imai, S. Lin, A. Poli (Eds.), Applied Algebra, Algebraic Algorithms and Error-Correcting Codes. XI, 350 pages. 2006.

Vol. 3855: E. A. Emerson, K.S. Namjoshi (Eds.), Verification, Model Checking, and Abstract Interpretation. XI, 443 pages. 2005.

Vol. 3854: I. Stavrakakis, M. Smirnov (Eds.), Autonomic Communication. XIII, 303 pages. 2006.

Vol. 3853: A.J. Ijspeert, T. Masuzawa, S. Kusumoto (Eds.), Biologically Inspired Approaches to Advanced Information Technology. XIV, 388 pages. 2006.

Vol. 3852: P.J. Narayanan, S.K. Nayar, H.-Y. Shum (Eds.), Computer Vision – ACCV 2006, Part II. XXXI, 977 pages. 2006.

Vol. 3851: P.J. Narayanan, S.K. Nayar, H.-Y. Shum (Eds.), Computer Vision – ACCV 2006, Part I. XXXI, 973 pages. 2006.

Vol. 3850: R. Freund, G. Păun, G. Rozenberg, A. Salomaa (Eds.), Membrane Computing. IX, 371 pages. 2006.